CASES IN COMPARATIVE POLITICS

THIRD EDITION

CASES IN COMPARATIVE POLITICS

THIRD EDITION

PATRICK H. O'NEIL, KARL FIELDS,
AND DON SHARE

W. W. NORTON & COMPANY

New York • *London*

Editor: Aaron Javsicas
Assistant editor: Carly Fraser
Project editor: Kate Feighery
Production manager, College: Eric Pier-Hocking
Composition: Matrix Publishing Services, Inc.
Manufacturing: Quebecor World—Fairfield division

Library of Congress Cataloging-in-Publication Data
O'Neil, Patrick H., 1966–
      Essentials of comparative politics / Patrick H. O'Neil, Karl Fields, and Don Share—3rd ed.
            p. cm.
      Includes bibliographical references.
      ISBN: 978-0-393-93377-2 (pbk.)

      1. Comparative government—Case Studies. I. Fields, Karl J. II. Share, Donald. III. Title.

JF51.O538 2009
      320.3—dc22   2009022518

      W. W. Norton & Company, Inc., 500 Fifth Avenue, New York, N.Y. 10110
                                    www.wwnorton.com

W. W. Norton & Company Ltd., Castle House, 75/76 Wells Street, London W1T 3QT

1 2 3 4 5 6 7 8 9 0

ABOUT THE AUTHORS

Patrick H. O'Neil is Professor of Politics and Government at the University of Puget Sound in Tacoma, Washington. He has a Ph.D. in Political Science from Indiana University. Professor O'Neil's teaching and research interests are in the areas of democratization, conflict and political violence. His publications include the books *Revolution from Within: The Hungarian Socialist Workers' Party and the Collapse of Communism* and *Communicating Democracy: The Media and Political Transitions* (editor).

Karl Fields is Professor of Politics and Government and Director of Asian Studies at the University of Puget Sound in Tacoma, Washington. He has a Ph.D. in Political Science from the University of California, Berkeley. Professor Fields's teaching and research interests focus on East Asian political economy, including government-business relations, economic reform, and regional integration. His publications include *Enterprise and the State in Korea and Taiwan*.

Don Share is Professor of Politics and Government at the University of Puget Sound in Tacoma, Washington. He has a Ph.D. in Political Science from Stanford University. He teaches comparative politics and Latin American politics, and has published widely on democratization and Spanish politics. His books include *The Making of Spanish Democracy* and *Dilemmas of Social Democracy*.

BRIEF CONTENTS

CONTENTS

6.   JAPAN   200

PREFACE

Cases in Comparative Politics can be traced to an ongoing experiment undertaken by the three comparative political scientists in the Politics and Government Department at the University of Puget Sound. Over the years the three of us spent much time discussing the challenges of teaching our introductory course in comparative politics. In those discussions we came to realize that each of us taught the course so differently that students completing our different sections of the course did not really share a common conceptual vocabulary. Over several years we fashioned a unified curriculum for Introduction to Comparative Politics, drawing on the strengths of each of our particular approaches.

All three of us now equip our students with a common conceptual vocabulary. All of our students now learn about states, nations, and different models of political economy. All students learn the basics about nondemocratic and democratic regimes, and they become familiar with characteristics of communist systems and advanced democracies. In developing our curriculum, we became frustrated trying to find cases that were concise, sophisticated, and written to address the major concepts introduced in Patrick H. O'Neil's textbook, *Essentials of Comparative Politics*. Thus, we initially co-authored six cases adhering to a set of criteria:

- Each case is concise, making it possible to assign an entire case, or even two cases, for a single class session.
- All cases include discussion of major geographic and demographic features, themes in the historical development of the state, political regimes (including the constitution, branches of government, the electoral system, and local government), political conflict and competition (including the party system and civil society), society, political economy, and current issues. This uniform structure allowed us to assign specific sections from two or more cases simultaneously.
- The cases follow the general framework of *Essentials of Comparative Politics* but could also be used in conjunction with other texts.

After the publication of the initial six cases (the United Kingdom, Japan, China, Russia, Mexico, and South Africa), we received positive feedback from teachers of comparative politics. Drawing on their comments and suggestions, we wrote new cases to accommodate individual preferences and give instructors more choice. We subsequently added cases on Brazil, France, India, Iran, the United States, and Nigeria. Based on feedback from instructors, this third edition adds Germany, bringing the total number of cases to thirteen.

Selecting only thirteen cases is, of course, fraught with drawbacks. Nevertheless, we believe that this collection represents countries that are both important in their own right and representative of a broad range of political systems. Each of the thirteen cases has special importance in the context of the study of comparative politics. Five of our cases (France, Germany, Japan, the United States, and the United Kingdom) are advanced industrial democracies, but they represent a wide range of institutions, societies, political economic models, and relationships with the world. Japan is an important instance of a non-Western industrialized democracy and an instructive case of democratization imposed by foreign occupiers. While the United Kingdom and the United States have been known for political stability, France and Germany have fascinating histories of political turmoil and regime change.

Two of our cases, China and Russia, share a past of Marxist-Leninist totalitarianism. Communism thrived in these two large and culturally distinct nations. Both suffered from the dangerous concentration of power in the hands of communist parties and, at times, despotic leaders. The Soviet Communist regime imploded and led to a troubled and incomplete transition to capitalism and democracy. China has retained its communist authoritarian political system but has experimented with a remarkable transition to a largely capitalist political economy.

The remaining six cases illustrate the diversity of the developing world. Of the six, India has had the longest history of stable democratic rule, but like most countries in the developing world, it has nevertheless struggled with massive poverty and inequality. The remaining five have experienced various forms of authoritarianism. Brazil and Nigeria endured long periods of military rule. Mexico's history of military rule was ended by an authoritarian political party that ruled for much of the twentieth century through a variety of nonmilitary means. South Africa experienced decades of racially based authoritarianism that excluded the vast majority of its population. Iran experienced a modernizing authoritarian monarchy followed by its current authoritarian regime, a theocracy ruled by Islamic clerics.

In writing the cases we have incurred numerous debts. First, and foremost, we wish to thank our wonderful colleagues in the Department of Politics and Government at the University of Puget Sound. By encouraging us to develop a common curriculum for our Introduction to Comparative Politics offering, and by allowing us to team-teach the course in different combinations, they allowed us to learn from each other. These cases are much stronger as a result. The university has also been extremely supportive in recognizing that writing for the classroom is as valuable as writing scholarly publications, and in providing course releases and summer stipends toward that end. Student assistants Brett Venn, Jess Box, and Liz Kaster proved extremely helpful in conducting research for our various cases; Irene Lim has, as always, supported us with her amazing technical and organizational skills. Our colleague Bill Haltom provided very helpful input throughout the project. Debby Nagusky contributed valuable copyediting assistance.

We very much appreciate the many helpful comments we have received from fellow instructors of comparative politics, including Emily Acevedo (California State University, Los Angeles), Josephine Andrews (University of California, Davis), Alex Avila (Mesa Community College), Jeremy Busacca (Whittier College), William Heller (Binghamton University), Robert Jackson (University of Redlands), Ricardo Larémont (Binghamton University), Mary Malone (University of New Hampshire), Pamela Martin (Coastal Carolina University), Mark Milewicz (Gordon College), John Occhipinti (Canisius College), Anthony O'Regan (Los Angeles Valley College), Paul Rousseau (University of Windsor), and José Vadi (Cal Poly, Pomona). We would especially like to thank Emmanuel J. Teitelbaum, from the Department of Political Science at the George Washington University, and Peter H. Loedel, Professor and Chair of the Department of Political Science at West Chester University, for providing insightful feedback on this most recent edition.

Many thanks to all the folks at Norton—Peter Lesser, Ann Shin, Roby Harrington, and Aaron Javsicas—who have contributed to the success of this project. Finally, we thank our students at the University of Puget Sound who inspired us to write these cases and provided valuable feedback throughout the entire process.

Don Share
Karl Fields
Patrick H. O'Neil

Tacoma, WA 2009

A note about the data: The data that are presented throughout the text in numerous tables, charts, and other figures are drawn from the *CIA World Fact* unless otherwise noted.

1 INTRODUCTION

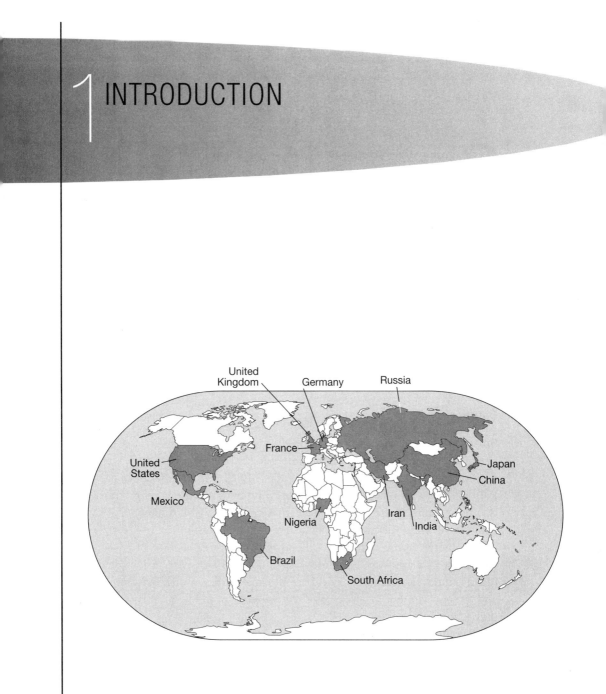

WHAT IS COMPARATIVE POLITICS?

Comparative politics is the study and comparison of politics across countries. Studying politics in this way helps us examine major questions of political science, for example, Why do some countries have democratic regimes whereas others experience authoritarianism? Why and how do regimes change? Why do some countries experience affluence and growth, but others endure poverty and decline? In this volume, we describe and analyze the political systems of thirteen different countries. We focus on their major geographic and demographic features; the origins and development of each state; and their political regimes, patterns of political conflict and competition, societies, political economies, and relationships with the world. In this introductory chapter, we summarize key terms and concepts that will help you compare the thirteen countries presented here as case studies in comparative politics.

Comparing States

States are organizations that maintain a monopoly of violence over a territory. The term *state* can be confusing because it sometimes refers to a subnational government (for example, the fifty states in the United States). Political scientists, however, use state to refer to a national organization. In this book, state is used in the latter, broader sense. Still, the concept of state is narrower than the notion of country, which encompasses the territory and people living within a state. As illustrated by our collection of cases, states can differ in many ways, including origins, length of existence, strength, and historical development.[1] Political scientists also distinguish between the state and the government, considering the **government** to be the leadership or elite that administers the state.

Two of the most obvious differences among states are their size and their population. The thirteen countries included in this book vary considerably in both respects. States also vary in their natural endowments, such as arable land, mineral resources, navigable rivers, and access to the sea. Well-endowed states may have advantages over poorly endowed ones, but resource endowments do not necessarily determine the prosperity of a state. Japan, for example, has become one of the world's dominant economic powers despite having relatively few natural resources. Russia and Iran, in contrast, are rich in natural resources but have struggled economically.

States also differ widely in their origins and historical development. Some countries (for example, China, France, and the United Kingdom) have long

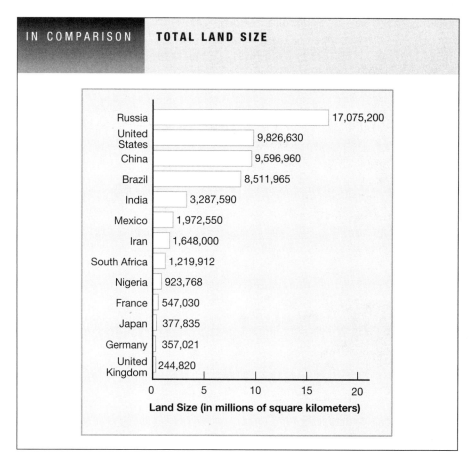

IN COMPARISON   **TOTAL LAND SIZE**

Russia — 17,075,200
United States — 9,826,630
China — 9,596,960
Brazil — 8,511,965
India — 3,287,590
Mexico — 1,972,550
Iran — 1,648,000
South Africa — 1,219,912
Nigeria — 923,768
France — 547,030
Japan — 377,835
Germany — 357,021
United Kingdom — 244,820

Land Size (in millions of square kilometers)

histories of statehood. Other political systems, like Germany, experienced the creation of a unified state only after long periods of division. Many countries in the developing world became states after they were decolonized. Nigeria, for example, became an independent state relatively recently, in 1960. With the end of the cold war in 1989 and the collapse of the Soviet Union two years later, a number of states emerged or reemerged. At the same time, Germany, which had been divided into two states during the cold war, became a single state in 1990.

States differ, too, in their level of organization, effectiveness, and stability. The power of a state depends in part on its **legitimacy,** or the extent to which its authority is regarded as right and proper. Political scientists have long observed that there are different sources of a state's legitimacy. State authority may draw on **traditional legitimacy,** in which the state is obeyed because it has a long tradition of being obeyed. Alternatively, a state may be considered legitimate because of **charismatic legitimacy,** that is, its identification with the magnetic appeal of a leader or movement. Finally, states may gain legitimacy on the basis of **rational-legal legitimacy,** a system of laws and procedures that becomes highly institutionalized. Although most modern states derive their legitimacy from rational-legal sources, both traditional and charismatic legitimacy often continue to play a role. In Japan and the United Kingdom, for example, the monarchy is a source of traditional legitimacy that complements the rational-legal legitimacy of the state. Some postcolonial states in the developing world have had considerable trouble establishing legitimacy. Often colonial powers created states that cut across ethnic boundaries or contain hostile ethnic groups, as in Nigeria and Iran.

States differ in their ability to preserve their sovereignty and carry out the basic functions of maintaining law and order. **Strong states** can perform the basic tasks of defending their borders from outside attacks and defending their authority from internal nonstate rivals. **Weak states** have trouble carrying out those basic tasks and often suffer from endemic internal violence, a poor infrastructure, and the inability to collect taxes and enforce the rule of law.

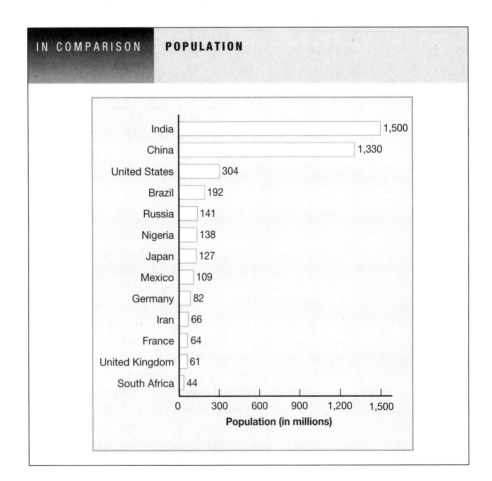

IN COMPARISON   **POPULATION**

India — 1,500
China — 1,330
United States — 304
Brazil — 192
Russia — 141
Nigeria — 138
Japan — 127
Mexico — 109
Germany — 82
Iran — 66
France — 64
United Kingdom — 61
South Africa — 44

Population (in millions)

> ## MONARCHIES AS A SOURCE OF TRADITIONAL LEGITIMACY IN MODERN DEMOCRACY
>
> By definition, monarchies are not democratic institutions. Among the thirteen cases in this volume, however, two vibrant democracies (Japan and the United Kingdom) have retained monarchs as head of state. How can a democracy justify having a hereditary monarch as head of state? In both Japan and the UK, the monarch serves not only as a significant link to the past but also as a reminder of the traditions that are cherished in each society. More important, both monarchs are bound by constitutions that limit their power almost entirely to symbolic functions. The monarchy has its critics in both countries, but most citizens support the presence of a head of state who is completely divorced from partisan politics.

High levels of corruption are often a symptom of state weakness (see "In Comparison: Perceived Corruption, 2008," p. 6). Taken to an extreme, weak states may experience a complete loss of legitimacy and power and may be overwhelmed by anarchy and violence. Political scientists refer to those relatively rare cases as **failed states.**[2]

Finally, states differ in the degree to which they centralize or disperse political power. **Unitary states** concentrate most of their political power in the national capital, allocating little decision-making power to regions or localities. **Federal states** divide power between the central state and regional or local authorities (such as provinces, counties, and cities). Unitary states, such as the United Kingdom and South Africa, may be stronger and more decisive than federal states, but the centralization of power may create local resentment and initiate calls for a **devolution** (the handing down) of power to regions and localities. Federal states, like Germany, Brazil, Mexico, Nigeria, Russia, and the United States, often find that their dispersal of power hampers national decision making and accountability.

Comparing Regimes

Political regimes are the norms and rules regarding individual freedoms and collective equality, the locus of power, and the use of that power. It is easiest to think of political regimes as the rules of the game governing the exercise of power. In modern political systems, regimes are most often described in written constitutions. In some countries, however, such as the United Kingdom, the regime consists of a combination of laws and customs that are not incorporated into any one written document. In other countries, such as China and Iran, written constitutions do not accurately describe the extraconstitutional rules that govern the exercise of power.

IN COMPARISON	PERCEIVED CORRUPTION, 2008

On a scale of 1 to 10, 1 = most corrupt; 10 = least corrupt.

Country	Score
Germany	7.9
United Kingdom	7.7
Japan	7.3
United States	7.3
France	6.9
South Africa	4.9
China	3.6
Mexico	3.6
Brazil	3.5
India	3.4
Nigeria	2.7
Iran	2.3
Russia	2.1

Source: Transparency International, www.transparency.org/policy_research/surveys_indices/cpi/2008 (accessed 26 December 2008).

Democratic regimes have rules that emphasize a large role for the public in governance and protect basic rights and freedoms. **Authoritarian regimes** limit the role of the public in decision making and often deny citizens' basic rights and restrict their freedoms. In the past quarter century, the world has witnessed a dramatic rise in the number of democratic regimes.[3] Over half the world's population, however, is still governed by nondemocratic regimes, which one leading research organization defines as either "partly free," sometimes called illiberal (meaning that some personal liberties and democratic rights are limited), or "not free," sometimes called authoritarian (meaning that the public has little individual freedom).[4]

COMPARING DEMOCRATIC POLITICAL INSTITUTIONS

Most political regimes, whether democratic or not, establish a number of political institutions. The **executive** is the branch of government that carries out the laws and policies of a given state. We can think of the executive branch as performing two separate sets of duties. On the one hand, the **head of state** symbolizes and represents the people, both nationally and internationally, embodying and articulating the goals of the regime. On the other hand, the **head of government** deals with the everyday tasks of running the state, such as formulating and executing policy. The distinction between those roles is most easily seen in, for example, Japan, the United Kingdom, Germany, India, and France, which have separate heads of state and heads of government. Other regimes, like those of Brazil, Mexico, Nigeria, South Africa, and the United States, assign the two roles of the executive branch to a single individual.

The **legislature** is the branch of government formally charged with making laws. The organization and power of legislatures differ considerably from country to country. In some political regimes, especially authoritarian ones like China and Iran, the legislature has little power or initiative and serves mainly to rubber-stamp government legislation. In other systems, like Germany or India, the legislature is relatively powerful and autonomous. **Unicameral legislatures** (often found in smaller countries) consist of a single chamber; **bicameral legislatures** consist of two legislative chambers. In those systems, one chamber often represents the population at large and is referred to as the **lower house,** and the other chamber (referred to as the **upper house**) reflects the geographical subunits.

The **judiciary** is the branch of a country's government that is concerned with dispensing justice. The **constitutional court** is the highest judicial body to rule on the constitutionality of laws and other government actions; in most political systems, the constitutional court also formally oversees the entire judicial structure. The power of a regime's judiciary is determined in part by the nature of its power of **judicial review,** the mechanism by which the court reviews laws and policies and overturns those seen as violations of the con-

A SPECTRUM OF REGIMES: FROM AUTHORITARIANISM TO DEMOCRACY

Our thirteen cases exemplify the broad spectrum of regime types. China has the most clearly authoritarian regime of them all, since it tolerates only one political power. Iran allows elections, but its unelected religious authorities severely circumscribe political parties and political institutions. Russia today (and Mexico during much of the twentieth century) is formally a democracy, but the power of state authorities (and in Mexico, the power of the dominant party) makes it effectively a semi-authoritarian system or illiberal democracy. The remaining cases in this volume more easily (if imperfectly in some instances) satisfy the criteria for being liberal democracies.

IN COMPARISON	FREEDOM HOUSE RANKINGS, 2008

On a scale of 1 to 7, 1 = free; 5 = partly free; 7 = not free.

Country	Ranking
United Kingdom	1
Germany	1
Japan	1
France	1
United States	1
South Africa	2
Brazil	2
India	2
Mexico	2
Nigeria	4
Iran	6
Russia	6
China	7

Source: Freedom House, www.freedomhouse.org/uploads/ chart116file163.pdf (accessed 26 December 2008).

stitution. Some regimes give the judiciary the power of **concrete review**, allowing the high court to rule on constitutional issues only when disputes are brought before it. Other regimes give the judiciary the power of **abstract review**, allowing it to decide questions that do not arise from legal cases, sometimes even allowing it to make judgments on legislation that has not been enacted. In France, the Constitutional Council has the power of abstract review, whereas in the United States the Supreme Court has the power of concrete review. The highest courts in England, by contrast, do not have power to overturn legislation under any circumstances.

The powers of these political institutions and the relationships among them vary considerably across regimes. The most important variation concerns the relationship between the legislature and the executive. There are three major models of **legislative-executive relations** within democratic regimes: parliamentary, presidential, and semi-presidential. The **parliamentary system** (seen among our cases in the United Kingdom, India, Germany, and Japan) features an executive head of government (often referred to as a prime minister) who is usually elected from within the legislature. The prime minister is usually the leader of the largest political party in the legislature. The prime minister and the **cabinet** (the body of chief ministers or officials in government in charge of such policy areas as defense, agriculture, and so on) are charged with formulating and executing policy. The head of state in such systems has largely ceremonial duties and is usually either an indirectly elected president or a hereditary monarch.

PARLIAMENTARY SYSTEMS

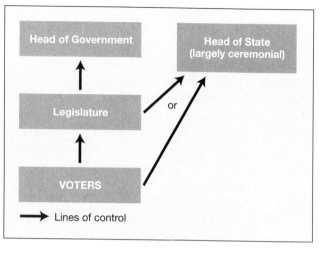

The **presidential system**, used by Brazil, Mexico, and the United States, combines the roles of head of state and head of government in the office of the president. These systems feature a directly elected president who holds most of the government's executive powers. Presidential systems have directly elected legislatures that to varying degrees serve as a check on presidential authority.

Scholars debate the advantages and disadvantages of these legislative-executive models.[5] Parliamentary systems are often praised for reducing conflict between the legislature and the executive (since the executive is approved by the legislature), thus producing more efficient government. In addition, when parliamentary legislatures lack a majority, political parties must compromise to create a government supported by a majority of the legislature. Parliamentary systems are also more flexible than presidential systems because when prime ministers lose the support of the legislature, they can be swiftly removed through a legislative "vote of no confidence." The appointment of

PRESIDENTIAL SYSTEMS

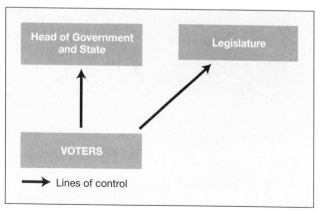

a new prime minister, or the convocation of new elections, can often resolve political deadlocks. But critics point out that parliamentary systems with a strong majority in the legislature can produce a very dominant, virtually unchecked government. Moreover, in fractious legislatures it can be difficult to cobble together a stable majority government.

Presidential systems are often portrayed as more stable than parliamentary systems. There are fixed terms of office for the president and the legislature, which is not the case in most parliamentary systems. Moreover, presidents are directly elected by the public and can be removed only by the legislature and only in cases of criminal misconduct. Nonetheless, presidential systems have been criticized for producing divisive winner-take-all outcomes, lacking the flexibility needed to confront crises, and leading to overly powerful executives in the face of weak and divided legislatures.[6]

In an attempt to avoid the weaknesses of parliamentary and presidential systems, some newer democratic regimes, like those of France and Russia, have adopted a third model of legislative-executive relations, called the **semi-presidential system**. This system includes both a prime minister approved by the legislature and a directly elected president, with the two sharing executive power. In practice, semi-presidential systems tend to produce strong presidents akin to those in pure presidential systems, but the exact balance between the executives varies from case to case.

Another political institution worth mentioning is the **electoral system**, which determines how votes are cast and counted. Most democratic regimes use one of two models. The most commonly employed is **proportional representation (PR)**. Among our thirteen cases, Germany, Brazil, and Russia employ this system. PR relies upon **multimember districts (MMDs)**, in which more than one legislative seat is contested in each electoral district. Voters cast their ballots for a list of party candidates rather than for a single representative, and the percentage of votes a party receives in a district determines how many of that district's seats the party will win. Thus, the percentage of votes each party wins in each district should closely corre-

SEMI-PRESIDENTIAL SYSTEMS

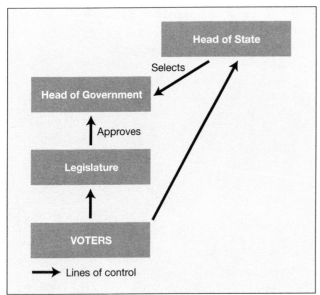

			Combinations of Political Institutions		
Country	Type of Regime	Type of State	Legislative-Executive System	Electoral System
Brazil	Democratic	Federal	Presidential	PR
China	Authoritarian	Unitary		
France	Democratic	Unitary	Semi-presidential	SMD
Germany	Democratic	Federal	Parliamentary	Mixed
India	Democratic	Federal	Parliamentary	SMD
Iran	Authoritarian	Unitary		SMD
Japan	Democratic	Unitary	Parliamentary	Mixed
Mexico	Democratic	Federal	Presidential	Mixed
Nigeria	Democratic	Federal	Presidential	SMD
Russia	Authoritarian	Federal	Semi-presidential	PR
South Africa	Democratic	Unitary	Parliamentary	PR
United Kingdom	Democratic	Unitary	Parliamentary	SMD
United States	Democratic	Federal	Presidential	SMD

spond to the percentage of seats allocated to each party. PR systems produce legislatures that often closely reflect the percentage of votes won nationwide by each political party. As a result, they tend to foster multiple political parties, including small ones.

A minority of democracies (mainly the United Kingdom and its former colonies, such as the United States, India, and Nigeria, as well as France, among the cases in the present volume) rely upon **single-member districts (SMDs)**. In these systems, there is only one representative for each constituency, and in each district the candidate with the greatest number of votes (not necessarily a majority) wins the seat. As opposed to PR systems, SMD votes cast for all but the one winning candidate are, in effect, wasted: that is, they do not count toward any representation in the legislature. SMD systems tend to discriminate against small parties, especially those with a national following rather than a geographically concentrated following.

As with the legislative-executive models, there is vigorous debate about which electoral system is more desirable.[7] PR systems are considered more democratic, since they waste fewer votes and encourage the expression of a wider range of political interests. The PR model increases the number of parties able to win seats in a legislature and allows parties concerned with narrow or minority interests to gain representation. SMD systems are often

HOW LEGISLATIVE-EXECUTIVE AND ELECTORAL SYSTEMS CAN INTERACT

In some parliamentary systems (for example, in the United Kingdom and, until recently, India), elections regularly produce a majority of seats in the legislature for one party. Such systems tend to use single-member district electoral systems, which usually favor the largest parties at the expense of smaller ones. In other parliamentary systems (for example, in Germany), elections rarely produce a parliamentary majority for any party. As a result, political parties often form coalition governments by dividing cabinet seats among coalition members. Those parliamentary systems tend to employ proportional representation electoral systems, which more often allow smaller parties to gain representaton in the legislature.

endorsed because they allow voters in each district to connect directly with their elected representatives instead of their party, making the representatives more accountable to the electorate. Supporters of SMD argue that it is beneficial to eliminate narrowly based or extremist parties from the legislature. They view SMD systems as more likely to produce stable, centrist legislative majorities.

Some democracies, including Germany, Japan, and Mexico, have combined SMD and PR voting systems in what is known as a **mixed electoral system**. Voters are given two votes: one for a candidate and the other for a party. Candidates in the SMDs are elected on the basis of a plurality; other seats are elected from MMDs and are allocated using PR.

COMPARING NONDEMOCRATIC REGIMES

Many nondemocratic regimes have institutions that on paper appear quite similar to those in democratic regimes. In most authoritarian regimes, however, the legislature, the judiciary, and the electoral system do not reveal much about the exercise of political power.

Nondemocratic regimes differ from one another in a number of important ways. Common forms of nondemocratic regimes include personal dictatorships, monarchies, military regimes, one-party regimes, theocracies, and illiberal regimes. A **personal dictatorship**, like that of Porfirio Díaz in Mexico (1876–1910), is based on the power of a single strong leader who usually relies on charismatic or traditional authority to maintain power. In a **military regime** (such as Brazil from 1964 to 1985 or Nigeria from 1966 to 1979), the institution of the military dominates politics. A **one-party regime** (like Mexico from 1917 to 2000) is dominated by a strong political party that relies upon a broad membership as a source of political control. In a **theocracy**, a rare form of government, though the one that characterizes present-day Iran, a leader claims to rule on behalf of God. An **illiberal regime** (as in present-day Russia) retains the basic structures of a democracy but does not protect civil liberties. In the real world, many nondemocratic regimes combine various aspects of these types. The apartheid regime in South Africa (1948–1994) had largely democratic political institutions but excluded the vast majority of its black population.

Communist regimes are one-party regimes in which a Communist party controls most aspects of a country's political and economic system. Specific Communist regimes (such as China under Mao Zedong or the Soviet Union under Joseph Stalin) have sometimes been described as **totalitarian**. Totalitarian regimes feature a strong official ideology that seeks to transform fundamental aspects of the state, society, and economy, using a wide array of organizations and the application of force. As the case of Nazi Germany illustrates, totalitarian regimes need not be Communist.

Nondemocratic regimes use various tools to enforce their political domination. The most obvious mechanisms are state violence and surveillance. The enforcement ranges from systematic and widespread repression (for example, the mass purges in the Soviet Union or contemporary Iran) to sporadic and selective repression of the regime's opponents (as in Brazil during the 1960s). Another important tool of nondemocratic regimes is **co-optation**, whereby members of the public are brought into a beneficial relationship with the state and the government. Co-optation takes many forms, including **corporatism**, in which citizen participation is channeled into state-sanctioned groups; **clientelism**, in which the state provides benefits to groups of its political supporters; and **rent seeking**, in which the government allows its supporters to occupy positions of power in order to monopolize state benefits. The nondemocratic regime that dominated Mexico for much of the twentieth century skillfully employed all of these forms of co-optation to garner public support for the governing party, minimizing its need to rely upon coercion. Finally, the mechanism of control that is most often employed in totalitarian regimes is the **personality cult**, or the state-sponsored exaltation of a leader. The personality cult of Stalin in the Soviet Union and that of Mao in China are prime examples, as is the cult of personality that developed around Ayatollah Ruhollah Khomeini, the leader of the Iranian revolution of 1979.

Comparing Political Conflict and Competition

Political scientists can compare and contrast patterns of political conflict and competition in both democratic and authoritarian regimes. In democratic regimes, for example, it is common to compare the nature of elections and other forms of competition among political parties (often referred to as the **party system**).

On the most basic level, political scientists can compare the nature of **suffrage**, or the right to vote. In democratic regimes and even in many nondemocratic ones, such as China and Iran, that right is often guaranteed to most adult citizens.[8] Another important feature of elections is the degree to which citizens actually participate by voting and by engaging in campaign activities (see "In Comparison: Average Voter Turnout, 1945–1998," below). Party systems also can be compared on the basis of the number of parties, the size of their membership, their organizational strength, their ideological orientation, and their electoral strategies.

A comparative analysis of political conflict and competition cannot focus solely on elections. In most political systems, much political conflict and competition takes place in **civil society**, which comprises the organizations outside the state that help people define and advance their own interests. In addition to political parties, the organizations that make up a country's civil society often include a host of groups as diverse as gun clubs and labor unions.

IN COMPARISON	AVERAGE VOTER TURNOUT, 1945–1998
Country (number of elections)	**Eligible Voters Voting (%)**
South Africa (1)	85.5
Germany (13)	80.6
United Kingdom (15)	74.9
Japan (21)	69.0
Iran (2)	67.6
France (15)	67.3
India (12)	60.7
Russia (2)	55.0
United States (26)	48.3
Mexico (18)	48.1
Brazil (13)	47.9
Nigeria (3)	47.6
China	NA

Source: "Turnout in the World: Country by Country Performance," International Institute for Democracy and Electoral Assistance, www.idea.int/vt/survey/voter_turnout_pop2.cfm (accessed 26 December 2006).

> ## ETHNICITY AS THE BASIS FOR AUTONOMY OR SECESSION MOVEMENTS
>
> In many of our cases (including Nigeria, the United Kingdom, India, China, Russia, and Iran), regions with a distinct ethnic identity have often sought either greater autonomy from the central state or outright independence. Sometimes states are able to weaken secession movements by granting greater political autonomy to regional ethnic groups. In other cases, like Scotland and the United Kingdom, increased autonomy has only fueled a desire for independence. Some regimes, including authoritarian ones like Iran and China and illiberal democracies like Russia, have viewed regionally based ethnic groups as a threat and have harshly repressed them.

Comparing Societies

The state and the regime exist in the context of their society, and societies differ from one another in ways that can strongly influence politics. For example, ethnic divisions exist within many states. **Ethnicity** refers to the specific attributes that make one group of people culturally different from others: for example, customs, language, religion, region, and history. Some states, like China, Japan, and Russia, are relatively homogeneous: one ethnic group makes up a large portion of the society. At the other extreme, countries like Nigeria, Iran, Mexico, and India have a great deal of ethnic diversity. Ethnic diversity can often be a source of political conflict, and even in relatively homogeneous societies the presence of ethnic minorities can pose political challenges (see "In Comparison: Ethnic and Religious Diversity," p. 16).[9]

Societies also differ in terms of their political cultures. **Political culture** can be defined as the patterns of basic norms relating to politics. Political scientists have learned a great deal about how political cultures differ in a variety of areas, including citizens' trust in government, respect for political authority, knowledge about politics, and assessment of their political efficacy (the ability to influence political outcomes).[10]

Political scientists also consider **national identity**, or the extent to which citizens of a country are bound together by a common set of political aspirations (most often self-government and sovereignty). Countries with a long history as a consolidated state often have higher levels of national identity than do states with a shorter history.

One interesting difference among societies is in the importance they place on religion. In most societies, religiosity has declined with economic prosperity and with the growth of secular values. France, Japan, Russia, and the United Kingdom are relatively secular societies in which most people do not

| IN COMPARISON | ETHNIC AND RELIGIOUS DIVERSITY |

Country	Largest Ethnic Group (%)	Second Largest Ethnic Group (%)	Largest Religious Group (%)	Second Largest Religious Group (%)
Brazil	55.0	38.0	80.0	20.0
China	92.0	8.0[a]	94–96.0	3–4.0
France[a]	NA	NA	83–88.0	5–10.0
Germany	91.5	2.4	34[e]	34[e]
India	72.0	25.5	81.0	12.0
Iran	51.0	24.0	89.0	9.0
Japan	99.0	1.0	84.0	16.0[d]
Mexico	60.0	30.0	89.0	6.0
Nigeria	29.0	21.0	50.0	40.0
Russia	81.5	3.8	54.0	19.0
South Africa	75.0	13.0	78.7	19.8
United Kingdom	81.5	9.6	71.6	2.7
United States	67.0[b]	14.0[c]	52.0	24.0

[a]The French census does not collect data on ethnicity.
[b]Based on the U.S. Census Bureau's 2003 estimate that about 14 percent of citizens are Hispanic.
[c]All other ethnic groups combined.
[d]All other religious groups combined.
[e]Protestants and Catholics have the same percentage of members in Germany.

view religion as very important; the United States continues to be an interesting exception in this regard. In Nigeria and Iran, religion is viewed as important by nearly all citizens.

Individuals and groups within a society can also be distinguished according to their political attitudes and ideologies. **Political attitudes** describe views regarding the status quo in a society, specifically, the desired pace and methods of political change. **Radical attitudes** support rapid, extensive, and often revolutionary change. **Liberal attitudes** promote evolutionary change within the system. **Conservative attitudes** support the status quo and view change as risky. **Reactionary attitudes** promote rapid change to restore political, social, and economic institutions that once existed. Since political attitudes describe views of the status quo, radicals, liberals, conservatives, and

POLITICAL ATTITUDES

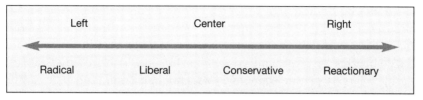

reactionaries differ according to their setting. A reactionary in the United Kingdom, for example, might support the creation of an absolute monarchy, a reactionary in Germany might desire a return to Nazism, and a reactionary in China might call for a return to Maoist totalitarianism.

Whereas political attitudes are particular and context specific, **political ideologies** are universal sets of political values regarding the fundamental goals of politics.[11] A political ideology prescribes an ideal balance between freedom and equality. The ideology of **liberalism** (as opposed to a liberal political attitude) places a high priority on individual political and economic freedoms, favoring them over any attempts to create economic equality. Private property, capitalism, and protections for the individual against the state are central to liberal ideology. **Communism**, in contrast, emphasizes economic equality rather than individual political and economic freedoms. Collective

POLITICAL IDEOLOGIES

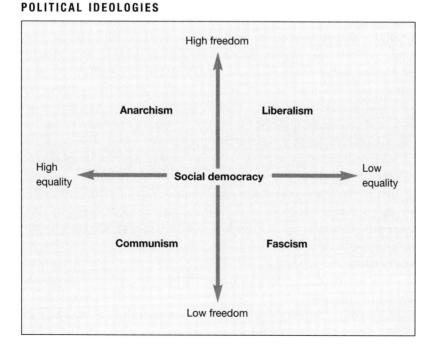

property (state ownership) and a dominant state are cornerstones of Communism. **Social democracy** (often referred to as democratic socialism) is in some ways a hybrid of liberalism and Communism in that it places considerable value on equality but attempts to protect some individual freedoms. Social democrats advocate a mixed welfare state in which an active state exists alongside a largely private economy. **Fascism**, like Communism, is hostile to the idea of individual freedom but rejects the notion of equality. **Anarchism**, like Communism, is based on the belief that private property and capitalism create inequality, but like liberalism it places a high value on individual political freedom.

The strength of each ideology differs across political systems. For example, opinion research demonstrates that citizens of the United States and, to a lesser extent, citizens of the United Kingdom have an unusually strong commitment to liberal ideology; large numbers of them support individualism and manifest a notable distrust of state activism. French and Japanese citizens tend to be less individualistic and are more supportive of an active role for the state in the economy. In China, the rise of capitalist economics has eroded popular support for Communist ideology.

Comparing Political Economies

The study of how politics and economics are related is commonly known as **political economy**; this relationship differs considerably in different political systems.[12] All modern states, however, intervene to some extent in the day-to-day affairs of their economies, and in doing so they depend on a variety of economic institutions. Perhaps the most important of these is the **market**, or the interaction between the forces of supply and demand that allocate goods and resources.[13] Markets, in turn, depend on the institution of **property**, the ownership of goods and services. In their attempt to ensure the distribution of goods and resources, states differ in their interaction with the market and their desire and ability to protect private property.

A major political issue in most societies, and a major point of contention among political ideologies, is the appropriate role of the market and the state in the allocation of goods and services. Some goods—for example, clean air and water—are essential to all of society but not easily provided by the market; these are often referred to as **public goods**. Other goods, such as the production of food and automobiles, are more feasibly provided by private producers using the market. In between those extremes is a large gray area. States differ in the degree to which they define a wide array of goods and services as public goods. As a result, government **social expenditures** (state provision of public benefits, such as education, health care, and transportation) vary widely among countries.

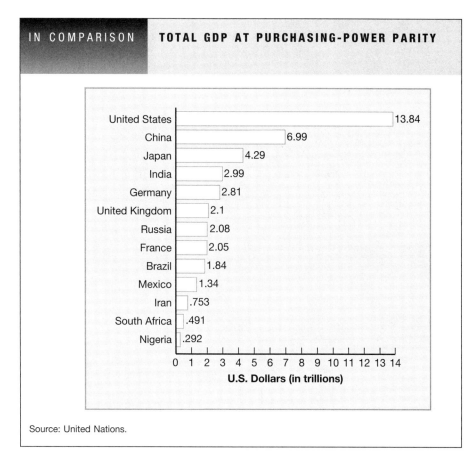

IN COMPARISON — TOTAL GDP AT PURCHASING-POWER PARITY

Country	U.S. Dollars (in trillions)
United States	13.84
China	6.99
Japan	4.29
India	2.99
Germany	2.81
United Kingdom	2.1
Russia	2.08
France	2.05
Brazil	1.84
Mexico	1.34
Iran	.753
South Africa	.491
Nigeria	.292

Source: United Nations.

In the political economic systems of countries such as the United States and the United Kingdom, where liberal ideology is dominant, the state plays a significant but relatively small role. In France, Germany, and Japan, however, the state has played a much larger role in the economy through state ownership (especially in France) and state planning (especially in Japan). Authoritarian regimes have typically had a heavy hand in economic matters, as has certainly been the case in China and Iran. Whereas China's Communist regime has gradually allowed growth in the private sector, the Iranian revolution of 1979 led to an increase in that state's involvement in the economy.

Economies also differ markedly in their size, affluence, rates of growth, and levels of equality. The most commonly used tool for comparing the size of economies is the **gross domestic product (GDP)**, the total market value of goods and services produced in a country in one year. GDP is often mea-

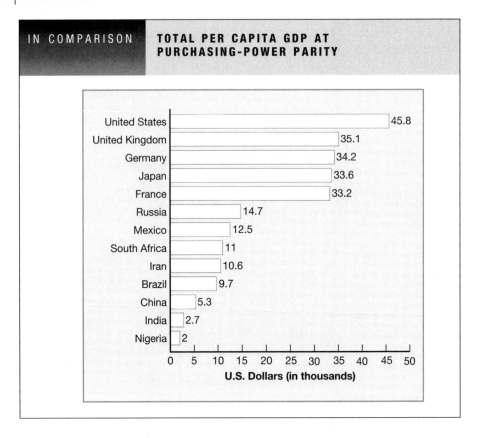

IN COMPARISON   **TOTAL PER CAPITA GDP AT PURCHASING-POWER PARITY**

sured in U.S. dollars at **purchasing-power parity (PPP)**, a mechanism that attempts to estimate the real buying power of income in each country using prices in the United States as a benchmark (see "In Comparison: Total GDP at Purchasing-Power Parity," p. 19). In terms of the overall size of the thirteen economies considered in this volume, the United States, China, Japan, and India dwarf the other cases. It is sometimes more useful, however, to look at **GDP per capita**, which divides the GDP by total population (see "In Comparison: Total Per Capita GDP at Purchasing-Power Parity," above). Because GDP is rarely distributed evenly among the population, the **Gini index** is the most commonly used measure of economic inequality, in which perfect equality is scored as 0, and perfect inequality is scored as 100. Endemic inequality has long been a characteristic of developing countries, such as Brazil, South Africa, Mexico, and India (see "In Comparison: Economic Inequality," p. 21). In wealthy countries like the United States, the economic boom of the 1980s and 1990s led to a growing gap between the rich and the poor and a surprisingly large increase in the percentage of the population in poverty.

It is also important to compare the GDP's rate of growth, often expressed as an average of GDP growth over a number of years. Nine of the thirteen countries considered in this volume enjoyed economic growth between 1975 and 2005, with China and India growing fastest (see "In Comparison: GDP Growth Rate, 1975–2005," p. 22).

The size and wealth of an economy, and even the distribution of wealth, are not necessarily correlated with the affluence or poverty of its citizens. The United Nations produces a Human Development Index (HDI) that considers a variety of indicators of affluence, including health and education ("In Comparison: Human Development Index Scores, 2006," p. 23). When considering GDP per capita and the HDI, one sees that the United States, the United Kingdom, Japan, and France are clearly the most affluent of the countries discussed in this volume.

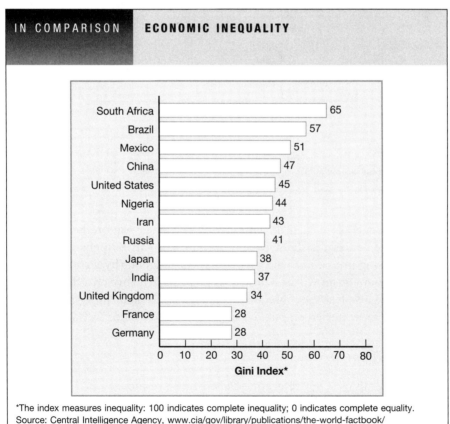

IN COMPARISON   ECONOMIC INEQUALITY

Country	Gini Index*
South Africa	65
Brazil	57
Mexico	51
China	47
United States	45
Nigeria	44
Iran	43
Russia	41
Japan	38
India	37
United Kingdom	34
France	28
Germany	28

*The index measures inequality: 100 indicates complete inequality; 0 indicates complete equality.
Source: Central Intelligence Agency, www.cia/gov/library/publications/the-world-factbook/ (accessed 26 December 2008).

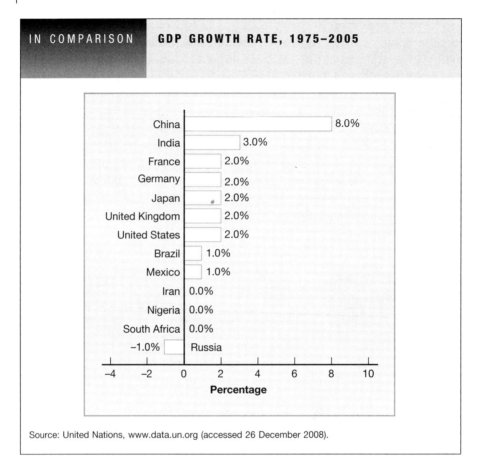

IN COMPARISON   **GDP GROWTH RATE, 1975–2005**

Source: United Nations, www.data.un.org (accessed 26 December 2008).

Governments often struggle with myriad challenges within their economic systems. One concern is the danger of **inflation**, a situation characterized by sustained rising prices. Extremely high levels of inflation (**hyperinflation**) can endanger economic growth and impoverish citizens who live on a fixed income. Governments also fear the consequences of high levels of unemployment, which can place a large burden on public expenditures and reduce the tax base.

The Global Context

A country's politics is not determined solely by domestic factors. Increasingly, international forces shape politics in the context of a rapidly expanding and intensifying set of links among states, societies, and economies. This phenomenon, known as **globalization**, has created new opportunities while posing important challenges to states. Cross-border interactions have long existed, but the trend toward globalization has created a far more extensive and intensive web of relationships among many people across vast distances. People are increasingly interacting regularly and directly through sophisticated international networks involving travel, communication, business, and education.

It is too early to predict the consequences of globalization for governments and citizens of states. Some observers have argued that globalization may eclipse the state, resulting in global political institutions, whereas others contend that states will continue to play an important, albeit changed, role.[14] Governments are increasingly restricted by the international system, because of both international trade agreements (like those promoted by the World Trade Organization) and the need to remain competitive in the international marketplace.

As a result of globalization, a host of international organizations regularly affect domestic politics, economics, and society. **Multinational corporations (MNC)**, firms that produce, distribute, and market goods or services in more

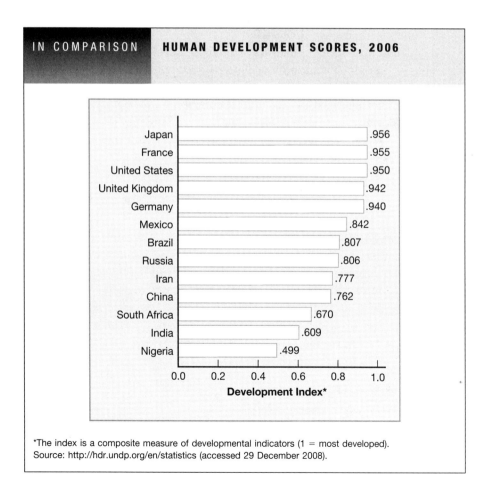

IN COMPARISON   HUMAN DEVELOPMENT SCORES, 2006

Country	Development Index*
Japan	.956
France	.955
United States	.950
United Kingdom	.942
Germany	.940
Mexico	.842
Brazil	.807
Russia	.806
Iran	.777
China	.762
South Africa	.670
India	.609
Nigeria	.499

*The index is a composite measure of developmental indicators (1 = most developed).
Source: http://hdr.undp.org/en/statistics (accessed 29 December 2008).

than one country, are increasingly powerful. They are an important source of **foreign direct investment**, or the purchase of assets in one country by a foreign firm. An array of nongovernmental organizations (NGOs)—Amnesty International and the International Red Cross, for example—are increasingly visible. Also active are **intergovernmental organizations (IGOs)**, which are groups created by states to serve particular policy ends. Some important examples of IGOs are the United Nations, the World Trade Organization, the European Union, the Group of 8 (G8), and the Organization of American States.

A final dimension of globalization, and another example of the growing interconnectedness of states, is the increasing movement of people both within and across borders. Relatively homogeneous societies like France and the United Kingdom have struggled in recent decades to integrate their growing immigrant populations. The United States has become dependent on immigrant labor from Mexico and elsewhere. China's opening to the world economy has drawn millions of rural citizens to its booming coastal cities. More than ever, states find that the environment of globalization limits the policy options open to their governments.

Globalization presents numerous challenges, but the cases in this volume also suggest that globalization has delivered enormous benefits. After World War II, Germany's integration into the European Union led to peace in a region often characterized by war, and it contributed to the rapid economic growth of Germany and France. Since the United Kingdom joined the European Union, the UK's economy has boomed. In China and India, integration into the world economy has lifted millions out of poverty.

CONCLUSION

This introduction briefly summarizes some key concepts and terms used by political scientists to compare political systems. The inquisitive student of comparative politics will find fascinating similarities in the thirteen cases that follow. The commonalities across cases give credence to the utility of the comparative enterprise and justify the analytic comparisons offered. But these countries are also diverse and always changing, reminding us of the daunting challenges facing comparative political study.

NOTES

1. For an excellent collection of essays on the state, see Peter B. Evans, Dietrich Rueschemeyer, and Theda Skocpol, eds., *Bringing the State Back In* (Cambridge: Cambridge University Press, 1985).

2. Robert I. Rotberg, "Failed States in a World of Terror," *Foreign Affairs*, 81, no. 4 (July/August 2002), pp. 127–40.

3. Samuel Huntington, *The Third Wave: Democratization in the Late Twentieth Century* (Norman, OK: University of Oklahoma Press, 1991).

4. Freedom House, www.freedomhouse.org/research/freeworld/2005/combined2005. pdf (accessed 2 February 2006).

5. See, for example, Alfred Stepan with Cindy Skach, "Constitutional Frameworks and Democratic Consolidation: Parliamentarism versus Presidentialism," *World Politics*, 46, no. 1 (January 1993), pp. 1–22.

6. Juan J. Linz and Arturo Valenzuela, eds., *The Failures of Presidential Democracy: The Case of Latin America* (Baltimore: Johns Hopkins University Press, 1994).

7. For an interesting contribution to the debate, see Benjamin Reilly, "Electoral Systems for Divided Societies," *Journal of Democracy*, 13, no. 2 (April 2002), pp. 156–70.

8. Nondemocratic regimes like the former Soviet Union or contemporary Iran often feature elections that impose serious limits on the political opposition. In the Soviet Union, only the Communist Party could run candidates. In Iran, the government has often excluded opposition candidates.

9. For a good overview, see Donald Horowitz, *Ethnic Groups in Conflict* (Berkeley: University of California Press, 2000).

10. Among the many works on public opinion and political participation, see Russell Dalton, *Citizen Politics: Public Opinion and Political Parties in Advanced Industrial Democracies* (Washington, DC: CQ Press, 2005).

11. For a good overview of political ideologies, see Leon Baradat, *Political Ideologies*, 9th ed. (Upper Saddle River, NJ: Prentice Hall, 2005).

12. For a classic treatment of political economy, see Charles Lindblom, *Politics and Markets: The World's Political Economic Systems* (New York: Basic Books, 1977). The field of international political economics studies the relationships between politics and economics on the international level and in political science, is a subfield of international relations.

13. Charles Lindblom, *The Market System: What It Is, How It Works, and What to Make of It* (New Haven, CT: Yale University Press, 2001).

14. For an example of the former, see Martin van Creveld, "The Fate of the State," *Parameters* (Spring 1996), pp. 4–18. For an example of the latter, see Saskia Sassen, "The State and Globalization," in Rodney Bruce Hall and Thomas Biersteker, eds., *The Emergence of Private Authority in Global Governance* (Cambridge: Cambridge University Press, 2002), pp. 94–106.

GLOSSARY OF KEY TERMS ⸻

abstract review   The power of judicial review that allows courts to decide on questions that do not arise from actual legal cases; sometimes occurs even before legislation becomes law.

anarchism   An ideology believing that private property and capitalism lead to inequality, but, like liberals, anarchists place high value on individual political freedom.

authoritarian regimes   Regimes that limit the role of the public in decision making and often deny citizens basic rights and restrict their freedoms.

bicameral legislatures   Legislatures with two chambers.

cabinet   The chief government ministers or officials in government, in charge of such policy areas as defense, agriculture, etc.

charismatic legitimacy   States that are considered legitimate because of their identification with an important individual.

civil society   Organizations outside of the state that help people define and advance their own interests.

clientelism   The state provides benefits to groups of its political supporters.

Communism   An ideology that places the emphasis on creating economic equality instead of individual political and economic freedoms.

Communist regimes   A type of one-party authoritarian regime, in which a Communist party controls most aspects of a country's political and economic system.

comparative politics   The study and comparison of politics across countries.

concrete review   The power of allowing the high court to rule on constitutional issues only on the basis of disputes brought before it.

conservative attitudes   Support the status quo and view change as risky.

constitutional court   The highest judicial body that rules on the constitutionality of laws and other government actions, and, in most political systems, formally oversees the entire judicial structure.

co-optation   When members of the public are brought into a beneficial relationship with the state and government.

corporatism   When citizens are forced to participate in state-sanctioned groups.

democratic regimes   Regimes with rules that emphasize a large role for the public in governance and that protect basic rights and freedoms.

devolution   When central states hand power down to lower levels of government.

electoral system   The system that determines how votes are cast and counted.

ethnicity   The specific attributes and society groups that make one group of people culturally different from others.

executive   The branch of government that carries out the laws and policies of a given state.

failed states   States that experience a complete loss of legitimacy and power, and are overwhelmed by anarchy and violence.

fascism   An ideology that is hostile to the idea of individual freedom and rejects the notion of equality.

federal states   States whose power is divided between the central state and regional or local authorities (such as states, provinces, counties, and cities).

foreign direct investment   The purchase of assets in one country by a foreign firm.

GDP per capita   A measure of affluence that divides Gross Domestic Product by total population.

Gini index   The most commonly used measure of economic inequality.

globalization   The process of expanding and intensifying linkages among states, societies, and economies.

government   The leadership or elite that operates the state.

gross domestic product (GDP)   The total market value of goods and services produced within a country over a period of one year.

head of government   The individual who deals with the everyday tasks of running the state, such as formulating and executing policy.

head of state   The individual who symbolizes and represents the people, both nationally and internationally, embodying and articulating the goals of the regime.

hyperinflation   Extremely high levels of inflation.

illiberal regime   Authoritarian regime that retains the basic structures of democracy but does not protect basic civil liberties.

inflation   A situation of sustained rising prices.

intergovernmental organizations (IGO)   Groups created by states to serve particular policy ends.

judicial review   The mechanism by which the court can review laws and policies and overturn those that are seen as violations of the constitution.

judiciary   The branch of a country's central administration that is concerned with dispensing justice.

legislative-executive relations   The relationship between legislatures and the executive.

legislature   The branch of government that is formally charged with making laws.

legitimacy   The extent to which the state's authority is regarded as right and proper.

liberal attitudes   Promote evolutionary change within the system.

liberalism   Ideology that places a high priority on individual political and economic freedoms, favoring them over any attempts to create economic equality.

lower house   The legislative house that usually represents the population at large.

market   The interaction between the forces of supply and demand that allocate goods and resources.

military regime   Authoritarian regime in which the institution of the military dominates politics.

mixed electoral system   Electoral system that combines single-member districts and proportional representation.

multimember districts (MMD)   When more than one legislative seat is contested in each electoral district.

multinational corporations (MNC)   Firms that produce, distribute, and market in more than one country.

national identity   The extent to which citizens of a country are bound together by a common set of political aspirations.

one-party regime   Authoritarian regime that is dominated by a strong political party that is able to create a broad membership as a source of political control.

party system   The nature of and competition among political parties.

personal dictatorship   Authoritarian regime that is based on the power of a single strong leader who usually relies on charismatic or traditional authority to maintain power.

personality cult   The state-sponsored exaltation of an authoritarian leader.

political attitudes   Views regarding the status quo in any society, specifically the desired pace and methods of political change.

political culture   Patterns of basic norms about politics.

political economy   The study of how politics and economics are related.

political ideologies   Sets of political values regarding the fundamental goals of politics.

political regimes   The norms and rules regarding individual freedom and collective equality, the locus of power, and the use of that power.

presidential system   Legislative-executive system that features a directly elected president with most executive powers.

parliamentary system   Legislative-executive system that features a head of government (often referred to as a prime minister) elected from within the legislature.

property   The idea of ownership of goods and services.

proportional representation (PR)   An electoral system where the percentage of votes a party receives in a district determines how many of that district's seats the party will gain.

public goods   Goods and services that benefit all of society and that are not easily provided by the market.

purchasing-power parity (PPP)   A mechanism that attempts to estimate the real buying power of income in each country, using United States prices as a benchmark.

radical attitudes   Support rapid, extensive, and often revolutionary change.

rational-legal legitimacy   Legitimacy based on a system of laws and procedures that become highly institutionalized.

reactionary attitudes   Promote rapid change to restore political, social, and economic institutions that once existed.

rent seeking   A process where the government allows its supporters to occupy positions of power in order to monopolize state benefits.

semi-presidential system   Legislative-executive system that features a prime minister approved by the legislature *and* a directly elected president.

single-member district (SMD)   The electoral system in which only one representative for each constituency and the candidate with the largest number of votes—and not necessarily a majority—wins the seat.

social democracy   An ideology that places considerable value on equality, but also attempts to protect some individual freedoms.

social expenditures   State provision of public benefits, such as education, health care, and transportation.

states   Organizations that maintain a monopoly of violence over a territory.

strong states   States that perform the basic tasks of defending their borders from outside attacks and defending their authority from internal non-state rivals.

suffrage   The right to vote.

theocracy   Authoritarian regime that has leaders who claim to rule on behalf of God.

totalitarian   Authoritarian regimes that feature a strong, official ideology that seeks to transform fundamental aspects of the state, society, and the economy using a wide array of organizations and the application of force.

traditional legitimacy   When the state is obeyed because it has a long tradition of being obeyed.

unicameral legislatures   Legislatures with a single chamber.

unitary states   States that concentrate most political power in the national capital, allocating very little decision-making power to regions or localities.

upper house   The legislative house that often represents geographic subunits.

weak states   States that have trouble carrying out the basic tasks of defending themselves against external and internal rivals, and often suffer from endemic violence, poor infrastructure, weak rule of law, and an inability to collect taxes.

WEB LINKS _____

CIA World Factbook **www.cia.gov/cia/publications/factbook**
Comparative Politics **web.gc.cuny.edu/jcp**
Freedom House **www.freedomhouse.org**

Inter-Parliamentary Union **www.ipu.org/english/home.htm**
Journal of Democracy **www.journalofdemocracy.org**
Political Science Resource Pages **www.psr.keele.ac.uk/area.htm**
World Bank **www.worldbank.org**
The WWW Virtual Library: International Affairs Resources
   www2.etown.edu/vl

2 UNITED KINGDOM

Head of state: Queen Elizabeth II
(since February 6, 1952)

Head of government:
Prime Minister Gordon Brown
(since June 27, 2007)

Capital: London

Total land size: 244,820 sq km

Population: 61 million

GDP at PPP: 2.1 trillion US$

GDP per capita at PPP: $35,100

Human development index ranking: 16

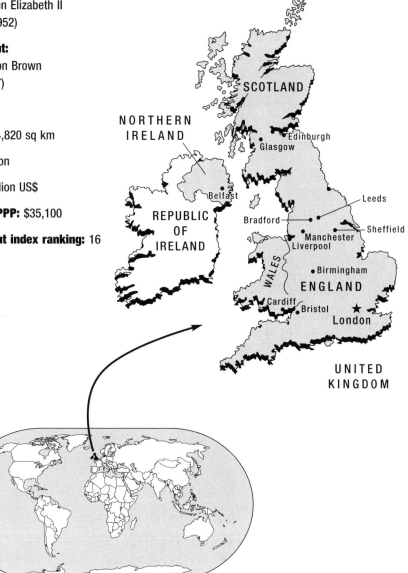

INTRODUCTION

Why Study This Case?

For many reasons, most introductory works about comparative politics begin with a study of the United Kingdom (UK). As the primogenitor of modern democracy, the UK's political system is at once strikingly unique and a model for many other liberal democracies. The UK is the world's oldest democracy. Its transition to democracy was gradual, beginning with thirteenth-century limitations on absolute monarchs and continuing incrementally to the establishment of the rule of law in the seventeenth century and the extension of suffrage to women in the twentieth century. The democratization process persists today, with reforms of the anachronistic upper house of the legislature, decentralization of power, and ongoing discussions about electoral reform. Unlike many other democracies, the UK cannot attach a specific date or event to the advent of its democracy. The UK is also unusual in that the main political rules of the game in that country have not been seriously interrupted or radically altered since the mid-seventeenth century.

The United Kingdom is one of only a handful of democracies without a written constitution. The longevity and stability of its democracy have thus depended to a large extent on both traditional legitimacy and a unique political culture of accommodation and moderation. Although its constitution is unwritten, many aspects of its democracy have been adopted by a number of the world's other democracies, especially in areas of the globe that were once part of the far-flung British Empire.

Finally, the United Kingdom deserves careful study because it is the birthplace of the Industrial Revolution, which turned it into the world's leading economic and political power for several hundred years. Some have attributed the UK's early industrialization to the emergence of liberal ideology. The UK was also the first major industrialized country to experience an extended economic decline after World War II, the reasons for which have been much debated.

The United Kingdom remains a fascinating case. In 1979, **Margaret Thatcher** of the **Conservative Party** was the first leader of an industrial democracy to experiment with neoliberal economic policies in an attempt to stem economic decline. The policies were very controversial within the UK but widely emulated in other democracies, including the United States. Even with Thatcher's resignation in 1990, the Conservatives (Tories) remained in power until the 1997 election when they were ousted by the **Labour Party**. Under the leadership of **Tony Blair**, and his successor **Gordon Brown**, the

Labour Party embraced many of the liberal policies executed by Thatcher and her conservative successors. These policies have become known as the **Third Way**.

Major Geographic and Demographic Features

Since 1801, the **United Kingdom of Great Britain and Northern Ireland** has been the formal name of the United Kingdom. Separated from France by the English Channel, Great Britain itself consists of three nations (England, Scotland, and Wales). These three nations plus the northeastern part of the island of Ireland constitute the United Kingdom. The remainder of Ireland is called the Republic of Ireland. Although it is confusing, citizens of the UK are often referred to as British or Britons even if they live in Northern Ireland. Most Welsh, Scots, and Northern Irish consider themselves British, but it would be unwise to call a resident of Edinburgh (in Scotland) or Cardiff (in Wales) English.

The United Kingdom is roughly the size of Oregon and about two thirds the size of Japan. It has approximately 60 million residents, nearly twice the population of California and about half that of Japan. The UK's population is not equally distributed among England, Scotland, Wales, and Northern Ireland. Five of six Britons live in England. The UK can be considered a multiethnic state because it contains Scottish, Welsh, and English citizens, who have distinct cultures and languages. Racially, however, the UK is relatively homogeneous; its nonwhite population, composed mainly of immigrants from the UK's former colonies, is only about 3 percent of the total. The majority of those immigrants come from the Indian Subcontinent, and about one third are from the Caribbean.

The UK's physical separation from the European mainland ended in 1994 with the inauguration of the Channel Tunnel, which links Britain and France. For much of British history, the country's isolation provided some protection from the conflicts and turmoil that afflicted the rest of Europe. A diminished fear of invasion may help explain the historically small size and minimal political importance of the UK's standing army (and the relative importance and strength of its navy). In addition, it may help explain the UK's late adherence to the European Union, its unwillingness to replace the British pound with the euro (the single European currency), and its continued skepticism about European unification.

Historical Development of the State

British citizens owe their allegiance to the Crown, the enduring symbol of the United Kingdom's state, rather than to a written constitution. The Crown sym-

\multicolumn{2}{c}{TIME LINE OF POLITICAL DEVELOPMENT}
Year	Event
1215	King John forced to sign Magna Carta, thereby agreeing to a statement of the rights of English Barons
1295	Convening of Model Parliament of Edward I, the first representative parliament
1529	Reformation Parliament summoned by Henry VIII, beginning process of cutting ties to the Roman Catholic Church
1628	Charles I forced to accept Petition of Right, Parliament's statement of civil rights in return for funds
1642–48	English Civil War fought between Royalists and Parliamentarians
1649	Charles I tried and executed
1689	Bill of Rights issued by Parliament, establishing a constitutional monarchy in Britain
1707	Act of Union put into effect, uniting kingdoms of England and Scotland
1721	Sir Robert Walpole effectively made Britain's first prime minister
1832–67	Reform Acts passed, extending right to vote to virtually all urban males and some in the countryside
1900	Labour Party founded in Britain
1916–22	Anglo-Irish War fought, culminating in establishment of independent Republic of Ireland, with Northern Ireland remaining part of the United Kingdom
1973	UK made a member of the European Economic Community (now the European Union)
1979–90	Margaret Thatcher served as prime minister
1982	Falklands War fought with Argentina
1997–2007	Tony Blair served as prime minister
2007	Gordon Brown becomes prime minister

bolizes far more than just the monarchy or even Her Majesty's government. It represents, of course, the ceremonial and symbolic trappings of the British state. In addition, it represents the rules (or regime) as well as the unhindered capacity (the sovereignty) to enforce and administer these rules and to secure the country's borders.

The evolutionary changes of the state over the past eight centuries have been thoroughgoing and not without violence. But in comparison with political change elsewhere in the world, the development of the modern British state has been gradual, piecemeal, and peaceful.

EARLY DEVELOPMENT

Although we commonly think of the United Kingdom as a stable and unified nation-state, the country experienced repeated invasions over a period of about 1,500 years. Celts, Romans, Angles and Saxons, Danes, and finally Normans invaded the British Isles, each leaving important legacies. For example, the Germanic Angles and Saxons left their language, except in Wales and Scotland and other areas that they could not conquer. Local languages remained dominant there until the eighteenth and nineteenth centuries. Today, we still refer to those areas as the UK's **Celtic fringe**.

In terms of the UK's political development, another important legacy was the emergence of **common law**, a system based on local customs and precedent rather than formal legal codes. That system forms the basis of the contemporary legal systems of the UK (with the exception of Scotland), the United States, and many former British colonies.[1]

The last wave of invasions, by the Normans, occurred in 1066. The Normans were Danish Vikings who occupied northern France. In Britain, they replaced the Germanic ruling class and imposed central rule. Politically, their most important legacy was the institution of feudalism, which they brought from the European continent. Under feudalism, lords provided vassals with military protection and economic support in exchange for labor and military service. Though hardly a democratic institution, feudalism did create a system of mutual obligations between lords and peasants on one level, and between monarchs and lords at another level. Indeed, some scholars have seen in these obligations the foundation for the eventual limits on royal power. The most important initial document in this regard is the **Magna Carta**, which British nobles obliged King John to sign in 1215 and which became a royal promise to uphold feudal customs and rights. The Magna Carta set an important precedent by limiting the power of British monarchs and subjecting them to the law. As a result, the United Kingdom never experienced the type of royal absolutism that was common in other countries (for example, in Russia), and this in turn helped pave the way for public control over government and the state.

The UK was fortunate to resolve relatively early in its historical development certain conflicts that other states would experience later in the modern era. A prime example is the religious divide. During the reign of Henry VIII (1509–47), a major dispute between the British monarch and the Vatican (the center of the Roman Catholic Church) had unintended consequences. When the Catholic Church failed to grant Henry a divorce, he used **Parliament** to pass laws that effectively took England out of the Catholic Church and replaced Catholicism with a Protestant church that could be controlled by the English state instead of by Rome.

The creation of a state-controlled Anglican Church led to a religious institution that was weaker and less autonomous than its counterparts in other European countries. Supporters of Catholicism fought unsuccessfully to regain power, and religion never plagued the UK as a polarizing force the way it did in so many other countries. Northern Ireland, where the split between Protestants and Catholics continues to create political division, is the bloody exception to the rule. A second unintended consequence of the creation of the Anglican Church was that Henry VIII's use of Parliament to sanction the changes strengthened and legitimized Parliament's power. As with the Magna Carta, institutional changes helped pave the way for democratic control—even if that result was not foreseen at the time.

THE EMERGENCE OF THE MODERN BRITISH STATE

Compared with its European neighbors, the United Kingdom had a more constrained monarchy. This is not to say that British rulers were weak. But in addition to the early checks on monarchic rule, three major developments in the seventeenth and eighteenth centuries decisively undermined the power of British sovereigns and are crucial to understanding why the UK was one of the first nations to develop democratic control.

First, the crowning of James I (a Scot) in 1603 united Scotland and England but created a political crisis. James was an absolutist at heart and resisted limits on his power imposed by Parliament. He sought to raise taxes without first asking Parliament, and his son Charles I, whose reign began in 1625, continued flaunting his royal power and eventually precipitated civil war. The **English Civil War** (1640–1649) pitted the defenders of Charles against the supporters of Parliament, who won the bitter struggle and executed Charles I in 1649.

For eleven years (1649–1660), England had no monarch and functioned as a republic led by Oliver Cromwell, whose rule soon became a military dictatorship. Parliament restored the monarchy in 1660 with the ascension of Charles II, but its power was forever weakened.

Second, when James II, a brother of Charles II, inherited the throne in 1685, the monarchy and Parliament again faced off. James was openly Catholic, and Parliament feared a return to Catholicism and absolute rule. In 1688, Parliament removed James II and sent him into exile. In his place, Parliament installed James's Protestant daughter Mary and her Dutch husband, William. A year later, Parliament enacted the Bill of Rights, institutionalizing its political supremacy. Since that time, monarchs have owed their position to Parliament. This so-called Glorious Revolution was a key turning point in the creation of the constitutional monarchy.

Third, in 1714, Parliament installed the current dynastic family by crowning George I (of German royalty). The monarch, who spoke little English, was forced to rely heavily on his **cabinet** (his top advisers, or ministers) and, specifically, on his **prime minister**, who coordinated the work of the other ministers. From 1721 to 1742, Sir Robert Walpole fashioned the position of prime minister into much of what the office is today. By the late eighteenth century, in large part in reaction to the loss of the colonies in America, prime ministers and their cabinets were no longer selected by monarchs but were instead appointed by Parliament. Monarchs never again had the power to select members of the government.[2]

THE BRITISH EMPIRE

The United Kingdom began its overseas expansion in the sixteenth century, and by the early nineteenth century it had vanquished its main European rivals to become the world's dominant military, commercial, and cultural power. Its navy helped open new overseas markets for its burgeoning domestic industry, and by the empire's zenith in 1870, the UK controlled about one quarter of all world trade and probably had the wealthiest economy. The dimensions of the British Empire were truly exceptional. In the nineteenth century, it governed one quarter of the world's population, directly ruled almost fifty countries, and dominated many more with its commercial muscle.

Paralleling the gradual process of democratization in the UK, the erosion of the British Empire was also slow and incremental. It began with the loss of the American colonies in the late eighteenth century, though subsequently the empire continued to expand in Asia and Africa. By the early nineteenth century, however, it had begun to shrink. Following World War I, the UK granted independence to a few of its former colonies, including Egypt and most of Ireland. With the conclusion of World War II, the tide had turned against the empire. International sentiment favoring self-determination for subject peoples, local resistance in many colonies, the costs of the war, and the burden of maintaining far-flung colonies helped spell the end of the British Empire. Independence was willingly granted to most of the remaining colonial possessions throughout Southeast Asia, Africa, and the Caribbean.

The United Kingdom managed to retain control of a few small colonies, and in 1982 it fought a brief war with Argentina to retain possession of the remote Falkland Islands. One of the UK's last colonial possessions, Hong Kong, was returned to China in 1997. Today, the **Commonwealth** includes the UK and fifty-four of its former colonies and serves to maintain the economic and cultural ties established during the UK's long imperial rule.

THE INDUSTRIAL REVOLUTION

The United Kingdom lays claim to being the first industrial nation, and industrialization helped support the expansion of its empire. The country's early industrialization, which began in the late eighteenth century and developed slowly, was based on its dominance in textiles, machinery, and iron production. By the mid-nineteenth century, most of the UK's workforce had moved away from the countryside to live in urban areas. While industrialization dramatically changed British politics and society, the process did not create the kind of political upheaval and instability that was seen in many late-developing nations, where it occurred more rapidly. Because the British were the first to industrialize, the UK faced little initial competition and therefore amassed tremendous wealth. Its early prosperity may have facilitated its first steps toward democracy.[3]

But the benefits of early industrialization may also have been factors in the United Kingdom's economic decline. As a world leader, the UK spent lavishly on its empire and led the Allied forces in World Wars I and II. Although the Allies won both wars, the UK was drained economically. The end of World War II also signaled the end of colonial rule, and the UK began to relinquish its empire. As the first industrialized country, the UK would also be one of the first industrialized nations to experience economic decline. When British industries faced new competition and obsolescence after World War II, the country found it increasingly difficult to reform its economy.

GRADUAL DEMOCRATIZATION

We have seen how Parliament weakened the power of the British monarchs, but at the same time we should note that Parliament itself originally represented the interests of the British elite: only the wealthy could vote. The UK had an "upper" **House of Lords**, which represented the aristocracy, and a "lower" **House of Commons**, which represented the interests of the lower aristocracy and the merchant class. In addition, by the time Parliament was established, British monarchs were no longer absolute rulers, although they continued to wield considerable political power. Two factors gradually democratized Parliament and further weakened monarchical power.

The first was the rise of political parties, which emerged in the eighteenth century as cliques of nobles but eventually reached out to a broader sector of society for support. The two largest cliques became the UK's first parties: the Conservatives (Tories) supported the monarch, and the **Liberals (Whigs)** opposed the policies of the monarch. The Whigs were the first to cultivate support among members of the UK's burgeoning commercial class, many of whom were still excluded from the political system.

The second was the expansion of suffrage. In 1832, the Whigs were able to push through a Reform Act that doubled the size of the British electorate, though it still excluded more than 90 percent of British adults. Over the next century, both parties gradually supported measures to expand the suffrage, hoping in part to gain a political windfall. The process culminated in 1928, when women over the age of twenty-one in the UK were granted the right to vote.

The gradual expansion of the vote to include all adult citizens forced the political parties to respond to demands for additional services. The new voters wanted the expansion of such public goods as health care, education, and housing, and they looked to the state to provide them. It was the Labour Party, as the main representative of the working class, that pushed for policies that would develop basic social services for all citizens, or what we commonly call the welfare state. The British workers who had defended the United Kingdom so heroically during World War II returned from that conflict with a new sense of entitlement, and they elected Labour to power in 1945. Armed with a parliamentary majority, the Labour government quickly moved to implement a welfare state. This was accompanied by the nationalization of a number of sectors of industry, such as coal, utilities, rail, and health care.

POSTWAR POLITICS AND THE EXPANSION OF THE STATE

The Labour Party initiated the welfare state, but British Conservatives generally supported it during much of the postwar period in what has been called the postwar **collectivist consensus**. By the 1970s, however, the British economy was in crisis, and a new breed of Tories (dubbed neoliberals) began to blame the UK's economic decline on the excesses of the welfare state.

When Margaret Thatcher became prime minister in 1979, she broke with traditional Tory support for the welfare state and pledged to diminish the state's role in the economy. She sought to lower taxes and cut state spending on costly social services, and she replaced some state services (in areas as diverse as housing and mass transit) with private enterprise. Her government thus marked the end of the postwar collectivist consensus. Yet in some ways, a new consensus has formed around Thatcher's reforms. Even the Labour Party, traditionally the staunch defender of an elaborate welfare state, has come to accept the Thatcherite view of more limited social expenditures and privatization.[4]

POLITICAL REGIME

The political regime of the United Kingdom is notable among the world's democracies because of its highly **majoritarian** features. Under the rules of British politics, the majority in Parliament has virtually unchecked power. Unlike political parties in other democracies, even parliamentary democracies, the majority party in the UK can enact policies with few checks from other branches of government. Again unlike other democracies, there are no formal constitutional limits on the central government, few judicial restraints,

TWO DOMINANT PRIME MINISTERS: THATCHER AND BLAIR

Margaret Thatcher and Tony Blair are arguably the United Kingdom's most important and controversial prime ministers since the end of World War II. Despite the fact that Thatcher, who served from 1979 to 1990, was a Conservative and Blair, who served from 1997 to 2007, a Labourite, they share some remarkable similarities. Defying the Conservative Party's traditional ties to the aristocracy, Thatcher was a grocer's daughter who came to political power through sheer force of will. She steered the Tories away from the party's traditional social paternalism and toward a more free-market economy. Blair reoriented the Labour Party away from its traditional hostility toward the free market and sought to make the party less dependent on its trade union supporters. Both of these leaders are credited with having reinvigorated political parties that were in crisis after having suffered from long periods of being out of government.

Once in office and armed with large majorities in the House of Commons, both leaders implemented important domestic reforms that were radical departures from the past. The Iron Lady, as Thatcher was dubbed, undertook a series of dramatic steps to reverse Britain's economic stagnation and to repeal the social democratic policies that had been created under the collectivist consensus. Her government privatized many state-owned businesses and allowed numerous ailing firms to go bankrupt. Thatcher also confronted and eventually defeated powerful trade unions during widespread strikes by unions that opposed her policies. One particularly controversial but popular policy was her decision to sell millions of public housing units to their occupants in order to create more private homeowners in the UK. Her boldest policy was the ill-advised introduction of the so-called poll tax, designed to move local governments' tax burden from property owners to all citizens. This legislation generated widespread resentment and even rioting. Blair's domestic reforms were no less dramatic, although they were less controversial. Although he continued most of Thatcher's economic policies, he implemented an ambitious set of constitutional reforms. Blair devolved power to regional and local governments (some of which had lost power under Thatcher), creating new legislatures in Scotland and Wales. He began to reform the archaic House of Lords, established a Supreme Court, and made the central bank (The Bank of Britain) independent of the government.

In their foreign policies, both leaders favored an extremely close relationship with the United States, often at the expense of relations with the UK's European allies. Thatcher and Blair also took the country into controversial wars. Thatcher launched a costly war against Argentina in 1982 to retake the distant Falkland Islands, and the UK's victory in that war temporarily buoyed Thatcher's political success. Blair joined the United States in the Iraq War, a move that was bitterly opposed by many within his own party and by a large majority of the UK public. As the war bogged down, Blair's popularity plummeted.

Thatcher and Blair were exceptional communicators with charismatic personalities that charmed the public. Thatcher was known for her tough, often blunt public statements and her fierce debating skills. Blair had a wit and charm that captivated Britons for over a decade. However, both were unpopular by the end of their time in office. Thatcher was viewed by many as insensitive and out of touch, and Blair was increasingly viewed as a spinmaster who often skirted the truth. Both of them stubbornly refused to budge from policies (like Thatcher's poll tax, or Blair's stance on the Iraq War) that were bitterly opposed by the British public.

After over a decade in power, Thatcher and Blair each resigned their positions without ever having lost an election. Thatcher quit when she faced growing opposition and a challenge to her leadership with the Conservative Party. After Labour won its third consecutive majority in the Commons, the increasingly beleaguered Blair agreed to step down and hand power to his longtime Chancellor of the Exchequer, Gordon Brown. One final similarity is worth noting: Thatcher and Blair handed power to competent but less charismatic party leaders who proved less controversial and less successful.

and no constitutionally sanctioned local authorities to dilute the power of the government in London. Only the historical traditions of democratic political culture, and, increasingly, restictions imposed by the European Union, keep the British government from abusing its power.

Political Institutions

THE CONSTITUTION

The United Kingdom has no single document that defines the rules of politics, but the constitution is generally understood to include a number of written documents and unwritten rules that most British citizens view as inviolable.[5] In 1215, the Magna Carta set a precedent for limits on monarchical power. Other documents include the 1689 Bill of Rights and the 1707 Act of Union, which united Scotland and England. What makes the UK's constitution particularly unusual is that it also consists of various acts of Parliament, judicial decisions, customs, and traditions. Since Parliament is viewed as sovereign, the democratically elected lower house of the legislature can amend any aspect of the constitution by a simple majority vote. This power extends to the very existence of the monarchy, the powers of regions or local governments, and the powers of the houses of Parliament. Unlike most other democratic regimes, the UK has no constitutional court.

The absence of written constitutional guarantees has consistently alarmed human rights advocates and has given rise to demands for a more formal constitution or, at the very least, *written* constitutional protections of basic rights.

ESSENTIAL POLITICAL FEATURES

- Legislative-executive system: parliamentary
- Legislature: Parliament
- Lower house: House of Commons
- Upper house: House of Lords
- Unitary or federal division of power: unitary
- Main geographic subunits: England, Scotland, Wales, Northern Ireland
- Electoral system for lower house: plurality
- Chief judicial body: House of Lords

Since 1973, when the UK became a member of the European Union, British citizens have increasingly appealed to European laws to protect their rights. In response to such concerns, in 1998 the government incorporated into law the European Convention on Human Rights, a document that now serves as a basic set of constitutional liberties.

Although it is a source of concern to some political analysts, others have lauded the UK's constitution for its unparalleled flexibility and responsiveness to the majority. Changing the constitution in most democracies is a cumbersome and often politically charged process. In the UK, however, changes can be implemented more quickly and without lengthy political battles. Admirers of the British constitution argue that it has delivered political stability since the late seventeenth century; in their view, a formal document does not necessarily make for a more democratic government.

THE CROWN

We can think of the **Crown**, the legislature, the judiciary, the prime minister, and the cabinet as the main branches of government in the United Kingdom. In most respects, we can think of the British Crown as the head of state. The Crown, embodied by the monarch, is the symbolic representative of the continuity of the British state. The monarch (currently Queen Elizabeth II) thus acts as a purely ceremonial figure, and on matters of importance she must act at the behest of the cabinet even though the cabinet is referred to collectively as Her Majesty's government. The British monarchy is a continual source of popular fascination, in part because the institution and all its pomp and circumstance appear to be a relic in the twenty-first century. The reality, however, is less glamorous. The British monarch today is essentially a paid civil servant: the government allocates a budget to cover the royal family's expenses, and the queen spends much of her time signing papers, dedicating public works, and performing diplomatic functions.

The UK's monarchy has survived for centuries precisely because it has agreed to act constitutionally. Since the nineteenth century, this has meant that it must always follow the orders of elected representatives. For example, although the monarch always selects the head of government, the choice must always be the leader of the majority party in the lower house of Parliament. Only in the unlikely event that no clear majority is present in the legislature could a monarch have any real influence on politics, and even in that case her choice would be severely constrained. Likewise, the monarch is officially the commander of the British armed forces, but it is the prime minister who has the power to declare wars and sign treaties.

The British monarchy is a hereditary institution, following the rule of primogeniture: the oldest son (or oldest daughter if there are no sons) inherits the throne. However, a cardinal principle of the UK's constitution is that Parliament may choose the monarch. In 1701, for example, Parliament imposed a new dynastic family (the Hanovers) to replace the reigning Stuarts. Since that time, only Protestants have been allowed to succeed to the throne. Since 1952, Elizabeth II has been queen, succeeding her father, George VI. Despite the series of high-profile scandals that have rocked the monarchy during her reign, polls consistently show that the institution remains highly popular, as evidenced by the public celebrations of the queen's golden jubilee (fifty years on the throne) in 2002. There have been occasional movements in the UK to eliminate the monarchy, but these have failed to garner much support. In spite of scandals and the costs of royalty, public support for the institution remains strong. A 2006 poll, for example, showed nearly three quarters of the public in favor of retaining the institution.[6]

The Branches of Government

THE PRIME MINISTER

Parliament is supreme in the United Kingdom's political system, but real power is concentrated in the prime minister and the cabinet. The prime minister is the head of government and, as in all parliamentary systems, must be an elected member of the legislature. He or she is the head of the largest party in the lower house, the House of Commons. Once named by the monarch (a mere formality), the prime minister selects his or her cabinet.

British prime ministers are probably the most powerful heads of government of any contemporary democracy. Because they can expect their parliamentary majority to approve all legislation, because party discipline in the UK is very strong, and because there are few checks on the power of the central government, prime ministers usually get their way. Prime ministers wield less power when their parties hold a slim majority (as was the case with John Major from 1990 to 1997) or when they are forced to depend on a coalition of parties (which is rare). Like any **member of Parliament (MP)**, prime ministers in the UK are elected to a maximum term of five years, but they alone can decide to call elections at any time before that term has expired. Prime ministers commonly call early elections to take advantage of favorable political conditions. After the UK's victory in the 1982 Falklands War, for exam-

STRUCTURE OF THE GOVERNMENT

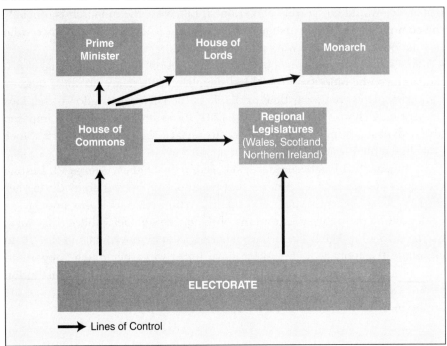

ple, Margaret Thatcher called an election despite the fact that she had two years remaining on her mandate.

Prime ministers are subject to a legislative **vote of no confidence**. This would occur if a government deemed a measure to be of high importance, but the legislature rejected that measure. In such situations, either the entire cabinet must resign (and be replaced by a new one) or new elections must be called. Although such a check on the government exists, it is rarely used; over the past seventy years, only one government has been toppled by a legislative vote of no confidence. In fact, the prime minister can use the threat of a no-confidence vote as a way to rally support. In March 2003, Tony Blair submitted a motion to the House of Commons to support the use of force against Iraq even though a prime minister may take the country to war without parliamentary approval. Yet he chose to submit his decision to the House of Commons, threatening to resign if he failed to win support. The tactic worked: despite widespread opposition to the war among Labour Party backbenchers, a large majority in Parliament supported the war.

Prime ministers play a number of roles. As leaders of their party, they must maintain the support of their fellow MPs, a condition that has plagued every prime minister since Thatcher. They must appear in the legislature weekly for a televised question period, during which they must defend government policies and answer questions from MPs—and in so doing display strong oratorical skills.[7] As head of government, the prime minister must direct the activity of the cabinet and smooth over differences among cabinet members; as a politician, he or she is expected to guide his or her party to victory in general elections. Even though the monarch is head of state and the nation, the prime minister is expected to provide national leadership. British prime ministers are also diplomats and world leaders, roles that Tony Blair especially relished, despite the objections of many of his own party members, particularly regarding the war in Iraq.

Prime ministers are always seasoned political veterans with, on average, more than two decades of experience in the House of Commons. As a result, British prime ministers are usually outstanding debaters, effective communicators, and skilled negotiators. In the British system, a political outsider has virtually no chance of becoming prime minister: one must move up the ranks of the party before gaining the highest office.

THE CABINET

Cabinets evolved out of the group of experts who originally advised Britain's monarchs. Contemporary British cabinets have about twenty members (called

---

PRIME MINISTER GORDON BROWN

The United Kingdom's current prime minister, Gordon Brown is the scholarly and taciturn son of a minister of a Church of Scotland. As is the norm in the UK, he spent decades training for his current job. After earning a Ph.D. in political science, he was first elected to parliament in 1983 and served for more than a decade as Tony Blair's Chancellor of the Exchequer. In 1997, Brown agreed not to contest the Labour Party leadership election, yielding to his close colleague, Blair.

Brown was widely credited with the sound economic policies that fueled the UK's economic boom during Blair's governments. As Blair's popularity waned, Brown was increasingly seen as leading the internal Labour Party opposition to Blair.

Upon taking office in 2007, Brown faced several immediate problems. First, the UK economy began to stagnate after a decade of strong growth. Brown failed to depart substantially from some of the more unpopular policies of his predecessor and was unable to establish his own political identity. Brown initially pledged to hold elections in order to win his own mandate, but clumsily reversed course when polls showed that Labour would lose. In the 2008 local elections, a revived Conservative opposition scored important victories that further embarrassed the government.

Perhaps most seriously, Brown has none of the charisma and charm that favored Tony Blair. As one leading observer wrote, "[Brown] is a lousy communicator. A failing in any leader, for Mr. Brown this weakness has proved catastrophic."[8]

ministers), all of whom must be members of Parliament. They are usually from the lower house but occasionally are members of the upper house, the House of Lords. The prime minister generally appoints leading party officials to the top cabinet positions.

As in most democracies, cabinet ministers in the United Kingdom preside over their individual government departments and are responsible for answering to Parliament (during question time) about actions of the bureaucracies they oversee. The most important ministries are the Foreign Office (which conducts foreign policy), the Home Office (which oversees the judiciary), and the Exchequer (whose minister, called the chancellor, oversees financial policy as head of the central bank).

One unwritten rule of cabinet behavior in the UK is **collective responsibility**; even when individual cabinet ministers oppose a given policy, the entire cabinet must appear unified and take responsibility for the policy. Cabinet ministers who cannot support a decision must resign and return to the legislature (in 2003, three members of Blair's cabinet resigned over the war in Iraq).

THE LEGISLATURE

The British legislature, called Parliament, is perhaps the most powerful legislature on earth, due in large part to the lack of constitutional constraints, which we have discussed above. The concentration of power is even more impressive when it is considered that of the two chambers of the legislature, the House of Commons and the House of Lords, only the former has any real power.

The House of Commons currently consists of 646 members of Parliament representing individual districts in the United Kingdom of Great Britain and Northern Ireland. Members are elected for a maximum term of five years, though new elections may be called before the expiration of the term. Government and opposition parties face each other in a tiny rectangular chamber, with the members of the government and the leaders of the opposition sitting in the front row. The other MPs, called backbenchers, sit behind their leaders. A politically neutral Speaker of the House presides.

Despite the enormous power of the House of Commons, individual legislators are far less powerful than their counterparts in the United States. They receive relatively paltry salaries and have very small staffs and few resources. In parliamentary systems in general, the largest party elects the prime minister as head of government; as a result, political parties, not individual members, are what matter. Thus, British legislators follow the lead of their party and, for fear of weakening party cohesion, do not undertake the type of individual initiative common to representatives in the United States. Moreover, parties designate certain members to serve as whips, who are charged with enforcing the party line.

Despite these limitations, MPs do perform important tasks. They actively debate issues, participate in legislative committees (though these are less powerful than their U.S. counterparts), vote on legislation proposed by the government, and have the power to remove the prime minister through a vote of no confidence. Finally, although the government initiates the vast majority of legislation, individual members propose measures from time to time.

Thus, despite the doctrine of parliamentary supremacy, the legislature in the UK mostly deliberates, ratifies, and scrutinizes policies that are proposed by the executive. The government is usually able to impose its will on its majority in the House of Commons. MPs vote with their parties more than 90 percent of the time. Nevertheless, even governments with large majorities occasionally lose the vote in the lower house, suggesting that MPs sometimes act independently.

The House of Lords is another uniquely British institution. Once the more powerful of Parliament's two chambers, it has gradually become virtually powerless, having lost most of its power nearly a century ago. The House of Lords was considered the *upper* house not only because it represented the top aristocracy but also because it was considered the more powerful of the two houses. As the UK underwent democratization, it made sense for a chamber of appointed members of the aristocracy to lose most of its power. True to the British desire to accommodate tradition, the House of Lords remains as yet another reminder of the UK's predemocratic past.

The House of Lords is composed of about 750 members, or peers, who have traditionally been appointed in several ways. **Life peers** are distinguished citizens appointed for life by the Crown upon the recommendation of the prime minister. Law lords are top legal experts, appointed for life, who play an important role in legal appeals. About a dozen top officials of the Church of England are also members of the House of Lords. The most controversial component of the House of Lords is composed of **hereditary peers**, members of the aristocracy (dukes, earls, barons, and so on) who until recently had been able to bequeath their seats to their offspring. In 1999, the Labour government eliminated virtually all of the hereditary peers as part of a reform of the upper chamber.

The House of Lords has no veto power over legislation, but it can delay some legislation up to one year and occasionally persuades governments to amend legislation. The most important role of the Lords has been as the UK's court of last appeal, and the legal expertise of some members of the Lords is often called on to improve legislation. However, legislation passed in 2005 created an independent Supreme Court that is due to be inaugurated in 2009 and that will deprive the Lords of most of its judicial influence. Currently, there is considerable debate in the UK about the future of the upper house and whether it should be directly elected and given greater powers.[9]

THE JUDICIAL SYSTEM

Compared with the United States and even compared with other parliamentary democracies, the judiciary in the United Kingdom has a relatively minor role. There is no tradition of judicial review (the right of courts to strike down legislation that contradicts the constitution) because the British parliament is always supreme: any law that is passed by the legislature is, by definition, constitutional. Thus the role of the courts in the UK is mainly to ensure that parliamentary statutes have been followed. Beginning in 2009 the UK will create a Supreme Court of the United Kingdom that will be the highest court of appeal on most legal matters.

Over the past couple of decades, however, a slow move toward greater political involvement of the courts has occurred. In part, this is because British governments have sought legal interpretations that would support their actions. A second factor in this development is the adoption of international laws, such as the European Convention on Human Rights, that codified for the first time a set of basic civil rights. These laws have given the courts new powers to strike down legislation as unconstitutional, though these powers have so far been used sparingly. Still, the days when we could speak of the UK as lacking judicial review may be slowly coming to an end.

Judges are selected from among distinguished jurists by the lord chancellor (the minister who heads the judiciary). They serve until retirement unless they are removed by Parliament (which has never happened). To the extent that the vast majority of judges come from relatively wealthy families and are educated at elite universities, it could be assumed that the judiciary has a conservative bias.

The legal system, based on common law and developed in the twelfth century, stands in stark contrast to the stricter code law practiced in the rest of Europe, which is less focused on precedent and interpretation. Like most democracies, the UK has an elaborate hierarchy of civil and criminal courts, and a complex system of appeals. The House of Lords, of which many members are distinguished jurists, is the highest judicial authority in the UK, though it does not serve the kind of constitutional-review function that is found in the U.S. Supreme Court.

The Electoral System

Like the United States, the United Kingdom uses the single-member district (SMD) system based on plurality, or what is often known as first past the post (FPTP). Each of the 646 constituencies elects one MP, and that member needs to win only a plurality of votes (that is, more than any other candidate), not a majority. Electoral constituencies are based mostly on population, and they average about 65,000 voters. Constituencies are revised every five to seven years by a government commission.

The implications of FPTP are fairly clear. First, as shown in the table below ("Consequences of the British Electoral System, 1987–2005"), the system helps maintain the dominance of the two main political parties, Labour and Con-

Consequences of the British Electoral System, 1987–2005			
Election Years	**% of Votes**	**Seats Won**	**% of Seats**
Labour			
1987	31	229	35.0
1992	34	271	42.0
1997	43	419	64.0
2001	41	412	62.5
2005	35	355	54.9
Conservative			
1987	42	375	58.0
1992	42	336	52.0
1997	31	165	25.0
2001	32	166	25.0
2005	32	197	30.0
Liberal Democrat			
1987	23	22	3.0
1992	18	20	3.0
1997	17	46	7.0
2001	18	52	8.0
2005	22	62	10.0
Others			
1987	4	24	4.0
1992	6	24	4.0
1997	9	29	4.0
2001	9	29	4.0
2005	10	32	5.0

Percentages do not always equal 100 percent due to rounding.

GOVERNING LONDON: "RED KEN" AND BORIS

As prime minister, Tony Blair reinvigorated the UK's system of local government that had been weakened under Conservative governments. Blair restored the post of Mayor of London that Thatcher had eliminated. The first occupant of that new office was Ken Livingstone, nicknamed Red Ken because of his identification with the radical left of the Labour Party. During his two terms in office, Livingstone was a controversial, enigmatic mayor, and he became one of the UK's most visible politicians. In order to reduce London's sclerotic traffic, Livingstone charged drivers a fee when they brought their vehicles into the city. In order to improve service and investment, he privatized much of the city's mass transit system. He was widely applauded not only for his response to the 2005 London terrorist bombings but also his ability to lure the 2012 Olympic games to the city. He was criticized, however, for a steady stream of imprudent and often incendiary political statements. Livingstone was narrowly defeated in 2008 by an equally controversial and flamboyant Conservative, Boris Johnson. Livingstone's defeat was viewed by many political analysts as being both a referendum on the increasingly unpopular Brown government and a backlash against some of Livingstone's more controversial policies.

servative. Second, the system consistently penalizes smaller parties. The Liberal Demo-crats, whose support is spread evenly across the country, regularly get between one fifth and one quarter of votes in many districts but can rarely muster enough votes to edge out the larger parties. In 2005, the Liberal Democrats won 22 percent of the vote but only sixty-two seats (about 10 percent of the total). With well less than three times as many votes as the Liberal Democrats, Labour won about five times as many seats! Small parties that are regionally concentrated, like the Scottish Nationalist Party, do somewhat better, but even they are underrepresented.

Third, the British electoral system has produced clear majorities in the House of Commons even when there was no clear majority in the electorate. Indeed, in the elections of 1951 and 1974, the party with the smaller percentage of the vote won the most seats because of the nature of the electoral system. Even in 1997, Labour won a huge (179-seat) majority in the Commons with only 43 percent of the vote. These distortions occur when more than two parties contest a seat, so that a majority of votes is wasted—that is, the votes are not counted toward the winning party. Since World War II, more than 60 percent of all seats have been won with a minority of votes.

In a system that gives virtually unchecked power to the party with the majority of seats, an electoral system that artificially produces majorities could be considered a serious distortion of democratic rule. It is no wonder that the parties most hurt by the electoral system (especially the Liberal Democrats) have called for electoral reform. The Labour government elected in 1997 appointed an independent commission to consider a more proportional electoral system. In 1998, the Jenkins Commission recommended a system that would be a mix of FPTP and proportional representation (PR), as is used in Japan, Russia, Mexico, and a number of other countries. Now that it is the chief beneficiary of the current system, however, Labour has been slow to act on the recommendations.

In contrast, regional legislatures in Scotland and Wales have adopted a mixed electoral system, and Northern Ireland uses a rare system known as single-transferable vote. Ironically, the governing Labour Party, which has benefited greatly from FPTP, favored a mixed system for the regional legislatures, fearing that FPTP would produce large majorities for the local nationalist parties.

Local Government

Unlike the United States, the United Kingdom has traditionally been a unitary state: no formal powers are reserved for regional or local government. Indeed, during the Conservative governments of Margaret Thatcher, the autonomy of municipal governments (known as councils) was sharply curtailed. The Labour government elected in 1997 has taken bold steps to restore some political power to the distinct nations that compose the United Kingdom and to local governments.

Although there has never been a constitutional provision for local autonomy, British localities have enjoyed a long tradition of powerful local government. Concerned that local governments, or councils (especially left-leaning ones in large urban areas), were taxing and spending beyond their means, Thatcher's Conservative government passed a law sharply limiting the ability of councils to raise revenue. The struggle between the central government and the councils came to a head in 1986, when Thatcher abolished the Labour-dominated Greater London Council as well as several other urban governments, a move deeply resented by urban British citizens. London was left with councils in each of its thirty-two boroughs, but it had no single city government or mayor. In 1989, Thatcher further threatened local governments by replacing the local property tax with a poll tax: that is, a flat tax levied on every urban citizen. The new policy shifted the tax burden from business and property owners to individuals (rich and poor alike) and was among the most unpopular policies of Thatcher's eleven years in power. In response, rioting broke out in London.

Thatcher's successor, John Major, abandoned the poll tax but continued to limit the financial autonomy of local governments. After 1997, Tony Blair restored considerable autonomy to municipal government, enacting reforms that allow Londoners to directly elect a mayor with significant powers and to choose representatives to a Greater London Assembly. Ironically, in the first such election, in 2000, a left-wing Labour opponent of the prime minister was elected (see "Governing London: 'Red Ken and Borris,'" p. 50). Nevertheless, Blair maintained the financial limitations on local government that were imposed during Thatcher's tenure.

Representation at the regional level has traditionally been very limited. Of the four nations that constitute the United Kingdom (England, Scotland, Wales, and Northern Ireland), only Northern Ireland had its own legislature— until political violence there caused the central government to disband it in 1972. Each of the four nations had a cabinet minister in the central government, called a secretary of state, who was responsible for setting policies in each region.

As it has with local government, the Labour Party has promoted devolution, or the decentralization of power, to the UK's regions. In 1997, Scotland and Wales voted in referenda to create their own legislatures to address local issues, though their powers are not uniform: Scotland's legislature is more powerful than that of Wales, a reflection of the much stronger nationalist tendencies in Scotland. Meanwhile, the 1998 **Good Friday Agreement** between Catholics and Protestants in Northern Ireland has allowed for the reestablishment of the Northern Ireland Assembly. Some observers view the development of these bodies as the first steps toward a federal UK.[10]

Despite these recent reforms, the UK remains a centralized, unitary state. Regional and local authorities clearly enjoy greater legitimacy and far more powers than in the past, but the central government still controls defense policy, most taxation power, and national economic policy, among other aspects of government. The central government also retains the power to limit (or even eliminate) local government if it so chooses.

POLITICAL CONFLICT AND COMPETITION

The Party System

In the United Kingdom's majoritarian parliamentary system, political parties are extremely important. The majority party controls government and can generally implement its policy goals, which are spelled out in the party manifesto.

From the end of World War II to 1970, the UK had a two-party system. The Conservative Party and the Labour Party together garnered more than 90 percent of the popular vote. The two large parties were equally successful during that period, with each winning four elections. After 1974, a multiparty system emerged, which included the birth of a stronger centrist Liberal Democratic Party and a surge of support for nationalist parties in Scotland, Wales, and Northern Ireland. But since the Conservatives and Labour continue to prevail, the current system is often called a two-and-a-half-party system, with the Liberal Democratic Party trailing far behind the other two parties.

The UK's party system differs regionally, even for national elections. In England the three major parties (Labour, Conservative, and Liberal Democrat) compete with one another. In Scotland, Wales, and Northern Ireland, important regional parties compete with the three national political parties. In the 2005 elections, the two leading parties together won about 67 percent of the vote, while the remaining votes were divided among a variety of parties. In total, eleven parties won seats in the House of Commons.

The two main parties may be losing votes as a result of the growth of smaller parties.[11] The percentage of the vote cast for parties other than the three major parties has steadily increased over the past three elections, and no party since 1935 has won a majority of the vote. However, the leading parties have not lost control of political power. Since 1945 every government has been run by the Conservatives (Tories) or Labour, and only between 1974 and 1979 did either party fail to have a majority in the House of Commons.

THE LABOUR PARTY

We have discussed the democratization of the United Kingdom as a gradual process that incorporated previously excluded groups into the political system. The Labour Party is a clear example of this, as it was formed in 1900 as an outgrowth of the trade union movement. Initially, it sought to give the British working class a voice in Parliament. Only after the mobilizing effect of World War I and the expansion of suffrage in 1918 was the Labour Party able to make significant progress at the polls. By 1918, it had garnered almost one quarter of the vote. Labour's turning point and its emergence as one of the UK's two dominant parties came with its landslide victory in 1945, just after the end of World War II.

Like virtually all working-class parties of the world, the British Labour Party considered socialism its dominant ideological characteristic. British socialists, however, were influenced by Fabianism, a moderate ideology that advocated working within the parliamentary order to bring about social democratic change. While Labour championed a strong welfare state and some state ownership of industry, the party's moderate politics never threatened to replace capitalism.

For most of its history, the Labour Party depended heavily on working-class votes, winning the support of about two thirds of the UK's manual laborers. Starting in the 1970s, however, the composition of the class structure began to change, with fewer Britons engaging in blue-collar jobs. At that point, the solid identification of workers with Labour began to erode, creating a serious challenge for the party.

By the mid-1970s, the Labour Party was badly divided between radical socialists who wanted the party to move to the left to shore up its working-class credentials and moderates who wanted it to move toward the political center. These divisions involved the party's relationship to the trade unions as well as its stand on economic and foreign policy. This internal division caused the more conservative elements to bolt the party in 1981. Most serious, the internal bickering led to the defeat of Labour in every election from 1979 to 1997.

In the 1980s and 1990s, the Labour Party began a process of ideological and organizational moderation. The party's constitution was rewritten to weaken severely the ability of trade unions to control party policy. Labour also abandoned its commitment to socialism and advocated a cross-class appeal. Tony Blair, who became party leader in 1994, consolidated these changes and advocated moderate free-market policies with ambitious constitutional reform, policies that were eventually known as the Third Way.[12] Blair's landslide victory in the 1997 elections marked the beginning of a period of party unity and electoral success that has been termed New Labour, and the election results of 2001 confirmed this success. Blair's victory in the May 2005 elections marked the first time in history that Labour had been elected to office three consecutive times.[13] However, those elections reduced Labour's majority by forty-seven seats, likely as a result of Blair's unpopular policy on Iraq. Blair promised to step down during his third term and hand power over to his Chancellor of the Exchequer, Gordon Brown. Brown had yielded to Blair in 1997 with the understanding that he would eventually assume the position of prime minister. In June 2007, Blair resigned, and the Labour Party endorsed Brown as Blair's successor.

THE CONSERVATIVE PARTY

If the Labour Party was never as leftist as some of its Continental counterparts, the Conservatives (Tories) similarly made for a rather moderate right. The UK's Conservatives emerged in the late eighteenth century and have come to be identified not only with the democratization of the UK but also with the origins of the British welfare state through the collectivist consensus. Because the Tories have usually been pragmatic conservatives and because they have always embraced democratic rule, the party has widespread respect and even electoral support among a wide range of voters. In 1997, about one third of the British working-class vote went to the Conservatives.

Just as the Labour Party developed severe internal ideological divisions beginning in the 1970s, the Tories became divided among advocates of traditional conservative pragmatism, advocates of a limited welfare state, and advocates of radical free-market reforms (known as neoliberals). The rise to power of Margaret Thatcher in the late 1970s marked the dominance of the neoliberal faction and the abandonment of support for the collectivist consensus. The party was further split over policy regarding the European Union, with the so-called Euroskeptics facing off against supporters of continued efforts at European integration.[14]

The Tories struggled in opposition after their defeat in the 1997 elections. A series of ineffective leaders attempted unsuccessfully to lead the Conservative Party back to power. The Tories gained thirty-three seats in the 2005 elections but failed to dislodge Labour. After the electoral results were announced, the Tories selected the young and charismatic **David Cameron** as party leader. Under Cameron's energetic leadership, the Tories were able to project a more centrist image and by 2007 had overtaken Labour in opinion polls.

THE LIBERAL DEMOCRATS

The Liberal Democratic Party was formed in 1988 through the merger of the Liberal Party and defectors from the Labour Party. Its ideology is a mixture of classical liberalism's emphasis on both individual freedom and a weak state and social democracy's emphasis on collective equality. The Liberals (Whigs) were displaced by the rise of the Labour Party in the early twentieth century. The current Liberal Democratic Party has been unable to recover the power and influence of the early Whigs. In recent years, the party has won between 17 and 22 percent of the vote but has not been able to break through the barriers imposed by the electoral system. As a result, one of the Liberal Democrats' chief issues is the reform of the electoral law. Without such reform, the future of the Liberal Democrats seems limited.

The Liberal Democrats have been consistent supporters of European integration and fierce opponents of the war in Iraq. Though viewed as a centrist party, the Liberal Democrats have often attacked Tony Blair's policies as too timid and have often called for increased taxation and social spending. Though generally viewed as closer to Labour than to the Conservatives, the party announced in 2004 that it would adopt a policy of strict neutrality vis-à-vis the two major parties and might be willing to form a coalition with either party should the 2005 elections result in a hung Parliament. Liberal Democrats were clearly hoping that the unpopular war in Iraq, backed by a majority of Labour and Tory members of Parliament (MPs), would lead the party to significant electoral gains in the 2005 elections. Indeed, the Liberal Democrats gained eleven seats and won 22 percent of the vote but still earned only about one tenth of the seats in the House of Commons.

In 2007, **Nick Clegg** was elected Liberal Democratic leader and became the UK's youngest party leader. In the 2008 local elections, the Liberal Democrats won a quarter of the vote and about the same percentage of local council seats. Whether Clegg can boost his party's fortunes enough to break the dominance of the two major parties remains to be seen.

OTHER PARTIES

Many small parties vie for seats in British elections, but few of them are successful. All parties must post a small deposit (about US$800), which is returned to parties that win more than 5 percent of the vote. The main impediment to the success of small parties remains the structure of the electoral system, since first past the post (FPTP) tends to work against small parties that cannot win a plurality of votes. Only regionally based parties—like the Scottish National Party, the Welsh Plaid Cymru, and several Northern Irish parties (for example, Sinn Féin)—have been able to concentrate enough votes in some districts to win seats in the legislature. Finally, while it has not gained any seats in Parliament, in recent years the extreme right-wing British National Party (BNP) has won a number of council elections in England on an anti-immigration platform. Some single issue parties, such as the United Kingdom Indpendence Party (UKIP), which opposes the UK's membership in the EU, have had limited success on the local level or in elections to the European Parliament.

Elections

British voters select all 646 members of the House of Commons during a general election. Elections must take place every five years but may take place before the end of the five-year term if the prime minister decides to call an early election, as often happens. Usually about 60 to 70 percent of the electorate votes in British general elections, below the European average but far above the U.S. turnout.

British campaigns are short affairs, usually lasting less than a month. The voter has a relatively simple choice: which party should govern? British parties are well disciplined and have clear, published policy manifestos. Compared with voters in the United States, voters in the United Kingdom are far more likely to know what each party stands for and how the parties differ. UK voters tend to focus on differences between parties rather than on differences between candidates. Candidates may not even reside in the district in which they run for office. The notion of one's candidate serving local (rather than party) interests first, that is, concentrating on bringing benefits (or pork) to local constituents to secure reelection, is of much less concern than it is in the United States.

Civil Society

As in virtually all democracies, in the United Kingdom various groups exist to articulate special interests (interests that benefit specific groups instead of the nation as a whole). British interest groups influence public policy and public opinion, but interest-group lobbying of MPs is far less prevalent than such lobbying is in the United States Congress because British parties are so highly disciplined. Interest groups must focus their attention on the party leadership (since parties, not individual MPs, make key policy decisions) and on the government bureaucracies, which often interpret and apply policies.

Perhaps the greatest influence of British interest groups comes through their participation in **quangos** (quasi-autonomous nongovernmental organizations). Quangos are policy advisory boards appointed by the government that bring government officials and affected interest groups together to help develop policy. First established in the 1960s and 1970s, quangos represent a move toward the neo-corporatist model of public policy making, in which government and interest groups work together to develop policy. Although attacked in the 1980s by Thatcher (who saw them as empowering special interests and weakening government), there are currently more than 5,000 such organizations working in different policy areas.

In sheer numbers, the **Trades Union Congress (TUC)**, a confederation of the UK's largest trade unions, is the most important British interest group. For much of the postwar period, the TUC dominated the Labour Party and was thus extremely influential during periods of Labour government. Yet a variety of factors has weakened the TUC over the past two decades. First, as is the case in all industrial democracies, the number of blue-collar workers is shrinking quickly, and the TUC has seen its membership plummet. Only twenty years ago, about one half of British workers belonged to trade unions; today, only about one quarter of workers are union members. Second, the Conservative governments of Margaret Thatcher sharply reduced the political power of the TUC by passing laws designed to restrict union activity. Third, reforms within the Labour Party in the 1990s severely eroded the TUC's control of that party. The TUC is still an important source of funding and electoral support, but the TUC-Labour link has been seriously weakened. The TUC can no longer dominate the selection of the Labour Party leader and no longer dominates the formation of Labour policy.

The most important business organization in the United Kingdom, and the main counterweight to the TUC, is the **Confederation of British Industry (CBI)**. Unlike the TUC, which has formal links to the Labour Party, the CBI has no direct link to the Tories. The main industrial and financial interests in the UK usually favor Conservative policy, however, and top business leaders have exercised considerable influence in past Conservative governments. Since taking power in 1997, the Labour Party has been careful to cultivate good relations with the CBI.

SOCIETY

The United Kingdom's social makeup is divided in many significant ways. The British state is both multinational and multiethnic; British society reveals class, religious, and even linguistic divisions. But while these divisions may appear rather sharp when viewed from the outside, compared with the social divisiveness in most other states the UK's divisions have been relatively benign. Over the centuries, the UK has demonstrated remarkable national unity and enviable social and political stability.

Class Identity

Class identity remains perhaps the most salient of all social divisions in the United Kingdom and the one perhaps most noticed by outside observers. Historically, political parties and many key policy debates have reflected class differences, not differences of ethnicity, region, or religion, as is the case in many other states. Certainly the social reforms of the twentieth century largely ameliorated the huge income disparities and rigid occupation-based class lines of nineteenth-century England that preoccupied both Karl Marx and Charles Dickens. But increased social mobility has not yet erased the perception of a two-tier society divided between an upper class and a working class.

Chief among the legacies of the class system has been the education system, which has long channeled a minority of the British elite into so-called public schools (which are, in fact, private schools originally designed to train British boys for public service). Graduates of these elite schools go on to Oxford or Cambridge University before pursuing white-collar careers in government or industry, careers enhanced by elitist old-boy networks. Class differences are also perpetuated by continued self-identification with either the upper class or the working class as manifested in preferred tastes and leisure activities (sherry versus warm beer, cricket versus football, opera versus pub) and variations in speech and accent. Some argue that under the neoliberal reforms of Margaret Thatcher and Tony Blair, class differences have finally

ETHNIC GROUPS

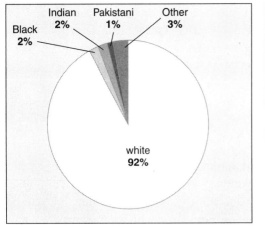

Black 2%
Indian 2%
Pakistani 1%
Other 3%
white 92%

RELIGION

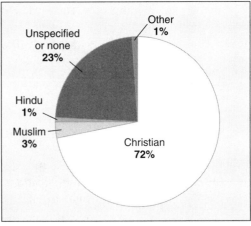

Unspecified or none 23%
Other 1%
Hindu 1%
Muslim 3%
Christian 72%

begun to break down. However, with a prosperous and vibrant white-collar southern England and a stagnant and struggling blue-collar north, regional disparities in income remain a source of social division.[15]

Ethnic and National Identity

Although we have noted that the United Kingdom is relatively homogeneous, religious, linguistic, and cultural divisions do exist and in some cases are becoming more significant (see "Current Issues," p. 68). The UK settled most of its religious differences early on, and its politics are more secular than those in the rest of Europe. Even today, however, Scots are mainly Catholic or Presbyterian, and the English are mostly identified with the Church of England. Compared with the United States, religiously oriented social issues in the UK, such as gay rights and abortion, have generally not become politicized.[16]

Religion remains a source of conflict in **Northern Ireland**, however, where the majority is Protestant (of Scottish or English origin) but some 40 percent of the population is Catholic. Northern Ireland comprises the northeastern portion of the island of Ireland (about 17 percent of the island's territory) that remained part of the United Kingdom following the creation of an independent Republic of Ireland in 1921. This religious divide was compounded by both national and class differences, with Catholics discriminated against in employment and education. Starting in the 1960s, members of the Irish Republican Army (IRA) turned to violence against British targets in the hopes of unifying the region with the Republic of Ireland, and the British army and illegal Protestant paramilitary organizations fought back. Nearly 4,000 individuals on both sides, many of them civilians, died in the conflict. In the 1990s, the British government and the IRA began talks in the hope of establishing peace, resulting in the 1998 Good Friday Agreement (see "Is Peace Possible in Northern Ireland?," p. 60), which bound the IRA to renounce its armed struggle in return for political reforms that would give the Catholic population greater say in local government. Since 1998, the region has been relatively peaceful for the first time in decades, although a series of killings in 2009 rekindled fear about a return of political violence.

Elsewhere, however, new divisions are emerging. Since the 1960s, former colonial subjects (primarily from Africa, the West Indies, India, and Pakistan) have immigrated to the United Kingdom in increasing numbers, giving British society a degree of racial diversity. For the most part, British society has not coped particularly well with this influx. Racial tension between the overwhelming majority of whites and the non-European minority (of less than 3 percent) has sparked conflict and anti-immigrant sentiment, both of which nonetheless remain moderate by American and Continental standards. Lacking proportional representation, the British electoral system has limited the

---

IS PEACE POSSIBLE IN NORTHERN IRELAND?

After years of negotiation, Northern Ireland's status seemed finally resolved by the 1998 Good Friday Agreement. Both the British and the Irish governments supported the decision, as did important Northern Irish political groups, including Catholic republicans, who favor Northern Ireland's unification with the Republic of Ireland, and Protestant unionists, who favor maintaining Northern Ireland's inclusion in the United Kingdom. Among other provisions, the Good Friday Agreement allows for the institution of a Northern Irish legislature and a voting system that ensures proportional representation (in the past, first past the post had effectively marginalized the Catholic minority).

With this agreement, violence by both republican and unionist paramilitary organizations virtually came to an end. However, one major sticking point remained. As part of the Good Friday Agreement, all paramilitary forces were expected to destroy their weapons. This stipulation was directed primarily toward the republican party (known as Sinn Féin) and its military wing, the Irish Republican Army, which retained a formidable arsenal. Even as the benefits of the peace became widespread and Sinn Féin assumed a role in local government, the party continued to resist the decommissioning of its military presence. Critics accused Sinn Féin of maintaining a ballots-and-bullets strategy, ready to take up arms if the democratic process did not go its way. Given the long and violent campaign waged by the IRA, immediate disarmament was not an easily achieved goal. Indeed, in the aftermath of the Good Friday Agreement, a car bombing by an IRA splinter group killed twenty-nine civilians in the town of Omagh in 1998.

As a result of the Sinn Féin's failures to decommission its military, the British government suspended Northern Ireland's legislature in October 2002. The IRA has not resumed a violent campaign, but the political future of the region remains uncertain. In October 2003, the IRA announced some limited destruction of weapons and was rewarded with new elections to the regional legislature that November. In July 2005, the IRA finally renounced the use of armed conflict, a move that was widely regarded as crucial to the achievement of a lasting peace in Northern Ireland. Perhaps the most visible sign of the success of the Good Friday Agreement was that the UK restored self-rule to Ulster in 2007. The first leader of the restored Northern Ireland government was the Protestant minister Ian Paisley, leader of the only mainstream Ulster party to oppose the Accord. His deputy leader was the former IRA terrorist, Martin McGuinness.[17]

---

impact of both the nonwhite and the far-right vote in most elections. Parliament has also sought to limit the nonwhite population by imposing quotas that restrict the entrance of nonwhite dependents of persons already residing in the UK. In spite of this, the UK continues to face growing rates of immigration, with some predicting that another 2 million immigrants will enter the country over the next decade. This will undoubtedly change the social dynamics and may increase xenophobic sentiment, strengthening parties like the British National Party (BNP). As discussed in the Current Issues section, the integration (or lack thereof) of the UK's Muslim population has been a growing concern since the 2005 terrorist attacks on London's transit system.

In addition to ethnic groups, the UK also comprises of a number of national groups, a fact outsiders tend to overlook. The United Kingdom of Britain and Northern Ireland is made up of four nations—England, Scotland, Wales, and Northern Ireland—with substantial cultural and political differences among them. Most citizens of the UK first identify themselves not as British but as belonging to one of these four nationalities.[18] (The U.S. equivalent to this would be a resident of Los Angeles identifying herself first as a Californian, not as an American.)

Long-standing yearnings for greater national autonomy have gained increasing political significance since the 1960s. Local nationalist parties—including the **Scottish Nationalist Party (SNP)** and the Welsh Plaid Cymru—with the support of the Labour Party have advocated devolution: that is, turning over some central-governmental powers to the regions. Tony Blair's Labour government delivered on its campaign promise of devolution in 1999 with the establishment of local legislatures for Northern Ireland, Scotland, and Wales. Some feared that rather than pacify nationalist tendencies, devolution would contribute to the eventual breakup of the country, most notably with an independent Scotland (see the discussion in the "Current Issues" section, pp. 68–69).

While persistent regional loyalties and the localization of government have challenged the British national identity, so, too, has the UK's growing dependence on the European Union. As the twenty-first century progresses, British identity (and perhaps even Scottish or Welsh identity) may be eclipsed or at least diluted by an increasing allegiance to Europe. Despite this diffuse loyalty, Britons remain generally very loyal to the Crown and to the notion of a sovereign British people.

Ideology and Political Culture

In terms of the goals of politics, British political values have been strongly influenced by the development of classical liberalism and the conviction that government's influence over individuals ought to be limited. However, the postwar goals of an expanded franchise of full employment and the creation of a welfare state led to a new consensus as many Britons embraced the social democratic values of increased state intervention and less individual freedom in exchange for increased social equality. Economic decline during the 1970s shifted the pendulum back toward personal freedom, which spurned consensus politics, rejected socialist redistributive policies, and advocated privatization.

The electoral success of the Labour Party in 1997 came on the heels of its new policy to reconcile social democratic and liberal ideologies, the so-called Third Way. While this may indicate that British voters did not fully embrace the stark individualism of the Thatcher revolution, much of Labour's success has come from embracing a "kinder, gentler" version of this neoliberal program. That said, most British—like their Continental neighbors—tend to be more socially and morally liberal than are citizens of the United States. The United Kingdom outlawed capital punishment and legalized abortion and homosexuality, all in the mid-1960s. Handguns were banned outright in 1998. Also, there is far less emphasis on religion and traditional family values.

British political culture is typically described as pragmatic and tolerant. Compared with other societies, British society is thought to be less concerned with adhering to overarching ideological principles and more willing to gradually tinker with a particular political problem. Scholars point to the incremental and ad hoc historical development of British political institutions, noting that there was no defining political moment in British history when founders or revolutionaries sat down and envisioned or established a political system or set of rules based on abstract ideals or theoretical principles. Political radicalism, on either the left or the right, is rare in the UK, with virtually all political actors embracing a willingness to seek evolutionary, not revolutionary, change. This pragmatism is bolstered by a classical liberal tolerance for opposing viewpoints, a strong sense of fair play, and a generally high level of consensus on the political rules of the game.

Although such general characterizations have some utility in accounting for British politics, British political culture in reality comprises multiple subcultures, as is the case in any complex modern or postmodern society. One can certainly still see evidence of an aristocratic culture among the political elite, who share a sense of superiority and noblesse oblige toward those they deem less able to rule, as well as a mass or working-class culture of deference to those in authority. The blurring of class lines has brought with it a greater sense of egalitarianism, however, particularly among the younger generation. These and other long-held values will likely continue to erode in a postindustrial and postmaterial United Kingdom that presumably grows more multiracial and Eurocentric and becomes more concerned with such issues as the environment and other global problems.[19]

POLITICAL ECONOMY

The United Kingdom is noteworthy for its contribution to the liberal economic model. Indeed, most political analysts would trace liberalism itself to the UK, where philosophers like John Locke spoke of the inalienable rights of "life, liberty and estate," setting the stage for such political innovations as the U.S. Declaration of Independence.[20] Yet liberalism in the UK has undergone a number of shifts over the past decades, from a greater emphasis on social democratic values after World War II to the neo-liberalism under Margaret Thatcher, which has been largely continued under the current Labour government.

LABOR FORCE BY OCCUPATION

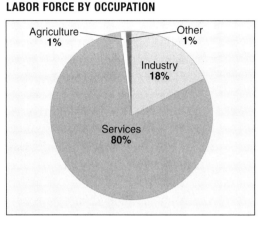

If there is a common theme that one finds in the UK's economy in the four decades since the end of World War II, it is decline. As we recall, during the Industrial Revolution, the UK was "the workshop to the world," the richest country on the planet. Yet over time, this position of dominance deteriorated. As of 2001, the UK's per capita GDP at purchasing-power parity ranked around twentieth in the world, behind once far poorer colonies like Ireland and Australia (though the UK's economy remains one of the ten largest in the world).

Why the decline? There is no single explanation, but one of the basic causes is the downside of early industrialization. Although the UK's early industrialization made the country the world's first industrial power, it also allowed the UK to be the first country to face the obsolescence of its technology and the difficulty of shifting to a new economic environment. A second factor is the burden of empire. Although industrialization helped fuel imperialism (and vice versa), the British Empire soon became a financial drain on the country rather than a benefit to it. Related to this is the argument that the UK's orientation toward its empire meant that it was slow to pursue economic opportunities with the rest of Europe when the Continent moved toward greater integration after World War II. Finally, many political analysts have argued that the collectivist consensus not only blocked meaningful economic reform in the UK for much of the postwar era but also focused the country on social expenditures while ignoring the simultaneous need to modernize the economy.

Where does this leave the UK's economy in the new century? Like other advanced democracies, the UK is a postindustrial economy. Although such industries as steel, oil, and gas still play an important role, nearly three quarters of the country's wealth is generated by the service sector, in particular, financial services and tourism. Privatization has significantly shrunk the role of the state in the economy, including the sale of a range of assets, among them public utilities and housing, British Airways, Rolls-Royce, and Jaguar. Tony Blair's Labour government sought to extend privatization to railroads, health care, and even the Underground (London's famous subway system). There have also been substantial changes in the welfare state, moving it from a system that provided direct benefits to the unemployed to one that sponsors "welfare to work" programs emphasizing training in order to find employment. These actions have all required a significant rethinking of Labour Party ideology. Even though Labour governments have tended to spend more on social welfare than do their Tory predecessors, the party has ended its traditional call for a greater role for the state in the economy (nationalization of industry was enshrined in the Labour Party constitution until 1995) and has distanced itself from its once close ties with organized labor.

To some observers, the Thatcher revolution and its preservation under Labour have helped the United Kingdom finally turn a corner: the UK's unemployment is half of what it was ten years ago, and the country has enjoyed a decade of strong economic growth. Until the recent economic downturn, the UK economy had performed much better than the economy of France, Germany, or Japan. However, as in many other countries, neoliberal economic policies have increased financial inequality throughout the UK, which has one of the highest levels of inequality in Europe. This inequality also has a regional element, with the country's south growing much faster than the north, which is the traditional home of heavy industry. Whether this gap is rising or falling is hotly debated. It has also been argued that welfare reform has been a costly program that has done little to ease unemployment.

Finally, there is the issue of the UK's economic relationship to the outside world. Historic ties notwithstanding, over the past half century the UK has become closely tied to the rest of Europe, with half of its trade going to other European Union (EU) member states. However, the UK has still not accepted the euro, which is the common currency of the EU and was fully introduced in most member states in 2002. British leaders and the public have been cool toward the idea of giving up the pound; they fear the change will undermine the country's sovereignty, placing important economic decisions (such as interest rates) in the hands of other member countries and EU bureaucrats. Opponents also argue that the British economy is significantly different from the economies on the Continent, and a single currency would reduce the UK's flexibility in responding to the different economic challenges that it faces. Supporters of the euro argue that if the UK were to make the change, the country would avoid the current fluctuations in the exchange rate between the euro and the pound. Adopting the euro would help trade (because there would no longer be the threat of a rising pound, making British goods too expensive for other Europeans) and promote investment (because investors would not worry about how exchange-rate volatility might affect their exports to the rest of Europe). Blair was a supporter of the euro and early in his tenure called for an eventual referendum on monetary union. However, he faced resistance not only from the public and the Conservatives but also from his own party, most notably from Chancellor of the Exchequer (and current Prime Minister) Gordon Brown. Adoption of the euro does not seem to be an option at this time, though Brown has kept open the idea that a referendum on the issue might be called. In the end, these issues tie into a much broader question: what is the UK's place in the contemporary international system?

Tony Blair and his chancellor of the exchequer, Gordon Brown, presided over a decade of unprecedented economic growth. Blair and Brown pursued market-friendly policies; they kept inflation low, limited public borrowing, and pledged not to raise income taxes on the wealthiest Britons. In late 2008, after Brown become prime minister, he abandoned such cautious policies to respond to the global financial crisis that hit the United Kingdom's economy particularly hard. Brown partially nationalized a number of private banks, announced an increase in income taxes for the wealthy, agreed to increase public borrowing, and announced a major increase in public spending.

FOREIGN RELATIONS AND THE WORLD

The United Kingdom's political future does not rest on domestic politics alone. Although the UK is no longer a superpower, it retains a relatively large army, has its own nuclear weapons, and boasts one of the largest economies in the world. It remains a major player in world affairs but is struggling to define its place and role in a post–cold-war world. The central difficulty lies in the UK's self-identity. As citizens of an island nation and a former imperial power, the British have long seen themselves as separate from Continental Europe, which was slower to adopt democracy and remains much more skeptical of the liberal values that first emerged in the UK. Rather than identifying itself with the Continent, the UK built its identity around its empire, orienting itself toward the Atlantic. When the empire eventually declined, the emergence of the United States gave the United Kingdom the sense that its power had in a way been resurrected in a former colony, whose citizens were imbued with liberal values and spoke a common language. Since the end of World War II, the United States has counted on the UK as its most dependable ally.[21]

The UK also remains willing to defend its interests militarily. In 1982, the Falkland Islands—a remote British territory of about 2,000 residents some 300 miles off the coast of Argentina—were seized by Argentina after a long-running dispute over ownership of the islands. The UK dispatched its military to retake the colony and succeeded in driving out the Argentine forces. In the process, more than 200 British soldiers and more than 600 Argentine soldiers were killed. Many observers may find the deaths of so many soldiers over two small and sparsely populated islands illogical, but it reflects the UK's postimperial identity and its desire not to surrender its international power. More recently, Tony Blair and Gordon Brown strongly supported the U.S.-led war in Iraq, and the UK was the only other country to contribute a significant military force to the conflict.

EUROPEAN UNION

Do you think our membership in the European Union is a good thing? Percent saying yes:

Country	Percent
Germany	60
France	48
United Kingdom	30

Do you trust the European Union? Percent saying yes:

Country	Percent
France	50
Germany	43
United Kingdom	29

Source: *Eurobarometer*, 69, 2008.

But despite the government's support of the war, the UK's Atlantic orientation is uncertain. Since 1989, most European countries have engaged in a new effort to expand and strengthen the European Union (EU), which has forged ever-closer political, economic, and social ties among its members. As noted earlier, the UK was late in warming to the idea of the EU, initially skeptical of membership and then later kept out by the French (who saw British membership as a Trojan horse through which the United States could influence Europe). The UK has continued to be less than enthusiastic about the EU, especially in respect to its ambitions for taking on more power and responsibilities, such as effecting monetary union or promulgating unified foreign policy. During the 1970s and 1980s, this attitude was less of a problem because the EU had entered a period of relative stagnation. In the past decade, however, many European leaders have moved forward to strengthen the EU to ensure regional stability and act as a counterweight to the "hyperpower" of the United States.

To many Britons, the notion of a stronger EU is unacceptable because they fear the EU will become an unwieldy superstate, undermining national sovereignty, draining the domestic budget, and imposing Continental values.[22] The fact that half the EU's budget is spent on agricultural subsidies, of which the UK gets relatively little, only underscores this suspicion. According to a 2008 poll only 30 percent of those surveyed in the UK thought that membership in the EU was a good thing, one of the lowest levels of support of any member state (see "In Comparison: European Union," p. 66). The UK's reluctance to adopt the euro is further evidence of this skepticism.

Others worry that if the UK remains skeptical of European integration, it will lose even more economic and diplomatic power. If the UK continues to opt out of monetary union and other EU measures, it may marginalize itself, becoming a peripheral player in the creation of a single European power.

In short, Britain's position vis-à-vis Europe remains ambiguous. The Conservatives made opposition to the euro and further European integration a centerpiece of their 2001 electoral campaign, but in 2005 their European policy was moved to the back burner. Once in power, the Labour Party backed away from its initial commitment to the euro, and during the 2005 campaign Blair promised a referendum on adoption of the euro but did not specify a date. Even the Liberal Democrats, the UK's most pro-European party, gave its European policies a low profile during the campaign, appearing to view its position on Europe as an electoral liability. The emergence of a new fringe party, the United Kingdom Independence Party, which advocates a complete withdrawal from the EU, sought to tap into widespread Euroskepticism in the UK and in May 2005 was able to field candidates in 500 of the UK's 646 electoral districts.[23]

If the United Kingdom continues to resist European integration, its relationship to the United States remains a powerful, if problematic, alternative. As we noted, the UK shares a strong historical affinity with the lone superpower. Even though the disparity in power between the two countries is enormous, British supporters of the Atlantic alliance argue that limited influence over the only superpower is superior to a more equal standing in a body like the EU, whose international authority is still rather limited.

But particularly in the aftermath of September 11 and the Iraq war, many Britons have come to the disappointing conclusion that the United States sees the United Kingdom not as a critical ally but rather as a junior partner that is expected to duly follow U.S. foreign policy and provide a veneer of multilateralism no matter what the United States wants to do. This perception has fueled British anti-Americanism much like that seen elsewhere in Europe today. As of 2003, one poll showed that fewer than half of Britons had a favorable view of the United States, down from more than 80 percent in 2000 (though this number still remains higher than in most of the rest of Europe). Nearly half of those surveyed also believed that the UK should act more independently of the United States.[24] The UK also finds itself in greater agreement with its European partners on the centrality of resolving the Palestinian-Israeli conflict in order to effect a lasting Middle East peace. This conflict between

European and U.S. foreign policies has left the UK in the middle, with diffuse and uneasy ties to both centers of power.

The United Kingdom, then, remains unique, as it was centuries ago. Its economic and political systems gave rise to liberalism but remain shaped by centuries-old institutions that have never been fully swept away. Its industrial strength once propelled it to empire status, though now it is overshadowed by its former colony across the Atlantic and an ever-converging Europe. In recent years, the UK has grappled with these issues, hoping to modernize old institutions yet retain its distinct identity and hoping, too, to retain its international stature while reevaluating its relationship to the United States and the rest of Europe. Will the United Kingdom break from its past, creating a new identity to meet its domestic and international challenges? This will be the critical issue in the UK's immediate future.

CURRENT ISSUES

THE FUTURE OF SCOTLAND

Northern Ireland is not the only region where a sector of the population has sought to leave the UK. Scotland was an independent state until the 1707 Act of Union, passed by the Scottish legislature despite widespread popular protest, fused it with England to form Great Britain. Scotland preserved its own legal system, its own church, and many of its own traditions. The Scottish Nationalist Party (SNP), formed in the 1930s, advocated Scottish independence but was relatively unsuccessful until fairly recently. In 1974, the SNP won about a third of all votes in Scotland and sent a record eleven representatives to the House of Commons in London. Both the discovery of oil in the North Sea in the 1960s and the opposition to Thatcher's economic policies in the 1980s helped reinforce the independence movement.

As a result of Tony Blair's push for devolution in 1998, Scotland received its own legislature and government, as well as broad powers over regional issues. Scotland has long had its own legal system, but Scotland and the rest of the UK increasingly differ on a variety of policies. For example, citizens of Scotland pay no tuition to attend university, unlike other UK citizens, and Scots pay less for health care and perscription drugs than do other UK citizens.

The Labour Party, in coalition with the Liberal Democrats, controlled the Scottish government from 1998 until 2007. The SNP capitalized on an economic revival in Scotland and widespread Scottish opposition to Blair's Iraq policy to win the 2007 regional elections. Alex Salmond, the SNP leader, became First Minister (leader) of the Scottish government, pledging to hold a referendum on independence from the UK in the future.[25]

Could Scotland become independent? First, it is not clear whether the United Kingdom would allow Scotland to declare independence.[26] The UK is a unitary state in which all power emanates from London, and the Scottish government was created (and could be revoked) by an act of the UK Parliament. Scotland lacks a military with which to defend its sovereignty. Second, Scotland is integrally linked to the UK. Because countless Scots live and work in the rest of the UK, and vice versa, creating distinct citizenship would be extremely complex. Scotland would lose its economic support from London and its military protection. Scotland sends fifty-nine members to the House of Commons in London; moreover, Tony Blair, UK Prime Minister Gordon Brown, and the speaker of the Commons are all Scots. Finally, it is not at all clear that a majority of Scots would support independence. Polls administered between 2005 and 2008 show that support for independence vacillates between a low of 25 percent to a high of 52 percent, with about 15 percent undecided.[27] In the 2007 Scottish elections, the SNP won a plurality in the Assembly but fell well short of a majority, with 47 of 129 seats.

THE IRAQ WAR

In the immediate aftermath of September 11, the U.S. government viewed the United Kingdom as one of its staunchest allies in the suppression of terrorism. Tony Blair lent his government's unqualified support to the U.S. war against Afghanistan, and British forces played a significant role in the conflict. Blair served as an important conduit between the United States and the rest of Europe, helping to articulate the fight against terrorism and its sponsors. This position was sorely tested with the subsequent war in Iraq. Whereas support for the 2001 war in Afghanistan was relatively easy to garner, the administration of President George W. Bush had a much more difficult time convincing its allies of the necessity and wisdom of deposing Saddam Hussein. Yet Tony Blair once again firmly backed the U.S. foreign policy, helping to convey to the rest of Europe the need and justification for the war. As a result, Blair not only put himself at odds with much of the European and international community but also invoked the hostility of much of the British public and members of his own party, including several members of his cabinet who resigned in protest. Though more than one hundred members of the Labour Party opposed the war, effectively calling for a vote of no confidence against the prime minister, the House of Commons (and most of the opposition Conservatives) eventually voted to support the Blair policy on Iraq. In the aftermath of the invasion of Iraq, Blair has faced harsh criticism. Critics charge him with bringing the UK into an intractable conflict based on questionable intelligence and with putting the country at risk of retaliatory acts of terror. These criticisms were bolstered by the July 2005 terrorist attacks in London.

Why did Blair support Bush's policy in the Iraq war? Common assertions claim that Blair, like many of his predecessors, sees the UK's relationship with the United States as vital, necessitating backing of U.S. policy regardless of the short-term cost. However, other observers have noted that the situation is more complex. Unlike many European politicians, Blair is noted for his moralistic attitude toward international relations, viewing the world in terms of good and evil in a manner more consistent with that found in U.S. politics.[28] This comes in part from Blair's strong religious faith: again, a departure from the largely unreligious UK. According to this theory, Blair backed the United States in Iraq not only because of the desire to remain close to the United States but also because, correctly or incorrectly, he believed the war was the morally right thing to do.

Blair's support for the Iraq War, whatever his motivation, severely weakened his popularity. His party, Labour, was "punished" by the electorate in the 2005 general election: it lost forty-seven seats despite a booming economy. At the same time, Labour retained its parliamentary majority; the Liberal Democrats, the only major party to oppose the war in Iraq, made some gains but failed to make significant electoral progress. As a top member of Blair's government, Brown supported the Iraq war, and since becoming prime minister he has defended the war but has accelerated plans to withdraw British troops from the region.

TERRORIST ATTACKS, RELIGIOUS MINORITIES, AND CIVIL LIBERTIES

Like the events of September 11, 2001, in the United States, the July 2005 bombings in London—in which Islamic extremists targeted the London transport system, killing fifty-two and injuring hundreds of commuters—focused the entire political system on preventing future attacks.

Much public scrutiny was directed toward the UK's Muslim community. The UK is a relatively homogeneous country in terms of ethnicity and religion, especially when compared with many of the other cases studied in this volume. Islam is currently the second-largest religion in the United Kingdom, after Christianity, but less than 3 percent of the population is Muslim. The vast majority of this population has ties to former UK colonies in South Asia. Muslims in the UK are heavily concentrated in urban areas, especially London where they make up about 9 percent of the population. After the terrorist attacks, the UK press began to highlight the presence of extremists within the Muslim community. Leaders of the Muslim community complained about the wave of anti-Muslim violence that resulted from the 2005 attacks. In this context, the Archbishop of Canterbury, the UK's most important religious official, raised a furor when he observed that many British Muslims did not "relate to the UK legal system" and suggested that adopting parts of sharia law (Islamic religious law) could help "maintain social cohesion."[29]

Another consequence of the terrorist attacks has been a series of attempts to improve the UK's law enforcement system. Despite fierce protests from the Liberal Democrats and many within the Labour and Conservative parties, in 2008 Gordon Brown's government narrowly passed a law that doubled to forty-two days the time that terrorist suspects could be held without being charged of a crime. The government also passed laws that criminalize the glorification of terrorism and the incitement of religious hatred. In an attempt to detect terrorist threats and reduce crime, the UK has employed the use of millions of surveillance cameras, and it is estimated that there is one surveillance camera for every fourteen citizens of the UK, making the UK the most electronically monitored society in the world.[30] These and other measures have given rise to concerns that civil liberties in the UK are in serious jeopardy.

NOTES

1. R. C. van Caenegem, *The Birth of the English Common Law* (Cambridge, UK: Cambridge University Press, 1989).
2. Jeremy Black, *Walpole in Power* (Stroud, UK: Sutton, 2001).
3. For a discussion of the link between economic and democratic development, see Barrington Moore, Jr., *Social Origins of Dictatorship and Democracy* (Boston: Beacon Press, 1966).
4. For a discussion of Thatcherism and its effects, see Earl Reitan, *The Thatcher Revolution: Margaret Thatcher, John Major, and Tony Blair, 1979–2001* (Lanham, MD: Rowman & Littlefield, 2003); for her own perspective, see Margaret Thatcher, *The Downing Street Years* (New York: HarperCollins, 1993).
5. For a discussion of the constitution in practice, see Peter Hennessy, *The Hidden Wiring: Unearthing the British Constitution* (London: Victor Collancz, 1995).
6. Monarchy Poll, MORI, 24 June 2006, www.ipsos-mori.com/content/polls-06/monarchy-poll.ashx (accessed 29 December 2008). For an interesting discussion of the value of the British monarchy to political life, see Vernon Bogdanor, *The Monarchy and the Constitution* (Oxford, UK: Clarendon Press, 1996).
7. British question time can be seen regularly on the public-affairs channel C-SPAN and can be accessed online at www.cspan.org.
8. "Captain Malaprop," *Economist*, 26 June 2008.
9. For more details, see "The House of Lords: Completing the Reform," Department for Constitutional Affairs, 7 November 2001, www.dca.gov.uk/constitution/holref/hoelreform.htm (accessed 3 August 2005).
10. "Breaking the Old Place Up," *Economist*, 4, November 1999.
11. Philip Lynch and Robert Garner, "The Changing Party System," *Parliamentary Affairs*, 58, no. 3 (June 2005), pp. 533–54.
12. Anthony Giddens, *The Third Way: The Renewal of Social Democracy* (Malden, MA: Blackwell, 1998).
13. On the 2005 elections, see Pippa Norris and Christopher Wlezien, "The Third Blair Victory: How and Why?" *Parliamentary Affairs*, 58, no. 4 (2005), pp. 657–83.

14. Mark Garnett and Philip Lynch, *The Conservatives in Crisis* (Manchester, UK: Manchester University Press, 2003).

15. An interesting discussion of the changing nature of class and civil society in Britain can be found in Peter A. Hall, "Great Britain: The Role of Government and the Distribution of Social Capital," in Robert D. Putnam, ed., *Democracies in Flux: The Evolution of Social Change in Contemporary Society* (New York: Oxford University Press, 2002), pp. 21–57.

16. Martin Durham, "Abortion, Gay Rights, and Politics in Britain and America," *Parliamentary Affairs*, 58, no. 1 (January 2005), pp. 89–103.

17. For an excellent overview of the success of and challenges facing the Good Friday accords, see "The Hand of History Revealed," *Economist*, 3 April 2008.

18. For further discussion, see the MORI/*Economist* poll results at www.mori.com/polls/2002/cre.shtml (accessed 5 August 2005).

19. For recent research on British political culture (especially as it relates to freedom equality), see William L. Miller, Annis May Timpson, and Michael H. Lessnoff, *Political Culture in Contemporary Britain* (Oxford, UK: Clarendon Press, 1996).

20. John Locke, *Two Treatises on Government: Of Civil Government Book II*, ch. 7, (1689; Electronic Text Center, University of Virginia, 2002), http://religionand democracy.lib.virginia.edu/library/tocs/LocTre2.html (accessed 5 August 2005).

21. Lawrence D. Freedman, "The Special Relationship: Then and Now," *Foreign Affairs*, 85, no. 3 (May/June 2006).

22. David Baker and Philippa Sherrington, "Britain and Europe: The Dog That Didn't Bark," *Parliamentary Affairs*, 58, no. 2 (April 2005), pp. 303–17.

23. See www.independenceuk.org/uk (accessed 3 August 2005).

24. Pew Research Center for the People and the Press, http://people-press. org/reports/display.php3?ReportID5175 (accessed 5 August 2005).

25. For an overview of the SNP argument on independence, see www.snp.org/independence (accessed 30 June 2008).

26. For a fascinating comparison of independence movements in Scotland and Quebec, see Peter Lynch, "Scottish Independence, the Quebec Model of Succession, and the Future of the Scottish National Party," *Nationalism and Ethnic Politics*, 11 (2005), pp. 503–31.

27. For a good summary of the polling on Scottish independence, see http://ukpolling report.co.uk/blog/scottish-independence (accessed 2 July 2008).

28. Peter Riddell, *Hug Them Close: Blair, Clinton, Bush and the "Special Relationship"* (London: Politico's, 2003).

29. http://news.bbc.co.uk/1/hi/uk/7232661.stm (accessed 30 June 2008).

30. http://news.bbc.co.uk/1/hi/uk/6108496.stm (accessed 15 June 2008).

GLOSSARY OF KEY TERMS

Blair, Tony   Labour prime minister from 1979 to 2007.

Brown, Gordon   Labour prime minister since 2007.

cabinet   Top members of the UK government who assist the prime minister and run the major ministries.

Cameron, David   Leader of the Conservatives and head of the opposition.

Celtic fringe   Refers to Scotland and Wales, which were not conquered by the Angles and Saxons.

Clegg, Nick   Leader of the Liberal Democrats, the UK's third-largest political party.

collective responsibility   Tradition that requires all members of the cabinet either to support government policy or to resign.

collectivist consensus   Postwar consensus between the UK's major parties to build and sustain a welfare state.

common law   Legal system based on custom and precedent rather than formal legal codes.

Commonwealth   Organization that includes the UK and most of its former colonies.

Confederation of British Industry (CBI)   The UK's most important group representing the private sector.

Conservative Party (Tories)   One of the UK's two largest parties, currently in opposition.

Crown   Refers to the British monarchy and sometimes to the British state.

English Civil War   Seventeenth-century conflict between parliament and the monarch that temporarily eliminated and permanently weakened the monarchy.

Good Friday Agreement   Historic 1998 accord between Protestants and Catholics in Northern Ireland that ended decades of violence.

hereditary peers   Seats in the House of Lords that were granted to aristocratic families in perpetuity but largely eliminated by recent legislation.

House of Commons   Lower house of the UK legislature.

House of Lords   Upper house of the UK legislature, whose reform is currently being debated.

Labour Party   Currently the governing party of the UK.

Liberals (Whigs)   The UK's historic first opposition party, and one of the UK's two major political parties until the early twentieth century.

life peers   Distinguished members of the society who are given lifetime appointments to the House of Lords.

Magna Carta   The 1215 document signed by King John that set the precedent for limited monarchical powers.

majoritarian   Term describing the virtually unchecked power of a parliamentary majority in the UK political system.

member of Parliament (MP)   An individual legislator in the UK House of Commons.

Northern Ireland   Northeastern portion of Ireland that is part of the United Kingdom, also known as Ulster.

Parliament   Name of the UK legislature.

prime minister   Head of government in the UK.

quangos   Quasi-autonomous nongovernmental organizations that assist the government in making policy.

Scottish Nationalist Party (SNP)   The party seeking Scottish independence, and currently in control of the Scottish regional government.

Thatcher, Margaret   Conservative prime minister from 1979 to 1990.

Third Way   Term describing recent policies of the Labour left that embrace the free market.

Trades Union Congress (TUC)   The UK's largest trade union confederation.

United Kingdom of Great Britain and Northern Ireland   Official name of the British state.

vote of no confidence   Legislative check on government whereby a government deems a measure to be of high importance, and if that measure fails to pass the legislation, either the government must resign in favor of another leader or new parliamentary elections must be called.

WEB LINKS

BritainUSA **www.britain-info.org** site of the British government in the United States

British Broadcasting Corporation **news.bbc.co.uk**

British Politics Group **www.uc.edu/bpg**

British Prime Minister **www.pm.gov.uk**

Conflict Archive on the Internet **cain.ulst.ac.uk** on conflict and politics in Northern Ireland, 1968 to the present

Foreign and Commonwealth Office **www.fco.gov.uk**

London University **www.ucl.ac.uk/constitution-unit** on constitutional reform

Parliament **www.parliament.uk**

Scottish Parliament **www.scottish.parliament.uk**

Welsh Assembly **www.wales.gov.uk**

3 UNITED STATES

Head of state and government:
President Barack Obama (since 2009)

Capital: Washington, District of Columbia

Total land size: 9,631,418 sq km

Population: 304 million

Total GDP at PPP: 13.84 trillion US$

GDP per capita at PPP: $45,800

Human development index ranking: 12

UNITED STATES

INTRODUCTION

Why Study This Case?

Some readers may believe that the United States is the standard against which to measure advanced industrial democracies. After all, the United States is governed by the oldest written constitution still in effect. It is the world's greatest military and economic power. Nevertheless, compared with other advanced capitalist democracies, the United States is best viewed as an anomaly full of paradoxes. It is a large and wealthy nation with a relatively weak state. The United States has a highly legitimate political regime and enjoys widespread adherence to the rule of law despite having a political system that was deliberately designed to prevent decisive and coherent policy making. U.S. citizens are deeply proud of their state but distrust it and its bureaucracy in far greater numbers than the citizens of other industrialized democracies distrust theirs. Its political system has long been dominated by two political parties, but those parties are themselves relatively weak, undisciplined, and fragmented. It has a vibrant civil society but very low voter turnout. The United States is a secular democracy in which religion continues to play a comparatively large role in politics and society. It began as a society of immigrants whose national identity is still in flux because of migration and geographic mobility. The United States has more wealth and more social mobility than any other democracy but is plagued by persistent inequality and the presence of an impoverished underclass that is more characteristic of developing countries. The United States leads the world in medical technology but has more citizens without medical insurance than any other advanced democracy. The United States, blessed with peaceful borders and isolation from major world conflicts, initially favored an isolationist foreign policy but has in recent decades intervened militarily in numerous global conflicts.

It is especially important to understand the unusual workings of the U.S. political system given the country's tremendous power in today's world. The importance of U.S. technology, culture, military power, and economic might is undeniable, and the projection of those strengths is often a source of both admiration and resentment by citizens of other countries.

As the United States enters the twenty-first century, it faces new challenges and new questions about its political system. A bitter dispute over a closely contested presidential election in 2000 raised serious doubts about the integrity of the electoral system and the fairness of the political system. A nation that had become assured of its military might and its sovereignty suddenly felt vulnerable after the terrorist attacks of September 11, 2001. The U.S.-led invasion of Iraq in 2003 has deeply polarized politics in the United States. Economic and international concerns have led many Americans to believe that their country's political and economic systems must undergo major changes in order to respond to the challenges of the future, which was reflected in the 2008 election of Barack Obama. A question for this case is, can the oldest constitutional democracy in the world deliver such change?

Major Geographic and Demographic Features

By 2009, the population of the United States was more than 300 million, third in the world after China and India. In terms of land size, the United States also ranks third in the world; it is slightly larger than Brazil and China but about half the size of Russia and slightly smaller than Canada. The United States occupies the central portion of the North American continent, between Canada and Mexico, spanning it from the Pacific Ocean to the Atlantic Ocean. It comprises forty-eight contiguous states (and the District of Columbia), Alaska (at the extreme northwest of the continent), and the island state of Hawaii, located about 2,100 miles west of the California coast. In addition, it possesses numerous overseas territories in the Caribbean and the Pacific. U.S. states are extremely diverse in area, population, geography, climate, and culture.

The United States is blessed with stunning geographic and climatic diversity. Almost half its territory is made up of agriculturally rich lowlands that have become the world's breadbasket. Its climatic diversity allows for the production of food year-round. The United States is divided by several major mountain ranges, but its extensive coastline and navigable river systems facilitate trade and commerce. The United States is richly endowed with natural resources, including minerals, gas, and oil.

For an industrial democracy, its population is unusual in some ways. Replenished by immigration, it has continued to grow more than the population of other industrialized democracies and currently has a birth rate higher than both China's and Brazil's. As a result, unlike Japan and some European countries, the United States does not face a labor shortage in the forseeable future.

The U.S. population is also more geographically mobile than is common in industrialized democracies. Despite a very high level of home ownership, it is estimated that about one in seven Americans moves from one house to another in a given year. In recent decades, this mobility has hurt the old industrial core of the Northeast and the Midwest, whose cities have lost population and wealth, and has favored the Southwest and the West.

Historical Development of the State

AMERICA AND THE ARRIVAL OF THE EUROPEAN COLONIZERS

The origins of the U.S. state can be found in the geographic expansion of European states in the early sixteenth century. A number of European countries began to explore and establish trading missions in the eastern part of the future United States. The French, the Dutch, the Spanish, and the English all attempted to form permanent settlements there.

English citizens migrated to America in search of land, which was becoming scarce in England, and religious freedom. **Puritans**, radical Protestants, constituted a large portion of the early English settlers in North America. English colonists began to establish permanent settlements in the early seventeenth century in present-day Virginia and Massachusetts. The Virginia colony began as a business venture and developed into a slave-based plantation society geared toward the production of tobacco and dominated by white landowners. The Massachusetts colonies were settled largely by Puritans and developed

TIME LINE OF POLITICAL DEVELOPMENT	
Year	Event
1607	First permanent English settlement in America
1754–63	Seven Years' War, ending the French Empire in America
1775–83	American Revolution
1776	Declaration of Independence
1781	Ratification of the Articles of Confederation
1788	Ratification of the U.S. Constitution
1803	Louisiana Purchase, expanding the U.S. frontier westward
1846–48	Mexican War, further expanding U.S. territory
1861–65	Civil War
1865	Ratification of Thirteenth Amendment to the Constitution, abolishing slavery
1903–20	Progressive Era
1933–38	Era of the New Deal
1955–65	Civil rights movement
2001–	War on Terror

NATIVE AMERICANS: "ETHNIC CLEANSING" AS THE BASIS FOR WESTERN EXPANSION

Though it is convenient to begin our discussion of the origins of the American political system with the establishment of the English colonies in the seventeenth century, more than 100 Indian tribes inhabited what is now the United States, and they had their own political regimes. With the arrival of Europeans, many Native American societies collaborated with or tolerated the colonists, while others violently resisted.

The chief cause of the declining indigenous population after the arrival of Europeans was disease, against which Native Americans lacked resistance. But Native American societies were also subject to military repression, murder, and forced relocation. One infamous example was the 1830 Indian Removal Act, initiated by President Andrew Jackson, which evicted the Cherokees and other tribes from their homelands in the southeastern United States and forced them to relocate on reservations in distant Oklahoma. The forced removal resulted in the death of thousands of Native Americans. The eviction of indigenous peoples by European colonizers in the United States bears numerous similarities to the Afrikaner treatment of blacks in South Africa.

---

into a society of small family farmers. Although Massachusetts was established by settlers who had been persecuted for their religious beliefs, the colonies themselves were characterized by religious intolerance and repression.

By 1640, England had established six of the thirteen colonies that would later form the United States. By the 1680s, the English established six additional colonies, including New York, which was taken from the Dutch, and Pennsylvania. The early colonists faced numerous challenges, including food shortages, disease, isolation from England, and understandable resistance by Native Americans. By the late seventeenth century, the British had begun to assert more control over their remote North American colonies. The British government, with the Navigation Act of 1651, sought to force the colonies to conduct their trade using only English ships, thereby creating colonial dependency. By the early eighteenth century, the British government had allowed elected legislatures to be established in the colonies, transplanting its own embryonic democratic institutions, and had imposed royally appointed colonial governors.

The colonies grew very rapidly, fueled by a high birth rate, the importation of enslaved Africans, mostly to the southern colonies, and continued immigration from England as well as other European countries. For Europeans, the lure of a seemingly endless supply of land was irresistible. Indeed, since colonial days America has been viewed by immigrants worldwide as a land of opportunity and promise.

Between about 1683 and 1763, the English colonists faced numerous foes. They fought indigenous tribes whose land they had taken. They also fought with the growing Spanish and French empires in America, who often allied themselves with Native American tribes and threatened to limit the English settlers' prospects for colonial expansion. In the Seven Years' War (1754–1763), the British effectively defeated the French Empire in North America and weakened the Spanish Empire (with Spain giving up claims to Florida in 1763). At the end of the Seven Years' War, Britain inherited a vast empire in America that would prove both costly and difficult to control.

THE REVOLUTION AND THE BIRTH OF A NEW STATE

The United States was the first major colony to rebel successfully against European colonial rule, leading one scholar to call it "the first new nation."[1] At its core, the American Revolution was caused by a conflict between two sovereignties: the sovereignty of the English king and Parliament and the sovereignty of the colonial legislatures that had been established in America. Both believed that they had the exclusive right to raise the taxes paid by the colonists. In the 1760s, the British Parliament had passed a number of taxes on colonists that sparked a spiral of petitions, protests, boycotts, and acts of civil disobedience on the part of the colonists. The British responded by disbanding the colonial legislatures and repressing protest with military force. In the Boston Massacre (1770), British soldiers attacked a mob of colonists, further fueling the colonists' opposition to British intervention in colonial affairs. Colonial militias clashed with British military forces, a precursor to the impending revolution.

In 1774, in response to British repression, anti-British colonial elites convened a Continental Congress in Philadelphia, which was made up of delegates from the colonies. It asserted the exclusive right of the colonial legislatures to raise taxes. The Second Continental Congress, meeting in 1775, created a Continental army, with **George Washington** at its command. In 1776, the Congress appointed a committee to draft a constitution and approve the **Declaration of Independence**.

The declaration of a new state and a new regime evoked an attack by a large and powerful British army. In the **American Revolution** (1775–1783), the colonists were greatly outnumbered but were aided by their knowledge of the terrain and an alliance with France, an enemy of England. With the defeat of the British at Yorktown, Virginia, in 1783, Britain granted independence to the thirteen rebellious American colonies.

THE CONSOLIDATION OF A DEMOCRATIC REPUBLIC AND THE DEBATE OVER THE ROLE OF THE STATE

A unique theme of the American Revolution was its opposition to a British state perceived as overbearing. Distrust of a strong state is still a feature of

U.S. politics, but it presented special challenges during the revolution. Fighting a war against the British required a central authority transcending the thirteen colonial governments, all of which had begun functioning under new constitutions. The **Articles of Confederation,** approved in 1781, created a loose alliance of sovereign states. It featured a unicameral legislature with a single vote for each state. The Confederation Congress assumed important powers regarding conflicts between states and the regulation of settlement to the west, but it required unanimity for the passage of all legislation, lacked a national executive, and did not have the ability to raise taxes or create a national currency. This weak central state made it difficult for the nation to conduct foreign relations, control inflation, and carry out international trade.

In response to those problems, a Constitutional Convention of state delegates was held in 1787 to consider a stronger national state. The resulting constitutional document was a compromise between advocates of a strong federal state and supporters of states' rights. The states ratified the new constitution in 1788, effectively creating a new national state and a new political regime.

The first U.S. Congress met in 1789. It passed legislation that strengthened the state, created a federal judiciary, and imposed a tariff on imports to fund federal expenditures. It also attempted to address the concerns of those who feared the power of a strong central state, by passing twelve amendments to the Constitution, ten of which were ratified by the states and became known collectively as the **Bill of Rights**. The ten constitutional amendments that constitute the Bill of Rights, passed by the first U.S. Congress, in large part aim to protect the rights of individuals against the state.

A major political division in the young American republic was between **Federalists**, led by President Washington's Secretary of the Treasury Alexander Hamilton, and **Democratic-Republicans**, led by the future president Thomas Jefferson. Hamilton, who advocated a strong central state, was responsible for consolidating the Revolutionary War debt incurred by the states, imposing a federal excise tax, and creating a federal bank to print and regulate currency. When Jefferson became president in 1801, he moved to reduce the power of the U.S. state by paying off the national debt, repealing the excise tax, and reducing the size of the federal bureaucracy and the military. At the same time, Jefferson was responsible for a massive increase in the territory of the United States when he acquired much of France's remaining North American territory in the **Louisiana Purchase** (1803). The Louisiana Territory extended America's westward borders to the Rocky Mountains and expedited future westward migration.

THE MOVE WEST AND EXPANSION OF THE STATE

With the Louisiana Purchase in 1803, acquisition of Florida from Spain in 1819, and end of the War of 1812 with Britain in 1815, Americans were free to move westward. This movement came at the expense of Native Americans. As Americans moved westward in search of land to be used for agriculture, the United States used legislation as well as military force to contain, relocate, or exterminate Native Americans. The westward expansion continued with the 1845 annexation of Texas, a Mexican territory prior to a successful separatist movement led by non-Hispanic Americans. The United States declared war on Mexico in 1846 (the Mexican War, also known as the **Mexican-American War**) to protect its acquisition of Texas and to lay claim to vast Mexican territories in present-day Arizona, California, Nevada, New Mexico, Utah, Colorado, and Wyoming. In all, the rapidly expanding United States gained one third of Mexico's territory through military conquest, further encouraging the flood of migrants westward.

CIVIL WAR AND THE THREAT TO UNITY

The American Revolution had temporarily united the English colonies, and under Washington's leadership and the work of Federalist leaders the foundations of a strong central state were constructed. But the Federalist project was always controversial, and the creation of a unified United States could not eliminate simmering regional differences that threatened to destroy the Union. These differences culminated in the **Civil War** (1861–1865). At its roots were the divergent paths of socioeconomic development in the southern and northern regions of the country. While the North experienced an industrial boom based on its prosperous cities, southern agriculture was still based on slave labor and export-oriented plantations.

In order to gain agreement on a federal constitution, the founders of the republic had largely sidestepped the issue of slavery. Slavery had been abolished in the North after the Revolution, but the Constitution tolerated it. A number of factors brought the issue of slavery to center stage by the mid-nineteenth century. First, the westward expansion of the United States raised the contentious issue of whether new territories would be "slave" states or "free" states. Then, in the first half of the nineteenth century, slavery was banned by England and most of Latin America, and the North increasingly viewed the South as an anachronistic threat to free-market capitalism based on individual liberty and a free labor market. Finally, the early nineteenth century saw the emergence of a rapidly growing abolition movement, largely in the North, which viewed slavery as both undemocratic and anathema to Christian values.

The 1860 election of Abraham Lincoln and the rise to power of the new anti-slavery Republican Party provoked the secession of eleven southern states and the commencement of the Civil War. The southern states formed a rebel state, called the Confederate States of America, and enacted their own constitution, which guaranteed the institution of slavery.

During the war, the North held important advantages over the South in terms of population (it was over twice as large), wealth, and industry. Nevertheless, the South had the advantage of playing defense on difficult terrain, and it hoped to prolong the war enough to wear down the northern invaders. The long and bloody conflict cost more than half a million lives before the South was defeated in 1865 and the Union was preserved. In the same year, the **Thirteenth Amendment** to the Constitution, abolishing slavery, was ratified.

The importance of the Civil War in the development of the U.S. state was immense. The federal government had increased spending and built a huge army in order to subdue the South. The federal government also gained enormous power through its role in reforming the South and reintegrating the southern states into the Union. This use of state power to end race-based slavery and promote democratic values set an important precedent.

THE PROGRESSIVE ERA AND THE GROWTH OF STATE POWER

The U.S. state used its newfound clout to promote democratic reform during the **Progressive Era** (1903–1920). Progressives sought to use state (national) power to restrict the power of big business, attack corruption, and address inequality. Under President Theodore Roosevelt (1901–1909), the federal government attacked monopolistic businesses and enhanced the ability of the Interstate Commerce Commission to regulate trade between states. In order to protect public land from private development, Roosevelt created a vast system of national parks. Under President Woodrow Wilson (1913–1921), laws were passed to curb further the power of large monopolies and to establish the centralized Federal Reserve System as a national lender of last resort. Perhaps the single greatest impetus for the growth of a centralized state was the adoption of the Sixteenth Amendment in 1913, which gave Congress authority to levy a national income tax. In addition, Wilson took the United States into World War I, despite considerable popular opposition, an act that dramatically increased the size and power of the state.

THE GREAT DEPRESSION AND THE NEW DEAL

The stock market crash of 1929 and the Great Depression devastated the U.S. economy. One quarter of the workforce lost their jobs, the GDP dropped by about one third, and there were massive bankruptcies and bank failures. The economic crisis was a pivotal factor in the 1932 election of the Democratic Party candidate Franklin Roosevelt and the implementation of a set of social democratic welfare policies known collectively as the **New Deal**.

The New Deal policies were aimed at ameliorating the economic crisis, but their long-term impact was to increase dramatically the power of the U.S. state. Despite opposition from conservatives and the Supreme Court, Roosevelt, with a Democratic majority in both houses of Congress, passed a series of unprecedented measures. Some of the most controversial pieces of legislation guaranteed workers the right to bargain collectively with employers, created state agencies to generate electric power, provided state payments to farmers who agreed to limit production, and heavily regulated the stock market. In order to carry out these policies, a massive extension of the state bureaucracy and the creation of numerous state agencies, such as the Securities and Exchange Commission and the National Labor Relations Board, were needed. Many of those agencies still exist today. The Social Security Act (1935) established the foundation for the U.S. welfare state (though much later and much less comprehensively than in many northern European countries), creating unemployment insurance, retiree pensions, and other social welfare measures.

The New Deal policies increased the role of the state, and the entry of the United States into World War II enhanced state power even further. The military grew rapidly, the state set wages and prices, and it directly intervened in private enterprise to serve the war effort. In wartime, the state trampled on civil liberties, censoring the press and sending thousands of citizens of Japanese ancestry to prison camps. After World War II, in the context of the cold war with the Soviet Union, the state took measures to persecute suspected Communists, firing them from government positions.

STRUGGLING FOR DEMOCRATIC RIGHTS: THE CIVIL RIGHTS MOVEMENT AND THE WAR ON POVERTY

Despite constitutional protections and the defeat of the South in the Civil War, U.S. democracy suffered from the legacy of slavery. Widespread discrimination against African Americans continued, most notably in the South but also in the North. After World War II (in which African Americans served and made valuable contributions), a growing **civil rights movement**, often backed by the federal government and the federal judiciary, advocated an end to all forms of racial discrimination.

The struggle for civil rights was only one of the popular reform movements that crystallized in the 1960s. During that decade, many U.S. citizens began to view economic inequality, gender discrimination, and environmental degradation by private business as impediments to democracy. In the mid-1960s, popular movements focused on those concerns combined with growing popular opposition to the **Vietnam War**, contributing to an atmosphere of unrest and rebellion.

Partly in response to popular pressure, the U.S. government attempted to address a number of socioeconomic problems. Under President John Kennedy (1961–1963), the federal government played a crucial role in imposing civil rights legislation on recalcitrant southern states. President Lyndon Johnson (1963–1969) announced a **War on Poverty**, with a dramatic increase in federal spending to combat economic inequality. Johnson launched new programs and founded new state institutions to protect the environment, build low-income housing, fund the arts, and redress racial discrimination. The growing state role in the economy and society continued even under the Republican president Richard Nixon (1969–1974), who imposed wage and price controls to stem inflation and signed into law a measure that provided food stamps to the poorest Americans.

In 1980, President Ronald Reagan (1981–1989) was elected on a neo liberal platform of ending the trend toward increased state involvement in the economy. Reagan viewed government as "the problem, not the solution," and rode to power on a wave of conservatism that was critical of the preceding decades of state-led social activism. Reagan cut social spending and reduced taxes while dramatically increasing defense spending. The reform of a welfare state widely viewed as bloated and inefficient continued under the Democratic president Bill Clinton (1993–2001) and the Republican persident **George W. Bush** (2001–2008), though during the Bush presidency this occurred alongside massive increases in spending on both defense and domestic policies.

In retrospect, it is clear that the United States was fortunate to build and consolidate its state under extremely favorable conditions. It did not have to contend with hostile neighbors and faced no appreciable external threats to its sovereignty. The development of the U.S. state during its first century also coincided with the steady success of the economy and the steady expansion of its power abroad.

POLITICAL REGIME

Because of their fresh experience with, and deep distrust of, authoritarian colonial rule, the founding fathers established a democratic regime governed by the **rule of law**. This means that government can act and citizens can be punished only as authorized by legal statute, all citizens are equal before the law, and no one is above the law, not even political leaders. Those concepts were framed in a written constitution establishing a democratic regime grounded in rational-legal legitimacy.

But the rule of law by itself was judged insufficient. The power of legitimate government in the hands of a misguided minority or even a well-intentioned majority could still lead to tyranny. Wariness about this possibility led the founders to establish a liberal democratic political system with institutions designed to weaken the power and authority of the state. Those institutions included federalism, the separation of powers, and the Bill of Rights. In a sense, the legitimacy of the state was based on its inherent weakness. But that raised a dilemma: How could a state and its elected government manage from a position of weakness the tasks of leading a new and growing nation facing a host of increasingly complex challenges?

The ongoing effort to resolve that dilemma required two regimes in the eighteenth century, a civil war in the nineteenth century, and a dramatic strengthening of central government authority in the twentieth century. In 1777, the Continental Congress established the new nation's first regime under the Articles of Confederation and Perpetual Union. The Articles called for a decentralized confederation of highly autonomous states that vested most authority in the individual states. The ineffectiveness and insufficiency of this confederal regime grew increasingly apparent as the new republic faced potential threats of internal rebellion and costly foreign trade disputes. By 1787, the Articles of Confederation had been jettisoned, replaced by an entirely new constitution, which became the codified embodiment of U.S. rule of law. Inaugurated in 1789, the Constitution established a representative democratic regime governed by a presidential system. The following section examines the institutional components of this regime, including the principles of federalism and separation of powers.

Political Institutions

THE CONSTITUTION

In a nation governed by the rule of law, the 1789 document constituting the regime became all important. The Constitution of the United States of America was passed in large part as a compromise: between less and more populous states, between northern merchants and southern planters, between slaveholders and those not holding slaves, and between Federalists (who supported a strong central government) and Anti-Federalists (who advocated states' rights and preferred the decentralized confederal status quo). But the founders and citizens on both sides of the debate shared two characteristics: a fear of too much government in the form of an overbearing central authority, and the recognition that the Articles of Confederation had provided too little government. The constitutional compromise was one of strengthened but nonetheless limited government checked by **federalism**, which divides governing authority between the national and state governments; the **separation of powers**, which prevents any one branch or office of government from dominating; and the Bill of Rights, which protects the freedoms of individual citizens. In an unprecedented way, the U.S. Constitution created, tempered, and buffered three sovereign spheres within a single political system: national, state, and individual.

The U.S. Constitution also stands out as the oldest written constitution still in force. Although it has been regularly interpreted by judicial action and occasionally amended (in total, twenty-seven times), it has been remarkably durable—indeed, it has proven difficult to even amend. Most of it remains fully in effect after more than 200 years, guiding U.S. politics and policy making under circumstances that could hardly have been imagined by its founders. For better or worse, it has served as the model for constituting the regimes of many newly established countries, and its guiding principles of federalism and

ESSENTIAL POLITICAL FEATURES
• Legislative-executive system: presidential
• Legislature: Congress
• Lower house: House of Representatives
• Upper house: Senate
• Unitary or federal division of power: federal
• Main geographic subunits: states
• Electoral system for lower house: plurality
• Chief judicial body: Supreme Court

separation of powers have become standards for numerous democracies.

The Branches of Government

At the national level, the power of government is shared by three institutions: a president; a bicameral legislature; and a judiciary, led by the Supreme Court, which has the power to interpret the Constitution. The framers put in place several institutions designed to check and balance the powers of each respective branch of government. For example, the upper chamber of the legislature (the **Senate**) is given the authority to approve or disapprove executive appointments and to ratify or not ratify treaties. Both the Senate and the **House of Representatives** (the House) can refuse to pass legislation and can impeach, convict, and remove from office a president or a federal judge (for grievous offenses). The executive (the president) can veto legislation passed by the legislature and appoint judges to the judiciary. The judges, once appointed, have virtually lifetime tenure and serve without political oversight. Most significantly, they have the power of concrete judicial review, meaning that they can interpret the Constitution and void any act of the other two branches that they deem unconstitutional if that act is brought before them in a court case. Ultimately, the framers sought to give Congress the upper hand, allowing it to override a presidential veto of legislation (with a two-thirds majority) and to overturn a decision of the Supreme Court by amending the Constitution.

The founders also intentionally gave each branch sources of legitimacy. Unlike a parliamentary system, in which executive authority and legislative authority are fused, and only members of parliament are directly accountable to voters, the U.S. system seats its president and members of the legislative chambers in separate elections. Separate branches and separate elections can also allow a third possible check on power: divided government, in which different parties control the executive and legislative branches. Although a single party has often dominated both, the United States has experienced divided

STRUCTURE OF THE GOVERNMENT

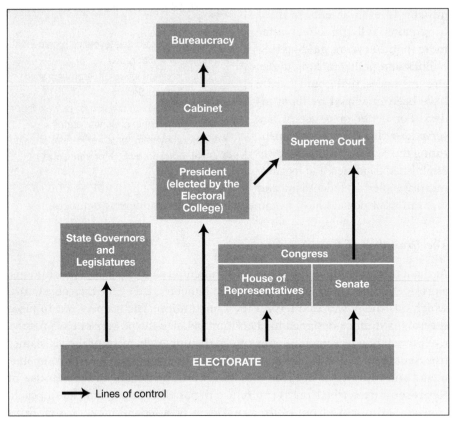

government over 40 percent of the time since 1830 and, since the end of World War II, nearly 60 percent of the time. Thus what politicians and analysts often criticize as the tendency for American policy-making "gridlock" is an intended consequence of the system of checks and balances. It fosters a state with weak autonomy and a relatively fragmented policy-making process. This formula has led some observers to argue that the United States would be better served by a parliamentary system, which can respond more decisively to threats or needs and can change the executive quickly when it has lost the support of the legislature.

On the other hand, this system reflects the powerful liberal sentiments of both its founders and U.S. political culture today. For many Americans, inefficiency is a price worth paying to keep state power in check. Moreover, in parliamentary systems, coalitions are often needed to form a majority, or a minority government must deal with its own sort of divided government. Coalition and minority governments, it is argued, can be far less stable and far less workable than the U.S. system.

THE EXECUTIVE

The U.S. president is both the head of state and the head of government. As such, the presidency is invested with a great deal of formal authority, and key presidents have expanded the power and influence of the office over time, particularly in the past century. The president is indirectly elected by the Electoral College (based on direct popular vote) to a fixed four-year term and may be elected only twice. Until the election of President **Barack Obama**, all U.S. presidents had been white men, and all but one have been Protestant Christians (John Kennedy was Catholic). Obama's election has clearly been a substantial departure from the norm in this regard.

As the head of state and the only leader elected to represent the entire citizenry, the president has traditionally taken the lead role in U.S. foreign policy (although treaties are subject to approval of the Senate). The president is also commander in chief of the military. As head of government, the president—similar to a prime minister—is responsible for managing the day-to-day affairs of the government and makes senior appointments to the executive and judicial branches (again, with approval of the Senate). Moreover, the president can initiate proposals for legislative action and veto legislative bills.

The president also manages an enormous bureaucracy, which has mushroomed over the years so that the civilian workforce now approaches 3 million employees, with the assistance of a **cabinet** composed mostly of the heads of key departments, offices, and agencies. Unlike its parliamentary counterparts, for which the cabinet is the government, the U.S. cabinet has no legal authority or standing; the influence of its officers and the institution, moreover, has varied from president to president. Some presidents come to rely upon a smaller inner cabinet (including, for example, the chief adviser of the National Security Council, a group of officials in the Executive Office of the President) or an informal "kitchen" cabinet of trusted advisers who may not be department heads. The U.S. bureaucracy is technically responsible to the executive branch and is further constrained by the legislature's control of its many budgets. In some respects, U.S. bureaucrats lack both the autonomy and the respect historically accorded to their counterparts in countries like France and Japan (*bureaucrat* and *bureaucracy* remain derogatory terms to most Americans).

With a few exceptions (such as Andrew Jackson in the 1830s and Abraham Lincoln in the 1860s), presidents prior to the twentieth century were relatively weak leaders who exerted little political influence. The White House and its Oval Office strengthened considerably over the course of the twentieth century, something seen in other executive institutions in the advanced democracies. In recent years, the public has expected, and presidents have sought to deliver, a strong executive offering genuine if not dominant leadership. Predictably, both the legislative and the judicial branches have sought to challenge and check this growing influence.

THE LEGISLATURE

The framers of the Constitution intended Congress to be the dominant branch of the U.S. government. In many ways, despite the growing influence of the presidency and the substantial clout of the Supreme Court, that remains the case. Scholars have argued that the U.S. Congress is "the only national representative assembly that can actually be said to govern."[2] They note that although most countries today have some form of national legislature, the legislatures in authoritarian systems do little more than affirm and legitimate the decisions of the political leadership. And although the parliamentary democracies of Western Europe and Japan possess the authority to say no to the executive (at the risk, in many cases, of having the parliament dissolved), those assemblies still lack the power even to modify, let alone initiate, legislation. Only the U.S. Congress has that authority.

The Constitution reserves the supreme power—the power to legislate—for Congress. It also gives Congress the power of the purse, that is, sole author-

DIFFERENT CHAMBERS, DIFFERENT ROLES

Given the differences in size, tenure, and assigned responsibilities, it is not surprising that the two chambers of Congress play different roles. The Senate is authorized to ratify treaties and approve presidential appointments, whereas the House is given exclusive power to originate tax and revenue bills. The Senate tends to be more deliberative, providing a forum for wide-ranging opinions and topics, whereas the House is more centralized and places strict limits on debate. Because they serve a larger and more diverse constituency, senators tend to be less specialized and less partisan and more hesitant to take a position that might offend any major portion of their broad base of voters. House representatives, in contrast, stand for election every two years and are by necessity more attuned to the needs and interests of their more narrowly defined constituencies. House members tend to be more specialized in their expertise and less reliant on a staff. The House is generally more politicized and partisan. Whereas senators are more likely to cross the aisle to form an alliance or vote with members of the opposing party on an important issue, representatives are generally more likely to vote along partisan lines.

ity to appropriate funds, to control the way in which its laws are implemented. Whereas the U.S. Congress never accepts the president's annual budget without making its own significant adjustments, governments in Britain and Japan can anticipate their parliaments' acceptance of their budgets without any changes.

Another indication of the framers' understanding of congressional power was their decision to divide the legislature against itself by making it bicameral. The House of Representatives consists of 435 members (a number that has remained unchanged since 1910) who are elected to two-year terms in single-member plurality districts. The number of seats and districts allotted to each state is determined by and distributed according to each state's population after each state is allowed one representative. For example, following the 2000 national census, California saw an increase in its allotment of House seats from fifty-two to fifty-three, and New York dropped from thirty-one to twenty-nine seats based on changes in population; Wyoming retained its single seat. In 1789, there was an average of 1 representative for every 30,000 people; in 1910, the average was over 200,000; since 2000, each member of Congress has represented more than 600,000 citizens on average.

There are 100 members of the Senate, each serving staggered terms of six years with one third of the body elected every two years. Since 1913, senators have also been elected in single-member plurality districts; prior to that, they were elected indirectly by the state legislatures. Each state is allotted two seats regardless of its population, making most senate districts far larger than those in the House. In California, for example, each senator represents approximately 18 million constituents, whereas each of North Dakota's senators represents just over 300,000 constituents.

THE JUDICIAL SYSTEM

The third branch of the U.S. government, the judiciary, was the least defined by the Constitution and initially was quite weak. But given the trust and legitimacy vested in the Constitution and the rule of law, it should not surprise us that the U.S. judiciary has come to play a prominent role in the American political system. Over time, the federal court system devised new tools of judicial authority and significantly broadened the scope of its jurisdiction. In 1789, Congress created the federal court system and authorized it to resolve conflicts between state and federal laws and between citizens of different states.

In the landmark decision of *Marbury v. Madison,* the Supreme Court in 1803 established its right of judicial review: the authority to judge unconstitutional or invalid an act of the legislative or executive branch or of a state court or legislature. Although this power of judicial review can be exercised by federal and state courts, the Supreme Court is the court of last resort, the court with the final word on the interpretation of the U.S. Constitution. This kind of judicial review is uncommon but not exclusive to the United States: Australian and Canadian courts also have such authority.

Federal judges are given essentially lifetime appointments, affording them substantial autonomy from both partisan politics and the executive and legislative branches of government. But the Court's power is checked by its reliance upon presidential appointments and Senate approval of nominees to the federal bench, as well as by legislative enforcement of its decisions. Nonetheless, the federal courts have played an increasingly influential role, particularly since the second half of the twentieth century, determining important policy outcomes in such areas as school desegregation and abortion and even determining the winner of the 2000 presidential election. In that case, the Court overturned a decision of a state supreme court (Florida's), and in so doing invalidated a partial recount of ballots in that hotly contested election. It is little wonder that appointments to the Supreme Court have become bitter political struggles as partisan forces seek to project their influence on this now prominent third branch of U.S. government.

The Electoral System

Nearly all elections in the United States are conducted according to a single-member district plurality system, in which there is one representative per district, and in which the seat is awarded to the candidate with the most votes (but not necessarily with a majority). This system has favored the emergence of two broadly defined parties and has effectively discouraged the survival of smaller and single-issue parties. Unlike a system of proportional representation, the plurality system in effect wastes votes for all but the dominant candidate, forcing coalitions to emerge to compete in the winner-take-all contests.

One way in which parties have sought to enhance their prospects for electoral success has been through the process of drawing up electoral districts, which are used to determine constituencies for Senate, House, and many state and local elections. State legislatures are required to adjust voting districts every ten years to reflect changes in population, and the dominant party in the legislature is able to control the process. Parties seek to influence electoral outcomes by redrawing the districts in ways that will favor their candidates and voting blocs. Political architects often employ **gerrymandering**, a process named after a Massachusetts governor, Elbridge Gerry, whose fellow party members crafted a district shaped like a salamander. Gerrymandering refers to the manipulation of district boundaries by one political party to favor the candidates of that party (nowadays achieved with the aid of sophisticated computer analyses of demographic data).

Although members of both chambers of Congress are elected directly by a popular vote, the president and the vice president are elected indirectly, by the Electoral College. The founders established the Electoral College as a means of tempering the particular interests (and feared ignorance) of voters. In this system, voters technically do not vote for a presidential candidate but vote instead for a slate of electors from their state, with the electors chosen or appointed by each party from each state. Each state receives a total of electoral votes equal to its combined number of senators and representatives. In addition, the federal District of Columbia has 3 votes, for a sum of 538 electoral votes (100 plus 435 plus 3). But unlike a plurality system, the Electoral College requires a majority (270) of votes to claim victory. If no candidate obtains a majority, the contest is determined by the House of Representatives (as was the case twice in the early nineteenth century).

National Election Results, 1992–2008					
	Legislative Elections				
Year of Election	House of Representatives* Total Seats: 435**		Senate* Total Seats: 100**		Presidential Elections* (party)
	Democrats	Republicans	Democrats	Republicans	
1992	258	176	57	43	Clinton (Democrat)
1994	204	230	48	52	—
1996	206	228	45	55	Clinton (Democrat)
1998	211	223	45	55	—
2000	212	221	50	50	Bush (Republican)
2002	204	229	51	48	—
2004	202	232	44	55	Bush (Republican)
2006	233	202	49	49	—
2008	257	178	56	41	Obama (Democrat)

*House terms of office are fixed at two years, with all seats elected every two years. Senate terms are fixed at six years, with one third of the seats elected every two years. Presidential terms are fixed at four years, with elections held every four years.
**When Democrats and Republicans together comprise less than the total number of seats, the Independent representatives account for the difference.

Because all but two states use a winner-take-all formula for awarding electoral votes, winning a plurality of the popular vote in a state earns a candidate all of the state's electoral votes. Thus, winning many states by large margins but losing key electoral-rich battleground states by narrow margins can lead to a popular victory but a loss in the Electoral College. This has happened three times in U.S. history, most recently in the controversial 2000 election between George W. Bush and Al Gore.

Even before the 2000 election, many observers had called for the elimination of the Electoral College, to parallel the elimination of the indirect election of senators nearly a century ago. Critics charge that this "quasi-democratic" vestige of the eighteenth century "undermines both respect for and the legitimacy of electoral results."[3] Nor is this the only electoral reform effort being proposed. Long-standing efforts to reform campaign finance are now being joined by bipartisan calls for changes in the logistics of voter registration, the actual mechanics of voting, and the way in which presidential primaries are conducted, along with a number of smaller issues.

One response to the frustration with the existing electoral and political systems has been the proliferation of state initiatives and referenda. Twenty-seven of the fifty states allow citizen-sponsored statewide ballots called initiatives, and legislature-proposed statewide ballots called referenda (with the ballots themselves often called propositions), in which voters are able to make direct decisions about policy. For example, in 2004 Colorado proposed changing their allocation of electoral college delegates from winner-take-all to proportional, though the measure failed to pass. The Constitution also authorizes a national ballot in the form of a national convention as one means of amending federal law, a method that has never been employed.

Local Government

The United States has a federal political system dividing authority between self-governing states and the national government that unites the states (hence, the name United States of America). The Constitution authorizes the national, or federal, government to manage both national commerce and foreign policy. Although the granting of those federal powers marked a significant centralization compared with the earlier Articles of Confederation, the states have retained significant powers, including responsibility for many direct social services (such as health, education, and welfare) and authority over internal commerce.

Over time, however, the national government has managed to increase its influence in many of the areas traditionally subject to state sovereignty. The federal government can review the constitutionality of state legislation, impose federal mandates, and make federal grants to states for such services as education and transportation, contingent upon the states' abiding by federal standards. States have given up their sovereignty only reluctantly, however, and in recent years groups advocating states' rights have called for limitations on federal power and returning greater political power to the states, or devolving it on them.

This federal structure of national and state authority has allowed states to experiment with a variety of policies in areas such as welfare restructuring, vehicle emissions standards, domestic partnerships, and educational reforms. But it has also resulted in a lack of standardization in those areas and varying levels of benefits and enforcement across the states. Not surprisingly, the greatest tension comes in areas of conflicting or overlapping authority. A tragic example was the government's response to the devastation caused by Hurricane Katrina in the southern Gulf Coast in 2005. Although state and local governments have first responsibility to respond to such a disaster, a state governor can invite the federal government to assist, something that, as one observer noted, the Louisiana governor initially refused to do "out of pride or mistrust or a desire to maintain some degree of control."[4] The lack of a timely response by the federal government further added to the frustration and confusion. These problems persist: as of 2008, tens of thousands of homes remain uninhabitable in New Orleans, public transportation is limited, and the population remains a quarter below its pre-storm level.

POLITICAL CONFLICT AND COMPETITION

Federalism and the separation of powers have had another important consequence: the multiple levels and branches of elected office in the U.S. political system mean that voters in the United States go to the polls far more often than do their counterparts in other democracies. Whereas a typical British or Canadian voter might cast on average four or five votes in as many years, a U.S. voter may go to the polls two or three times as often and cast dozens, if not hundreds, of votes in local, state, and national primary and general elections involving hundreds of candidates for dozens of offices and additional issues presented as initiatives and referenda.

Although this surplus of contests and contestants may be an indication of the health of democracy in the United States, some critics have pointed to it as a cause of "voter fatigue" and one of several reasons for the strikingly lower levels of voter turnout compared with turnout in other democracies. Levels of voter turnout are on average lower in the United States than in all other advanced democracies considered in this volume. Although voter turnout has actually increased in the past two presidential elections—59 percent in 2004 and 62 percent in 2008, the highest level since 1968—only about 40 percent of eligible Americans vote regularly.

Suffrage in the United States, as in other democracies, has expanded over time. Limited originally to white male landholders, the franchise was extended first to nonpropertied white males. It was extended to African American men by the end of the Civil War (though full participation was not possible until Congress passed the **Voting Rights Act** in 1965) and to women in 1920. Most recently, the voting age was lowered from twenty-one to eighteen in 1971.

The Party System

Another factor sometimes blamed for declining rates of voter turnout is the weakness of political parties. Formerly bottom-up organizations linking party members tightly together in purposive grassroots campaigns, political parties in the United States have evolved over time into top-down, candidate-driven national organizations with much looser ties to voters and citizens. American political parties today tend to be weaker and more fragmented than are their counterparts in most other countries.

But with much talk recently about the ideological and even geographic polarization of American voters into "red" (Republican) states and "blue" (Democratic) states, it is clear that the U.S. two-party system has certainly endured even as it has evolved. The U.S. plurality system has fostered a two-party system in which the Democratic and Republican parties have won virtually all votes and political offices since their rivalry began nearly 150 years ago.

THE DEMOCRATIC PARTY

The Democratic Party has its roots in the Democratic-Republican Party, which formed in the 1790s with southern agrarian interests as its base. Andrew Jackson led a splinter group to presidential victory in 1828, calling it the Democratic Party and portraying it as the party of the common man. The Democrats dominated the political scene until 1860 and for most of the years between 1932 and 1968.

As a coalition party, like its Republican rival, the Democratic Party is difficult to characterize fully in terms of a set of philosophical principles or even policy preferences. It may be said, however, that the party tends to embrace policies that support minorities, urban dwellers, organized labor, and working women. Although less so than European social democrats, Democrats in the United States generally perceive state intervention designed to temper the market and enhance equality as both legitimate and necessary. As has been the case with social democratic parties in Britain and elsewhere, however, neoliberal trends since the 1980s have weakened the Democratic coalition, causing conflict over traditional New Deal–type social welfare programs providing such benefits as affirmative action. The party has also struggled with divisive social issues like abortion and gay marriage, which are often opposed by working-class and immigrant communities that would otherwise be drawn to the Democratic Party.

THE REPUBLICAN PARTY

The Republican Party, familiarly called the Grand Old Party (GOP), is in fact not as old as its rival. It first contested elections in 1856 on an anti-slavery platform that also appealed to northern commercial interests. With Lincoln's presidential victory in 1860, the party dominated national politics until the 1930s, when the Great Depression brought that era of its supremacy to an end. By the late 1960s, the GOP had regained the presidency and by the 1990s had obtained congressional majorities as well.

The Republican Party currently brings together a coalition that includes both economic and moral conservatives. It draws support disproportionately from rural dwellers, upper-income voters, evangelical Christians, and voters tending to promote individual freedom over collective equality, such as owners of small businesses and libertarians. Although there are fewer registered Republican voters than Democratic voters, registered Republicans have tended to vote more regularly than do their rivals. Americans identify themselves with both parties in roughly equal numbers, with approximately one third of adults expressing a preference for each of the two parties and most of the remaining one third identifying themselves as independents. As with the Democrats, Republicans are often divided over those who favor greater liberalism in economic and moral issues, as opposed to those whose cultural or religious preferences call for a greater state role in social issues.

THIRD PARTIES

If fully one third of Americans do not identify themselves with either party, is there political space for a third party? Certainly single-member plurality systems in other countries, such as the United Kingdom, have yielded more than two parties. But in the U.S. setting, establishing the kind of presence essential for national viability has proved difficult, if not prohibitive, for smaller parties. Moreover, the dominant parties have all the advantages of incumbency, including the ability to establish and preserve laws discouraging financing third-party candidates and including them on the ballot.

That said, third parties have emerged on the U.S. political scene occasionally as protest voices. In that sense, third parties and their candidates can claim to have had an impact on the political process even if few of them have had any prospect of national electoral success. Among the third-party movements, the Populists of the late nineteenth century and the Progressives of the early twentieth have been the most successful. More recently, protest voices have emerged from each side of the political spectrum: Ross Perot's populist United We Stand Party earned nearly 20 percent of the presidential vote in 1992, and Ralph Nader's pro-environment Green Party garnered nearly 3 percent in 2000. In both cases, one can argue that the third-party candidates took crucial votes from the losing candidate. Nader, for example, garnered nearly 100,000 votes in Florida in the 2000 election. If only 1 percent of his supporters had voted for Gore instead, Gore would have won Florida and the national election. This result had the effect of suppressing third-party candidates in the 2008 presidential election, though they are likely to re-emerge in the future.

A factor contributing to the lack of third-party success in the United States is that the dominant parties have routinely embraced key elements of the more successful third-party movements, bringing at least some of the disaffected voters back into the two-party fold, even as they weaken the third parties.

Elections

In the United States, in contrast to countries that have parliamentary systems, terms for all elected offices—and therefore the sequencing of elections—are fixed. Each state determines the conduct of the elections, including the rules for any primary elections: that is, preliminary direct elections that are held in many states and are designed to narrow the field of candidates. Since the 1950s, electioneering in the United States has shifted from campaigning done almost exclusively by party leaders and grassroots party workers to highly centralized and professionalized media campaigns. Election contests today are hugely expensive and marked by media sound bites, talk-show interviews, televised debates, and advertising blitzes, all guided by polls and sophisticated demographic studies.

No campaigns are more illustrative of this American-style electioneering than those for the U.S. presidency. As voters have apparently become less loyal to either party, and in many cases less interested in voting and participating at all, the parties and their candidates have redoubled their efforts (and expenditures) to capture this top political prize. In total, the 2008 presidential candidates raised over $1.7 billion and spent more than $1.3 billion, far more than that spent on campaigns in any other country. Campaigns begin early, with an extensive season of primaries, and involve an all-out effort to both promote the candidate and denigrate the opponents, all in an attempt to mobilize new voters and persuade the undecided voters.

Civil Society

Observers since the nineteenth-century French political philosopher Alexis de Tocqueville have marveled at the vibrancy of U.S. civil society and the willingness of its citizens to become civically engaged. Recently, however, analysts have pointed to an apparent weakening of that civic commitment, noting low voter turnout and other signs of growing political apathy among U.S. citizens as evidence of a broader, generational decline in social capital.[5] Others argue, however, that the participation of individuals and the organized groups that represent their interests has perhaps not declined as much as it has simply changed: individual citizens associate with one another and seek to influence politics and policy in a variety of new and nontraditional ways.[6]

But precisely because the U.S. policy-making process is so complex and allows so many points of access—including individual officeholders at the national, state, and local level, legislative committees, regulatory agencies, and the initiative process—it has been difficult for individual citizens to influence the political process. As U.S. political parties have grown weaker and less cohesive, various special-interest groups have emerged and expanded their influence. The remarkable proliferation and enormous influence of these groups in the United States sets this case apart from that of other democracies.

Interest groups are often organized around a single issue or a cluster of issues and therefore typically do not officially affiliate with a particular party or candidate. These organized interests can include a single corporation or business association, public interest groups, and even state or local governments. Perhaps most well known are the political action committees (PACs), political fund-raising organizations authorized by law to raise money for political causes. Although forbidden to support individual candidates, PACs were long permitted to raise unlimited amounts of money in support of political parties. Although a 2002 campaign-finance law banned so-called soft-money, or unregulated donations, even to political parties, organized interests quickly discovered a loophole. Thus was born a new type of tax-exempt organization (known as a 527, for the section of the federal tax code governing its behavior) that can raise unlimited campaign funds as long as the funds are spent on voter mobilization and issue advocacy and do not specifically promote a candidate or a party. Besides seeking to finance campaigns, these interest groups, as well as business corporations and wealthy individuals, exercise their influence through various lobbying techniques, both legal and questionable, to promote the interests of their constituencies.

SOCIETY

Ethnic and National Identity

The first American colonists were largely English-speaking Protestants, but early in the country's history its society was diversified by the importation of enslaved Africans and a steady stream of immigration from Europe. In the

ETHNIC GROUPS   **RELIGION**

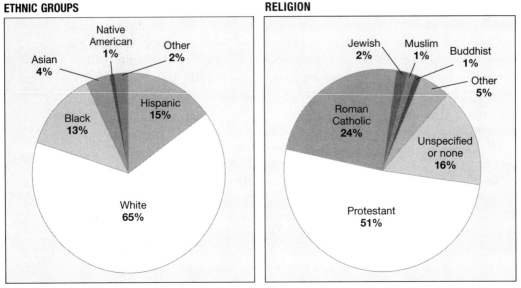

Source: CIA World Factbook, 2008.

mid-nineteenth century, a wave of Asian immigration was spurred by the California gold rush, and another major migration from southern and eastern Europe began in the 1880s. In the 1920s, Congress reacted to the new immigrants by imposing a series of restrictive immigration quotas that favored immigrants from northern Europe. With the amended Immigration and Nationality Act of 1965, Congress abandoned those quotas. As a result, immigration surged again, with the bulk of the new immigrants arriving from Latin America and Asia. The influx of non-European immigrants, especially **Hispanics**, has become an important issue in U.S. politics (see "Current Issues," p. 110). As of 2008, about 13 percent of U.S. citizens were born abroad (in Canada, the figure is 20 percent).

Contrary to the common perception of the United States as a peaceful **melting pot** of cultures, immigrants have always faced resentment and discrimination. The debate about the impact of immigrants on U.S. society has deep roots in American history, with changes depending on which group of immigrants were predominant at the time (Catholics, Asians, Hispanic).

Ideology and Political Culture

Much debate centers around the distinctiveness of U.S. ideology and political culture. There is broad consensus, however, that the attributes discussed below characterize the dominant U.S. ideology.

INDIVIDUALISM AND FREEDOM

Although citizens of other industrial democracies are more likely to view freedom as resulting from government policy, Americans are more likely to view
their individual freedom in terms of what the state cannot do to them. As a
result, whereas many other democracies attempt to specify in their constitutions what the state should provide its citizens, the U.S. Constitution emphasizes citizens' protections from the state.

Like classic liberal thinkers, Americans tend to eschew collective or societal goals in favor of personal or individual goals. Consequently, the role of
private property in U.S. society is especially important, and taxes, which are
viewed as the state's appropriation of private property, are highly unpopular.
Individualism may be one factor that has weakened political parties in the
United States and limited their ideological coherence.

PARTICIPATORY CIVIL SOCIETY

An often-observed feature of U.S. political culture is Americans' participation
in a plethora of voluntary groups that can be referred to collectively as civil
society. Even in the nineteenth century, Tocqueville noted that Americans
were "forever forming associations."[7] The rich web of civic organizations in
the United States exemplifies the notion of self-government and political
equality and performs a host of tasks that in other societies might be carried
out by the state. In their classic work *The Civic Culture*, Gabriel Almond and
Sidney Verba found that American citizens, far more than citizens in other
democracies, believed that participation in community affairs is part of good
citizenship.[8]

Some leading scholars have expressed alarm about what they see as a rapid
decline in the amount of participation in traditional civic groups. Moreover,
scholars have noted that the nature of civil society is changing in the United
States, with less participation in local grassroots organizations and the emergence of national, professionally managed lobbies (such as the National Rifle
Association and the Sierra Club). The terrorist attacks of September 11, 2001,
and concerns about environmental issues may be reviving civic participation,
especially among younger Americans, but there is still a debate about whether
civil society is in danger.

POPULISM

Populism, the idea that the masses should dominate elites and that the popular will should trump professional expertise, is a key feature of the U.S. creed.
As a result, Americans believe in electing public officials at virtually all levels
of society, including some law-enforcement officials and judges, and many
states have seen an explosion of public initiatives that give the electorate a
direct say in a variety of policy issues.

EQUALITY OF OPPORTUNITY, NOT OUTCOME

A deep-seated aspect of U.S. political culture, rooted in the frontier mentality of early America, is the belief that all Americans have, and should have, an equal opportunity to become prosperous and successful. In the nineteenth century, Tocqueville observed that the United States had a far more egalitarian class structure than did Europe. Although assessments of economic equality and social mobility were certainly exaggerated even in early America—women were second-class citizens, and many others, like African Americans, were excluded altogether—the notions of equality of opportunity and social mobility have endured as part of a fundamental ethos.

Opinion research confirms that Americans today hold true to the notion of equality of opportunity but place less value on equality of actual economic outcomes, believing that success is a function of individual effort. Today the reverse of what Tocqueville observed in the nineteenth century is true: disparities of income are greater in the United States than in most of Europe,

IN COMPARISON	ECONOMIC EQUALITY

Do you think economic success is beyond our control? Percent saying no:

Country	Percent
United States	64
Canada	64
United Kingdom	56
France	48
Japan	47
Brazil	41
Mexico	39
Nigeria	35
Russia	33
Germany	31
South Africa	31
China	30
India	18

*Data on Iran not available.

Source: Pew Center for the People and the Press, 2007.

and they are growing quickly. Indeed, Americans tend to oppose state policies aimed at redistributing income to benefit the poor, and compared with their counterparts in other advanced democracies Americans are more likely to blame the poor for not taking advantage of opportunities open to them. For example, Americans far more than Europeans believe that hard work is likely to lead to success.

Despite growing inequality and persistent poverty, Americans evince confidence about their future. Most believe they are better off than their parents, two thirds think that they will achieve the American dream of self-improvement at some point in their lifetime, and 80 percent think that they can start out poor and become rich through their own labors.[9]

ANTI-STATISM

The U.S. public has historically viewed its state with relatively high levels of trust and pride. Paradoxically, a deep-seated liberal distrust of "excessive" state power is also a prominent feature of the political culture. The American Revolution began as a rebellion against a powerful British state that was seen as abusing its authority through the unjust taxation of its citizens. The United States is unique in that anti-statism became a founding principle of the new regime. The founders of the U.S. regime consciously sought to embed in the system myriad checks on the power of the central state (a devolution of much power to state and local governments, a powerful and independent judiciary, separations of powers, and so on). As a result, Americans are skeptical of state efforts to promote social welfare, an outlook that largely explains the relatively small size of the U.S. welfare state. Compared with citizens in other advanced democracies, far fewer Americans believe it is the responsibility of the state to provide basic food and housing for every citizen.

THE IMPORTANCE OF RELIGIOUS VALUES

The United States is also unusual among the advanced democracies in the importance it continues to place on religion. A far higher percentage of its citizens belong to a church or other religious organization than do the citizens of other advanced democracies, and Americans are more likely to believe that there are clear guidelines about what is good or evil.

Some scholars have argued that the high levels of religiosity in the United States stem from the early separation of church and state, which in effect turned religious organizations into voluntary civic groups that competed for membership.[10] In the United States, new religious groups (most recently, evangelical denominations) constantly emerge to attract congregants who might be disillusioned with more established denominations. Indeed, one could argue that the absence of a state religion led Americans to associate religion with democracy, whereas in other countries state religions have been viewed

IN COMPARISON	RELIGIOUS VALUES

Must one believe in God to be moral? Percent answering yes:

Country	Percent
Brazil	83
Nigeria	82
South Africa	74
India	66
United States	57
Mexico	53
Germany	39
Japan	33
Canada	30
Russia	26
United Kingdom	22
France	17

*Data on Iran not available.

Source: Pew Center for the People and the Press, 2007.

as inimical to democracy. The importance of religion in the United States has been linked to what has been called **utopian moralism**, the tendency of Americans to view the world in terms of good versus evil. At the same time, the "free market" for religion and anti-statism often complicates the quest for moral clarity. On many moral issues, such as homosexuality, Americans are uncomfortable both with sanctioning behavior they may see as immoral and with restricting personal behavior.

Finally, it is interesting to see how these values have tracked over time in surveys, the findings of which may run counter to our perceptions of conservative American political culture. Surveys on American values over the past twenty years have shown that the public has grown much more tolerant of homosexuality and gender and racial equality and has become slightly less religious, particularly among the young. Americans (unlike most Europeans) continue to believe that personal success is determined by individual actions (rather than events beyond their control), reflecting the central tenet of American individualism.[11]

POLITICAL ECONOMY

The United States has the world's largest national economy, surpassed only by the combined economies of the European Union. With less than 5 percent of the world's population, the United States contributes 20 percent to its economic output, compared with 11 percent for China, the second-largest producer.[12] In the 1990s, while many of the world's economies struggled the United States enjoyed the longest period of sustained economic growth in its history. Since the 1970s, inflation and unemployment have been relatively low—though this is clearly changing in the face of economic difficulties.

In general, the U.S. state plays a smaller role in the market than do the governments of most other industrialized democracies. The proportion of GDP spent by the state has hovered around 35 percent, less than in most European countries (for example, Sweden's state consumes over 50 percent of GDP); that figure has not varied much over time.[13] Studies of global economic freedom rank the U.S. economy in the top five globally.[14] The United States also has some of the lowest tax rates among the industrialized democracies. However, what the United States does not provide by way of direct state expenditures it often distributes in the form of various tax breaks for home ownership, children, or student loans, to name a few. As a result, some observe that the notion of a weak U.S. welfare system is misleading; rather, benefits are often in the private sector and supported by a complicated system of tax breaks. Such a system, however, tends to benefit the middle class much more than the poor, who lack the resources to take advantage of tax exemptions and might more easily benefit from public goods, such as nationalized health care.

Although private enterprise is the main engine of the U.S. economy, the state does play a significant role. Starting with the New Deal reforms of the 1930s, the state's role in the economy increased to prevent a market collapse and promote equity. Since the 1980s, governments have attempted at times to scale back the role of the state in the economy. The Reagan administration, for example, deregulated many sectors of the economy (including telecommunications and the airlines) to make them more competitive; under Clinton, welfare revisions also devolved many of these responsibilities to the states. Government regulation of the economy has become a contentious issue as

LABOR FORCE BY OCCUPATION

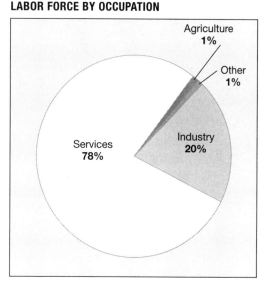

Agriculture 1%

Other 1%

Industry 20%

Services 78%

some deregulated sectors (like the savings and loan and mortage industries) have experienced massive bankruptcies and economic scandals, notably in the housing market. Currently, much of the U.S. state's intervention in the economy is aimed at improving the business climate. Over the past forty years, the tax burden has shifted from corporations to individuals while the state has granted huge subsidies to agribusiness and given generous tax breaks to corporations. At the same time, in contrast to many European countries, the state has done little to support trade unions. In spite of a Republican administration, under George Bush the size of the state grew faster than any time since the 1970s, though this has largely to do with military spending.[15]

Despite its impressive record of economic growth, the United States faces numerous political and economic challenges in the twenty-first century. Foremost is the persistent and growing inequality. Since the Social Security Act of 1935, the U.S. state has provided a safety net of welfare measures, but the provisions have been less extensive than those of other advanced democracies. The United States spends about 15 percent of its GDP on social expenditures, lower than almost any other advanced democracy (only Ireland's is lower). Legislation in the 1960s expanded welfare measures to include some health-care coverage for the poor and the elderly but stopped short of providing universal health care for all citizens. During the Reagan administration, welfare spending per poor recipient fell by one fifth. Under President Clinton, there was bipartisan support for measures aimed at cutting welfare expenditures, and with some notable exceptions (such as prescription benefits for the elderly), social expenditures have stayed flat or declined. As a result, income inequality in the United States has become a serious and growing problem. While the main measure of inequality, the Gini index, has remained relatively flat in many countries around the world, the United States has seen a dramatic increase over the past two decades. In 1980, the U.S. Gini index stood at 30, where it had been since the late 1960s. By way of comparison, this number is the equivalent of the European Union's Gini index in 2007. Since the 1980s the U.S. Gini number has risen to 45, similar to China and many countries in Africa.[16] The United States has the largest number of millionaires in the world but also a large number of poor for a country of its wealth (hence the high degree of inequality). About 12 percent of the country's citizens lives below the poverty line, including approximately 20 percent of its children (the highest percentage among the advanced democracies). This poverty is particularly concentrated among African Americans and Hispanics, indicating the way in which poverty in the United States is compounded by migration and racism. Persistent racial divisions in the United States remain one of the greatest challenges to reducing inequality.

Related to the problems of inequality and poverty is the growing budget deficit over the past two decades. While U.S. social expenditures are small compared with those of other advanced democracies, the low level of taxation, growing numbers of elderly, and costs of defense and the wars in Iraq and Afghanistan have translated into far greater expenses than state revenues. This budget deficit has been funded by borrowing. As a result, the United States has a gigantic national debt of almost $10 trillion, which is 70 percent of GDP, a level not seen since World War II. If at some point the United States is no longer able to sustain this debt through borrowing (often from foreign sources, such as China), the result could be economic decline and the inability to sustain military commitments abroad.

Finally, the U.S. economy also faces the challenges of globalization that are common to the other cases in this book. Both Democrats and Republicans have pushed for freer world trade, though there has been pressure in the other direction of late. President Clinton signed the North American Free Trade Agreement (NAFTA), which has further integrated the economies of the country's largest trading partners: Canada and Mexico. The subsequent administration pushed for expanding free trade agreements with much of Latin America. During the presidential campaign of 2008, however, Democrats in particular singled out NAFTA as a cause of job losses and economic decline, and both parties have frequently pointed to China as a cause of American economic woes. Global economic difficulties and recession currently confronts most countries. How will this affect personal and government debt, growth, inequality, and poverty in the United States? How will it affect economic relations between the United States and the rest of the world? We will get a better sense of this as events unfold in the near future.

FOREIGN RELATIONS AND THE WORLD

The United States remains the most powerful actor in world politics, due in large part to the size of its military and its economy. The United States plays a major role in a number of multilateral institutions, such as the International Monetary Fund, the World Bank, and the United Nations.

The United States spent its first century after independence relatively removed from world affairs. Governing a country blessed with geographic remoteness from most of the world's major conflicts, U.S. presidents generally sought to avoid what President Thomas Jefferson called "entangling alliances." The rapid growth of the population and the economy drove the projection of U.S. power beyond its borders, however, in what some Americans came to view as the nation's **manifest destiny**. In the early nineteenth century, President James Monroe (1821–1825) warned European powers to stay out of the entire Western Hemisphere (this became known as the Monroe Doctrine). Later in the century, the United States extended its borders and its power through economic and military means, with victories in the Mexican War (1846–1848) and the Spanish-American War (1898) and with the annexation of Hawaii (1898).

By the early twentieth century, the United States was the dominant foreign power in Latin America and expanded its influence there under President Theodore Roosevelt. Roosevelt, who bragged that he "took" Panama from Colombia in 1903 to build the canal there, preferred economic domination and the threat of U.S. military action (what he called the Big Stick) as a means of influence, rather than officially acquiring territory. Roosevelt's visit to Panama in 1906, the first-ever foreign trip by a U.S. president, boldly ended the era of isolation.

The long-held preference for avoiding entanglements in Europe was forsaken when the United States belatedly entered World War I. The creation of a national military draft enabled a significant increase in military capability, and the Allied victory resulted in a national sense of pride and confidence. At the same time, revulsion at the deaths of a hundred thousand Americnas created a strong popular desire to return to isolationism and avoid future wars. The United States entered World War II only after the Japanese attack on Pearl Harbor, Hawaii, in December 1941. Involvement in World War II was a major turning point in the nation's foreign policy. The United States created a massive army, and its participation was a decisive factor in the Allied victory against the Axis powers. The controversial U.S. decision to deploy its nuclear arsenal against Japan in 1945 heralded its new status as a global superpower.

Almost immediately after World War II, the United States moved to counter the influence of its wartime ally, the Soviet Union, in a growing conflict that came to be known as the cold war. Under the Marshall Plan (1947–1952), the United States invested heavily in the rebuilding of Western Europe, in large part to immunize the region against Communism. The United States also formed an alliance of industrialized democracies, the North Atlantic Treaty Organization (NATO), in 1949 to ensure the provision of mutual defense in the event of a Soviet attack. In the second half of the twentieth century, the United States acted frequently through direct invasion or covert action to deter Communist threats (real or perceived) in Asia and Latin America.

The U.S. record in its quest to contain the global spread of Communism was mixed. In the Korean War (1950–1953), it succeeded in protecting South Korea from Communist invasion, and it later helped topple numerous governments it viewed as dangerous (such as Guatemala's in 1954 and Chile's in 1973). The United States was unable to prevent a Communist victory in China in 1949, however, though it intervened to preserve the government of Taiwan, and it failed in the Vietnam War (1961–1973), a protracted, costly, and politically unpopular conflict that did not prevent a Communist takeover of Vietnam. Similarly, despite an attempted invasion and decades of covert action and economic pressure, the United States failed to overthrow the Communist regime of Fidel Castro in neighboring Cuba.

The fall of the Berlin Wall in 1989 and the subsequent collapse of the Soviet Union effectively brought the cold war to an end and left the United States as the only world power. This post-Soviet era nonetheless produced serious new challenges. As the undisputed global leader, the United States was called upon to help resolve ethnic violence that erupted in the Balkans and elsewhere. America's cold-war involvement in global conflicts and its enhanced power in the post–cold-war era created considerable global resentment of the United States. In the 1990s, the United States intervened militarily in the Persian Gulf (to repel the Iraqi invasion of Kuwait) and in the Balkans (to stem ethnic violence), both times taking part in international peacekeeping efforts. After the terrorist attacks on the United States of September 11, 2001, President George W. Bush declared a "war" against global terrorism and announced that the United States would use unilateral preemptive force against all possible terrorist threats to the United States. This **Bush doctrine** was viewed by many countries, including some U.S. allies, as a rejection of international law and the United Nations. Some critics viewed it as a dangerous projection of U.S. nationalism and a reassertion of the nineteenth-century view of manifest destiny.[17] As a result, anti-Americanism, a long-standing sentiment that goes back even to the period of isolationism, rose dramatically around the world.

In October 2001, in the first manifestation of the Bush doctrine, the United States led a coalition of forces that invaded Afghanistan and toppled the regime that had harbored Al Qaeda, the organization responsible for the September 11 attacks. The Bush doctrine was further called on in March 2003 with the U.S.-led invasion of Iraq. The Bush administration claimed that Iraq was a threat to the United States and the world because of its possession of weapons of mass destruction and because it, too, harbored terrorists (neither of which turned out to be correct). By the end of 2008, the wars in Iraq and Afghanistan had cost 100,000 civilian lives and the deaths of more than 4,000 U.S. soldiers, and the United States has allocated close to $1 trillion through 2009 for war and security-related expenditures. Contrary to expectations, however, these conflicts became less of an issue in the 2008 presidential elections, as improvements in Iraqi security and a decline in the American economy shifted public attention. Some political analysts hope that the new administration will be able to facilitate a drawdown of troops from Iraq and improve frayed relations with much of the world, which has grown critical of the unilateralist policies of the Bush administration. However, tense relations with Russia, Iran, and at times China mean that the United States will continue to face challenges in the international system.

CURRENT ISSUES

CULTURAL DIVERSITY AND U.S. NATIONAL IDENTITY

The current wave of immigration is a hot political issue. In California, for example, voters in 1994 passed an initiative denying state services to illegal immigrants and their children. Some observers have gone so far as to argue that the very size of Mexican immigration in particular will undermine the fundamental values of the United States, claiming that this group is so large and distinct that it will resist assimilation.[18] Others disagree, noting that since the founding of the United States, various waves of immigrants have been viewed as a threat to American political culture but over time have been assimilated. Even those observers who agree that the current flow of immigration differs in many important respects from those of the past generally disagree with the assessment that Mexican immigration poses a threat to U.S. society.[19] Much evidence points to the fact that Hispanic immigrants are speaking English and otherwise assimilating into U.S. culture: more than 90 percent of second-generation Hispanics are either bilingual or mainly English speakers, and many intermarry with non-Hispanic partners. As one scholar has concluded, "Hispanic immigration is part and parcel of broader American patterns of assimilation and integration. Their story, like that of the Irish, Jews, and Italians before them, is an American story."[20]

Similarly, the public shows mixed views of immigration. After the September 11, 2001, attack, there was a sharp increase in support for restricting immigration, but this support has steadily declined in recent years.[21] More generally, several scholarly studies indicate that the relatively weak level of social expenditures in the United States has much to do with its cultural diversity. In short, while citizens may be willing to support immigration, they also appear to be much less willing to redistribute wealth to those who they feel are not like them.[22] Indeed, the rise of the welfare state in the United States coincides with heavy restrictions on immigration after World War I and II, and the rollback of the welfare state with the rapid increase in immigration starting in the 1980s. The United States continues to be a melting pot of cultures fed by a steady stream of immigrants, but Americans remain ambivalent and deeply divided about this aspect of their society. If economic difficulties persist over the long term, this may increase pressure for restrictions on immigration, as immigrants become the flashpoint for anxieties about economic security. That said, it is projected that by 2042 minorities in the United States will in fact become the majority population.

BOOM AND BUST IN THE U.S. ECONOMY

The U.S. economy has a bad hangover. Over the course of the 2000s there was an enormous boom in the housing market, facilitated by economic growth and looser (and often unethical and illegal) practices in the loan markets. While home ownership has long been an important symbolic part of the American economy, in recent years a large market grew for speculative residential property. Buyers purchased larger homes and/or second homes on the prospect that they could quickly sell, or "flip," these properties for a substantial profit. In addition, rising housing prices gave many Americans the ability and incentive to borrow against the growing equity in their homes. All of this fed into a bubble economy, where psychological perceptions that one could get rich quick began to override warning signs that the market could not sustain such expansion and growth. By 2006, the bubble began to burst, taking much of the consumers' confidence with it. As of late 2008, home sales had reached a ten-year low, prices had fallen by as much as a third in some markets, and many homeowners found themselves saddled with loans for more than their houses were worth—the first national housing crash since the Great Depression. This decline in the housing market has in turn affected, for example, credit and employment as consumers cut back their spending and financial institutions cut back their loans or went under. This has had a ripple effect on the global economy, which depends on the United States for much of its exports, leading to economic difficulties worldwide, from Europe to Asia.

What is the long-term repercussion of the bubble? Some speculate that it may take several years before the United States can clear these financial problems, leading to reduced growth worldwide. It may also affect the role that the United States plays in the international community, severely restricting its ability to influence international relations through economic or other means. Could the housing market be the first sign in the decline of the United States as the dominant economic force in the global economy? If so, what might be the implications for international growth and globalization?

NOTES

1. Seymour Martin Lipset, *The First New Nation: The United States in Historical and Comparative Perspective* (New York: W. W. Norton, 1979), p. 2.
2. This quotation and its subsequent elaboration are drawn from Theodore J. Lowi et al., *American Government: Power and Purpose,* 7th ed. (New York: W. W. Norton, 2002), p. 162.
3. Lowi et al., *American Government,* p. 454.
4. Nicholas Lehman, "Insurrection," *New Yorker,* 26 (September 2005), pp. 66–67.
5. Robert Putnam, *Bowling Alone: The Collapse and Revival of American Community* (New York: Simon and Schuster, 2000).
6. See, for example, the recent Pew Internet and American Life Project, www.pewinternet.org (accessed 27 January 2006).
7. Quoted in "Degrees of Separation," Survey: America, *Economist,* 14 (July 2005).

8. Alan Abramowitz, "The United States: Political Culture under Stress," in Gabriel Almond and Sidney Verba, eds., *The Civic Culture Revisited* (Boston: Little, Brown, 1980), p. 179.

9. "Degrees of Separation."

10. Lipset, *The First New Nation*, pp. 180–81.

11. *Trends in Core Values and Political Attitudes 1987–2007*, Pew Center for the People and the Press, http://people-press.org (accessed 2 August 2008).

12. See IMF World Economic Outlook database, 2008, www.imf.org.

13. Graham K. Wilson, *Only in America? The Politics of the United States in Comparative Perspective* (Chatham, NJ: Chatham House, 1998), p. 61.

14. Heritage Foundation, Index of Economic Freedom 2008, www.heritage.org (accessed 19 February 2009).

15. Richard Kogan, *Federal Spending, 2001 Through 2008*, Center on Budget and Policy Priorities, March 2008, www.cbpp.org/3-5-08bud.htm (accessed 2 August 2008).

16. For details, see the CIA World Factbook, www.odci.gov (accessed 5 August 2008).

17. This is the argument of Anatole Lieven, *America, Right or Wrong: An Anatomy of American Nationalism* (New York: Oxford University Press, 2005).

18. Samuel P. Huntington, *Who are We? The Challenges to America's National Identity* (New York: Simon and Schuster, 2004).

19. Tamar Jacoby, ed., *Reinventing the Melting Pot: The New Immigrants and What It Means to Be American* (New York: Basic Books, 2004).

20. Robert A. Levine, "Assimilation, Past and Present," *Public Interest* (Spring 2005), p. 108.

21. "Fewer Americans Favor Cutting Back Immigration" Gallup, July 10, 2008. www.gallup.com (accessed 19 February 2009).

22. Alberto Alesina and Edward Glaeser, *Fighting Poverty in the US and Europe: A World of Difference* (Oxford, UK: Oxford University Press, 2006).

GLOSSARY OF KEY TERMS

American Revolution   Conflict between Britain and the American colonists that resulted in U.S. independence (1775–1783).

Articles of Confederation   A weak, confederal regime that governed the colonies after 1781. It was replaced by the U.S. Constitution after 1790.

Bill of Rights   Ten amendments to the Constitution passed by the first United States Congress in 1789.

Bush doctrine   President George W. Bush's declaration that the United States would use military force to preempt potential terrorist threats to U.S. security.

Bush, George W.   President of the United States from 2001 to 2009.

cabinet   The appointed officials that serve the executive in overseeing the various state bureaucracies.

civil rights movement   The movement (1955–1965) designed to address the legacy of slavery by ending various forms of racial discrimination.

Civil War   Conflict between the Southern, slave-holding states and the North.

The victory of the North preserved the unity of the United States and resulted in the abolition of slavery.

Declaration of Independence   The declaration of independence from Britain, issued by the Continental Congress in 1776.

Democratic-Republicans   Early opponents of a strong federal state, led by Thomas Jefferson.

federalism   A system in which significant state powers, such as taxation, lawmaking, and security are devolved to regional or local bodies.

Federalists   Early advocates of a strong federal state in the United States, led by Alexander Hamilton.

gerrymandering   Dividing up electoral districts in such a way as to favor one political party or marginalize certain groups.

Hispanics   Residents of the United States who trace their ancestry to Spanish-speaking countries in Latin America.

House of Representatives   The lower house of the U.S. congress (legislature).

Louisiana Purchase   The 1803 purchase of territory from France that greatly expanded U.S. territory westward.

manifest destiny   View held by many Americans throughout U.S. history that the U.S. was destined to lead the world.

melting pot   The diversity of cultures that has historically characterized U.S. society.

Mexican-American War   The 1846 conflict between Mexico and the United States that resulted in the U.S. acquisition of much of the current Southwest of the United States.

New Deal   A set of policies between 1933 and 1938 that used state intervention to stimulate the economy and to counter the effects of the Great Depression.

Obama, Barack   President of the United States, elected in 2008.

populism   A key feature of U.S. ideology, the idea that the masses should dominate elites, and that the popular will should trump those with professional expertise.

Progressive Era   The period from 1903–1920 when progressives sought to use the state to limit the power of private business.

Puritans   Radical protestants, who comprised a large portion of the original American colonists.

rule of law   All citizens are equal before the law and no one is above the law, including political leaders.

Senate   The upper house of the United States Congress (legislature).

separation of powers   A system in which there are significant and independent sources of power within the executive, legislative, and judicial systems.

Thirteenth Amendment   The Constitutional amendment that abolished slavery.

utopian moralism   The tendency of Americans to view the world in terms of good versus evil.

Vietnam War   The protracted, costly, and ultimately unsuccessful attempt to defeat Communism in Southeast Asia (1959–1975).

Voting Rights Act   1965 legislation that eliminated barriers that had been imposed by some states to prevent African Americans from voting. It was seen as a major victory in the struggle for civil rights.

War on Poverty   President Lyndon Johnson's use of state spending to combat inequality.

Washington, George   Commander of the U.S. forces during the Revolutionary War, and first president of the United States.

WEB LINKS

C-SPAN **www.cspan.org** public service media focused on U.S. politics

Library of Congress **http://thomas.loc.gov**

National Archives **www.archives.gov** repository for government documents

Project Vote Smart **www.votesmart.org** on elections, elected officials, and candidates

Real Clear Politics **www.realclearpolitics.com** politics blog

Roll Call **www.rollcall.com** news source focused on Congress

University of Michigan **www.lib.umich.edu/govdocs/psusp.html** US politics resources

4 FRANCE

Head of state: President Nicolas Sarkozy
(since May 17, 2007)

Head of government:
Prime Minister François Fillon
(since May 17, 2007)

Capital: Paris

Total land size: 547,030 sq km

Population: 64 million

GDP at PPP: 2.047 trillion US$

GDP per capita at PPP: $33,200

Human development index ranking: 10

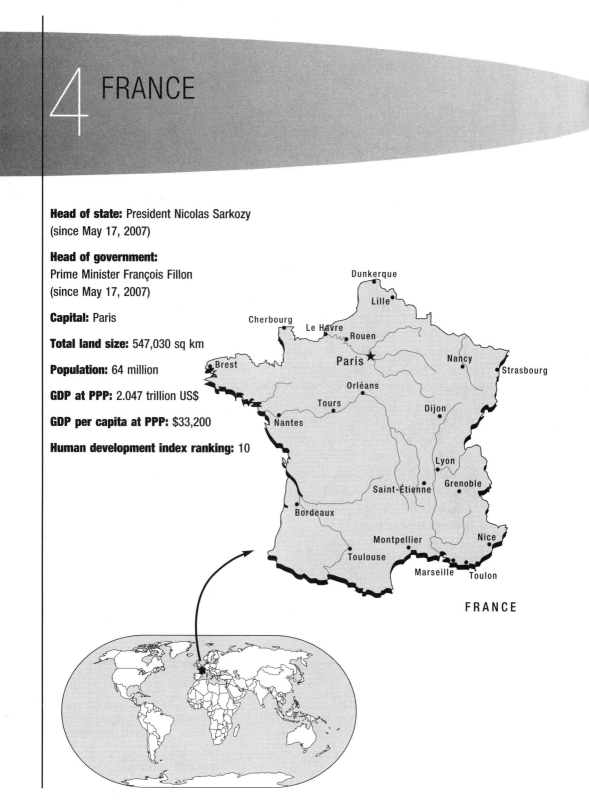

FRANCE

INTRODUCTION

Why Study This Case?

In a fundamental sense, comparative politics is the comparative study of political regimes. The term **regime**, fittingly, comes from the French word for *rule* or *order* and refers to the norms and rules that govern politics. These norms and rules are institutionalized—often embodied in a constitution—but can and do change as a result of dramatic social events or national crises. Regimes express fundamental ideals about where authority should reside and to what end this authority should be employed.

The French case offers a fascinating study of regimes. In little more than two centuries, France has endured a remarkable range of regimes, including both authoritarian (from absolute monarchy to revolutionary dictatorship) and democratic (such as parliamentary and semi-presidential). During this period, France has been governed by no less than three monarchies, two empires, five republics, a Fascist regime, and two provisional governments and has promulgated fifteen separate constitutions. A popular nineteenth-century joke had a Parisian bookseller refusing to sell a copy of the French constitution to a would-be customer, claiming he did not sell periodicals.[1] The most dramatic transition was, of course, the **French Revolution** (1789–1799) in which French citizens overthrew the **ancien régime** (the European old order of absolute monarchy buttressed by religious authority) and replaced it, albeit briefly, with a democratic republic guided by the Declaration of the Rights of Man and of the Citizen.

France can claim title to the birthplace of modern democracy on the European continent, but democracy has not come easily. The French Revolution embraced a set of universal rights for all people and redefined French subjects as citizens. But French revolutionaries concluded that the state had to be strong enough to destroy the old regime, impose the new, and forge a strong national identity. French republicanism established a short-lived revolutionary dictatorship that was followed by Napoléon Bonaparte's **coup d'état**—a forceful and sudden overthrow of government. Over the next seven decades, French reactionaries battled radicals, and France oscillated between empires, monarchies, and republics, with two more revolutions as well.

Not until the present **Fifth Republic** (established in 1958) has France seemed able to break this alternating cycle of stern authoritarian rule and chaotic, or at least dysfunctional, democracy. Although revolution is no longer politics-as-usual and today's French citizens are more centrist, French political life is far from mundane. French citizens remain skeptical, if not cynical, about politics and politicians and vigorously divided on issues such as immigration, European integration, unemployment, and the proper role of the state. Whereas most established democracies have vested their constitutions with a certain sanctity and have only cautiously amended them, France's willingness to write and rewrite the rules of the political game offers us a fascinating study in comparative politics and gives us insights into French politics and its political culture.[2]

Major Geographic and Demographic Features

France is a large country roughly the size of Texas. By European standards, it is substantial, twice the area of Great Britain; in Europe, it is third in size only to Russia and Ukraine. France seems even larger than it is because of its span across much of Western Europe; it shares borders with six countries and is at once an Atlantic, continental, and Mediterranean country.

Although this geography has facilitated foreign commerce, it has also exacerbated French feelings of vulnerability. Protected by mountains to the southwest (the Pyrénées) and the southeast (the Alps), no such natural barriers exist on its border with Belgium and Germany to the north and northeast. Through the centuries, this corridor has been the locus of repeated invasions and confrontations. Abundant mineral resources (in the Saar region) and productive farmland (in Alsace-Lorraine) have raised the stakes and aggravated the conflicts. Vulnerability has also motivated France's preoccupation with establishing a formidable standing army and a strong centralized state (unlike England, which had a strong navy but a weak army). The French solution to its geographic vulnerability after World War I was the construction of the Maginot Line, a series of concrete fortifications along the Franco-German border designed to prevent the next war. Nazi forces, however, simply skirted the defenses and invaded France through Belgium. The French solution after World War II—integration with its long-standing German nemesis in the form of the European Union—has proved much more effective.

Within France, there are no significant geographic obstacles to transportation or communication. A number of navigable rivers have, over the centuries, been supplemented by canals and a highly developed rail system. This ease of internal travel and communication, combined with France's natural mountain and ocean boundaries, has given the French a strong sense of national identity and facilitated France's economic and political integration.

At the hub of this national integration—both literally and organizationally—lies the capital, Paris. For centuries, Paris has served as the administrative, commercial, and cultural nucleus of France. Generations of Parisian bureaucrats have imposed taxes, corvée (mandatory labor assessments), and even the Parisian dialect of French on all regions of the country. In addition to this linguistic homogeneity, more than 80 percent of all French are at least nominally Catholic.

This national unity should not be exaggerated, however. Although metropolitan Paris is home to roughly one sixth (10 million) of France's 60 million citizens, "provincial" life, with its more rustic and relaxed lifestyle, is mythologized by many French people over the hustle and bustle of urban life. One enduring effect of this view is that while the number of farmers has shrunk in France, they have a disproportionate amount of power and have strongly influenced not only domestic politics but also those of the European Union. The preservation of rural life as a symbol of being French has lead to conflicts over agricultural subsidies and globalization, complicating domestic and international politics. Similarly, although French citizens are proud of their national heritage, many are likewise proud of their regional differences. Generally speaking, southern France is more rural, conservative, religious, and agrarian—and relatively less prosperous—than is northern France, which is more urban, politically liberal, secular, and industrial.

Historical Development of the State

Whereas French history offers us valuable insights into the study of regimes, this same history is also an essential primer on the rise of the modern nation-state. From Louis XIV's declaration *L'état, c'est moi* (I am the state) to Napoléon's establishment of bureaucratic legal codes and the rule of law, the development of the French state offers an archetype for the emergence of a powerful state, one paradoxically combined with a public that views mass demonstrations against authority as an important tool of political change.

ABSOLUTISM AND THE CONSOLIDATION OF THE MODERN FRENCH STATE

In carving out the Holy Roman Empire in the early ninth century, Charlemagne, leader of a Germanic tribe known as the Franks, established a realm encompassing much of Western Europe. In doing so, he unified the area we know as France earlier than would occur in any of the other European states, including Britain. But with Charlemagne's death, Frankish control was rexduced to an assortment of small feudal kingdoms and principalities well within the confines of what is now France. As with feudal kings elsewhere, the Frankish rulers sought to increase their holdings, stature, and security by squeezing wealth from their subjects. In the United Kingdom, struggles among the aristocracy led to a gradual decentralization of power, as signified by the Magna Carta. In France, however, feudalism led to absolute monarchs, who centralized authority and developed bureaucracies capable of taxing the subjects and administering the other affairs of state.

Absolute monarchy—the stage in the evolutionary development of Europe between the more decentralized feudal monarchies of the Middle Ages and the constitutional governments of the modern era—made several important con-

TIME LINE OF POLITICAL DEVELOPMENT

Year	Event
800 C.E.	"France" first emerges as an independent power under Charlemagne
1661–1715	Absolute monarchy culminates in rule of Louis XIV
1789	French Revolution launched with storming of the Bastille in Paris
1799	Napoléon Bonaparte seizes power and brings revolution to an end
1848, 1871	Popular uprisings lead to the Second and Third Republics
1940	Third Republic replaced by Vichy (German puppet) regime
1946	The weak Fourth Republic is established
1954	French leave Vietnam in defeat
1958	Threat of civil war over Algeria returns Charles de Gaulle to office, leading to the ratification of his presidency and the Fifth Republic by referendum
1968	The Events of May rioters in Paris demand social and educational reforms
1969	De Gaulle resigns
1981	François Mitterrand and Socialists elected
1986	First period of "cohabitation" between Socialist president Mitterrand and neo-Gaullist prime minister Jacques Chirac
1992	Slim majority of French voters approve Maastricht Treaty, establishing the European Monetary Union (within the European Union) and the euro
2005	In referendum, French voters reject proposed European Union constitution

tributions to the modern French state.[3] Many of the responsibilities that we associate with a modern state, such as education, welfare, and transportation, were at that time handled by the family, the church, an odd assortment of local authorities, or simply not at all. But three primary duties—making and executing laws, waging war and providing defense, and raising money to defend the state—became the responsibility of the French kings.

In carrying out those responsibilities, these monarchs did not ignore the social classes outside the court. In fact, the crown initially allied with and—

as its autonomy grew—ultimately employed each relevant class, or "estate," in carrying out its duties. The Catholic clergy, or First Estate, had primary responsibility for administering the legal system; the landed aristocracy, or Second Estate, prosecuted the king's wars; and financiers from the commoners who made up the commercial class, or Third Estate, gathered the taxes that paid for the luxuries of the court, the military, and the rest of the state apparatus. In order to co-opt these groups initially, in the fourteenth century the monarchy established an assembly known as the **Estates General**, with representatives from each of the three estates.

By the fifteenth century, Louis XI had sufficiently centralized his authority such that he could wage expansive wars, doubling the size of his kingdom to roughly France's current borders. He was also able to weaken the influence of the nobility and largely ignore the Estates General. His successors over the next three centuries reinforced these trends, forging a centralized state with a reputation for administrative efficiency that has largely persisted to this day. The pinnacle of this absolutist authority came during the rule of Louis XIV, who dubbed himself the Sun King and famously declared that he alone *was* the state. Although that was an overstatement, the absolutist French state of the seventeenth century was remarkable, indeed the envy of all Europe. France had a standing professional army, a mercantilist state-run economy, a ruthless tax system, and the extravagant palace of Versailles. In fact, the Sun King never even convened the Estates General.

Neither war nor court life came cheap, and the drains on the royal coffers, combined with the system of taxation, had by the eighteenth century reduced the French commoners to famine and bankrupted the state. In a desperate attempt to shore up support and seek essential funding, Louis XVI convened the long-dormant Estates General in 1789. Although each estate was to have one vote (allowing the more conservative clergy and nobility to override the commoners), the more numerous representatives of the Third Estate argued that all three houses should meet together as one assembly (allowing the commoners to prevail). The king resisted, stirring the anger and protests of the commoners. In this revolutionary environment, rising bread prices in Paris prompted Parisians to storm the Bastille, the old Paris jailhouse, on July 14, 1789, launching the French Revolution.

THE FRENCH REVOLUTION, DESTRUCTION OF THE ARISTOCRACY, AND EXTENSION OF STATE POWER

In the early days of the revolution, the Third Estate established the **National Assembly**, and that body issued the Declaration of the Rights of Man and of the Citizen. Inspired by the French political thinkers Jean-Jacques Rousseau and Baron de Montesquieu, and by the example of the American Revolution, this document was a powerful and influential statement on liberty that proclaimed the natural rights of the individual in opposition to the tyranny of monarchy. The revolutionaries concluded that the ancien régime, with its hereditary and religious privileges, must be destroyed and replaced. No longer should birth or faith determine justice, public office, or taxation. "Liberty, Fraternity, Equality" became the rallying cry of the revolution.

Rather, in the new French republic, sovereignty was to rest with the people and their elected representatives, church and state were to be separate, and all male citizens could claim the natural and universal rights of both freedom and equality before the law. These revolutionary pronouncements have obviously had a profound effect on French politics and the constitutions of nearly all modern nation-states since then. In addition, the revolution fostered nationalism and patriotism as an expression of the natural right of the French nation-state to exist on terms established by its own citizens. A rational, "scientific" state would be the revolutionaries' goal. But unlike their American counterparts, who feared the tyranny of any centralized authority, French revolutionaries never questioned a powerful, centralized state, who would control it, and toward what ends it would serve.

Indeed, the new republic embraced what we might now call a technocratic form of rule, embracing the Enlightenment and the early stages of the Scientific Revolution to modernize and transform their society, sweeping away old institutions. In spite of its absolutism, the ancien régime, like most states of that period, inhibited trade and development by its lack of a number of basic standards. In response, the French Revolution became a catalyst for standardization and reform, perhaps best captured in the metric system, introduced in 1795 and soon adopted by most of the world (the United States and the United Kingdom being notable exceptions). Calendar and monetary reforms were similarly embraced by the French revolutionaries. These reforms and standardization were important not only because they changed France and much of the rest of the world, but also because they institutionalized the idea that the state could play an important role in directing expertise, science, and technology toward the good of the country as a whole. This idea continues to be an important part of French meritocratic politics and technocratic economic policies, as we shall see.

In 1791, French moderates wrote a new constitution limiting the monarchy and setting up a representative assembly that in many ways resembled Britain's constitutional monarchy. But this middle-ground effort was undermined both by monarchists on the right (conservative nobles and clerics) and by radical anti-clerical republicans on the left. Led by a militant faction known as the Jacobins, the radicals seized power and launched a class war known as the **Reign of Terror**, in which many who stood in the way of this radical vision of republicanism were executed (including the monarchy). As in other later revolutions, such as in the Soviet Union and China, terror bred turmoil and paranoia such that the very perpetrators of the revolution were themselves devoured by the violence. The Jacobins' ruthless leader, Robespierre, became the guillotine's final victim as the Reign of Terror came to an end in 1794. Although the violence ended, this ideological and cultural division between two poles—conservative, Catholic, and rural versus progressive, secular, and urban—would resonate in French politics for centuries and in some ways persists today.

In the wake of the Reign of Terror, moderates established a weak and ineffectual government that limped along for five more years and two more constitutions. In 1799, General Napoléon Bonaparte seized power in a coup d'état that brought the decade of revolutionary turmoil to an end. Unlike the revolution that had swept away the former social and political institutions, Napoléon's coup retained and indeed codified key elements of the revolutionary order. The Napoleonic Code documented the principles that all men are equal before the law; that the people, not a monarch, are sovereign; and that the church and state are separate domains. Further enhancing France's long bureaucratic tradition, Napoléon established a meritocratic civil service open to all citizens and a system of elite schools to train these functionaries.[4]

THE RETURN TO ABSOLUTISM IN POST-REVOLUTIONARY FRANCE

Napoléon's strong state became even stronger when he was proclaimed emperor for life in a national referendum in 1804, and the First Republic gave way to the First Empire. Clearly, French citizens preferred the peace, stability, and order of Napoleonic France to the republican chaos that had preceded it. Although the French also valued their civil and property rights, over time Napoléon's rule increasingly resembled the tyranny of the absolute monarchy that had justified the revolution. Napoléon ruled for another ten years, then abdicated the throne for a year in the wake of a series of military defeats at the hands of the hostile conservative monarchies that surrounded France. After a brief return, Napoléon was permanently defeated in 1815 by the British at the Battle of Waterloo and died in exile, remembered by most French as a national hero.

With military support from the victorious European powers, absolute monarchy, not democracy, replaced Napoléon's empire, and the bitter ideological divisions of the revolutionary era reemerged. The church and the aristocracy reasserted their privileges until a popular revolt in 1830 forced the crown to establish a constitutional monarchy and promise to pay more respect to the interests of the rising bourgeoisie. A third revolution, in 1848, ended monarchical rule, established universal male suffrage, and constituted the short-lived Second Republic, with a directly elected president—the first such office in Europe. Elsewhere in Europe executive power was held by monarchs and prime ministers. In this development one sees the ongoing French preference for a strong executive, albeit one who is directly chosen by the people; it reflects an amalgam of monarchical and revolutionary values. In 1848, the people elected as their first president Napoléon's nephew Louis-Napoléon, who quickly followed in his uncle's footsteps, using a national referendum to proclaim himself emperor. In 1852, Louis-Napoléon (now called Napoléon III) replaced the Second Republic with the Second Empire. Napoléon III ruled for nearly two decades, presiding over a period of peace and rapid industrial growth.

Both peace and prosperity came to an end with France's defeat in the Franco-Prussian War of 1870–1871, in which Napoléon III was captured and the Second Empire came to an end. Not surprisingly, the absence of central authority once again led to violent conflict between conservative monarchists and radical republicans. Although conservatives came to dominate the National Assembly, radicals in Paris, inspired by Marx, established a short-lived rival government known as the Paris Commune, until French troops crushed the uprising. While unsuccessful, the Commune would continue to inspire Communists and anarchists worldwide for decades to come; it was in reference to the Commune that Marx and Engels first spoke of a dictatorship of the proletariat that could serve as a model for future revolutions. Interestingly, then, France contributed to the emergence of not only liberal democratic ideas but also Communist ones, though in both cases the regimes themselves foundered in France.

DEMOCRATIZATION AND THE WEAK REGIMES OF THE THIRD AND FOURTH REPUBLICS

Out of the ashes of the Second Empire emerged France's Third Republic, which survived seventy years, until the outbreak of World War II. Its endurance should not be mistaken, however, for either strength or legitimacy. The Third Republic was weakened by the persistent and seemingly irreconcilable splits among among various ideological factions, ranging from monarchists to anarchists. These divisions made stable government almost impossible, with successive governments often lasting less than a year. Despite weak government, the powerful bureaucracy remained and, allied with French business interests, continued to promote economic development.

Political divisions were further polarized by the devastation of World War I, during which more than 1.5 million French people died, and the economic depression that followed. These crises provided fertile ground for both Communism and fascism, as political extremists of the left and the right proffered Stalinist Russia and Nazi Germany, respectively, as preferable alternatives to France's weak and immobilized Third Republic.

This debate was preempted by France's swift defeat at the hands of the overwhelming Nazi military force in the opening weeks of World War II. The

Nazi victors collaborated with the French right in setting up the puppet Vichy regime, named after the town in central France where the government was based. Even many French moderates ended up supporting this fascist government, reasoning that the Nazis were better than the threat of a Communist government.[5] Other French citizens, however, including members of religious groups and Communists, resisted (both from within France and outside of the country) the Nazi occupation. Although the resistance effort was diverse and at best only loosely linked, the man who came to lead the military resistance and ultimately embody the French anti-Nazi movement was General Charles de Gaulle, who led French forces in England following his retreat from France in 1940.

After World War II, de Gaulle's heroic stature as leader of the resistance effort and his role in France's provisional government made it natural that he would play an important political role in the new Fourth Republic. However, de Gaulle believed that one of the main weaknesses of the previous regime was that too little power had been invested in the presidency, a view not shared by other political leaders. As a result, de Gaulle withdrew from politics. After the war, the new Fourth Republic, based on an electoral system of proportional representation and parliamentary government with a weak prime minister, was frequently as paralyzed as the Third Republic had been. No single party or even a stable coalition of parties was able to form a government for long—twenty governments were formed in just twelve years—and thus no political leader was in a position to make difficult choices.

During this period there was significant progress in such areas as postwar reconstruction and the creation of the European Union (EU). The regime, however, could not effectively deal with its colonial legacy, as independence movements in many colonies grew powerful. This was particularly acute in the case of Algeria: a North African and Muslim country that had been under French control for over a century. It was also home to some 1 million French and European settlers. Growing Algerian resistance to French rule had led to significant violence between Algerians, settlers, and the French military. By 1958, French Communists had demanded immediate independence for Algeria, and French generals in Algeria responded by establishing a provisional government and threatening military action against France itself if Algeria did not remain French. Under these dire circumstances, the government called on de Gaulle to return to politics and seek a way out of the crisis.[6]

THE RECOVERY OF STATE POWER AND DEMOCRATIC STABILITY UNDER THE FIFTH REPUBLIC

As he had a decade earlier, de Gaulle insisted that he would serve only if the French people would authorize and accept a new constitution that established a strong executive and addressed the other ills of the Third and Fourth Republics. The new constitution was put to a referendum and accepted. De

Gaulle, who had served briefly as the last **prime minister** of the Fourth Republic, became the first president of the new Fifth Republic, in 1958.

We conclude this discussion of the historical development of the French state by noting de Gaulle's significant impact on the republic and his ten-year tenure as its leader. Using his sweeping executive authority, from 1958 to 1968 de Gaulle granted Algeria independence, established France as an independent nuclear power, withdrew it from the military command structure of the North Atlantic Treaty Organization (NATO), promoted European integration, nationalized a number of key industries and private firms, and established a substantial welfare state.

Although he averted civil war, revitalized the French economy, and restored French national pride, de Gaulle was also criticized (particularly by the left) as an authoritarian demagogue. He failed to command the loyalty of a new generation that had no memories of World War II or his role in it. In

---

CHARLES DE GAULLE: A TWENTIETH-CENTURY NAPOLÉON?

Although the two were dramatically different in stature (Napoléon was famously short; de Gaulle was over six feet, five inches tall) and dissimilar in many other ways, Charles de Gaulle (1890–1970) is often compared to his earlier counterpart. Like Napoléon, he was a career military man who arrived on the French political scene at a time of crisis and saw himself as a savior of France. Also like Napoléon, de Gaulle graduated from a military academy with a predilection for the use of artillery. In the early weeks of World War II, he led a French tank division against Hitler's attacking armies. When his superiors sued for peace, General de Gaulle opposed the action and escaped first to England and then to Algeria. He became a leader in the resistance movement and in 1944 formed the Free French provisional government that governed liberated France until 1946.

Charged with constituting the Fourth Republic after the war, de Gaulle argued for the establishment of a strong executive that could rebuild war-devastated France and avoid the problems of the weak, polarized Third Republic. French voters rejected his proposal and instead opted for a strong assembly and a largely symbolic presidency. De Gaulle resigned and left politics, warning (accurately) that the Fourth Republic would be no better than its predecessor. Economic problems at home and colonial crises abroad (first in Vietnam and then, most acutely, in Algeria) brought France to the brink of civil war, its government having become immobilized. Amid these crises, de Gaulle returned to the political scene—as Napoléon had in his time—and demanded, and received by referendum, a new constitution that established a strong presidency and formed France's Fifth Republic. Wielding great power, de Gaulle avoided civil war, decolonized Algeria, revived the French economy, and to a great extent restored French prestige. De Gaulle served for eleven years. He then resigned after his constitutional reform proposals in response to the 1968 Paris riots were defeated. He withdrew (again) from politics and died the following year.

1968, many young Parisians took to the streets in what came to be known as **The Events of May**. Students erected barricades and demanded educational changes, and workers seized factories and called for sweeping social reforms. De Gaulle was able to weather these protests, but in the end had lost his mandate. When he turned to the public to galvanize support by presenting a referendum on various constitutional reforms, the president was defeated; he stepped down from office in 1969.

It might be expected that de Gaulle's departure would have signaled the end of the Fifth Republic, so tightly connected was it to de Gaulle himself. But rather than prompting a new round of polarized debate, revolution, and yet another constitution, the regime held and remains the current regime of France. Although the French had rejected a leader, they chose not to reject his vision of a republic led by a strong national executive. Since de Gaulle, a series of powerful presidents have each contributed to the image of France as a country with a strong bureaucracy, an independent foreign policy, and an economic system tightly connected to the state. However, over the past decade there has been a growing sense inside France that the country is in crisis, or at least adrift, with low economic growth and a growing, yet marginalized, immigrant population. The 2007 election of President **Nicolas Sarkozy** strongly reflected these concerns, as his supporters and detractors alike focused on issues of reform, immigration, and law and order. Does President Sarkozy represent a break from the past? Is France at a turning point? And is change really necessary or wanted in France? We shall consider these questions as we look at the institutions and policies of this important European state.

POLITICAL REGIME

Political Institutions

THE CONSTITUTION

As noted earlier, France has experienced different types of authoritarian regimes (from absolute monarchy to revolutionary dictatorship) as well as a broad range of democratic regimes (both parliamentary and semi-presidential). The French Third (1875–1940) and Fourth (1946–1958) Republics were purely parliamentary regimes. Many French viewed those regimes as weak and ineffective because fractious legislatures often resulted in a revolving door of prime ministers (with twenty cabinets in less than twelve years during the Fourth Republic). When fragmented legislatures disagreed with government policies, governments collapsed.

France's current regime, the Fifth Republic (1958–present), is codified in the constitution of 1958. That document was very much the product of

Charles de Gaulle's reaction to the perceived instability of the previous two regimes. The central goal of de Gaulle's 1958 constitution was to eliminate the pure parliamentary system and enhance the power of the executive vis-à-vis France's traditionally powerful and fractious legislature. France thus developed a semi-presidential executive system that was innovative at the time and subsequently adapted elsewhere, such as in Russia. The

ESSENTIAL POLITICAL FEATURES

- Legislative-executive system: semi-presidential
- Legislature: **Parlement**
- Lower house: Assemblée nationale (National Assembly)
- Upper house: Sénat (Senate)
- Unitary or federal division of power: unitary
- Main geographic subunits: regions
- Electoral system for lower house: single-member district majority
- Chief judicial body: Cour de cassation (Supreme Court of Appeals)

Fifth Republic created a system whereby political power is shared by the legislature, a directly elected president, and a prime minister who reports to both the president and the legislature.

The French constitution has proved durable and has seen relatively few significant amendments over the past fifty years. Most notable changes have involved the presidency; in 1962 the constitution was modified to allow direct election of the president, and in 2000 the president's term was reduced from seven to five years to limit divided government (which we will speak of shortly).

The Branches of Government

THE PRESIDENCY

Unlike a presidential system, the French **semi-presidential** system includes a dual executive: the president is head of state, and the prime minister is head of the government. However, the constitution of 1958 is ambiguous when it comes to differentiating the powers of the president and the prime minister.[7] Indeed, the French president has relatively few formal powers, but during the course of the Fifth Republic the president has, by precedent, acquired powers somewhat beyond those specified by the constitution.

The constitution envisions the French president as a head of state who is to be above the parties. But unlike the United Kingdom's merely symbolic head of state, French presidents hold important political powers, though they are far less explicit powers than held by their U.S. counterparts. Much of the authority of the French presidents results from the prestige and precedent of de Gaulle and from the fact that the president is the only directly elected political figure, providing a national mandate.[8] Moreover, French presidents are elected for long terms (five years) and can be reelected without term limits.

STRUCTURE OF THE GOVERNMENT

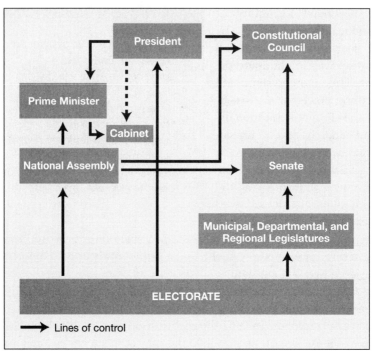

According to the constitution of the Fifth Republic, presidents do not directly govern. Rather, they appoint a prime minister, who must be approved by a majority of the lower house of the legislature; he is supposed to select a cabinet (called the **Council of Ministers**) and preside over the day-to-day affairs of the government. In practice, when French presidents enjoy a majority in the legislature, they select both the prime minister and the members of the cabinet.

The 1958 constitution would appear to create a potential conflict between a directly elected president and a legislature dominated by the opposition. This is because the constitution requires the legislature to approve the president's choice of prime minister. Many observers predicted that this feature was a recipe for political disaster. The French system has worked rather smoothly, however, due in part to the fact that from 1958 to 1986 the same party dominated the presidency and the legislature, thus reducing the possibility of intra-executive conflict. During those years, the French president developed the important informal powers he wields today. As noted below, however, even when presidents have lacked a majority in the legislature, they have compromised by appointing prime ministers from the opposition. What might happen should a president refuse to compromise is not entirely clear.

Presidents and Prime Ministers Since 1959

President	Dates in Office	Terms	Party	Prime Ministers (Dates)
Charles de Gaulle	1959–69 (resigned in second term)	two	N/A	Michel Debré (1959–62) Georges Pompidou (1962–68) Maurice Couve de Murville (1968–69)
Georges Pompidou	1969–74 (died in office)	one	Gaullist	Jacques Chaban-Delmas (1969–72) Pierre Messmer (1972–74)
Valéry Giscard d'Estaing	1974–81	one	Union pour la Démocratie Française (UDF)	Jacques Chirac (1974–76) Raymond Barre (1976–81)
François Mitterrand	1981–94	two	Parti Socialiste (PS)	Pierre Mauroy (1981–84) Laurent Fabius (1984–86) Jacques Chirac (1986–88) Michel Rocard (1988–91) Edith Cresson (1991–92) Pierre Bérégovoy (1992–93) Edouard Balladur (1993–95)
Jacques Chirac	1995–2007	two	neo-Gaullist	Alain Juppé (1995–97) Lionel Jospin (1997–2002) Jean-Pierre Raffarin (2002–2005) Dominique de Villepin (2005–2007)
Nicolas Sarkozy	2007–present		Union pour un Mouvement Populaire (UMP)	François Fillon (2007–present)

The constitution of the Fifth Republic does give the president some formal constitutional tools in addition to those that have become institutionalized over time through precedent. Presidents direct the armed forces. They cannot veto legislation, but they can ask the lower house to reconsider it. They can submit referenda directly to the people. They must sign all laws and decrees. Presidents also have the power to dissolve the legislature and call new elections, a power that has been employed on five occasions, usually to obtain or reinforce legislative majorities to the president's liking. The president also enjoys a powerful staff, whose members help him develop and initiate policy and work with the prime minister and the cabinet.

Perhaps the most important power of the president is the authority to appoint the prime minister, though the appointment is subject to legislative approval. Moreover, presidents have simply asserted the power to remove prime ministers and cabinet members even if those officials have support in the legislature, although the constitution does not specify this authority. In short, the prime minister has become a sort of chief aide whose goal is to carry out the president's political agenda. Consequently, the president—not the prime minister—chairs the weekly meetings of the Council of Ministers.

In the early years of the Fifth Republic, it was often argued that because of the power and prestige of the president, France was developing a republican monarchy.[9] Even during de Gaulle's time, however, the presidency was hardly omnipotent; recall that de Gaulle resigned after the electorate rejected his 1969 referendum. President **François Mitterrand**, despite serving for fourteen years, was twice forced to "cohabitate" with an opposition prime minister; this divided government severely limited his power. President **Jacques Chirac** was similarly stymied when the opposition controlled the lower house and prime minister's office from 1995 to 2002. It was this divided government that led to the change in the president's term of office, syncing presidential and legislative elections in the hope that voters would support a single party for both institutions. So far this has been the case, which may promise a more consistently powerful presidency in future.

THE PRIME MINISTER

French prime ministers are appointed by the president but serve with the support of both the president and the legislature. As opposed to many parliamentary systems in which the prime minister is drawn from among the members of parliament, Article 23 of the French constitution prevents members of the legislature from serving simultaneously as prime minister. This creates a disconnect between the legislature and the prime minister, and it ties the prime minister more strongly to the president. On paper, the constitution appears to make the prime minister the most powerful politician in France. In practice, when presidents enjoy a majority in the legislature, French

---

"SARKO" THE AMERICAN?

Whether Nicolas Sarkozy will be a successful president, it is clear that his election marks a departure from the past presidents and typical French leadership. While postwar presidents have been a product of elite education and extensive experience in the public sector, Sarkozy's biography is quite the opposite. The son of a Hungarian immigrant, Sarkozy came not from the ranks of the *enarques*, but rather had an undistinguished educational background and became a private lawyer. Whereas many other political elites were groomed inside the civil service, Sarkozy ran for elected office early, became a city councilor in his twenties, a city mayor, a member of the National Assembly, and by 1993 a member of the government cabinet. During that time he developed a reputation for favoring greater reform and being critical of French political culture as too risk averse and reliant on state power. During his stint as Minister of the Interior he also became known for his tough positions on immigration and crime, most notably during the 2005 riots. Sarkozy broke with the traditional mold of the French president; he was more of an energetic self-made man whose personality and behavior struck many, unfavorably, as so-called American. Indeed, Sarkozy (or Sarko, as some wags nicknamed him), openly expressed his admiration for the United States.

Since taking office, Sarkozy has laid out numerous reforms, though the extent to which he will be able to carry these through remains uncertain. He assembled around him a diverse cabinet, including members of the Socialist Party and the first women cabinet member of North African origin—and few *enarques*. But he also became mired in public controversy over his ostentatious lifestyle, divorce, and remarriage, which has cost him time and public credibility. Sarko must now buckle down.

---

prime ministers are chiefly responsible for cultivating support for presidential policies from within the legislature, rather than setting policy themselves. Prime ministers may be removed with a **motion of censure** (effectively a vote of no confidence), though this requires an absolute majority of the 577 members of the lower house.[10]

When presidents lack a majority in the legislature, leading to the appointment of a prime minister from an opposing party—**cohabitation**—the prime minister assumes a much greater degree of power, since she or he does not feel bound to subordinate policy matters to a president from another party. Under these conditions, the explicit powers of the prime minister as laid out in the constitution become prominent, effectively creating a parliamentary system with a more ceremonial president. However, the 2000 constitutional amendment that modified presidential terms may have well brought cohabitation to an end, since presidential and parliamentary elections now occur at roughly the same time. It is possible that in the future voters could split their ticket, favoring one party for the legislature and the candidate of another party for the president, leading again to cohabitation and a strong prime minister. So far, that has not been the case, nor do many observers expect it in the future.

THE LEGISLATURE

France has a bicameral legislature, composed of the 577-member Assemble nationale (National Assembly) and a 321-member upper house, the **Sénat** (Senate). Deputies in the National Assembly are elected for five-year renewable terms, and senators are elected for six-year terms. The constitution of the Fifth Republic clearly weakened the legislature vis-à-vis the executive. As a result, the French legislature is weaker than its counterparts in most advanced democracies, but it still plays an important role.

The constitution gives the legislature the right to propose legislation, but most bills (about 80 percent) originate with the executive. The constitution gives the government considerable control over the workings of the legislature, including control of the agenda and the schedule of parliamentary activity. One particularly important instrument is the **blocked vote**, which limits the legislature's ability to amend legislation. French legislators also have no power to introduce bills or amendments that affect public spending; only the government may introduce such legislation. Moreover, if the Parliament does not approve finance bills and the annual budget within seventy days, they automatically become law.

Another unique feature of the constitution allows governments to submit legislation as motions of confidence. In such cases, the proposed laws are passed unless the legislature can muster a motion of censure against the government. This is not an easy task (as it requires an absolute majority), and one that could trigger new elections. This feature was used frequently during the 1980s and 1990s as a way of passing important legislation without legislative debate. The constitution's Article 38 also grants the legislature the right to enable the government to legislate via decrees, known as ordinances, though this has only been used sparingly. Finally, the constitution limits the number and powers of the legislative committees that served as powerful legislative tools of previous regimes.

In spite of these limitations, the legislature has gradually asserted itself more forcefully. Since the 1970s, it has conducted a weekly questioning of government ministers (though not the president) that is somewhat similar to the British routine. The French parliament now regularly amends legislation, and the executive no longer asserts its right to reject all amendments. In 1995, the legislative session was extended from six months to nine months, and extended special sessions have become fairly common. Legislative committees have become more important in proposing and amending legislation, and motions of censure, while unlikely to pass, are used by the opposition as a way to bring controversial issues to the floor for debate. In April 2008, the government faced a motion of censure over sending more troops to Afghanistan, which was used by the opposition Socialists as a way to criticize President Sarkozy's call for stronger military ties to the United States and NATO.[11]

The French upper house, the Senát, is clearly the weaker of the two legislative chambers. It is elected indirectly by an electoral college of local government officials and members of the lower house. This indirect election helps deprive it of popular legitimacy, and its legislative powers are limited to delaying legislation passed by the lower house. Important legislation has been passed over the objection of the Senát, most notably during the Socialist governments from 1981 to 1986, when the more conservative Senát opposed much of the legislation enacted by the leftist government. The Senát's main power resides in its ability to reject constitutional amendments, which require the consent of both houses. The Senát is widely seen as somewhat obsolete and unrepresentative, composed of elderly conservatives (more than half the members are over sixty years old). As with the British House of Lords, there have been regular calls for constitutional reform of the upper house, but unlike in the UK, there have been few constitutional changes since de Gaulle's failed attempt in 1969.

THE JUDICIAL SYSTEM

As in most democracies, the French judiciary is divided into several branches, including civil, criminal, and administrative. The French judicial system is based on Continental European **code law**, in which laws are derived from detailed legal codes rather than from precedent (as in common law used in the United States, Canada, and the UK). During Napoléon's rule, French laws were systematically codified, and much of that original code remains in place today. The role of judges is simply to interpret and apply those codes. Consequently, judges in France have less discretion and autonomy than those in the common law systems.

The French court system also operates very differently from that in the United States or Canada. Judges play a much greater role in determining whether charges should be brought, and they assume many of the roles of prosecuting attorneys. In France, judges, not lawyers, question and cross-examine witnesses. Because the 1958 constitution created a semi-presidential system with built-in potential for deadlock of the legislature and the executive, the Fifth Republic also created a **Constitutional Council** to settle constitutional disputes.[12] The Constitutional Council is comprised of nine members, who are appointed for a single nine-year term by the president and heads of the National Assembly and Senate. Former presidents of France also serve as members of the Council, for life, once they have left office. The Council is empowered to rule on any constitutional matter, so long as there is a request from either the government or the head of or at least sixty members of either house of the legislature. In its early years, the Constitutional Council tended to act rarely and usually backed presidential actions. In recent decades, however, it has shown more independence; in 2008, the Constitutional Council rejected legislation that would have allowed for the indefinite imprisonment of dangerous criminals even after their terms had been served. One role that the Constitutional Council does not serve is that of a court of last appeal for cases from lower courts; that function is held by other judicial bodies.

The Electoral System

France's electoral system is majoritarian rather than proportional, thus looking more like the United States, Canada, and the United Kingdom than Continental Europe. However, the use of a two-round runoff between candidates distinguishes it from the plurality-based system found in those countries. French presidents are directly elected in two rounds of voting every five years. Unless a candidate gets over 50 percent of the vote in the first round (which has never happened in the Fifth Republic), a second round of balloting two weeks later pits the top two candidates against each other.

France also employs a two-round electoral system for its single-member district elections of members of the National Assembly. In each district, candidates with over 12.5 percent of the vote face off in a second round of balloting (again, unless a candidate gains over 50 percent of the votes in the first round). During the Socialist administration of François Mitterrand, France experimented with proportional representation for lower-house elections, as it had in the Fourth Republic, but returned to single-member districts two years later. Using two rounds of voting does ensure that winning candidates have a majority of the vote in each district, but it still delivers disproportionate outcomes common in single-member district elections. In 2007, for example, President Sarkozy's party won 54 percent of the lower-house seats with only 46 percent of the nationwide vote.

By using two rounds of voting for presidential and lower-house elections, the French system encourages more parties and candidates than do single-member district systems in Canada, the UK, or the United States. At the same time, the second round of elections still uses a winner-take-all format, and the 12.5 percent threshold for entry into the second round of legislative elections severely limits the number of parties that actually win. The National Front, for example, won nearly 5 percent of the vote in the first round of the 2007 elections, but not a single seat. The complexity of a two-round system can create a rather confusing electoral landscape, as parties and individuals compete for seats with the expectation not necessarily that they can win, but rather that a good showing in the first round can translate into leverage to be used against more powerful parties. Small parties or coalitions or candidates may throw their support behind a stronger rival as part of a political deal. Still, these calculations can backfire, as they did in the 2002 presidential elections, when candidates on the left fragmented their vote—with a disastrous outcome. We shall speak more about this below.

Local Government

France is usually considered a prototypical unitary state with all power concentrated in Paris, the capital and largest city. Furthermore, compared with most of its neighbors, France has experienced relatively little separatism or demands for greater regional autonomy (an independence movement on the island of Corsica is a rare exception). Whereas this is a generally accurate picture, France also has a long history of localism and regionalism that should not be discounted and three levels of local government—region, department, and commune—that have enjoyed increasing power over time.

There are twenty-six regions in France, four of which are overseas. The regions' primary responsibilities are regional planning and economic development. The regions are led by a council, elected every six years. At the next level there are 100 departments, with responsibility in such areas as health services and infrastructure. For nearly two centuries, power in the departments resided with a **prefect** appointed by the central government, but a series of reforms in 1982 transferred a great deal of power to a directly elected council. Finally, at the municipal level there are directly elected councils and mayors who handle the main tasks of these communities. Since the 1982 reforms, local governments have been given some control over taxes and revenues, and as a result their powers have slowly grown. However, their share of the budgetary pie remains very small.

Other Institutions: The French Bureaucracy

The development of the French state is associated with the creation of one of the world's earliest and most efficient bureaucracies, the legacy of which can be seen in contemporary French politics. Compared with that of most other democracies, where the notion of bureaucracy conjures up the image of inefficiency and red tape, the civil service in France retains a high profile and considerable prestige, as well as an important springboard to elected office. One gateway to the bureaucracy is the **École Nationale d'Administration (ENA)**, a state educational institution the primary mission of which is to train civil servants. Indeed, the highest category of civil servants are usually recruited through ENA and several other elite state institutions.

This specialized training combined with few barriers between civil service and politics means that the links between the bureaucracy and elected office are strong and considered normal. The *enarques,* as graduates of ENA are known, commonly move between the civil service and elected or appointed political office. Former President Chirac graduated from ENA in 1959 and was a civil servant for nearly a decade before running for office; his last prime minister, Dominique de Villepin, also was an *enarque* with a long career within the state—indeed, Villepin never held any elected office, including that of the prime minister itself. This blurry line between state and politics extends to the economy as well, which has long been subject to state guidance and partial state control. Career bureaucrats often move from the civil service to positions within business: a transition that is known as ***pantouflage***—literally, putting on slippers. The largest private companies in France remain dominated by *enarques,* though this has declined of late.[13] The impact of the civil service on French life thus is hard to overstate. By one estimate, over half the population either works for, or has a parent, child, or spouse who works for, the public sector; of course, such a large state comes with a cost in the form of wages and benefits, and as the French population ages, supporting the civil service and its retirees will be an increasingly costly proposition.

POLITICAL CONFLICT AND COMPETITION

The Party System

De Gaulle was deeply suspicious of political parties, blaming them for much of the political turmoil of the Third and Fourth Republics. The single-member district system helped narrow the field of parties and often produced stable majority governments. By the 1960s, the badly fragmented party system of the Fourth Republic had been replaced by a less fragmented multiparty system that featured a **bipolar** alternation of coalitions of the center right and the center left.[14] By the late 1970s, the political blocs of the right, composed mainly of the **Rally for the French Republic (RPR)** and the **Union for a Popular Movement (UMP)**, and the left, composed mainly of the **French Communist Party (PCF)** and the **French Socialist Party (PS)**, each earned about half the vote in French elections. The four major parties together won over 90 percent of the vote. The electoral system helped this dominance of the two major blocs, as the single-member district system, with its two rounds of voting, required coalition building in the second round.

Since the 1980s, the **four-party, two-bloc system** has been in transition. One important ideological change has been the spectacular demise of the PCF on the left and the emergence of the **National Front (FN)** on the right, changing the prospects for electoral coalitions. In addition, constitutional changes may have brought cohabitation to an effective end, also transforming the power of political parties to act as a counterweight to the president. The French system may be coalescing into a more standard two-party system, though the two-round electoral system probably means that smaller parties will continue to play a role in French political life. In addition, the institution of the presidency also encourages party formation as a springboard for presidential campaigns, while weakening the internal coherence of the parties themselves. Below we discuss the main ideological groups in the party system.

THE FRENCH LEFT

The Communist Party and the Socialist Party have been the dominant parties of the French left since the end of World War II. The Communist Party played a major role in the French resistance to the Nazi occupation and was rewarded at the polls after the war. The Communists had long been a party staunchly loyal to Moscow, and supported the Soviet Union's invasion of Czechoslovakia in 1968 (though it drifted away from its allegiance by the 1970s). Historically, the PCF had a very strong base of support among French workers and in France's trade union movement, and for much of the post–World War II period it did well in local and national elections, usually winning about 20 percent of the vote. This did not translate into significant national power, even though the PCF participated in government coalitions led by the rival Socialist Party and briefly held cabinet positions in Socialist governments. Rather than giving the PCF credibility, government experience only tarnished its image as a principled party of the opposition; the collapse of the Soviet Union undermined the appeal of its ideology. By 2007, the PCF polled only 4 percent of the votes in the first round of parliamentary elections.

The Socialist Party, formed in 1905, was also long divided into social democratic and Marxist camps. In the 1930s, the Socialists were elected to power and led a brief and ill-fated government. After World War II, the Socialist Party reemerged, though it regularly gained fewer votes than the Communists and stagnated. Its fortunes began to change, however, when François Mitterrand became its leader in 1971. Mitterrand forged an electoral alliance with the stronger Communists and eventually eclipsed them with a more moderate social democratic ideology. This strategy was vindicated by the 1981 election of Mitterrand to the presidency, the first (and to date only) leftist president of the Fifth Republic. Mitterrand's long presidency (1981–1995) was marred by his party's loss of its legislative majority in 1986 and by his need to cohabit with a conservative prime minister during most of his two terms in office. Subsequently the Socialist Party won a legislative majority in 1997, and though they were defeated in the 2002 and 2007 legislative and presidential elections, they remain a powerful political party that is certain to return to power. At present, the Communist Party, along with the Green Party and Radical Party, command some attention but few seats.

THE RIGHT

Unity has also long proved elusive for the French right, though like the left this may now be over. In the past, the most important force on the right consisted of those who consider themselves the political heirs of General Charles de Gaulle, often called Gaullists or neo-Gaullists. But since de Gaulle never associated himself with any party, his heirs created various competing parties of the right that were more often than not divided by personality and presidential ambitions. The two most important forces were the Rally for the French Republic (RPR), created by Jacques Chirac, and the **Union for French Democracy (UDF)**, an alliance of five center-right parties founded by Chirac's rival, former president Valéry Giscard d'Estaing. These parties differed in part over the role of the state and their view of the European Union, but over the years, the differences mostly disappeared. In 2002, President Chirac encouraged most of the center right to cohere as a single party, the Union for a Popular Movement (UMP). Under the current president of France, Nicolas Sarkozy, the UMP has continued to move in a more liberal direction; like the Socialist Party, however, the UMP supports a strong state role in economic development and extensive social benefits.

Unity among France's two main conservative parties was partly spurred by the emergence and surprising success of the National Front on the far right. A small if noisy party, the National Front's major policy focus has been a reduction in immigration and expulsion of illegal immigrants. Led by the fiery **Jean-Marie Le Pen**, the FN made its first real mark in national politics when proportional representation was briefly introduced in the 1980s, enabling it to win its first seats in the lower house. The party reached its peak with 15 percent of the vote in the 1997 legislative elections, but due to the single-member district system has never won more than a single seat in the lower house. Nevertheless, in the 2002 presidential elections Le Pen benefited from the divided votes among various leftist candidates to actually make it into a runoff with President Chirac. In the second round, Le Pen won less than 20 percent of the vote as voters recoiled from the possibility of a Le Pen presidency. But the factors that make the National Front a success, particularly fears over immigration, remain. To a large extent these fears have been successfully coopted by the UMP, which has emphasized law and order and greater controls over immigration and immigrants.

Elections

THE PRESIDENTIAL ELECTIONS OF 2007

Toward the end of his second term, President Chirac had lost much of his popular support. This was due in part to public fatigue (Chirac had been in office since 1995), allegations that he and his government were deeply corrupt, and a greater sense that the government was incapable of carrying out needed reforms. Indeed, many expected that in 2002 he would lose to the candidate of the Socialist Party, but he was saved by the fragmentation on the left that led to the runoff against Le Pen. Chirac thus chose not to run for a third term in 2007, leaving the elections open to a new generation of candidates. On the left, the Socialist Party fielded Segolene Royal, an *enarque* who nonetheless had a long service in elected office, having first entered the National Assembly in 1988. Royal had also served in several cabinet positions in previous governments. Also notable was Royal's gender, a women in a country where female representation in the National Assembly is low by European standards. On the right, the UMP's Nicolas Sarkozy also represented a break from the past (see "'Sarko' the American?," p. 131). The 2007 presidential elections between Royal and Sarkozy mobilized the population to a degree perhaps not seen for many years; voter turnout was higher than at any time since 1974, and the campaign turned on questions of reform, liberalization, immigration, and improving law and order. More broadly, the campaign was about change, with Sarkozy arguing that the country faced a crisis that required dramatic actions. In spite of his polarizing nature, Sarkozy won handily over Royal. The question now is whether the president can deliver, something we shall discuss in the following sections.

REFERENDA

The constitution of the Fifth Republic allows the president to call national referenda. President de Gaulle held five referenda, staking his reputation and political capital on each one. Referenda were used to approve controversial policies, such as independence for Algeria, and to approve the direct election of the president. When de Gaulle lost a 1969 referendum aimed at reforming the upper house of the legislature, he resigned. Since then, referenda have been used less frequently, though often utilized regarding changes to the European Union. In 1972, President Pompidou used a referendum to approve the enlargement of the European Union, and in 1992 President Mitterrand asked voters to approve the EU's Maastricht Treaty. More recently, in 2005 President Chirac submitted a proposed European Constitution to a referendum. Voters delivered a resounding rejection of the document despite Chirac's support for it. The defeat weakened Chirac, and since that time the government has not been willing to submit further EU treaty reforms to a national vote (it is not required by the constitution). France has suggested, however, that it might require a public referendum on a Turkish membership in the EU, if it is offered. As such a referendum would surely fail, this has engendered consternation among other EU members as well as Turkey.

Civil Society

As early as the 1830s, the French scholar Alexis de Tocqueville noted the weakness of French civil associations. Most scholars argue that French interest groups and associations remain weaker than those in most advanced democracies, a function of the powerful state and the emphasis on so-called mass action over organized lobbying. Nevertheless, trade unions and business organizations are two important elements of civil society that are worth discussing in detail.

LABOR UNIONS

Observers of French politics, particularly its numerous strikes, commonly speak of how powerful the French labor unions are. This is misleading. In fact, French labor unions have traditionally had a long history of being "divided, weakened, and quarrelsome."[15] Less than 10 percent of the French workforce belongs to a union, one of the lowest rates in Europe. And unlike the powerful trade unions found elsewhere on the continent, French labor unions have usually been divided along partisan lines. The most powerful French union confederation includes the **General Confederation of Labor (CGT)**, historically linked to the PCF; in contrast, the **French Democratic Labor Confederation (CFDT)** and Force Ouvrire (FO) have tended to have a more centrist or anti-Communist orientation. Paradoxically, it is in part the weakness and fragmentation of French unions that explain the large number of strikes that occur in France. More powerful unions could effectively engage in productive bargaining with employers or the government, but lacking this authority, public demonstrations and work stoppages have become a vital tool to express discontent, something that capitalizes on the French tendency toward mass action and public protest. But despite their weakness, unions continue to play a key role in French society and in the management of the country's major welfare organizations (health care, retirement, and social security). They are also strongly represented in France's public-sector workforce and are a force to be considered when any French government attempts to reform welfare benefits, as has been attempted of late.

PRIVATE ENTERPRISE

Compared with French labor, the business sector is well organized, with large firms represented by MEDEF (French Enterprise Movement), and smaller firms represented by CGPME (General Confederation of Small and Medium-Size Enterprises). Both have tended to support lower taxes on business, more flexible laws regarding the hiring and firing of workers, and a reduced role for government in the economy. Business has generally supported parties on the right like the UMP. Since large numbers of France's business leaders are *enarques*, French business often has privileged access to the state bureaucracy. Not surprisingly, MEDEF has been a strong supporter of Sarkozy's call for economic reforms; CGPME has been less enthusiastic, fearing deregulation that will remove many of the barriers that currently protect small businesses from competition.

ORGANIZED RELIGION

France is formally a Catholic nation, and despite minorities of Muslims, Protestants, and Jews, over 80 percent of the French are nominally Catholics. Yet despite the predominance of a single religion, France has long been an anti-clerical society, dating back to the Revolution, when the church was seen as a tool of monarchical power. Church and state have been formally separate since 1905, under what is known as **laïcité** (which roughly translates as secularism). Under *laïcité*, no religion could receive state support, and religious education was restricted. The church continues to play a role in important social rituals (marriage, births, funerals), but not in the day-to-day lives of most French citizens. The church lacks an important or central role in French politics, which has no Christian democratic party as found in other Catholic countries, such as Italy or Germany. The church can, however, rally to the defense of its own institutional issues: in the 1980s, church opposition forced the Socialist government to back away from plans to impose stricter government control over religious schools.

As the Catholic Church has waned in power, other religions, particularly Islam, have grown. France has thus seen a rapid growth in mosques and Islamic educational and cultural institutions, something that has made many French nervous. For many of these institutions the Union of Islamic Organizations acts as an umbrella group, and in 2002 the government created the French Council of the Muslim Faith to act as an intermediary between the government and Muslim leaders. This has had limited success in building state-faith relations, and tensions remain.

SOCIETY

Ethnic and National Identity

In its ethnic identity, France is a relatively homogeneous society. Historically this was not the case, and it continues to change in the present. In centuries

RELIGION

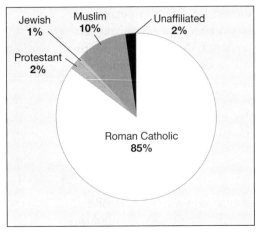

Jewish 1%
Muslim 10%
Unaffiliated 2%
Protestant 2%
Roman Catholic 85%

past, many parts of France maintained distinct ethnic identities, which included their own languages and cultures: Gascon, Savoyard, Occitan, Basque, and Breton, to name a few. Over time, these unique communities were largely assimilated into a single French identity, though certain ethnic groups, particularly Basques and Corsicans, have retained stronger language and cultural ties.

Assimilation was in part connected to the particular role that the French state played in the development of national identity. One of the important facets of the French Revolution was the idea of a set of universal rights that identified people as citizens rather than subjects of the state. This form of republicanism was unlike that of the American Revolution, where democracy was predicated on an individualism that demanded a weak state and federalism. French revolutionaries believed in the necessity of a powerful state to destroy the institutions of the past and serve the people in building the future. A powerful state thus became a key instrument in solidifying and expressing French national identity and patriotism in a way in which it did not in the United States.[16] In contrast to U.S. policy, in France rivals for public loyalty were eradicated or brought under control of the state.

This relationship between state and nation is now being challenged by changes in both religious and ethnic identity. In the past, laïcité served to subordinate religious identity to the state, and ethnic identities were downgraded through assimilation and nationalism. In fact, French identity is so primary that the national census does not record such basic information as ethnicity and religion (and is forbidden by law to do so). This became a point of debate in the 2007 presidential campaign, during which the candidates and the public were divided over whether recording such information would help address social issues or exacerbate division.

Why this question should emerge is that these identities are becoming more salient. In the past few decades, France has seen an influx of people from outside of Europe, notably Africa, the Middle East, and Southeast Asia. Data are sketchy, but it is assumed that France has the largest immigrant population in Europe; around 10 percent are foreign born. By way of contrast, in the United States the number of foreign born is about 12 percent, and in Canada the number is approximately 20 percent. As in many countries, immigrants to France and their children often find themselves marginalized due to a lack of education, language barriers, and/or persistent discrimination.

Many immigrants are concentrated in housing projects on the outskirts of Paris and other large cities, with poor social services, employment opportunities, or transportation. This ghettoization compounds the sense of disconnect from French life and has led to violence. In 2005, France saw a month of heavy rioting across France's immigrant suburbs, culminating in a state of emergency and approximately $200 million in damages. A second set of riots, not as large though more violent, occurred in 2007.

Within this debate over immigration, the future of the Muslim community takes center stage. Currently, France has the largest Muslim population in Europe outside Turkey: about 5 to 6 million people (approximately 10 percent of the population, including foreign born and those born in France). The growth of a large Muslim population has been disconcerting for a country that historically has been overwhelmingly Catholic, if now only nominally so. This situation is not unlike that of other Western countries but is compounded by the particular position of the French state. *Laïcité* means that Muslims are expected to place their faith below that of national and patriotic identity as

IN COMPARISON   RELIGION AND GOVERNMENT

Should religion and government be kept separate? Percent saying yes:

Country	Percent
France	72
Canada	71
Germany	67
Brazil	67
United Kingdom	66
India	58
Nigeria	57
United States	55
Russia	55
South Africa	45
Japan	33
Mexico	38
China	21

*Data on Iran not available.
Source: Pew Center for the People and the Press, 2007.

part of the assimilation process. Yet many Muslims believe that the French state should be more accommodating to their needs, rather than vice versa. Furthermore, in the face of persistent marginalization, many Muslims turn to their faith as a source of identity and meaning.

In the past few years, one prominent example of this conflict was over the headscarf. Growing expressions of Muslim identity have been a challenge to *laïcité*, in particular whether girls could wear a headscarf in public schools. Many French on both left and right argued that educational institutions, as part of the state, could not allow the wearing of the headscarf without violating the principle of *laïcité*. After a long discussion, France passed a law in 2004 that forbade the wearing of any "conspicuous religious symbol" in schools, whatever the faith. The ban has been overwhelmingly popular among the non-Muslim French population, but the French Muslim population is more divided.[17] Whether such steps will help bring minorities into the mainstream or further marginalize them is open to debate. Many French would point out that the United Kingdom's much more multicultural approach (for example, female Muslims in the British police force may wear headscarves) has not prevented similar problems of marginalization, and that the Muslim community in the UK is much more radicalized than it is in France.

How to resolve these conflicts over immigration and religion? President Sarkozy has argued in favor of positive discrimination, which would give advantages to immigrants and their children: this is a radical position in a country whose revolution was based on the notion that all humans are inherently equal and thus not entitled to special treatment. At the same time, Sarkozy has favored greater restrictions on immigration, a greater emphasis on integrating immigrant populations, and a greater emphasis on so-called law and order (which is widely understood to mean a focus on crime committed by immigrants and their offspring and to many observers is a not-particularly-subtle expression of racism). Multiculturalism remains taboo in France, and the current policy path seems to be to provide more opportunities for immigrants to assimilate themselves into the French polity. This may work, or it may leave increasing numbers of immigrants and their offspring behind.

Ideology and Political Culture

The role of the state in shaping French national identity can be seen in the country's ideological landscape and political culture. Ideological divisions in France are much more fragmented than are those in other European countries, where there tend to be a few coherent and persistent parties that dominate the political scene. Divisive historical events, the weakness of civil society, the importance of the state, Gaullist hostility toward political parties, the two-round electoral system, and semi-presidentialism have all played a part in creating a system in which individual political leaders, rather than ideological groupings, have been central.

As a result, although we can speak generally of left and right, social democratic or liberal, in fact the ideological divisions are much more diverse and reflect a range of experiences, such as the battles over the French Revolution and the role of the Catholic Church in French life. In many cases, these values cannot be classified as an ideology at all but rather fall under the term *populism*, or a set of ideas that is suspicious of organized power and places faith in the common man. From the revolution to Napoléon to de Gaulle, French leaders have often appealed to the masses by seeking to transcend ideology and speak for the people. This populism has helped keep civil society and ideology weak by fostering an ongoing mistrust of such institutions as political parties.

The residual strength of populist ideas explains not only why ideological divisions in France are as much within groups as between them but also why one of the most notable elements of French political culture is the tendency toward mass protests. With civic organizations being too weak to articulate public concerns and with individuals being faithful to the populist notion that the people must struggle against those with power, one of the most common forms of political activity in France is mass protest: marches, demonstrations, and strikes. For example, France regularly averages more than 1,000 workers' strikes per year, compared with fewer than 200 in the United Kingdom.[18] That said, French respondents to political surveys tend to put themselves more on the left of the political spectrum than do those in the United States, UK, or Canada.[19]

At the same time, France's populism and faith in the power of mass action is combined with a strong sense of national and patriotic identity and a pride in the French state, with a belief that France is exceptional among countries—not unlike the American vision of itself. This has led to frequent conflict with the United States, a rival with a similar notion of its own exceptionalism but whose ideology of individualism runs counter to the French vision.

POLITICAL ECONOMY

The political economy of France shares with its continental neighbors a strong state role in the economy. Part of this is a function of modern social democratic policies, whereas other elements can be traced over the course of several centuries. As far back as the sixteenth century, the absolute monarchy levied heavy taxes on the populace to support a large bureaucracy. At the same time, the French economy was highly mercantilist domestically, divided into a number of smaller markets, each subject to internal tariffs and nontariff barriers. Exports constituted a relatively small portion of the economy.[20] Although the French Revolution and the reign of Napoléon rationalized many of these structures, by the twentieth century France was lagging behind many of its neighbors in terms of economic development. The country retained a large agricultural sector, had few large firms, and had experienced a relatively low level of urbanization. As one scholar described Paris in 1948, it was "empty of vehicles, needed neither traffic lights nor one-way streets"; electrical services and major consumer goods like refrigerators were little known. He concluded, "France had not really entered the twentieth century."[21]

In the aftermath of World War II, the French government set out to rapidly transform the economy. This took the form of what the French termed **dirigisme**, which can be explained as an emphasis on state authority in economic development—a combination of both social democratic and mercantilist ideas. Dirigisme involved the nationalization of several sectors of the economy (such as utilities), the promotion of a limited number of "national champion" industries to compete internationally (such as Airbus), the creation of a national-planning ministry, and the establishment of the ENA and similar schools to ensure the education of bureaucrats who would be able to direct the economy.

True to its objectives, the dirigiste system helped bring about a transformation of the French economy. Economic wealth grew rapidly, along with increased urbanization. Through the help of economic subsidies from the European Union, France was also able to change its agricultural sector from one of small farms to one of large-scale production. Whereas in the 1950s France's per capita GDP was approximately half that of the United States, within twenty years it had surpassed its historical rivals, the United Kingdom and Germany.[22] Dirigisme, however, came with costs, including a large public sector, an expansive welfare system, and a heavy tax burden. By 2007, total government expenditures consumed 50 percent of France's GDP compared with around 40 percent in Canada and 30 percent in the United States.

As with many other economic systems around the world, in the past twenty years this model has been put to the test. By the mid-1980s, unemployment had risen to over 10 percent, a rate that has persisted and is disproportionally concentrated among the young. Economic growth, which had been double that of the United States from

LABOR FORCE BY OCCUPATION

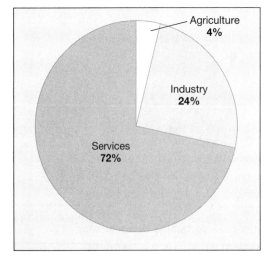

Agriculture 4%

Industry 24%

Services 72%

the 1950s to the 1970s, fell to around 2 percent, the lowest in the EU. As a result of this slow growth, France's GDP has stagnated, once again falling below the United Kingdom and Germany. France also faces the European-wide dilemma of an aging population, compounded by a large public sector workforce that can retire early with generous benefits. As the French population has grown older, it is thus using an ever greater share of the welfare system, while fewer young workers are available to fund those expenditures.

The French government has found it difficult to respond to these challenges. Part of the reason is a function of political culture. As the dirigist model faces internal stresses, it is also being buffeted by international competition from the United States, Asia, and within the EU itself. Increasing globalization presents new opportunities for France's economy, but for many French, globalization is seen as risky economic liberalism extended to the international level. Tellingly, when the French speak of economic liberalization or globalization, they speak of an Anglo-Saxon model, by which they mean the United Kingdom and the United States. Many French thus are suspicious that domestic economic reforms will essentially Americanize France, undermining their core identity. France is awash in discussions that the country is in decline and must carry out radical change if it is to survive in a changing world. It was Sarkozy's very call for a rupture with the past that help him win the presidential election.

President Sarkozy has proposed a number of changes, including pension reform, expanding the work week past thirty-five hours, lowering taxes, deregulating business, and liberalizing the labor market. These will be easier said than done; the previous government backed off on reforms in 2006 after a wave of strikes, and President Sarkozy has already faced numerous protests in 2007 and 2008 against these reforms. Meanwhile, the global economic recession only makes reforms that much more difficult. There are, however, several elements working in favor of reform. First is the general consensus that reform is necessary, even if there is less appetite for the reforms themselves. Second is the fact that in spite of the structural problems of the French economy, in many ways it is highly competitive. The United States may have a higher GDP per capita, for example, but that is due in part to the fact that Americans work much longer hours than do the French. But when measured in terms of productivity, the French produce more, per hour of labor, than do Americans, British, or Canadians.[23] The challenge now will be to reform old institutions and capitalize on French economic strengths while assuring the public that French identity itself will not get lost in the process.

Another interesting facet of the debate about the future of the French economy can be seen in the struggle over agriculture. Though the percentage of the French population engaged in agriculture has shrunk dramatically in the past fifty years, agriculture still plays a central role in French identity. French

DECLINISM IN FRANCE

For the past few years, there has been a growth industry in France of books decrying the country's current state and predicting its demise unless steps are taken. One best seller by historian and economist Nicolas Baverez, *La France qui tombe* (*Falling France*), claims that the country's greatest period was in the 1970s, and that since then it has been unable to adapt to a changing European and international environment. This crisis, he has argued, is not merely economic but also intellectual. Member of Parliament Pierre Lellouche's *Illusions Gauloises* (*Gallic Illusions*) similarly criticizes France's focus on its external forces (the United States, the UK, and the EU) rather than emphasizing its own internal problems and need for reform. Journalists Denis Jeambar and Jacqueline Remy, in their book *Nos enfants nous haïront* (*Our Children Will Hate Us*) criticize the '68-ers (as baby boomers are commonly called in France) for protecting their interests above all else and thus stifling change. The discussion of declinism helped pave the way for a Sarkozy presidency, but whether France is "in decline" depends on what we mean by this term. France remains a highly developed and internationally competitive country with some of the highest standards of living in the world. And all countries, including the United States and the UK, have experienced their own declinist debates on numerous occasions, only to reform and rebound. Catastrophe sells but is no predictor of the future.

culture is strongly tied to the concept of rural and agricultural life, and this is also bound up with national identity: locally or nationally produced food is central to the French self-image and to international prestige (think of French wines or cheeses).

The French identity has been sustained in part, however, by large subsidies from the EU, through what is known as the Common Agricultural Policy (CAP). Created in part to satisfy French conditions for joining the EU, it became one of the EU's main expenditures. The CAP consumes over 40 percent of the EU's budget, with France the largest single recipient. Whereas countries with large agricultural sectors have done well under the CAP, member states with smaller or more efficient farms have resented the costs of the CAP. Outside the EU, the United States and less developed countries have long opposed the CAP's tariff barriers and import quotas, which limits non-EU agricultural products. The growing cost of the CAP (especially with enlargement), combined with pressure from non-EU countries, has intensified this conflict in recent years. But in spite of the pressure, the French government has resisted restructuring the CAP. French farmers have also turned the issue into one of anti-globalization, arguing that reduced support and open trade will lead to the "McDonaldization" of French food.[24] In a country where agriculture is central to national identity, such arguments carry weight.

FOREIGN RELATIONS AND THE WORLD

Our discussions have already touched on the idea that France views itself as a product of revolution with universal application, such as the American Revolution before it or the Russian Revolution after. With such a view, France has long seen itself as having a special mission in the international system, that is, to export its revolution's core ideas. Such thinking was part of the legitimizing force of the French empire in the eighteenth century, when the concepts of egalitarianism and the importance of the nation-state spread from France across Europe. Modern nationalism as we understand it, in the form of mass volunteer armies and patriotic fervor, was first associated with the French Revolution and Napoléon Bonaparte. Today, the historical struggles for national identity across Europe are often traced to the Napoleonic Wars.

France's unique view of its place in the world has persisted to the present, and this role was brought into sharp focus with the rise of two rivals to universal authority: the United States and the Soviet Union. With the onset of the cold war, France saw itself as caught between two superpowers, both of whom claimed that their ideological mission represented the ultimate political destiny for the rest of the world, including France. During the cold war, France played an important role in two Western European institutions: the European Union (EU) and the North Atlantic Treaty Organization (NATO). In the case of the EU, France was a founding member, along with Germany, Italy, Belgium, the Netherlands, and Luxembourg, in 1951. Recall how radical this proposal was at the time, since France and Germany had concluded a bitter war only a few years earlier. But France's motivation was not driven by a sense that its role in the international system had past, requiring it to subsume its powers into a larger, supranational organization. Rather, France saw in the EU the potential to extend its own authority, as a counterweight to the United States and the Soviet Union. With a French-German motor at its core, the EU could be a superpower in its own right, changing a bipolar international system into a multipolar one.

Thus, the French have always viewed the EU somewhat differently than have other member states, particularly Germany and the United Kingdom. For Germany, the EU has been seen as a necessary instrument to prevent another major war by openly refuting the primacy of nationalism and patriotism. For the United Kingdom, the EU is an ongoing threat for precisely the same reason. But for France, the EU has always been an instrument through which French ideals could be pursued. Indeed, under de Gaulle, France consistently blocked the UK's membership in the EU, viewing it as a Trojan horse for American interests.

Even NATO, explicitly created to counter Soviet power, was viewed by the French in these terms. For de Gaulle, America's domination of NATO reduced the likelihood that the organization could function as an expression of French policies and values. As a result, the French relationship to NATO was much more distant. Seeking to enhance a European position that would be more independent of the United States, France withdrew from the central military command of NATO in 1966 and developed its own independent nuclear capacity. France failed to achieve its objective of developing Europe as a superpower independent of the United States, but it continued to seek its own path and authority in the international system, both independently and through the EU.

The end of the cold war and the emergence of the United States as the sole superpower brought a new set of issues and concerns to French foreign policy. Even before 2001, French officials worried about what they termed the United States' "hyperpower". This hyperpower was no longer fettered by the cold war and in the absence of any restrictions would be free to act unilaterally, attempting to remake the world in its own image. Moreover, American military hyperpower would be further enhanced by globalization, which at its core was seen an internationalization of Anglo-Saxon values and institutions. As a French foreign minister put it, the United States was like a fish in the sea of globalization, uniquely suited to swim in its waters. For some French observers, then, the end of the cold war and the rise of U.S. hyperpower not only were a challenge to France's international role but also represented an existential crisis, undermining France's place in the world order.[25]

This tension has been evident since September 11, 2001. Although France expressed strong support for the United States after the terrorist attacks, relations between the two countries grew more tense, especially over the U.S. decision to go to war with Iraq. The debate over the war related to a number of factors important to French foreign policy. First, France saw the war as a clear expression of U.S. hyperpower, a unilateralism that rejected international institutions and thus marginalized other countries. Opposition to the war was therefore driven in part by a desire to have a say, and by the belief that U.S. force should be part of a multilateral process. The administration of George W. Bush rejected such calls, seeing France's arguments as an attempt simply to stymie U.S. power. A second factor was that France has traditionally cultivated a strong relationship with the Middle East, establishing far friendlier relations with many Arab states than with the United States. Not surprisingly, then, as with the United States moved closer to war, France became one of the strongest voices of protest, opposing a United Nations resolution authorizing force.

The Iraq war badly damaged diplomatic relations between the United States and Europe, particularly France. However, these relations may be on the mend with the election of President Sarkozy. Unlike his predecessor, Sarkozy is unabashedly pro-American and has sought to reconnect the country more strongly to the United States: for example, he proposed that France rejoin the NATO command structure that it left in 1966. Sarkozy has emphasized the need for a more muscular role for French foreign policy, calling for a modernization of the military and taking a more assertive position on such issues as Iran's nuclear program. Sarkozy's vision is one where France plays a stronger international role through its own diplomatic and military authority, a renewed partnership with the United States, and a leadership position in the European Union. It may be the last issue, however, that proves most difficult to achieve.

For many Europeans, the EU represents an important achievement in bringing security and prosperity to the continent. For France in particular, the EU has been a way for the country to amplify its power within this growing body. At an extreme, some observers imagined a fully federal Europe, with a unified foreign and security policy, that could become a superpower to rival the United States or a rising China. But there are obstacles to this vision and France's place in it. First, the expansion of the EU eastward has brought in a number of countries whose view of the international system is quite different from that of France. Having experienced the cold war from under Soviet control, they view the United States less as a rival than a liberator. This proved problematic in the run up to the Iraq War, when several East European states backed the U.S. intervention, much to France's chagrin. This reconfirmed France's suspicion of further enlargement, a concern that more, and more diverse, members would dilute French influence inside the EU. The French have thus emerged as strongly opposed to possible EU membership for Turkey, a Muslim country (albeit with a secular state) that has a population as large as France. As mentioned earlier, it has been proposed that Turkish accession would require a referendum in France (which would certainly fail), and President Sarkozy has expressed strong opposition to Turkey inside the EU.

The issue of enlargement is also tightly connected to institutional changes within the EU and France's perception of these changes. In the past, French leaders have favored an expansion of EU power as an extension of their own power. But with enlargement and the growing diversity of the EU there has been a need for institutional reform (essentially, an EU constitution) that would give more power to all member states but reduce the authority of such founding members as France. This has caused consternation in France and played an important role in the country's rejection of the 2005 referendum on the constitution. From having long viewed the EU as central to the French role in Europe and the world, it became clear that for many French the EU has become a threat to their authority and even a symbol of globalization. As of 2007 nearly 40 percent of French surveyed argued that the EU was headed in the wrong direction, a larger number of dissenters than in any other EU member.[26] France thus finds that even familiar institutions may be changing into something they do not understand and are beyond ability their ability to control. The question now is whether the French will embrace this uncertainty or retrench.

CURRENT ISSUES

THE CHALLENGE OF HIGHER EDUCATION

France is often seen as a country of intellectuals and scholars that reveres knowledge in a way few other countries do. Institutions like ENA further reinforce this idea of a state that emphasizes meritocracy and technocracy: that is, rule by merit and technical expertise. Higher education is highly centralized and free to those who are talented enough to be accepted. That said, it is surprising to find that, by many standards, higher education in France is in poor shape. Top institutions like ENA accept only a fraction of university students, leaving the remainder to make their way through institutions that are overenrolled and poorly funded, with large classes and high dropout rates. Furthermore, there are concerns that the French university system is not serving as an important engine of innovation and growth. Two separate studies do not place any French university among the top twenty in the world, and they place only three or four (depending on the study) among the top 100 research institutions in the world.[27]

Under the Sarkozy presidency there have been proposals to transform higher education in France in several ways. None of these may seem particularly radical, but for France's centralized institutions they could in fact amount to dramatic change. First, universities have been allowed to raise private funds; while the notion of an endowment funded by private donors is common in the United States, in Europe it is largely unheard of. Second, there are proposals to give students more freedom in choosing to which schools they can apply and to give universities more leeway in deciding which students they may accept. Traditionally, students could only attend nearby universities, and the universities were forbidden from rejecting students who had passed entrance exams. Third, the government has suggested basing funds on regular evaluations of a university's performance, determined by its endowments and the job success of its graduates.

Interestingly, one of the greatest sources of opposition to these reforms have been students. Although many understand that the current system could improve by providing a better education, there remains resistance to changes that in effect will increase competition between schools and competition between students. Surveys indicate that many young French still hope to land a job in the state sector, and they view their degree less as an important bundle of skills to be used in the job market than as a necessary credential that should translate into a secure public sector job. As a result, proposals for reforms in education and the labor market to create more flexibility in both have resulted in student demonstrations. As one European magazine noted, the interesting contrast with the protests of 1968 is that back then youth sought to dramatically change the current order. In France today, however, students are protesting to keep the current order from being changed.[28]

NOTES

1. Rolf H. W. Theen and Frank L. Wilson, *Comparative Politics: An Introduction to Seven Countries* (Upper Saddle River, NJ: Prentice-Hall, 2001), p. 101.

2. Britain has no single document defining its democratic regime but has a constitutional order dating at least to the seventeenth century. The United States has had only one constitution, which it has amended only twenty-six times in more than two centuries. Japan has never changed its postwar constitution.

3. For a useful discussion of these contributions, see James B. Collins, *The State in Early Modern France* (Cambridge, UK: Cambridge University Press, 1995).

4. Malcolm Crook and John Dunne, "Napoléon's France: History and Heritage," *Modern and Contemporary France*, 8 (2000), pp. 429–31.

5. John Hellman, "Memory, History, and National Identity in Vichy France," *Modern and Contemporary France*, 9 (2001), pp. 37–42.

6. For more, see Serge Bernstein, *The Republic of de Gaulle, 1958–1969* (Cambridge, UK: Cambridge University Press, 1993).

7. Gino Raymond, "The President: Still a 'Republican Monarch'?" in Gino Raymond, ed., *Structures of Power in Modern France* (New York: St. Martin's Press, 2000), pp. 1–18.

8. From 1958 to 1962, presidents were indirectly elected by an electoral college composed of elected officials. De Gaulle sought direct election of the presidency in order to enhance his own power, as well as that of the institution of the presidency.

9. Robert Elgie, *The Role of the Prime Minister in France, 1981–1991* (New York: St. Martin's Press, 1993).

10. See "Procedures for Raising an Issue of Government Responsibility, French National Assembly," www.assembleenationale.fr/english/government_responability.asp (accessed 13 August 2008).

11. John Lichfield, "Sarkozy's Military Plans 'Put Independence at Risk,'" *The Independent* (9 April 2008), www.independent.co.uk (accessed 19 January 2009).

12. Alec Stone, *The Birth of Judicial Politics in France* (New York: Oxford University Press, 1992).

13. William Wright, "FN Focus on France: ENA Loosens its Grip on Power," Financial News Online, 29 October 2007, www.efinancialnews.com/assetmanagement/peoplemoves/content/2349055738 (accessed 15 August 2008).

14. See Alistair Cole, "The Party System: The End of Old Certainties," in Raymond, *Structures of Power in Modern France*, pp. 19–36.

15. Susan Milner, "Trade Unions: A New Civil Agenda?" in Raymond, *Structures of Power in Modern France*, pp. 37–69.

16. For a discussion of the differences between the United States and France, see Robert A. Levine, *Assimilating Immigrants: Why America Can and France Cannot*, Rand Occasional Paper (Santa Monica, CA: Rand, 2004).

17. Justin Vaïsse, "Veiled Meaning: The French Law Banning Religious Symbols in Public Schools," U.S.-France Analysis Series, Brookings Institution, March 2004, p. 5, n. 16.

18. Mark Carley, "Developments in Industrial Action," EIROnline, www.eurofound. europa.eu/eiro/2005/06/update/tn0506101u.htm (accessed 19 January 2009).

19. World Values Survey 1999, www.worldvaluessurvey.org (accessed 19 January 2009).

20. Douglass C. North and Robert Paul Thomas, *The Rise of the Western World: A New Economic History* (Cambridge, UK: Cambridge University Press, 1973), ch. 10.

21. David S. Landes, *The Wealth and Poverty of Nations: Why Some Are So Rich and Some So Poor* (New York: W. W. Norton, 1998), p. 468.

22. Angus Maddison, *The World Economy: A Millennial Perspective* (Paris: OECD, 2001), pp. 132, 185.

23. United States Bureau of Labor Statistics, "Comparative Real Gross Domestic Product Per Capita and Per Employed Person (July 2007), www.bls.gov/fls/flsgdp.pdf (accessed 15 August 2008).

24. José Bové and François Dufour, *The World Is Not for Sale: Farmers against Junk Food* (London: Verso, 2001).

25. See Hubert Vedrine, *France in an Age of Globalization* (Washington, DC: Brookings Institution, 2000); see also Philip Gordon and Sophie Meunier, *The French Challenge: Adapting to Globalization* (Washington, DC: Brookings Institution, 2001).

26. European Union, *Eurobarometer*, 69 (June 2008), p. 18, http://ec.europa.eu/public_ opinion/archives/eb/eb69/eb_69_first_en.pdf (accessed 15 August 2008).

27. See the Times Higher Education Top 200 World Universities, www.timeshigher education.co.uk (accessed 19 January 2009); also Academic Ranking of World Universities, Shanghai Jiao Tong University, www.arwu.org/rank2008/en2008.htm (accessed 19 January 2009).

28. Kim Rahir, "Liberté Egalité and Job Securité," *Der Spiegel* (March 15, 2006), www.spiegel.de/international/spiegel/0,1518,406157,00.html (accessed 19 January 2009).

GLOSSARY OF KEY TERMS

absolute monarchy   That stage in the evolutionary development of Europe between the more decentralized feudal monarchies of the Middle Ages and the constitutional governments of the modern era.

ancien régime   European "old order" of absolute monarchy buttressed by religious authority.

bipolar   Alternation between coalitions of center-right and center-left.

blocked vote   Forces the legislature to accept bills in their entirety and allows amendments only if approved by the government.

Chirac, Jacques   President from 1995–2007.

code law   Laws that are derived from detailed legal codes rather than from precedent.

cohabitation   An arrangement when presidents lack a majority of legislative power and appoint an opposition prime minister who can gain a majority of support in the legislature.

Constitutional Council   Empowered to rule on any constitutional matter at the request of the government, the heads of each house of the legislature, or a group of at least sixty members of either house.

Council of Ministers   The cabinet selected by the prime minister.

coup d'état   Forceful and sudden overthrow of government.

dirigisme   An emphasis on state authority in economic development; a combination of social democratic and mercantilist ideas.

École Nationale d'Administration (ENA)   National Administrative School.

Estates General   Weak French assembly representing the clergy, nobles, and commoners prior to the French Revolution.

The Events of May   1968 Parisian riots in which students and workers called for educational and social reforms.

Fifth Republic   France's current regime (1958–present).

four-party, two-bloc-system   A system that required coalition building in the second round of the two-round, single-member district system.

French Communist Party (PCF)   One of the dominant parties of the French left since the end of World War II.

French Democratic Labor Confederation (CFDT)   A smaller confederation backed by the Socialist Party.

French Revolution   1789–1799; overthrow of French absolute monarchy and establishment of the First Republic.

French Socialist Party (PS)   Dominant party of the French left.

General Confederation of Labor (CGT)   The most powerful French union confederation, it is linked to the French Communist Party.

laïcité   The subordination of religious identity to state and national identity—state over church.

Le Pen, Jean-Marie   Created the National Front in 1972.

Mitterrand, François   Leader of the French Socialist Party starting in 1971, president of France from 1981 to 1995.

motion of censure   An act of legislature against the government, requiring new elections when proposed legislation submitted as matters of confidence are not passed.

National Assembly   Lower house of the French parliament.

National Front (FN)   A political party on the far right that was created by Le Pen in 1972.

pantouflage   Literally putting on the slippers; used to describe the move of administrative elite from the bureaucracy to the top echelons of the private sector.

parlement   France's bicameral legislature.

prefect   Government-appointed local official.

prime minister   Appointed by the French president and approved by the majority of the lower house of the legislature to select a cabinet and preside over the day-to-day affairs of government.

Rally for the French Republic (RPR)   Formed by Jacques Chirac as the more nationalist, socially conservative, EU-skeptic force of the French right.

regime   Norms and rules that govern politics.

Reign of Terror   Seizure of power and class war launched by radical Jacobins in revolutionary France (1793–1794).

Sarkozy, Nicolas   President of France since 2007.

semi-presidential   A legislative-executive system that shares political power among the legislature, a directly elected president, and a prime minister responsible to *both* the president and the legislature.

Sénat   France's 321-member upper house of legislature.

Union for a Popular Movement (UMP)   A single cohesive party of the center-right formed in 2002 with Chirac's encouragement.

Union for French Democracy (UDF)   An alliance of five center-right parties founded in 1978 by Chirac's rival and former president Giscard d'Estaing as a more neo-liberal force of the French right.

WEB LINKS

Assemblée nationale **www.assemblee-nat.fr**
Constitutional Council **www.conseil-constitutionnel.fr**
Information on national, regional, and local governments
     www.politicalresources.net/france3.htm
Ministry of Foreign Affairs **www.diplomatie.gouv.fr/en**
Le Monde diplomatique **mondediplo.com**
President **www.elysee.fr/elysee**
Prime Minister **premier-ministre.gouv.fr/en**

5 GERMANY

Head of state: President Horst Koehler
(since July 1, 2004)

Head of government:
Chancellor Angela Merkel
(since November 22, 2005)

Capital: Berlin

Total land size: 357,021 sq km

Population: 82 million

GDP at PPP: $2.81 trillion US$

GDP per capita at PPP: $34,200

Human development index ranking: 22

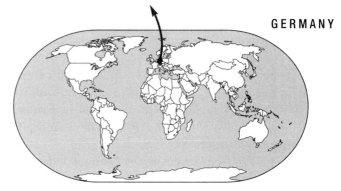

GERMANY

INTRODUCTION

Why Study This Case?

Germany commands a prominent position in the world and a pivotal position in Europe. It is the world's largest exporting nation, Europe's biggest economy, the European Union's most populous country, and an integral member of Europe's economic, political, and security organizations. Situated in the heart of the Continent, Germany today in many ways typifies the political, social, and cultural values and institutions of Europe and offers a useful window into understanding the political institutions and public policies shared broadly by many of its European neighbors. By and large, Germans embrace social democratic political and economic values, champion postmaterialist concerns for the environment and the pursuit of leisure, and vigorously promote European integration even as they seek to enhance the competitiveness of Germany's capitalist economy and to strengthen its national security. But in other fundamental ways, Germany sits apart from its European neighbors and poses interesting puzzles for the comparative political scientist.

Unlike many of its western and northern European counterparts, the German state is federal; sovereignty and nationhood came very late to Germany. The modern institution of the nation-state finds its origin in Europe, in no small part with the 1648 Peace of Westphalia, which affirmed the principle of national sovereignty at the end of Europe's bloody Thirty Years' War. But even though this treaty was inked on German soil, it would take another 220 years before a German nation-state was established. Once forged in the nineteenth century, German nationalism took on powerful and ultimately virulent and destructive force in the twentieth century at the hands of Nazi fascists. The disastrous consequences of this hypernationalism led the allies who defeated Germany to divide the nation in 1945, a division perpetuated for over three decades by the cold war. Despite reunification of East and West Germany in 1990, many Germans today remain hesitant to promote nationalism and are among Europe's strongest advocates of greater European integration and the European Union. Although it can claim a thoroughly Western and European heritage, German modernization in many ways better resembles the experience of Japan than that of Britain, France, or the United States. Germany is a latecomer to both modern capitalism and democracy, with both imposed externally.

The very successes of German industrialization, democratization after World War II, and peaceful reunification have left the country uncertain about its own future. Globalization poses new challenges to Germany's vaunted welfare state. Immigration has raised old questions about race and national identity; the end of the cold war changed Germany's role as a linchpin of East-West relations; the expansion of the European Union eastward has weakened the central role that the country historically played in the organization. Germany remains a major power, but its role in the post–cold war international system seems muted, a reflection of a country still troubled by its past and uncertain what responsibilities it must shoulder in the future.

Major Geographic and Demographic Features

With an area slightly smaller than Montana or Japan, even reunified Germany cannot be considered large on a global scale. But its substantial population (over 80 million), economic vitality, and location in the heart of Europe have placed it at the center of European affairs for many centuries. German topography has enhanced this centrality. Situated on the plains of Northern Europe, it shares contiguous borders with nine European countries. With the exception of the Alps to the south and the Baltic and North Seas to the north, Germany possesses no natural boundaries. Unlike England, Japan, or even France, which relied upon natural barriers to offer protection from foreign predators and to create a strong sense of national identity, Germany found itself externally vulnerable and internally divided. This central location, accessibility, and internal incoherence meant that many of Europe's conflicts over the centuries were carried out on German soil and that Germans, unlike the British or Americans, did not have the luxury to remain aloof from the military and political affairs that surrounded and too often engulfed them. This predation by foreign armies only perpetuated Germany's continued political disunity, its sense of vulnerability, and its propensity for military preparedness.

Often the victim of foreign affairs, the German state, once it finally achieved political unity and military capacity in the nineteenth century, took its defense into its own hands and at times engaged in aggressive expansion. A lack of natural resources—with much of Germany's coal, iron, and some of its most productive farmland located in disputed border regions—also inspired German imperialism and military aggression as a means of obtaining resources. The German empire's late nineteenth century "scramble for Africa" and Nazi Germany's call for *lebensraum* (living space) were justified in these terms. This same sense of vulnerability and the bitter lessons learned from nearly a century of aggression have also propelled postwar German overtures for European integration. Just as Germans in the nineteenth century recognized that German safety and interests were well served by unification, Germans in the postwar era have concluded that German and European security and prosperity are well served by the peaceful integration of Europe.

The absence of geographical barriers also encouraged the migration of Germans and the diffusion of German culture into surrounding regions over time. These German migrants spread the German language and culture well beyond the boundaries of what now constitutes Germany. What at times became bitter conflicts over disputed territories with France (Alsace-Lorraine), Denmark (Schleswig), Czechoslovakia (Sudetenland), and Poland (Silesia) stem in no small part from the diffusion of ethnic groups and rival claims to these border regions.[1] The absence of natural borders has also meant that language, physical characteristics, and shared cultural values have been more important national markers in Germany than elsewhere, a cultural theme enhanced and elaborated by German intellectuals over the centuries. Although it now hosts Europe's largest immigrant population, Germany proper today remains quite homogeneous. Over 90 percent of the population is ethnically German, with ethnic Turks making up 2.5 percent and the remaining 6 percent a variety of other European nationalities.

Historical Development of the State

The economic, social, and political forces that swept modernization through much of Western Europe trickled far more slowly into the region that we now know as Germany. National unity, industrialization, and democracy all came later to Germany than to its Western European neighbors. Scholars agree that this relative backwardness profoundly shaped the German state. In France and England, feudalism gave way to states centralized by absolute monarchies that established standardized legal and administrative systems and fostered a coherent sense of nationalism. By contrast, national sovereignty and a centralized state eluded Germany until the nineteenth century. Although the German state was long in coming, once established it loomed very large in Germany's rush to modernize.[2] As the idea of a German nation became institutionalized in a sovereign state, this unity born of national identity had powerful force. Centuries of decentralization and disunity gave way to intense periods of authoritarian militarism and mercantilism, first under the leadership of the state of Prussia in the late nineteenth century and then again under Nazi direction in the 1930s and 1940s. This relatively late unification and catch-up economic development meant that development of the state preceded industrialization, fostering state-led mercantilist development and authoritarianism.

Relative backwardness also placed Germany behind in the race for colonies and raw materials to feed industrialization, which fostered a voracious and aggressive imperialism that led ultimately to the **Third Reich** (empire), fascist Nazi expansionism, and military defeat. As a democratic and decentralized federal state no longer plagued by disunity, postwar Germany vigorously promoted European integration and pursued a costly program of complete

TIME LINE OF POLITICAL DEVELOPMENT

Year	Event
800–900 C.E.	Loose confederation of German principalities forms Holy Roman Empire; later known as the First Reich
1871	Otto von Bismarck unifies Germany; later dubbed Second Reich
1918	Germany defeated in World War I
1919	Weimar Republic formed under difficult conditions
1933	Hitler and Nazis rise to power, establishing the Third Reich
1945	Hitler and Nazis defeated in World War II
1945–49	Germany divided among allies into four occupied zones
1948	Berlin blockade and airlift
1949	Founding of Federal Republic of Germany (FRG) in the west and German Democratic Republic (GDR) in the east
1952	FRG joins European Coal and Steel Community
1955	FRG joins NATO, and GDR joins Warsaw Pact
1957	FRG participates in founding of European Economic Community
1961	Construction of the Berlin Wall
1969	FRG Chancellor Willy Brandt launches policy of Ostpolitik
1989	Fall of the Berlin Wall
1990	Germany unified with GDR incorporated into FRG
1993	Germany becomes a founding member of the European Union

German unification. As the original German and French architects of integration hoped, the success of the former effort has largely tempered fears that a reunified Germany would pursue militarist expansionism or any undue unilateral political influence.

THE ABSENCE OF A STRONG CENTRAL STATE DURING THE HOLY ROMAN EMPIRE, 800–1806

Charlemagne founded what came to be known as the Holy Roman Empire in western and central Europe in 800 C.E. By the middle of the ninth century, a collection of German, Austrian, and Czech princes acquired nominal control of this loosely constituted empire, or **reich**. A feudal empire, it consisted of an odd assortment of hundreds of principalities, city-states, and other local political entities with varying degrees of autonomy and legitimacy, but there was virtually no allegiance to the center. This weak confederation waxed and waned in size and influence over the next thousand years, persisting until the time of Napoléon in the nineteenth century. Whereas comparable feudalism gave way to centralized states in England and France, the Holy Roman Empire remained politically disunified.

The empire took political form with the office of a weak emperor, which rotated among princes, and the imperial *Reichstag*, or, congress. This precursor of the contemporary German parliament began as a royal court composed of prominent princes and dukes who met irregularly to elect the emperor. By the fifteenth century, the Reichstag had become slightly more representative, with lesser princes and free cities also seated. However, the dominant princes, lesser princes, and urban representatives met in separate bodies, which made the Reichstag more divided, weaker, and less representative than its British counterpart. Indeterminate boundaries, centuries of entrenched localism, and mutual suspicions and prejudices among these localities hampered any efforts of unification.

Although religion had earlier served an important role in unifying much of Europe under the banner of Christianity, by the sixteenth century it too had become a divisive force within the Holy Roman Empire in the form of the Protestant Reformation. In 1517, the German monk and professor Martin Luther publicly displayed his writ of complaints about certain Catholic practices and doctrines. Among many other significant outcomes, this revolt split the previously religiously unified Holy Roman Empire and its German core. This religious divide took on political significance, leading to separate and often competing state churches in German locales, giving new sources of legitimacy to these local chieftains and additional justification for resisting unification. The Reformation also touched off the Thirty Years' War (1618–1648), a religious conflict between Catholics and Protestants that was fought largely on German soil. For reasons beyond religion, the protracted war came to envelope most of Europe before ending with the Peace of Westphalia in 1648. This settlement affirmed the sovereignty of local political entities, thereby preserving decentralized German authority and further weakening the Holy Roman Empire.

THE UNIFICATION OF THE GERMAN STATE, THE RISE OF PRUSSIA, AND THE SECOND REICH, 1806–1918

Napoléon's invasion of Germany in 1806 effectively destroyed the empire, inadvertently began the process of German unification, and unleashed the forces of German nationalism that would ultimately lead to the rise of Nazi fascism. Napoléon's offensive wiped out many of the empire's sovereign principalities (there were some 300 at the time) and compelled others to merge with their larger neighbors for protection. Ultimately, only **Prussia** to the east and Austria to the south were strong enough to resist Napoléon's onslaught and avoid inclusion in the confederation of defeated territories formed by Napoléon. After his defeat in 1815, German allies under Prussian leadership set up a loose confederation of some forty sovereign mini-states that formed for the first time the semblance of a German state.

Over the course of the eighteenth and nineteenth centuries, the kingdom of Prussia in eastern Germany gradually acquired the autonomy, capacity, and legitimacy that allowed it to emerge as a viable core for a modern German state. A series of generally enlightened monarchs established an authoritarian state administered by an efficient and loyal bureaucratic staff, supported by a conservative and wealthy landed aristocracy known as **Junkers**, and defended by a large and well-trained standing army. (Voltaire once commented that "while some states have an army, the Prussian army has a state.") As important as the state's monopoly on violence was its mercantilist promotion of economic growth through the development of national infrastructure, the expansion of education among its subjects, and the enhancement of trade. Prussia established a customs union with neighboring German states that by 1834 included all but Austria. This highly capable and autonomous state managed to defend itself from aggressors, expand its territory, grow its economy, and thereby enhance its legitimacy beyond Prussia as it successfully competed with Austria for ascendancy in unifying Germany.

This unification was not accompanied by greater liberalization in the political regime, which can be explained in part by the relative weakness of Germany's commercial and industrial middle class. Much as in China during the early twenty-first century, the educated and intellectual elite of nineteenth-century German society comprised fewer merchants and entrepreneurs and more bureaucrats, judges, and professors largely employed by the state. Though modern in their thinking and in many ways even liberal in their outlook, this portion of society saw the state (in their hands) as a positive and essential instrument in building German national unity, wealth, and power. German intellectuals argued that individual freedom was a luxury or indeed a weakness not fit for the forging of German national identity. It would be militarist and mercantilist "blood and iron," not liberal elections, that would unify Germany.

By the 1860s, Prussia had forceful and capable leadership, a powerful military, and a growing industrial economy. Impressive war victories over Denmark, Austria, and ultimately France drew other German states into the cause and led in 1871 to the establishment of a national German empire, or what came to be known as the Second Reich. Although the Prussian king was crowned emperor of all Germany, the key figure in the process of expansion and unification was Count Otto von Bismarck, prime minister, or chancellor, of Prussia. A politician, military officer, and member of the Junker landed class, he led a so-called revolution from above in which regime change came not from the lower disenfranchised classes, but rather from an alliance of iron and rye—that is, between the industrialists and the landed aristocracy. Through the savvy use of diplomacy, war, and political machinations, the Iron Chancellor—as he came to be known—dominated German politics for two decades and brought about the first unified modern German state.

Not surprisingly, unified Germany's first national constitution established an authoritarian monarchy with only the trappings of liberal democracy. Sovereignty remained vested in the emperor, or *Kaiser* (derived from the Latin Caesar), and political power flowed from him. Although the constitution established a federal structure in which all of the states were to have equal influence (a nod to the long-standing regional autonomy of the German states), it ensured the dominance of Prussia by mandating that the Prussian prime minister would always become imperial chancellor. Similarly, although the constitution gave nominal deference to the notion of political equality (thus addressing the demands of the small but growing liberal middle class) by granting universal male suffrage for elections to the *Reichstag* (national parliament), it retained aristocratic privilege in Prussian state elections. In addition, the imperial chancellor, the bureaucracy, and the military answered only to the emperor as head of state, not the constitution. The emperor appointed the imperial chancellor, and the Reichstag could not dismiss the government. The emperor, chancellor, and their unelected administrators controlled foreign affairs and the military.

The Iron Chancellor took no chances that the constitution's nominal democratic allowances would get in the way of his force-draft modernization drive. Bismarck bullied or circumvented the Reichstag in those few areas it did have some authority (such as the budget). He encouraged the creation of multiple political parties and then skillfully played them off of each other. Through the promotion of patriotism and German culture and the expansion of national wealth and empire, Bismarck enhanced the popularity and legitimacy of his authoritarian rule. The core of this support remained the landed gentry, military, and industrial elite, but the middle and lower classes were "largely swept along" by growing prosperity and appeals to national pride as Germany's international stature grew.[3] Groups opposing his authoritarian rule (including Catholics, liberals, social democrats, and Marxists) were met at times with coercion and other times cooptation. This policy of an "iron fist in a velvet glove" kept the peace through the deft use of both violence and the granting of social welfare benefits, such as health insurance and old-age pensions.

But if democracy found infertile ground in modernizing Prussia, catch-up industrialization proved much more successful. In 1890, Bismarck was eased out of office, and Emperor Kaiser Wilhelm II assumed personal control, continuing the policy of rapid industrialization and imperialist expansion. By the early twentieth century, Germany had surpassed Britain in iron production and had become a leading industrial power. Society became more complex as both the middle and working classes grew in size and political strength, with the socialist movement capturing one third of German votes by 1912. As socialist opposition grew, some traditional sectors of German society, such as small capitalists and landed aristocrats, embraced nationalism and anti-Semitism.

German patriotism, however, prevailed over these social divisions and differences. Frustrations associated with Germany's efforts to expand its empire and suspicions about the intentions of its neighbors stoked feelings of nationalism and unfulfilled destiny and contributed to German willingness to bring about World War I (1914–1917). But as the war pressed on and took a particularly heavy toll on Germany, these differences once again rose to the surface. Political liberals, Catholics, and others began to question openly why they lent their support to an authoritarian government waging war against countries that provided their citizens democratic rights. Workers wondered why they could fight and die but not have an equal vote in the parliament. As the war ground to its bitter conclusion, the emperor made assurances of reform, but these promises offered too little and came too late. German defeat in 1918 combined with urban uprisings prompted the emperor to abdicate and proclaim Germany a republic.

POLITICAL POLARIZATION AND THE BREAKDOWN OF DEMOCRACY DURING THE WEIMAR REPUBLIC, 1919–1933

The political vacuum that followed the collapse of the Second Reich proved to be particularly infertile ground for the establishment of Germany's first republic. One scholar concluded that with radical Communists on the left, reactionary monarchists and militarists on the right, and no historical experience with liberal democracy, German society could claim "virtually no republicans."[4] No one was prepared for the sudden departure of the emperor, and few had considered how Germany ought to be constituted as a republic with no monarchy. The seeds of cynicism and elitism sown in this era would grow into the extremism and fascist totalitarianism that would spell the republic's doom in less than two decades.

In the face of these and other difficulties, politicians met in the city of Weimar in 1918 to draft a constitution. Promisingly, the majority of socialists retreated from their revolutionary goals and participated in the process. The **Weimar Republic** featured a remarkably democratic constitution that offered universal suffrage for all adults (ahead of both Britain and the United States), universal health insurance and pensions, and the right to employment or unemployment compensation. Drafters of the constitution looked to the British parliamentary system as a model, retaining a bicameral parliament with a strong, popularly elected lower house (*Reichstag*) and a weaker upper chamber (*Reichstrat*) representing the states. But they mistakenly saw the British monarch as the key to the system's stability and replaced the German kaiser with a strong president, a measure that would ultimately doom the republic. This resulted in a dual executive, semi-presidential system (similar to the current Russian and French systems) in which the president as head of state was directly and popularly elected, could nominate the chancellor as head of government, and could rule through emergency decree under threatening circumstances.

The Weimar Republic also adopted a proportional representation electoral system for the Reichstag with no minimum threshold of votes, which fostered a proliferation of parties, many of them small and representing narrow interests. This meant that no party ever won an outright majority in the Reichstag, and increasingly weak and short-lived coalitions became the norm. Between 1919 and 1933, Germany had more than twenty governments, often functioning as minority coalitions unable to cobble together a majority of seats.

By the mid-1920s, Weimar Germany had achieved some stability, with moderate parties in the center managing to counterbalance the more radical and reactionary fringes (including a failed coup attempt in 1923 by a young firebrand reactionary named Adolph Hitler). The Weimar Republic faced anything but ordinary circumstances, however, struggling with internal and external challenges that might have doomed even the most stable and resilient regime.[5] These challenges included the humiliation and burden of the Versailles Peace Treaty concluding World War I, which imposed upon Germany billions of dollars of reparations, military demobilization, the forfeiting of portions of German territory to France, and the loss of its overseas colonies; devastating hyperinflation brought on by war reparations and postwar economic turmoil (the inflation rate at one point in 1923 was 26 billion percent); and the consequences of the Great Depression, which caused widespread unemployment in Germany (nearly a third of German workers were unemployed by 1932).

Those opposed to the Weimar regime were able to blame the democratic parties that authored the constitution for all of these ills. A threatened middle class, defeated soldiers, and unemployed workers all proved ripe for recruitment into extreme nationalist and radical Communist movements as the Weimar Republic began to unravel. By 1930, moderate center parties favoring liberal democracy lost their majority in parliament. Germany's Communist Party, which received only 2 percent of the popular vote in the 1920 Reichstag election, had by 1932 garnered 17 percent. In 1928, the **National**

Socialist (Nazi) Party, led by **Adolf Hitler**, running on a platform of militarism and anti-Semitism, commanded less than 3 percent of the vote, but by 1932 obtained 37 percent, the highest total for any party during the Weimar period.

Under conditions of increasing instability, German state capacity weakened as violence replaced legislative politics and Communist and Nazi militias fought regularly in the streets. Following the 1932 election, conservative President Hindenberg and his nationalist supporters faced the difficult choice of forming a coalition government in alliance with moderate parties against the Nazis, declaring martial law and attempting to forcibly shut down the Nazis, or allying with Hitler and the Nazis in an effort to tame them. Hindenberg chose the latter option. In 1933, Hitler used this alliance and mounting disorder to first secure the office of chancellor and then gain passage of the Enabling Act, which yielded the Reichstag's powers to the chancellor, effectively dissolving the constitution and bringing the Weimar Republic to an end.

FASCIST TOTALITARIANISM UNDER THE THIRD REICH, 1933–1945

Unfettered by constitutional restrictions, Hitler moved swiftly to establish the Third Reich, replacing the democratic institutions of the Weimar Republic with those of a Nazi-led fascist totalitarian regime. Although the term *fascism* is often misused to describe the ideologies or motives underpinning various authoritarian regimes and political movements, the term accurately describes the corporatist (rejecting individual freedom), hierarchical (rejecting social equality), and hypernationalist values driving Hitler's Nazi Party. The Nazis imprisoned political opponents, required a loyalty oath of all civil servants, banned opposition political parties, and placed all social organizations including clubs and churches under restrictions or direct party control. Hitler employed state terror and a state-supervised mercantilist economy to achieve the regime's ideological goals of restoring German national power, expanding the German empire, and destroying those political ideologies and ethnic groups that threatened his vision of Aryan supremacy.

It is difficult for us to understand in hindsight how a totalitarian political regime with such reprehensible means and ends could be successful, popular, and even legitimate. For many Germans facing social chaos and economic collapse, the stability, order, and national wealth and pride Hitler promised were far more important values than either freedom or equality. Hitler identified and vilified scapegoats for Germany's ills, resurrected the flailing economy, and united the divided country. With extraordinary charisma, Hitler delivered heroically and almost miraculously on his promises to rearm the nation, reclaim lost territories, and restore Germany's pride, power, and prestige. The Nazi propaganda machine effectively used pageantry and propaganda to amplify Hitler's inherent speaking magnetism. As with other totalitarian regimes, such as Stalin's Russia and Mao's China, Hitler did not hesitate to use terror at the hands of an extensive security apparatus to intimidate opponents and destabilize and atomize society. In increasingly bold and aggressive measures, Hitler rearmed Germany (in violation of the Versailles Treaty), annexed Austria, occupied Czechoslovakia, and in 1939 invaded Poland, provoking World War II.

But by invading Russia in 1941, Hitler attempted one too many miracles and pushed Nazi aggression, racism, and ultimately genocide beyond the bounds that the world and increasingly Germans themselves would tolerate. Like Napoléon before him, Hitler's vaunted war machine proved no match for the harsh Russian winter or the bravery of the Russian people. But before the Nazi war machine was ultimately defeated in 1945, it had exterminated some 6 million Jews and millions of other noncombatants on racial and ethnic grounds. The war brought more than 50 million casualties in Europe alone. Among those casualties was Hitler himself, who committed suicide in a Berlin bunker in 1945, a week before Russian, American, British, and French allies would overrun and occupy a defeated Germany.

FOREIGN OCCUPATION AND THE DIVISION OF THE GERMAN STATE, 1945–1949

In 1945, Germany found itself utterly defeated, its industry, infrastructure, society, and polity completely in ruins. Germans often describe this complete institutional vacuum from which it would begin to rebuild as zero hour (*Stunde Null*), a starting from scratch. The German state surrendered sovereignty to the four Allied Powers (Britain, France, the United States, and Russia), each of which occupied a portion of the country. The capital, Berlin, was similarly quartered. Territories that had been seized and annexed by the Nazis were carved off and returned to neighboring countries, while parts of Germany were annexed by Poland.

Although initial plans called for cooperation among the four occupying forces in moving toward the reestablishment of German sovereignty, the cold war intervened leading to a de facto division between the Soviet-occupied eastern zone and the regions in the west occupied by the other three powers. In an obvious step toward establishing a separate West German state, the three Western allies established a common currency for their three zones in 1948. The Soviet Union reacted by blocking land access from the West German sector into West Berlin (located in the eastern sector) that same year. Western allies in turn responded to this blockade with the Berlin Airlift, which delivered vital supplies to West Berlin by air for nearly a year. The Western allies also ordered the West Germans to convene a separate constitutional assembly, something the Germans were reticent to do for fear such a move would permanently institutionalize a divided German state. This convention led not to a constitution (deemed too permanent) but to the **Basic Law**, which established the **Federal Republic of Germany** (**FRG**, or West Germany) in 1949 as a democratic and demilitarized state. The Soviets quickly responded by setting up the **German Democratic Republic** (**GDR**, or East Germany) in the same year. "Independence" for both German states did not, however, bring complete sovereignty; each Germany remained beholden to its cold war patron, exercising what one scholar has labeled semi-sovereignty.[6] Both the United States and the Soviet Union reserved the right to control much of their respective client's foreign policy and even to intervene in domestic matters as deemed necessary, authority neither patron fully relinquished until the reunification of the German states in 1990.

In West Germany, as in defeated Japan, Western allies and German reformers took steps to weaken those institutions seen as responsible for Nazi militarism, including sweeping de-Nazification. Reformers also devolved authority from the central state to Germany's federal regions and strengthened democratic institutions. They reformed and broadened the party system and encouraged coalitions in an effort to prevent the emergence of narrowly defined interests and ideologies. These measures included bringing together Catholic and Protestant political interests in separate but like-minded wings of the newly established Christian Democratic Union, healing a political divide that had persisted since the time of the Reformation in the sixteenth century.

In the context of the cold war, the United States sought to rebuild the West German economy as an engine of economic revitalization for Western Europe. Like Japan, Germany took up this task of capitalist economic development with seemingly miraculous success, growing rapidly to become one of the wealthiest countries in the world. At the same time, strong democratic leadership brought stable constitutional democracy and a prosperous social democratic political economy to the Federal Republic. Effective chancellors included Konrad Adenauer (1949–1963) who sought to integrate Germany into the Western alliance and bind it to its former military foes in Europe by joining the Coal and Steel Community and NATO, and Willy Brandt (1969–1974), who introduced a pragmatic policy of reconciliation with East Germany known as *Ostpolitik*. Despite political competition among thriving democratic parties, general consensus prevailed across the political spectrum favoring domestic policies of comprehensive social welfare programs and a state-regulated marketplace and a foreign policy promoting growing European integration and pragmatic measures to ease tensions with East Germany and ultimately embrace unification.

In the German Democratic Republic, Stalinist totalitarianism replaced fascist totalitarianism. Because the Soviets blamed the capitalist system both in Germany and more globally as responsible for the Third Reich and both world wars, their first step was to eliminate East Germany's capitalist economy and replace it with a new socialist system presided over by a totalitarian Communist Party state. By the end of the 1940s, the Eastern portion of Germany possessed political and economic systems almost identical to those of its Soviet mentor. With economic growth rates over the first two postwar decades nearly as impressive at those of its western counterpart, East Germany became the economic showcase of the Communist bloc. But like its Soviet mentor, the East German socialist economy ultimately could not keep pace with the capitalist West. Its failure to do so was demonstrated by the grim reality of life in the Democratic Republic. The East German state retained power by force and terror, manifested in its reliance on the *Stasi* (secret police) to squelch dissent, the construction of the fortified Berlin Wall surrounding West Berlin in 1961, and the summary execution of those caught trying to flee.[7]

In fact, Soviet leader Mikhail Gorbachev's efforts to revitalize Communist rule and the economy in the Soviet Union through his 1980s' reforms of perestroika and glasnost had their more immediate effects not on the Soviet Union but on its central European allies, including East Germany. These political and economic reforms threatened to undermine the Stalinist foundation on which the East German system was built. In early 1989, Hungary opened its borders with Austria, and East Germans vacationing in Hungary quickly took advantage of this breech in the Iron Curtain to leave for the West. Over the next six months, some 2 percent of the East German population emigrated to West Germany. This led to a rapid weakening of the Democratic Republic's legitimacy and its capacity to control events. Gorbachev urged the East German leadership to follow the Soviet reforms, further threatening the regime as the entire Communist system seemed to be crumbling around them. As public protests in East Germany grew and the pace of the exodus to the west picked up, the economy ground to a halt and the party-state lost its capacity to govern. The East German leaders stepped down and announced on November 9, 1989, the opening of the border between East and West Berlin. Crowds swarmed both sides of the Berlin Wall as the gates were opened, and this tangible and iconic image of the beginning of the end of Germany's division and the collapse of the Iron Curtain was televised across the world.

REUNIFICATION OF THE GERMAN STATE, 1990–PRESENT

The collapse of the East German state and the euphoria shared by all Germans propelled events much more rapidly than anyone could have anticipated. East and West German leaders prepared for a gradual process of thawing and increased contacts, but it quickly became apparent that the only source of stability would be a quick process of unification. The flood of Germans migrating from East to West prompted hurried negotiations leading to full reunification in 1990, less than one year after the fall of the wall. In effect, **reunification** meant the incorporation of East Germany into the Federal Republic, with the adoption of the West German Basic Law as the constitution of a unified Germany and West Germany's capitalist economic system imposed on East Germany. Although the Basic Law called for a new constitution and national referendum upon reunification, thus far, no such action has been taken.

The 1990 merger probably averted a much more disastrous political implosion of East Germany, but the long-sought reunification proved much more difficult and costly than the early optimists had bargained for. The early euphoria of national unification gave way to the cold, hard reality of bringing together two sovereign nation-states that shared a language (for the most part) and a pre–World War history and culture, but little else. The huge inequality in living standards, infrastructure, and income between the western and eastern portions of Germany has been tempered in the two decades since unification, but despite huge transfers of wealth these inequalities are still not resolved. Since reunification, the government has spent nearly US$2 trillion on eastern Germany in an effort to modernize its infrastructure and stabilize its economy. Following reunification, inefficient and bloated state-owned enterprises collapsed and shrank, leading to massive layoffs. Although unemployment in the former East Germany has declined, it remains at nearly 20 percent, twice the figure of the former West Germany.

POLITICAL REGIME

For students of political science, Germany's political regime since 1949 (often called the **Bonn Republic**, since Bonn was West Germany's capital from 1949 to 1990) is a fascinating example of constitutional engineering. Its founders sought to prevent the breakdown of democracy that doomed the Weimar Republic. Thus, the Bonn Republic's architects sought a better balance between local and national power, between the legislature and the executive, between political stability and representative democracy, and between the power of the state and the rights of individuals. They created an innovative political system that also contained some elements of continuity with Germany's institutional past. The German political system has more checks and balances, and is thus less efficient and decisive, than is the British Westminster model, but to date it has proved remarkably stable and effective.

Political Institutions

THE CONSTITUTION

The Basic Law (intended to serve as West Germany's temporary constitution until its unification with East Germany) was amended in 1990 to incorporate East German states and has become Germany's permanent constitution. The

ESSENTIAL POLITICAL FEATURES

- Legislative-executive system: parliamentary
- Legislature: Parliament
- Lower house: Bundestag (Federal Diet)
- Upper house: Bundesrat (Federal Council)
- Unitary or federal division of power: federal
- Main geographic subunits: länder (states)
- Electoral system for lower house: mixed single-member districts and proportional representation
- Chief judicial body: Federal Constitutional Court and Federal Court of Justice

Basic Law is founded on five principles, designed to avoid both the chaos of the Weimar Republic and the authoritarianism of the Third Reich.[8] First, where Hitler had destroyed the power of German states, the Bonn Republic Basic Law created a system of cooperative federalism, in which the federal government and state governments would share power. Second, the Basic Law guaranteed an elaborate set of basic political, social, and economic rights. Third, to counter the powerful Weimar president, the Bonn Republic established a weak, indirectly elected head of state. Fourth, political power was concentrated in the head of government, the chancellor, elected by and directly responsible to the legislature. Fifth, the Bonn Republic established a powerful and independent judiciary to check the government. Each of these constitutional features will be discussed in more depth in the following sections.

The Basic Law can be amended by a two-thirds majority in both houses. In an attempt to prevent excessive concentration of state power, however, some constitutional features, such as Germany's federal system and individual rights, cannot be altered.

The Branches of Government

THE HEAD OF GOVERNMENT AND THE CABINET

German democracy is often referred to as chancellor democracy since the **federal chancellor**, or prime minister, is the most powerful political figure and the chief executive authority in Germany. The Basic Law made the office of the chancellor far more powerful vis-à-vis the head of state to create a stronger, more stable, and more democratic regime than the Weimar Republic.

As is typical in a parliamentary system, the head of government is elected by the lower house of the legislature (the Bundestag) and has always been the leader of the largest party in the legislature. As leader of the largest party or coalition, chancellors expect to see most of their government's policy proposals approved by the legislature. Chancellors appoint and oversee the cabinet, the group of ministers (currently fifteen) who head government departments. Cabinet ministers need not be members of the legislature (though most are). Chancellors may create or eliminate cabinet posts at will. Chancellor Helmut Kohl, for example, created a Minister of the Environment,

Conservation, and Nuclear Safety; his successor, Gerhard Schroeder, combined the ministries of Economics and Labor. Chancellors may fire cabinet ministers at any time, although chancellors who preside over coalition governments may threaten the stability of the government when dismissing a cabinet member from a party that is a coalition partner. Indeed, all German cabinets since 1949 have been coalitions of at least two parties, and coalition

German Chancellors and Their Coalitions, 1949–2008

Bundestag Election Year	Governing Coalition	Chancellor (Party)
1949	CDU/CSU–FDP, DP	Konrad Adenauer (CDU)
1953	CDU/CSU–FDP, DP	" "
1957	CDU/CSU, DP	" "
1961	CDU/CSU–FDP	" " (to 1963)
		Ludwig Erhard (CDU)
1965	CDU/CSU–FDP (to 1966)	Ludwig Erhard (CDU, 1965–66)
	CDU/CSU–SPD (1966–69)	Kurt Kiesinger (CDU, 1966–69)
1969	SPD-FDP	Willy Brandt (SPD)
1972	SPD-FDP	Willy Brandt (SPD, to 1974)
		Helmut Schmidt (SPD, to 1976)
1976	SPD-FDP	Helmut Schmidt (SPD)
1980	SPD-FDP (1980–82)	Helmut Schmidt (SPD, 1980–82)
	CDU/CSU–FDP (1982–83)	Helmut Kohl (CDU)
1983	CDU/CSU–FDP	" "
1987	CDU/CSU–FDP	" "
1990	CDU/CSU–FDP	" "
1994	CDU/CSU–FDP	" "
1998	SPD-Greens	Gerhard Schroeder (SPD)
2002	SPD-Greens	" "
2005	CDU/CSU–SPD	Angela Merkel (CDU)

Key to Party Acronyms:
CDU/CSU (Christian Democratic Union/Christian Social Union)
SPD (Social Democratic Party)
FDP (Free Democratic Party)
DP (Deutsche Partei, conservatives)

Source: Adapted from Simon Green, et al., *The Politics of the New Germany* (New York: Routledge, 2008), p. 63.

partners often designate their preferred candidate to occupy the cabinet posts allotted to them.

The actual power of German chancellors has varied over time, depending in part on their ability to dominate their own parties. Two recent German chancellors, Helmut Kohl and Gerhard Schroeder, were especially dominant political figures. Kohl was the unquestioned leader of his party, had few powerful rivals, and oversaw German reunification. Schroeder also came to dominate his party and his coalition partners, the Greens.

Chancellors have at their disposal considerable resources, including the chief of the chancellery, a chief of staff with broad powers over the government. In addition to naming the cabinet, the chancellor makes numerous political appointments to government posts.

THE HEAD OF STATE

Like most parliamentary systems, Germany's head of state (the **federal president**) is separate from the head of government. In contrast to the Weimar Republic, when the substantial powers of a directly elected president were abused to facilitate Hitler's rise to power, the Basic Law made the president an indirectly elected and almost entirely ceremonial figure who performs mainly symbolic tasks. The president may formally sign bills into law, must sign treaties, and can pardon convicted criminals—but usually only takes such actions at the behest of the chancellor. Presidents can, however, refuse to sign laws they believe contravene the constitution. They formally nominate candidates to become chancellor but are expected to select the head of the majority party in the legislature, or absent a majority, the head of the largest party in the legislature. Those candidates, moreover, must receive a majority of the votes in the lower house of the legislature. In the case of a badly fragmented legislature, the president could conceivably exercise some significant discretion in deciding on a nominee, but to date this situation has not occurred. Presidents also decide whether to dissolve the legislature and call new elections when lacking a majority.

German presidents are elected for a maximum of two five-year terms by a special Federal Convention that includes all members of the lower house of the legislature and an equal number of individuals selected by Germany's state legislatures. Presidents are intended to be consensus choices who are highly respected elder statesmen, and they are expected to behave in scrupulously nonpartisan fashion once in office.

The president, Horst Kohler, a conservative, was elected in 2004; he is a highly respected economist and former head of the International Monetary Fund. Kohler has been a somewhat controversial president. In 2006, he refused to sign a Consumer Information Law passed by the legislature because he viewed the legislation as violating states' rights as enshrined in the Basic Law.

STRUCTURE OF THE GOVERNMENT

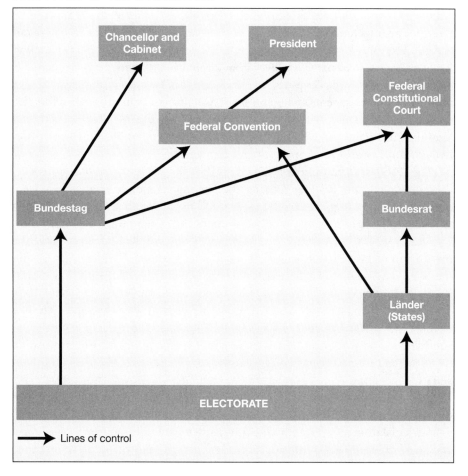

Kohler was narrowly reelected in May 2009. Traditionally there has been little real opposition to incumbent presidents seeking a second term.

THE LEGISLATURE

In parliamentary systems, the legislature is normally the center of political power. Germany's bicameral legislature, Parliament, is a powerful institution, but the Basic Law weakened the legislature's power vis-à-vis the chancellor in order to avoid problems that undermined the Weimar Republic. The lower house, the **Bundestag** (Federal Diet), represents the population; the upper house, the **Bundesrat** (Federal Council), represents Germany's sixteen states.

The Bundestag is the more powerful of the two houses. It has 598 deputies who are Germany's only directly elected public officials at the federal level. Deputies are elected for a maximum of four years, though elections can occur earlier. The Bundestag's chief power is its capacity to elect the chancellor. Because no German party has ever won a majority of seats in the legislature, members of the lower house select a chancellor (normally the head of the party with the most seats) who can form a majority coalition among the parties in the legislature. The current chancellor, **Angela Merkel**, was elected after the 2005 elections, when her conservative party was able to form a majority legislative coalition with the Social Democrats.[9]

The Bundestag can remove the chancellor, but only through a "constructive" vote of no confidence. During the Weimar Republic chancellors were often removed from power by the legislature, usually with votes from extreme parties of the right and left who were unable to agree on a new chancellor. The result was a succession of weak chancellors, political paralysis, and the imposition of presidential rule that facilitated the rise of Hitler. As a result, the Basic Law allows the Bundestag to remove a chancellor only if a majority of its members can (constructively) approve a replacement. There have been only two constructive votes of no confidence since 1949, and only one of those (in 1982) was successful. Chancellors may also call for a motion of confidence, and if that motion fails to win a majority, the legislature can be dissolved and new elections can be convened. (This occurred most recently in 2005.)

While the Bundestag must approve all federal laws, the government (not the legislature) initiates most legislation. The lower house can amend and debate legislation submitted by the government. In addition, the lower house can question members of the government during weekly question hours, similar to question periods in the United Kingdom. Members submit written questions to ministers ahead of time but can ask supplementary questions during the debate. The Bundestag includes powerful legislative committees that have the ability to question government ministers and to investigate government activities; they also have the expertise to challenge bills submitted by the government.

The upper house, the Bundesrat, is made up of sixty-nine members who are appointed by the governments of Germany's *länder* (states). Each state appoints between three and six members, depending on its population, and the minister-president (state prime minister, or governor) is usually the head the state delegation. Within the Bundesrat, delegations of representatives cast their ballots as a bloc, following the instructions of the state government.

All legislation is submitted to the upper house before being sent to the lower house. The Bundesrat must approve all laws that affect the states (including laws that require states to implement policies of the federal government), giving it an effective veto power over about one third of all legislation. For all other legislation, the Bundesrat's opposition can be overridden by the lower house. When the two houses disagree, joint committees often convene to negotiate a compromise. The Bundesrat must also approve all constitutional amendments.

The Bundesrat has traditionally served as an important check on the federal government because it has very often been controlled by opposition. Since state elections do not coincide with federal ones, the outcome of state elections can alter the balance of power in the upper house. In 2003 a nine-month battle took place over the Social Democratic Party (SPD) Agenda 2010 legisla-tive program (a controversial package of economic reforms). The SPD-Green coalition in the lower house locked horns with the Conservative-dominated Bundesrat. When in 2005 the SPD lost power in Germany's most populous state, thus further eroding its position in the upper house, the SPD government pushed for early elections.

THE JUDICIAL SYSTEM

In an effort to avoid a repeat of the Weimar Republic, the architects of the Basic Law sought to create an independent judiciary that could safeguard the constitution. The result was the **Federal Constitutional Court** that serves as the ultimate guardian of the Basic Law. The Constitutional Court settles disputes between states, and between the federal government and states. It also adjudicates disputes about elections and hears cases when citizens believe their constitutional rights have been violated. The court only acts in response to cases brought before it by either house of the legislature, by lower courts, or by individual citizens. The court has the power of abstract review, meaning that it can review pending legislation on the request of one third of the members of either house of the legislature.

There are sixteen members of the Constitutional Court, divided into two chambers (called Senates). Each house of the legislature selects half of the members of each chamber, and judges must be approved by a two-thirds majority. Judges are elected to a single twelve-year term and must retire by age sixty-eight.

The Constitutional Court has been an important, active, and highly respected institution in German politics. It has ruled on some controversial issues, such as its upholding of the ban on the Communist and Neo-Nazi parties in 1952, its approval of West Germany's treaty with East Germany in 1973, and numerous decisions restricting legalized abortion.

The Federal Constitutional Court is entirely independent from the government and from the rest of Germany's legal system that handles criminal and civil matters. For all nonconstitutional issues, Germany employs a system of code law, wherein judges interpret and apply complex legal codes, rather than relying upon precedent or common law. Germany has an elaborate system of courts at the state level, and a top tier of courts at the federal level. For all nonconstitutional matters, the Federal Court of Justice of Germany is the highest ordinary court in Germany and the highest appeals court.

The Electoral System

The Basic Law created an innovative mixed electoral system that has since been emulated by other democracies, including three of the cases in this volume (Russia, Japan, and Mexico). Its authors sought a system that would combine the fairness of proportional representation with the voter-representative link that is a feature of single-member district systems. In addition, the framers of the Basic Law envisioned a system that would represent diverse political interests but avoid the legislative fragmentation and instability that characterized the Weimar Republic.

Half of the seats of Germany's lower house are elected by proportional representation (PR). Seats are awarded to parties from their party lists according to the proportion of the vote won by each party. The entire country serves as one large PR district. The remaining seats are elected using 299 single-member districts, where seats are allocated according to first-past-the-post criteria (that is, the candidate with the most votes wins the seat). Thus, when voting for the Bundestag, Germans vote once for a national party list and once for a representative in their district. The proportional representation seats are subject to a 5 percent threshold; to win seats from PR lists, a party must win at least 5 percent of the vote nationally, or win three single-member districts seats. That threshold has successfully limited the number of parties in the Bundestag, including small extremist parties, and has prevented the kind of fragmentation and polarization that plagued the Weimar Republic.

The German electoral system contains one additional feature that is often confusing for German citizens and students of German politics alike. If results from the single-member district produce a Bundestag with a membership that does not accurately reflect each party's national support (as determined by the PR list vote), additional seats can be awarded to parties that are underrepresented. In the 2005 election, the two largest parties (the CDU/CSU and the SPD) did particularly well in the single-member districts, giving them more seats in the Bundesrat than their national percentage of the vote would indicate. The German system allowed them to keep their "overhang" seats, and the list system was used to award additional seats to parties whose percentage of the national vote merited greater representation in the lower house. Consequently the number of seats in the Bundestag can change from election to election. The minimum number of seats is 598; after the 2002 elections, there were 603 members of the lower house, and following the 2005 elections there were 614.

The implications of Germany's electoral system are profound. First, political parties are strengthened because the national party lists are drawn up by party leaders. Parties are thus directly responsible for selecting half of the lower house, and they can more easily enforce internal discipline. Proportional representation means that parties (at least those large enough to win 5 percent of the vote or three single-member districts) can have a voice in the legislature. Only once since 1949 have the centrist Free Democrats been able to win a single-member district seat, but they have won PR seats in every election. Because of the electoral system, a small party like the Free Democrats has had far more influence in Germany than the UK's Liberal Democrats, even though the Liberal Democrats consistently win a higher percentage of the vote. The presence of more parties in Germany has also meant that no German political party has ever won a legislative majority. Whether this is a positive or negative feature can be debated. The absence of a clear majority can sometimes lead to prolonged negotiations after elections (as was the case after the 2005 elections). The German political system, however, represents a wide range of political views, and the need to form coalitions means that political compromise is a built-in feature. The German electoral system is certainly complex, but it has produced stable and effective governments; turnout for elections, moreover, has been consistently high.

Local Government

The Basic Law provides for a system of federalism that is a rarity among Western Europe's mostly unitary systems. Germany's sixteen states share power with the federal government, which controls some areas, such as defense and foreign policy; the states have exclusive power over education, administration of justice at the state level, culture, and law enforcement. For all remaining areas not covered by the Basic Law, power is given to the states. German states implement much of the legislation passed by the federal government. States also have a direct check on the federal government via their representation in the upper house. Unlike U.S. states, German *länder* and municipal governments do not possess the power to raise taxes, and they are dependent on revenues allocated by the federal government. States control over half of German government spending.

Each German state has its own unicameral legislature (elected for four years), which in turn selects a **minister-president** (governor). Minister-presidents are often powerful figures in German politics, and German chancellors have often built their political careers in state politics.

POLITICAL CONFLICT AND COMPETITION

The Party System

As in most parliamentary systems, political parties are the central political actors in German politics. The founders of the Basic Law believed that a highly structured party system could prevent the kind of charismatic authoritarian leadership that doomed the Weimar Republic. The Basic Law thus envisions representation of the people through political parties, rather than through direct elections for a head of government or head of state, or referenda (which are not permitted at the federal level). As a result, the German state provides about one third of the budget of the major political parties, in addition to free advertising on public television and radio during campaigns.

Since 1949, Germany has had a remarkably stable system of political parties, even taking into account reunification and emergence of new political forces in the 1980s and 1990s.[10] From 1957 to 1983, the party system was dominated by two large forces (the center-right CDU/CSU and the center-left SPD) and one smaller party (the liberal FDP). During that period, those three parties won all the seats in the Bundestag. In the early 1980s, the Greens were able to break into the legislature and occupy political space to the left of the SPD. Reunification in 1990 led to a fifth political force composed mainly of former East German Communists (currently named The Left).

The two German political parties that have provided every chancellor since 1949 (the CDU/CSU and the SPD) have been characterized as **catch-all parties**. During the Weimar Republic, parties aimed their appeals at narrow constituencies based most often on social class or religion. Aided by the climate of the cold war, the dramatic postwar economic recovery, and the advent of television, catch-all parties represented a more modern, mass party that appealed more broadly to voters of all types. Such parties therefore presented a more centrist image.

THE CHRISTIAN DEMOCRATS

The notion of a modern catch-all party was best illustrated by the creation in 1945 of the **Christian Democratic Union (CDU)**.[11] Together with its Bavarian ally, the Christian Social Union (CSU), it emerged as a pro-business, anti-socialist, Christian political party that for the first time in German history appealed to both Catholics and Protestants. The CDU established itself both as a strongly pro-West party with close ties to the United States and as a staunch supporter of a European union.

Two CDU chancellors, Konrad Adenauer and Helmut Kohl, were dominant figures in the history of the CDU/CSU. Under Konrad Adenauer's long chancellorship (1949–1963), the CDU/CSU was able to steer the German right in a modern, market-oriented, and pro-European direction.

ANGELA MERKEL: GERMANY'S FIRST FEMALE CHANCELLOR

Germany's current chancellor, Angela Merkel, is the first woman to hold that position and the first to be raised in the former German Democratic Republic. The daughter of a Protestant pastor, she was trained as a scientist (she has a doctorate in chemistry and physics) and managed to avoid membership in the Communist Socialist Unity Party. She was elected to the Bundestag in 1990, during the first elections that included East Germany. She gained a series of ministerial posts under Helmut Kohl's chancellorship in the 1990s. In 2002, the CDU passed her over for the nomination to oppose SPD Chancellor Gerhard Schroeder.

After being elected head of the CDU in 2000, Merkel pushed hard to change the Conservative's traditional policy orientation. On the one hand, she moved the party toward the center on such social issues as immigration and the environment. On the other hand, she encouraged the party to adopt free-market policies more similar to those of Britain's Conservatives. Under her leadership, the CDU has promoted tax cuts and reforms to the health care system, and it has been closer to the United States in foreign policy.

Helmut Kohl, who was chancellor from 1982 to 1998, was responsible for Germany's rapid reunification after the fall of the Berlin Wall in 1989. Voters initially rewarded the CDU/CSU under Kohl for its support of reunification. By 1994, however, they punished it for the consequent economic and social costs of his policies. Kohl's political comeback was derailed in the late 1990s when he admitted to accepting illegal campaign contributions. Although the CDU/CSU is a pro-business party, it has broadly accepted Germany's welfare state, and some of its members even opposed market-oriented reforms proposed by the Social Democrats in recent years.

THE SOCIAL DEMOCRATS

Unlike the CDU, the **Social Democratic Party (SPD)** is an old party (it was founded in 1863) and was a major actor during the Weimar Republic.[12] The SPD had a Marxist orientation and defined itself as a party of the working class. In part because of its radical orientation, the SPD won less than 30 percent of the vote in the first two elections of the new democracy.

Party leaders realized they needed to broaden the SPD's appeal. At its 1959 party convention, the SPD renounced Marxism and adopted a strategy to market the party to Germans of all social classes. This approach paid immediate electoral dividends. The SPD's vote grew steadily through the 1950s and 1960s; by 1966, the SPD had gained enough respectability to be included in a Grand Coalition government with the CDU/CSU. In 1969, the SPD finally formed the first coalition government of the left under SPD leader Willy Brandt. He promoted better relations with the Communist bloc and increased worker par-

---

THE INDECISIVE BUNDESTAG ELECTIONS OF 2005

After Chancellor Gerhard Schroeder's Social Democrats were defeated in the pivotal state of North Rhine-Westphalia in May 2005, the opposition gained a majority in the upper house. In a controversial move, Schroeder then intentionally lost a motion of confidence and asked the president to dissolve the legislature and convene new elections.

The results of the 2005 elections were equally controversial. With a typically high turnout of about 78 percent, no party came close to winning a majority of seats. The governing Social Democrats lost 29 seats, and the main opposition party, the CDU/CSU, lost 22 seats. The centrist Free Democrats and The Left gained seats. Both major parties claimed victory. The CDU/CSU claimed it had won the most seats, but the SPD countered that the CDU and CSU were formally separate parties, and that therefore the SPD was actually the largest party and should head any new coalition. The CDU could not cobble together a majority, even with support from the centrist FDP. The SPD was unable to form a majority coalition with smaller parties to its left. After lengthy negotiations, a coalition between the CDU/CSU and SPD was formed. In November 2005, Merkel was elected chancellor by the Bundestag; cabinet posts were split evenly between the two parties.

---

ticipation in the management of private enterprise. The SPD continued its success between 1974 and 1982, under the chancellorship of Helmut Schmidt.

Hurt by its ambivalent support for reunification, the SPD found itself out of power until the election of Gerhard Schroeder in 1998. Schroeder formed a coalition with the Greens and backed some controversial environmental policies, such as a phasing out of nuclear power, a proposed speed limit on Germany's *autobahn* (expressways), and new taxes on carbon emissions. On economic matters, Schroeder represented the more conservative wing of the SPD, and his call for fundamental reforms to Germany's welfare state and his foreign policy alienated the SPD left, led by Oskar Lafontaine, who would eventually take his supporters out of the SPD to form a party called The Left. The SPD-Green alliance narrowly won the 2002 elections, but Schroeder's gamble of calling early elections in 2005 backfired: the SPD narrowly lost the election, and although his party entered government as a junior coalition member, Schroeder lost the chancellorship.

In 2008, the Social Democrats selected the popular foreign minister Frank-Walter Steinmeier, a longtime aid to Schroeder, to lead the party in the 2009 general elections.

THE FREE DEMOCRATS

The **Free Democratic Party (FDP)** has been a staunch defender of free-market economic and civil liberties and has consistently drawn support from professionals and upper-middle class Germans. Since 1949, support for the FDP has ranged from a low of just under 6 percent (1969) to a high of about thirteen percent (1961). Nevertheless, from 1949 to 2008, the FDP was a junior coalition partner in thirteen of eighteen German governments, making it a crucial "hinge" party that could determine the nature of coalition governments.

In the early years of German democracy, the FDP was a natural ally of the conservatives, given its support of free-market policies. In the late 1960s, the FDP found common cause with the Social Democrats over social reforms and foreign policy. In general, the FDP has been less socially conservative than the CDU/CSU but less supportive of the welfare state than the SPD.

In the past decade, the FDP has faced new challenges. It has suffered internal divisions, and its advocacy of civil liberties, personal freedoms, and a less cumbersome bureaucracy has been supplanted somewhat by the rise of the Greens.[13] The FDP has been unable to join a coalition government since 1998, although it managed to poll almost 10 percent in the 2005 elections.

THE GREENS

In the 1970s, some Germans became disenchanted with the three main parties, all of whom shared a broad consensus on promoting rapid industrial growth via the market economy. While coalescing around environmental policies (especially opposition to nuclear energy), the **Greens** represented a host of postmodern issues, such as women's rights, gay rights, pacifism, and grass-roots democracy.[14] It initially viewed itself as an "anti-party party" that would not behave like the established parties and would not compromise its principles in pursuit of power.

The Greens won their first Bundestag seats in 1983, bringing with them a fresh style of politics. Green members of the Bundestag wore blue jeans, sported long hair, and boasted a less hierarchical internal party structure. From the start, the Green movement was divided between moderates (known as realos) and radicals (known as fundamentalists, or fundis). The moderates sought to achieve Green goals by entering into coalition governments and exercising political power. The radicals feared that such tactics would compromise Green values and destroy the distinctive identity of the movement.

Electoral realities tipped the balance of power within the Greens toward the moderates: in 1990, the West German Greens failed to reach the 5 percent threshold and were shut out of the lower house (although the East German Greens, known as Alliance 90, were able to win seats). The Greens reevaluated their previous opposition to electoral alliances, and in the 1994 and 1998 elections a new alliance of East and West Greens (known as Alliance 90/The Greens) increased its share of the vote and won Bundesrat seats. In a controversial decision, the Greens entered a coalition government as junior partners of the SPD in 1998 and again in 2002, gaining control of three cabinet seats. By entering government, the Greens and their leader, Joschka Fischer (who became vice chancellor and foreign minister), gained new respectability and a high profile but also became subject to new political contradictions and pressures. The Greens' traditional pacifism clashed with the SPD-Green government's policy of German intervention in Kosovo and Afghanistan, leading some members to abandon the party. Even a policy to phase out nuclear power by 2020, spearheaded by a Green Environment Minister, disappointed radicals within the party, who sought a more immediate end to nuclear power.

The 2005 elections failed to deliver a victory for the SPD-Green coalition, and the Greens left the government, even though the Greens lost only one seat in the Bundestag. In 2008, the Greens entered a first-ever coalition with the conservative CDU in the Hamburg state government, demonstrating a further willingness to compromise to advance some of its policy goals.

THE LEFT

The newest political formation with seats in the Bundestag is **The Left** (*Die Linke*), founded in 2007 through a merger of the heirs of the former East German Communists and some leftists who abandoned the SPD.[15] After reunification, the remnants of East Germany's Communist Party reformed into the renamed Party of Democratic Socialism (PDS). The party performed poorly in the 1990 elections and struggled to surpass the 5 percent threshold in subsequent elections, winning only two single-member district seats in the 2002 elections. After the merger with disgruntled Social Democratic defectors, led by the charismatic Oskar Lafontaine (a former SPD party chairman), The Left's political fortunes increased, as did its appeal in the west of Germany. In 2005, The Left won almost 9 percent of the votes and fifty-one seats.

The platform of The Left is still evolving, but the party opposes the policies of privatization and tax cuts that have been pursued by recent German governments, and it has been a fierce opponent of both the SPD and CDU/CSU foreign policy. In a posture reminiscent of the early Greens, The Left has called itself Germany's only real opposition party, vowing not to enter into coalitions with any of the major political parties. However, The Left has entered into coalitions with the SPD at the state level and currently shares power with the SPD in Germany's capital, Berlin.

OTHER PARTIES

Because of Germany's history with totalitarianism, the Basic Law was designed to prevent the emergence of extremist parties on the left or right, and there has been less tolerance in Germany of parties that are deemed to be anti-system than in other European democracies. Far right parties, for example the National Democratic Party (NDP), were tolerated in Germany,

Seats in the Bundestag, 2008		
Party	**Number of Seats**	**Percent of Seats**
CDU/CSU (Conservatives)	226	36.8
SPD (Social Democrats)	222	36.2
FDP (Free Democrats)	61	9.9
The Left	54	8.8
Alliance 90/Greens	51	8.3
Total	614*	100

*Of this total, 299 seats were awarded in single-member constituencies. The other 299 seats were awarded via the national party PR list. The extra 11 seats are "overhang" seats that were awarded to two parties (9 for the SPD and 2 for the CDU) to make their legislative seats equivalent to their proportion of the national vote.

and they have won seats in state legislatures. But they never surpassed the 5 percent threshold at the federal level. The Communist left was banned by the Constitutional Court in the 1950s, and until reunification no party of the extreme left was able to win seats in the legislature.

Elections

The sixteen German federal elections since 1949 have enjoyed consistently high voter turnout, ranging from a low of 77.7 percent in 2005, to a high of 91.1 percent in 1972, although turnout has been decreasing since the 1970s. German campaigns have traditionally centered around parties and their platforms, but in recent elections they have become more Americanized, that is, more about personalities and slick advertising. Because of the dominance of the CDU and SPD, German campaigns inevitably become a battle between titans. For example, in the 1998 electoral campaign, the SPD attacked CDU Chancellor Kohl for having underestimated the costs of reunification, labeling Kohl the "unemployment chancellor." In 2002, the SPD played up Chancellor Schroeder's popular opposition to the Iraq war, while the CDU attacked rising fuel taxes under the SPD-Green coalition government. In the 2005 campaign, the focus became the economy, with the CDU's Merkel calling for tax cuts and faster reform of the economy, and the SPD proposing a tax on wealthy Germans.

Civil Society

German citizens did not greet the return of democracy with much civic enthusiasm. The experience of Nazism and Germany's defeat in World War II rendered most Germans apathetic about politics. In the early decade of the Bonn Republic, opinion polls showed lingering support for authoritarian ideas. Germany's only real experience with democracy during the Weimar Republic had been short-lived, unsuccessful, and traumatic.

Nevertheless, we have seen that Germans after 1949 regularly turned out in large numbers to vote, and that they overwhelmingly rejected parties on the political extremes. With Germany's spectacular economic recovery, Germans came to support democratic politics, and German civil society began to germinate. Recent opinion surveys reported that more than half of all Germans were interested in politics, over half had signed a petition, over a third had attended a lawful demonstration, and almost 10 percent had joined in some type of boycott. A 2007 study showed that Germany had the second-highest level of protest activity in Western Europe.[16]

LABOR UNIONS AND BUSINESS ORGANIZATIONS

In comparative perspective, trade unions in postwar Germany have been both strong and influential. The Federation of German Labor (DGB) represents most of Germany's trade unions, and during the postwar period about two thirds of workers were unionized. The DGB enjoyed a close relationship with the Social Democratic Party and played a key role in German policy making.

German trade unions, however, have experienced a rapid decline in membership since the 1990s. Between 1991 and 2006, the DGB lost almost half its membership for a variety of reasons. Reunification flooded the labor market, unemployment soared, and economic growth rates declined. Over half of German workers are presently covered by collective bargaining agreements between unions and employers, but that percentage has dropped considerably and rapidly over the past two decades.

German business is also highly organized. The Federal Association of German Employers (BDA) and the Federation of German Industry (BDI) are powerful groups with close ties to the CDU. This level of organization can be traced to Germany's use of neocorporatism, which we discuss in the section on political economy below.

OTHER GROUPS

German society experienced growth of a variety of political groups in the 1960s and 1970s, as was the case in many Western democracies. These groups challenged various aspects of the German model of economic growth, including its reliance on nuclear energy, pollution, the status of women, and the dominance of the major political parties. Some of the groups were later integrated into the Greens, reflecting the centrality of political parties in the German system; other groups remained autonomous from the party system.

The German women's movement has been particularly influential. In the Bonn Republic, women have organized regarding unequal pay, access to legal abortion, and other political rights. In the 1980s, the Greens established a quota for female candidates, spurring most other political parties to adopt similar policies.

German churches have also been an important interest group since 1949. Before reunification, over 90 percent of West Germans belonged to either the Catholic or Protestant Church, and the German state provided those churches with generous economic support. Of the two churches, the Catholic Church has been more outspoken on social issues and has a closer relationship to the CDU/CSU. In Communist East Germany, the Protestant Church was an important political actor as one of the few autonomous organizations permitted. The influence of organized religion is likely to decline in the future as religiosity and church attendance has declined. Moreover, the inclusion of East Germans, over half of whom are nonreligious, has weakened the power of organized religion.

SOCIETY

Ethnic and National Identity

As with many other European countries, Germany is relatively homogeneous in terms of its ethnic identity. Although unification came late to Germany, a strong shared cultural and even national identity has bound Germans together for a much longer period. Important cultural figures, such as Beethoven, Wagner, and Goethe, helped generate the idea of a single German people, even if

ETHNIC GROUPS

RELIGION

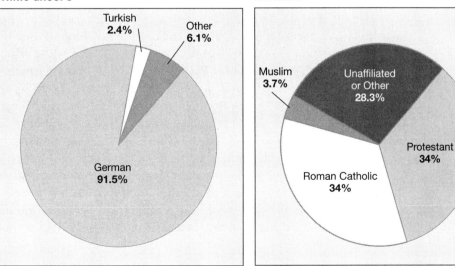

what bound these individuals together was not territory, constitutions, or regimes. Interestingly, then, a shared German identity developed long before there was a single German state; indeed, a single state, encompassing all Germans, has never existed (except under the Nazi regime). Austria, Switzerland, Lichtenstein, and Luxembourg are also countries where German is a state language. One result of this gap between national identity and a single state has been a weak German attachment to the state and state symbols. Such attachments were further weakened by the effects of World War II, wherein nationalism became the fuel for war and genocide. That war also destroyed the Jewish population of Germany, further reducing its ethnic and cultural diversity, while large portions of eastern Germany were annexed by Poland.

At the level of national identity, there remain important distinctions across the country, again a reflection of late unification. Recall that Germany can be seen as a fusion of two different systems: the Prussian empire in the north, and a series of "free states" and kingdoms in the south. This distinction remains important particularly in the state of Bavaria, which still calls itself a *freistaat* (a republic) indicating both its historical role as an independent country before unification and a sense that the region remains separate from (and superior to) much of the rest of Germany.

Bavaria is noted for its high level of economic development and the still-strong role played by Catholicism. Indeed, the current Pope, Benedict XVI, hails from Bavaria and is noted for his religious conservatism (a source of pride for many Bavarians). In contrast, northern and eastern Germany is overwhelmingly Protestant, though religious affiliation or identity is much weaker. It may be a stretch to think of Bavarians (or any other German cultural subgroups) as a distinct ethnic identity, but these groups do identify themselves by custom, dialect, and even particular stereotypes regarding attitudes and behavior.

These distinct, if relatively weak, identities have become more diverse over the past fifty years, through immigration and unification. First, unification with East Germany brought into the country a new population whose historical experiences were quite different. For West Germans, the aftermath of World War II brought de-Nazification, a deep suspicion of national pride, and an emphasis on democratic institutions. In contrast, East Germans largely avoided de-Nazification, as the Communist government instead redirected public identity toward the East German state and gave little attention to such events as the Holocaust. At the time of unification, Germany's population in the East embodied an identity that had been shaped by fifty years of socialism: that is, strongly secular and having a complicated relationship to nationalism. Germans as a result often speak of the differences between *Ossi* and *Wessi;* how distinct these differences are, or will remain, we shall discuss more below.

Another second factor that has transformed national and ethnic identity has been the role of immigration. Germany's postwar economic growth created a demand for labor that the country could not meet; as a result, Germany turned to **gastarbeiter** (guest workers) to fill this role. Guest workers, primarily from Turkey, were expected to stay only temporarily in Germany and were therefore not part of any formal plan for naturalization. Far fewer guest workers returned home than was expected, and eventually entire families and children became part of the German population. By 2000, the total number of individuals of Turkish origin was over 2 million. This growing Turkish population has created significant challenges for the German state and nation. In the past, German identity, including citizenship, centered on notions of race. As such, descendants of ancient German communities in Russia, for example, could gain citizenship, while Turkish children born and raised in Germany had no similar rights. Since 2000, the citizenship laws in Germany have been reformed to recognize and integrate non-German immigrants, but their social integration is far more difficult. Many Germans still have difficulty imagining nonethnic Germans as so-called true Germans, and concerns about political Islam have added a new tension to the situation. Some Germans worry that the country's failure to integrate its Muslim population is leading to the development of a "parallel society" disconnected from democratic institutions and susceptible to fundamentalism.[17]

Ideology and Political Culture

We have already alluded to many of the central facets of German ideology and political culture. German political identity is complicated both by the legacies of late unification and by the rise of fascism. The war and de-Nazification led to a strong undercurrent of national shame and the conclusion that nationalism and even patriotism were values that, at least for Germany, were dangerous and unacceptable. For most of the postwar period, then, the emphasis on democratic institutions was less an expression of national or patriotic identity than a belief that such institutions were a necessary bulwark against extremism and a recurrence of past policies. German political culture emphasized a greater pride in the country's economic achievements than in the state or nation, both of which had taken on negative connotations.

Over the past thirty years, a significant percentage of the population (30 to 40 percent) has consistently stated that they are not proud of their country; compare this with France and the United Kingdom, where close to 10 percent of the population responds with this answer. Germans show overwhelming support for democracy, even if their confidence in their own democratic institutions (such as the legislature) is rather low. The former citizens of East Germany still show lower levels of support for democratic institutions (compared to West Germans), as well as a weaker awarenss that they have particular democratic rights (such as free speech).[18] Some of this is understandably generational, as these differences between westerners and easterners are much smaller among people under twenty-five. The concern about a lingering *mauer im kopf* (Berlin Wall of the mind) still separating the two peoples seems to be fading. Ideologically, too, there is similarly strong support among eastern and western Germans for a political regime that emphasizes collective well-being over individual rights and favors a system that combines capitalism with consensus.

One dramatic shift in Germany's political culture was the rise in postmaterialist values (such as participation, feminisim, the environment, and other quality-of-life issues) and a decline in bread-and-butter materialist concerns (such as economic growth, jobs, and order). In 1973, only 13 percent of Germans felt postmaterialist concerns were a priority, but 43 percent took that position in 1995.[19] Postmaterialist values have become more pronounced in all advanced democracies, but they are by far the strongest in Germany—perhaps explaining why Germany has had one of the world's most successful Green parties.

POLITICAL ECONOMY

If Germany must still carry the legacy of Nazism and war, casting a shadow over its national identity, then it is in the area of its economy in which Germany can be rightly proud. Many observers would assert that the *wirstschaftswunder* (economic miracle) of the 1960s was in part a way in which Germany could reinvest national energy and identity around institutions and projects that were removed from the symbols of the fascist past. This is similar to Japan, both cases in which imperialism was replaced by occupation and demilitarization, followed by rapid industrial growth with the support of the United States.

The German political economic structure is manifestly capitalist, but within a social democratic mold. German political culture strongly emphasizes the importance of collective rights within the context of private property and the marketplace. This can be found across both the left and the right, with those on the left influenced by social democratic ideas of the state role in the economy and those on the right shaped by Christian democratic values that similarly favor a "moral" marketplace.

One of the most important institutional expressions of this emphasis on consensus in the economy is German **neocorporatism**. By *corporatism* we mean a system in which the ordinary elements of civil society, such as unions, are sanctioned by the state and given authority to represent particular groups.

This can be found in some authoritarian countries, and was part of the Nazi system of totalitarian control. In contrast, neocorporatism is a democratic variant in which business, labor, and the state work within an explicit framework to guide the economy toward particular goals. While many European countries have elements of neocorporatist policy making, Germany has a particularly strong model. Beginning in the 1960s, in an attempt to stimulate economic growth, German governments sought to bring business and labor groups together to negotiate labor agreements and to coordinate economic policy. For decades the German state regularly coordinated meetings between the main labor and business representatives. Beyond regular meetings, one particularly controversial aspect of German neocorporatism is the policy of **codetermination**, advocated by the Social Democrats, in which unions are given half of all seats on the board of directors in Germany's largest private firms.

LABOR FORCE BY OCCUPATION

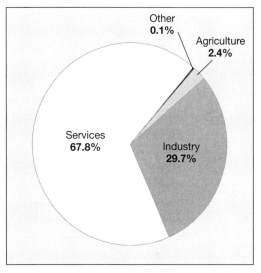

The neocorporatist model has been credited with fostering rapid growth rates and with limiting conflict between labor and business. However, the model has not been without its critics. German business resisted codetermination and unsuccessfully fought it in the courts. German unions became extremely powerful, often at the expense of other civil society groups that were not part of the neocorporatist system. Critics on the left also argued that neocorporatism did not really give workers power over major economic decisions.

These concerns have been negligible for most of the postwar period, as Germany developed a sophisticated economy (the fifth largest in the world) and one of the world's most prosperous societies. German industry is famous for its advanced industrial and consumer products, such as automobiles and chemicals, and built much of its economic structure around exports. However, by the 1990s the economic miracle began to show signs of strain for several reasons. First, one of the results of neocorporatism and a high degree of social expenditures has been the growing cost of labor. Over time, the German workforce has become less competitive as costs have risen. Second, globalization and the rise of other regional economies have also rivaled German exports with their lower costs and increasing technical sophistication. German firms, too, have in many cases chosen to invest overseas rather than at home. This has been particularly dramatic in Eastern Europe, where German capital could find an inexpensive yet relatively productive workforce close to home. The expansion of the European Union eastward has only increased this investment, thus increasing concerns among Germans. Finally, although Germany has spent an enormous amount of money revitalizing eastern Germany (over $100 billion per year since 1990), the region remains much weaker in terms of productivity, entrepreneurialism, and investment. Assumptions that massive government spending on infrastructure and new technologies would lead to significant private investment and growth in the east have not been borne out.

Growing concerns about the potential decline in German competitiveness in the global economy have led to reforms, although not without resistance. In 2003, the Social Democratic government proposed what was known as Agenda 2010, a series of measures meant to liberalize the economy. Agenda 2010 met with fierce resistance from labor unions in particular, limiting its implementation. However, changes that did occur included restructuring unemployment benefits, the generosity of which had led to a large number of permanently unemployed recipients. In addition, the increased pressures of the global economy have forced many labor unions to recognize that increased flexibility may be the only way to compete in the global market.

That said, Germany has a long road ahead of it. Economic difficulties across Europe and the United States, alongside a strong Euro, have hurt German exports; these concerns have weakened support for further reform. Unemployment remains high, GDP growth has been on the decline since 2006, and Germany faces a growing underclass—which is particularly disconcerting for a country that has prided itself on its concern for equity.[20] There is widespread pessimism about the future performance of the economy, but Germany's consensus-based policies make significant reform difficult to enact.

FOREIGN RELATIONS AND THE WORLD

As in many other areas of German politics, the country's position in the international system is complicated and freighted with history. For the past half century, the legacy of Germany's role in World War II and subsequent de-Nazification has been a strong sentiment of pacifism and a wariness of national pride or patriotism. Even though Germany regained its sovereignty and rebuilt its military after World War II, it made the conscious decision to bind its foreign policy to larger international institutions and objectives. Germany became a member of the North Atlantic Treaty Organization (NATO) and a strong partner of the United States, which saw Germany as the front line of the cold war and a possible war with the Soviet Union. As a result, the United States could rely on Germany even in controversial decisions, such as the deployment of American nuclear missiles on German soil. In addition to NATO, Germany became one of the central actors within the European Union.

IN COMPARISON	**MILITARY FORCE**

Sometimes military force is necessary to maintain order in the world. Percent who agree:

Country	Percent
India	90
Brazil	84
United States	77
South Africa	72
Mexico	72
Canada	71
United Kingdom	67
France	67
China	66
Russia	61
Japan	60
Germany	41

*Data on Iran not available.

Source: Pew Center for the People and the Press, 2007.

Indeed, many viewed the EU as driven by a French-German "axis" that provided much of the impetus for integration. Resolving age-old animosities between France and Germany, and binding Germany to international military commitments, was seen as a way to solve "the German problem" once and for all. At the same time, Germany developed a strong pacifist streak, contributing to the emergence of the Green Party (which was as much anti-war as environmentally focused), and remained literally divided into East and West Germany.

The collapse of the Soviet Union and the East German regime placed "the German question" back on the table for the first time in decades. There were widespread fears that German reunification, combined with the dramatic changes in East-West politics, would set the stage for a resurgent and potentially dangerous Germany. In retrospect, these concerns were unfounded. If anything, a great deal of energy and effort were directed inward for integrating East Germany into the country as a whole and modifying institutions to accommodate these dramatic changes.

But this does not mean that German foreign policy is the same as it was during the cold war. Although Germany has remained a central actor in NATO and the EU, it has also sought to play a more independent role in foreign affairs. This has led to mixed results. In the 1990s, Germany was an important player in brokering the breakup of Yugoslavia, providing support for Croatia and Slovenia in their quest for independence. This raised concerns that Germany was siding with its former wartime allies and that this support contributed to the brutal wars that followed. In 1999, violence between Kosovar Albanians and the Serb-controlled Yugoslav government led NATO to carry out airstrikes against Yugoslavia, with German participation—its first military action since World War II. Germany has several thousand troops in Kosovo and Bosnia, and since 2001 has also played a combat role in Afghanistan. In all of these situations, however, the German military has avoided a direct combat role—even in Afghanistan, where its troops are not in the front lines of battle against the Taliban. Germany has taken on a greater—albeit limited and cautious—role in the international system. Indeed, even its international deployments to date have required constitutional review.

A lack of clarity about Germany's international role has become particularly evident within the European Union and in Europe's relationship to Russia. Since the formation of the European Union, Germany has been one of the central engines of integration, working in partnership with France to expand the European Union. Germany was also an important actor in securing EU membership for many of the former Communist countries of Eastern Europe, where Germany has long had strong ties. Much of the impetus driving Germany forward within the EU was the desire to solidify relations with France and build a strong Europe that would avert war. This is one of the European Union's greatest accomplishments; the notion that EU members would wage war against each other now seems absurd, even though the last conflict occurred just over fifty years ago.

With these accomplishments has come increased uncertainty about Germany's future role in the international system. Most notably, while German foreign policy has become increasingly independent of the United States, this has not translated into a greater leadership role in the European Union. France and Germany's traditional partnership inside the EU has, in fact, become more strained of late, affected in part by France's increased focus on the Mediterranean and Middle East while Germany's attention has been directed eastward—each reflecting their traditional spheres of influence. A clear example of these difficulties was seen in the brief war between Georgia and Russia in 2008. One might expect that given its own history and ties to former Communist countries, Germany might have supported a strong EU position against Russian occupation of Georgian territory. But Germany is also highly dependent on Russian energy: nearly a quarter of German energy is in the form of natural gas, and nearly half of that comes from Russia. This creates worries that poor relations with Russia could have a disastrous effect should the latter ever choose to turn off the taps. As a result, the European Union found itself divided over how to respond to Russia, with Germany urging a more cautious approach. This disagreement has continued to shape debates within the EU over whether to pursue trade talks with Russia (which Germany has favored). In the future, relations between Russia and Europe as a whole are likely to remain strained, even as German dependence on Russian energy is likely to increase. This raises the possibility of an increasingly fractured policy toward Russia from within the European Union, with Germany losing its ability to act as a leader in this area.

German foreign policy remains uncertain and unclear. At one level, the country emerged from the cold war unified, with a strong belief in the importance of democracy, peace, and international institutions. At another level, however, Germany seems to lack a clear sense of its own mission in Europe or the world as a whole and the extent to which it should take the lead and bear the possible repercussions of such a leadership role. It may take another generation before Germans can clearly articulate their role in Europe and the world.

CURRENT ISSUES

TERRORISM AND ISLAM IN GERMANY

Germany is no stranger to terrorism. From the 1970s to the 1990s, Germany faced its own homegrown terrorism in the form of the Red Army Faction, which used bombings and kidnappings in its attempt to bring about a revolution. In addition, Germany was frequently the battleground for the conflicts in the Middle East. Best known are the events surrounding the 1972 Munich Olympics, when terrorists from the Palestinian group Black September took a number of Israeli athletes hostage, a standoff that ended in a botched rescue mission and seventeen deaths.

Since September 11, 2001, there has been growing concern that Germany is once again becoming a central launching point, if not a target itself, for terrorism. Much of the planning for the September 11th attacks was done in Germany; Mohammad Atta, one of the central planners, received his graduate education in Germany and coordinated the attacks from Hamburg. Radicalization among some of Germany's Turkish population and Germany's participation in the war in Afghanistan raise the possibility that Germany may be next. In 2007, two bombs were placed on German trains but failed to explode; a group planning attacks on U.S. military installations and other American institutions in Germany was arrested. Clearly the threat of terrorism is very real, as is the threat that the fear of terrorism will worsen relations between ethnic Germans and the Muslim and Turkish communities in Germany. The fundamentalist organization Hizb ut-Tahir, which promotes the creation of a single pan-Islamic state, has been active in Germany. Although the organization disavows violence, it has been banned from public activities; it operates openly, however, elsewhere in Europe. Even such basic issues as the construction of new mosques in Germany have led to strident conflict. Such divisions could further alienate Muslim and non-Muslim Germans and create the opening for dangerous radicalization among some citizens.

THE GENDER GAP IN GERMANY

It is often assumed that Germany, a strongly social democratic country, emphasizes gender equity, perhaps akin to that found in the Scandinavian countries. Germany has long had a strong women's movement, as anecdotal evidence would seem to prove: for example, Prime Minister Angela Merkel seems to be strong evidence that there is no glass ceiling for women in Germany. Moreover, approximately a third of the Bundestag is comprised of women, a far greater presence than in the EU on average. But in general the country is less egalitarian than we might think. Much of this is a function of German culture, which still stresses the importance of women in raising children as opposed to being in the workforce. As a result, the state has been less generous in such areas as child care, and German women's pay is nearly a quarter below that of men, among the lowest rates in the European Union. Given the weakness of state support and lower wages, many women feel that they are forced to choose between family and career, with the result that the country has a very low fertility rate. Prime Minister Merkel herself has no children.

While gender inequality has long been the norm in Germany, it has become a growing source of debate, particularly when linked to the prospects of a declining German population. The government has increased the amount of pay for parental leave and proposed expanding child care nationwide, with the hope that such reforms will not only increase the birthrate but also encourage women to stay in the workforce to help reinvigorate the economy. Also necessary, however, is a cultural shift in the perception of women's role at home and in the workforce, a discussion that is just now beginning.[21]

NOTES _____

1. These disputes in many cases continue to simmer. See, for example, Mark Landler, "Lawsuit Reopens Old Wounds in Polish-German Dispute," *New York Times*, 25 December 2006, p. A1.
2. See Michael Hughes, *Nationalism and Society: Germany, 1800–1945* (London: Edward Arnold Press, 1988).

3. Monte Palmer, *Comparative Politics: Political Economy, Political Culture, and Political Interdependence* (New York: Wadsworth, 2005), p. 139.

4. Arnold J. Heidenheimer, *The Government of Germany* (New York: Crowell, 1967), p. 15. Or as Dahrendorf describes the Weimar Republic: "a democracy without democrats." See Ralf Dahrendorf, *Society and Democracy in Germany* (New York: Doubleday, 1967).

5. On the Weimar Republic, see M. Rainer Lepsius, "From Fragmented Party Democracy to Government by Emergency Decree and National Socialist Takeover: Germany," in Juan Linz and Alfred Stepan, eds., *The Breakdown of Democratic Regimes: Europe* (Baltimore: Johns Hopkins Press, 1978), pp. 34–79.

6. See Peter Katzenstein's discussion of West Germany's "semi-sovereignty," in Peter Katzenstein, *Policy and Politics in West Germany: The Growth of a Semi-Sovereign State* (Philadelphia: Temple University Press, 1987).

7. For an excellent discussion of the Stasi, see Timothy Garton Ash, *The File* (New York: Vintage, 1998).

8. Adapted from M. Donald Hancock and Henry Krish, *Politics in Germany* (Washington, D.C.: CQ Press, 2009), pp 80–103.

9. For an insightful analysis of Merkel's rise to power, see Sarah Elise Wilarty, "Angela Merkel's Path to Power," *German Politics*, 17, no. 1 (March 2008), pp. 81–96.

10. On the German party system, see Charles Lees, "The German Party System(s) in 2005: A Return to Volkspartei Dominance," *German Politics*, 15, no. 4 (December 2006), pp. 361–75.

11. A good treatment of the CDU is "Ulrich Lappenküper, "Between Concentration Movement and People's Party: The Christian Democratic Union in Germany," in Michael Geller and Wofram Kaiser, eds., *Christian Democracy in Europe Since 1945*, Vol. 2 (New York: Routledge, 2004), pp. 25–37.

12. On the SPD, see William Paterson and James Sloam, "Is the Left Alright? The SPD and the Renewal of German Social Democracy," in *German Politics*, 15, no. 3 (September 2006), pp. 233–48, and Dan Hough and James Sloam, "Different Road Maps, Similar Paths? Social Democratic Politics in the UK and Germany," *German Politics*, 16, no. 1 (March 2007), pp. 26–38.

13. On the Free Democratic Party, see "Liberals in the Wilderness," *Economist* (27 August 2005), www.economist.com/world/europe/displaystory.cfm?storyid= E1_QPNSTQP (accessed 30 December 2008).

14. On the Greens, see Margit Mayer, *German Greens: Paradox Between Movement and Party* (Philadelphia: Temple University Press, 1998), and Mark Hertsgaard, "Green Power," *The Nation* (30 January 2006), pp. 21, 22.

15. Jonathan Olsen, "The Merger of the PDS and WASG: From Eastern German Regional Party to National Radical Left Party?" *German Politics*, 16, no. 2 (June 2007), pp. 205–21.

16. Taehyun Nam, "Rough Days in Democracies: Comparing Protests in Democracies," *European Journal of Political Research*, 46, no. 1 (January 2007) pp. 97–120.

17. "Paving the Way for a Muslim Parallel Society," *Der Speigel* (29 March 2007).

18. See, for example, the World Values Survey 1981–1999; "Views of a Changing World 2003," Pew Center for the People and the Press.

19. Russell J. Dalton, *Citizen Politics* (New York: Chatham House, 2002), p. 84.

20. Olaf Groh-Samberg, "Increasing Persistent Poverty in Germany," DIW Berlin Report, no. 4 (2007). www.diw.de/english/products/publications/weekly_report/ volume_2007/55079.html?weekly_report_diw (accessed 30 December 2008).

21. "Equality Between Men and Women, 2008," European Union, Employment, Social Affairs and Equal Opportunities, http://ec.europa.eu/social/ (accessed 30 December 2008).

GLOSSARY OF KEY TERMS

Basic Law   Germany's current constitution.

Bonn Republic   Nickname of the Federal Republic of Germany, named after West Germany's capital city.

Bundesrat   Upper house of Germany's legislature.

Bundestag   Lower house of Germany's legislature.

catch-all parties   Parties that attempt to attract voters of all classes and are, therefore, generally centrist in their platforms.

Christian Democratic Union (CDU)   Germany's largest conservative party.

codetermination   System requiring that unions occupy half of all seats on the boards of directors of Germany's largest private firms.

federal chancellor   Germany's prime minister and head of government.

Federal Constitutional Court   Germany's powerful court that interprets the Basic Law.

federal president   Germany's indirectly elected and largely ceremonial head of state.

Federal Republic of Germany (FRG)   The official name of democratic West Germany during the postwar division of Germany.

Free Democratic Party (FDP)   Small centrist party that has often formed part of governing coalitions.

gastarbeiter   "Guest workers" or foreign workers allowed to reside temporarily in Germany to provide much-needed labor.

German Democratic Republic (GDR)   Official name of Communist East Germany during the postwar division of Germany.

Greens   Germany's environmental party.

Hitler, Adolf   Nazi leader who led the Third Reich and led Germany to defeat in World War II.

Junkers   Politically powerful Prussian landed aristocrats.

länder   German states.

The Left   The furthest left of Germany's major parties; an alliance of leftist Social Democrats and remnants of former East German Communists.

Merkel, Angela   Germany's current conservative chancellor.

minister-president   Governor of a Germany state.

National Socialist (Nazi) Party   Hitler's fascist party.

neocorporatism   A political economic model in which business, labor, and the state work within an explicit framework to guide the economy toward particular goals.

Prussia   The most powerful German state before Germany's unification,.

reich   The German term for empire.

reunification   The 1990 integration of East and West Germany.

Social Democratic Party (SPD)   Germany's oldest party, located on the center-left.

Third Reich   The name Hitler gave to his fascist totalitarian regime (1933–1945).

Weimar Republic   Germany's first democratic republic (1919–1933), the collapse of which led to Hitler's totalitarian regime.

WEB LINKS

Germany's Christian Democratic Party **www.cducsu.de**

Germany's Free Democratic Party **www.fdp-fraktion.de**

Germany's Green Party **www.gruene-bundestag.de**

Germany's Left Party **www.linksfraktion.de**

Germany's legislature **www.bundestag.de**

Germany's Social Democratic Party **www.spd.de/**

Information about Germany **www.deutschland.de/** a one-stop portal

Major daily newspapers of Germany **www.deutschland.de/unterrubrik.
php?lang=2&category1=157&category2=160&category3=199**

6 JAPAN

Head of state: Emperor Akihito
(since January 7, 1989)

Head of government: Prime Minister Aso Taro
(since September 24, 2008)

Capital: Tokyo

Total land size: 377,835 sq km

Population: 127 million

GDP at PPP: 4.29 trillion US$

GDP per capita at PPP: $33,600

Human development index ranking: 8

INTRODUCTION

Why Study This Case?

Japan offers an important case for the study of contemporary politics, perhaps foremost to educate a Western audience about what Japan *is not*. Too much of our understanding of Japan is shaped or at least shadowed by dangerously misleading stereotypes. For example, *Japan is not*

- *small:* It has a landmass greater than Germany or Great Britain; a population larger than that of all non-Asian countries other than the United States, Brazil, Russia, and Nigeria; and an economy third only to those of the United States and China.
- *defenseless:* Despite the constitution's famous **Article 9**, which renounces war, Japan possesses a **Self-Defense Force** second only to the U.S. military in terms of technical sophistication and boasts defense expenditures comparable to or greater than those of all member countries of the North Atlantic Treaty Organization except the United States.
- *unique,* or at least no more so than any other country: In terms of political stability, state involvement in the economy, cultural conformity, and even ethnic homogeneity, Japan may be quite different from the United States, but in these and other ways it is more often the United States that is exceptional, not Japan.

If Japan is more "normal" than we might have assumed, it nonetheless remains an intriguing case that defies generalization and begs further investigation.

Politically, an authoritarian vanguard of low-ranking nobles launched a sweeping revolution from above in the latter half of the nineteenth century, modernizing Japan under the mercantilist slogan **"rich country, strong military."** As in Germany during the same period, the aristocracy and its militarist successors waged wars of imperialist expansion in the name of the Japanese emperor during the first half of the twentieth century, leading ultimately to stunning defeat at the hands of the United States in 1945. U.S. occupiers then launched a second revolution from above, replacing authoritarian rule with a remarkably liberal and democratic constitution written entirely by the Americans (in just six days!) and wholly unaltered by the Japanese in more than six decades.

For nearly the entire period beginning with the formation of the conservative **Liberal Democratic Party (LDP)** in 1955 through the present, the LDP has governed Japan. Moreover, elected politicians have historically been subservient to Japan's nonelected career civil servants, who write most of Japan's laws. Has externally imposed democracy taken root in Japan? If not, how do we characterize this type of governance? If so, what lessons might Japan offer for more recently imposed democratic nation-building efforts elsewhere?

Economically, under conditions of state-directed industrialization, imperialism, and war, Japan's authoritarian leaders forged a highly centralized economy in the first half of the twentieth century. Concerned about Japan's economic stability in a heightening cold war, the United States carried out only halfhearted economic restructuring, in contrast to intense U.S. efforts placed on Japan's political reform. Japan therefore extended into peacetime its wartime mercantilist economy, which linked career bureaucrats, conservative politicians, and a big-business elite (what analysts have called neocorporatism without labor) and was spectacularly successful for several decades.[1] By the 1980s, Japan had achieved and in many cases had surpassed the levels of technological prowess, commercial competitiveness, and economic prosperity of the advanced Western industrialized nations.

By the early 1990s, however, this seemingly invincible economy had begun a dramatic and persistent decline. If Japan's state-led expansion draws comparisons with Prussian modernization or French dirigisme, Japan's more recent economic experience invites comparisons with Great Britain's earlier postwar economic slide. Japan is well into its second decade of stagnant or slow economic growth and lagging industrial production. For much of this period, banks have been in crisis and unemployment has climbed as the stock market has plummeted. How does one account for this dynamic of rapid growth followed by precipitous decline? What have been the causes of Japan's economic success and its more recent failures? If its mercantilist policies persisted throughout the past century, can they be held responsible for both the rise and the decline of the nation's economy? Must Japan change, and if so, how and when?

Finally, Japan may not be unique, but its balancing of freedom and equality certainly differentiates it to some degree from many other countries. By all measures, Japanese citizens enjoy a very high level of income equality, but this has been managed with low levels of taxation, social services, and other state measures designed to redistribute income (what one political scientist describes as "equality without effort").[2] By the same token, the civil and personal freedoms enshrined in Japan's postwar constitution are unrivaled by all but the most liberal Western regimes, yet Japanese politics remains elitist, its society conformist, and its economy mercantilist.

Even the less stereotypical and more nuanced generalized features of Japan's economy now face the prospect of unprecedented if not revolutionary change. In the wake of the country's recent economic failures, long-standing corporate practices, such as lifetime employment for white-collar workers, are fading. In the face of persistent government scandal and a growing popular sense of political inefficacy, policy making in a previously harmonious Japan is becoming far more fractious and perhaps even more pluralist. Is Japan facing a third revolution, this time from below? Only by understanding what this country is and where it has come from will we be able to make sense of where it may be going.

Major Geographic and Demographic Features

Even though Japan may not be a particularly small country (it is slightly larger than Germany), its topography and demography certainly make it seem small and have given the Japanese a keen sense of vulnerability and dependency. Although the Japanese archipelago includes nearly 7,000 islands (including several of disputed sovereignty), few are inhabited, and nearly all Japanese reside on one of the four main islands: Hokkaidō, Honshū, Kyūshū, and Shikoku. Even on the main islands, mountainous terrain renders only 12 percent of the land inhabitable, and 80 percent of all Japanese live in an urban setting, with half the population crowded into three megametropolises: Tokyo, Ōsaka, and Nagoya. This means that most of Japan's 127 million inhabitants are crammed into an area about twice the size of New Jersey, making Japan one of the most densely populated countries in the world.

Land (both inhabitable and arable) is not the only scarce natural resource in Japan. Although it has maintained rice self-sufficiency through heroic levels of subsidies for inefficient domestic producers and trade restrictions on foreign rice (Japanese consumers pay about four times the world market price for their rice), Japan remains dependent on imports for nearly three fourths of its food. This critical dependence extends as well to most of the crucial inputs of an advanced industrial economy, including virtually all of its oil and most of its iron ore, thus compelling modern Japan to focus on external trade relations and making it particularly sensitive to the vagaries of such trade.

Japan's external focus has sharpened at important historical junctures because of its relative proximity to the Asian mainland. The Korean peninsula in particular served as a ready conduit to ancient and medieval Japan for importing language, technology, religion, and even the popular culture of Korea, China, and places beyond. Over time, Japan adopted (and adapted) from its mainland mentors traditions as varied as Buddhism and bowing, chopsticks and Chinese written characters. At the same time, Japan feared its vulnerability at the hands of its powerful neighbors to the west (particularly China and, later, Russia), and Japanese cartographers and rulers identified the Korean peninsula as a dagger poised at the heart of Japan.

Japan's fears of vulnerability were not unfounded. In the thirteenth century, a formidable force of Mongols and Koreans mounted two separate attacks on Japan, both of which were repulsed in part by typhoons (named kamikaze, or "divine wind" by the Japanese) that blew the attacking ships off course. These incursions and subsequent struggles for power within Japan led rulers first to practice for several hundred years and then to impose for two and a half centuries a formal policy of *sakoku*, or xenophobic isolation. This ended only when Western imperialists forcibly opened Japan in the nineteenth century, reaffirming Japanese fears of weakness.

Japan's insular status has certainly contributed to its racial, ethnic, and linguistic homogeneity and its cohesive national identity. This cultural uniformity, however, should not be overstated. Although today virtually all citizens of Japan identify themselves as Japanese, this image masks the earlier assimilation of the indigenous Ainu (now found almost exclusively on Hokkaidō) and the Okinawans. In recent decades, Japan has witnessed an influx of Asian migrant workers (predominantly from Southeast Asia, China, and South Asia) who continue to face varying degrees of political discrimination and social marginalization.

Historical Development of the State

Despite the many cultural oddities that European traders and missionaries discovered when they first arrived in sixteenth-century Japan, they had actually stumbled upon a nation and society the historical development of which bore striking similarities to the development of their own countries. As in Europe, isolated tribal anarchy had gradually given way to growing national identity and the emergence of a primitive state. Aided by clearly defined natural borders and imperial and bureaucratic institutions borrowed from neighboring China, the Japanese state grew in both capacity and legitimacy, particularly after the seventh century C.E. Imperial rule was first usurped and then utilized by a feudal military aristocracy that came to rule over an increasingly centralized and sophisticated bureaucratic state for many centuries even as it allowed the emperors to continue to reign symbolically.

Whereas weakening feudalism gave way to powerful modernizing monarchs and then to middle-class democracy in Europe, Japan's version of centralized feudalism persisted until Western imperialism provided the catalyst for change in the nineteenth century. A forward-looking authoritarian oligarchy rejected feudalism but consciously retained the emperor as a puppet to legitimate its forced-draft efforts to catch up with the West. These oligarchs, borrowing this time not from China but from the institutions of modern European states, established a modern Japanese state that grew in autonomy and capacity as it became a formidable military and industrial power. Once again, this new course of imperial expansion and military conquest ended with defeat, this time at the hands of the Americans in 1945, who defanged Japan's militarist state but allowed its mercantilist bureaucracy to remain intact.

Year	Event
645 C.E.	China-inspired Taika political reforms introduced
1192	Minamoto Yoritomo declared first shogun
1603	Tokugawa Shogunate established
1853–54	Forced opening of Japan by Commodore Matthew C. Perry
1867–68	Meiji Restoration
1894–95	First Sino-Japanese War
1904–05	Russo-Japanese War
1918–31	Era of Taisho democracy
1937–45	Second Sino-Japanese War
1941	Pacific War begins
1945	Japan's defeat and surrender in World War II
1945–52	U.S. occupation of Japan
1955	Formation of the Liberal Democratic Party (LDP)
1993	LDP briefly loses majority in Diet's House of Representatives
2007	LDP loses majority in Diet's House of Councillors

TIME LINE OF POLITICAL DEVELOPMENT

Although modernization brought dramatic changes to Japan, several themes or continuities emerge from this process that are relevant to the development of Japan's modern state and its contemporary politics. First, at critical junctures in its history, outside influence or foreign pressure (what the Japanese call *gaiatsu*) has brought change to Japan. Second, in the face of this pressure, the Japanese have often chosen not to reject or even resist the external influence but rather have chosen to adopt and then adapt it, deftly assimilating what they perceive as valuable foreign innovations. Third, for many centuries and arguably to the present, Japan's ruling elite has maintained a persistent division of labor between rulers and reigners. This division of responsibility has preserved the autonomy and strengthened the political capacity of those rulers controlling power while enhancing the continuity of the regime and the legitimacy of the state by retaining symbolic reigning authority. Fourth, Japan early on established a highly effective and respected bureaucratic leadership, which has guided the state and pursued economic development as a means of achieving national sovereignty and state legitimacy. This leadership has established a close working relationship between national bureaucrats and private business and a favorable attitude toward state intervention in the economy.

PREMODERN JAPAN: ADAPTING CHINESE INSTITUTIONS

As early as the third century C.E., shifting coalitions of tribal hunters and early rice cultivators had formed a primitive state in southern Honshū under the leadership of a tribal chieftain whose legitimacy rested on a claim of divine lineage descending from the sun goddess. By the seventh century, Japan had come under the powerful cultural influence of Tang-dynasty China, an influence that cannot be overstated. Among the most significant and lasting of its cultural exports were Buddhism, Confucianism, the Chinese written language (which by that time had become the dominant script of all Asia), and the trappings of material culture (including modes of dress, architectural styles, and even chopsticks).

Tang China also had a profound influence on political reforms in seventh-century Japan, inspiring the country's leaders to establish an administrative system modeled on the Tang imperial state. To finance this new bureaucracy, the state introduced sweeping land reform, purchasing all land and redistributing it among peasants so that it could be taxed. Although Buddhist religious doctrines and Confucian social values thrived, the Tang-inspired Taika administrative and land reforms did not take hold as well as the other borrowings. The meritocratic civil bureaucracy soon evolved into a hereditary, self-perpetuating ruling elite supported by a declining tax base. Squeezed mercilessly, the peasants, either for survival or protection, were forced to sell out to local wealthy officials, who had managed to arrange tax immunity for their own lands.

From the eighth to the twelfth century, political power and wealth steadily shifted from the central government to independent rural landowners, and the urban-centered imperial system gradually disintegrated into a formalistic body concerned only with the trappings and rituals of state. The territorial nobles or lords, known as daimyo, governed both the lands they occupied and the former peasants who had become their serfs and their warrior retainers, or **samurai**.

As their power grew, the landed aristocrats became increasingly dissatisfied with the ineffectual rule of the court. Over the course of the next 400 years, from the thirteenth through the sixteenth century, power was completely transferred to this military aristocracy. Different clans vied for supremacy, and ascendant clans established a government known as the *bakufu* (literally, "tent government," referencing its martial origins). This was a period of continual warfare based on attempts at establishing a line of succession and a semblance of unity through military conquest, during which the emperor was largely disregarded. But in Japan, unlike Europe, the imperial household was neither "absolutely" empowered nor completely displaced. The emperor had become not so much a person as a symbol; whoever spoke in the name of the imperial chrysanthemum crest spoke with legitimate authority. The best comparison to a Western experience is perhaps that of the powerful European kings who sought claim to spiritual authority through papal anointing. The emperor became a puppet in the hands of aspiring daimyo, who never destroyed the emperor but forced him to anoint the strongest among them **shogun**, or dominant lord.

TOKUGAWA SHOGUNATE: CENTRALIZED FEUDALISM

By the end of the sixteenth century, the feudal wars had come to a head, and Japan was slowly and surely unified by the **Tokugawa** shogunate, which imposed an enforced peace for the next two and half centuries. Successive shoguns from the Tokugawa clan ruled over this feudal hierarchy in the name of the emperor, successfully shoring up its own authority and keeping the daimyo in check through an effective strategy of divide and rule at home and *sakoku*, or closed-country isolation abroad.

The power of a local daimyo rested, in turn, on the size and productivity of the hereditary fief or feudal domain he controlled, the peasants who tilled the land, and—most important—the number of samurai the domain could support. The warrior retainers lived with their lords in the castle towns that served as the fortresses and administrative centers from which the lords governed their domains. But as the Tokugawa-enforced peace settled over the countryside, the samurai were gradually converted from warriors to civil officials with fiscal, legal, and other administrative responsibilities. These samurai-turned-bureaucrats tackled civilian tasks in the same devoted, selfless manner in which they had been trained to carry out their martial responsibilities. It is difficult to overstate the value of this cadre of efficient, skilled, disciplined, and highly respected bureaucrats as the country faced the challenges of abrupt modernization in the nineteenth and twentieth centuries.

Although Tokugawa Japan's political system was remarkably stable, its social organization and economy developed what proved to be volatile contradictions. Tokugawa society was strictly hereditary and rigidly hierarchical; individuals were born into a particular station and could neither move between classes nor for the most part even advance within their own class. The samurai class was at the top of the hierarchy, but not all samurai were equal. Theirs was a diverse warrior class, ranging from the wealthy and powerful shogun and daimyo to the lowly retainers barely getting by on a subsistence stipend of rice. Next on the social rung were the peasants, who formed the bulk of the remaining subjects, followed by artisans and craftsmen, and finally—at (or near) the bottom of the social hierarchy—the merchants.[3] As in other Confucian societies, commercial activities, including moneylending, and those people who participated in them were viewed with great disdain. Despite being socially despised, however, these merchants had established sophisticated and lucrative trading networks throughout Japan by the nineteenth century. Moreover, they had established themselves as the financiers of the lifestyles of the upper ranks of the samurai, who over time grew increasingly indebted to them.

When Commodore Matthew C. Perry steamed into Edo Bay with his fleet of U.S. warships in 1853, he unsuspectingly came upon this system, which was apparently stable but internally ripe for change. The ruling class had status and privilege but was heavily indebted and, in the case of many low-ranking samurai, even impoverished. The merchants were wealthy but socially disdained, lacking both political power and social status. Many Japanese, particularly among the lower ranks of the samurai, had become dissatisfied with what they saw as an increasingly ineffectual if not redundant Tokugawa government and were ready for revolt. Perry did not cause this revolt, but he certainly facilitated it.

The forceful entry of American and (subsequently) European powers into Japan and the pressure they placed on the shogunate created a crisis of legitimacy for Tokugawa rule. Virtually free from foreign military threats and isolated from external innovations during the centuries of enforced isolation, the Tokugawa government lacked the military capacity to resist the unfair trade demands of the Americans and Europeans. The regional daimyo, however, judged these demands as unacceptable and thus revolted.

A decade of political chaos ensued, prompting a revolution launched not from below, by restive peasants or even aspiring merchants, but from above, by a handful of junior samurai officials. Much like Germany's nineteenth-century modernizers, this aristocratic vanguard was committed to sweeping change cloaked in traditional trappings. They recognized that the maintenance of Japanese independence required the end of the feudal regime and the creation of a modern economic, political, social, and perhaps most important, military system capable of holding its own against the Western powers. But rather than deposing the symbolic leader of the old regime, the modernizers launched their reforms in the name of the sixteen-year-old emperor Meiji, ostensibly "restoring" him to his rightful ruling position.

MEIJI RESTORATION: REVOLUTION FROM ABOVE

The vanguard of junior samurai who led the **Meiji Restoration** in 1867 and 1868 came to be known as the **Meiji oligarchs**. What began as a spontaneous xenophobic rejection of the Western threat quickly spawned regime change, a movement for positive reform that involved emulation of and catching up with the West. These oligarchs were well ahead of the rest of Japanese society, establishing the foundations of the modern Japanese state.

Their first priority was to make Japan a strong and wealthy state capable of renegotiating the inequitable treaties the West had imposed on the country. Under the slogan "rich country, strong military," they promoted their mercantilist view that there needed to be a strong relationship between economic development and industrialization, on the one hand, and military and political power in the international arena on the other hand. They dismantled the feudal state, deposing the shogun and converting the decentralized feudal domains to centrally controlled political units. They jettisoned the feudal economy, abolishing hereditary fiefs, returning land to the peasants, and converting samurai stipends to investment bonds. Perhaps most surprisingly, they destroyed their own class, ending samurai privileges.

In 1889, the oligarchs adopted an imperial constitution (patterned after the German constitution), which was presented as a "gift" from the emperor to his subjects. It specified not the rights and liberties of the citizens but the duties and obligations that the subjects owed the emperor and the state. The constitution created some of the formal institutions found in Western democracies, including a bicameral parliament known as the **Diet**, but its members were chosen by a limited franchise and exercised little real authority. The constitution vested all executive power in the emperor, who appointed the cabinet ministers (just as reigning emperors had previously appointed the ruling shogun) and retained supreme command over the military. The oligarchs further legitimized this power structure by promoting an emperor-centered form of Shintoism as the mandatory state religion and by inculcating both national patriotism and emperor worship in the education system.

Buttressed by the traditional and charismatic legitimacy of a reigning emperor and the rational-legal legitimacy of an equally symbolic (and largely powerless) parliament, the oligarchs had obtained both the authority and the autonomy to promote painfully rapid development and to create a modern military. The highly capable agents for carrying out these goals were threefold:

1. *Bureaucracy:* This revolution from above was envisioned by a handful of elites, but it was carried out by a modern, centralized bureaucracy recruited on the basis of merit. Although the civil service was open to all, it was staffed almost entirely by former samurai who were literate, respected, and had served their feudal lords in similar administrative capacities for generations.

2. *Zaibatsu:* Believing they did not have the luxury to wait for the emergence of an entrepreneurial class, the oligarchs fostered and financed the establishment of huge industrial conglomerates, known as *zaibatsu*, or financial cliques. In so doing, Japan's leaders forged the first of the enduring ties between big business and the state that have persisted to the present.

3. *Military:* Although the military was created initially for defense, the country's resource dependency, the voracious appetite of the *zaibatsu*, and the

example of Western imperialism soon launched Japan on its own successful wave of imperial warfare.

By the end of World War I, the Meiji oligarchs had realized many of their initial goals. In foreign policy, they had successfully renegotiated the inequitable treaties with the West, which now recognized Japan as a rising world power. Japan had not only defeated both imperial China (1894–1895) and czarist Russia (1904–1905), but had also acquired colonies in Taiwan (1895) and Korea (1910). In the economic realm, by this time Japan had established a fragile but rapidly growing economy.

But Japan's foreign policy and economic successes were not matched in the domestic political realm. By the 1920s, Japan was becoming a nation of diverse economic and political interests that could no longer be easily subsumed under a single banner or slogan, and pressure to change the highly authoritarian system was building. The desire for change became increasingly apparent during the reign of the Taisho emperor (1912–1926), particularly in the era of Wilsonian democracy after World War I. By that time, the original Meiji oligarchs had passed from the scene, and efforts by their bureaucratic and military successors to maintain the Meiji political system faced challenges from a middle class demanding democratic rights, laborers organizing for better working conditions, and peasants rioting against onerous taxes.

In an era that came to be known as **Taisho democracy** (1918–1931), efforts by these groups and their liberal political proponents to institute democracy were significant but short-lived and ultimately unsuccessful. Different groups increasingly sought to exercise influence in the political realm, with some success, including the election of the first commoner as prime minister in 1918, the granting of universal male suffrage by 1925, and the establishment of political parties.

THE MILITARIST ERA: IMPERIAL EXPANSION AND DEFEAT

By the end of the 1920s, a number of events had stymied Japan's first attempt at liberal democracy. The Great Depression and the rising global protectionism of the 1930s dealt trade-dependent Japan a harsh blow, leading to increased labor agitation and political unrest as the economy weakened. This domestic instability combined with anti-Japanese sentiment in China led to rising nationalist and fascist sentiments at home and reemerging militarism and adventurism abroad. As in Europe and elsewhere, the emergence of such forces led in the early 1930s to a period of political polarization and increased political violence, with democracy the chief victim. One critic labeled this period an era of government by assassination.

The era of Taisho democracy ended with the Japanese army's seizure of Manchuria in 1931 and the assassination of the last elected head of the government by naval cadets in 1932. Over the next decade, the military steadily expanded its control of the state, ruling in an often uneasy alliance with the bureaucracy and the *zaibatsu*. Although most historians are not comfortable labeling the Japanese militarist state fascist, the emperor-based system lent itself to the establishment of a near-totalitarian state, one with many similarities to the European fascist states. The state sought to bring under its auspices or otherwise eliminate virtually all pluralist groups and autonomous organizations, censoring the press, repressing all forms of political dissent, crushing political parties and other forms of free association, and gaining almost complete control over industrial production.

Also, like its fascist allies in Europe, Japan promoted an ultranationalist emperor-based ideology and expansionist foreign policy, with the intent of extending its empire. It annexed Manchuria in 1932, invaded China proper in 1937, and launched full-scale war in December 1941 with the attack on Pearl Harbor and rapid expansion into Southeast Asia. At the height of its power, Japan's so-called Greater East Asian Co-Prosperity Sphere of conquered lands included most of the eastern half of China (including Manchuria), Sakhalin and some of the Aleutian Islands, Korea, Taiwan, the Philippines, Indochina, Thailand, Malaya, Burma, Indonesia, and portions of the South Pacific. As in Europe, Allied forces met, stemmed, and turned back the aggression by 1944. Costly but stunning defeats at sea and on land, followed by the destructive U.S. firebombing of Japanese cities in early 1945 and the atomic bombing of Hiroshima and Nagasaki in August prompted Japan's unconditional surrender on September 2, 1945.

U.S. OCCUPATION: REINVENTING JAPAN

Japan's defeat and destruction were devastatingly complete: militarily, industrially, even psychologically. One historian estimates that the war cost Japan some 2.7 million lives (nearly 4 percent of its population) and that by war's end many more millions were injured, sick, or seriously malnourished.[4] Under these conditions, it was once again foreign (more specifically, American) pressure that provided the impetus for revolutionary change in Japan. Although the seven-year occupation was technically an Allied operation, it remained overwhelmingly a U.S. enterprise managed by a single individual: the Supreme Commander of Allied Powers in Japan, General **Douglas MacArthur**.

Like the arrival of Commodore Perry's ships nearly a century earlier, the American occupation of Japan is significant both for what it changed and what it did not change. The initial plan called for demilitarization to exorcise Japan's militant feudal past and then democratization to establish American-style democratic values and institutions. Demilitarization proceeded swiftly and included not only the purging of all professional military officers, key wartime politicians, and *zaibatsu* leaders but also the disbanding of the ultranationalist associations and political parties. These thoroughgoing purges destroyed the military class and replaced entrenched politicians with technocrats (in most cases, former bureaucrats) and *zaibatsu* families with professional managers. Most dramatically, the new "Japanese" constitution (quickly drafted by MacArthur's staff and adopted by the Diet in 1947 almost unaltered) included Article 9, the so-called peace clause, by which Japan would "forever renounce war as a sovereign right" and never maintain "land, sea, and air forces, as well as other war potential."

Changing the status of the emperor—in the eyes of the Japanese as well as constitutionally—and eliminating the institution as a political force were key to MacArthur's democratization efforts. The constitution reduced the emperor's stature from godlike and inviolable to simply symbolic, and it transferred sovereignty to the Japanese people. Other measures of this regime change included extending suffrage to women; clarifying relations among the prime minister, the cabinet, and the two houses of the Diet; guaranteeing civil rights and freedoms; breaking up the *zaibatsu* and imposing antitrust measures; encouraging labor unions and other interest groups; redistributing land to the peasants; and reforming the education system.

The two-stage approach of demilitarization and democratization remained largely in place for the first two years of the occupation. But continued economic hardship (due in part to war reparations and a policy of little economic aid) combined with the newfound freedom of socialist and Communist activists pushed Japan rapidly toward the left. This political shift and the onset of the cold war (compounded by the Communist victory in China in 1949 and the outbreak of the Korean War in 1950) led to a "reverse course" in occupation policies.

The earlier desire to refashion Japan as weak and docile in the manner of an Asian Switzerland gave way to a plan that would make Japan a full, albeit still unarmed, ally of the West. The deconcentration of industry was scaled back in order to rebuild the economy, and labor strikes were prohibited. Leftist labor activists were purged and in some cases (re)jailed even as numerous conservative politicians were released from prison and rehabilitated. Notably, in all of the twists and turns of occupation policy, the wartime bureaucracy of technocratic planners was left intact, in part because the American occupiers needed

IRON TRIANGLE

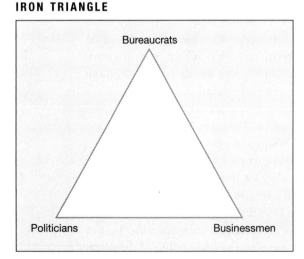

it, and in part because they saw the bureaucracy as only the instrument, not the agent, of war.

Today, some occupation reforms are universally considered to have been both successful and beneficial. Others largely failed, whereas still others remain highly controversial and even contradictory. For instance, on paper Japan has one of the most liberal political systems in the world. But by default and design, Japan's postwar state featured a core elite of experienced bureaucrats closely allied with conservative politicians (many of whom were former bureaucrats) and big-business executives. This ruling triad, or **iron triangle**, has remained largely intact through good times and bad.

POLITICAL REGIME

Is Japan a democracy? The continuing dominance of a ruling triad of bureaucrats, politicians, and businessmen has led to much controversy on this issue. In important ways, Japan's political structures and procedures are democratic. The rights and liberties enshrined in Japan's 1947 constitution certainly exceed those of the U.S. Constitution and are perhaps unrivaled. Its citizens are well protected by the rule of law, and its electoral system is probably no more corrupt than that of other advanced liberal democracies. Unlike the United States, Japan has successful socialist and Communist parties, arguably resulting in a greater range of political debate and choice than in the United States.

Yet these formal institutions and procedural safeguards of democracy do not tell the whole story. Although democratic practices seldom live up to the ideals of political pluralism in any democratic regime, the initial dominance and persistent power of the postwar bureaucracy and its conservative political and corporate allies have led some analysts to conclude that Japan's democracy is dysfunctional, if not an outright mockery. For most of the postwar era, the conservative Liberal Democratic Party (LDP) has dominated the legislature and has in turn been overshadowed in policy making by nonelected career civil servants. Long-standing political practice and informal levers and linkages of power have constrained the full functioning of this imported democracy. This

ESSENTIAL POLITICAL FEATURES

- Legislative-executive system: parliamentary
- Legislature: Diet
- Lower house: House of Representatives
- Upper house: House of Councillors
- Unitary or federal division of power: unitary
- Main geographic subunits: prefectures
- Electoral system for lower house: mixed single-member district and proportional representation
- Chief judicial body: Supreme Court

dualism becomes more apparent upon examination of the formal institutions and substantive procedures of Japanese democracy.

Political Institutions

THE CONSTITUTION

"We, the Japanese people. . . ." The opening phrase of Japan's unamended 1947 constitution reveals what are perhaps its two most significant aspects: its American imprint and the transfer of sovereignty from the emperor to the Japanese people. Although America's allies were calling for the prosecution of Emperor Hirohito as a war criminal, General Douglas MacArthur insisted that the emperor renounce his divinity but be allowed to retain his throne, to offer continuity and legitimacy to both the occupation government and the new democratic regime. The constitution reduces the emperor's godlike stature to that of a "symbol of the State and of the unity of the people with whom resides sovereign power." In order to empower Japanese citizens, the American framers of the Japanese constitution constructed an elaborate system of representative institutions, including universal suffrage, a parliamentary legislature in which the cabinet is responsible to the Diet (rather than the emperor), and an independent judiciary. The constitution also introduced a greater measure of local autonomy, increasing the role of local elected officials.

The Branches of Government

THE HEAD OF STATE

Although invested by the Meiji Constitution with total authority, the imperial institution was always controlled by de facto rulers. The 1947 constitution eliminated even this derivative authority, making the role of the emperor wholly symbolic. Unlike the British monarch, the Japanese emperor is technically just a symbol of the Japanese state, not the head of state. Like the British queen, however, this standard-bearer of the world's oldest imperial dynasty continues to play a significant role in symbolizing the unity and continuity of contemporary Japan. The emperor also performs purely formal tasks, such as appointing the prime minister (who is elected by the Diet) and appointing the chief justice of the Supreme Court (who is designated by the government), and he receives foreign ambassadors and represents the nation on many important ceremonial occasions at home and abroad.

The Japanese throne is both hereditary and patrilineal; therefore, no female heir is permitted to rule in her own right. Emperor Hirohito (who reigned from 1926 to 1989) was succeeded by his eldest son, Akihito, who became Japan's 125th emperor. Although polls show that recent generations

STRUCTURE OF THE GOVERNMENT

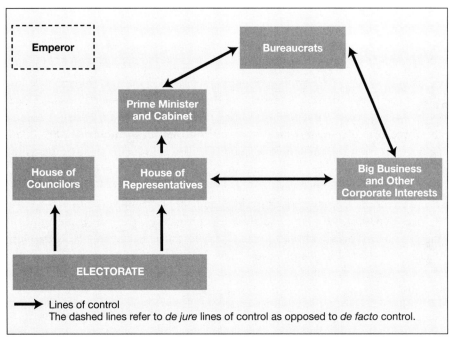

Lines of control
The dashed lines refer to *de jure* lines of control as opposed to *de facto* control.

of Japanese citizens, like their British counterparts, find themselves increasingly less connected to the throne, significant events such as the passing of Hirohito and the birth of a prospective heir generate enormous public interest and a deeper sense of attachment than the polls seem to indicate. Furthermore, Japan's royal family has faced none of the scandal that has recently challenged the British royals.

THE PRIME MINISTER AND THE CABINET

The prime minister serves as head of government and draws from the Diet cabinet members who serve as ministers, or heads, of Japan's seventeen bureaucratic ministries and other key agencies. The prime minister is always chosen from the lower house and is elected by the members of the Diet. But because the LDP has almost always held a parliamentary majority (more recently, dominating the ruling coalition), its candidate for prime minister (always the party president of the LDP) has typically been elected. This selection process has enhanced the role of LDP internal politics at the expense of parliamentary politics and has diminished to some extent the significance of the office of prime minister.

Successful candidates to the office of prime minister have therefore been required not only to belong to the right party but also to curry sufficient favor and rise high enough in a dominant faction within that party. Thus prominent and prospective LDP party leaders are more concerned with factional ties, personal connections, and back-room bargaining than with promoting a particular policy agenda. Faction leaders have typically brokered this selection process and rotated the office of LDP president (and prime minister) among various factions relatively frequently. Therefore, although Japanese prime ministers are usually experienced and savvy politicians, they tend to be older, have less policy expertise, and, with notable exceptions, serve for far shorter tenures than do their counterparts abroad.[5] Recent prime ministers are good cases in point. The three prime ministers who succeeded **Koizumi Junichiro** (2001–2006) include a son and grandson of former LDP prime ministers, had an average age of 64 when assuming office, and in the case of the first two served for only one year each. None, including current Prime Minister **Aso Taro**, has faced a general election, instead relying on factional support within the LDP to secure the presidency of the party and thus ascend to the office of prime minister (though parliamentary elections must be held every four years). This frequent turnover of elected heads of government makes them very dependent on the expertise, experience, and connections of the unelected bureaucrats within the ministries over which they ostensibly preside.

THE LEGISLATURE

The 1947 constitution declares Japan's Diet the "highest organ of state power" and claims exclusive law-making authority for the bicameral parliament. The Japanese Diet has two directly elected chambers: the House of Representatives and the House of Councillors. The **House of Representatives**, the lower house, has 480 members elected for a four-year term. As in other parliamentary systems, the government typically dissolves the lower house prior to the expiration of the term to call elections from a position of strength. Alternatively, a vote of no confidence can force dissolution, as it did most recently in 1993 (one of only four successful postwar no-confidence votes). General elections have taken place on average every two to three years since 1947. The upper chamber, the **House of Councillors**, comprises 242 members, elected for fixed six-year terms (staggered so that half the chamber stands for election every three years). Unlike the lower house, the upper house cannot be dissolved, but the House of Councillors passed a historic and unprecedented no-confidence vote in 2008, following the 2007 victory of the opposition Democratic Party of Japan in upper chamber elections.

As in other parliamentary systems, Japan's lower house is far more powerful than the upper, though the House of Councillors remains more consequential than the British House of Lords, as the 2007 upset election victory of the opposition Democratic Party of Japan (DPJ) and its control of the upper chamber has proven. Although the House of Representatives can override any upper house decision on significant legislation with a two-thirds majority vote in the lower house, the DPJ's control of the House of Councillors has allowed it to embarrass the LDP government and obstruct or at least slow its efforts on a number of domestic and foreign policy issues, including logistical support of the U.S.-led war efforts in Afghanistan in 2007 and domestic health and energy issues in 2008.

The Diet convenes for only about eighty days each year, a session roughly half that of the British Parliament. The brevity of the session has enhanced the role and responsibility of the standing committees. Many veteran politicians have established both expertise in particular policy areas and close ties to bureaucrats and interest groups having jurisdiction over or interest in those policy areas. This has given individual legislators a degree of influence over policy formerly reserved for bureaucratic experts and has simultaneously weakened party discipline in voting. The importance of pursuing **pork-barrel projects** for home-district constituencies has also weakened allegiance to the government. So despite their long-standing dominance of the Diet, LDP governments have been hesitant to provoke the objections of their own members. This has meant that LDP governments have promoted change only gradually, if at all; an inclination only strengthened by the fact that it now faces a divided parliament.

THE JUDICIAL SYSTEM

The 1947 constitution established for Japan a court system with a high degree of judicial independence from the other branches of government. In practice, however, the LDP has used its political dominance, appointment powers, and other administrative mechanisms to manipulate the courts and ensure judicial decisions in accordance with its political interests. This has been made easier because, unlike the dual system of federal and state courts in the United States, the Japanese system is unitary, with all civil, criminal, and administrative matters under the jurisdiction of a single hierarchy. At the top is the constitutional court, or Supreme Court, whose fifteen members are appointed by the cabinet.

Although politicians in all democracies seek to influence the courts, this combination of a unitary judicial system dominated by a single conservative party has rendered Japan's courts particularly subservient. Perhaps not surprisingly, even though the Supreme Court is invested with the constitutional power of judicial review, it has used this authority sparingly and has been extremely hesitant to declare laws unconstitutional.

The Electoral System

As with other political institutions in Japan, the electoral system is both cause and consequence of the LDP's long-standing reign. Postwar LDP governments maintained grossly disproportionate voting districts and established electoral rules that clearly favor the party's interests.[6] Despite reforms enacted by two short-lived opposition coalition governments in the mid-1990s, the LDP has continued to press its advantages.

Representatives in the two chambers of the Diet are elected according to different rules. Although the membership of the weaker House of Councillors has varied slightly during the postwar period, its electoral rules were not affected by the 1990s reforms and have remained largely unchanged. The 242 councillors serve fixed six-year terms, with half facing election every three years. Elected according to a mixed system, 98 are chosen from party lists using proportional representation (PR) in a nationwide election. The remaining 149 are elected from forty-seven multimember districts (MMD) that coincide with Japan's forty-seven prefectures. Each district returns from two to eight members, but rather than drawing from a party list, voters have a single, nontransferable vote that they cast for an individual candidate. In other words, rather than first-past-the-post in a single-member district (SMD), as in Great Britain and the United States, the top several-past-the-post (ranging from two to eight members) are elected from each district.

Prior to 1994, the electoral system that was used to determine membership in the House of Representatives resembled the second part of the system used for the upper house.[7] Two significant consequences of the old system should be mentioned. First, because contenders ended up competing for seats not just against opposition candidates but also against members of their own party, the system produced mini-parties; that is, factions within the LDP and other parties large enough to put forth multiple candidates. Therefore, the most important electoral battles were fought within the LDP, among individuals sharing essentially the same conservative ideology and policy positions. Second, unable to rely upon simple party or factional affiliations or even policy positions alone to succeed, candidates were compelled to form local party machines, known as **koenkai**, to generate essential votes and campaign funds.

In the wake of a series of notorious scandals, unpopular tax measures, and precipitous economic decline, thirty-eight years of unchallenged LDP rule gave way in 1993 when a group of LDP legislators defected from the party to support a vote of no confidence. The opposition coalition that replaced the LDP government lost no time in reforming the electoral system, restructuring the rules governing lower house elections seven months after coming to office. These reforms eliminated the old system and established a new mixed system similar to that of Germany and Mexico. Under the new system, the lower chamber still has 480 seats, but 300 of them are elected from single-member districts (SMDs). The remaining 180 are chosen by PR from eleven regional blocs, in which seats are assigned to the parties according to their share of the total blocwide votes. As in the German system, candidates may run in their own districts and be included in a regional party list, to safeguard their seats in the event of defeat in the home SMD.

This anti-LDP coalition government intended the reforms to shift electoral competition away from highly personalized factional politics within the LDP to national party politics between two dominant parties offering genuine policy alternatives. Although the PR portion of the ballot provides some seats for smaller parties able to garner the minimal threshold of votes, nearly two thirds of the seats are chosen from single-member districts, favoring well-organized and well-established big parties, as in the United States and Great Britain. The 1994 reforms also reapportioned districts to reflect demographics more accurately, giving more equitable clout to the much more numerous (and typically less conservative) urban voters in an effort to weaken the disproportionate clout of rural voters, who are among the LDP's most loyal supporters. Reflecting the continued elitism of Japanese politics, the reforms were less successful in dealing with (and in fact less concerned about) political corruption, which the Japanese call **money politics**—precisely the issue that the public and foreign observers most hoped would change. Although anti-corruption measures were implemented, as in other capitalist democracies, individual candidates and the corporations and other interest groups that woo them have discovered plenty of loopholes to keep campaign funds flowing.

Because the government registers voters, practically all eligible voters in Japan are registered. Accordingly, voter turnout in national elections has been relatively high, usually between 60 and 80 percent. But significantly, even as the system has become more competitive and politicians have increased their clout vis-à-vis the bureaucracy, voter turnout has declined. Although there are a number of reasons for the decline, popular distrust of politicians and disillusionment with the political process and the Japanese state are paramount.

Local Government

Japan is divided into forty-seven administrative divisions, known as prefectures, each with its own elected governor and legislature. Japan is nonetheless a unitary—not a federal—system, in which most political power is invested in the central government. The prefectural governments decide many local issues and are able to raise sufficient taxes to cover about one third of their expenditures (what the Japanese call 30 percent autonomy). These subnational governments depend on the central government, however, for the remainder of their budget. Central authorities delegate all local authority (at the prefectural and municipal levels) and can, and sometimes do, retract that authority. The national government can override the decision of any local governor and has done so most notably in the case of Okinawa, whose elected local officials have attitudes toward the overwhelming U.S. military presence there that differ significantly from those of national leaders. Okinawans are not alone, however, in wishing for the devolution of more authority and increased local autonomy.

Other Institutions: Bureaucracy and the Iron Triangle

The Japanese state's most influential, yet entirely extraconstitutional, institution of policy-making authority remains the bureaucracy. As in other liberal democracies, the Japanese bureaucracy staffs the dozen or so ministries comprising the Japanese state but is at once both smaller in size and greater in

---

THE POWER AND PRESTIGE OF JAPAN'S BUREAUCRACY

Analysts point to several reasons that bureaucrats have been so powerful and respected in Japan. First, the Japanese state has a long-standing tradition whereby people who have formal authority do not necessarily exercise power. Rulers and ruled alike are accustomed to legitimate governance by people who may not be vested with formal authority. Nonelected administrators, for example, have long exercised such power in Japan. Second, whereas U.S. occupation authorities jailed wartime politicians, purged the military, and broke up the *zaibatsu*, the experienced bureaucrats continued to administrate Japan uninterrupted and unscathed. Third, this political vacuum prompted many veteran bureaucrats to move into leadership positions in Japan's conservative postwar political parties, giving them significant political influence. Chief among these was **Yoshida Shigeru**, a former Foreign Ministry bureaucrat who served as prime minister through most of the occupation and beyond (from 1946 to 1954, with a short hiatus) and profoundly shaped the postwar bureaucracy-dominant political system. Fourth, the legitimacy and prestige of this dominance have been enhanced by the strictly meritocratic nature of hiring and advancement within the bureaucracy. As these bureaucrats advance, only the very best are promoted to senior leadership positions; the bureaucrats who have been passed over are dismissed from the ministry. Senior civil servants exercise extensive policy authority in potent ministries, such as the Ministry of Finance and the Ministry of Economy, Trade, and Industry (formerly and famously known as the Ministry of International Trade and Industry, or MITI).

This orderly promotion-and-dismissal policy also helps explain the willingness of the bureaucrats to work so hard for apparently so little and offers a final reason for the remarkable reach and power of the Japanese bureaucracy. Each year, a contingent of dismissed but nonetheless highly qualified bureaucrats in their forties and fifties undergo *amakudari* ("descent from heaven") either to try their hand in politics (overwhelmingly as LDP Diet members) or, more commonly, to take senior positions in the very corporations they previously regulated. All but a handful of Japan's postwar prime ministers were former top bureaucrats. Likewise, the corporations that employ retired civil servants gain not just their skills but also their connections. At any given time, Japan's policy elite do not just share a common outlook but often have attended the same prestigious schools and may have worked for decades in the same ministry.

influence than any of its Western counterparts. Ministers appointed to head these ministries are often not experts in their assignments but rather obtain their appointments based on political criteria and must rely almost entirely upon the career civil servants within their ministries to formulate, facilitate, and ultimately implement and enforce laws and policies. In each ministry, an administrative vice minister with some twenty-five to thirty years of experience in that particular ministry heads these efforts, presiding over a staff of Japan's brightest, who willingly subject themselves to grueling workweeks for relatively meager compensation (see "The Power and Prestige of Japan's Bureaucracy," p. 220).

Enduring linkages among senior bureaucrats, conservative politicians, and corporate executives form what has been referred to as an iron triangle, in which the determination and implementation of policies are often facilitated not by negotiations, hearings, and parliamentary votes but by informal discussion (known as **administrative guidance**) between former colleagues and during after-work drinking sessions among friends. This web of informal connections within the Japanese state consists of hundreds of triangles involving veteran politicians with particular policy expertise, bureaucrats in a particular ministry or division, and the private-sector representatives of interest groups in that policy area. Although ruling bureaucrats have traditionally dominated these associations, the reigning Diet has legitimated the work of the bureaucracy and assured that its policies would not go beyond the range of public tolerance. LDP governments have also made sure that the party's most important constituents, including corporations (from which it received massive campaign funds) and rice farmers (on whose overrepresented vote it depended), were well taken care of with producer-oriented industrial and financial policies and protectionist trade policies. Representatives of Japan's large corporations in turn offered firsthand policy advice to the bureaucrats and generally accepted the business-friendly policies and guidance they received in return.

Events in recent years have led some scholars to argue that this "well-oiled, conservative regime" is now undergoing a "regime shift," in which politicians, interest groups, and even Japanese citizens are gaining political influence at the expense of the bureaucracy and even the elitist triangle.[8] They point to a series of recent bureaucratic scandals and bunglings that have tarnished the reputation and prestige of the bureaucracy, including kickbacks; an AIDS-tainted transfusion cover-up that led to hundreds of deaths; and poor handling of such national crises as the extended economic downturn, a religious cult's gassing of the Tokyo subway system in 1995 with a deadly poison, and the Kobe earthquake that same year. They note that politicians were able to take advantage of these and other problems, briefly dislodging the LDP from office and pursuing both electoral reforms and, more recently, administrative changes designed to give the prime minister new leverage over the bureaucracy. Politicians have also gained increasing policy expertise in their own right, making them less dependent on their bureaucratic counterparts in policy making.

Where, then, does power reside in the Japanese state? Even though Japan, unlike the United States, lacks the formal separation of powers between state and national government and between the executive and legislative branches, it is fair to say that there is no single locus of power in the Japanese state. Even during the era of the bureaucracy's greatest strength, from the 1950s through the 1970s, powerful prime ministers such as Yoshida Shigeru and Tanaka Kakuei still often held sway over the bureaucracy.[9] Some of Japan's most famous and successful corporations, such as Sony and Honda, achieved their status in part because they defied bureaucratic dictates. And while each bureaucratic ministry may have substantial authority within its own domain, these independent fiefdoms are subject to no overriding direction or guidance.

Scholars critical of this Japanese state have described it as headless and susceptible to the kind of uncoordinated drift that led not only to a quixotic war against the United States half a century ago but also to unsustainable trade surpluses with virtually every industrialized country and an inability to reform a twentieth-century mercantilist economy so that it may cope with the challenges it faces in a twenty-first-century globalized economy.[10] Will Japan be able to change, and if so, what will be the impetus? Because elements within the iron triangle have demonstrated little willingness or incentive to change, many observers argue that one must look beyond this ruling triad and perhaps even beyond Japan to locate the forces and pressures capable of bringing about change.

POLITICAL CONFLICT AND COMPETITION

The Party System and Elections

Like Mexico, Sweden, or Italy, postwar Japan offers an example of a predominant party system. In this case, the Liberal Democratic Party (LDP) has dominated all others since it formed as a merger of existing conservative parties in 1955. Its closest rival, the Japan Socialist Party (JSP), is similarly the product of a merger of leftist parties that same year and served for decades as the perennial loyal opposition, until the major reshuffling in 1993. The JSP regularly garnered fewer than half as many votes as the LDP in parliamentary elections and, thanks to LDP gerrymandering, obtained even fewer seats.

During this period, several other parties joined the JSP in opposition by taking advantage of Japan's former electoral system to carve out niches in the Japanese electorate among voters who felt excluded by both of the larger parties. These included the Japan Communist Party (JCP), which consistently embraced policies to the left of the JSP, and the more moderate Democratic Socialist Party (DSP) and Clean Government Party (CGP, or New Komeito), which occupied a middle ground between conservative, pro-business LDP politics and the socialist (and pacifist) platform of the JSP. These three and a couple of other short-lived parties typically accounted for roughly 20 percent of the popular vote.

This remarkably stable one-and-a-half-party system, an important component of the equally stable iron triangle, remained intact for nearly four decades. But in 1993, LDP corruption scandals and inept, unpopular government reactions to Japan's drastic economic downturn led to a political revolution of sorts. To understand the causes and the nature of this revolt and why it was so long in coming, it is necessary first to examine LDP party politics.

THE LIBERAL DEMOCRATIC PARTY

With the exception of an eleven-month period from 1993 to 1994, the LDP has dominated the Diet from 1955 to the present. The nature of this rule has led some observers to conclude that the LDP is woefully misnamed: it is conservative, not liberal. Its internal politics are highly authoritarian, not democratic. Its factional divisions, moreover, make it a collection of mini-parties, not a single party.

The LDP can perhaps best be understood as a highly pragmatic electoral machine in which ideological consistency has never taken priority over winning. It has established electoral rules and engaged in campaigns and elections with the express purpose of staying in power by maintaining a majority (or at least a healthy plurality) of seats in the parliament. But it has also been more than a political machine for members of the parliament. The LDP's persistent lock on the government has meant that the campaign for the LDP presidency has in almost all cases been the contest for the office of prime minister.

Two organizational features have been key to the LDP's continued dominance, but they have also caused the party significant problems and prevented effective internal reform. The first of these features is the factions, or mini-parties, that have formed within the LDP. Japan's former electoral system compelled contenders for seats in the parliament to compete against candidates not only from other parties but also from their own party. This intraparty competition meant that candidates had to vie for the support of patrons within the party, who provide members with campaign funds, official party endorsements, appointed positions within the party and the government, and other favors. These faction leaders in turn count on the support of their faction members in the party's all-important presidential elections. Five LDP factions emerged in the mid-1950s, have been led by successive generations of LDP kingpins, and have largely survived to the present.

But even unswerving factional loyalty did not guarantee LDP parliamentary candidates electoral success in their home district under the old system. Because several LDP candidates ran in each district, persuading voters to vote for the LDP was not enough. A sufficient number of voters had to vote for each LDP contender to guarantee that each surpassed the threshold in these multi-member districts. In order to help individual candidates obtain enough votes and to ensure that no single contestant received too many votes (therefore "wasting them"), each candidate constructed a local support group, or party "machine," known as a *koenkai*. The *koenkai* are made up of influential district members able to gather votes in their community or, more recently, among members of a particular professional or other special-interest group within the district.

In the same way that the LDP candidates promised allegiance to their factional patron in exchange for support from above, so they promised policy favors and other pork-barrel enticements in exchange for the votes and campaign donations delivered by their *koenkai*. And just as the factions have outlived individual leaders, so have the *koenkai* been multigenerational. It is not uncommon for an entire *koenkai* to throw its full support behind the son, grandson, or other successor of a retiring member of parliament.

Although these multiple levels of patron-client relations have certainly contributed to the LDP's long-term political dominance, the gifts, favors, and huge sums of money required to lubricate the system and manage the LDP's intense intraparty competition (in which purse size, not policy preference, matters) have fostered a system of money politics, which has made Japanese election campaigns among the most expensive in the world. Put simply, the LDP has been foremost a vote- and money-delivery system, with money being the single most powerful way of obtaining votes. Both money and votes have been secured through expanding circles of corporatist co-optation of businesses and other large interest groups as well as through clientelist currying of favor among local communities and individuals by means of pork-barrel projects, favors, and gifts. As in any democracy, pork-barrel projects in the home district, such as bridges and schools, deliver votes, and the lucrative contracts and licenses awarded to corporations to build these projects bring campaign donations. But LDP politicians and their supporters also attend the funerals, weddings, graduations, and other important events of their loyal constituents (on average over thirty each month), honoring them with their presence and an appropriate (monetary) gift.

Campaign strategies and money politics, both hugely expensive, have plagued the LDP with scandals throughout its history. The most successful politicians are precisely those who are able to generate enough money and connections to rise to the top.

THE 1993 REVOLT

Persistent—indeed, mounting—corruption scandals, combined with general dissatisfaction with LDP governance, prompted widespread calls from outside and, to some extent, from inside the party for electoral and campaign reforms. With the LDP old guard continuing to resist, several prominent members of the LDP bolted the party in 1993, taking with them a substantial number of the members of their LDP factions. These renegades formed several new parties and left the LDP with (barely) less than a majority of seats in the lower house.

The leader of one of these parties, Hosokawa Morihiro, managed to piece together a coalition government of all the opposition parties except the Communists, which remained unified just long enough (nine months) to enact electoral reforms. A second minority coalition survived for ten weeks, its government cut short when the JSP (renamed the Social Democratic Party, or SDP), in an act of political expediency, joined its longtime rival the LDP to form a majority coalition. The deal earned the JSP/SDP the office of prime minister. This coalition lasted from 1994 until 1996, by which time the LDP had embraced newly enacted electoral reforms and was powerful enough in its own right to form a series of coalition governments in which it once again called (most of) the shots. The opposition, too, has retooled and, under pressure from the new winner-take-all single-member district (SMD) system to unite, has begun to coalesce around the centrist Democratic Party, which nonetheless remains a distant second behind the LDP in parliamentary seats and popular vote.

Major Political Parties

Party	Ideology	House of Representatives Election, 2005 (Number of Seats)
Liberal Democratic Party (LDP)	Right	296
Democratic Party (DP)	Center	113
Clean Government Party (CGP)	Center	31
Social Democratic Party (SDP)	Left	7
Japan Communist Party (JCP)	Left	9
Other		33
Total		480

Can the humbled but renewed LDP retain the loyalty of Japanese voters? The five-year tenure of LDP Prime Minister Koizumi from 2001 to 2006 seemed to bode well for the LDP. Koizumi, with his raffish hairdo and populist style, was in many ways the antithesis of the traditional LDP politician. He secured the LDP presidency without the explicit backing of any major LDP faction and won three consecutive elections with promises to halt Japan's economic malaise and take on the country's conservative bureaucratic and political elite (including his own LDP) and their deeply entrenched constituencies. LDP party rules required the popular prime minister to step down in 2006 after five years as party president, but his government can take credit for a number of modest reforms, including the privatization of Japan's Postal Savings System, which wrested the world's wealthiest bank from the control of Japan's powerful bureaucrats (see "Koizumi, Japan Post, and the Iron Triangle," below). But Koizumi's tenure has been succeeded by LDP politics as usual, including factional infighting, corruption scandals, and colorless prime ministers. These have included Abe Shinzo, who was forced out of office in 2007 after just one year in the wake of corruption charges and the 2007 upper-

KOIZUMI, JAPAN POST, AND THE IRON TRIANGLE

When Japan's Meiji modernizers looked to the West in the nineteenth century seeking to adopt institutions to promote their modernization efforts, one of the first they seized upon was Britain's postal savings system. It offered banking through neighborhood post offices and channeled deposits large and small into state coffers where the funds could be reinvested in industrial development. Although a dozen other countries also copied the British model, **Japan Post** has proven the most successful by far, with holdings growing in recent years to over US$3 trillion, making it the largest bank in the world. Because Japan's powerful bureaucracy controlled the purse strings of this huge financial institution, Prime Minister Koizumi made privatization of Japan Post one of the key measures in his efforts to reform and weaken Japan's iron triangle. Not surprisingly, Koizumi's plan faced resistance not just from the Ministry of Finance and other bureaucrats, but also from the LDP old guard who worked with bureaucrats to channel these monies into pork-barrel projects in their home districts. In 2005, when LDP members of parliament (MPs) refused to support his privatization bill, Koizumi responded by dissolving the House of Representatives, calling snap elections, and nominating new ninja ("assassin") candidates to contest seats held by those who rejected his privatization bill, both from the opposition Democratic Party and his own LDP. Koizumi and his LDP "assassins" won a landslide victory (see "Major Political Parties," p. 225), giving the LDP an outright majority in the lower house and permitting Koizumi to pass his landmark bill, which authorized a ten-year privatization plan for Japan Post.

house election defeat; Fukuda Yasuo, the son of a former LDP prime minister who also stepped down after a one-year tenure; and Aso Taro, who is the current prime minister.

DEMOCRATIC PARTY OF JAPAN

With the popularity of post-Koizumi LDP governments flagging, opposition parties, including the largest opposition party—the Democratic Party of Japan (DPJ)—have sought to capitalize on the LDP's hard times. Led by former LDP kingpin Ozawa Ichiro, the DPJ came together in the late 1990s as the merger of several of the 1993 breakaway parties from the LDP. Because the party's primary goal is simply to unseat the LDP government, it is difficult to draw much distinction between the DPJ's calls for liberalization, devolution, and breaking up the iron triangle and similar efforts made by Koizumi's LDP government and at least the lip service of his LDP successors to do likewise.

That said, the DPJ has made substantial gains in recent years, particularly in the upper House of Councillors where it outpolled the LDP in elections in 2004 for half the seats (though the LDP managed to maintain its overall majority). The DPJ followed up on this with an even more dramatic and significant electoral victory for the other half of the seats contested in 2007, giving the DPJ outright control of the upper house and depriving the LDP of a majority for the first time since the party's inception. This situation of a divided parliament has politically emboldened the DPJ and afforded it the legislative means to stymie a number of LDP policy measures, if not yet allow it to give serious challenge to the LDP government and its control of the more powerful lower house.

Civil Society

Because the reforms that brought about Westernization and democracy were imposed from above (and, in many cases, from *outside*), Japan has a centralized bureaucratic society rather than a civil society in which citizens voluntarily organize and participate in political, economic, and social affairs. Like other authoritarian systems, the Meiji and militarist states fostered corporatist and mercantilist institutions to harness Japan's industrial society in the service of modernization and imperialism. Although the U.S. occupiers destroyed many aspects of Japanese authoritarianism and carried out sweeping political, social, and economic reforms, they retained the bureaucracy and, out of fears of Communism, squelched many of the nascent civic groups they had initially fostered.

In pursuing economic development and political stability, the postwar Japanese state organized or co-opted interest groups that were important to these goals, such as business and agricultural interest groups, and formed associations for facilitating their political participation. In exchange for their support, these groups have had their interests well represented (and protected) and have prospered. This symbiotic relationship has since been expanded to include many other smaller groups and constituencies in a system of distributional welfare that has prolonged LDP bureaucratic rule, at the increasing expense of both economic health and political flexibility. In addition, labor unions, consumers, and other groups that have often been prominent in the politics of industrialized countries have been notably absent from these arrangements and have in many ways borne the burden of the corporatist system, which is sometimes referred to as Japan, Inc.

The third leg of the iron triangle is made up of Japan's large corporations and the large industrial groupings or conglomerates (**keiretsu**) to which they belong. These players have been both proponents of and participants in Japan's postwar development. Big business exercises political influence through Keidanren (Federation of Economic Organizations), which voices the concerns of large corporations and offers policy recommendations to the government. Keidanren has been the conduit through which most campaign contributions have been channeled from large businesses to LDP coffers and therefore has inclined the government to champion business-friendly policies, such as cheap access to capital, investment incentives, and various forms of market protection. Since the economic downturn of the 1990s, businesses have bridled at these campaign contributions and have complained about the use of growing corporate taxes to subsidize inefficient farmers and pork-barrel projects. Analysts point to this divergence of interests as yet another sign of the weakening of the iron triangle.

The other pillar of LDP support has been the agricultural sector, whose highly organized political interests are channeled through local agricultural cooperatives to the national "peak organization" Nōkyō (Central Union of Agricultural Cooperatives). Agriculture's key political contribution has been its capacity to provide the LDP with a dependable and geographically concentrated bloc of votes. In exchange, LDP government and bureaucratic policies have favored farmers with protection from agricultural imports, price supports, and relatively low taxes. Although urbanization and electoral redistricting have to some extent weakened the significance of the rural farm vote, Japanese farmers remain an important political force.

Big business and agriculture are not the only interest groups to have offered their campaign contributions and votes to the LDP in exchange for favorable policies and a share of the benefits of Japan's postwar economic boom. Small and medium-size businesses make up most of the Japanese economy, despite their unsung status when compared with such high-profile large firms as Toyota and Sony. The smaller manufacturers and retailers have been very well organized and have parlayed their electoral support into tax breaks, subsidies, and protection from larger firms. For example, the ubiquitous mom-and-pop corner grocery stores effectively kept large retailers out of Japan's neighborhoods for many years. Another group worth mentioning is the half million construction firms in Japan, most of which are small, unproductive, and well cared for by an inefficient and corrupt government bidding system for public works.

Japan's faltering economy and growing corruption scandals involving the LDP and its supporters have cast new light on the economic and political costs of the country's corporate welfare system. Critics argue that the LDP's varied and growing host of constituencies has led to distributional tyranny, fueled Japan's economic crisis, and stifled political change. Corporatist arrangements have also long excluded interests that were deemed potentially harmful to the goals of rapid industrialization, including trade unions, consumers, and women's groups. Because of this, Japan's major labor organizations, including RENGO (Japanese Trade Union Confederation) and the teachers' and public employees' unions, have had adversarial relations with the LDP and have supported the more left-leaning political parties, such as the Socialists and Communists. As Japan's postindustrial and postmaterialist society grows more complex and the political marketplace more competitive, many observers hope that an increasing number of interests will use constitutional guarantees to establish a broader range of civic associations.

SOCIETY

Ethnic and National Identity

Few national populations view themselves as racially and ethnically homogeneous as do the Japanese. With immigrants constituting only 1 percent of the population, this perception is grounded in demographic reality. Nonetheless, those of foreign ancestry in Japan make up some 5 percent of the population. The notion of a racially pure and monoethnic Japan was largely fostered by the Japanese state from the Meiji period onward as it sought to forge a Japanese nation from the culturally and even linguistically diverse feudal domains of nineteenth-century Japan and to establish Japanese racial superiority over the peoples of its far-flung empire in the first half of the twentieth century.

Japan's strong ethnic and national identity has come at the expense of several minority groups that have been prevented from developing a Japanese identity and enjoying the full privileges of citizenship as Japanese nationals with a separate ethnic heritage. These minorities include the indigenous Ainu in the north and Okinawans in the south; descendants of Koreans, Chinese,

ETHNIC GROUPS

RELIGION

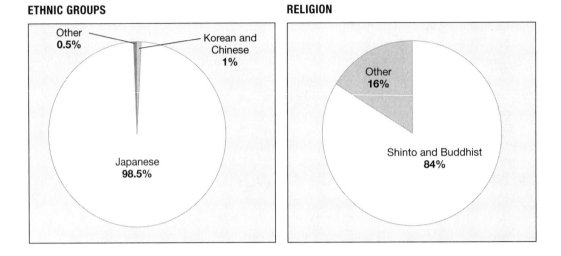

and Southeast Asians; and the children of mixed ancestry and foreigners. Although not racially separate, the 2 million *burakumin* (social outcasts), whose ancestors worked in the "unclean" occupations, are also seen as a minority group and have faced intense prejudice. Discrimination against these minority groups has been widespread and persistent. Those individuals who have sought to assimilate by taking on Japanese names, mastering the Japanese language, and adopting Japanese cultural mores have generally remained socially marginalized and culturally scorned.

If cultural assimilation is difficult, the naturalization process is nearly as arduous. Being born in Japan does not automatically confer citizenship or voting rights. Non-Japanese can become citizens only after adopting a Japanese name and enduring a series of interviews that include home visits and consultations with neighbors to ensure that the candidate has sufficiently assimilated Japanese culture. This is a process that many find invasive and humiliating. In addition, permanent residents who do not choose citizenship are fingerprinted and required to carry alien-registration identification.

However, economic necessity may bring about the social integration and mobility that cultural obstacles and state policy have prevented. With both a rapidly aging population and dwindling fertility, Japan faces the prospect of having some 30 percent fewer people by mid-century than it has today and a proportionally smaller workforce. Economists and demographers argue that if Japan is not prepared to overcome both its racism and its sexism, which have prevented immigrants and women from fully contributing to the workforce, the country may close the door on its last, best chance to regain its status as an economic powerhouse.

Ideology and Political Culture

Japan's historical experiences with Shintoism, Buddhism, Confucianism, feudalism, militarism, and bureaucratism have certainly shaped the norms and values that guide Japanese political behavior. So have its experiences with the West, from imposed inequitable treaties and democratic institutions to military defeat and the embrace of Western popular culture. In efforts to attribute political behavior to culture, scholars often point to the group conformity and social hierarchy that pervade most aspects of Japanese life. The basic unit of Japanese society is not the individual but the group, as manifested in such institutions as the family, the company, the political faction, and the nation. Japanese are socialized to defer to the needs of the group and to make decisions through consensus rather than majority vote. Similarly, hierarchy governs most social relationships in Japan, and Japanese are most comfortable in settings in which their social standing in relation to others is clear. Inferiors yield to their superiors' authority, and superiors are obliged to care for their subordinates' needs. Promotion in firms, bureaucratic ministries, and LDP factions is more often based on seniority and personalized patron-client relationships than on merit.

Japan has undergone political and economic modernization, but on its own (not fully Western) terms. Individual freedom and social equality remain less important than one's acceptance by the group and one's rightful position in that group's hierarchical division. Japan's remarkably equitable distribution of wealth (on par with that of the European social democracies) has little to do with cultural norms of egalitarianism or explicit government policy. In fact, Japan has had a weak labor movement, and its conservative governments have promoted the low taxation and public spending policies that typically foster inequality. Rather, Japan's economic and social equality can be attributed in large part to (1) World War II, which reduced all of Japanese society to poverty levels; (2) postwar occupation reforms, including land reform; breakup of the huge *zaibatsu* conglomerates; purges of the political, military, economic, and aristocratic elite; and empowerment of labor unions to bargain collectively for improved working conditions; and (3) Japan's rapid and sustained postwar economic growth, which showered unprecedented prosperity on virtually all social groups in Japan. These factors have consistently weakened the salience of issues of redistribution of wealth as an ideological cleavage in Japan, contributing to the weakness of the Japanese left and shoring up support for the LDP and its pro-growth policies. In a recent poll, nearly three fourths of respondents identified themselves as having a political stance ranging from conservative to neutral, whereas less than one fourth saw themselves as progressive or close to progressive.

The recent economic malaise (combined with an ongoing generational change in values) may lead to greater diversity of political attitudes and ideologies in Japan. The fading of guaranteed permanent employment (so-called lifetime employment) for Japan's corporate *sarariman* (white-collar salaryman) and rising unemployment among college graduates (and indeed an increasing number of college and even high-school dropouts) have led to disillusionment with business and politics as usual and to mounting calls for change. Such disillusionment is particularly strong among Japanese youth, who have no memory of wartime hardship or postwar poverty and place more value on individual fulfillment through leisure diversions and risky entrepreneurial opportunities rather than long hours and long years of work for the sake of a company. Younger Japanese have less incentive to remain loyal to a company that can no longer promise them job security, and they have little patience for the corruption and authority of long-in-the-tooth LDP bureaucratic rule. In short, change may be initiated by a younger generation that is far more willing and likely to switch both their jobs and their political loyalties.

POLITICAL ECONOMY

Japan's sudden introduction to the global political economy in the nineteenth century fostered the development of a mercantilist political economic system concerned with neither liberal freedom nor Communist equality. Compelled by U.S. gunships to open the country's borders to "free" trade with the West, the Meiji oligarchs recognized that Japan must either modernize quickly or, like China, be overrun by Western imperialism. State-led economic development became not a means of serving the public but rather a means of preserving national sovereignty. The oligarchs' national slogan, "rich country, strong military," reflected Meiji modernizers' awareness from the outset of the strong relationship between economic development and industrialization, on the one hand, and military and political power in the international arena on the other.

Despite the tumultuous change that Japan experienced in the twentieth century, the basic structure of its catch-up mercantilist political economy persists. Forged under conditions of military rigor, refined during the U.S. occupation, and perfected under the aegis of American mil-

LABOR FORCE BY OCCUPATION

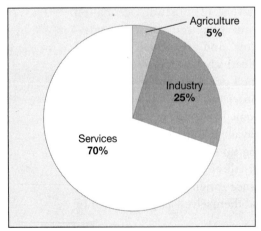

Agriculture
5%

Industry
25%

Services
70%

itary and economic protection, this developmental model propelled Japan from the ashes of devastating military defeat to become the second-largest economy in the world. Not surprisingly, scholars and policy makers alike have sought to understand this developmental "miracle," and the investigation of the model of Japan's **capitalist developmental state** has become an important field of academic study and policy analysis.[11] Japan's capitalist developmental state differs significantly from the liberal capitalist system that Americans often presume to be the only "true" form of capitalism. Like France's dirigiste system of state intervention in the economy, Japan's political economic system permits a far higher level of state guidance of private firms and competitive markets than do the systems in the United Kingdom or the United States. This guidance has included a host of formal and informal economic measures often grouped under the term *industrial policy*. Industrial policies are formulated and implemented by Japan's elite economic bureaucracy, after consultation and coordination with the private sector. Measures include imposing protective tariffs and nontariff barriers on imports, encouraging cooperation and limiting "excessive" competition in strategic export sectors, and offering low-interest loans and tax breaks to firms willing to invest in targeted industries.

Government guidance has not always worked well or as planned. But for many decades, state-led developmental capitalism kept Japan's economy strong, prosperous, and internationally competitive. The prewar family *zaibatsu* were replaced by professionally managed *keiretsu* conglomerates with ready access to cheap capital. Workers agreed to forgo disruptive labor strikes in exchange for promises of permanent employment, ensuring management a skilled and disciplined workforce. As early heavy-handed policies of protectionism and explicit control proved unwieldy, bureaucrats came to rely more upon informal directives known as administrative guidance and subtle incentives more suitable for the increasingly internationalized Japanese economy. After growing at an average rate of over 10 percent per year during the 1950s and 1960s, Japan's economy still managed to grow over 5 percent per year during the 1970s and 1980s, substantially faster than the economy of any other advanced industrial democracy. The flagship automotive and consumer-electronics companies within Japan's large conglomerates became multinational giants and household names, and the fruits of Japan's rapid growth lifted the income of and opportunity for nearly all Japanese.

By the 1980s, Japan's very prosperity was masking what now, in hindsight, is much easier to detect as serious structural problems within the model. As the international political economy was becoming ever more integrated and hypercompetitive, the cost of doing business in Japan was mounting. Japan's multinational automotive and electronics exporters felt this competitive pressure first but kept their heads above water by shifting production overseas and drastically cutting costs at home. Most of Japan's companies were not able to react so nimbly, however, nor was the government prepared to tolerate the kind of unemployment that would have resulted from the wholesale transfer of production abroad. Rather than face global competition, inefficient industries used their influence within the iron triangle to seek protection. They obtained it from a government that had become accustomed to looking after not just economically strategic industries but also politically strategic industries. This government assistance led to waste, overcapacity, and overpricing.

These corporate welfare measures, combined with a rapid jump in the value of Japan's currency, propelled its stock and real estate markets skyward in the latter half of the 1980s. This led to dangerous overvaluation of both securities and land. At one point in the early 1990s, Japan's stock market was valued at fully half of all the world's stock markets combined. At its peak value, the land under the emperor's palace grounds in central Tokyo was worth as much as the land of the entire state of California! Japan was awash in overinflated assets and easy money, leading companies, banks, the Japanese Mafia, and even the government to invest in grossly overpriced assets and risky (even foolish) business ventures. When this asset bubble burst in 1992, the value of stock and property plummeted, growth slowed, and already uncompetitive companies were left with huge debts (and dwindling assets and production with which to repay them). The Japanese labeled these firms **zombies**: essentially dead but propped up by banks and a political system unwilling to force them into bankruptcy. The government slid deeper into debt as it sustained not just these insolvent firms but also the banks that carried their debts (valued in the trillions of dollars) even as it attempted to stimulate individual consumption. Although Japan has recently begun moving, in fits and starts, toward economic recovery, it continues to struggle in its second decade of slow to no growth and slow to no reform of its political economic system.

There is no question that the cooperation between government and business and the state's laserlike focus on economic development fostered Japan's postwar economic boom, but that boom was sustained by a political economic structure that is collapsing under its own weight. Producer-oriented industrial and financial policies and protectionist trade measures secured the continuation of LDP rule and guaranteed bureaucrats the autonomy to focus on development. But such policies also sowed the seeds of destruction in Japan's well-oiled conservative political economy. The corporate welfare that sustained the politicians' positions and the bureaucrats' vision came at the expense of a competitive Japanese economy and led to the collapse of Japan's vaunted lifetime employment. That same welfare, moreover, has offered little relief or consolation to Japan's battered consumers. Although the destructive inefficiencies were tolerable during the boom years, they have become a political albatross to the still-powerful LDP and a potential millstone for the Japanese economy.

Just as the loosening of the iron triangle may gradually be bringing political competition to Japan, so, it is hoped, will the slow privatization of state-owned financial institutions, the painful weaning of firms from government protection, the loosening of the bonds of companies to their *keiretsu* alliances, and the weakening of employees' ties to their firms bring much-needed market competition and efficiency into the Japanese economy. But precisely because changes are painful, even the reformer Prime Minister Koizumi struggled to deliver on his bold promises of structural reform in the face of conservative bureaucratic and political resistance. More recent LDP governments have been both weaker and less motivated to pursue economic reforms, leading many observers to conclude that the key to substantial economic liberalization remains political reform.

FOREIGN RELATIONS AND THE WORLD

Despite the vicissitudes of Japan's external relations, its foreign affairs have been marked by several continuities worth noting. First, though insular, the Japanese have been inveterate adopters and adapters of things foreign. From Chinese ideograms to American popular culture, the Japanese have at key periods in their history pragmatically adopted and adapted foreign elements that they deemed beneficial. Second, the Japanese have generally maintained a hierarchical perception of the world, in which international entities (countries, empires, races), like internal entities (family members, classes, companies), are seen and ranked in hierarchical terms. Third, Japan's island status and catch-up strategy of mercantilist development have given the Japanese a very strong and sharply delineated sense of nationalism, which has made Japanese citizens highly responsive to calls for sacrifice on behalf of the nation when faced with a foreign challenge.[12]

Given these continuities, it should not surprise us that advocates of change in Japan are calling for *gaiatsu* (foreign pressure) or even a "third opening" of Japan (after Perry and MacArthur) as the impetus for change. Although the country's external dealings over the past century and a half have been the source of understandable anxiety and much military disaster, they have also been the impetus for beneficial change. By the same token, Japan's growing international stature has meant that both its economic success and its more recent problems have been spilling over into the rest of the world, with a variety of consequences.

If one were to view Japan's international relations as a series of concentric circles, the most immediate and significant circle would include Japan and its Asian neighbors. These Asian neighbors have felt most acutely both the cost and the benefit of Japan's military, economic, and cultural expansion. Under the promise (or guise) of a Greater East Asian Co-Prosperity Sphere, Japan first expanded its empire to Taiwan and Korea, then to the Chinese mainland, Southeast Asia, and the Pacific Islands. Japan brought oppressive colonial rule, imperial exploitation, and military destruction wherever it went but also built the economic infrastructure, transferred technology and training, and exported its version of developmental capitalism to several of its longer-held colonies. Moreover, Japan brought much of Asia into what it termed in the 1930s a **flying geese** pattern of economic development, with Japan at the head of a flock of dependent Asian economies. Japan offered leadership by exploiting its comparative advantage in advanced industries and then passing its skills on to the next tier as newer technologies became available. The second tier would do the same for the third, providing a ladder of industrial progress for (and Japanese dominance of) all of Asia.

Since Japan's defeat and its embrace of American-directed pacifist prosperity, the rest of Asia has viewed Japan with understandable ambivalence. On the one hand, though its constitution renounces war, Japan has never been required to atone for or even acknowledge its colonial and wartime legacies in the way that Germany has faced and frequently reexamined its Nazi past. The Japanese imperial army forced thousands of Korean and other Asian so-called

YASUKUNI

Located in a peaceful wooded setting in central Tokyo, *Yasukuni* Shrine was established as a national memorial during the nineteenth century to honor soldiers and others who had lost their lives fighting on behalf of the emperor. The U.S. occupation's mandate that the emperor renounce his divinity and that there be a complete separation of church and state forced the Japanese to privatize what had been a national shrine. In accordance with Shinto beliefs, the memorial offers a permanent resting place for the 2.5 million spirits of those who died in armed conflict and are enshrined there. The shrine has stirred much controversey because it honors among others the spirits of those convicted of war crimes during World War II, and it operates an on-site museum honoring Japanese war heroes that presents a highly sanitized if not revisionist interpretation of World War II. Most controversially, many Japanese politicians, including former Prime Minister Koizumi have paid regular visits to this "private" shrine in the face of acrimonious complaints from the leaders of foreign countries, particularly China and Korea, who see their nations as victims of Japan's aggression. Koizumi's successor, Abe Shinzo, an ardent nationalist who had visited *Yasukuni* in the past, did not visit during his year long tenure as prime minister nor have his successors, Fukuda Yasuo or Aso Taro.

comfort women to serve as sexual slaves for its troops in the field, and—like most conquering armies—committed a host of other war-related atrocities. Koreans, Chinese, and other Asians are troubled that Japanese textbooks have largely glossed over these events and that many of Japan's conservative politicians and prime ministers have made annual pilgrimages to *Yasukuni* Shrine, a controversial Shinto shrine honoring Japan's war dead (see *"Yasukuni,"* p. 236). Chinese and Korean patriots regularly take to the streets demanding Japanese apologies and threatening boycotts of Japanese products.

On the other hand, the past benefits and future fruits of investment in and trade with the world's second-largest economy make it difficult for the rest of Asia to turn its back on Japan. Despite memories of war, many Asians are more interested in educational opportunities in Japan or employment in a Japanese factory than they are in an apology for past offenses. Despite historical tensions, its own economic woes, and the growth of other economies in the region, Japan remains by far the lead goose as the region's largest provider of trade, technology, and investment capital.

But Japan's very real economic clout in Asia must be placed in the broader context of its continued economic—and, particularly, military—dependence on the United States. Within the context of Japan's overwhelming defeat in World War II and America's decades-long struggle with the Soviet Union, this patron-client relationship made good sense and good foreign policy for both the United States and Japan. For the United States, Japan offered a shining (if still superficial) example to the world of American-sponsored liberal capitalist democracy and was certainly worth the cost of military protection and the toleration of mercantilist trade policies. For their part, most Japanese (with notable exceptions on the left and the right) were content to develop the economy under this military and economic protection.

During the 1950s and 1960s, the United States and Japan were happy with their roles in the relationship. The United States sponsored Japan's return as a member in good standing of the U.S.-sponsored world trading system and cold war alliance, and Japan turned its full attention to rebuilding its economy. But by the 1970s, its very success as dutiful client led to a divergence in Japan's economic and security relations with its American patron. Whereas both the United States and Japan have been willing to retain a relationship of military protection and dependence, Japan's rapid economic growth has made it a full-fledged economic competitor. Over the past three decades, the United States and Europe have engaged in trade wars with Japan and have increased their demands that Japan end its economic protectionism and shoulder the burdens of an economic colleague, demands to which Japan has acceded, albeit at times reluctantly.

Japan, the rest of Asia, and the rest of the world have changed too much to allow the persistence of Japan's status quo. Critics inside and outside Japan express frustration over the country's split personality as economic giant and political pygmy and call for Japan to become a "normal" or "ordinary" country. These terms mean different things to different advocates but typically entail the liberalization of Japan's economy and society, opening the country's borders to trade, investment, immigrants, and students, as well as the militarization of Japan, developing the ability to both defend itself and contribute to regional and global security. We have already discussed the obstacles to and prospects for economic and social change in Japan. Here, we turn finally to Japan's security and its political role in the world.

Despite a constitution that prohibits the use or threat of war in resolving conflicts (Article 9) and the presence of 33,000 U.S. troops on its soil, Japan is not without its own means of defense. It currently has a Self-Defense Force (SDF) of some 240,000 personnel and an annual military budget of nearly US$50 billion, ranking it fourth in the world in terms of military expenditures. Although sentiment in Japan since World War II has been decidedly pacifist, rising tensions on the Korean peninsula and the growing capacity of China's military (which ranks third in the world in expenditures) have shifted public opinion quite dramatically. Although only 33 percent of Japanese respondents in a 2007 opinion poll favored changing Article 9 of the constitution for reasons related to defense, this is nearly twice the percentage who advocated such a change in 2003 and four times the percentage in a 2001 poll.

At the same time, the United States and other countries are pressuring Japan not only to bear more of the burdens of its own defense but also to participate more fully in regional and global peacekeeping operations. They criticize Japan's so-called checkbook diplomacy, by which, for example, Japan offered US$13 billion to compensate for its inability to participate militarily in the Gulf War of 1991. Conservative Japanese governments have responded, using this convergence of *gaiatsu* (foreign pressure) with their own political and ideological interests to bolster the technological sophistication of Japan's military and the capacity to project force beyond its borders. Despite a great deal of controversy at home, Koizumi deployed naval refueling ships to the Indian Ocean in support of U.S. operations in Afghanistan in 2001 and later sent more than five hundred troops to help rebuild Iraq. In 2007, the parliamentary opposition in the upper house forced Prime Minister Fukuda's government to withdraw the support ships and resort to a scaled-back version of the policy to resume the refueling efforts in 2008.

But while a growing minority of Japanese is willing to accept a greater role for Japan's armed forces, most Japanese, and certainly most Asians, remain highly wary of Japanese militarism. Advocates of a nonmilitarized Japan argue that the country can and indeed has projected its power and influence abroad in a host of beneficial ways and that striving for militarized "normalcy" is contrary both to the intent of Japan's pacifist constitution and to the interests of Japan and the world. They argue that Japan need not be a military power to be a global power and point to numerous areas in which Japan has already shown global leadership. They note that Japan has been among the world's top donors of international aid, giving over US$10 billion in foreign-development assistance annually. They contend that Japan ought to focus its efforts on areas of global benefit, such as technology transfers to developing countries and for the challenge of global warming, rather than engage in a dangerous and costly arms race with China or other countries.

Can Japan use its unique constitutional restrictions to create a new kind of nonmilitary hegemony? More fundamentally, can it implement the economic and political reforms necessary to right its economic ship in time to maintain its international influence? Will these reforms come from above, from below, from the outside, or perhaps not at all (or not in time)? In this, as in other areas, Japan's capacity and willingness to change in the twenty-first century will prove crucial to its future security, as well as to its economic prosperity and political stability.

CURRENT ISSUES

DIVIDED GOVERNMENT

One of the reasons that prediting future Japanese foreign (and domestic) policy has become so difficult is because Japanese policy making has entered uncharted waters. Long accustomed to a legislative process that remained an internal and harmonious affair among wisened bureaucrats and willing LDP politicians, the ruling LDP government finds itself facing a divided parliament for the first time in its history. Capitalizing on voter dissatisfaction with bureaucratic scandal and LDP unresponsiveness, the opposition Democratic Party of Japan (DPJ) gained enough seats in the 2007 upper house elections to secure a majority.

Although the constitution allows the more powerful lower house to override an upper house vote with a two-thirds majority (which the LDP and its Clean Government Party coalition partner can still muster), on several key issues the DPJ has embarrassed and even hobbled the ruling LDP's efforts to push through its policy agenda. The House of Councillors stymied plans to renew Japan's Maritime Self-Defense Force refueling mission in 2007. In 2008, the DPJ challenged high-profile government legislation on an unpopular gas tax and then passed an unprecedented no-confience motion over a health insurance plan. Although a no-confidence motion, coming from the upper house, is nonbinding on the prime minister's government, the opposition seeks with these efforts to weaken support for the government and ultimately force a dissolution of the lower house and a general election.

PERCENTAGE OF THE POPULATION OVER AGE 65

Year	Japan	United States	Germany	France	Italy	United Kingdom
1990	12.05	12.39	14.96	13.99	15.32	15.72
1995	14.54	12.47	15.47	15.09	16.62	15.74
2000	17.37	12.30	16.40	15.97	18.07	15.75
2010	22.54	12.89	20.19	16.62	20.63	16.95
2020	27.85	16.29	22.51	20.45	23.85	20.21
2030	29.57	20.17	27.70	23.85	28.58	24.34
2040	33.23	21.00	30.92	26.16	34.53	27.24
2050	35.65	21.09	30.97	26.73	35.87	27.31

Source: "International Comparison: Ratio of 65 Years Old and Over among Total Population," Statistics, Web Japan: Gateway for All Japanese Information, http://web-japan.org/stat/stats/01CEN2C.html (accessed 16 July 2005)

While this divided government has frustrated the ruling LDP and slowed legislation, those hoping for greater democracy in Japan point to this "cohabitation" of parliament by opposing parties as a healthy sign and vindication that political reforms over the past two decades may slowly be taking hold.

ARTHRITIC JAPAN

Policy gridlock may not be good news as Japan seeks to cope with an economic challenge that is not yet as acute as the structural problems that prolonged its recession but could be even thornier. Japan finds itself at the forefront of a problem facing many advanced industrial societies: the convergence of an aging population and dwindling fertility rates. Like Italy, Germany, and other European societies, Japan has a population aged sixty-five and older that is rapidly increasing relative to the rest of its society. As noted in the table above ("In Comparison: Percentage of the Population Over Age 65"), the ratio of Japanese senior citizens to the total population was only 12 percent in 1990 and is currently less than 20 percent but is expected to climb to more than 35 percent by 2050. By mid-century, demographers predict, Japan will have 1 million centenarians and 30 percent fewer people overall, and nearly 1 million more people will die each year than are born.

The graying of Japan's population brings economic challenges that the United States and other countries certainly face as well, including health and financial care. But the most acute problem that Japan faces, far more so than other advanced countries, is that of a declining workforce. The size of Japan's workforce peaked in 1998 and is expected to decline rapidly as fewer and fewer Japanese reach maturity each year to replace retiring and dying workers. Japan is certainly not alone in this problem, but whereas most advanced societies have expanded their labor pools by more fully integrating women and immigrants into the workplace, Japan has not been willing to embrace either group. In fact, experts have argued for years that one of the quickest boosts to Japan's economic slowdown would be the expansion of work opportunities for women, particularly in management and other professional roles. Only 40 percent of Japanese women currently work (compared with nearly 47 percent in the United States and 48 percent in Sweden). But resistance to expanding women's role in the workforce remains high in this traditionally patriarchal society.

Even if Japanese women were fully empowered, economists and demographers agree that the only long-term hope for stabilizing Japan's population and workforce is to increase and sustain immigration over many years. Absent this source of workers, consumers, and taxpayers, experts predict that Japan's economy will not just decline but may very well collapse! As its traditional views toward the role of women have kept women at home, Japan's conservative attitudes toward ethnic purity and the insular nature of Japanese society have severely restricted immigration. Whereas the United States accepted an average of 1 million immigrants a year during the 1990s, it took Japan a quarter century to absorb 1 million immigrants into its society. Moreover, most of these immigrants are brought in from other Asian countries to fill low-paying "dirty, dangerous, and difficult" jobs. Japan has done little to attract immigrants with specialized knowledge and skills, once again handicapping its economy. These issues pose the question of whether Japan is willing or indeed even able to make the changes necessary to assume its global responsibilities or compete internationally in a twenty-first-century world that has changed so considerably while many aspects of Japan have not.

NOTES

1. T. J. Pempel and Keiichi Tsunekawa, "Corporatism without Labor: The Japanese Anomaly," in Philippe Schmitter and Gerhard Lehmbruch, eds., *Trends toward Corporatist Intermediation* (New York: Sage, 1990).

2. Margaret A. McKean, "Equality," in Takeshi Ishida and Ellis S. Krauss, eds., *Democracy in Japan* (Pittsburgh: University of Pittsburgh Press, 1989), p. 203.

3. There was also an underclass or outcast segment of society known as the *eta* or *burakumin*, discriminated against for their work in the ritually impure trades, such as tanning and butchering.

4. John Dower, *Embracing Defeat: Japan in the Wake of World War II* (New York: W. W. Norton, 1999), p. 45.

5. Prime ministers have served, on average, just over two years. The obvious recent exception to this is the five-year tenure of Koizumi Junichiro from 2001 to 2006. Cabinet members turn over even more frequently than prime ministers, with an average tenure of less than one year (finance ministers have averaged approximately sixteen months).

6. Although the population of voting districts was relatively balanced when districts were originally set up after the war, the LDP never reapportioned them even as the countryside became depopulated. In exchange for their voting loyalty, farmers were assured high prices for their rice and were given voting clout as much as three times greater than that of urban voters, who were less likely to vote for the LDP. In the 1990 lower house elections, for example, opposition parties won nearly 54 percent of the popular vote but garnered only 44 percent of the seats.

7. Under the old system, all representatives were elected from multimember districts (MMDs) in which voters had a single nontransferable vote (SNTV) that they cast for a specific candidate instead of a party list. This unusual MMD/SNTV system created a variety of incentives and consequences, both for the LDP, which benefited immensely from the rules, and for opposition parties struggling to compete.

8. T. J. Pempel, *Regime Shift: Comparative Dynamics of the Japanese Political Economy* (Ithaca, NY: Cornell University Press, 1998).

9. Tanaka, the consummate Japanese politician, was perhaps also Japan's most influential and successful. He fostered a powerful LDP faction in the early 1970s and served as prime minister from 1972 to 1974 but was forced to resign and ultimately convicted of financial misdeeds involving huge sums of money.

10. See, for example, Karel van Wolferen, *The Enigma of Japanese Power* (New York: Alfred Knopf, 1989).

11. The seminal study in this field is Chalmers Johnson, *MITI and the Japanese Miracle: The Growth of Industrial Policy, 1925–1975* (Stanford, CA: Stanford University Press, 1982).

12. Clyde Prestowitz, *Trading Places* (New York: Basic Books, 1988), pp. 82–94.

GLOSSARY OF KEY TERMS

administrative guidance   Informal policy negotiations among Japanese bureaucrats and corporate executives.

amakudari   Literally "descent from heaven," in which retiring Japanese senior bureaucrats take up positions in corporations or run for political office.

Article 9   Clause of Japan's postwar constitution requiring Japan to renounce the right to wage war.

Aso Taro   Current LDP prime minister, serving since September of 2008.

capitalist developmental state   Japan's modern neo-mercantilist state, which has embraced both private property and state economic intervention.

Diet   Japan's bicameral parliament.

flying geese   Model of regional economic development imposed on Asia in the 1930s with Japan at the head of a flock of dependent Asian economies.

House of Councillors   Upper and weaker chamber of Japan's parliament.

House of Representatives   Lower and more powerful chamber of Japan's parliament.

industrial policy   Government measures designed to promote economic and industrial development.

iron triangle   Conservative alliances among Japan's elite bureaucrats, conservative politicians, and big-business executives.

Japan Post   Japan's national postal system, including the world's largest savings institution, which began privatization in 2005.

keiretsu   Japan's large business conglomerates.

koenkai   Japan's local political support groups or political machines.

Koizumi Junichiro   Populist Japanese LDP prime minister (2001–2006).

Liberal Democratic Party (LDP)   Japan's conservative political party, which has governed Japan for all but one year since the party's inception in 1955.

MacArthur, Douglas   U.S. general who presided over the seven-year occupation of Japan (1945–1952).

Meiji oligarchs   Vanguard of junior samurai who led Japan's nineteenth-century modernization drive.

Meiji Restoration   Japan's 1867–1868 "revolution from above" that launched Japan's modernization in the name of the Meiji emperor.

money politics   Informal system of gifts, favors, and huge sums of money required to lubricate Japanese politics.

pork-barrel projects   Government appropriation or other policy supplying funds for local improvements to ingratiate legislators with their constituents.

"rich country, strong military"   Mercantilist slogan promoting Japan's nineteenth-century modernization efforts.

sakoku **("closed country")**   Tokugawa Japan's policy of enforced isolation from the seventeenth to the nineteenth centuries.

samurai   Japan's feudal-era warrior retainers.

Self-Defense Force   Japan's military, ostensibly permitted only defensive capacity.

shogun   Dominant lord in feudal Japan.

Taisho democracy   1920s' era of tentative democratization in Japan.

Tokugawa   Military clan that unified and ruled Japan from the seventeenth to the nineteenth centuries.

Yasukuni   Controversial Shinto shrine honoring Japan's war dead.

Yoshida Shigeru   Influential Japanese LDP prime minister from 1946 to 1954, with a brief hiatus.

zombies   Japanese firms rendered essentially bankrupt during Japan's recession but propped up by banks and politicians.

WEB LINKS

Japanese Constitution **www2.gol.com/users/michaelo/Jcon.index.html**
Japanese Prime Minister and Cabinet
  www.kantei.go.jp/foreign/index-e.html
Japanese Statistical Data **web-japan.org/stat/index.html**
  This site, affiliated with Japan's Ministry of Foreign Affairs, provides regularly updated statistical information in twenty-three different categories, including aging, crime, elections, media, women, and others.
National Diet of Japan **www.lib.duke.edu/ias/eac/Kokkai.htm**
  Includes useful links to House of Councillors and House of Representatives, with extensive information on membership, relative strength of parties, and electoral and legislative procedures.

7 RUSSIA

Head of state: President Dmitri Medvedev
(since May 7, 2008)

Head of government:
Prime Minister Vladimir Putin
(since May 8, 2008)

Capital: Moscow

Total land size: 17,075,200 sq km

Population: 141 million

GDP at PPP: 2.08 trillion US$

GDP per capita at PPP: $14,700

Human development index ranking: 67

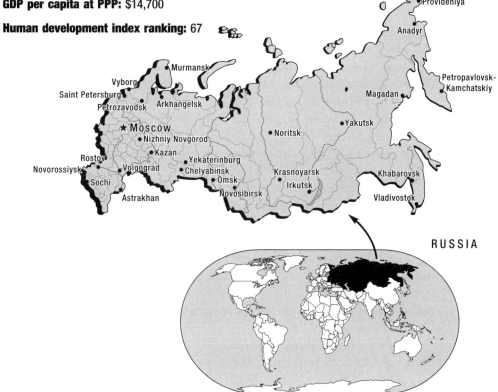

INTRODUCTION

Why Study This Case?

For decades, Russia stood out from all other countries in the world. Established in 1917, the Soviet Union (which included present-day Russia and many of its neighbors) was the world's first Communist state. The Soviet Union served as a beacon for Communists everywhere, a symbol of how freedom and equality could be transformed if the working class could truly gain power. It provoked equally strong responses among its opponents, who saw it as a violent, dangerous, and power-hungry dictatorship. The rapid growth of Soviet power from the 1930s onward only intensified this tension, which eventually culminated in a cold war between the United States and the Soviet Union following World War II. Armed with thousands of nuclear weapons and ideologically hostile, these two states struggled to maintain a balance of power and avoid a nuclear holocaust. Until the 1980s, many observers believed that humanity would eventually face a final, violent conflict between these two systems.

Yet when the Soviet Union's end finally came, it was not with a bang but a whimper. In the 1980s, the Soviet Union saw the rise of a new generation of leaders, who realized that their system was no longer primed to overtake the West, economically or otherwise. The general secretary of the Soviet Union's Communist Party, Mikhail Gorbachev, attempted to inject limited political and economic reforms into the system to overcome these problems. His reforms, however, seemed only to exacerbate domestic problems and polarize the leadership and the public. Gorbachev's actions resulted in the actual dissolution of the Soviet Union and the formation of fifteen independent countries, one of which is Russia.

How would Russia be reconstructed from these ruins? Like many of the other post-Communist countries, Russia had to confront the twin tasks of forging democracy and establishing capitalism in a country that has had little historical experience of either process. How does a nation go about creating a market economy after Communism? How does it go about building democracy? Russia proved a fascinating studying in the quest to build new institutions that reconcile freedom and equality in a manner far different from that of the previous regime. We can learn a lot from Russia's attempt at meeting this awesome challenge.

Nearly twenty years on, the prospects for Russian democracy and development look increasingly dubious. After a decade of incomplete and chaotic political and economic reform, the country has increasingly moved away from a liberal economic system and liberal democracy, under the leadership of President—and now Prime Minister—**Vladimir Putin**. During the Putin presidency, Russia saw the weakening of democratic institutions. This included the state, where central and regional sources of political power were restricted, and ever-greater authority concentrated in the hands of the president. Limitations on federalism, electoral reform, and other changes all were directed at reducing political power beyond the presidency. Within society as well, steps were taken to restrict civil society, with the state bringing the mass media under control and increasingly preventing independent political parties or nongovernmental organizations from functioning. An incipient democratic ideology has been replaced by a focus on Russian nationalism, with anti-Western overtones and an emphasis on the country's humiliation by outside forces and its need to reassert its authority and role within the region and the world.

Similarly, the economy, which in the 1990s experienced a drastic and incomplete shift to private property and market forces, has seen both institutions increasingly curtailed. Powerful economic leaders whose fortunes rose during this period, the **oligarchs**, have in most cases been divested of their wealth, driven from the country, or imprisoned. Assets, particularly natural resources, have been renationalized in many cases or transferred to individuals close to Putin. Although economic growth has characterized the past few years, it is largely propelled by a rise in oil and gas prices. In economics and politics, the country has fallen under control of the *siloviki* (men of power), individuals who, like Putin, have their origins in the security agencies. And yet Putin's consolidation of power and limitations on democracy and the market garnered tremendous public support. Tired of the chaos of market reforms, cynical about post-Communist politics, and angry about Russia's loss of power in the world, the people appreciated Putin's promise to restore order and Russian pride. To a large extent, he succeeded.

In 2008, President Putin stepped down from power, having served the two-term limit on the office. His handpicked successor, Dimitri Medvedev, easily won the presidential election and promptly appointed Putin to be his prime minister. Given Medvedev's non-*siloviki* background and the power inherent in the presidential office, some expected that this transfer of power could represent a break with the Putin era. But for now, Putin appears to still call the shots, which raises the question of the extent to which the ostensible functions of political institutions in Russia even matter. In many ways, Russia has become as opaque as it was under Communism, a worrying sign for the rest of the world. In the next few pages we will look at the past, the promise, and the present of Russian politics and political change, with an eye toward where this country may be headed in the future.

Major Geographic and Demographic Features

As we study Russia's geography, the first thing we notice is the country's vast size. Even when viewed separately from the various republics that made up the Soviet Union, Russia is nearly four times the size of the United States and covers eleven time zones. Yet much of this land is relatively unpopulated. With some 141 million people, Russia's population is far smaller than that of the United States or the European Union (with around 300 million and 500 million, respectively). Much of the Russian population is concentrated in the western, geographically European part of the country. Russia's east, Siberia, is a flat region largely uninhabited because of its bitterly cold weather. Siberia represents an interesting comparison to the American frontier experience. While Americans moved westward toward the Pacific Ocean in the nineteenth century to find new lands to settle, Russians moved eastward toward the same ocean. Alaska was part of the Russian Empire until it was sold to the United States in 1867. But Russian and American experiences of the frontier were quite different. In America, the amenability of the climate and soil helped spread the population across the country and reinforce a sense of pioneer individualism. In contrast, the harsh conditions of Siberia meant that only the state could function effectively in much of the region, where it developed infrastructure and created populated communities. Many of the people who, to some extent, settled Siberia, before and after 1917, were political prisoners sent into exile.

Because of Russia's vast size and location, the country has many neighbors. Unlike the relative isolation of North America, Russia shares borders with no fewer than fourteen countries. Many of these countries were part of the Soviet Union and are considered by Russians to remain in their sphere of influence (not unlike the way in which many Americans view Latin America). But Russia also shares a long border with China, a neighbor with whom it has often had poor relations. Russia also controls a series of islands in the Pacific that belonged to Japan until 1945, a situation that remains a source of friction between the two countries. Russia has long felt uneasy about its neighborhood. Over the centuries, unable to rely upon oceans or mountains as natural defenses, it has been subject to countless invasions from Europe and Asia. Physical isolation has never been an option.

While Russia may suffer from some intemperate climates and uneasy borders, it benefits in other areas. The country is rich in natural resources, among them wood, oil, natural gas, gold, nickel, and diamonds. Many of these resources are concentrated in Siberia and are thus not easy to extract, yet they remain important and have been central in the recent growth of the Russian economy.

Historical Development of the State

FOREIGN INVASION, RELIGION, AND THE EMERGENCE OF A RUSSIAN STATE

Any understanding of present-day Russia and its political struggles must begin with an understanding of how the state has developed over time. While ethnically Slavic peoples have lived in European Russia for centuries, these peoples are not credited with founding the first Russian state. Rather, credit is usually given to Scandinavians (Vikings) who expanded into the region in the ninth century C.E., forming a capital in the city of Kiev. Nonetheless, the true origins of the Russian state remain open to debate. This issue is highly politicized, as many Russians reject the notion that foreigners were first responsible for the organization of the Russian people. The dispute even involves the very name of the country. Scholars who believe in the Viking origin of the Russian state argue that the name Russia (or **Rus**) comes from the Finnish word for the Swedes, *Ruotsi,* which derives from a Swedish word meaning "rowers." Those who dispute this claim argue that the name is of a tribal or geographic origin that can be traced to the native Slav inhabitants.[1]

Whatever its origins, by the late tenth century the Kievan state had emerged as a major force, stretching from Scandinavia to Central Europe. It had also adopted **Orthodox Christianity**, centered in Constantinople (modern-day Istanbul). Orthodoxy developed distinctly from Roman Catholicism in a number of practical and theological ways, among which was the perception of the relationship between church and state. Roman Catholics came to see the pope as the central leader of the faith, separate from the political power of Europe's kings. Orthodoxy, however, did not draw such a line between political and religious authority, a situation that, some argue, stunted the idea of a society functioning independently of the state.

Another important development was the Mongol invasion of Russia in the thirteenth century. The Mongols, a nomadic Asian people, first united under Genghis Khan and controlled Russia (along with much of China and the Middle East) for over two centuries. During this time, Russians suffered from widespread economic destruction, massacres, enslavement, urban depopulation, and the extraction of resources. Some scholars view this occupation as the central event that set Russia on a historical path separate from that of the West, one leading to greater despotism and isolation. Cut off from European intellectual and economic influences, Russia did not participate in the Renaissance, feel the impact of the Protestant Reformation, or develop a strong middle class.

Not all scholars agree with this assessment, however. For some, the move toward despotism had its impetus not in religion or foreign invasion but in domestic leadership. Specifically, they point to the rule of Ivan the Terrible

TIME LINE OF POLITICAL DEVELOPMENT

Year	Event
1237–40	Mongols invade
1552–56	Ivan the Terrible conquers the Tatar khanates of Kazan and Astrakhan; establishes Russian rule over the lower and middle Volga River
1689–1725	Peter the Great introduces reforms, including the subordination of the church, the creation of a regular conscript army and navy, and new government structures
1798–1814	Russia intervenes in the French Revolution and the Napoleonic Wars
1861	Edict of Emancipation ends serfdom
1917	Monarchy is overthrown and a provisional government established; Bolsheviks in turn overthrow the provisional government
1918–20	Civil war takes place between the Red Army and the White Russians, or anti-Communists
1938	Joseph Stalin consolidates power; purges begin
1953	Stalin dies
1956	General Secretary Nikita Khrushchev denounces Stalin
1985	Mikhail Gorbachev becomes general secretary and initiates economic and political reforms
1991	Failed coup against Gorbachev leads to the collapse of the Soviet Union; Boris Yeltsin becomes president of independent Russia
1993	Yeltsin suspends the parliament and calls for new elections; legislators barricade themselves inside the parliament building, and Yeltsin orders the army to attack parliament; Russians approve a new constitution, which gives the president numerous powers
1994–96	In war between Russia and the breakaway republic of Chechnya, Chechnya is invaded, and a cease-fire is declared
1996	Yeltsin reelected
1999	Yeltsin appoints Vladimir Putin prime minister and resigns from office; Putin becomes acting president
1999	Russia reinvades Chechnya following a series of bomb explosions blamed on Chechen extremists
2000	Putin elected president
2004	Putin reelected
2008	Medvedev becomes president; Putin becomes prime minister

(1533–1584), who came to power in the decades following Russia's final independence from Mongol control. Consolidating power in Moscow rather than Kiev, Ivan began to assert Russia's authority over that of foreign rulers and began to destroy any government institutions that obstructed his consolidation of personal power. In a precursor to the Soviet experience, Ivan created a personal police force that terrorized his political opponents. Though Ivan is viewed in much of Russian history as the unifier of the country, many historians see in him the seeds of repressive and capricious rule.[2] Whatever his legacy, it was with Ivan's rule that we can see the emergence of a single Russian emperor, or **czar** (from the Latin word *Caesar*), who exercised sovereignty over the nation's lands and aristocrats.

We might argue that no one factor led to Russia's unique growth of state power and its dearth of democratic institutions. Religion may have shaped political culture in a way that influenced how Russians viewed the relationship between the individual and the state. Historic catastrophes like Mongol rule may have stunted economic growth and cut the country off from the developments that occurred elsewhere in Europe. Political leadership might also have solidified certain authoritarian institutions. None of these conditions, individually, may have had a strong influence on the country's development, but taken together they served to pull Russia away from the West. This interpretation of events has been reemphasized of late in Russian politics.

Ivan's death left Russia with an identity crisis. Did it belong to Europe, one of numerous rival states with a common history and culture? Or did differences in history, religion, and location mean that Russia was separate from the West? Even today, Russia continues to confront this question. Some rulers, most notably Peter the Great (1689–1725), saw Westernization as a major goal. This was typified in the relocation of the country's capital from Moscow to St. Petersburg, to place it closer to Europe. Peter consulted with numerous foreign advisers in his quest to modernize the country (particularly the military) and to carry out administrative and educational reforms. In contrast, reactionaries like Nicholas I (1825–1855) were hostile to reforms. In Nicholas's case, the hostility was so great that in the last years of his reign even foreign travel was forbidden. Reforms, such as the emancipation of the serfs in 1861, proceeded over time but lagged behind the pace of changes in Europe. As Russia vacillated between reform and reaction, there was continuity in the growth of a centralized state and a weak middle class. Industrialization came late, emerging in the 1880s and relying heavily on state intervention. This inconsistent modernization caused Russia to fall behind its international rivals.

THE SEEDS OF REVOLUTION

The growing disjunction between a largely agrarian and aristocratic society and a highly autonomous state and traditional monarchy would soon foster revolution. As Russia engaged in the great power struggles of the nineteenth and twentieth centuries, it was battered by the cost of war, and national discontent grew. In 1904, Russia and Japan came into conflict as each sought to gain control over portions of China. To Russia's surprise, Japan asserted its military strength and quickly proved itself the more modern power, defeating Russia. In 1905, Russia experienced a series of domestic shocks in the form of protests by members of the growing working class, who had migrated to the cities during the rapid industrialization of the previous two decades. The Revolution of 1905 forced Nicholas II to institute a series of limited reforms, including the creation of a legislature (the **Duma**). Although these reforms did quell the revolt, they were not revolutionary (the changes themselves were limited), nor did they bring stability to Russia. Shortly thereafter, the czar began to weaken the very rights and institutions he had agreed to. Meanwhile, many radical political leaders refused to participate in these new institutions and sought the removal of the czar himself.

World War I was the final straw. The overwhelming financial and human costs of the war exacerbated domestic tensions, weakening rather than strengthening national unity. As the war ground on, Russia faced food shortages, public disturbances, and eventually a widespread military revolt. The czar was forced to step down in March of 1917, and a non-Communist, republican leadership took control, unwisely choosing to remain in the war. This provisional government had little success asserting its authority. As disorder and public confusion grew, Communist revolutionaries, led by Vladimir Ilich Lenin (1870–1924), staged a coup d'état. This was no mass rebellion but rather an overthrow of those in power by a small disciplined force. After a subsequent civil war against anti-Communist forces, Lenin began transforming Russia, which was renamed the Soviet Union: the first Communist state in world history.[3]

THE RUSSIAN REVOLUTION UNDER LENIN

In many aspects, Lenin's takeover was a radical, revolutionary event, but in other ways the new Communist government fell back on the conservative institutions of traditional Russian rule. Under Lenin, local revolutionary authority (in the form of **soviets**, or workers' councils) was pushed aside, though it was given superficial recognition in the new name of the country: the Union of Soviet Socialist Republics. Similarly, although the Communist Party embraced Russia's multinational character by creating a federal system around its major ethnic groups, the new republics had little power. Authority was vested solely in the Communist Party, which controlled all government and state activity. Alternative political parties and private media were banned. A secret-police force, the **Cheka**, was formed to root out opposition; it would later become the **KGB**, the body that would control domestic dissent and supervise overseas surveillance. The "commanding heights" of industry were nationalized, that is, seized by the state in the name of the people. Managing all of this newfound power was a growing bureaucratic system, composed of the ***nomenklatura***—a term that refers to the politically influential jobs in the state, society, or economy and the Communist Party appointees who staffed them. The Communist state took on an enormous task of managing the basic economic and social life of the country. This helped justify the state's high degree of capacity and autonomy.

Yet even under Lenin's harsh leadership, the Soviet state did not reach its zenith. For the Soviet leadership, 1917 was intended to be simply a first step in a worldwide process. The historian Mary McAuley writes evocatively of Soviet telephone operators ready to receive the call that revolution had broken out elsewhere in the world in response to their triumph.[4]

As the years passed without other successful revolutions, the Soviet Union had to confront the possibility that it alone might have to serve as the vanguard of world revolution. Its focus had to shift so that domestic politics, not spreading revolution, would be paramount. Yet many old revolutionaries (those who had taken part in the 1917 events) had little interest in the day-to-day affairs of the party and state. One exception was Joseph Stalin (1879–1953), whose power over the party grew after Lenin died. By appointing loyal followers to positions of power and slowly consolidating his control over party and state institutions through increasingly brutal means, Stalin was able to force out other revolutionary leaders. One by one, those who had fought alongside Lenin in the revolution were removed from power, demoted, exiled, imprisoned, and/or executed.

STALINISM, TERROR, AND THE TOTALITARIAN STATE

By the late 1930s, Stalin had consolidated control over the Soviet party-state and was thus free to construct a totalitarian regime that reached across politics, economics, and society. As a central-planning bureaucracy was created to allocate resources and distribute goods, the last vestiges of private property were wiped away. The impact of this was particularly dramatic in agriculture, which was forcibly collectivized. Farmers often destroyed their livestock and crops rather than surrender them to the state, and many wealthy peasants were executed. Agricultural production collapsed, and as many as 7 million lives were lost in the resulting famine. In industry, the government embarked on a policy of crash industrialization in an attempt to catch up with and overtake the capitalist countries.

Power was thus centralized to a degree unknown before Soviet rule.[5] This growing power of the bureaucratic elite was enforced by the secret police, who turned their attention to anyone suspected of opposing Stalin's rule, whether outside the party or within. Millions of people were imprisoned or executed. Terror became a central feature of control, and the innocence or guilt of those arrested was often largely irrelevant. Finally, Stalin's power was solidified through a cult of personality that portrayed him as godlike, incapable of error and infinitely wise.

STABILITY AND STAGNATION AFTER STALIN

With Stalin's death, the Soviet leadership moved away from its uses of unbridled terror and centralized power, and Stalin's excesses were publicly criticized to a certain extent. The basic feature of the Soviet system, however, remained in place. Power was vested in the **Politburo**, the ruling cabinet of the Communist Party. At its head was the general secretary, the de facto leader of the country. Government positions, such as national legislators, the head of the government, and the head of state, were controlled and staffed by the Communist Party and simply implemented the decisions of the Politburo. The economy also remained under the control of a central-planning bureaucracy, and although Russians were no longer terrorized, security forces continued to suppress public dissent through arrest and harassment. All basic aspects of Soviet life were decided by the *nomenklatura*. The party elite became, in essence, a new ruling class.

For a time, this system worked. The state was able to industrialize rapidly by controlling and directing all resources and labor. Moreover, in its infancy, Soviet rule enjoyed a high degree of legitimacy among the public. Even in the darkest years of Stalin's terror, citizens saw the creation of roads, railways, massive factories, homes and schools, and the installation of electricity, where none had existed before. If freedom was nonexistent, a rough level of equality was created, and many people were given education, jobs, health care, and retirement benefits, often for the first time. The Soviet people saw their standard of living increase dramatically.

But by the 1960s, some party leaders had begun to realize that a system so controlled by a central bureaucracy would become too institutionalized and conservative to allow necessary change or innovation. General Secretary Nikita Khrushchev, who took office in 1953 after Stalin's death, made an initial attempt at reform. But Khrushchev was thwarted by the party-state bureaucracy and was forced from his position by the Politburo in 1964. He was replaced by Leonid Brezhnev, who rejected further reform and placated the *nomenklatura* by assuring them that their power and privileges were protected. Under these conditions, economic growth slowed, and those in power became increasingly corrupt and detached, using their positions to gain access to scarce resources. Public cynicism grew as economic development declined. In the 1960s, it was still possible to believe that Soviet development might match or even surpass that of the West. But by the 1980s, it was clear that in many areas the Soviet Union was in fact stagnating or falling behind.

THE FAILURE OF REFORM AND THE COLLAPSE OF THE SOVIET STATE

Upon Brezhnev's death, in 1982, a new generation of political thinkers emerged from the wings, seeking to transform the Soviet state. Among its members was Mikhail Gorbachev, who became general secretary in 1985. Unconnected to the Stalinist period, Gorbachev believed that the Soviet state could be revitalized through the dual policies of **glasnost** (political openness) and **perestroika** (economic restructuring). Gorbachev believed that a limited rollback of the state from public life would encourage citizen participation and weaken the *nomenklatura*'s powerful grip. Similarly, it was thought that economic reforms would increase incentives and reduce the role of central planning, thus improving the quality and quantity of goods. Overall, the ruling bodies expected that the Soviet people would be better off, and that the legitimacy of the Communist Party would be restored.

In hindsight, we can see that the attack on state power was disastrous for the Soviet system. Gorbachev unleashed forces he could not control, leading to divisive struggles inside and outside the party. Nationalism grew among the many ethnic groups in the various republics, with some going so far as to demand independence. Critics attacked the corruption and incompetence of the party, calling for greater democracy, and others demanded a greater role for market forces and private property. Still others were disoriented by the changes, upset by the implication that the Soviet past had in fact been a historical dead end.[6]

Party leaders became polarized over the pace and scope of reform. Among them was **Boris Yeltsin**, an early protégé of Gorbachev's who was sidelined as his calls for change grew more radical. Ejected from the Politburo, Yeltsin was elected president of the Russian Soviet Socialist Republic (the largest republic in the ostensibly federal Soviet system). The moderate Gorbachev was now under attack from two sides: Yeltsin and other reformers who faulted Gorbachev's unwillingness to embrace radical change, and conservatives and reactionaries who condemned his betrayal of Communism. The very institutions of the party-state, unresponsive and unchanged for decades, began to unravel. In some ways, the Soviet Union began to resemble the chaotic Russia of pre-1917, and the tensions eventually came to a head. In August 1991, a group of antireform conservatives sought to stop the disintegration of Soviet institutions by mounting a coup d'état against Gorbachev, hoping that the party-state and the military would join their ranks. With Gorbachev under arrest by the conspirators, Yeltsin led the resistance, famously denouncing the takeover while standing atop a tank. The army refused to back the coup, and it unraveled within two days.

As the coup collapsed, so did Gorbachev's political authority. The public blamed him for the chaos that had led up to the takeover (in fact, the conspirators were members of his cabinet, appointed to solidify his power). Moreover, Gorbachev was eclipsed by Yeltsin, whose authority was bolstered by his heroic stance against the coup. Yeltsin seized the opportunity to ban the Communist Party, effectively destroying what remained of Gorbachev's political base. In December 1991, Yeltsin and the leaders of the various Soviet republics dissolved the Soviet Union, and Yeltsin became president of a new, independent Russia. He held this position until 1999, when he named his prime minister, the otherwise unknown Vladimir Putin, acting president. Putin won the presidential elections in 2000 and again in 2004; he stepped down in 2008. In 2008, Putin was replaced by Dimitri Medvedev who, as with Putin before him, was relatively unknown until he was chosen by Putin to run for the office.

POLITICAL REGIME

Any sense that Russia could be considered a democracy has in the past few years come to an end. Certainly, the country enjoys a much higher degree of freedom than did its Soviet predecessor. But while a number of democratic structures have been built since 1991, they remain weakly institutionalized and increasingly restricted or ignored by the president. It is hard to speak of Russia as even an illiberal democracy, since it has few elements of democracy that in fact function to any meaningful degree. Whereas in the past decade democratic institutions and civic organizations were weak and uninstitutionalized, under the Putin era they were effectively stifled. An illiberal regime presumes the existence of democratic institutions whose power and legitimacy are uncertain. In Russia now, it is difficult to point to any institutions among state or society that are allowed to contribute to democratic activity in any meaningful way. As we consider Russia's political regime, therefore, we need to keep in mind the extent to which any of these powers or responsibilities as elucidated by the constitution jibe with politics in reality.

Political Institutions

THE CONSTITUTION

The Russian constitution is a document borne of violent conflict. Russia emerged in the aftermath of a failed coup d'état by opponents of radical reform. This history is different from the recent history of most other Eastern European Communist countries, where Communist leaders were removed from power through public protest and elections. Although the Soviet state was dissolved, many elements of the old regime, including its political leaders, remained intact and in power. Boris Yeltsin thus faced a set of political institutions that were largely unchanged from those of the previous era. This carryover led to conflict. Most problematic was the battle between President Yeltsin and the existing parliament. At first, the parliament was a bicameral body consisting of the Congress of People's Deputies and the Supreme Soviet, both of which remained packed with former party members. The parliament initially supported Yeltsin but soon clashed with him over the speed and scope of his economic reforms.

As Yeltsin sought increased reform, the parliament grew so hostile that it sought to block

---

ESSENTIAL POLITICAL FEATURES

- Legislative-executive system: semi-presidential
- Legislature: Federal Assembly
- Lower house: State Duma
- Upper house: Federation Council
- Unitary or federal division of power: federal
- Main geographic subunits: republics, provinces, territories, autonomous districts, federal cities (Moscow and St. Petersburg)
- Electoral system for lower house: proportional representation
- Electoral system for upper house: appointed by local executive and legislature
- Chief judicial body: Constitutional Court

---

his policies (including constitutional reform) and impeach him. In September 1993, Yeltsin responded by dissolving the parliament. Yeltsin's parliamentary opponents barricaded themselves in their offices, attempted to seize control of the national television station, and called for the army to depose the president. The army sided with Yeltsin, however, containing his opposition and suppressing the uprising with force. This support paved the way for Yeltsin to write a new constitution, which was enacted in 1993. Though the new constitution formally swept away the old legislative order, it could hardly be described as an auspicious beginning for democracy and facilitated the development of a system that emphasized presidential power.

The Branches of Government

THE KREMLIN: THE PRESIDENCY AND THE PRIME MINISTER

For centuries, Russians have referred to executive power, whether in the form of the czar or in the form of the general secretary, as the **Kremlin**. Dating back to the eleventh century, the physical structure known as the Kremlin is a fortress in the heart of Moscow that has historically been the seat of state power. Today, much of the Kremlin's power is vested in the hands of the presidency, as elaborated in the 1993 constitution. That constitution created a powerful office through which the president could press economic and political changes despite parliamentary opposition. Under Yeltsin and Putin, the result was a semi-presidential system in which the president serves as head of state while a prime minister serves as head of government. Power is divided between the two offices, but the president has held an overwhelming amount

WHO IS VLADIMIR PUTIN?

Vladimir Putin's rapid rise to power caught virtually every observer by surprise, since not many were aware of his existence just a few years before his election to the presidency. Putin was born in 1952 in Leningrad (now St. Petersburg) and studied law at the state university there. From his early years, he showed an interest in the security services; in 1975, upon graduation, he joined the KGB, which is the Soviet intelligence agency. What exactly Putin did during his time in the KGB is unclear. It is known that from 1984 to 1990 he was stationed in East Germany, where he learned German and was charged with recruiting KGB agents and keeping tabs on opposition movements in that country.

In 1991, Putin left the KGB to work for the new mayor of Leningrad, Anatoly Sobchak, who had been one of Putin's college professors and supported Yeltsin during the 1991 coup. In 1994, Putin became deputy mayor of the city (by then renamed St. Petersburg) and was soon after made deputy chief administrator for the Kremlin, charged in part with helping to implement presidential decrees. In 1998, Yeltsin made Putin head of the Federal Security Service and in 1999 appointed him prime minister.

In December 1999, Yeltsin resigned from office, naming Putin acting president in advance of the 2000 presidential elections. During that time, Putin was viewed as a decisive actor, in contrast to the increasingly unstable (and often drunk) Yeltsin. Of particular importance for Putin's career was the second Chechen war, which he initiated in 1999 after a series of terrorist apartment-house bombings in Russia killed more than three hundred people. After becoming president, Putin filled many of the top posts in his administration with the so-called *siloviki* (men of power) whose careers began in the military or the KGB. At the same time, he effectively marginalized any rivals to power, either inside or outside government. Even as he finished his two terms in office, he managed the election of the new president, viewing Medvedev as someone unlikely to check Putin's power base. Putin's current role as prime minister and head of the political party United Russia means that it is clear he will continue to play a prominent role in Russian politics, with many political analysts expecting that he will return to the president's office in due course. Putin continues to enjoy overwhelming support from the public for his tough leadership. (He is known for his coarse language and aggressive manner.) Many Russians believe that Putin saved the country from collapse and has restored its place in the world.

of executive power. The president is directly elected to serve a four-year term, may serve no more than two terms, and may be removed only through impeachment. Vladimir Putin was elected in 2000 after serving as Boris Yeltsin's last prime minister and was reelected in 2004, having faced little serious competition for the office. His successor, Dimitri Medvedev, was similarly selected by Putin to run for the office in 2008 and won easily, since other candidates were effectively barred from running for the office.

On paper, the president's powers are numerous. It is the president, not parliament, who chooses and dismisses the prime minister and other members of the cabinet. The lower house of parliament, the State Duma, may reject the president's nominee, but if it does so three times, the president must dissolve the Duma and call for new elections. The president cannot dissolve the Duma in the year following parliamentary elections, however, or in the last six months of his term. The president also appoints leaders to seven federal districts that constitute all of Russia, allowing him to oversee the work of local authorities.

The president may propose and veto bills and can issue decrees, which are laws that do not require legislative approval, are often not made public, and may not be challenged by citizens in the courts. President Yeltsin frequently relied on decrees to bypass his obstreperous legislature, and even with a more compliant body, Putin often used the power of the decree to enact law.[7]

Another source of power lies in the president's control of important segments of the state. The president has direct control over the Foreign Ministry,

STRUCTURE OF THE GOVERNMENT

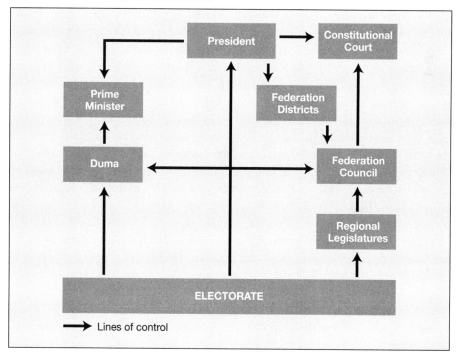

Lines of control

the Defense Ministry, and the Interior Ministry (which handles the police and domestic security) as well as the armed forces. The president also controls the successor to the KGB, the **Federal Security Bureau (FSB)**, which manages domestic and foreign intelligence. Presidential control over these so-called power ministries allows the office a great deal of influence in foreign affairs and domestic security.

As in the United States and other presidential or semi-presidential systems, it is difficult to remove the Russian president; impeachment is possible only on a charge of high treason or another grave crime. The impeachment process must first be approved by the high courts, after which two thirds of both houses of parliament must vote in support of the president's removal. In 1999, the parliament attempted to impeach President Yeltsin on various charges, including his 1993 conflict with the legislature, economic reform, and the war in **Chechnya**. None of the charges passed.

In contrast to that of the president, the prime minister's role is to supervise those ministries not under presidential control and to propose legislation to parliament that upholds the president's policy goals. The Russian prime minister and other members of the cabinet, unlike their counterparts in many other parliamentary systems, are not appointed from and need not reflect the relative powers of the various parties in parliament. Because of the president's ability to choose the prime minister and other members of the cabinet, there is less of a need to form a government that represents the largest parties in parliament. Under Putin, Russian prime ministers were largely career bureaucrats chosen for their technical expertise or loyalty to the president rather than party leaders who have climbed the ranks in parliament. However, the appointment of Putin to be prime minister "under" Medvedev raised many questions about the nature of the semi-presidential system in Russia. In advance of the 2008 presidential elections Putin made it clear that he expected to become prime minister in return for his selection of Medvedev to run for president, and that, in contrast to the past, he now viewed the prime minister's office as the real locus of power. While there have been no constitutional changes since the elections, it is clear that Putin's personal authority has moved with him to the prime minister's office. Putin continues to wield significant power, as was seen in the war with Georgia (see "Current Issues," p. 281). This has lead to a great deal of confusion inside and outside of Russia as to where executive power really lies. It has also become clear that Putin's personal authority has trumped institutional authority, making our understanding of Russian politics through reference to the constitution problematic.

THE LEGISLATURE

Given the power of the Russian presidency, does the national legislature have any real role? Its lack of effectiveness is certainly consistent with the Soviet past. Under Communist rule, the legislature served as little more than a rubber stamp, meeting for a few days each year simply to pass legislation drafted by party leaders. Today, Russia's parliament has little direct influence over the course of government, but it would be an exaggeration to say that nothing has changed since Soviet times.

Russia's bicameral parliament is known officially as the Federal Assembly. It comprises a lower house, the 450-seat State Duma, and an upper house, the 178-seat **Federation Council**. Members of both houses serve four-year terms, with power residing in the lower house. The Duma has the right to initiate and accept or reject legislation and may override the president's veto with a two-thirds vote. The Duma also approves the appointment of the prime minister, though repeated rejections can lead to its dissolution. As in other legislatures, the Duma can call a vote of no confidence in opposition to the prime minister and his government. Should a no-confidence vote pass, the president may simply ignore the decision. If a second such vote passes within three months, however, the president is obliged to dismiss the prime minister and cabinet and call for new Duma elections.

In the instances of prime-ministerial approval and votes of no confidence, then, the Duma wields unpredictable weapons. The Duma's opposition to the prime minister (and, by extension, the president) could lead to its own dissolution. Under the right circumstances, however, the Duma's opposition could lead to elections that strengthen the position of opposition parties. Of course, the exact opposite could also occur. Thus far, the Duma has not put this power to use, though in 1998 the Yeltsin administration was forced to withdraw a candidate for prime minister after he was rejected twice. In that case, the president feared new elections would only bring more anti-Yeltsin representatives into the Duma.

Another area in which the Duma can wield some power is in the drafting of legislation. During the Yeltsin administration, the majority of legislation originated in the Duma, much of it dealing with substantial public issues. This changed under the Putin administration, however, and most legislation now originates with the president or prime minister, in keeping with most European parliamentary systems.

The legislature's powers have become increasingly theoretical over the past decade. As the Duma became dominated by a single party loyal to Putin (see "The Electoral System," p. 263), it has receded from any significant political role. This is not to say that its constitutional functions could not again become important should the balance of power inside Russia shift. For now, however, that is not the case.

As the upper house, the Federation Council holds are even less power than does the Duma. The Federation Council primarily serves to represent local interests and act as a guarantor of the constitution. The body represents each of the eighty-nine federal administrative units, with two representatives from each. Since 2002, one representative has been selected by the governor of each region and another by the regional legislature. Prior to that time, governors and the heads of the regional legislatures served directly in the Federation Council. Although the Federation Council does not produce legislation, it must approve bills that deal with certain issues, including taxation and the budget. Other Duma legislation may also be considered by the Federation Council if it acts within two weeks of the proposal's passage by the lower house. If the Federation Council rejects legislation, the two houses compromise to approve it, or the Duma may override the upper house with a two-thirds vote. The Federation Council also has the ability to approve or reject presidential appointments to the Constitutional Court, declarations of war and martial law, and international treaties; as a result, it often weighs in publicly on international relations, though with little direct influence. Over the past decade, we have not seen the Federation Council serve as a particularly powerful institution inside the Russian state.

THE JUDICIAL SYSTEM

One of many tasks that Russia faces in the coming decades is the establishment of the rule of law. By this we mean a system in which the law is applied equally and predictably, with no individual being exempt from its strictures. Prior to Communist rule, Russia had not developed any real traditions of a law-bound state: the czar acted above the law, viewing the state, society, and economy as his subjects and property. This continued into the Soviet era. Under Stalin, any legitimate legal structures were undermined by the arbitrary use of terror and the vast secret police force that maintained its own courts and jails. While these excesses were curbed after Stalin's death, the legal system remained an important means by which opposition to the Communist regime could be checked. Moreover, no constitutional court existed. By definition, the party represented the true expression of the people's will and therefore by definition could not act in an unconstitutional manner. In reality, the party was not representative of the people's interests. The lack of legal safeguards served only to undermine public confidence in the political order.

Given the history of weak legal institutions, it has been difficult to generate the rule of law in the post-Communist era. Since 1991, Russia has faced an explosion in corruption, as economic and political change created opportunities to generate fortunes and allowed those with political power to gain access to new sources of wealth. Organized crime has also become a serious problem, with criminals actively trafficking in drugs, prostitution, money laundering, and private-business "protection." Meanwhile, the public has lost faith in the state to protect it or mete out justice.

At the top of the Russian legal structure lies the **Constitutional Court**. First developed under Mikhail Gorbachev's reforms in the late Soviet era, the Constitutional Court has nineteen members, nominated by the president and confirmed by the Federation Council to serve fifteen-year terms. As in other countries, the court is empowered to rule on such matters as international treaties, relations between branches of government, violations of civil rights, and the impeachment of the president. It has the power of both abstract review (the ability to rule on constitutional issues even when a case has not been brought before it) and concrete review (the ability to rule on specific cases). One role the Constitutional Court does *not* play is that of a court of last appeal for criminal cases; this is the responsibility of the Supreme Court.[8]

At the start of the Putin administration, the president promised to implement what he called a "dictatorship of law," though the result tended to be more dictatorship than law. A decade later, the country remains mired in what President Medvedev has called "legal nihilism," wherein legal codes are not respected and courts are frequently used to settle political vendettas. The international corruption-watchdog group Transparency International ranks countries on a 10-point scale, with 1 being the most corrupt; in 2004, Russia was given a rating of 2.2, having dropped significantly over the past few years from an already poor standing. Russia now shares the dubious distinction of corruption far worse than India or China and commensurate with unstable Nigeria.[9]

Similarly, while the Constitutional Court could serve as a tool of political stability, it has shown little action of late. In the 1990s, local authorities often flouted national laws, while in the past few years it is the executive who has shown similar disdain for the rule of law. In 2008, the Constitutional Court was further distanced, literally, from political power when President Putin signed a degree moving the court from Moscow to St. Petersburg. Members of the court opposed the move, complaining that it would reduce their effectiveness.[10]

The Electoral System

Like Russia's other institutions, its electoral structure has changed dramatically over the past fifteen years. In the late Soviet period, the president of Russia was indirectly elected by the republic's Congress of People's Deputies. Just prior to the 1991 coup, the presidency was made a directly elected office; Yeltsin won the election and retained the office when Russia became an independent country. Since that time, Russians have elected their president directly. Elections were held in 1996, when Yeltsin was reelected; in 2000 and 2004, when Putin came to office; and in 2008, when President Medvedev was elected. Presidential elections are relatively straightforward: if no candidate wins a majority in the first round, the top two candidates compete against each other in a second round. A president can serve no more than two terms.

In 2000 and 2004, Putin won a majority (over 70 percent in 2004), eliminating the need for a runoff. In 2008, in spite of the overwhelming public support for Medvedev as Putin's anointed successor, the state nevertheless tightly controlled the election. Candidates were barred from running, the media was effectively closed to opposition candidates, and challengers to Medvedev were regularly harassed. As with Putin, Medvedev won with over 70 percent of the vote.

The Duma has also held regular elections. Between 1990 and 1993, these elections were conducted using a plurality system of single-member districts (SMDs), as in the United Kingdom and the United States. With the 1993 constitution, however, Russia adopted a mixed system similar to that found in Japan and Germany. That is, half the seats in the Duma were elected through a plurality system, and the other half were selected in multimember districts (MMDs) using proportional representation (PR), in which the share of the vote given to a party roughly matches the percentage of seats it is allotted. In addition, Russia relied upon a 5 percent threshold for the PR section of the ballot to keep smaller parties out of the parliament.

Under Putin, this system was again changed to consolidate political power. This change makes for an interesting study of the effects of electoral systems, in that the change was away from SMD and toward pure PR. Often we assume that PR allows for greater diversity in parties and ideology, since smaller groups can win a share of the seats in the legislature. Since the collapse of the Soviet Union, however, political parties have not proven to be a major problem for the presidency, since they are weakly institutionalized and tend to coalesce around leaders rather than ideologies (see "The Party System and Elections," p. 266). What the Putin administration found irritating, however, was that the SMD portion of the ballot allowed for independent candidates, often representing regional or particular interests, to win a seat in the Duma and advance their agenda. In 2003, for example, nearly half of the SMD seats in the Duma were won by independent candidates. As a result, the 2007 Duma elections were held solely under PR. Furthermore, the party threshold was raised from 5 to 7 percent, making it even more difficult for small parties to enter to Duma. Electoral reforms also prevented parties from forming an electoral bloc to compete as a single group to overcome the threshold.

Local Government

One of the greatest battles within the institutional framework of Russia over the past fifteen years has been between the central government and local authorities. Just as tensions between Soviet central power and the republics contributed to the dissolution of the Soviet Union, so, too, has Russia confronted centrifugal tendencies since 1991. Like the Soviet Union that preceded it, Russia is a federal system that has a bewildering array of 89 different regional bodies: 21 republics, 50 *oblasts* (provinces), 6 *krays* (territories), 10 autonomous *okrugs* (districts), and 2 federal cities (Moscow and St. Petersburg).

Each of these bodies has different rights, not only for each category but also within the bodies in each category. The twenty-one republics, for example, represent particular non-Russian ethnic groups and enjoy greater rights, such as the ability to have their own constitution and a state language alongside Russian. In the early 1990s, several republics went so far as to make claims of sovereignty that amounted to near or complete independence; in Chechnya, the result was outright war against the central authorities, which was brought under control only after years of warfare and terrorism. In contrast, many other federal bodies are much weaker. This difference is commonly termed **asymmetric federalism**, a system in which power is devolved unequally across the country and its constituent regions, often as the result of specific laws negotiated between a region and the central government. Each of the eighty-nine territories, regardless of its size or power, has its own governor and local Duma; as described above, the governor appoints one representative to the Federation Council, and the Duma appoints the other.

As in other areas, the Putin administration took several steps in recent years to reduce regional power and make the territories comply with national laws and legislation. First, a number of regional laws and agreements between the central and local governments were changed or annulled, compelling the regions to revise their laws and agreements to bring them in accordance with the Putin administration. In some cases these local laws were clearly unconstitutional, but in many other cases these changes were simply to reduce local power. In addition, in 2000 the government created seven new federal districts that encompass all of Russia and its constituent territories. Each district region is headed by a presidential appointee, who serves to bring the local authorities more directly under presidential control. It was alongside this reform that Putin also barred the regional governors and heads of local Dumas from serving directly in the Federation Council. Previously, membership comprised the governors and Duma heads of each region.[11]

Finally, in 2004, all local governors became directly appointed by the president, with their appointments subject to confirmation by the local legislatures. Prior to that time they had been directly elected by the citizens in the region. While these changes have severely curtailed federalism in Russia, local offices continue to have power. Many local mayors remain directly elected, and regional governors, while now appointed by the president, still can prove to be a thorn in the side of the national government, particularly in those regions that had established significant amounts of autonomy under Yeltsin.

POLITICAL CONFLICT AND COMPETITION

The Party System and Elections

The Russian transition from a one-party system has not been easy. Russia has yet to see the institutionalization of political parties with clear ideologies and political platforms. In most democracies, parties serve to articulate and aggregate preferences and hold elected officials accountable. It is hard to say that such a system currently exists in Russia. Instead, multiple parties rise and fall between elections, for a number of reasons. The relative weakness of ideology among the public (see "Society," p. 272) contributes to some extent. A second factor is the power of the presidency. Largely divorced from the legislature and its party politics and standing alongside a weak prime-ministerial office, the presidency has contributed to the creation of parties that largely serve one individual's presidential ambitions. Making clear distinctions between the parties, or even keeping track of them, is thus difficult.[12] However, we can create a few categories.

COMMUNIST AND LEFTIST PARTIES

Since 1991, the strongest and most institutionalized party has been the **Communist Party of the Russian Federation (CPRF)**, successor of the Soviet-era organization. Though banned by Yeltsin in 1991, the party was allowed to reorganize and draws support from a substantial portion of the population that is ambivalent about or hostile to the political and economic changes that have taken place since the 1980s. The CPRF has done consistently well since the 1993 elections, when it captured 10 percent of the Duma's seats; in the 1995 elections it increased this share to one third, becoming the largest single party in the Duma. Although its vote share subsequently declined, it remains the second-largest party in the Duma. The CPRF's head, Gennady Zyuganov, has come in second in every presidential election since 1996 (though in recent years this has meant less than 20 percent of the vote).

The CPRF differs from most other post-Communist parties in Eastern Europe; many of these parties broke decisively from their Communist past in the 1990s and successfully recast themselves as social democratic organizations. In contrast, the CPRF remains close to its Communist ideology, though it has recently attempted to move in a more nationalist direction and to capitalize on nostalgia for the Soviet Union. However, the party has not shown any significant opposition to the Putin or Medvedev administrations, nor is it able to establish its nationalism as particularly distinct from that of the Putin/Medvedev governments. As the Russian population ages, the CPRF runs the risk of losing its base of support as its core of older backers die out.

LIBERAL PARTIES

In spite of Russia's move toward capitalism, liberalism has made relatively few inroads into political life, and even these have declined of late. Liberalism has had a standard-bearer in **Yabloko**, however, formed in 1993 by Grigory Yavlinsky, a former economic adviser to Mikhail Gorbachev. As a party, Yabloko has been pro-Western and pro-market economy, favoring stronger ties to the North Atlantic Treaty Organization and the European Union. Traditionally Yabloko drew support from white-collar workers and urban residents in the major cities, and its orientation can be described as somewhere between liberalism and social democracy. Similar to Yabloko is the **Union of Right Forces (URF)**, which was founded by Boris Nemtsov and Anatoly Chubais, former members of Boris Yeltsin's cabinet. In the 1990s these two parties tended to gain around 5 to 10 percent of the vote in the Duma elections; by the 2000s, this began to decline such that by the 2007 elections with the removal of SMD seats in Russia, both parties lost all of their representation in the Duma. In the aftermath of these elections, Yavlinsky stepped down from Yabloko's leadership, and there continue to be discussions about merging Yabloko, URF, and other oppositional movements into a single viable party.

Why has liberalism found such rocky soil in Russia? Several factors are at work. First, given the historically statist and collectivist nature of Russian politics, a liberal political ideology is not likely to find a wide range of popular support. Second, Russia's middle class, a likely base of liberal support, remains relatively small. Third, Yabloko and URF were tainted by accusations that they were instruments of the oligarchs, individuals who became rich in the aftermath of Communism, often through connections to the government. Finally, the difficult economic and political transition after Communism is viewed by many Russians as a humiliation forced on them by the West. As such, political parties that embody Western values have little resonance with the public: indeed, with the rise of nationalism in Russia, such parties are often viewed as tools of the West or traitors to Russia.

NATIONALIST PARTIES

During the 1990s, one of the most infamous aspects of the Russian party spectrum was the strength of nationalism, as manifested by the ill-named **Liberal Democratic Party of Russia (LDPR)**, headed by Vladimir Zhirinovsky. Neither liberal nor democratic, the LDPR espoused a wild rhetoric of xenophobia and anti-Semitism, the reconstitution of the Soviet Union (by force if necessary), and a general hostility toward liberal capitalism and democracy.[13] In the 1993 elections, many observers were shocked by the LDPR's electoral strength and its gain of 14 percent of the seats in the Duma. Subsequently, the LDPR's fortunes waned to the point where it barely met the 5 percent PR threshold in the 1999 elections. In recent elections, however, the LDPR has staged something of a comeback and now stands as the third-largest party in the Duma. This resurgence can be attributed in part to the LDPR's consistent support for Putin and his government: indeed, many observers suspect that the LDPR is effectively funded by the government to serve as a pseudo-opposition that can be controlled. The LDPR's current manifesto speaks of the period between 1965 and 1975 as the "best years" of the country, but the manifesto is otherwise unremarkable and has lost much of the reactionary content that characterized the party a decade ago. The standard-bearer for extreme nationalism is now the tiny National Bolshevik Party, which spouts an ever-changing mixture of Communist and fascist ideas. Headed by former émigré Eduard Limonov, the party is a staunch opponent of United Russia and Putin, and it is noteworthy for its strong youth following and public demonstrations. The party was banned in 2007 and a number of its members arrested, but the party continues to stage small protests.

PARTIES OF POWER AND UNITED RUSSIA

Although the **parties of power** have consistently represented the largest segment of parties in the Duma, they cannot be described in ideological terms. Russia's parties of power can be defined as those parties created by political elites to support their political aspirations. Typically, these parties are highly personalized, lack specific ideologies or clear organizational qualities, and have been created by prime ministers during or following their time in office. For example, the Our Home Is Russia Party was created in advance of the 1995 Duma elections as a way to bolster support for Prime Minister Victor Chernomyrdin and President Yeltsin. Lacking any specific ideology, the party nevertheless took the second-largest share of seats (after the CPRF). Once Chernomyrdin left office, in 1998, the party's share of support rapidly declined. Subsequently, in the 1999 elections, two contending parties of power emerged. Fatherland–All Russia was formed to advance the presidential aspirations of former prime minister Yevgeny Primakov and Moscow mayor Yuri Luzhkov. Meanwhile, Unity was created to bolster Putin's campaign. After Unity beat Fatherland–All Russia handily in the Duma elections, Primakov and Luzhkov withdrew from the presidential campaign, and in 2001 the two parties merged to form United Russia, essentially climbing on the bandwagon of power. Drawing on Putin's popularity and the government's increased control over the electoral process, United Russia swept the 2003 elections. In 2008, as Putin left the presidency, he formally became head of the party.

It seems likely that United Russia is the final manifestation of these parties of power, given that it has now had a decade to gain control over various segments of the state and economy and to eliminate its rivals in the process.

United Russia boasts a cult of personality around Putin, a youth wing that advances the cause of the party and harasses its opponents, and party membership as a means for individual access to important jobs in the state and economy. In that sense, the party has developed a strongly corporatist tendency, and it seems likely to institutionalize its control for the long term.[14] Future aspirants to office are thus more likely to work their way up through United Russia than to form their own party of power.

Overall, the 2007 Duma elections showed that these could no longer be considered democratic, even in the most generous definition of the term. Smaller parties were shut out of the electoral process in favor of United Russia and those few parties (CPRF and LDPR) tolerated by Putin. The media, largely in the hands of the state, also gave overwhelming support to United Russia. International observers concluded that the elections were not fair and did not meet basic standards for democratic procedures.[15]

Civil Society

As with political parties, civil society in Russia has developed in fits and starts, created largely from scratch. Prior to the 1917 Russian Revolution, civil society was weak, constrained by low economic development, authoritarianism, and feudalism. With the revolution, what little civil society did exist quickly came under control of the Soviet authorities, who argued that only the party could and should represent the so-called correct interests of the population. A wide range of corporatist institutions were thus created to link the people to the party, through the workplace, media, culture, and even leisure activities. The few remnants of independent organized life, such as religion, were brought under tight control. With the advent of glasnost in the 1980s, however, civil society slowly began to reemerge. The first independent group that resulted from liberalization may have been the fan club of a Moscow soccer team, established in 1987. By late 1989, tens of thousands of groups had appeared and were playing an important role in eroding Soviet rule.

After 1991, civil society grew dramatically in Russia. But this growth also highlighted tensions in society; of late, civil society has again come under state pressure. One notable area is that of religion. Historically, Russians have been overwhelmingly, if nominally, Orthodox Christians, with smaller numbers belonging to other faiths. Although Soviet-imposed atheism seriously weakened the role of religion, in recent years Orthodox Christianity has to a degree reclaimed a role in public life. Other religious movements also have emerged or reemerged, ranging from Islam and Buddhism to evangelical Christians and various New Age groups. For example, in the 1990s the Japanese religious group Aum Shinrikyo had its second-largest following in Russia. This became particularly worrisome to authorities after the group used nerve gas attempting to cripple the Tokyo subway system and was found to be pursuing other weapons of mass destruction.

As the Russian government has turned more toward nationalism as a source of legitimacy, it has also emphasized Orthodox Christianity as a central part of what makes Russia unique (and distinct from the West and Western liberalism). The church, in turn, has supported the restoration of its special relationship to the state and sought to restrict evangelical or other groups from proselytizing in the country. In 1997, the Russian government placed restrictions on the ability of new religious groups to proselytize or build seminaries and educational programs; despite this restriction, however, many religious groups continue to actively function, though they may find it difficult to formalize their religious activity. It remains difficult for many religious groups to build houses of worship or rent facilities.

This leads us to the broader observation that through such regulations the government is seeking to co-opt civil society, pulling it into a tighter orbit around the state by legislating what kinds of organizations can and cannot exist and what they can and cannot say. The government has been particularly aggressive in opposing civic groups that are openly critical of the government. Tools to control civil society include the tax code, used to investigate sources of income; the process of registering with the authorities, which can be made difficult; and police harassment and arrest on various charges ranging from tax evasion to divulging state secrets. In 2006, the government passed its toughest measures against nongovernmental organizations, requiring that all such organizations be approved by the government, restricting their funding from foreign sources, and making the organizations subject to regular inspections and pre-approval for any activity. A number of foreign nongovernmental organizations have been forcibly closed by the Russian authorities; others have left, citing their inability to work. The result, as the organization Human Rights Watch put it, is that the Russia state is destroying nongovernmental organizations by choking them on bureaucracy.[16]

The final obstacle to civil society in Russia is the means through which it can express itself, most notably the media. The collapse of Communism saw the emergence of a lively Russian media that for the first time was able to speak critically on an array of issues. Many of the most powerful segments of the media, however, such as radio and television, remained in the hands of the state or came under the control of oligarchs with ties to Yeltsin. Indeed, Yeltsin's victory in the 1996 elections was attributed in part to the strong support he received in the media, whose owners feared the repercussions should the Communist candidate come to power. Similarly, the media came to support Putin during his consolidation of power, viewing him as the successor to Yeltsin who would preserve the power of the oligarchs. In spite of this sup-

CIVIL SOCIETY AND THE "OTHER RUSSIA"

The strongest manifestation of Russian civil society and opposition to the current government is a loose movement known simply as the Other Russia. First formed in 2006, it has brought together a number of individuals and groups from across the political spectrum who are united by their opposition to the current political system. Most notable among them is former world chess champion Garry Kasparov (who also ran for president in 2008), former prime minister Mikhail Kasyanov, and Eduard Limonov of the National Bolshevik Party.

The diversity of the membership has been problematic for the movement, however, since more mainstream organizations, such as Yabloko and the Union of Right Forces, have been unwilling to associate themselves with more extremist leaders like Limonov. In spite of these difficulties, Other Russia has managed to present itself as the strongest opponent to the government, staging several protests in 2006 and 2007, the latter of which was forcibly broken up by the police with numerous individuals detained. That said, if Other Russia is the most prominent expression of civil society in Russia, it remains a minor force. News coverage of the organization is nonexistent, with the exception of media reports that suggest the group is threatening to overthrow the government, and public support for the organization is minimal.

port, Putin soon put strong economic pressure on much of the independent media, employing economic and legal tactics to acquire them and curb their editorial independence. During the past decade, all of the largest private television stations have come under direct state ownership or indirect state-controlled firms. To be fair, previous to Putin's tactics, these were hardly objective stations. Most of them served as the mouthpiece of their oligarch owners. But with nationalization, the Russian media has become much less diverse and are clearly oriented toward supporting those in power. Although a few open media outlets remain, particularly newspapers, their audience pales in comparison with radio and TV audiences, and they are often under pressure from the Kremlin to provide a pro-government slant or to not cover subjects that the government dislikes. Those that continue to pursue independent journalism find that their livelihoods and even lives can be at stake. Between 1996 and 2006, eighty-eight journalists were killed in Russia, second only to Iraq in deaths of journalists worldwide.[17] This statistic includes the noted journalist Anna Politkovskaya, whose work on the Chechen conflict in particular had raised the ire of the government. Politkovskaya was shot near her apartment in 2006, which the government blamed on a former Russian oligarch living in the West.

SOCIETY

Ethnic and National Identity

The Soviet Union, like the Russian Empire before it, was an ethnically diverse country made up of a number of republics, each representing a particular ethnic group. The dissolution of the Soviet Union, however, eliminated much of this ethnic diversity. Today, Russia is overwhelmingly composed of ethnic Russians, part of a larger family of Slavic peoples in Eastern Europe who are linked by similarities in language (and, to a lesser extent, culture and religion). Inside and outside the borders of the former Soviet Union there are Slavic peoples, such as Ukrainians, Poles, Belarusians, Serbs, Czechs, and Slovaks. In some areas, there is a strong affinity among the Slavs; in others, animosity is more the norm.

Over 80 percent of the Russian population is ethnically Russian, and although there are scores of minority groups, none represents more than 4 percent of the population. These minorities include other Slavic peoples, indigenous Siberians who are related to the Inuits of North America, and many others whose communities were absorbed into Russia as part of its imperial expansion over time. Russia is also dominated by a single religious faith, Orthodox Christianity, a branch of Christianity that is separate from the Roman Catholicism and Protestantism that dominate Europe.

NATIONAL IDENTITY AND CITIZENSHIP

The fact that ethnic Russians make up an overwhelming percentage of the Russian population has not helped the country avoid ethnic conflict. As in many other countries, some of Russia's ethnic groups have developed nation-

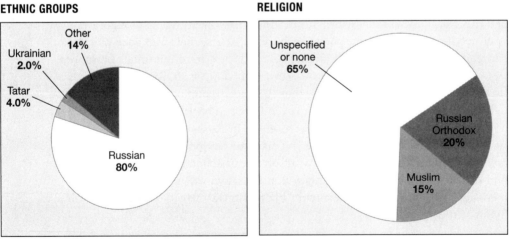

ETHNIC GROUPS

Other 14%
Ukrainian 2.0%
Tatar 4.0%
Russian 80%

RELIGION

Unspecified or none 65%
Russian Orthodox 20%
Muslim 15%

THE CAUCASUS

Source: University of Texas Austin, www.lib.utexas.edu/maps/common
wealth/chechnya_rev01.jpg (accessed 2 January 2009).

alist aspirations and seek greater autonomy from the central authorities, even
to the point of outright independence. Serious ethnic conflicts have been most
prominent among non-Russian populations in the mountainous region known
as the **Caucasus**, in southwestern Russia, near the Black Sea and Turkey. This
area is home to a diverse mixture of non-Slavic peoples with distinct languages, customs, and religious faiths. Whereas only about 10 percent of the
Russian population is Muslim, Islam is the dominant faith in many parts of
the Caucasus.

Most notable is the case of Chechnya. With the collapse of the Soviet Union
in 1991, the various republics broke off to form independent states. Chechnya, however, was not a republic in its own right but rather part of now-
independent Russia. Many Chechens believed that they, too, should have the
right of independence and so began to agitate for an independent state. The
conflict eventually led to outright war between Russian military forces and
Chechen rebels, in which much of the Chechen capital was demolished and
tens of thousands of civilians were killed or left homeless. During the mid-
1990s, an uneasy peace allowed Chechnya to function as a de facto independent country; in 1999, however, Russian forces reinvaded Chechnya in the
aftermath of a series of apartment-house bombings in Russia that may or may
not have been the work of Chechen rebels. Indeed, it was the second invasion
of Chechnya during Putin's tenure as acting president that helped pave the
way for his 2000 presidential victory. Although Russian forces regained con-

trol over the region, the conflict continued, most notably with a series of acts of terrorism. These included the seizure of an elementary school in Beslan in 2004, which concluded with an open firefight between Chechen terrorists and Russian forces, in which more than three hundred people died, many of them children. Ethnic conflict in the Caucasus has also spilled over into Russia's neighbors, most recently in Georgia, where ethnic conflict has drawn these two countries into war (see "Current Issues," p. 281).

Ideology and Political Culture

Not only political parties but also political ideologies in Russia are very much in flux. Beginning in 1917, essentially one ideological viewpoint was legally tolerated: that of Communism. Alternative views on the relationship between freedom and equality were long suppressed by the Soviet system. People could read Marx but not Jefferson or any other political thinker who had a different view. Since 1991, Russia has experienced a much greater diversity of ideas, but in many ways those ideas have not made a deep impact on political life. This is particularly true in the case of democratic values. Surveys taken between 2006 and 2008 found that a majority or plurality favored Putin's increased state control over the media and nongovernmental organizations and viewed democracy as a system of order and prosperity, rather than as a system of individual rights. (See, for example, "In Comparison: Russian Democracy," below.)

What values, then, can we speak of in Russia today? During the past decade we have seen the growing importance of nationalism as a central political value in Russia. This is not surprising; in a number of post-Communist coun-

Russian Democracy

Do you think the democratic system accepted in the West is suitable for Russia? Percent who agree:

Answer	Percent
Definitely no	15
Probably no	36
Probably yes	28
Definitely yes	7
Don't know	14

Source: Levada Center, nationwide survey, 18–21 January 2008, N = 1600.

tries, the decline of Communism ideology has meant that leaders have attempted to recast political legitimacy around the idea of patriotism and nationalism. In Russia, the government has actively promoted this trend by resurrecting symbols of the old Soviet regime, by downplaying the ruthlessness of the Stalin era, by evoking nostalgia for the Soviet Union's superpower status, and by asserting that Russia is not truly Western but somehow different (and thus not subject to such Western notions as pluralism). This sense of restoring a "great Russia" from the humiliation of the 1990s has found an eager audience among many Russians, but it runs the risk of even worse relations with Europe and the United States.

POLITICAL ECONOMY

How does one build capitalism, with its private property and open markets, in a country that historically has had little of either? This was the challenge that faced Russia as it moved away from Communism, and as in other areas, the results have been mixed: the new economic system is no longer Communist, nor is it liberal. Russia's economy has taken an upturn of late, but what this portends for the future development of the country is uncertain.

Like other former Communist countries, Russia undertook a series of dramatic reforms in the 1990s to privatize state assets and to free up market forces. Looking to the lessons of Poland and acting on the advice of Western economic advisers, Russia opted for a course of **shock therapy**, rapidly dismantling central planning and freeing up prices with the hope that these actions would stimulate competition and the creation of new businesses. The immediate result was a wave of hyperinflation: in 1992 alone, the inflation rate was over 2,000 percent. Savings were wiped out, the economy sank into recession, and tensions between President Boris Yeltsin and the parliament deepened, helping to foster the violent clash between the two branches of government in 1993. The Gross Domestic Product (GDP) contracted dramatically; only in the late 1990s did it begin to grow again.

Also during the late 1990s, Russia began the process of privatization, which was equally problematic. Privatization started with the distribution of vouchers to the public so that Russians could purchase shares that would give them ownership in formerly state-owned businesses. In many cases, however, businesses were not sold off to a large number of shareholders but became subject to **insider privatization**, with the former directors of these firms acquiring the largest shares. Therefore, wealth was not dispersed but concentrated in the hands of those who had strong economic and political connections. Despite the power of this old *nomenklatura* elite, however, a small number of new businessmen quickly emerged from various ranks of society, taking advantage of the environment to start new businesses and buy old ones,

LABOR FORCE BY OCCUPATION

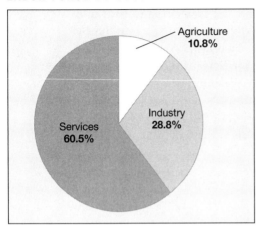

Agriculture
10.8%

Industry
28.8%

Services
60.5%

amassing an enormous amount of wealth in the process. It is this group that came to be known as the oligarchs. They were noted for their control of large amounts of the Russian economy (including the media), their close ties to the Yeltsin administration, and the accusations of corruption surrounding their rise to power.

The problem of the oligarchs was compounded in 1996, when the government instituted the loans-for-shares program. Strapped for cash (and fearful of a Communist Party victory in the 1996 presidential elections), the Yeltsin administration chose to borrow funds from the oligarchs in return for shares in those businesses that had not yet been sold off by the state—in particular, the lucrative natural-resources industry and the energy sector. Overall, foreign investment played a very small role in the Russian privatization process.

Debate continues over whether the particular policies of marketization and privatization were a mistake. Critics argue that market reforms failed to take into account the institutional constraints of Russia, among them the absence of private enterprise, a weak civil society and a risk-averse culture, the absence of the rule of law, and the centralization and large scale of industry. Moreover, the privatization process was not geared toward encouraging foreign investment and a greater distribution of assets but toward empowering a narrow elite that could support those in power. Other observers retort that given the weakness of the economic and political institutions in Russia, no reform was likely to be easy and that, if anything, Russia suffered from reforms that were too conservative rather than too radical. Despite these differences of opinion, Russia's ongoing economic problems are not simply the result of economic reform. Many of them are a function of the Soviet order that had reached a crisis stage, a condition that any policy would have been forced to confront.

The economic reforms of the 1990s left Russia in a difficult situation as Putin came to power. The government faced high rates of poverty, a great deal of inequality, the disproportionate power of the oligarchs, widespread corruption and organized crime, and an inefficient state. During this period the country's GDP declined by around 40 percent. Many analysts looked to Putin as a president who could rebuild the state and restore confidence in the economy, and now, ten years later, they see him as the architect of the country's economic transformation.

What has changed in the Russian economy? One of Putin's first steps was to act against the oligarchs and divest them of power. Using a variety of tools, one by one the oligarchs were stripped of their assets, many of which they had gained under the loans-for-shares scheme. A number of the most prominent oligarchs left the country to avoid imprisonment; others wound up in jail under dubious charges—including Mikhail Khordokovsky, at the time the richest man in Russia. This destruction of the oligarchs was extremely popular among the public, as many of the assets were renationalized and brought under Putin's control. In other cases, firms were redistributed among the *siloviki* who were close to Putin, forming a new economic elite around the security services—what some have referred to as "KGB, Inc."

As Putin stepped down from the presidency, he could point to a number of economic successes. The country now enjoys GDP growth similar to that of China (after many years of near negative growth) and the emergence of a new middle class and upper class, as per capita GDP has risen sharply and poverty declined. The economic situation is better than at any time since the collapse of the Soviet Union. However, we should be clear about the sources of this economic progress: 90 percent of the country's exports are oil, gas, and metal, all of which benefited from a dramatic rise in the international mar-

---

IN COMPARISON   FREE MARKETS

People are better off in free markets. Percent who agree:

Country	Percent
Nigeria	79
China	79
India	76
South Africa	74
United Kingdom	72
Canada	71
United States	70
Germany	65
Brazil	65
France	56
Mexico	55
Russia	53
Japan	49

*Data on Iran not available.

Source: Pew Center for the People and the Press, 2007.

kets. This in turn has provided the overwhelming majority of the country's GDP and government revenues. In contrast, foreign direct investment remains limited, disinclined by the high degree of corruption and political intervention in many areas of the economy, while small and medium-sized businesses are similarly hindered. Nor have Russia's traditional strengths in science been translated into new economic fields, in spite of the government's call for Russia to take the lead in such areas as nanotechnology.[18] Some observers now view Russia as moving toward a "resource trap" economy, as found in Iran or Saudi Arabia, where natural resources empower the state, weaken public control, and stifle other forms of economic development.[19] As in other resource-rich countries, in spite of Russia's national wealth, the country's overall standard of living is lower than its GDP would lead us to believe. The UN's Human Development Index places Russia at 67, just above Brazil (whose GDP is half that of Russia). What are the long-term implications for the Russian economy now that oil prices have fallen?

FOREIGN RELATIONS AND THE WORLD

Like the United Kingdom, Russia has struggled to deal with its position as a former superpower. Yet unlike the United Kingdom, Russia has been forced to confront this change suddenly and dramatically. Not long ago, the Soviet Union was one of the world's most powerful countries, boasting an impressive military, a nuclear arsenal, and a network of allies around the world. One of Mikhail Gorbachev's reforms was to reduce hostility between the Soviet Union and the West to foster greater cooperation between the superpowers. Little did he (or others) expect that this reconciliation would create such turmoil. The collapse of the Soviet Union has left Russia in an odd situation as it considers its role in the international community. Russian pride was dealt a blow when the Soviet Union splintered and the United States emerged as an unequaled international military power. In recent years, this has led to increasing international tension, with some viewing the advent of a new cold war. Why has reconciliation between Russia and the West failed?

The answer includes several elements. One factor was the slow eastward expansion of the North Atlantic Treaty Organization (NATO) and the European Union (EU). NATO was founded in 1949 as an international alliance that stood in opposition to the Soviet Union, but since 1989 many post-Communist countries have sought membership in it to cement their relationship with Western Europe and the United States. Russia has cooperated with NATO to some extent but has also been critical of it, still viewing it as an organization opposed to Russian interests. One specific source of tension was the 1990s wars in the former Yugoslavia, in which Russia expressed greater sympathy with the Serbs, a Slavic people who share the culture and Orthodox Christianity of many Russians. In contrast, NATO eventually intervened on behalf of the Muslims in Bosnia and Kosovo. Russia also saw NATO's eastward expansion, incorporating a number of former Communist countries, as an incursion into their traditional sphere of influence and territory. In spite of Russian pressure, from 1999 on a number of former Soviet satellites and even former republics of the Soviet Union itself have joined NATO, bringing the organization up to the border of Russia. To be certain, NATO has changed its international role since the collapse of Communism, providing support in such areas as the war in Afghanistan. However, for Russia the organization remains a force created to contain Russia, and its active role in the former Yugoslavia has only intensified Russian hostility.

Just as Russia confronts an ever-larger NATO alliance on its border, it must also contend with the enlargement of the European Union. In May 2004, the EU accepted ten new countries into its ranks, including three (Estonia, Latvia, and Lithuania) that had once been part of the Soviet Union, bringing the EU, as with NATO, up to the borders of Russia. And as with NATO, there are no expectations or beliefs that Russia will join the EU. Russian membership in the European Union would require the country to surrender its self-perception as an independent world actor and transfer sovereignty to international institutions. It would also necessitate substantial reform of all levels of domestic institutions and demand a political solution to the ongoing crisis in Chechnya. At the same time, EU integration further marginalizes Russia from Europe. Already, formerly Communist EU candidate countries have reoriented their economies, turning them away from the Russian market; the political, cultural, intellectual, and even linguistic ties that once linked Russia to Eastern Europe are quickly disappearing.

Finally, Russia's relations with the West have been significantly strained by increased Russian nationalism. The expansion of NATO and the European Union has exacerbated the situation, though underlying this is the more fundamental issue of the collapse of the Soviet Union and the sense of loss and humiliation that resulted for many Russians. Furthermore, the Russian government has actively cultivated these feelings as a way to build legitimacy—recall our earlier discussion of nationalism replacing ideology as a unifying force in the country. In 2005, public demonstrations in Ukraine ousted the former pro-Russian government, bringing this country much closer to the West. In 2008, the former Serbian province of Kosovo declared independence, which Russia strongly opposed; in contrast, many Western countries recognized Kosovo. Around the same time, Russia and the United States tangled over a proposed missile shield, based in Eastern Europe, that would be built to protect the United States and Europe against an Iranian nuclear missile. Although the missile defense system is too small to act as a deterrent to Russia, Russia argued that it was in fact a first step in a much larger system directed toward them.

While Russia's relationship with the United States and Europe has soured, Russia has attempted to create its own sphere of influence. Part of this effort can be seen in the **Commonwealth of Independent States (CIS)**, a loose integrationist body that incorporated many former Soviet republics after 1991. While the CIS has little formal power, Russia has used it as a body to coordinate its relationship with a number of former Soviet republics, particularly in Central Asia. It has also become militarily involved in several conflicts across the former Soviet Union, most recently in the Caucasus. In addition, Russia has sought to improve ties with China and countries in the Middle East, notably Iran, where it was actively involved in developing that country's nuclear program. Finally, while Russian influence in Europe has diminished, Russia has reoriented itself toward Asia and the Middle East in the search for new alliances.

Russia may have lost its traditional forms of influence in Europe, but the growing role of Russian oil and gas supplies has given the country some leverage over the region. In several instances, Russia has turned off resources to countries (like Ukraine) to express displeasure over their political or other disputes. Given that Europe depends heavily on Russian energy, Russia's resources can be a significant economic weapon, though one that cannot be wielded with any particular nuance.

At the military level, Russia has limited power. Though it holds a vast arsenal of nuclear weapons, its military has shrunk so dramatically that it can no longer assume any significant international role. Russia's soldiers are underpaid and untrained, and much of their equipment is outdated, in spite of recent increases in military spending. There have also long been concerns that Russia's weapons of mass destruction—chemical, biological, and nuclear—are not as tightly secured as they should be, raising the threat of proliferation or terrorism. Although Russia appears to be restoring control and efficacy over its military, it remains a shadow of its former self. Of course, for many of its smaller and weaker neighbors, even that shadow is worrisome.

Russia has historically vacillated between the poles of internationalism and nationalism, engagement and isolationism. Russians have long argued whether their country is somehow separate from Europe and the West, different in culture, religion, and historical traditions. During the 1980s and 1990s, Russia began to move into the European and liberal democratic orbit, albeit in a chaotic fashion. Yet in spite of greater individual connections to the outside world, such as international travel, as a whole Russia has become less engaged with Europe and North America. What are the long-term implications of this disengagement? It was once said about the United Kingdom that they had lost an empire but not yet found a role in the international system. The same could be said about Russia, and for now, at least, Russia's role seems to be one that seeks to recapture the glory of the past, while pressing questions about the future remain unresolved.

CURRENT ISSUES

THE WAR WITH GEORGIA AND ITS AFTERMATH

The open questions about the future of Russia and its relations with the outside world were brought into sharp focus by the brief war with Georgia in 2008. The origins of this war are complicated. When the Soviet Union collapsed in 1991, Georgia, a republic in the Caucasus, gained independence. But like much of the region, its territory was a diverse mixture of peoples, particularly along the northern border with Russia, where ethnic Abkhaz and Ossetians live, each with their own distinct language and culture. Conflict between these populations and the Georgian government led to open warfare. Russia eventually intervened militarily, ending the conflict but essentially asserting control over Abkhazia and South Ossetia. Over time, these regions grew increasingly integrated into Russia, with much of their populations taking Russian citizenship and Russians taking leadership positions inside the regions. For all intents and purposes, Abkhazia and South Ossetia functioned as independent states or regions of Russia.

In 2003, public protests in Georgia brought about a dramatic change in government, with the election of President Mikhail Saakashvili. Western educated, Saakashvili advocated NATO membership and the reintegration of Abkhazia and South Ossetia. Russia continued to consolidate its control over these regions, arguing that their demands for independence were no different from that of Kosovo from Serbia (which the West supported and Russia opposed). Increasing tensions and cross-border attacks finally led to war. In August 2008, Georgian forces attempted to take South Ossetia, and Russia responded in kind, effectively destroying much of the Georgian military, attacking military bases and other installations across the country, and seizing control of Georgian territory. It also formally recognized Abkhazia and South Ossetia as independent countries (as of this writing only Nicaragua has followed suit).

In the aftermath of this conflict, there is much blame to go around and many questions are unanswered. Critics have accused the Georgians of failing to accommodate non-Georgians after independence, thus stoking the ethnic conflicts that led to this war. In addition, many have criticized President

Saakashvili for the invasion of South Ossetia, which was certain to bring about a massive Russian response. Others suggest that the conflict was provoked by Russia as a way to finalize its control over the region, which had been deepening for some time. Whomever is to blame, the result has been a rupture between Russia and NATO, increased European support for the U.S. missile defense program, and the specter of a new cold war or further Russian intervention in the region. Russia may have won this battle, but at the cost of isolating itself even further from the West.

NOTES

1. Hakon Stang, *The Naming of Russia*, Meddelelser Occasional Paper, no. 77 (Oslo: University of Oslo, 1996), www.hf.uio.no/east/Medd/PDF/Medd77.pdf (accessed 26 July 2005); see also Nicolas Riasanovksy, *A History of Russia* (New York: Oxford University Press, 1963).
2. For a fascinating Soviet-era interpretation of Ivan's leadership, see the Sergei Eisenstein film *Ivan the Terrible* (1945).
3. For a discussion of this period, see Richard Pipes, *Three "Whys" of the Russian Revolution* (New York: Vintage, 1995).
4. Mary McAuley, *Soviet Politics: 1917–1991* (New York: Oxford University Press, 1992), pp. 26–27.
5. See Robert Conquest, *The Great Terror: A Reassessment* (New York: Oxford University Press, 1991), and Anne Applebaum, *Gulag: A History* (New York: Doubleday, 2003).
6. For a discussion of the last days of Soviet rule, see David Remnick, *Lenin's Tomb: The Last Days of the Soviet Empire* (New York: Random House, 1993).
7. Oleh Protsk, "Ruling with Decrees: Presidential Decree Making in Russia and Ukraine," *Europe–Asia Studies*, 56 (July 2004), pp. 637–60.
8. See Alexei Trochev, "Implementing Russian Constitutional Court Decisions," *East European Constitutional Review* (Winter/Spring 2002), pp. 95–102, and "Less Democracy, More Courts: A Puzzle of Judicial Review in Russia," *Law and Society Review* (September 2004), pp. 513–48.
9. Transparency International Annual Report 2007, www.transparency.org (accessed 7 May 2009).
10. RIA Novosti News Service (Russia), 4 May 2008.
11. Duckjoon Chang, "Federalism at Bay: Putin's Political Reforms and Federal-Regional Relations in Russia," unpublished paper, 2005.
12. For more on political parties in Russia, see Michael McFaul, "Party Formation and Non-Formation in Russia," *Working Papers*, 12 (May 2000), Carnegie Endowment for International Peace, www.ceip.org/files (accessed 27 July 2005).
13. See Vladimir Petrovich Kartsev and Todd Bludeau, *Zhironovsky* (New York: Columbia University Press, 1995).
14. Peter Rutland, "Oil and Politics in Russia," paper presented at the 2006 American Political Science Association Conference.
15. See the statement by the Organization for Security and Cooperation in Europe, 12 December 2007, www.oscepa.org (accessed 7 May 2009).

16. Human Rights Watch, "Choking on Bureaucracy: State Curbs Independent Civil Society Activism," February 2008, www.hrw.org (accessed 7 May 2009).
17. International News Safety Institution, "Killing the Messenger," March 2007, www.newssaftey.com (accessed 7 May 2009).
18. "Dubna's Tale," *Economist*, 31 July 2008.
19. Steven Fish, *Democracy Derailed in Russia: The Failure of Open Politics* (Cambridge, UK: Cambridge University Press, 2005).

GLOSSARY OF KEY TERMS ▬▬▬▬▬▬▬▬▬▬

asymmetric federalism   A system where power is devolved unequally across the country and its constituent regions, often the result of specific laws negotiated between the region and the central government.

Caucasus   Southwest Russia, near the Black Sea and Turkey, where there is a diverse mixture of non-Slavic peoples with distinct languages, customs, and a much stronger historical presence of Islam than Orthodox Christianity.

Chechnya   Russian republic that has been a source of military conflict since 1991.

Cheka   Soviet secret police created by Lenin; precursor to the KGB.

Commonwealth of Independent States (CIS)   A loose integrationist body that incorporates most former Soviet republics.

Communist Party of the Russian Federation   Successor party in Russia to the Communist Party of the Soviet Union.

Constitutional Court   Highest body in the Russian legal system, responsible for constitutional review.

czar   Russian word for emperor (from *Caesar*).

Duma   Lower house of the Russian legislature.

Federal Security Bureau (FSB)   Successor to the KGB, the Russian intelligence agency.

Federation Council   Upper house of the Russian legislature.

glasnost   Literally, openness. The policy of political liberalization implemented in the Soviet Union in the late 1980s.

insider privatization   A process in Russia where the former *nomenklatura* directors of these firms were able to acquire the largest share.

KGB   Soviet secret police agency charged with domestic and foreign intelligence.

Kremlin   Eleventh-century fortress in the heart of Moscow that has been the historical seat of Russian state power.

Liberal Democratic Party of Russia (LDPR)   Political party in Russia with a nationalist and anti-democratic orientation.

nomenklatura   Politically sensitive or influential jobs in the state, society, or economy that are staffed by people chosen or approved by the Communist Party.

oligarchs   Russian people who are noted for their control of large amounts of the Russian economy (including the media), their close ties to the government, and the accusations of corruption surrounding their rise to power.

Orthodox Christianity   A variant of Christianity separate from Roman Catholicism and Protestantism, originally centered in Byzantium (now roughly modern-day Turkey).

parties of power   Russian parties created by political elites to support their political aspirations. Typically lacking any ideological orientation.

perestroika   Literally, restructuring. The policy of economic liberalization implemented in the Soviet Union in the 1980s.

Politburo   Top policy-making and executive body of the Communist Party.

Putin, Vladimir   President of Russia from 1999 to 2008; prime minister from 2008.

Rus   Origin of the word *Russia,* thought to refer to Vikings who settled the region in the ninth century CE.

shock therapy   A process of rapid marketization.

soviets   Name given to workers' councils that sprang up in 1917.

Union of Right Forces (URF)   Political party in Russia with a liberal-democratic orientation.

Yabloko   Small party in Russia which advocates democracy and a liberal political economic system.

Yeltsin, Boris   President of Russia from 1991 to 1999.

WEB LINKS

Carnegie Endowment for International Peace, Russian and Eurasian
    Program **www.carnegieendowment.org**
Moscow Times **www.moscowtimes.ru/index.htm**
Radio Free Europe/Radio Liberty **www.rferl.org**
Russian and East European Network and Information Center
    http://inic.utexas.edu/reenic/countries/russia.html
Russian Public Opinion Research Center **http://wciom.com/**
Transitions Online **www.tol.cz**

8 CHINA

Head of state: President Hu Jintao
(since March 15, 2003)

Head of government: Premier Wen Jiabao
(since March 16, 2003)

Capital: Beijing

Total land size: 9,596,960 sq km

Population: 1.330 billion

GDP at PPP: 6.99 trillion US$

GDP per capita at PPP: $5,300

Human development index ranking: 81

CHINA

INTRODUCTION

Why Study This Case?

Napoléon Bonaparte is said to have described China as a sleeping giant. Centuries later that description continues to resonate, though with every passing year it seems less and less appropriate. Today, China is indeed stirring after centuries of slumber, with repercussions that are transforming the world. But it is not simply these changes that draw our attention; after all, China is not the first, nor the only, country to undergo dramatic change. Rather, it is that these changes are taking place in a country that we tend to speak of in superlatives, qualities no other country can easily match.

The first of China's superlatives is its history, which extends back at least 4,000 years. Several millennia before most modern nations and states existed in even rudimentary form, China had taken shape, creating a relatively unified country and people. To be certain, China was torn apart innumerable times during this process by civil strife and external invasion. Yet in spite of these difficulties, a continuous Chinese civilization has existed for thousands of years and directly shapes and informs modern Chinese society and politics.

Second is the sheer size of China's population. China is the most populous country in the world, with more than 1.3 billion people. This is four times the population of the United States and, with the exception of India (whose population also exceeds 1 billion), no other country's population even comes close to China's. Overpopulation has been both a source of concern for the Chinese government and a lure for foreign businesses that have dreamed for centuries of the profits that could be gained if they could somehow tap this vast market.

This leads to a third superlative quality, China's recent and rapid development. In centuries past, China was one of the most powerful empires in the world, easily dominating its much smaller neighbors. China saw itself as the center of the world. Over time, this superiority led to isolation and from isolation to stagnation. Foreign imperialism in the nineteenth century forced China open but also led to war and revolution. By the time of the Communist takeover in 1949, foreign powers had finally been expelled, and China once again enjoyed a period of isolation. But starting in the late 1970s, the ruling Chinese Communist Party introduced more liberal economic policies while maintaining its tight control over political power. Known as **reform and opening**, these changes led the country to a period of economic growth unmatched in the world. In the three decades after reform and opening began in 1978, China's GNP grew at an average rate of just under 10 percent a year—

double the rate of the other fast-growing Asian tigers, such as South Korea and Singapore, and quadruple the average growth rates of the United States, Japan, and the United Kingdom.

A bold symbol of China's amazingly rapid economic development is the fact that six of the ten tallest buildings in the world can now be found in China. Visitors to the city of Shanghai stand awestruck before the massive skyscrapers that line the banks of the Huangpu River. Political reform, however, has been much more limited, and public protests for change, such as the **Tiananmen Square** protests in 1989, have garnered violent reactions from the Communist regime. In this sense, China stands in contrast to Russia, whose initial transition from Communism made way for greater democracy but came at the expense of economic decline and marginalization from the rest of the world.

As a result of reform and opening, millions of Chinese have risen out of poverty over the past several decades, but economic reforms also have led to the closure of many inefficient state-owned businesses, jeopardizing the livelihoods of millions of workers. China is thus engaged in a precarious race to reform itself before the shock of these changes overwhelms the country. Economic modernization is not only transforming the physical and social landscape of the country but also reshaping international finance, trade, and the environment. China, moreover, is becoming a central factor in globalization. Indeed, the recent flood of cheap Chinese exports into the world market has displaced numerous workers outside of China, raised concerns in advanced countries about the safety of its food and toy exports, and substantially lowered rates of global inflation. Its voracious consumption of oil and other raw materials is part of international discussions about global shortages and global warming. China now claims sixteen of the world's twenty most polluted cities and is facing an environmental crisis of unprecedented proportions that has already spread well beyond its borders. Now that the giant is awake, its development will have profound effects on the world.

Major Geographic and Demographic Features

In addition to boasting the largest population in the world, China, not surprisingly, is also one of the largest countries in terms of landmass, exceeded only by Russia, Canada, and the United States. Its physical size allows for a range of climates and geographic features. The southwestern portion of the country, including Tibet, is known for its mountain ranges (the Himalayas and the Altai), and most of the northwestern Xinjiang region is desert. The northeastern portion, bordering Mongolia and Russian Siberia, is marked by bitterly cold winter temperatures. Most of the Chinese population, therefore, lives in the southern and seaboard portions of the country, where the climate is more temperate and there is greater rainfall, yielding the majority of China's arable land. Intersecting this region are the two lifelines of China: the Yellow (*Huang He*) and Yangtze (*Chang Jiang*) Rivers, which flow east toward the Pacific Ocean. The Yangtze has garnered much domestic and international attention due to the Three Gorges Dam project, which was completed in 2008. The largest ever constructed, this dam generates millions of kilowatts of electricity (something desperately needed in China) and will help prevent the flooding that has been a recurrent problem. Critics point out that the dam has destroyed countless historic sites, displaced millions of people, and caused major environmental damage. Moreover, failure of a dam this size would have catastrophic results.

Given the country's large population and landmass, the Chinese are a puzzlingly homogeneous population, with over 90 percent of the population considered part of the main ethnic group, known as Han. This stands in contrast to the persistence of ethnic diversity in Europe, Africa, and South Asia, even within individual countries. What explains the difference? The answer lies in the geography. The southern portion of the country is not only more amenable to human habitation but also free of the extreme geographic barriers, such as high mountains and deserts, that impede travel and migration. Historically, the Yellow and Yangtze Rivers connected much of the country, allowing knowledge, foods, animals, and culture to spread more easily than in other parts of the world. Such connections helped foster the emergence of a single Han identity, though not always intentionally. The lack of land barriers made it much easier for early empires to develop and bring a large area under their control. China was first unified as early as 221 B.C.E., and with political centralization the diverse cultures and languages of southern China were slowly absorbed into the larger Han identity. It is at this point in history that we can begin to speak of the emergence of a singular Chinese state.

Historical Development of the State

The paradox of China's political development is how a country with such an ancient civilization and such early political centralization could become such a weak state by the nineteenth century, lacking both the capacity and autonomy to resist Western imperialism. But a closer examination reveals that China's early development and later weakness are closely related. The country's first political leaders can be traced to the Shang dynasty, which reigned from the eighteenth to the eleventh century B.C.E., two thousand years before European states appeared in their earliest forms. It was during this time that written Chinese (characters) emerged. Power in the country was decentralized, however, and feudal wars between various rivals were commonplace. It was only much later, during the Qin dynasty (221–206 B.C.E.), that a single

TIME LINE OF POLITICAL DEVELOPMENT

Year	Event
1700 B.C.E.	Beginning of Chinese civilization under Shang dynasty
221 B.C.E.	Unification of China under Qin dynasty
1839–42	First Opium War
1911	Overthrow of Qing dynasty
1919	May Fourth movement
1921	Founding of Chinese Communist Party (CCP)
1934–35	Long March
1937–45	Sino-Japanese War
1949	Founding of the People's Republic of China (PRC)
1958–60	Great Leap Forward
1966–76	Cultural Revolution
1978	Deng Xiaoping launches reform and opening
1989	Tiananmen Square massacre
2001	China's accession to the World Trade Organization (WTO)
2008	China hosts the Beijing Summer Olympics

Chinese empire (and the name China) was born. During this period, China first experienced political centralization, with the appointment of nonhereditary officials to govern provinces, the minting of currency, the development of standard weights and measures, and the creation of public works, such as roads, canals, and portions of the famous Great Wall.

CENTRALIZATION AND DYNASTIC RULE

Sovereign power was centralized and expanded by the Han dynasty (206 B.C.E.–. 220 C.E.), a reign marked by great cultural development, the rise of domestic and international trade, foreign exploration, and conquest. At this time, China was far ahead of Europe in its understanding of timekeeping, astronomy, and mathematics. The philosophy of **Confucianism** influenced the imperial leaders, with its emphasis on a fixed set of hierarchical roles, meritocracy, and obedience to authority. Confucianism in turn helped foster the development of the Chinese civil service, a corps of educated men chosen on the basis of exams testing their familiarity with Confucian thought. The notion of a professional bureaucracy based on competitive exams did not emerge elsewhere in the world for centuries.

With the collapse of the Han dynasty, China was divided for nearly four centuries, until the Sui and Tang dynasties (591–907 C.E.). These dynasties restored the unity of the empire: the bureaucratic institutions of the Han period were resurrected, and the economic and cultural life once again flourished. The institutionalization of the bureaucracy also helped foster the development of a gentry class made up of landowners and their children, who were groomed from birth to join the bureaucracy. This bureaucratic class became the glue that held China together. Subsequent dynasties continued to rely upon the bureaucracy to maintain Chinese unity, even when new dynasties were established by foreign conquerors, as under the Yuan (Mongols) and the Qing (Manchus). Such continuity helped foster economic development and innovation, which continued to advance faster than in Europe and other parts of the world.

AFFLUENCE WITHOUT INDUSTRIALIZATION—AND THE FOREIGN CHALLENGE

At the advent of the Ming dynasty (1368–1644), China still led the world in science, economics, communication, technological innovation, and public works. Although such knowledge offered the foundation for Chinese modernization and industrialization, these processes did not take place. During these three centuries, as Europe experienced the Renaissance, international exploration, and the beginnings of the Industrial Revolution, Chinese innovation and economic development began to stagnate. By the mid-1400s, the Chinese empire had banned long-distance sea travel and showed little interest in developing many of the technological innovations it had created. Why did this occur?

There are several possible reasons. One argument is cultural. Confucian thought helped establish political continuity and a meritocratic system in China, but over the centuries these ideas became inflexible and outdated. During the early twentieth century, bureaucratic examinations were still based on 2,000-year-old Confucian texts. Rigid Confucian ideology placed China at the center of the world (and universe), viewing any new or outside knowledge as unimportant and rejecting changes that might disrupt the imperial system.

A second argument is economic. During the early centuries of the Chinese Empire, entrepreneurialism was the main path to wealth. But with the rise of the bureaucratic elite, this role became a more powerful means of personal enrichment, particularly through rent-seeking and corruption. The financial rewards of public employment led many in the upper classes to divert their most talented children to the civil service. It also concentrated economic power in the hands of the state, while business activity was stunted by a Confucian disdain for commerce and steep, arbitrary taxation (naturally, the bureaucracy opposed any reforms that might threaten its privileges).

A third argument is geographic and furthers the points above. The geographic factors that facilitated early unification and continuity also limited competition, since there was less danger that a lack of innovation might lead to destruction by outside forces. In Europe, by contrast, innumerable states continuously vied for power, making isolation impossible and conservatism a recipe for economic and military defeat. No one power in Europe could ban seafaring or abolish the clock; states that resisted progress and innovation soon disappeared off the map. China, however, could reject technology and embrace isolation since there were no rival powers to challenge such policies. In short, a combination of cultural, economic, and geographic forces allowed China's lengthy isolation.

Europe's economic and technological development continued, and its age of exploration and conquest began just as China was closing itself to the outside world. The Portuguese first reached China by 1514, and during the sixteenth and seventeenth centuries other European traders sought to expand these initial contacts. These remained tightly controlled by the Chinese, however, and attempts to expand connections were futile. In perhaps the most famous example, a British trade mission led by Lord Macartney was rebuffed by the Chinese emperor, whose reply to King George III read: "I set no value on objects strange or ingenious, and we have no use for your country's manufactures."[1]

But the Chinese Empire was losing its ability to ignore the outside world, and external forces were beginning to test China's power. The First Opium War (1839–1842), with Great Britain, resulted in a resounding Chinese defeat, forcing China to cede Hong Kong to the British and pay restitution. Various Western powers quickly demanded similar access, and subsequent wars with the French and the Japanese only further extended the control of imperial powers over the country. Foreign pressures in turn contributed to growing domestic instability.

THE EROSION OF CENTRAL AUTHORITY: CIVIL WAR AND FOREIGN INVASION

By the beginning of the twentieth century, the centralized authority of the Chinese state, developed over two thousand years, effectively crumbled. In 1911, a public revolt finally swept away the remnants of the Qing dynasty, and China was declared a republic, but it soon fell under the control of regional warlords. In the midst of this chaos, two main political organizations formed to compete for power. The Nationalist Party, also known as the **Kuomintang (KMT)**, slowly grew in strength under the leadership of **Sun Yat-sen**. The party was aided by student protests in 1919, known as the **May Fourth movement**. These nationalist revolts rejected foreign interference in China and called for modernization, radical reform, and a break with traditional values and institutions, including Confucianism.

The second organization was the **Chinese Communist Party (CCP)**, formed in 1921 by one of the leaders of the May Fourth movement. Though the KMT's Sun had been educated in the United States, both parties received support from the recently established Soviet Union. In fact, the Soviets saw the KMT as a more likely contender for power than the CCP and hoped to move the KMT into the Soviet orbit. Following Sun's death in 1925, relations between the KMT and the CCP unraveled. Chiang Kai-shek, head of the KMT's armed forces, took control of the party and expelled pro-Soviet and pro-CCP elements. Chiang also ensured that both warlords and the CCP were brutally suppressed in areas under KMT control. By 1928, the KMT had emerged as the effective leader of much of the country, while the CCP was pushed out of the cities and into the countryside. The KMT quickly shed any pretense of democracy, growing ever more dictatorial and corrupt.

During the repression of the CCP, power within the party began to pass into the hands of **Mao Zedong** (1893–1976). Deviating from the Marxist convention that revolutions be led by the urban proletariat, Mao believed that a Communist revolution could be won by building an army out of the peasant class. Mao and the CCP established their own independent Communist republic within China, but KMT attacks forced the CCP to flee westward in what came to be known as the **Long March** (1934–1935). In this circuitous retreat, the CCP and its loyal followers traveled over 6,000 miles and lost many lives (indeed, of the 100,000 who set out on the Long March, only 10 percent arrived at their final destination, in Yan'an). The Long March represented a setback for the CCP but secured Mao's leadership and strengthened his idea that the party should reorient itself toward the peasant majority. The CCP fostered positive relations with the peasantry during the Long March, which contrasted strongly with the more brutal policies of the KMT. The revolutionary ideology of the CCP and its call for equality drew all classes of Chinese to its ranks.

In 1937, both the KMT and the CCP faced a new threat as Japan launched a full-scale invasion of the country after several years of smaller incursions. The two parties formed a united front, though they continued to battle each other even as they resisted the Japanese advance. While the war weakened KMT power, which was based in the cities, it bolstered the CCP's nationalist credentials and reinforced its ideology of a peasant-oriented Communism of the masses. The war also forged a strong Communist military, the **People's Liberation Army (PLA)**, geared to fight the enemy and win public support. This birth of Chinese Communism through peasant guerilla warfare is quite different from the Soviet experience, in which a small group of urban intellectuals seized control of the state through a coup d'état. In fact, the CCP and PLA comprised a new state and regime in the making.

THE ESTABLISHMENT AND CONSOLIDATION OF A COMMUNIST REGIME

Japan's defeat at the end of World War II found the CCP much strengthened and the KMT in disarray. The Communists now commanded the support of much of the countryside, while the KMT's traditional urban base of support was shattered by war and tired of corruption. Communist attacks quickly routed the KMT, and in 1949 the Communist forces entered Beijing unopposed and established the People's Republic of China (PRC). Chiang and the remnants of the KMT fled to the island of Taiwan, declaring themselves the true government of China—which the United States recognized (rather than the PRC) until 1979. Taiwan continues to function independently of China, though the PRC has never recognized it and asserts that eventually the so-called renegade province will return to mainland control.

The new Communist regime faced the challenge of modernizing a country that was far behind the West and ravaged by a century of imperialism and war. The CCP's assets, forged during the war, were its organizational strength and a newly established reservoir of public legitimacy. Forming a close alliance with the Soviet Union, China began a process of modernization modeled after the Soviet experience under Joseph Stalin: nationalization of industry, collectivization of agriculture, and central planning. At the same time, the CCP began to ruthlessly repress anyone viewed as hostile to the revolution, including landowners, KMT members and sympathizers, and others suspected of opposing the new order. Several million were killed.

EXPERIMENTATION AND CHAOS UNDER MAO

Within a few short years, however, China had diverged from the typical Soviet-style path of Communist development. This difference resulted partly from growing tensions between the Soviet Union and China and partly from the particular ideological facets of Chinese Communism that had developed in the wake of the Long March. Stalin died in 1953, bringing to an end his ruthless terrorizing of the Russian people. His successor, Nikita Khrushchev, openly denounced Stalin in 1956, taking tentative steps toward allowing greater personal liberty and bringing an end to the unbridled use of violence against the public.

In China, too, some liberalization took place. Mao's **Hundred Flowers campaign** of 1956 encouraged public criticism and dissent, though it soon ended and the most prominent critics were removed from their positions of authority. Mao and other Chinese leaders began to see Soviet de-Stalinization as a retreat from Communist ideals and revolutionary change, and they upheld China as the true vanguard of world revolution. China's own experience in constructing peasant-based Communism in a largely agrarian country provided China's leaders with justification for assuming this leadership role. After all, its experiences were not dissimilar to the many anti-imperial struggles taking place across the less developed world at the time.

China's first major break from the Soviet model was the **Great Leap Forward** (1958–1960). Departing from the model of highly centralized planning, Mao reorganized the Chinese people into a series of communes; these communes were to serve all basic social and economic functions, from industrial production to health care. Each commune was to set its own policies for economic development within the guidelines of general government policy. In Mao's view, revolutionary change could be achieved by putting responsibility directly into the hands of the public, which would move the country rapidly into Communism. State capacity was thus devolved, albeit within an authoritarian system.

In the absence of clear directives and organization, the Great Leap Forward quickly faltered. For example, a campaign to increase steel production led not to the creation of large foundries staffed by skilled employees, as had happened in the Soviet Union, but produced a million backyard furnaces built by unskilled communes, which consequently produced worthless metal. Overall economic and agricultural production declined, leading to disorder, famine, and the deaths of tens of millions of Chinese. In the face of this debacle, Mao stepped down as head of state in 1959 (though he remained head of the CCP), and China recentralized production and state control. Poor relations with the Soviet Union compounded these setbacks, which culminated in 1960 with the Soviet withdrawal of technical and financial support.

From this, Mao drew the conclusion that the problem was not that the CCP had been too radical but that it had not been radical enough. Soviet history proved, Mao reasoned, that without an unwavering commitment to radical change, revolution would quickly deteriorate into conservatism (as Mao saw occurring in China). He thus sought to place himself back at the center of power and reignite revolutionary fervor through the construction of a cult of personality. This was first captured in the publication of *Quotations from Chairman Mao,* the Little Red Book of Mao's sayings that became standard reading for the public.[2]

In 1966, the cult took shape as Mao and his backers accused the CCP itself of having "taken the capitalist road" and encouraged the public (particularly students) to "bomb the headquarters"—that is, to challenge the party-state bureaucracy at all levels. Schools were closed, and student radicals, called the **Red Guard**, took to the streets to act as the vanguard of Mao's **Cultural Revolution**. Authority figures (including top party and state leaders, intellectuals, teachers, and even parents) were attacked, imprisoned, tortured, exiled to the countryside, or killed. Historic buildings, writings, and works of art condemned as "bourgeois" and "reactionary" were destroyed.

By weakening all social, economic, and political institutions in China, Mao made himself the charismatic center of all authority and wisdom. The result of this new vision was years of chaos and violence as the country slid into near civil war among various factions of the state, society, and the CCP. State capacity and autonomy largely disappeared. The only remaining institution having any authority, the PLA, was finally used to restore order. The excesses of the Cultural Revolution were largely curbed by 1968, though factional struggles within the party continued until Mao's death, in 1976.

REFORM AND OPENING AFTER MAO

With Mao's death, the incessant campaigns to whip up revolutionary fervor ended, and the party came under control of leaders who had themselves been victims of the Cultural Revolution. Most important was **Deng Xiaoping** (1904–1997), a top party leader from the earliest years of the CCP who had been stripped of his posts (twice) during the Cultural Revolution. In the race to take control of post-Mao China, Deng outmaneuvered Mao's widow, Jiang Qing, and her allies (known as the Gang of Four) and consolidated power. By 1979, Deng had set the nation on a very different course.

In contrast to Mao's emphasis on revolutionary action for its own sake, Deng pursued modernization at the expense of Communist ideology, in what became known as reform and opening. The government encouraged the gradual privatization of, first, agriculture and, then, business; it also cultivated foreign relations with capitalist countries, continuing a process that began under Mao with U.S. president Richard Nixon's visit to China in 1972. It also expanded foreign investment and trade while de-emphasizing ideology. To quote Deng, "Whether a cat is black or white makes no difference. As long as it catches mice, it is a good cat." Ironically, the destruction of much of the party-state under the Cultural Revolution made these pragmatic reforms easier. China began to embrace the market economy, with all of its benefits and difficulties.

One reform that did not take place, however, was political. In spite of the downgrading of Communist ideology, the CCP still maintained complete control over political life, and attempts at public debate in the 1970s were quickly silenced. Although reform and opening lifted millions out of poverty, by the 1980s serious problems had emerged, among them inflation, unemployment, and widespread corruption (particularly within the CCP). As with the May Fourth movement and the Red Guards of the Cultural Revolution, students once again played a major role in expressing discontent over this situation. In the 1989 Tiananmen Square demonstration, hundreds of protesters were killed for daring to openly call for political reforms (see "Gate of Heavenly Peace," p. 296).

The regime's swift and violent response to the protest and its vigilant suppression of even hints of political unrest in the two decades since Tiananmen have been combined with continued economic reform and opening. Deng's formula of persistent political authoritarianism to preserve the Communist

GATE OF HEAVENLY PEACE

The broad plaza that fronts the Forbidden City (the former imperial palace) in the heart of Beijing known as Tiananmen or "Gate of Heavenly Peace" Square has been the site of numerous significant political events, including the 1919 May Fourth movement, the declaration of the PRC's founding in 1949, and huge Red Guard tributes to Mao Zedong during the 1960s' Cultural Revolution. In April 1989, students once again gathered at the Square to mourn the death of Hu Yaobang, a former general secretary of the CCP who had been dismissed after student protests in 1987. The eulogy quickly grew into a general protest against corruption and a call for political reform. These were calls not for an end to Communist rule but for greater public participation in decision making, not unlike what was occurring at the same time in the Soviet Union under Mikhail Gorbachev.

The demonstrators' ranks swelled rapidly. On the historically significant May 4, an estimated 100,000 students and other citizens marched in the streets of Beijing, and by May 17 an estimated one million people had occupied Tiananmen Square. Martial law was declared, but many protesters remained, and on June 4 (now known in China simply as *liusi* or "6/4" much as Americans refer to "9/11"), the party leadership brought in the military. Although those gathered at the square itself were permitted to leave, hundreds of protesters were killed in clashes around Beijing that day and in other major Chinese cities. Over the next few months, thousands of students and others connected to the protests were arrested, and students throughout China were required to attend Communist ideology indoctrination courses. Two decades later, security at Tiananmen Square remains extremely tight.

regime's political monopoly plus increasing economic freedoms prevails: after Deng's passing in 1997 with his successor, **Jiang Zemin**, and under Jiang's successor, current leader **Hu Jintao**.

POLITICAL REGIME

Despite China's three decades of economic reform and global trends of democratization, the country remains stubbornly authoritarian. In fact, approximately half of the world's population that does not democratically elect its leaders resides in China.[3] Certainly China's historical legacy of over 2,000 years of centralized authoritarian rule (legitimized by Confucian precepts) has buttressed the current regime. But to understand the nature and resilience of China's Communist authoritarianism, we must examine the ways in which political control is organized and exercised in a Communist party-state. In spite of China's economic liberalization, its Communist party-state retains the essential organizational structure that the Chinese Communist Party (CCP) adopted from the Soviet Union. Though China's reformist leaders have almost fully rejected Marx in their embrace of market freedoms, their decision to retain a closed political system is very much in accord with Lenin's vision of the Communist party-state. Lenin contended that for the Communist revolution to succeed in Russia, a self-appointed Communist Party elite, enlightened with wisdom and imbued with revolutionary fervor, would need to serve as a vanguard on behalf of the masses. This group alone would have the organizational capacity and resolve to lead the revolutionary transition from feudalism and capitalism to state socialism and ultimately utopian Communism. The need to allow the process to unfold, Lenin argued, justified the party in maintaining a political monopoly and serving as a "dictatorship of the proletariat."

This ideological and organizational logic has had several consequences for the exercise of political control in China (as was true in the Soviet Union and other Communist party-states). Most important, it means that political authority flows from the party elite to those within the party, the state, and society, who are expected to submit to this authority. We examine each of these in turn.

Political Institutions

THE PARTY

The CCP is governed according to Lenin's principle of **democratic centralism**, in which "the individual Party member is subordinate to a Party organization, the minority is subordinate to the majority, the lower level organization is subordinate to the higher level, each organization and all members of the whole Party are subordinate to the Party's National Congress and the Central Committee."[4] And while party leaders have a moral obligation to provide opportunities for party members to discuss, consult, and even criticize, in fact, leaders impose all important decisions on those below them, who are expected to fully abide by decisions made at the center. In short, centralism always prevails over democracy.

THE STATE

The party elite exercises control over state (and party) officials through the *nomenklatura* system, by which party committees are responsible for the appointment, promotion, transfer, and firing of high-level state, party, and even public-industry personnel (in China's case, this comprises some 10 million positions). The party also maintains direct control over the government and

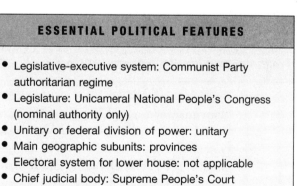

ESSENTIAL POLITICAL FEATURES

- Legislative-executive system: Communist Party authoritarian regime
- Legislature: Unicameral National People's Congress (nominal authority only)
- Unitary or federal division of power: unitary
- Main geographic subunits: provinces
- Electoral system for lower house: not applicable
- Chief judicial body: Supreme People's Court

Parallel Organization of the Chinese Communist Party and the Chinese Government

Party Office or Organ	Officeholder or Number of Members or Departments	Corresponding Government Office or Organ	Officeholder or Number of Members or Departments
Chairman	Office abolished in 1982	President (head of state)	Hu Jintao
General secretary	Hu Jintao	Premier (head of government)	Wen Jiabao
Politburo Standing Committee (PSC)	9 members	State Council Standing Committee	10 members
Politburo	24 members	State Council	43 members
Central Committee (CC)	198 members	National People's Congress Standing Committee	159 members
National Party Congress	2,979 members	National People's Congress (NPC)	2,120 members
Central Military Commission (CMC)	8 members	Central Military Commission	7 members
CMC chairman	Hu Jintao	CMC chairman	Hu Jintao
Secretariat	Large staff of the party cadre	State Council General Office	Large staff of civil servants
Party departments	Approximately 46 departments	Bureaucratic ministries	Approximately 46 ministries, bureaus, and commissions
Central Discipline Inspection Commission	121 members	Supreme People's Court	1 president and 8 vice presidents

Source: Adapted from Melanie Mannion, "Politics in China," in Gabriel Almond et al., *Comparative Politics Today: A World View* (New York: Pearson/Longman, 2004), p. 428.

bureaucracy through a political structure of "organizational parallelism," in which all government executive, legislative, and administrative agencies are matched or duplicated at every level of organization by a corresponding party organ (see "Parallel Organization of the Chinese Communist Party and the Chinese Government," above). These CCP bureaus supervise the work of the state agencies and ensure that the interests of the party prevail. This means that although the Chinese state has a premier, a parliament, and bureaucratic ministries, party officials and organizations orchestrate the policy process and direct the votes of all party members who hold elected and appointed government and state offices (typically more than four fifths of all officeholders).

SOCIETY

Scholars describe ruling Communist parties as "greedy institutions" that are not satisfied with simply controlling the political process but seek to control all aspects of public and even private life. This was particularly true during the Maoist era of mass campaigns and totalitarian penetration of society. Control was maintained through the ***danwei* (unit)** system, which gave all Chinese citizens a lifetime affiliation with a specific industrial, agricultural, or bureaucratic work unit that dictated all aspects of their lives, including housing, health care, and other social benefits. This organizational plan was reinforced by the ***hukou* (household registration)** system, which tied all Chinese to a particular geographic location. Economic liberalization and the freedoms of private employment are gradually breaking down these traditional methods of social control, however, and China now has a **floating population** of some 150 million itinerate workers (more than the entire population of Russia) who have abandoned their rural hukou to seek employment in China's cities and have no danwei affiliation. But the authoritarian party-state has proven remarkably effective at keeping pace, drawing on the same Internet and cell phone technology that has hastened China's social mobility to maintain and even enhance its social control through high-tech surveillance and censorship.

We need to be very careful, however, not to overestimate the authoritarian grasp of China's political leaders. Despite these herculean efforts at control, the opening of the economy and the growing complexity of Chinese society have inevitably weakened China's authoritarian regime. Economic and financial decentralization has given local authorities and private firms the autonomy to resist central policies and develop greater independence. These changes, combined with the long-standing inefficiency of China's enormous bureaucracy and growing problems of corruption and nepotism at all levels of government (as well as the sheer size, diversity, and backwardness of much of China), also call state capacity into question. These centrifugal pressures for decentralization and general weakening of the party's power have led scholars to label China's current political regime one of "fragmented authoritarianism." Before exploring the potential consequences of this fragmentation, we first examine the political institutions of China's authoritarian rule.

THE CONSTITUTION

China is ostensibly governed by a constitution that is designated "the fundamental law of the state" that vests formal authority in both party and state executive and legislative offices. However, under the conditions of elite author-itarian rule in China, political power has not been highly institutionalized. Just as the party always prevails over the state, so Mao Zedong and his suc-cessors have been little deterred by any checks or balances inherent in the formal institutions of either the party or the state. China's supreme leaders have relied as much or more on their informal bases of power (including per-sonal connections, age, experience, and patronage) than on their formal posi-tions or titles. Although there has been collective agreement among current leaders to avoid a return to the tyranny of the Maoist era, political rule in post-Mao China has remained largely vested in a single "paramount" leader surrounded by a key group of twenty-five to thirty-five highly influential polit-ical elites. Though these leaders hold key positions in the party and the state, their stations simply affirm (but do not decide) their status and authority.

More fundamentally, the personal and particular nature of political rule has meant that the Western notion of the rule of law (in which all citizens are equal under the law and are protected from arbitrary state power) has generally not prevailed in China. Most significantly during the Maoist period but even to the present, the country's legal issues have been highly politicized. Most legal institutions have been subject to the ideological priorities of the party-state and the personal motivations of its leaders. Reform and opening, however, have had growing influence on legal reform as foreign investors, local entrepreneurs, and now the World Trade Organization (WTO) have begun pressing the Chinese authorities to abide by contracts and to respect property rights. This newfound legal adherence is spilling over into other aspects of policy making and portends an even greater role for some of China's other formal political institutions discussed below.

Communist Party Institutions and Organs

Although the National Party Congress "elects" its Central Committee (CC), which in turn "selects" the Politburo, in fact the nine or so members of the Politburo Standing Committee (PSC) make up the top political leadership of China. The PSC convenes in weekly meetings headed by the general secretary of the party, currently Hu Jintao. PSC members are "elected" by the twenty-five or so Politburo members, but it is the PSC (that is, its dominant senior members) that typically makes national decisions. The Politburo effectively serves as China's governing cabinet, with each member of the Politburo responsible for a particular set of policy areas or issues that roughly corre-sponds to the ministerial portfolios of the State Council.

Technically, the Politburo, the PSC, and the general secretary are all "elected" by the CC of the National Party Congress, but in reality party lead-ers determine the makeup of both the Politburo and the PSC prior to the actual casting of ballots. When the two hundred or so CC members vote, they do so on a ballot on which all candidates run unopposed. The CC typically meets annually and carries out the ongoing approval and endorsement of the National Party Congress between its sessions. Despite the largely ceremonial role of the CC, its members constitute the pool of China's party officials who are groomed for top leadership. However, in this system of largely informal power, membership in the CC simply confirms the elite status that these party leaders have already earned through personal connections and patronage ties.

The CC in turn is elected by the **National Party Congress**, which is the party's cumbersome legislative body, parallel to the government's National People's Congress. With nearly 3,000 members, it is far too unwieldy and meets too infrequently to conduct any real policy making. Instead, its "plenary," or full, sessions have been used as the venue for announcing changes in policies and leadership and formally endorsing the ideological "line" of the party. In recent decades, the National Party Congress has regularly convened at five-year intervals. There have been a total of 17 party congresses from the founding of the party in 1921 through the Seventeenth National Party Congress held in 2007. This latest session reelected Hu Jintao for another five-year term as general secretary and unveiled Hu's policy of "scientific development and the creation of a harmonious society," party-speak for the continuation of economic reform but with more concern for the growing wealth and welfare gap between urban and rural China.

Delegates to the National Party Congress ostensibly represent the more than 73 million members of the CCP organized at the provincial and local levels. In both the National Party Congress and its CC, delegates are left with few if any choices of candidates for the higher-level bodies, and their senior leaders heavily influence the choices they can make. Since 1982, however, members of the CC have been elected by secret ballot, and since the late 1980s there have actually been more candidates than seats available for the CC.

There are several other party organs worth noting. Like the government, the CCP also staffs its own bureaucracy, known as the Secretariat. The Secretariat oversees the implementation of Politburo decisions and, just as important, the distribution of propaganda in support of these decisions through its Propaganda Department. Given the important political role of China's military, party leaders have used the Central Military Commission (CMC) to retain tight control over the armed forces. The CMC reports directly to the Politburo and has always been chaired by China's paramount leader or his designee. Significantly, Hu Jintao's predecessor Jiang Zemin first relinquished his positions as general secretary of the CCP in 2002 and as president of the People's Republic of China (PRC) in 2003, but retained his office of chairman of the CMC for another year. A final party organ, the Central Discipline Inspection

Commission, is charged with maintaining party loyalty and discipline and rooting out corruption.

Each of the institutions discussed above is part of the central party structure located in Beijing. Each province also has a party committee with a secretary and a standing committee with departments and commissions in the pattern of the central party apparatus. Below this level, the party is represented by comparable organizations at the county, city, district, township, and village levels. The lower-level party leaders have often exercised a degree of autonomy, with potentially significant consequences for the devolution of authority and the political liberalization of China.

The Branches of Government

Although the national constitution designates China's legislature—the **National People's Congress (NPC)**—the highest organ of the state, government and state institutions remain subservient to party oversight. Nonethe-

STRUCTURE OF THE GOVERNMENT

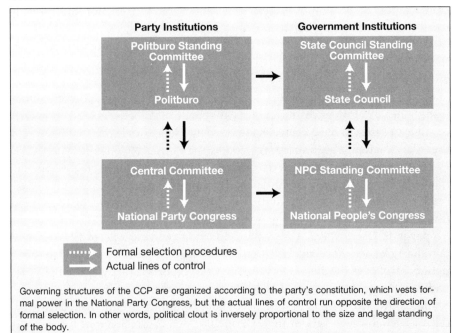

Governing structures of the CCP are organized according to the party's constitution, which vests formal power in the National Party Congress, but the actual lines of control run opposite the direction of formal selection. In other words, political clout is inversely proportional to the size and legal standing of the body.

less, day-to-day responsibilities for managing the affairs of the country are largely in the hands of the executive State Council's ministries and commissions.

THE HEAD OF STATE

The president of the PRC is China's head of state, an entirely titular office. During the reform era, the supreme leader or his designee has always held this office. Jiang Zemin held the office from 1993 to 2003 concurrently with his positions as general secretary of the CCP and head of the CMC. As noted above, Jiang has resigned from all three of these positions, handing them one by one to his designated successor and current leader, Hu Jintao.

THE STATE COUNCIL

The State Council, China's executive branch, is the primary organ of daily government activity and is led by the premier (who serves as head of government). The premier is recommended by the party's Central Committee and then formally elected by the NPC, which has never yet failed to choose the recommended candidate. The premier, currently **Wen Jiabao**, is typically the second- or third-ranking member of the PSC. With the assistance of several vice premiers, the premier and his cabinet of ministers and commissioners (collectively, the State Council) govern China. The council oversees the work of China's forty or so bureaucratic ministries and commissions, which manage the country's economy, foreign relations, education, science, technology, and other affairs of the state. The ministers who lead each ministry or commission may also serve as vice premiers or hold party offices as members of the Politburo or even the PSC. Like the CCP's Politburo, the State Council also has its own standing committee, which meets twice weekly.

Historically, the State Council's primary responsibility was the management of China's socialist economy, devising the annual and five-year economic plans and managing the state-owned enterprise system. But learning perhaps from the Soviet Union's failed efforts at perestroika, China's State Council has shown more administrative flexibility in adapting to the needs of a more open economy. Under the guidance of its party counterparts, the council's ministries and commissions formulate and implement most of China's laws and regulations.

THE NATIONAL PEOPLE'S CONGRESS

The State Council is formally appointed by China's parliament, the National People's Congress (NPC), which serves as China's legislative branch. NPC elections are held every five years, a schedule observed faithfully only since Mao's death. The NPC's nearly 3,000 delegates represent both geographic and functional constituencies (for example, industry and the military). As with many other government and party organs, delegates are generally selected by party officials and run unopposed, rather than being democratically elected from below. The NPC typically meets annually for about two weeks and "elects" a standing committee of approximately 150 members, usually headed by a member of the PSC. This NPC Standing Committee then meets regularly as a legislative assembly roughly every two months throughout the year.

Despite having the constitutional authority to pass laws and even amend the constitution, the NPC has never had an independent or influential role in policy making. Rather, it has most often served to ratify policies already determined by central leaders. In more recent years, however, as China's economy and society have become more complex, the NPC and its standing committee have gradually become venues for delegates to offer opinions, express dissatisfaction with government policy, and even occasionally cast dissenting votes. Rival party leaders have also used the body in recent years either to promote or to slow the reform process. As its constituent committees and specialized policy groups have become more knowledgeable and sophisticated, the NPC has started to shape these policies of reform. The full NPC is, of course, still far from a democratic parliament. Like its party counterpart, the institution is too large and meets too seldom and too briefly to exert substantial influence. And while its standing committee is gaining substance, it, too, remains far weaker than both the executive State Council and (of course) the CCP.

THE JUDICIAL SYSTEM

Under China's system of authoritarian rule, the law is subject to the leaders, not the other way around. In fact, for the most part the PRC's legal system did not function under Mao, and no criminal code existed prior to 1978. Legal reforms since that time have established a judicial system, but it remains subservient to the party hierarchy, which routinely protects officials from the law. Party leaders have often applied corruption or abuse-of-office statutes selectively and have fabricated or exaggerated crimes in order to snare political opponents or hold up one deviant as an example to others.

China has come under severe criticism from human rights groups both for its eagerness to employ capital punishment for a variety of crimes (including corruption, smuggling, theft, bribery, and rape) and for its extensive incarceration of political prisoners. Observers estimate that some 300,000 prisoners are being held in labor reeducation camps with no access to the legal system. Amnesty International noted that during one of China's periodic "strike hard" campaigns, Chinese authorities executed more criminals (1,781) in three months than did the rest of the world in the previous three years.[5] Amnesty International also contends that an estimated 50,000 practitioners of the outlawed **Falun Gong** meditation sect have been detained as political prisoners, with many of them and numerous other prisoners of conscience subjected to torture and other inhumane conditions.

Local Government

Unlike both Japan and Europe, which experienced decentralized feudalism in the not-so-distant past, China has been unified and ruled centrally for over 2,000 years. This has led successive authoritarian regimes, including the current one, to resist notions of federalism, believing that unity and stability are possible only under strong central leadership. Central control over such a huge and diverse nation has been far from complete but has been managed in China through the central structure of parallel party and government rule replicated throughout the descending levels of government. This includes 27 provinces, almost 3,000 counties, 45,000 townships, and nearly 1 million villages![6] Each level is modeled on the central government, with party and government councils, administrative departments, and congresses at the provincial, county, and township levels.

But if China's authoritarian rule has always been somewhat fragmented, the increased social and political demands brought on by reform and opening are making their mark on local politics. In an effort both to shore up the legitimacy of Communist rule and to address growing discontent within local communities, central political leaders have been experimenting over the past two decades with gradually increasing measures of local democratization. Initial ventures, during the 1980s, granted rural villages the right to secret ballot elections for county-level government congresses; later they were allowed to popularly elect relatively powerless "village committees" and "village heads." But by the late 1990s, increasingly brazen farmers, workers, and entrepreneurs had begun demanding the right to elect their local party secretaries, who are the real locus of power at the village level.[7] Although this political liberalization has not yet "trickled up" in any formal way, its impact on the nearly 1 billion Chinese still living in local villages ought not to be underestimated.

Other Institutions: The People's Liberation Army

Chairman Mao famously stated, "Political power grows out of the barrel of a gun." Later he claimed that he had not meant that military might is the means of obtaining political power but rather that "the Party commands the gun, and the gun must never be allowed to command the Party."[8] Although the CCP has sought to abide by Mao's admonition, the People's Liberation Army (PLA), which comprises China's army, navy, and air force, has played a significant role not just in China's revolutionary history but also in contemporary Chinese politics. Mao used the prestige and heroic stature the PLA garnered in battle prior to 1949 to add legitimacy to the Communist party-state once the PRC was established. The PLA played a key role in economic reconstruction in the 1950s, brought the Red Guard to heel during the chaotic Cultural Revolution, and smashed the protests at Tiananmen Square in 1989. The crackdown on the Tiananmen Square demonstration left hundreds (some say thousands) of protestors dead, capturing the world's attention. In the reform period, party leaders have sought to narrow both the economic and the political roles of the military. Party leaders have forced the military to sell off its extensive industrial and commercial interests, reduce its manpower, and upgrade the PLA's professionalism and technological prowess. Even with its new "leaner" status, the PLA remains the world's largest military force, with some 2.5 million troops and a military budget of nearly US$50 billion. The party established the Central Military Commission (CMC) first within the party and later as a government agency to guarantee party-state control over the gun. This control seems more certain now than perhaps at any other time in PRC history.

POLITICAL CONFLICT AND COMPETITION

The Party System: The Chinese Communist Party

Although reform and opening have created new avenues of economic and social mobility in China, membership in the Chinese Communist Party (CCP) remains essential for acquiring political influence and status. Because it offers the primary path to political advancement and is an obligatory credential for many careers and appointments, membership in the CCP is both sought after and selective. In 2007, there were over 73 million registered members in the party, roughly 7 percent of China's adult population. Between 2 million and 3 million new members are accepted into the CCP every year. Significantly, over a quarter of its current members are under age thirty-five, one fifth have college degrees, and over 3 million are capitalists!

While party membership has always been the chief pathway to elite recruitment, over time different sectors of society have gradually been targeted for inclusion in the party as the needs and priorities of the party-state have evolved. Mao Zedong's most significant contribution to Communist doctrine was his inclusion of peasants as an integral component of Communist revolution. Whereas Lenin described the Russian peasants as backward "vermin," Mao glorified the peasants' role in the Chinese revolution and recruited peasants to take political office in the new People's Republic of China. During the 1950s, the CCP sought to first create and then recruit a sector of industrial workers to establish a more orthodox (Marxist) Communist party. During the Cultural Revolution, the keys to political advancement were ideological purity and a background untainted by either feudal or bourgeois heritage.

Since Mao's death, China's reformist leaders have successively broadened the definition of political correctness in an effort to co-opt those deemed important to the reform program into the ranks of the party. Deng Xiaoping emphasized that an "ability to catch mice" (expertise), and not the "color of the cat" (political correctness), was the true measure of contribution to China's progress. He welcomed professionals, scholars, and intellectuals into the party. In a move that was sure to have Marx rolling in his grave, Jiang Zemin broadened the definition of the CCP in a 2001 policy known as the **"Three Represents"** to include not just workers and peasants, but even private entrepreneurs! Such moves have led critics to wonder how long a ruling party founded on the principle of destroying the very social class it has now chosen to embrace can endure.

But even as increasing numbers of scholars and other interested observers inside and outside China predict the collapse of CCP rule, it has managed thus far to resist both external challenges and internal decay.[9] Although the CCP's original heroic stature and revolutionary legitimacy may have little hold on China's younger generations, recent party leaders have effectively employed a mixture of authoritarian controls, patriotic nationalist appeals, and economic benefits to maintain the party's monopoly of political power.

The Succession and Circulation of Elites

One of the greatest challenges to perpetuating the CCP's political dominance has been the issue of political succession. As in most authoritarian systems, China faces the problem of having no institutionalized "vice office" to ease the transition to a successor when the top leader dies. The passing of longtime leader Mao Zedong in 1976 led to a leadership crisis and caused a rancorous struggle among several elite factions. In an effort to avoid repeating this problem, Deng Xiaoping did not assume formal leadership positions in either the party or the government when he came to power two years later and launched his reforms. Although he retained his position on the Politburo Standing Committee until 1987 and chaired the Central Military Commission until 1989, Deng's only other official title, until his death in 1997, was honorary president of the China Bridge Players Society.[10] From behind the scenes, he served as the paramount leader of China. "Third-generation" leader Jiang Zemin followed a variant of this model. After some ten years, in 2002, 2003, and 2004, respectively, Jiang stepped down from his positions as party general secretary, national president, and chairman of the CMC. Each of these positions was surrendered to his "fourth-generation" successor, Hu Jintao, who in 1992 had already been tapped by Deng Xiaoping as Jiang's successor.

In explaining the apparent success of this smooth transition from the third to the fourth generation of party leaders and the continued resilience of China's authoritarian rule, scholars point to a number of factors. These include the willingness and ability of the party elite to follow established norms of succession, promote elites within the party based more on merit than on personal or factional connections, and carefully balance the co-opting of elites and masses by repressing organized opposition to the party.[11] The party-state's careful management of this increasingly complex society is the focus of the next section.

Civil Society

Because the CCP claims to represent all legitimate social interests, officially there is no civil society in China. By definition, any organized interests outside the party are illegitimate and potentially harmful. Accordingly, the party-state has organized a number of mass organizations to control society and mobilize social groups to fulfill national goals. Legitimate "mass organizations" formed by the CCP include, among others, the Women's Federation and the All-China Federation of Trade Unions. Such groups are led by party officials and assist the party-state in disseminating information and implementing policies. In addition, the government organized numerous nongovernment associations during the reform period to facilitate state control of emerging economic and social interests, including small and large businesses, laborers, and other sectors. Although these are still firmly under state control, scholars point to these interest groups as potential elements of an independent Chinese civil society.

By far, the CCP's greatest gamble to date has been its 2001 decision to welcome capitalists as members of the party. In a move of political expediency that would have been incomprehensible to both Marx and Mao, Jiang Zemin argued that under the current conditions of "socialism with Chinese characteristics," the CCP ought to represent not just the interests of workers and peasants but also those of the private agents of China's "advanced productive forces." This open (if awkward) embrace of what was long considered socialism's class enemy acknowledges the growing economic influence (and political potential) of China's capitalist class, with private companies now accounting for some 70 percent of China's GDP. China's leaders recognize that, one way or another, capitalist interests will be heard. However, their determination that such interests be heard from within the party rather than from without may indeed have "revolutionary" consequences.

It should also be noted, however, that the illegality of independent civil associations has not prevented their emergence. This was perhaps most apparent in the 1989 demonstrations of students and their supporters at Tiananmen Square. But there have been many other efforts both prior to and since that event to organize social interests outside the official confines of the party-state (in fact, the events at Tiananmen Square in 1989 were the site's third such protest during the reform era).

To date, all significant attempts to form unauthorized political or social interest groups have been swiftly repressed. A decade following the crushing of the student movement at Tiananmen Square, the party-state launched a repression campaign against practitioners of the meditative martial arts movement Falun Gong. Founded in 1992, this traditional Chinese martial arts sect was initially promoted by the party-state as a safe domestic alternative to potentially threatening Western social and religious movements. But as the

IN COMPARISON	IS THE STATE TOO POWERFUL?

The state controls too much of our daily lives. Percent of survey respondents who agree:

Country	Percent
Brazil	76
Germany	74
India	71
Mexico	68
United States	65
France	65
United Kingdom	64
South Africa	63
Canada	59
Nigeria	59
China	39
Russia	36
Japan	34

*Data on Iran not available.
Source: Pew Center for the People and the Press, 2007.

movement rapidly gained adherents and grew in stature and organizational capacity, it caught the attention of the state, which began to impose restrictions. In response, Falun Gong began to mount larger demonstrations and rallies, including a daylong silent protest in 1999 outside the Beijing residential compound of China's top leaders that involved some 10,000 adherents. This prompted a swift crackdown in which the regime labeled the sect an evil cult, banned the organization, and arrested some 5,000 practitioners. Human rights groups charge that many of the arrested have been tortured and in some cases executed, with their corpses rendered for organ harvesting. Despite the persecution, Falun Gong still claims some 60 million Chinese followers (although the regime puts the number of participants at less than 2 million). The party-state's determination to squelch a social movement that claims no political agenda demonstrates both the extent of state paranoia and the remarkable organizational capacity and compelling attraction of this social movement under daunting circumstances.

The increasing complexity and openness of China's twenty-first-century society—coupled with the inevitable growing pains of its ongoing economic revolution—almost guarantee that this cycle of subversive rebellion, state repression, and renewed social resistance will continue to grow. Scholars point to a growing variety of increasingly motivated and articulate social groups—unemployed state employees, displaced farmers, migrant workers, environmentalists, members of underground Christian "house" churches, and many others—that are no longer easily subsumed under Mao's category of the masses and who have stepped up their demands even in the face of state repression. Peasant protests against onerous taxes, local corruption, and environmental hazards, and urban workers' strikes against layoffs and horrific working conditions are both increasingly common and well organized. The Chinese government officially acknowledged some 87,000 such protests in 2005 alone.

Potentially even more destabilizing is China's floating population of migrant workers, estimated now at 150 million and predicted to grow to 350 million by 2025. These nomadic laborers have little job security, no legal residency beyond their abandoned villages, and no authorized access to housing, health care, or education. Likewise, China now boasts over 300 million netizens—more than any other country in the world—who regularly surf and blog, severely testing the regime's capacity to monitor their networking activities and censor their access to politically dangerous resources on the web.

Although none of these groups is yet an organized social movement like Falun Gong or a political separatist movement like those active in China's western border regions (see "Xinjiang and Tibet: Separatism or Assimilation?," p. 311), some observers predict that such grassroots movements could combine with ongoing intellectual dissidence to rekindle demands for democ-

XINJIANG AND TIBET: SEPARATISM OR ASSIMILATION?

For millennia, China has struggled to maintain sovereignty over its border regions, particularly its western frontiers. This remains true in the twenty-first century, as China faces demands for increased autonomy from the Turkic Uighur minority in the northwestern province of Xinjiang and from Tibetans in the southwest. Advocates for greater autonomy in both regions can point to periods of independence during the first half of the twentieth century and much longer periods of separation from the Chinese empire in the centuries before. But the Chinese Communists moved quickly after 1949 to consolidate control over these two sparsely populated regions and used an uprising in Tibet in 1959 to eliminate opposition to Chinese sovereignty and force the Tibetan hereditary religious and political leader, the Dalai Lama, into exile in India. Muslim Uighurs and Buddhist Tibetans have long resented Chinese Communist control, and proponents of a "Free Tibet" and an "East Turkestan" continue to champion independence or at least greater autonomy. These voices are primarily from outside of China's borders, although internal acts of terrorism and violence have been regular occurrences.

Chinese Communist leaders have always viewed sovereign control of both regions as vital and nonnegotiable. The recent discovery, moreover, of extensive fossil fuel reserves in Western China and the strategic position of these regions as China looks farther westward to Central Asia and the Middle East has made full control of the regions even more important to Chinese authorities. In both regions, the regime has countered separatist efforts with an effective pacification strategy that has combined co-optation, assimilation, and repression. In recent years, the government has pumped billions of dollars into the regions, improving transport and communication infrastructure, including construction of the world's highest (and most expensive) railway (to Tibet) and citywide broadband in Xinjiang's larger cities. This investment has provided jobs, income, and opportunities to locals, particularly the educated elite. But it has also brought waves of ethnic Han Chinese, who now outnumber the local population in Xinjiang and claim the lion's share of new jobs created in both regions. Although the population of the less-accessible Tibet is still over 90 percent ethnic Tibetan, locals in both regions complain that it is only a matter of time before the dominant Han Chinese culture overwhelms the indigenous languages, cultures, and perhaps even faiths. When resentment and complaints turn violent, as they did in both regions most recently in the run up to the 2008 Summer Olympics, the regime has not hesitated to react with harsh repression.

ratization and the end of CCP rule. Others counter that the party-state's control of the Internet, cell phones, and other media resources through its censorship and the extensive reach of its security apparatus have largely managed to keep a lid on social unrest and thwart the emergence of an autonomous civil society. They note that although Western observers and political leaders denounced the brutal state repression of Tibetan protests in 2008 (and threatened a boycott of the Beijing Summer Olympics), Chinese authorities were able not only to control almost completely what its own citizens heard and saw but also to portray the protests to its own people as a violent Tibetan threat to Chinese sovereignty and as Western exploitation of a national tragedy.

Can this juxtaposition of an increasingly open economic system and a persistently closed political system endure? Although there is much debate over whether China's authoritarian political system is moving toward greater liberalization or inevitable collapse, most observers conclude that this volatile combination is far too contradictory to prevail for long.

SOCIETY

Ethnic and National Identity

Though the Chinese commonly view themselves as a homogeneous society, China is not without ethnic diversity. China is populated mostly by Han Chinese (who make up more than 90 percent of the total population), but it recognizes at least fifty-five minority nationalities. Although minorities comprise only a small percentage of the population, many reside in strategic "autonomous areas" (such as Tibet and Xinjiang) that make up more than 60 percent of China's territory and have a long and often violent history of resistance to the Chinese state. Even among Han Chinese there is tremendous linguistic diversity, as the map on p. 313 illustrates. For thousands of years, Han Chinese have shared a written language, but Han speakers are divided into eight main language groups and hundreds of dialects. The majority of Chinese (about 800 million) speak Mandarin, but many also speak some form of Wu (90 million) or Yue (also known as Cantonese; 70 million).

Since the twentieth century, Beijing has sought to make Mandarin (and, specifically, the Beijing dialect of Mandarin) the official language of government and education. Despite these attempts, Mandarin is not spoken universally in rural China, and its use has actually declined in prosperous urban areas along China's southern coast. Indeed, the inability of China's Communist regime to impose a uniform national language calls into question its overall capacity to rule and suggests that local resistance to central control is stronger than often assumed.

Ideology and Political Culture

Chinese political culture is in a state of flux, and much of it will remain unknown until more extensive public-opinion data (banned until very recently) are available. During the rule of Mao Zedong, the party-state attempted to

CHINESE-LANGUAGE DIALECTS

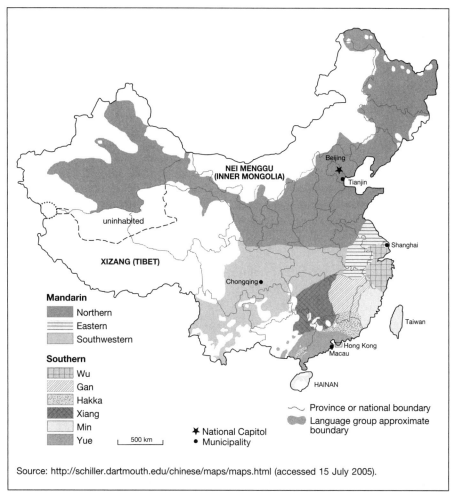

Mandarin
Northern
Eastern
Southwestern

Southern
Wu
Gan
Hakka
Xiang
Min
Yue

✱ National Capitol
● Municipality

500 km

◠ Province or national boundary
Language group approximate
boundary

NEI MENGGU
(INNER MONGOLIA)

Beijing
Tianjin

uninhabited

Shanghai

XIZANG (TIBET)

Chongqing●

Taiwan

Hong Kong
Macau

HAINAN

Source: http://schiller.dartmouth.edu/chinese/maps/maps.html (accessed 15 July 2005).

reshape China's traditional political culture through massive propaganda, mobilization, and repression. The importance of Communist ideas has waned since the time of Mao's death, especially as a capitalist economy has come to replace state socialism. Communist ideology still maintains strong rural influence, but China's cities reflect a growing diversity of information and ideas.

TRADITIONAL CENTRALIZED AUTHORITARIANISM

Mao viewed China's "poor and blank" population as ripe for the party-led makeover of political culture, but traditional Chinese political culture was far more resilient than Mao had imagined. Before the Communists took power in 1949, China had a long history of centrally imposed authoritarian politics.

ETHNIC GROUPS

RELIGION

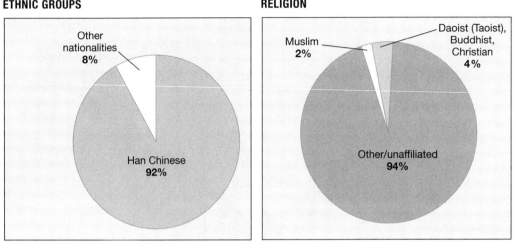

Mao's Communists moved the capital from Nanjing back to Beijing (which had been the imperial capital for centuries) and in doing so directly connected their rule to traditional Chinese authoritarianism. In many ways, the Communist regime replicated elements of the rigid and hierarchical imperial system. For example, China still administers extremely competitive national examinations that determine university admission, and under Communist rule the tradition of respect for one's elders was reflected in the elevated average age of party leaders. Despite significant efforts by some to improve the status of Chinese women, the male domination of China's Communist leadership continues to expose the traditional paternalism of Chinese politics.

CONFUCIANISM

One significant influence over the political culture and ideology of the Chinese people has been the thought of the scholar Confucius (551–479 B.C.E.). Under the tenets of Confucianism, the role of government is to impose a strict moral code and to foster "correct" thought. Key to the Confucian view of the world are the ideas of hierarchy and subservience to one's superiors, with respect radiating out from one's family (the elders) to the national leader (the emperor).

MAOISM

While Mao's ideas were firmly rooted in Marxism-Leninism, Mao gave those ideas a decidedly Confucian spin. He believed that the key to revolutionary prosperity lay in the ability of the Communist Party to create a "new socialist man" and to alter the way people think. While building on traditional Chinese political culture, Mao introduced some radical concepts. For example, instead of rallying to the traditional Confucian notion of harmony, Mao promoted constant class struggle. Maoism emphasized the collective over the individual, again drawing on traditional Confucian notions. However, where traditional Chinese values favored loyalty to the extended family, Mao sought to transfer that loyalty to the larger community, as embodied by the party, the state, and, locally, the work unit (*danwei*). The Communists also claimed to promote egalitarianism, thus improving the lot of the nation's poor, peasants, and women.

In Mao's view, revolutionary thought (as decreed by the party leadership) could replace Chinese values, and the party could promote these ideas through constant propaganda and slogans, mass campaigns, and the education system, which included intensive sessions of "thought reform" and "self-criticism." Likewise, economic development could be "willed" through massive acts of peasant-driven voluntarism. Mao regularly favored political correctness ("Red") over technical expertise ("expert"), often at great cost to China's economy, most infamously during the Great Leap Forward and the Cultural Revolution.

Given the dearth of modern opinion research in Communist China, it is impossible to know whether Maoism has changed Chinese political culture or merely reinforced traditional Chinese characteristics. The ease with which the Chinese have embraced capitalist reforms, increased individualism, and allowed the growth of inequality suggests that Mao's ideas were accepted more out of deference to central authority than out of any deep convictions. Since Mao's death, the importance of Maoism and indeed Communism has waned. China's current leaders neither demand nor desire the type of mass mobilization that was a hallmark of Mao's China. The current leadership instead prefers a largely depoliticized public that is more common in the authoritarian regimes of developing countries, as it was in pre-Communist China.

NATIONALISM

Nationalism was a dominant feature of twentieth-century China and has perhaps become even more important today, as the nominally Communist party-state seeks new sources of legitimacy for retaining its monopoly of political power. The country's long and powerful imperial past (and its humiliation at the hands of foreigners in the nineteenth and twentieth centuries) has bred a strong sense of national pride. Mao's Communists capitalized on this sense of nationalism by melding the struggle for Communism with the bitter struggle to expel the Japanese occupiers during World War II. Fierce nationalism, often manifested as xenophobia, is a cornerstone of Chinese political culture and is frequently used by Communist leaders to maintain support for the political system. Chinese hostile reaction to the inadvertent U.S. bombing of China's embassy in Yugoslavia in 1999 and the downing of a surveillance plane in 2001, widespread anti-Japanese street protests in 2005, and angry Chinese

---

BEIJING SUMMER OLYMPICS 2008: CHINA COMES OF AGE

After an unsuccessful bid for the 2000 Olympics, China learned in 2001 that it had been selected to host the 2008 Summer Olympics in Beijing. Proud Chinese citizens at home and advocates of "constructive engagement" with China abroad all celebrated the decision. They argued that as with Japan, which hosted the 1960 Tokyo Olympics, China's Olympic sponsorship would mark its "coming of age," would help consolidate the gains of its three decades of economic and cultural opening, and like South Korea, which hosted the 1988 Seoul Olympics, would likely spur its authoritarian regime to move toward greater political openness.

But by 2008, China found its position in the limelight increasingly uncomfortable, as groups at home and abroad hoping to influence China's foreign and domestic policies took advantage of the increased scrutiny and the potential leverage this brought to advocate and bring about change. Human rights groups criticized China's ongoing support of the authoritarian Sudanese regime and its policy of genocide in Darfur. Calls increased for boycotting the Olympics as China's plans for a triumphal global torch relay became what some described as a public relations disaster, coinciding with a violent Chinese crackdown on Tibetan unrest. Each new stop on the torch's journey provided a new media-saturated venue for large-scale human rights protests against Chinese policy and increasing nationalist anger among Chinese citizens who saw the protests as unfair foreign meddling.

Tragically, it was a devastating earthquake in the central Chinese province of Sichuan that shifted the attention of the media, Chinese nationalists, and even human rights advocates. The 8.0 earthquake claimed the lives of more than 70,000 and left nearly 5 million Chinese homeless. The world turned its attention to the plight of the victims of the quake and watched the heroic efforts of rescue teams and Chinese locals. Although muted criticism abroad and some demonstrations and unrest within China persisted throughout the Olympics, the event was by nearly all accounts a national success, if not an obvious catalyst for political change.

---

reactions to foreign protests leading up to the 2008 Summer Olympics are recent manifestations of this Chinese nationalism. Indeed, China's hosting of the Beijing Olympics was both manifestation and confirmation of the key role of patriotism and nationalism in twenty-first century China (see "Beijing Summer Olympics 2008: China Comes of Age," above).

CHALLENGES TO CHINA'S COMMUNIST POLITICAL CULTURE

There is growing evidence that the strict party control of Chinese political culture is steadily eroding. The widespread support for the pro-democracy student movement in Tiananmen Square in 1989 was the first major sign that the Communist Party no longer had a monopoly on political ideas (even as the party's crushing of the protests demonstrated that the state retained a monopoly of force). Subsequent years have seen steady growth in dissent and protest by China's rural poor, disgruntled industrial workers, and disaffected ethnic minorities. The spiritual success of Falun Gong and China's thousands of illegal Christian "house churches" has frightened the Chinese government with its ability to attract and mobilize followers independent of state control. Internet usage vital to China's economic growth has exploded in China and created a venue for Chinese political opposition. For better or worse, booming trade and tourism have released a flood of Western ideas and values. In sum, it is unclear how long China's leaders can depend on a largely passive and compliant public, especially as rapid economic growth and globalization create new tensions, problems, and opportunities.

POLITICAL ECONOMY

From 1949 to 1978, China adopted a Soviet-style Communist political economic model. In choosing this model, Mao Zedong and the Chinese Communist Party (CCP) leadership consciously opted for equality over freedom, promising all Chinese an "**iron rice bowl**" (cradle-to-grave health care, work, and retirement security), as well as retaining state ownership of all property and full control of the economy through central planning. State bureaucrats assigned targets and quotas to producers at all levels of the economy and allocated basic goods to consumers.

As in the Soviet Union, this centrally planned political economic model favored the development of heavy industry at the expense of consumer goods. It also led to the creation of a massive state economic policy-making bureaucracy not present in capitalist political economies. Between 1949 and 1952, the state gradually nationalized most private industries and mobilized the economy to recover from the eight years of war with Japan and four years of civil war. By 1952, the Communist state had redistributed land to more than 300 million landless peasants. In the mid-1950s, peasants were strongly encouraged to form larger agricultural cooperatives, pooling land, equipment, and labor and sharing profits; such cooperatives gave the state greater political control over the countryside.

Despite the agrarian roots of the Chinese revolution, Mao and the CCP sought to emulate Stalin's successful crash indus-

LABOR FORCE BY OCCUPATION

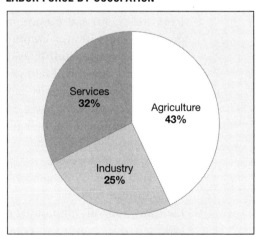

Services 32%

Agriculture 43%

Industry 25%

trialization policy by launching the Great Leap Forward (1958–1960). Mao believed that Communist-led mass campaigns could be marshaled for rapid industrial growth, and to pursue that goal he favored a policy of **Reds versus experts**: that is, politically indoctrinated party cadres (Reds) over those with economic training (experts). Vowing to progress "twenty years in a day" and to catch up with the industrialized West in fifteen years, Mao promoted the creation of small-scale, labor-intensive industry (so-called backyard industries) in both cities and the countryside. The Great Leap Forward further collectivized agriculture by creating gigantic communes that became party-controlled providers of education, health care, public works, and industrial production. The Great Leap Forward was a gigantic failure. The diversion of energy to inefficient industry from agriculture and a drop in food production caused by the forced collectivization of farm production were largely responsible for a three-year famine that killed as many as 30 million people.

By the early 1960s, Mao had been marginalized from the realm of economic policy making, and most of his Great Leap policies had been abandoned. Large-scale agricultural communes were disbanded, and peasant households were allowed to operate as independent producers, supplying their goods directly to the state and selling their surplus on the free market. Industries began to emphasize expertise over political correctness and material over moral incentives.

Responding to his own marginalization, Mao attacked these new policies as "capitalist" and in 1966 launched the Great Proletarian Cultural Revolution. The persecution unleashed during the next decade targeted those with the most expertise; the impact on the economy was devastating. Once again, Mao's disastrous policies were shelved.

In the mid-1970s, China's was still a poor and isolated economy. After the death of Mao in 1976, and under the leadership of Deng Xiaoping, economic reform began gradually as the Chinese Communist leadership shifted its focus from the traditional Communist goal of equity to creating rapid economic growth.[12] Agricultural communes were disbanded and replaced with the **household responsibility system**, a euphemism for largely private farming. Individual farmers still had to sell a set amount of their produce to the state but were free to sell any surplus on the open market. Food production improved dramatically, and famine became a thing of the past. Industries were decentralized; in their place, "collective" and "town and village" enterprises were allowed greater economic freedom and encouraged to generate profits. The importance of China's state sector gradually diminished, dropping from about 80 percent in 1980 to under 20 percent by 1996. By the mid-1980s, private industry was permitted (though initially heavily regulated), and the state gradually eliminated price controls. Hoping to end China's economic isolation, the government created **special economic zones** in 1979, offering tax breaks and other incentives to lure foreign investment to a handful of coastal enclaves.

By the 1990s, China's socialist command economy had been transformed into a "socialist market economy." The reforms have sparked three decades of astounding economic growth. Over this period, China's economy expanded nearly 10 percent annually, and its GDP grew tenfold. Hundreds of millions of people have been lifted out of poverty, but China remains a poor country. Its per capita GDP at purchasing power parity in 2007 was only $5,300, compared with $45,800 in the United States, $14,700 in Russia, and $12,800 in Mexico.

The reforms have created both rapid growth and huge problems. First, as China's enterprises have become more profit oriented, they are free to lay off unproductive labor. As a result, Mao's "iron rice bowl" has given way to massive unemployment. The Chinese leadership is betting that China's growing private sector will be able to absorb the unemployed. Second, after decades of Communist emphasis on equality, the reforms of the past two decades have made China much less equal, magnifying inequality between individuals, between urban and rural Chinese, and between regions.[13] China's Gini index (a measure of inequality where a score of 0 equals perfect equality and 1 equals total inequality) rose from .39 to .47 in the two decades from 1988 to 2007. Most direct foreign investment has been concentrated along China's eastern coast, especially in Guangdong Province, Shanghai, Beijing, and Tianjin, while China's poorer interior has received very little of this investment. The growing inequality is partly responsible for the estimated 150 million Chinese who comprise China's floating population and has been blamed for rising crime rates.[14] The Chinese no longer enjoy guaranteed access to health care, and even the traditional benefit of free universal education has eroded.

Third, rapid industrial development has created huge resource shortages and environmental damage for China. A fourth of the country is desert and three fourths of its forests have disappeared. Its rivers are drying up, and the water and air that remain are filling with harmful chemicals. Half a billion Chinese lack access to safe drinking water, and an equal number breathe dangerously unsafe air—the Chinese are literally "choking on their own success."[15] And increasingly, China's problem has become the world's problem: China surpassed the United States in 2008 as the world's largest emitter of greenhouse gases, and China's voracious economy is consuming world resources at an unprecedented rate. Finally, China's exports, the engine of its growth, are also causing problems as China's trade surplus with its trading partners grows and controversy mounts concerning the safety and quality of its products.

In China's increasingly competitive economic environment, state-owned enterprises (SOEs) have struggled. The state attempted to restructure the SOEs through mergers and consolidation, and the number of such firms has been reduced from 100,000 in the mid-1990s to about 60,000 a decade later. The private sector produces 74 percent of industrial output, but the state sector is still enormous and continues to suffer from inefficiency, corruption, and surplus labor—while consuming a disproportionate amount of credit granted by state-owned banks. The Chinese state subsidizes unprofitable state industries, in large part through the state-owned banking system, because it wants to avoid politically dangerous levels of unemployment.

RURAL UNEMPLOYMENT AND TRANSITION

Seventy percent of China's population lives in the countryside. Early economic reforms largely benefited the rural areas, but more recent reforms have focused primarily on China's cities, and much of rural China remains desperately poor and largely neglected. Prices for agricultural goods are low, taxes are high, school is expensive, health care is poor, and the modern consumer amenities that are increasingly available in urban China are mostly absent in rural areas. As a way of favoring industrialization, China has kept prices for farm products artificially low, and as the country modernizes its agriculture, hundreds of millions of Chinese have migrated to the cities to escape rural poverty. In China, such immigration is technically illegal, and rural Chinese who migrate to cities face harsh conditions and discrimination. The state has been unable to stem the tide, however, despite recent promises to redress the imbalance between urban and rural benefits from reform and opening.

THE GROWTH OF A FOREIGN PRESENCE

China's entry into the World Trade Organization (WTO) in 2001 has brought both benefits and new challenges to its economy. WTO membership requires China to further liberalize its economy, and domestic firms, especially SOEs, face growing competition from foreign enterprises. Most recently, even China's debt-ridden state-banking sector has begun to feel the harsh winds of foreign competition. Despite the tremendous liberalization of the Chinese economy, the country's economic system remains substantially closed. China's economy is freer than Russia's but is still more restricted than the economies of Mexico, Japan, the United Kingdom, and the United States.

FOREIGN RELATIONS AND THE WORLD

During much of their long history, the Chinese viewed themselves as economically and culturally superior to the rest of the world. When nineteenth-century incursions by more economically advanced Western powers shattered that perception, Chinese society entered an extended period of crisis and self-doubt. The defeat of the Japanese in 1945 ended the humiliation of Japan's brutal occupation of China, and in 1949 the victorious government sought to restore China's past grandeur. China's return to isolation reached its zenith during the Cultural Revolution, when Mao Zedong attacked all foreign cultural and economic influences. China was not only isolated from Western capitalist nations and most of its neighbors but also estranged from its erstwhile mentor, the Soviet Union, beginning in the late 1950s—when Soviet and Chinese policies diverged after Stalin's death.

Since Mao's death in 1976, China has steadily emerged from decades of isolation under the policy of reform and opening. U.S. President Richard Nixon's historic visit to China in 1972 marked the beginning of China's opening to the West and the rest of the world. By the end of the 1970s, the United States and most other countries had normalized relations with Communist China and had, in effect, ceased to recognize the anti-Communist regime in Taiwan. Today, China's military might, the size of its economy, and its status as a permanent member of the United Nations Security Council make it an important international power. However, the country's long legacy of isolation continues to color its foreign relations and inform its official rhetoric.

Throughout the 1990s, China continued to improve its relations with much of the world, signing major accords with the European Union, Russia, Japan, and the Association of Southeast Asian Nations (ASEAN). These treaties are part of what the Chinese leadership has referred to as "strategic partnerships."[16]

Despite persistent bitter memories of the brutal Japanese occupation during World War II, China has to a large extent made peace with Japan. The two nations now share substantial and mutually important economic relations, although Japan's unwillingness to apologize for its past to China's satisfaction continues to fuel strong anti-Japanese sentiment in China. Bitter rivalry with India, with whom China fought a border war in the early 1960s, has been replaced by a growing trade relationship and a 2005 agreement to resolve outstanding border disputes. These two regional nuclear powers are poor countries with populations exceeding 1 billion, and the potential for a dangerous confrontation between them has diminished in recent decades. India has recognized Chinese sovereignty over Tibet but has also provided refuge for the Dalai Lama and the exiled Tibetan government. China once supported Pakistan in its conflict with India but is now officially neutral. In 2001, China and Russia signed their first friendship treaty in fifty years; in 2008, they resolved their final border disputes, bringing to an end what had been a long-standing cold war rivalry for world Communist leadership.

China has played an important role in the growing global concern about the nuclear capabilities of North Korea, its neighbor and traditional ally. North Korea shows only vague interest in the Chinese model of gradual economic liberalization and maintains a closed state and a Communist political economy similar to Maoist China's policies. Nevertheless, since the end of the cold war, China has been North Korea's only reliable ally and its chief source of economic aid. This special relationship has given China a key role in diplomatic efforts to address North Korean threats. China must balance this relationship with its now-booming trade and investment ties with capitalist South Korea.

Ever since President Nixon's visit, China's volatile relationship with the United States has been characterized by periodic tension and mistrust. When U.S. pilots mistakenly bombed the Chinese embassy in Belgrade in 1999, China's leadership responded with bellicose rhetoric that alarmed U.S. leaders. In 2001, China and the United States faced off over China's capture of a U.S. surveillance plane that was forced to make an emergency landing on Chinese soil, with China's leaders making statements that incited nationalist sentiment and smacked of the Maoist era. Since the events of September 11, however, relations between China and the United States have steadily improved.[17] Although some Chinese intellectuals viewed the attacks on the United States as understandable retaliation for so-called U.S. imperialist behavior, China supported the U.S. invasion of Afghanistan and the broader war on terrorism (though not its invasion of Iraq in 2003).[18]

At the heart of Sino-U.S. relations is the nearly US$400 billion in two-way trade and the substantial direct investment ties that bind the two countries. China is currently America's second-largest trading partner (behind Canada), and the United States is first on China's trade list. But one central question threatens this relationship: Does China pose a threat to world peace? Although China's leaders speak often of China's "peaceful rise," some scholars have pointed to Chinese leaders' frequent outbursts of nationalist, anti-U.S., and anti-Japanese rhetoric. They doubt that economic liberalization and increased trade will moderate Chinese behavior toward its neighbors and make it a more peaceful member of the international community. They point to China's huge and growing demand for natural resources and the territorial disputes and questionable alliances these resource needs have fostered. Others point to these same economic interdependencies and China's remarkably successful staging of the 2008 Olympics as growing evidence that China's growth has given it both the need and the confidence to fully participate as a peaceful leader of the international community.

CURRENT ISSUES

THE TAIWAN QUESTION

By far the most serious threat to China's peaceful rise is the potential conflict over the future of Taiwan, which is located only 100 miles off the Chinese mainland. After the victory of the Communists in 1949, Nationalist troops under Chiang Kai-shek retreated to Taiwan, which prospered as a capitalist authoritarian state and, during the cold war, gained the military protection of the United States. But at the urging of the PRC, Taiwan lost its United

Nations seat in 1971. The United States (along with most other nations) effectively ceased to recognize Taiwan after formal diplomatic relations were established with China in 1979. By the 1980s, Taiwan appeared increasingly vulnerable to Chinese attack.

The Chinese leadership has always regarded Taiwan as a renegade province of the mainland, and it has always sought the full reintegration of Taiwan into the PRC.[19] China has continually threatened Taiwan, first with bombardment and subsequently with harsh rhetoric and military displays. The Chinese have repeatedly claimed that they would view any declaration of independence by Taiwan as an act of war. Tensions over Taiwan have continued to grow since it democratized in the late 1980s. In late 1995, the PRC sought to intimidate voters in Taiwan's presidential election with aggressive military exercises and veiled threats. The United States' unique relationship with Taiwan and continued promises of military protection and weapons sales has often proved to be a thorn in the side of Sino-U.S. relations. Despite the continued tension between Taiwan and China, however, Taiwanese investment in and trade with China, estimated at US$500 billion in 2007, is quickly drawing the economies closer together.

The case of Hong Kong may provide a model for peaceful resolution of the Taiwan issue. Hong Kong is a tiny territory that was ceded by the Chinese to the United Kingdom in the mid-1800s, largely as a result of China's losses in wars intended to open China to foreign trade. The United Kingdom ruled Hong Kong as a colony for over 150 years, and it became a successful capitalist economic powerhouse on the doorstep of Communist China. In the 1980s, China and the United Kingdom agreed on a plan that would relinquish Hong Kong to Chinese sovereignty in 1997 under the principle of "**one country, two systems**." The Chinese guaranteed Hong Kong virtually total autonomy for a transitional period of fifty years, a pledge that it has thus far respected in most regards. China has argued that a Hong Kong–style reintegration of Taiwan into the PRC would involve little or no disruption for the Taiwanese. However, China's manhandling of social unrest in Tibet and Xinjiang has left many of Taiwan's citizens unpersuaded.

HUMAN RIGHTS AND FOREIGN RELATIONS

China's repeated violations of human rights from Tiananmen to Tibet have been a source of tension between China and the rest of the world. The Chinese view any criticism of their domestic politics as foreign meddling, and they tend to react defensively. American attempts to link China's human rights behavior to trade benefits were deeply resented by the Chinese and have been largely abandoned since the mid-1990s. China's main trading partners have been reluctant to focus too much attention on human rights issues as their economic stakes in China increase. Free-trade advocates contend that increased trade and contact with the West—constructive engagement—not economic sanctions, will most effectively improve human rights in China. Others contend that globalization will increase economic disparities and tensions within China and that the leadership may respond with even greater political repression. Whether or not China's entry into the World Trade Organization and hosting of the Olympics have led the regime to pay more attention to human rights or given it the confidence to turn a deaf ear to foreign pressure remains a topic for debate. To date, China has been remarkably successful in balancing its economic reform and opening with harsh political repression.

NOTES

1. Qianlong, letter to George III (1793; Internet Modern History Sourcebook, Fordham University, 1998), www.fordham.edu/halsall/mod/1793qianlong.html (accessed 16 June 2005).
2. For a list of quotations, see Mao Tse-tung, *Quotations from Chairman Mao Tse-tung*, www.marxists.org/reference/archive/mao/works/red-book (Mao Tse-tung Internet Archive, 2000) (accessed 18 June 2005).
3. Bruce Gilley, "The Limits of Authoritarian Resilience," *Journal of Democracy*, 14 (2003), p. 18.
4. China Internet Information Center, "China's Political System: The Party in Power," www.china.org.cn/english/Political/25060.htm (accessed 19 August 2003).
5. See Amnesty International, "China: 'Strike Hard' Anti-Crime Campaign Intensifies," press release, 23 July 2002, http://web.amnesty.org/library/Index/engASA17029 2002?Open (accessed 17 November 2003).
6. The first figure includes twenty-three actual provinces and the four "municipalities," or megacities of Beijing, Shanghai, Tianjin, and Chongqing.
7. Charles Hutzler, "Elections: Winding Road to Reform," *Far Eastern Economic Review* (5 September 2002), p. 27.
8. Mao Tse-tung, "Problems of War and Strategy," in *Selected Works*, vol. 2 (Beijing: Foreign Language Press, 1965), p. 225.
9. See, for example, Gordon G. G. Chang, *The Coming Collapse of China* (New York: Random House, 2001), and Minxin Pei, "Contradictory Trends and Confusing Signals," *Journal of Democracy*, 14 (2003), pp. 73–81.
10. Like many Chinese, Deng Xiaoping was an avid bridge player.
11. Andrew J. Nathan, "Authoritarian Resilience," *Journal of Democracy*, 14 (2003), pp. 6–17.
12. Gordon White, *Riding the Tiger: The Politics of Economic Reform in Post-Mao China* (Stanford, CA: Stanford University Press, 1993).
13. Tony Saich, "China's New Leadership: The Challenges to the Politics of Muddling Through," *Current History*, 101 (September 2002), pp. 250–55.
14. Michael Dorgan, "Growing Rich–Poor Gap, Economic Growth, Spur Crime in China," *Knight Ridder/Tribune Business News*, 27 March 2002.
15. Joseph Kahn and Jim Yardley, "As China Roars, Pollution Reaches Deadly Extremes," *New York Times*, 26 August 2007.
16. Zhang Y. S. Wankun, "Patterns and Dynamics of China's International Strategic Behaviour," *Journal of Contemporary China*, 11, no. 31 (May 2002), p. 235.
17. David Shambaugh, "Sino-American Relations since September 11: Can the New Stability Last?" *Current History*, 101 (September 2002), pp. 243–49.

18. Ying Ma, "China's America Problem," *Policy Review*, 111 (February/March 2002), pp. 43–56.
19. Kurt M. Campbell and Derek J. Mitchell, "Crisis in the Taiwan Strait?" *Foreign Affairs*, 80 (July/August 2001), p. 14.

GLOSSARY OF KEY TERMS

Chinese Communist Party (CCP)   Authoritarian party that has ruled China from 1949 to the present.

Confucianism   Philosophy attributed to Chinese sage Confucius (551–479 B.C.E.) emphasizing social harmony.

Cultural Revolution   Mao's radical movement launched in 1966 to regain political control from rivals resulting in a decade of social and political chaos.

danwei **(unit)**   Maoist program providing all Chinese citizens lifetime affiliation with a work unit governing all aspects of their lives.

democratic centralism   Communist Party doctrine subordinating individual members to the party organization.

Deng Xiaoping   China's paramount leader (1978–1997) who launched China's policy of economic reform and opening.

Falun Gong   Meditative martial arts movement founded in 1992 and banned by Chinese government in 1999 as an "evil cult."

floating population   China's roughly 150 million itinerant peasants who left the countryside seeking urban employment.

Great Leap Forward   Mao's disastrous effort (1958–1959) to modernize China through localized industrial production and agricultural communes.

hukou **(household registration)**   Maoist program that tied all Chinese to a particular geographic location.

household responsibility system   Deng's 1980s' highly succesful rural reform program that lowered production quotas and allowed the sale of surplus agricultural produce on the free market.

Hundred Flowers campaign   Period from 1956 to 1957 in which Mao encouraged intellectuals to offer criticism of national policy, followed by crackdown on critics.

Hu Jintao   China's current Communist Party leader and head of state.

iron rice bowl   Mao's promise of cradle-to-grave health care, work, and retirement security that has largely disappeared under reform and opening.

Jiang Zemin   Deng's successor in the 1990s as Communist Party leader and head of state.

Kuomintang (KMT)   China's Nationalist Party founded by Sun Yat-sen and led by Chiang Kai-shek, who was overthrown by Mao's Communists in 1949 and forced to flee to Taiwan.

Long March   The Communist Party's 3,000-mile heroic retreat (1934–1935) to northwestern China during its civil war with the Chinese Nationalist KMT.

Mao Zedong   Leader of the Chinese Communist revolution who dominated Chinese politics from the founding of the PRC until his death.

May Fourth movement   Student-led anti-imperialist cultural and political movement growing out of student demonstrations in Beijing on May 4, 1919.

National Party Congress   Chinese Communist Party's cumbersome legislative body.

National People's Congress (NPC)   China's national legislature.

"one country, two systems"   China's guarantee to Hong Kong of fifty years of domestic autonomy as a "special administrative region" after the British colony was returned to China in 1997.

People's Liberation Army (PLA)   China's military.

Red Guard   Radicalized youth who served as Mao's shock troops during the Cultural Revolution.

Reds versus experts   Mao's policy favoring politically indoctrinated party cadres (Reds) over those people who had economic training (experts).

reform and opening   Deng's economic liberalization policy, starting in the late 1970s.

special economic zones   Enclaves established since 1980 by the Chinese government that have offered tax breaks and other incentives to lure foreign investment.

Sun Yat-sen   Founder of China's Nationalist Party (Kuomintang) and considered the father of modern China.

"Three Represents"   Jiang Zemin's 2001 policy co-opting private entrepreneurs into the CCP.

Tiananmen Square   Historic plaza in Beijing where the Chinese party-state crushed the 1989 pro-reform demonstration.

Wen Jiabao   China's current premier and head of government.

WEB LINKS

China General Information Base **www.chinatoday.com/general/a.htm**
   Unofficial site offering useful general information.

China's Political System **www.china.org.cn/english/Political/25060.htm**
   Official government site describing the political structure, fundamental laws, rules, regulations, and practices of China since its founding.

A Country Study: China **lcweb2.loc.gov/frd/cs/cntoc.html**
   Library of Congress's *Country Studies Series* presents a description and analysis of the historical setting and the social, economic, political, and national security systems of China.

9 INDIA

Head of state: President Pratibha Patil
(since July 2007)

Head of government:
Prime Minister Manmohan Singh
(since May 2004)

Capital: New Delhi

Total land size: 3,287,590 sq km

Population: 1.15 billion

GDP at PPP: 2.99 trillion US$

GDP per capita at PPP: $2,700

Human development index ranking: 128

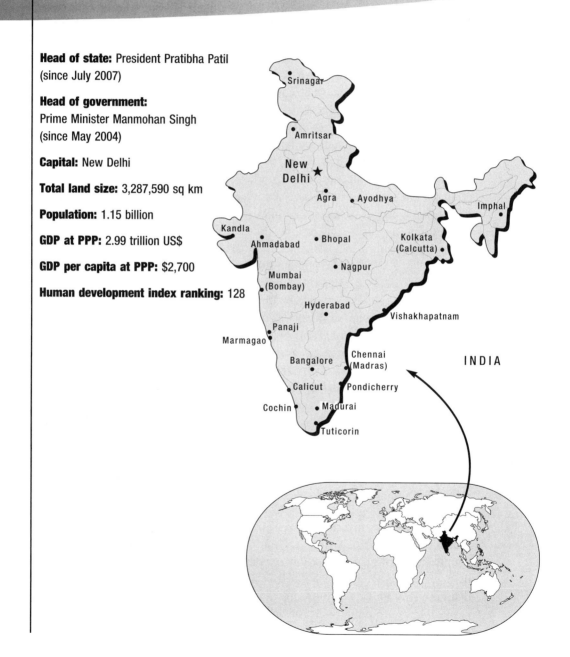

INTRODUCTION

Why Study This Case?

India presents a remarkable and instructive case for the study of comparative politics. This South Asian nation will, within several decades, eclipse China as the world's most populous country. Already it is the world's largest democracy, with more voters in a typical election (some 400 million) than the entire population of any other country in the world except China.

Besides being the largest, India is also one of the most improbable of democracies, and herein lies one of the key puzzles of the case. Scholars most often associate democracy with critical levels of prosperity, mass literacy, urbanization, and national unity. India seemingly disproves each of these factors. One fourth of all Indians live on less than US$1 a day, and less than half of all Indian women are literate. Paradoxically, poor and illiterate Indians—most often living in rural areas, not cities—are three times as likely to vote as the national average. And despite the backwardness of rural India, satellite dishes have brought television to more than 80 percent of the country's half million villages (though less than a third of rural households own a television).

Most puzzling, perhaps, is how democracy can survive and thrive in a country so dangerously divided by history, language, religion, and **caste**. India has thousands of years of history as an authoritarian, hierarchical culture that has stratified, segmented, and compartmentalized its society. Today, more than 1 billion Indians speak some 325 distinct languages with over 1,500 dialects.[1] They worship over 5,000 gods, and six separate religions have at least 50 million adherents each. Caste divisions still segregate India socially, economically, and culturally. At times, these ethnic and social divisions have erupted into violent conflict and dramatic threats of secession. Given these circumstances, some observers marvel that the country can even stay together, let alone accommodate the cacophony of demands that present themselves.

Others argue that democracy may not be so much the puzzle as the solution. A ponderous but flexible democracy may be the only way of holding this patchworked nation together. Prior to gaining its independence in 1947, India had already been introduced to—if not allowed to participate in—the liberal practices of its British imperial master. As a sovereign nation, India fully adopted the political institutions of British democracy: the Westminster parliamentary model. This system has taken root and flourished, but it remains distinctly Indian. India thus offers comparative political scientists a useful petri dish for studying the transferability of democratic institutions to a postcolonial setting and the challenges facing such a transplant.

In recent years, the greatest challenge to Indian democracy and political stability has come from persistent religious conflict and increasing fundamentalism. As this case will demonstrate, Sikh and Muslim separatism and Hindu chauvinism have threatened the very democratic system that has sought, so far successfully, to accommodate them. India prevailed in its struggle for colonial independence in large part because of one devout Indian's ability to combine the Hindu concept of nonviolence with the liberal notions of tolerance and the separation of religion and state. The charismatic leadership of Mahatma (Mohandas K.) Gandhi and the political secularism of his followers successfully united an ethnically diverse colony in the common cause of democratic nation building.

But as has been the case in nearly all other postimperial countries, modernization has come neither quickly nor easily to India. This huge and still impoverished nation must juggle the maintenance of its notable democracy with the challenges of development and increasing globalization. Although India's urban centers can boast a prosperous and technically savvy elite minority that stands very much in the twenty-first century, its rapid economic development over the past two decades has left much of the rest of the nation behind. So to the many other divisions threatening India's democracy and political integrity, we must add the inequalities of income and opportunity.

To some extent, India shares with most other less developed and newly industrializing countries the multiple and simultaneous threats of ethnic conflict, political instability, and economic inequality. In that regard, India offers insight into the challenges and opportunities that developing countries face. India is important not just because of its relative ability to manage these challenges democratically, but also because its sheer size and growing international prominence guarantee it will have increasing influence in the rest of the world.

Major Geographic and Demographic Features

India looms large in both size and population, surpassed only by China as Asia's largest and most populous country. The country divides relatively neatly into two triangles stacked on top of each other, with the sharp angles pointed to the north and the south. The northern triangle is home to territorial disputes that have led to three wars with Pakistan to the west and ongoing tension with China to the east. The northernmost state of Jammu and Kashmir at the apex of the northern triangle is claimed by both Pakistan and India and remains a volatile tinderbox of ethnic and nationalist dispute. The southern triangle forms a huge peninsula that juts into the Indian Ocean, historically buffering the area from India's neighbors but opening the region to Western trade and, ultimately, imperial conquest.

Both India's climate and its politics have been profoundly shaped by geography. The Himalayas serve as towering sentinels on the northern border, shielding the subcontinent (comprising India, Pakistan, and Bangladesh) over the millennia from Siberian winds and Central Asian invaders. The Himalayas (Sanskrit for "abode of snow") are also the source of India's two most important river systems: the Indus, long the cradle of Indian civilization, and the Ganges, a river Hindus value as sacred and worship as a goddess. These rivers and the sheltered climate of India's northern plains have made the north remarkably fertile, sustaining dense levels of civilization.

Crop production in southern India is no less important but riskier because of its dependence on the monsoons: the four summer months of heavy rains. A successful monsoon season—neither too little nor too much rain—can make the difference between drought or flood and famine or feast for many Indians. The **green revolution** of the 1960s and 1970s, with its technologically enhanced crops and cropping methods, improved production dramatically, particularly in the arid regions of the Northwest. Nonetheless, India's rapidly growing population remains highly dependent on an agricultural economy, often called a "gamble in rains."[2]

Although India possesses a wide range of natural resources, its per capita endowment of oil, timber, minerals, and petroleum reserves is relatively low. More than half of all Indians remain dependent on an agrarian livelihood; only China has more peasants. And only China has more people. The United Nations predicts that India will surpass China as the world's most populous country by 2035 and will continue to grow until 2050, when, it is estimated, its population will peak at roughly 1.8 billion, or, more than one fourth the world's total.

The product of numerous waves of empire building, India's population is racially, ethnically, and linguistically diverse. The simplest division of Indian society is between the Aryans to the North and the Dravidians to the South, though this division is amplified by linguistic differences. In the North, most Indians speak some variety of Indo-Aryan, which is part of the Indo-European family of languages. Most common among these is **Hindi**, now one of two national languages, the other being English. Most people in the South speak one of four major dialects of the Dravidian language, almost completely distinct from Hindi. English has become the only universal language, but one that is spoken in large part by the elite. Even so, there are more English speakers in India (33 million) than in Canada, a fact of which Western companies drawn to India for the **outsourcing** of a growing range of business processes are well aware.

Historical Development of the State

Civilization on the Indian subcontinent predates a unified Indian state by several thousand years. Three religious traditions and nearly 1,000 years of for-

TIME LINE OF POLITICAL DEVELOPMENT

Year	Event
1857–58	Sepoy Mutiny put down, and formal British colonial rule established
1885	Indian National Congress created
1947	India gains independence from Britain; India and Pakistan partitioned
1948	Mahatma Gandhi assassinated
1947–64	Jawaharlal Nehru serves as prime minister until his death
1971	India-Pakistan War leads to creation of Bangladesh
1975–77	Indira Gandhi institutes emergency rule
1984	Indira Gandhi launches military operations at Amritsar and is assassinated by Sikh bodyguards
1984–86	Rajiv Gandhi serves as prime minister
1991	Rajiv Gandhi assassinated
1992	Ayodhya mosque destroyed
1996	Electoral victory of the Bharatiya Janata Party (BJP) leads to the rise of coalition governments
1998	Nuclear weapons tested in violation of the Nuclear Non-Proliferation Treaty
2002	Muslim-Hindu violence breaks out in Gujarat
2004	Congress-led coalition defeats BJP coalition; Manmohan Singh becomes prime minister
2005	India and United States begin negotiating controversial nuclear agreement
2007	Pratibha Patil is elected India's first female president
2008	Muslim terrorist bombings in Mumbai and other Indian cities

eign domination mark the contours of the gradual formation of a sovereign Indian state.

HINDUISM, BUDDHISM, AND ISLAM

Over 3,000 years ago, nomadic Indo-Aryans began migrating eastward from Persia into the northern and central plains of present-day India, subduing the darker-skinned Dravidians, many of whom moved southward. From the fusion of the two cultures emerged the customs, philosophical ideas, and religious beliefs associated with **Hinduism**. Like other traditional religions, Hinduism governs not just worship practices but also virtually all aspects of life, including the rituals and norms of birth, death, marriage, eating, and livelihood. For roughly the next 2,000 years, India enjoyed relative freedom from outside influence as Hindu traditions, such as polytheism, reincarnation, and the social and political hierarchy of caste, infused Indian society (see "Indian Caste System," below).

It was under the auspices of Buddhism—a second religious tradition, originating in India in the sixth century B.C.E.—that rulers commenced India's

INDIAN CASTE SYSTEM

Like many other premodern societies, India's was divided and compartmentalized for thousands of years according to such categories as birth, region, occupation, and social obligations. However, India's "caste" system (the term derived from the Portuguese *casta*, meaning species or breed) was at once more complex and more flexible than often portrayed. The term *caste* is typically used to refer to two different but related types of social divisions. The first of these affiliations is known as *jati*, which refers to the thousands of separate but not wholly rigid occupational and regional groups and subgroups that divide Indian society (Gandhi, for instance, means greengrocer). Each category possessed its own detailed rules for the social behavior and interactions involved in such activities as eating, communicating, and marrying. More generally, Indian society was also divided into four broader castes, or *varnas*, including Brahmans (priests), Kshatriyas (warriors and rulers), Vaishyas (traders and merchants), and Sudras (peasants and laborers). At the bottom of— technically outside—the hierarchy were the so-called **untouchables**. These included two groups: those who performed duties deemed unclean, which involved handling the dead and disposing of human waste, and those aboriginals who lived outside village life, in the mountains or forests (often referred to as "tribals"). The touch or even shadow of these outcastes was considered polluting by high-caste Hindus. Long sanctioned and legitimized by the Hindu religion, British colonial bureaucrats painstakingly cataloged these various classifications and hierarchies in an effort to enhance social order, rendering the castes increasingly rigid over time. In independent India, Hindu elites have used these social divisions to establish political patronage networks and to justify and enhance their dominant position in the caste system. Critics of the divisive and exploitative consequences of caste, however, have made efforts to ease the discrimination associated with it and, in particular, its deleterious effects on the untouchables. Mahatma Gandhi worked tirelessly on their behalf, referring to them as harijans, the children of God. India's 1950 constitution not only banned the status known as untouchable but also legislated special "reservations," or affirmative actions, designed to improve the status of these "scheduled castes and tribes." Calling themselves *Dalits* (Suppressed Groups), they now number some 140 million people, or 16 percent of the population.[3]

first efforts at nation building. Spreading Buddhism's message of peace and benevolence to subjects of all ethnic groups and social ranks, dynastic rulers unified much of what is now India by the fourth century B.C.E. and remained in power for several hundred years. The development of the silk route by the first century C.E. spread Buddhism eastward to China and beyond. At home, however, Hinduism gradually reemerged as the state religion and has remained India's dominant faith, with over 80 percent of Indians identifying themselves as Hindu. Today, Hinduism is the world's third-largest religious tradition, after Christianity and Islam.

India's 2,000 years of relative isolation gave way to a millennium of foreign domination beginning with marauding Muslim invaders in the eighth century. (Foreign invasion and occupation did not end until India gained its independence from British imperialism and colonialism in 1947.) The arrival of this third religious tradition at the hands of martial Muslim rulers never fostered the kind of tolerance shared by Hindus and Buddhists. But the introduction of Islam to India gave birth to a new religious tradition, **Sikhism**, which combines Hindu and Muslim beliefs. It also sowed the persisting seeds of mutual animosity among India's Hindus, Muslims, and Sikhs. A final wave of Muslim invaders, descendants of Genghis Khan known as **Mughals** (Persian for "Mongol"), ruled a relatively unified India for several hundred years beginning in the sixteenth century. But by the eighteenth century, Mughal rule had weakened at the hands of growing internal Hindu and Sikh dissatisfaction and expanding Western imperialism.

BRITISH COLONIALISM

The lucrative spice trade beckoned European powers to the Indian Ocean, beginning with the Portuguese and the Spanish in the sixteenth century and then the Dutch and the British by the seventeenth century. Lacking a strong, centralized state, India was vulnerable to foreign encroachment, and the British in particular made significant commercial inroads. In 1600, the British crown granted a monopoly charter to the private East India Company, which over the years perfected an imperial strategy of commercial exploitation. This private merchant company first cultivated trade, then exploited cheap labor, and ultimately succeeded in controlling whole principalities. It did so through a strategy of setting up puppet Mughal governorships, known as nabobs, with British merchant advisers at their side. This **nabob game** greatly facilitated the plundering of Indian wealth and resources.

The British introduced the concept of private property and the English language, and with it science, literature, and—perhaps most revolutionary—liberal political philosophy. Also, as the East India Company lost its monopoly on Indian trade, a growing number of British merchants sought Indian markets for British manufactures, particularly cotton cloth. With British cotton selling at less than half the price of local handmade cloth, this "free" trade put millions of Indian cloth makers out of work. Communication and transportation technology—the telegraph, print media, the postal system, and the railroad (the British laid some 50,000 miles of track)—did much to unify India and give its colonial subjects a shared recognition of their frustrations and aspirations. This was particularly true of those native Indians employed in the colonial military and civil service who were beginning to develop and articulate a sense of Indian nationalism.

Growing economic frustration, political awareness, and national identity led to the **Sepoy Mutiny** of 1857–1858, a revolt sponsored by the Indian aristocracy and carried out by sepoys (Indian soldiers employed by the British). Incited to arms by the revelation that their British-issued guns fired bullets greased in either pork lard or beef tallow (offensive to Muslims and Hindus, respectively), the mutinous Indians failed in large part because they were too divided, both by British design and by the long tradition of religious animosity that split the Hindu and Muslim conscripts. The failure convinced the growing number of Indian nationalists that independence from British colonialism would first require national unity. To British authorities, the mutiny signaled the weakness of nabob rule, the threat of Indian anti-colonialism, and the dangers of liberal ideas and institutions in the hands of the locals. In 1858, the British Parliament passed the Government of India Act, which terminated the East India Company's control of India and placed the territory under direct and far more harsh colonial rule. Under this British **raj** (rule), civil servants and British troops replaced private merchants and puppet nabobs, and British talk of eventual Indian self-rule gave way to calls for the "permanent subjection of India to the British yoke."[4] The colony of India became the "brightest jewel in the crown of the British empire."[5]

THE INDEPENDENCE MOVEMENT

By the end of the nineteenth century, calls for self-rule had become louder and more articulate, though they were still not unified. Two local organizations came to embody the anti-colonial movement: the **Indian National Congress** (**INC**, also referred to simply as Congress or Congress Party) founded in 1885, and the **Muslim League**, founded in 1906. But hopes for a gradual transfer of power after World War I were instead met with increased colonial repression, culminating in a 1919 massacre in which British troops opened fire on unarmed civilians, murdering hundreds and wounding more than 1,000 innocent Indians.

This massacre galvanized Indian resistance and brought **Mahatma (Mohandas K.) Gandhi**, a British-trained lawyer, to the leadership of Congress and the broader independence movement (see "Gandhi and the Indian Independence Movement," p. 335). Gandhi led successful protests and nationwide boycotts of British commercial imports and employment in British institutions, such as the courts, schools, and civil service. Perhaps most success-ful of these protests was his 1930 boycott of British salt, which was heavily taxed by the colonial raj. In declaring the boycott, Gandhi led a group of fol-lowers on a well-publicized 200-mile march to the sea to gather salt, a viola-tion of the British monopoly. Upon their arrival, Gandhi and many others were jailed, and the independence movement garnered national and interna-tional attention.

Gandhi's integrity and example, the charismatic draw of his remarkable strategy of nonviolence, and the growing repressive and arbitrary nature of colonial rule swelled the ranks of the independence movement. Among those who joined was a younger generation of well-educated leaders schooled in the modern ideas of socialism and democracy. Chief among them was **Jawahar-lal Nehru,** who succeeded Gandhi as the leader of the INC and became inde-pendent India's first prime minister.

Weakened by both economic depression and war, Britain was in no shape to resist Indian independence and entered into serious negotiations toward this end following World War II. The biggest obstacle to independence became not British foot-dragging but disagreements and divisions among India's many interests, most particularly Hindus and Muslims. Fearful that Muslims, who constituted 25 percent of the population, would be unfairly dominated by the Hindu majority, Muslim leaders demanded a separate Muslim state. Negoti-

GANDHI AND THE INDIAN INDEPENDENCE MOVEMENT

Mohandas K. Gandhi, affectionately known by Indians as *Mahatma*, or Great Soul, was born in 1869 and studied law in Britain. He first experienced racism while practicing law in South Africa and was thrown out of the first-class compartment of a train because of his skin color. That event prompted his tactics of revolutionary nonviolent resistance, first practiced against South African discrimination and then perfected in India after his return there in 1914. Upon his return, he adopted the simple dress, ascetic habits, and devout worship of a Hindu holy man and devel-oped his philosophies of satyagraha (holding firmly to truth) and ahimsa (nonvio-lence, or love). He argued that truth and love combined in nonviolent resistance to injustice could "move the world." He also taught that Western industrial civilization must be rejected in favor of a simpler life. He led a charismatic nationalist move-ment embodied in his example of personal simplicity and campaigns for national self-sufficiency. The movement was punctuated by dramatic instances of nonvio-lent resistance, hunger strikes, and periods of imprisonment. Successful in his cam-paign to end colonialism, even the Great Soul could not prevent either Hindu-Muslim violence or, ultimately, the partition of Pakistan and India, despite his best efforts. Five months after India achieved independence, a Hindu militant assassinated Gandhi to protest his efforts to keep India unified.

ations collapsed as civil war broke out between militant adherents of the two faiths.

Against this background of growing violence, the British chose **partition**, creating in 1947 the new state of Pakistan from the Muslim-dominated northeast (what would become independent Bangladesh in 1971) and from the northwest and forming independent India from the remaining 80 percent of the colony. This declaration led to the uprooting and transmigration (in effect, ethnic cleansing) of over 12 million refugees—Muslims to Pakistan, Hindus and Sikhs to India—across the hurriedly drawn boundaries. It is estimated that as many as 1 million Indians and Pakistanis were killed in the resulting chaos and violence.[6] Among the victims of this sectarian violence was Gandhi himself, assassinated in 1948 by a militant Hindu who saw the leader and his message of religious tolerance as threats to Hindu nationalism. Not surprsingly, the ethnic violence that marked partition and the birth of the Indian nation continues to plague Hindu-Muslim relations in contemporary India and India's relations with neighboring Pakistan.

INDEPENDENCE

Like many of the other newly minted countries that would became part of the postwar decolonization movement, independent India faced a host of truly daunting challenges. In India, these included settling some 5 million refugees from East and West Pakistan, resolving outstanding territorial disputes, jump-starting an economy torn asunder by partition in an effort to feed the country's impoverished millions, and creating democratic political institutions from whole cloth. This last task, promised by Nehru and his INC, had to be carried out in the absence of the prosperity, literacy, and liberal traditions that allowed democracy to take hold in the advanced democracies and seemed to many an unlikely prospect. Given India's particular circumstances and its kaleidoscopic social, political, and economic interests—what one author called "a million mutinies now"[7]—such an endeavor seemed particularly foolish.

But unlike many other postcolonial countries, India brought to the endeavor of democratization several distinct advantages. First, its lengthy, gradual, and inclusive independence movement generated a powerful and widespread sense of national identity. Although India had not experienced a thoroughgoing social revolution in the style of Mexico or China, most Indians had come to identify themselves not just by their region, caste, or even religion but also as citizens of the new republic. The legacy of Gandhi's charismatic outreach to all Indians, including outcastes, Muslims, and Sikhs, brought much-needed (if perhaps ultimately short-lived) unity to its disparate population.

Second, although Indians did not control their own destiny under the British raj, the Indian intellectual class was well schooled in both the Western philosophies and the day-to-day practices of liberal democracy. Generations of the Indian elite had not just been taught in the British liberal tradition; many of them had also served faithfully in the colonial bureaucracy. By the time of independence, Indians for most practical purposes were in fact governing themselves, albeit following the dictates of a colonial power. Indeed, their appreciation of and aptitude for the virtues of democracy made its denial under British imperial rule seem all the more unjust.

Moreover, independent India inherited not just liberal ideas and traditions, it also inherited a sophisticated and generally well-functioning central state apparatus, including an extensive civil service and standing army. The comparison between a relatively democratic India and the more authoritarian Pakistan and Bangladesh is significant. Although all three shared a common British colonial heritage, the territories that would come to constitute Pakistan and Bangladesh had not developed India's degree of centralized state administration during the colonial period. In addition, the Muslim League was much less successful than the Indian National Congress in bringing effective political organization to these regions. When it came time to assert state authority over their respective territories, independent Pakistan and Bangladesh turned more readily to an authoritarian military and bureaucracy, whereas India was able to rely, at least more frequently, upon democratic political parties and politicians.[8]

Finally, the long-standing role of the INC as the legitimate embodiment of the independence movement and Nehru as its charismatic and rightful representative gave the new government a powerful mandate. Like Nelson Mandela's African National Congress, which took its name from its Indian predecessor and swept to power in South Africa's first free election in 1994, Nehru led the INC to a handy victory in India's first general election in 1951. This afforded the INC government the opportunity to implement Nehru's vision of social democracy at home and mercantilist trade policies abroad. The INC would govern India for forty-five of its first fifty years of independence, led for nearly all those years by either Nehru, his daughter, or his grandson.

A NEHRU DYNASTY

Uncle Nehru, as Jawaharlal Nehru was affectionately called, led the INC to two subsequent victories: in 1957 and 1962. But by his third term, Nehru had realized the intractability of many of India's economic and foreign policy challenges and his own inability to transform the nation as quickly as he had hoped. As one scholar observed, "In India, nothing changed fast enough to keep up with the new mouths to be fed."[9] Nehru died in office in 1964, and with his death the INC began to lose some of its earlier luster and its ability to reach across regional, caste, and religious divisions to garner support.

Within two years, Nehru's daughter, **Indira Gandhi** (no relation to Mahatma), assumed leadership of a more narrowly defined INC and became

India's first woman prime minister. Far more authoritarian than her father, Gandhi's first decade of rule divided the party between her supporters and her detractors. With her popularity within the party weakening in the 1970s, Gandhi sought support from India's impoverished masses with a populist campaign to abolish poverty. Although the program was highly popular and initially successful, the global oil crisis reversed many of the early economic gains. Riots and strikes spread throughout India, with citizens of all classes complaining of the dangerous dictatorship of the "Indira raj."

Facing declining support, charges of corruption, and calls to step down, Gandhi instead chose in 1975 to suspend the constitution by declaring martial law, or **emergency rule**. The Indian constitution does authorize such a measure, and during the two years of emergency rule, riots and unrest ceased and economic efficiency improved. Nonetheless, Gandhi's swift suspension of civil liberties, censorship of the press, banning of opposition parties, and jailing of over 100,000 political opponents (including many of India's senior statesmen), chilled Indian democracy and prompted widespread (albeit largely silent) opposition to her rule.

When Gandhi surprisingly lifted emergency rule in 1977 and called for new elections, virtually all politicians and the overwhelming majority of voters rallied to the cause of the new Janata (People's) Party in what was seen as an effort to save Indian democracy. This Janata coalition formed the first non-Congress government in thirty years of independence. Although key supporters shared a common interest in rural causes and the party drew its strength largely from rural constituencies, the coalition was unified primarily by its opposition to Gandhi's emergency rule. After two years of factional disputes and indecisive governance, the INC was returned to office—with Gandhi as its leader. Indian voters had spoken, indicating their preference for the order and efficiency of Gandhi's strong hand over the Janata Party's ineptitude.

During Indira Gandhi's second tenure, persistent economic problems were compounded by increasing state and regional resistance to central control and growing ethnic conflict. Demands for the devolution of central authority were sharpest in the Sikh-majority Punjab in northern India, whose leaders had become increasingly violent in their political and religious demands. Violence escalated, and demands for an independent Sikh state of Khalistan heightened. In 1984, Gandhi declared martial law, or **presidential rule**, in the state of Punjab. This state-level equivalent of declaring emergency rule is also constitutionally authorized, permitting the federal government to oust a state government and assume national control of that state. Gandhi then launched a military operation on the Golden Temple in **Amritsar**, Sikhism's holiest shrine. Sikh separatists' firebrand leader and some 1,000 of his militant followers ensconced in the temple were killed in the operation, and loyal followers swore vengeance. The vengeance came months later, when Gandhi's Sikh bodyguards assassinated her. In what was to become a motif of communal violence, the assassination sparked violent retribution as angry Hindus murdered thousands of innocent Sikhs throughout India.

Indira presided over Indian politics for almost as long as did her father, Nehru, who led the INC and governed India for some seventeen years. But whereas Nehru's legacy was one of national inclusion and consensus building among a wide range of regional interests, Gandhi's rule was far more divisive, intolerant, and heavy-handed. The Indian state she bequeathed to her son Rajiv, who replaced her as leader of the INC, was more centralized and its party politics far more divided. This was not, however, necessarily a negative experience for Indian democracy. For the first time, a viable political opposition was emerging, one capable of standing up to the powerful INC.

Widespread sympathy in the wake of Gandhi's assassination made it natural for the INC to select her younger son, Rajiv (her older son and heir apparent, Sanjay, having been killed in a plane accident), and it assured the Congress Party its largest (and last) majority in the 1984 election. Rajiv Gandhi governed for five years, beginning the shift of India's economic focus away from the social democratic and mercantilist policies of his mother and grandfather. He promoted more liberal market measures, which have been expanded in the decades since. Ethnic violence and political divisiveness persisted, with trouble simmering between Hindus and Muslims in the Punjab and in new hot spots in the border region between India and Bangladesh to the east and between Hindus and ethnic Tamil separatists to the south. During a 1991 campaign, two years after Rajiv Gandhi had been turned out of office by a weak opposition coalition, he was assassinated by a Tamil suicide bomber. The Nehru dynasty thus ended (at least for the time being), and coalition governments became the norm.

COALITION GOVERNMENTS

The decline of the INC's dominance has led to a series of coalition governments typically headed by a national party, such as Congress, but shored up by regional partners. Coalitions of all political stripes have maintained the reforms begun under Rajiv Gandhi and the INC, including economic liberalization and increased political devolution to state governments. The INC's strongest competition has come from the **Bharatiya Janata Party (BJP)**, a party with the potential for nationwide scope and appeal. The BJP has been able to articulate a Hindu nationalist vision, an alternative (some would say a dangerous one) to the vision of a secular India established by the INC at the time of India's founding. Drawing its strength initially from upper-caste

Hindu groups, by the late 1990s the BJP was attracting Hindus of all castes under the banner of Hindu nationalism.

The event that began to galvanize support for the BJP was yet another incident of sectarian violence at yet another temple site. The Babri Mosque, located in the northern Indian city of **Ayodhya**, had been built by Mughals on a site alleged to be the birthplace of the Hindu god Ram. The site was deemed sacred by Muslims and Hindus and for decades has been a point of controversy for local adherents of both faiths. By the 1990s, various Hindu nationalist groups had seized on Ayodhya as both a rallying political issue and a gathering place. In 1992, BJP supporters and other Hindu extremists destroyed the mosque, vowing to rebuild it as a Hindu shrine. This act ignited days of Hindu-Muslim rioting and violence and the killing of many Indians across the country. Repercussions have persisted. In 2002, on the tenth anniversary of the event, in the city of Godhra in the western state of **Gujarat**, Muslims set fire to railcars carrying Hindu activists back from a ceremony at Ayodhya, killing fifty-eight people. Hindu retaliatory violence incited by religious militants in the state of Gujarat killed thousands. The issues continue to simmer, with extremist elements in both the Muslim and Hindu camps regularly taking aim at each other. The year 2008 proved particularly violent, with Muslim terrorist bombings in several of India's large urban centers and a dramatic assault on Mumbai led by a Pakistani-based group that targeted wealthy Indians, Westerners, and Jews.

This communal violence has served to harden positions on both sides and polarize political support. A BJP coalition that had come to power in 1998 remained in office until 2004, when it was turned out by a surprisingly resurgent INC and assorted coalition partners. Organizations loosely affiliated with the BJP have continued to promote divisive Hindu nationalist rhetoric to garner support and have sponsored violence and discrimination against a variety of minority religious and ethnic groups. During its six years in office, however, the BJP coalition governed relatively moderately. It did so both to retain its coalition partners and to promote India's national goals of economic growth and stable relations with neighboring countries. These current domestic and international priorities will be taken up in subsequent sections.

Significantly, the leader of the INC at the time of its surprise return to office in 2004 and reelection in 2009 was **Sonia Gandhi**, the Italian-born widow of Rajiv Gandhi. Although she would have been the logical choice to assume the office of prime minister (and extend the Nehru dynasty), the BJP made her foreign birth a divisive campaign issue. Thus, she stepped aside and allowed **Manmohan Singh** to become the country's first Sikh prime minister. It should be noted, however, that Sonia Gandhi continues to lead the INC and has a son, Rahul, who gained a Congress seat in parliament in 2004, and a daughter, Priyanka, who has also shown political ambitions. Although many judge the younger sister to be more politically astute, analysts predict that Rahul will someday lead the INC, like his mother, father, and grandfather before him.[10]

POLITICAL REGIME

With an electorate approaching 700 million voters, India can easily claim title to the world's largest democracy. But is this democracy genuine? And does it work? Certainly in form it is democratic. Its constitution and other political institutions were modeled explicitly on Britain's Westminster parliamentary system, and few changes to the original blueprint have been enacted. With the exception of Indira Gandhi's authoritarian interlude of the 1970s, the institutions seem in practice to function more effectively and legitimately in India than in many other former British colonies that share a similar institutional inheritance. Indian democracy nonetheless differs in important ways from that of its colonial mentor and other advanced Western industrialized democracies.

Why has democracy fared better in India than, for example, in neighboring Pakistan, a country that shares with India many of the same cultural and historical legacies? Although a full answer to this question is beyond the scope of this work, the well-established stability and near-universal legitimacy of the political institutions discussed below provide an important part of that answer. Three generations of Indian politicians and citizens from across the ideological spectrum have been schooled in the lessons of parliamentary democracy. They function and participate in a system that maintains civil parliamentary debate, a politically neutral bureaucracy, an independent judiciary, and firm civilian control over the military.

Political Institutions

THE CONSTITUTION

Perhaps befitting India's size and population, its constitution is one of the world's longest, enshrining in writing the fundamental principles of Britain's unwritten constitutional order of parliamentary democracy. It establishes India as a federal republic, reserving significant authority for the state governments. During its nearly fifty years of hegemonic rule, the Indian National Congress (INC) limited the autonomy of state governments. The weakening of the INC and the onset of coalition governments have spurred a process of devolution, allowing regional political parties and the states they represent to wrest significant authority from the **Center** (a term referring to India's national government and its capital in New Delhi).

Two controversial tenets of the Indian constitution have certainly enhanced the power of the Center. The first of these authorizes the central

ESSENTIAL POLITICAL FEATURES

- Legislative-executive system: prime ministerial
- Legislature: Parliament
- Lower house: House of the People
- Upper house: House of States
- Unitary or federal division of power: federal
- Main geographic subunits: states
- Electoral system for lower house: single-member district plurality
- Chief judicial body: Supreme Court

government to suspend or limit freedoms during a "grave emergency," when India faces threats of "external aggression or internal disturbance." This emergency rule (nationwide martial law) was invoked twice during international conflicts, with China in 1962 and with Pakistan in 1971. More controversially, Indira Gandhi invoked this clause to institute emergency rule from 1975 to 1977, using it as a blunt (but nonetheless effective) tool against her political opponents. After her defeat in the subsequent election, the constitution was amended to limit such a decree to conditions of external aggression or domestic armed rebellion.

Indira Gandhi was not the only prime minister to invoke the second measure, that of presidential rule, which allows the central government to oust a state government and assert direct rule of that state. National governments have employed this measure on more than 100 occasions when ethnic unrest, local resistance, or simply a political stalemate has rendered a state, in the judgment of the Center, ungovernable. Although these measures may seem unusual and have at times been imposed for purposes of political expediency, the violence, disorder, and corruption often associated with regional Indian politics have made presidential rule an important and generally legitimate tool of the central government.[11]

The Branches of Government

THE PRESIDENT

Because India is a republic, its head of state is a president, not a monarch; as in most other parliamentary systems, moreover, the president's role is largely symbolic. The president is authorized to appoint the prime minister, but as with the monarchs of Britain and Japan, this appointment is simply a ceremonial affirmation of the leader of the dominant party or coalition in the parliament. Similarly, while it is the president's role to declare national or state emergency rule, this declaration can be made only on the advice of the prime minister.

The substantive exception to these symbolic tasks has been the president's role following elections that have produced no majority party (which happens more often nowadays). Under these circumstances, the president seeks to identify and facilitate the formation of a workable governing coalition. If that is not possible, the president dissolves the parliament and calls new elections. An electoral college, made up of the national and state legislators, elects presidents to five-year renewable terms, though many presidents have in effect been appointed by powerful prime ministers. The current president, Pratibha Patil, was elected in 2007 and serves as India's first woman president. Nominated by the governing Congress coalition, her election was unusually contentious because of opposition BJP fears that if an upcoming election returned no majority party, Ms. Patil would give her patron, the INC, the first chance to form a coalition government.

THE PRIME MINISTER AND THE CABINET

As in the British system, the Indian prime minister and cabinet constitute the executive branch. The prime minister, as head of the government, is responsible for managing the day-to-day affairs of government and is the state's most important political figure. The prime minister has typically been the leader of the party with a majority in the lower house of the legislature or, more recently, a leader from within a coalition of parties that can garner sufficient support

STRUCTURE OF THE GOVERNMENT

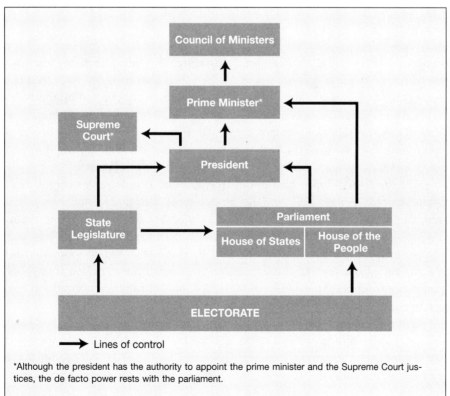

Lines of control

*Although the president has the authority to appoint the prime minister and the Supreme Court justices, the de facto power rests with the parliament.

to constitute a majority, or even a minority, government. To remain in office, the prime minister must retain the confidence of the lower house and may choose to dissolve it at any point and call elections to solidify support for the government.

The prime minister chooses members of the parliament to serve in a Council of Ministers that presides over all government ministries and departments. From this larger council, a smaller and more manageable group of the fifteen to twenty most important ministers meets weekly as a cabinet to formulate and coordinate government policy. The current prime minister, Manmohan Singh, is the country's first Sikh to serve in that office and began his tenure in 2004 and was reelected in 2009 as leader of Congress-led coalitions.

During the years of Congress dominance, the three generations of Nehru prime ministers wielded overwhelming executive power. Although this was most apparent during Indira Gandhi's authoritarian tenure, her father and even her son were also dominant prime ministers who left their personal imprints on the office and on Indian politics. Even during the more recent era of coalition governments in which the prime minister's influence has weakened, the office remains the primary source of policy making and political power.

THE LEGISLATURE

As is true in many parliamentary systems, the lower house, or **House of the People**, dominates India's bicameral legislature. This lower chamber seats 545 members, all but 2 of whom are elected by voters for terms not to exceed five years (the final 2 seats are reserved for Anglo-Indians appointed by the president). Although its size may seem to weaken its effectiveness, India's huge population remains relatively underrepresented. Each representative serves nearly two million people, four times that of a member of the U.S. House of Representatives and twenty times that of a member of Britain's House of Commons!

Like the British lower house, the House of the People serves primarily as a chamber of debate between the government and the opposition. It has adopted many of the rituals and institutions of its colonial model, including a neutral Speaker of the House who presides over Question Time. Seen during the era of the INC's dominance as little more than window dressing for the party in power and its prime minister, the lower house has had an increasingly important political role since the emergence of multiparty coalition governments and the strengthening of regional parties.

As its name denotes, the upper house, or **House of States**, represents India's twenty-eight states and seven territories. All but 12 of its 250 members are elected (the remaining 12 being appointed by the president) to fixed six-year terms. Although the upper chamber technically possesses most of the same powers as its lower counterpart—including the right to introduce legislation—

in practice it has been much weaker. Only the House of the People can introduce bills to raise revenue, and any financial measure the House of States votes
down can be enacted with just the support of the lower house. Any other dead-
locked legislation is put to a majority vote of a joint session, ensuring that the
more numerous lower chamber has the upper hand. Most significantly, the
prime minister and cabinet are responsible only to the lower house, which can
force the prime minister from office by a vote of no confidence.

THE JUDICIAL SYSTEM

Unlike Britain and more like the United States, India has a Supreme Court
with a bench of twenty-six justices, who are appointed by the president and
may serve until age sixty-five. Typically, the most senior judge serves as chief
justice.

India's Supreme Court is a constitutional court with the authority of judicial review (the right to rule on the constitutionality of acts of the parliament).
This power to interpret the constitution is limited, however, by the comprehensive nature of the Indian constitution. Its power has also been limited by
the parliament's ability to reverse court decisions by amending the constitution, as it has done on a number of occasions (ninety-two times in six decades).
With the exception of the two-year period of Indira Gandhi's emergency rule
in the 1970s, when the judiciary was seen as having yielded to the prime minister's political influence both in the appointment of justices and in the suspension of constitutionally guaranteed civil rights, the Supreme Court has
enjoyed (and earned) a reputation for fairness and independence.

The Electoral System

As with many of its other political institutions, India's electoral system closely
resembles the British model. At the national level, voters use a plurality system to elect representatives to the House of the People, as in Britain and the
United States. The country is divided into 543 single-member districts (SMDs),
in which the candidate who earns a plurality of votes on the first ballot is
elected. The districts are based primarily on geography and population, but
some districts are reserved for the scheduled castes and tribes, or so-called
untouchables. Members of the upper house are elected for staggered six-year
fixed terms by the state legislatures, with seats apportioned according to each
state's population.

Whereas this plurality system in the United States and Britain has favored
the emergence of few or two nationally based large parties and has penalized
smaller parties, this is increasingly not the case in India. The INC certainly
used the electoral system to its advantage during its period of dominance,
winning clear majorities of seats in the House of the People in most elections

even though it never won a majority of the popular vote (nor has any other party in India's history) and often received little more than a plurality. The largest of the other parties, including the Janata Party and the Bharatiya Janata Party (BJP), have also benefited, winning a higher percentage of seats than votes. The weakening of the INC's hegemony since the 1990s has splintered the national vote, however, and has given new significance to regional parties based on caste or on linguistic or religious identity. This has meant that while two parties tend to dominate each electoral district, these regional and caste-based parties are not nationally dominant.[12] Recent House of the People elections have seated representatives of nearly forty different political parties, none with a majority of the seats and ten parties with over ten seats each (see "House of the People Election Results, 2004 and 2009," p. 352).

Local Government

India's extensive regional diversity and the sectarian conflicts troubling India at the time of its founding led the framers of India's constitution to establish a federal republic that preserved substantial powers for both the various states and the central government. The Center's constitutional powers to declare a national emergency or impose presidential rule on an obstreperous state are muscular examples of central authority. The federal government is also authorized to challenge any state legislation that contradicts an act of the parliament and can even change the boundaries of states as it sees fit. But like their American counterparts, in the day-to-day management of government affairs Indian states retain a great deal of jealously guarded autonomy. Public policies concerning health, education, economic and industrial development, and law and order are largely determined at the state level and vary significantly from state to state. The rise of coalition governments and the growing influence of regional parties in national affairs has only strengthened state power.

India is now divided into twenty-eight states and seven territories, whereas the original division had fourteen states and six territories. This expansion is in large part a nod to powerful state interests and speaks to an important way in which India's federalism differs from the American model. State borders in India reflect in most cases linguistic or ethno-religious differences, which pit regional interests against the Center. This conflict has been most pronounced in states such as Punjab, dominated by the Punjabi-speaking Sikhs, and **Kashmir**, where Urdu-speaking Muslims constitute a majority. However, other ethnic groups have also wielded the mechanisms of state authority to assert state interests against the federal government.

Perhaps the best comparison with Indian federalism is not the United States but rather the historically diverse and linguistically distinct European Union (EU).[13] Like the English and the Greeks, the Hindi speakers of Bihar in the north and the Tamil speakers of Tamil Nadu in the south converse in mutually unintelligible tongues and share little common history and equally little interaction. Like the citizens of Sweden and Portugal, their customs, cultures, and traditions vary widely, as do their social and economic profiles. Bihar is impoverished and largely illiterate, whereas Tamil Nadu is relatively more prosperous and technologically advanced. There are no similarly intense contrasts in the United States.

Comparison of India with the EU also points to one of the crowning accomplishments of India's democratic resilience. For all of the local conflict and secessionist violence that India has experienced, the Center has held, and the strife has remained localized. With larger populations and religious, linguistic, and territorial disputes sufficient to rival any of those that led to the numerous wars of Europe (and ultimately prompted the formation of the EU), India has for the most part managed these disputes peacefully and democratically. This is no small feat. And as state-based regional political parties and movements in India continue to strengthen and call for increased devolution, it gives hope not only to the emerging democratic federal system in Europe but also to that in Iraq, Russia, and other areas threatened by centrifugal dissolution.

POLITICAL CONFLICT AND COMPETITION

Despite occasional heavy-handed government restrictions on civil rights and periodic demonstrations of communitarian intolerance and even violence, Indian politics remains vibrant, open, and generally inclusive. Voter turnout typically averages around 60 percent for parliamentary elections. The nonpartisan Freedom House in 2008 deemed India "free," with ratings of 2 in its political rights and 3 in civil liberties (on a scale of 1 to 7, with 1 the most free).[14]

In fact, given India's size and diversity, some might argue that political competition has been too inclusive. As one Indian journalist complained, "Everyone in India gets a veto."[15] The competition and conflict—typically but not always healthy—reflect the dualism and diversity of India: a prosperous, cosmopolitan, and highly literate minority voting side by side with roughly two thirds of the electorate who cannot read, have their roots in rural villages or urban slums, and may survive on less than US$1 a day. Both are important components of Indian democracy.

The Party System

During the first few decades of independence, India's party system was stable and predictable. Like Japan's Liberal Democratic Party or Mexico's Partido Revolucionario Institucional, the Indian National Congress presided over a one-party-dominant system that effectively appealed to a broad range of ideological and social groups and co-opted numerous disaffected constituencies, including the poor and minorities. More recently, this system has become far more fragmented, complex, and unpredictable as national opposition parties and regional and even local interests have gained ground in both state and national elections.

THE CONGRESS PARTY

More than just a political party, the Indian National Congress (INC), from its founding in 1885, became the flagship of national independence, commanding widespread appeal and support across the political and even ethnic spectrums. After independence, Jawaharlal Nehru and the INC pursued a slightly left-of-center political ideology of social democracy. This included social policies of "secularism" (more a program of religious equal opportunity than a separation of religion and state) and social reform, continuing the efforts of Gandhi to eliminate caste discrimination.

The party's economic program was marked by democratic socialism, including national five-year plans and state ownership of key economic sectors. These policies earned the support of workers, peasants, and particularly members of the lower castes. At the same time, the INC retained the support of business by respecting private property and supporting domestic industry with mercantilist policies of import substitution. It remained for decades the only party with national appeal.

The INC's dominance began to weaken after Nehru's death, as disagreements grew between Indira Gandhi and party elders in the late 1960s. These disagreements led to divisions within the party and to Gandhi's capture of the dominant faction, known as Congress (I) for Indira, during the 1970s. Gandhi made populist promises to India's poor, vowing to abolish poverty through government programs but never delivered on those promises. By the 1980s, the INC had begun to move away from its traditional priorities of democratic socialism and religious neutrality. Indira Gandhi began promoting Hindu nationalism, and her son Rajiv launched neoliberal economic reforms. These legacies have outlived their architects and have been embraced even more enthusiastically by other political parties.

By the late 1980s, the INC had surrendered its position of primacy, and the single-party-dominant system gave way to a regionalized multiparty system and coalition governments. During this time, the INC alternated rule with various permutations of Hindu nationalist coalitions, controlling the government in the first half of the 1990s and then returning to power in 2004. Although the INC continues to embrace in principle the neoliberal reform program first launched by Rajiv Gandhi, its most recent return to government was in large part a result of its progressive appeal to India's peasantry, a nod to both Nehru's democratic socialism and Indira Gandhi's populism.

THE BHARATIYA JANATA PARTY

As opposition to the INC grew during Indira Gandhi's 1970s autocratic interlude, a number of contending parties began to emerge or take on new importance. A coalition of some of these opposition parties, under the name Janata
(People's) Party, ultimately wrested the government from the INC in the late
1970s. One of the smallest of these coalition partners was Jana Sangh, a Hindu
nationalist party that left the Janata coalition in 1980 and changed its name
to the Bharatiya Janata Party (BJP), or Indian People's Party.

The BJP's popularity climbed rapidly as support for secularism gave way
to increasing sentiment for ethnic and religious parties. The BJP won only
two seats in the House of the People elections of 1984, but increasing Hindu
nationalist sentiment (manifested most violently in clashes with Sikhs at
Amritsar in 1984 and with Muslims in Ayodhya in 1992 and in Gujarat in
2002) allowed it to expand its representation to 161 seats by 1996 and form
a coalition government, led by Atal Behari Vajpayee. Although the first BJP
coalition lasted only twelve days, by 1998 the BJP had become the largest
party in the parliament, and Vajpayee and his BJP-led coalition governed from
1998 until turned out of office in the 2004 elections. Despite recent decline in
support (the BJP held on to only 116 seats in 2009), it remains, with the INC,
one of India's two largest parties.

From its founding, the BJP has been an outspoken advocate of Hindu
national identity. It is a member of a larger constellation of more than thirty
loosely tied Hindu nationalist organizations known collectively as the RSS
(the Hindi acronym for National Association of Volunteers). These religious,
social, and political associations vary widely in their acceptance of violence
and militancy in promoting Hindu nationalism, but all embrace **Hindutva**,
or Hindu-ness, as India's primary national identity and ideal. Whereas some
of the more moderate RSS member organizations promote benign patriotism,
other reactionary or fundamentalist association members teach a Hindu chau-
vinist version of Indian history and condone and even train their members in
violent tactics of religious and racial discrimination.

Similarly, the BJP itself has both moderate and militant elements. Its elected
national leaders tend to downplay the BJP's religious ties, promote the BJP as
a more honest alternative to the INC, and emphasize its neoliberal economic
policies of privatization, deregulation, and foreign investment. This reputation
of honesty and neoliberalism has appealed in particular to India's growing middle class, which is more interested in economic freedom and prosperity than in
secular equality. This predominantly Hindu middle class has become frustrated
with what it perceives as the reverse discrimination of the INC's secular policies of tolerance of minority religion and caste-based affirmative action.

The extremist and fundamentalist elements in the BJP are more overtly
anti-Muslim, contending that India's Muslims were forced to convert by for-

eign invaders and would naturally revert to their native Hinduism in an India permitted to promote its true heritage. They are more prone to violence, praising the assassin of Mahatma Gandhi and the combatants of Ayodhya and Gujarat as heroes and protectors of Indian heritage. Their leaders have been more successful politically at the local and state levels (particularly in the region of India's so-called cow belt in the Hindu-majority north) but have also become important allies in the BJP's efforts to form national ruling coalitions.

The most successful and controversial of the regional BJP leaders is the charismatic and outspoken chief minister (governor) of the state of Gujarat, **Narendra Modi**. Swept to power in the wake of the anti-Muslim violence in Gujarat in 2002, Modi was reelected in 2007 and clearly has national aspirations beyond his home state of Gujarat. At the same time, the strident Hindu nationalism championed by Modi and other hard-liners is offensive to many of the allied parties that formed the BJP's governing coalition prior to 2004. National party leaders recognize that the BJP cannot win national elections on the narrow platform of Hindu nationalism, and this has led to squabbling over leadership and continued divisions within the party.

PARTIES OF THE LEFT

India's so-called Left Front consists of a collection of Communist and other left-leaning parties whose popularity seems unfazed by the declining success of Communist parties and countries elsewhere in the world. These parties together have managed to garner on average between 7 and 10 percent of the national vote and typically over fifty seats in the House of the People. This bloc of seats has given the Communist parties a decisive role in the making and breaking of recent coalitions and therefore a certain leverage in government policy, despite their minority status. Following the 2004 general elections, the INC-led coalition required the support of four Communist parties in order to gain a voting majority in parliament. The fragile nature of this arrangement became apparent in parliamentary wrangling in recent years over a controversial nuclear cooperation treaty between India and the United States. Supported by the Congress Party, the deal was adamantly opposed by its erstwhile Communist allies who threatened to withdraw, and then ultimately withdrew, their support from the coalition in 2008. This forced the INC to form ad hoc alliances with other small parties to assemble a majority and to avoid a vote of no confidence that would bring the government down and force a new election.

The leftist parties have, in large part, remained successful because of their willingness to evolve and seek alliances with other parties. Although both of the two largest leftist parties, the Communist Party of India and the Communist Party of India (Marxist), initially supported violent revolution, over the years both have ultimately embraced peaceful means to achieve Communism. More recently, both have come to look and act much more like social democratic parties, embracing a mixture of state and private ownership and even promoting foreign investment. Like nearly all other parties in India, these leftist parties rely upon strong local and regional bases of support. The lion's share of party leadership and voting strength has come from the states of **Kerala** in the far south and West Bengal in the far east. Not all political movements on the left, however, have been willing to work within the democratic system. Chief among these radical groups is the Maoist (or guerrilla Communist) insurgency known as **Naxalism**. Named for the region in West Bengal where the movement originated in the late 1960s, the movement has grown in recent decades, particularly in rural areas in several of the poorest states of north-cental India. Naxalite recruits are drawn primarily from the low castes, outcastes, and tribal natives largely excluded from India's recent and dramatic economic growth.

REGIONAL PARTIES

The declining dominance of the INC and the rise of coalition governments have given new prominence to regional and local political parties, which have come to dominate in many states and tip the balance in national elections. Moreover, as INC-supported secularism has waned, ethnic, linguistic, and religious identities have become increasingly important rallying points for political interests that are often concentrated by region. For example, states with predominant ethnic or religious identities, such as the Dravidian Tamils in the southern state of Tamil Nadu and the Punjabi Sikhs, have often been led by these regional and state parties. Other parties draw support from lower-caste Indians in several of India's poorer states. In only one of India's six most populated states does either the INC or the BJP hold a majority in the state parliament.

The localized parties also often have sufficient voting strength to control small but influential blocs of seats in the national parliament. In the 2004 election, the INC and the BJP secured less than half the total vote, with state and special-interest parties winning nearly 40 percent. This reflects in one sense a devolution of central power that could be healthy for Indian democracy. But given the diversity of India's interests, it also speaks to the secessionist aspirations and highly localized interests of Indians and may be a sign of dangerous centrifugal forces.

Elections

Campaigns and elections are essential procedures in any viable democracy and are oftentimes dramatic theatrical events. Certainly this is true of India, where all aspects of an election must be measured in superlatives. For instance, in the spring of 2004 nearly 400 million of the eligible 690 million voters flocked to the 700,000 polling stations to cast votes (using over 1 mil-

House of the People Election Results, 2004 and 2009		
Party or Coalition	2004 Seats	2009 Seats
Indian National Congress (INC)	145	206
Bharatiya Janata Party (BJP)	138	116
INC and allies (United Progressive Alliance; UPA)	217	262
BJP and allies (National Democratic Alliance; NDA)	185	159
Left Front (LF)	59	24

lion new electronic voting machines). They selected their favored parliamentary candidates from the thousands of choices, representatives of one of six "national" parties or the dozens of regional ones. The task was so huge that polling was spread out over four weeks as election officials and their machines migrated across the country, harvesting votes. Indeed, this four-week election process was longer than the government-limited three-week campaign that preceded it.

Perhaps most amazing was the outcome itself, again testament to the authenticity of Indian democracy. Prior to the 2004 election, it was a foregone and universally held conclusion that the BJP-led coalition would retain its majority and extend its six-year tenure. With strong national economic growth and thawing relations with Pakistan over the troubled issue of Kashmir, the governing coalition called early national elections to capitalize on these successes, campaigning under the motto "India Is Shining." In the weeks prior to the election, BJP leaders were already busy divvying up potential cabinet posts, and INC leaders were offering justifications and finger-pointing for their party's anticipated weak showing.

But Indian voters had different plans, allowing the INC to edge ahead of the BJP with just over one-fourth of total seats. With its coalition partners, the INC gained control of 40 percent of the seats, and, after several days of negotiations, the INC expanded the coalition to include a number of regional, state, and left-of-center parties and secured the outside support of the Communist Party of India. The INC formed a majority coalition government, with Manmohan Singh as prime minister and returned both the coalition and Singh to office in 2009 (see "House of the People Election Results, 2004 and 2009," above).

Civil Society

As the dominance of the INC has faded and political authority has become decentralized, more—and more diverse—interests and elements of Indian society have demanded political influence. Although India has conventional civil organizations representing business, labor, and even peasants, these groups tend not to be particularly effective in influencing policy. Labor unions are organized by political party and are therefore fragmented and limited in their effectiveness, although they have done much to champion the interests of labor. Business certainly influences both politics and politicians—corruption is a serious problem among members of India's parliament—but this influence has been held in check by both traditional Hindu and more modern socialist biases against private business. Peasants are plentiful and at times vocal, but their political demands tend to be episodic and particular.

Communal interests representing ethnic, religious, and caste groups have been far more influential in Indian politics than have other factors. Hindus, Muslims, and Sikhs all have well-organized groups representing their political interests, and each supports its own political party or parties. This is also true of the **Dalits**, or untouchables, who have their own political party and constitute one of India's largest mass movements. Although there is good reason to be concerned about the destabilizing and divisive potential of these religious- and caste-based groups, there is also evidence that their multiple demands have often been addressed substantially (if not fully met) through the political process, thereby defusing civil discord and strengthening the legitimacy of the system.

Less traditional divisions and demands are also taking shape in contemporary Indian civil society, including significant environmental and women's movements. Environmental protests include resistance to development projects, such as the Narmada dam and deforestation, and advocacy of redress for industrial accidents, such as the Union Carbide disaster in Bhopal in 1984. Women's movements bridging class and ethnic divisions have organized to protest so-called dowry deaths, which claim the lives of as many as 25,000 Indian women annually.

Another important voice of Indian civil society is the media establishment, arguably one of the largest and most active in the world. It comprises 40,000 newspapers and other periodicals, including some 4,000 dailies, all of which enjoy a significant degree of editorial and political freedom. These figures are all the more impressive when one remembers that nearly a third of Indian men and over half of Indian women are illiterate. Given these figures, India's extensive radio and television networks are even more important conduits of information and have been subject to more careful government scrutiny and control. This oversight has become increasingly difficult, however, as satellite television—now available in 80 percent of India's half million villages—has introduced new competition into the market. India's substantial investment in networking the entire country with broadband cable will also certainly expand avenues for civic communication.

SOCIETY

Ethnic and National Identity

Contemporary India is a "complicated jigsaw" of astounding ethnic and social diversity pieced together by centuries of imperial conquest.[16] Independent India has sought to create from this patchworked imperial raj a unified and secular nation-state. This effort has required of India and its citizens a measure of social tolerance that has not always been available, seemingly leaving the country on the edge of disintegration. Yet for all the communitarian conflict and threats of secession, national unity has prevailed. Before noting the political culture that has at least to some degree preserved this unity, we turn first to the ethnic and social divisions that threaten it.

When the lighter-skinned Indo-Aryans migrated into what is now northern and central India thousands of years ago, they pushed the native, darker-skinned Dravidians southward. Each culture retained separate linguistic and cultural identities that persist to some extent today. Roughly two thirds of Indians (virtually all in the north) speak some variation of the Sanskrit-based language brought by the Indo-Aryans, which now forms some ten distinct languages. The most common of these is Hindi, one of two official national languages, which is spoken by over one third of all Indians. Approximately one fourth of all Indians speak one of the four main Dravidian languages. In all, the constitution recognizes fourteen languages, but at least another thirty languages claim over 1 million speakers each. The only other national language is English. Although only some 3 percent of the population speaks English fluently, as in other polyglot former colonies it has become an essential medium for national politics and commerce.

ETHNIC GROUPS

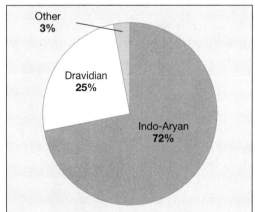

RELIGION

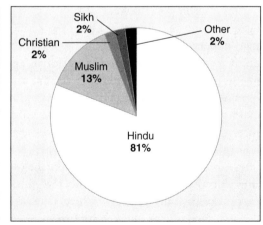

These divisions are at once exacerbated and moderated by religious differences. Although more than 80 percent of Indians share a common faith, regional and linguistic groups practice their Hinduism in various different ways. The promotion of Hindu nationalism has brought a degree of unity to these groups, but at the expense of some 12 percent of Indians who are Muslim, 2 to 3 percent who are adherents of Sikhism (an amalgam of Hindu and Muslim theologies), and the comparable percentage who are Christian. These religious differences have often acquired political significance, leading at times to assassinations, violent pogroms and bitter reprisals, secessions and threats of secession. The most dramatic flare-ups of sectarian violence have been between Hindus and Muslims, including the initial partitioning of Muslim Pakistan and Hindu India and ongoing territorial disputes in Kashmir as well as the events at Ayodhya in 1992, Gujarat in 2002, and the spate of attacks in 2008. Less dramatically but perhaps even more significantly, India's democracy has fostered the emergence and growth of religious-based political parties that have rallied around these nationalist and separatist sentiments.

As if the linguistic and religious differences were not sufficiently divisive, the hierarchical separation of Indian society into castes remains the most significant of India's social divisions. Although industrialization and urbanization have made the caste system today more permeable and flexible than it once was, it remains socially, politically, and economically important. Although neither class identity nor income inequality are as severe in India as in many other developing countries, those in the lower ranks of India's caste system are typically also the poorest, with the scheduled castes and hill tribes the poorest of the poor. In an effort to redress discrimination against these suppressed groups, or *Dalits*, the government has established affirmative action programs reserving for them jobs, scholarships, and even seats in the parliament.

Although not fully effective in leveling the playing field, these measures have helped the *Dalits* achieve a degree of social mobility and even political organization (including the formation of a regional political party). These policies have become contentious, angering many higher-caste Hindus, who see the measures—along with special protections afforded to minority religious groups—as reverse discrimination. The Hindu nationalist Bharatiya Janata Party (BJP) has seized on this issue in expanding its constituency among the growing Hindu middle class and stirring the embers of Hindu fundamentalism.

Ideology and Political Culture

As with many other elements of Indian politics, India's political culture defies generalization. Nonetheless, two somewhat contradictory values are worth mentioning. On the one hand, Indians tend to identify themselves and their

FEARS ABOUT FOREIGN INFLUENCE

Our way of life must be protected from foreign influence.
Percent saying yes:

Country	Percent
India	92
Nigeria	85
South Africa	80
Russia	77
Brazil	77
Mexico	75
China	70
Japan	64
United States	62
Canada	62
United Kingdom	54
Germany	53
France	52

*Data on Iran not available.
Source: Pew Center for the People and the Press, 2007.

politics locally. Indians are tied most importantly to family, occupational group, and their immediate regional linguistic and religious associates. These immediate ties tend to segment and even fragment politics in India, which promotes political awareness and cooperation locally but also causes political friction and even violence between groups. Although such localization may limit the scope of conflict, it also constrains the kind of mobilization that could address pressing national needs.

On the other hand, despite their cultural diversity and contentious politics, Indians continue to identify themselves as Indians and generally support—and see themselves as an important part of—Indian national democracy. So while the bonds of national unity are less powerful than local ties, India's "bewilderingly plural population" nonetheless sees itself as "capable of purposeful collective action."[17] Gandhi and Nehru remain national heroes for most Indians who take their role as citizens seriously and see Indian democracy as legitimate.

Some see in this combined sense of local power and political efficacy a dangerous tendency toward identity politics in Indian democracy. Nehru's secular nationalism has ceded ground to political movements that mobilize supporters in the name of religion or region. Majority Hindus perceive themselves as threatened by minority religions, the prosperous middle class depicts itself as victim of India's poorest outcastes, and Punjabi Sikhs and Kashmiri Muslims clamor for independence. Globalization has further created a sense that Indian identity as a whole is under threat and must be defended. Yet democracy and unity prevail, speaking to India's remarkable capacity to adopt and adapt foreign institutions for its own use. An Indian adage claims that "democracy is like cricket—a quintessentially Indian game that just happened to have been invented elsewhere." There is no question that India has made democracy its own.

POLITICAL ECONOMY

By the time India finally obtained its independence from British imperialism, it had had quite enough of the West's version of liberal free trade. For nearly four decades, successive (mostly INC) governments adopted a foreign policy of mercantilist economic nationalism, promoting **import-substitution industrialization** and restricting foreign investment and trade. Governments also promoted social democratic policies domestically to limit the private sector, redistribute wealth, and give the state the leading role in guiding the economy. These policies achieved several significant results. By the late 1970s, through the technological gains of the green revolution, India had become one of the largest agricultural producers in the world and for most years since then has been a net exporter of food. India established a relatively large—if not broad—middle class, and some niches in the economy and some regions of the country truly prospered.

By the mid-1980s, however, frustration with poverty, corruption, and continued slow growth at home, coupled with the popularity of export-led growth and structural adjustment programs abroad, led successive governments to adopt neoliberal policies of economic reform. Piecemeal efforts during the 1980s to dismantle nearly four decades of mercantilist protectionism gave way to substantial liberalization following a balance of payments crisis in 1991. Although the process was more gradual than the "shock therapy" adopted in Poland or Russia and the results have been less thorough than the reform and opening of China, measures to liberalize foreign trade and investment and to privatize the economy have been significant. Governments weakened India's notorious **license raj**, the mercantilist holdover requiring licensing and approval processes for operating a business and importing and exporting prod-

---

THE LICENSE RAJ AND THE "HINDU RATE OF GROWTH"

Referring to India's relatively slow rate of development during its early decades of independence, an Indian economist famously compared what he called the "Hindu rate of growth" with the more rapid pace of its East Asian neighbors. Although the phrase would seem to implicate India's non-Confucian culture, most observers agree that the greatest obstacle to Indian growth has been (and in important ways remains) India's huge bureaucracy with its associated red tape and corruption. India's "license-permit-quota raj" was the legacy of an extensive British colonial civil service superceded by independent India's far larger state bureaucracy. To carry out his social democratic vision for India, Nehru established an interventionist state that pursued socialist and mercantilist economic policies, including protectionist measures promoting import-substitution industrialization and far-reaching regulations designed to protect consumers and lift India's poorest. The result was a highly bureaucratized and politicized system of licenses, permits, and quotas governing virtually all aspects of the Indian economy.

Although some of the most stifling aspects of the license raj were reduced or eliminated with the 1991 liberalization program, much of India's wealth is still "sponged up or siphoned off by a vast tumorous bureaucracy."[18] It still takes an average of three months to secure the permits necessary to start a business in India and much longer than that to secure a license to import a computer. Because Indians have found it so difficult to work within this system, most have little choice but to work around it by paying bribes, which have come to be expected "at almost every point where citizens are governed, at every transaction where they are noted, registered, taxed, stamped, licensed, authorized, or assessed."[19]

---

ucts (see "The License Raj and 'Hindu Rate of Growth,'" above). Restrictions on foreign investment have been eased, and many state-owned companies have been sold to the private sector.

The results of the liberalization effort are impressive. In the two decades since the reforms were launched, economic growth in India averaged nearly 6 percent per year (twice the rate for the previous twenty years). In the past few years, economic expansion has neared the frenzied rates of neighboring China, with growth averaging closer to 10 percent per year (and inflation rates to match). Even as the population has continued to grow (too) rapidly, the total number of poor Indians is declining. Trade and investment are up, and Western outsourcing (moving the production of goods and services to another country to take advantage of cheap labor or other savings) has brought jobs and growth to some segments of the Indian economy.

Yet huge economic problems persist. Fully one quarter of India's population remains mired in poverty, living on less than US$1 per day. Half of India's children under the age of five are under-weight, and the total number of malnour-ished Indians has hardly dropped in the past ten years. Fully one fourth of the world's undernourished reside in India. Corruption and protectionism persist, and the pollution accompanying India's industrial expansion threatens to undermine the development success India has achieved to date. The World Bank predicts that by 2020, India's water, air, and soil resources will be under greater threat than those of any other nation. An Indian auto manufacturer is now pro-ducing the Nano, priced at $2,500 and billed as "the world's cheapest car." The Indian capital, Delhi, adds 1,000 cars a day to its roads.

LABOR FORCE BY OCCUPATION

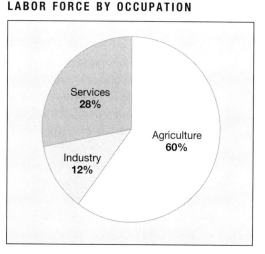

Comparing India's development trajectory with neighboring China's is instructive.[20] Although China was poorer than India when both countries were established in the late 1940s and remained so through the 1970s, China has dramatically outperformed India since then. Its growth rates have hovered near 10 percent for the past thirty years, population growth has slowed, and trade and investment have skyrocketed. In recent years, China's annual increases in trade have exceeded India's total annual trade.

Part of the explanation for this difference rests in two challenges that con-tinue to perplex India: too many people and too little education. Whereas the growth rate of China's population has slowed to less than 1 percent per year, India's remains closer to 2 percent. This has meant fewer mouths to feed in China and more wealth to spread around. The World Bank has concluded that extreme poverty has been nearly eradicated there.

In addition, China has done a far better job of providing basic education for its citizens. More than 90 percent of Chinese adults are literate, compared with less than 60 percent of Indians. More troubling, less than half of Indian women are literate, compared with over 85 percent of Chinese women. Econ-omists and demographers argue, however, that there may be a silver lining for India: if India can educate its citizens, particularly its women, population pressures will ease as women gain more control over reproductive choices and families deem it rational to limit family size. More important, this demo-graphic liability could become an asset as mouths to feed develop into skilled, competitive workers in the twenty-first-century global economy.

Like China and many other developing countries that have been drawn into the global economy, India faces an additional problem. Although the economy is growing, it is doing so unevenly. Much has been made of India's recent information technology (IT) boom, and for good reason. Several large Indian computer firms are now globally competitive, and Western companies have flocked to such cities as Bangalore in the south and Hyderabad in the north to take advantage of India's wealth of service workers and English-speaking engineers.

But the IT industry remains largely irrelevant to most Indians. As a whole, it employs fewer than 2 million workers out of a labor force of some 500 million and makes up only 5 percent of India's GDP. Six of India's twenty-eight states receive virtually all of India's foreign investment. Thus it has created for India a dual economy that exacerbates both regional and class tensions. An elite, urban, prosperous, and Westernized middle-class minority sits precariously on top of a huge lower class that is largely rural, illiterate, and in many cases unemployed or underemployed.

If India is to eliminate or at least address this persistent poverty and inequality, stay ahead of its rapid population growth, and perhaps catch up to China and other competitors, scholars and policy makers agree that it must do several things. Among them are improving conditions for its rural population; improving roads, telecommunication, and other aspects of the infrastructure; increasing foreign investment; and above all providing elementary education and basic health care, particularly to Indian girls and women.

There is evidence that this can be done. The state of Kerala, in southwestern India, boasts female literacy rates of nearly 90 percent and fertility rates and population growth far lower than the national average. These are the result, however, not of neoliberal market reforms but of several decades of socialist state policies in education, health care, and land reform that have generally emphasized equality over freedom and state intervention over free-market policies. Although India is not likely to return fully to the social democratic policies of the 1950s, its voters in 2004 chose the INC and its leftist coalition partners with a mandate not to forget them—the majority of Indian voters whom recent economic growth has in many ways left behind.

FOREIGN RELATIONS AND THE WORLD

Once India had gained its independence, Jawaharlal Nehru charted for the country a foreign policy of "peaceful coexistence" with its neighbors and "non-alignment" in the superpower cold war that was just then taking shape in the postwar world. In fact, Nehru became a leader of the nonaligned movement of postcolonial developing countries seeking to create a neutral "third world" separate from the American-led Western nations (the first world) and the Soviet-led Eastern bloc (the second world). Unfortunately, the ethnic politics of partition and the geopolitics of big-power relations derailed this course. In the decades that followed, India fought three wars with neighboring Pakistan and maintained frosty relations with both Communist China and capitalist United States. With the end of the cold war, however, and under conditions of much higher (nuclear) stakes (first China, then India, and finally Pakistan joined the United States as nuclear powers), India's relations have recently thawed with all three of these countries. With growing economic and political clout, India is beginning to command the respect of an emerging great power in both the region and the world.

PAKISTAN AND THE KASHMIR DISPUTE

No issue has haunted India's foreign relations as much as the legacy of partition. The bitter division of India into Muslim Pakistan and Hindu India in 1947 not only soured relations between these erstwhile partners in the independence struggle but also left jagged and festering wounds in the very boundaries between them. At the center of the conflict is the contested region of Kashmir, which is situated on the northern portion of the border between the two countries and is claimed in whole by both nations. On one side of the conflict is the Indian state of Jammu and Kashmir; on the other, is the Pakistani-administered state of Kashmir. At the time of partition, Kashmir was the largest of three principalities that had not committed themselves

Source: "A Good Vote in the Angry Valley," *Economist*, 30 December 2008, www.economist.com/world/asia/displaystory.cfm?story_id=12868164 (accessed 15 January 2009).

to joining either India or Pakistan. The majority of its subjects were Urdu-speaking Muslims whose ethnic sentiments leaned toward Pakistan, but its prince was a Hindu who hoped Kashmir would remain independent. This ambivalence gave way to armed conflict—the first of three undeclared wars between India and Pakistan—within months of the partition.

A year of armed conflict ground to a halt in 1949, and the line of conflict has remained the de facto border between the two countries (see "Pakistan and the Kashmir Dispute," p. 361). Pakistan launched a second war in 1965, hoping to sever Kashmir from the rest of India, but the Pakistani advantage of surprise was no match for India's superior forces, and the hostilities ended in three weeks. The third war was waged not over Kashmir but over the struggle for independence in Bangladesh, which was then East Pakistan. Although the original partition created one Pakistan, its eastern and western halves were linked only by a shared religion and were divided by language, culture, and—most troubling—nearly 1,000 miles of Indian territory. Backed by newly acquired Soviet armaments, India came to the aid of the secessionist movement in 1971, forcing Pakistan to accept liberation and Bangladeshi independence.

The Kashmir region remains the world's most militarized border dispute. The level of tension has waxed and waned, but as one author notes, the cease-fire line has continued "to serve as a target range" claiming thousands of lives each year.[21] With nuclear weapons now potential ammunition for both sides, many political analysts hope that caution will prevail over the "pathological politics" of ethnic hatred.[22] There is reason for hope. Substantive peace talks on a negotiated and more permanent settlement of the Kashmir conflict and other territorial disputes resumed in 2004. The two countries have once again permitted limited cross-border travel, signed an agreement to reduce the risk of an accidental nuclear war, and are discussing a gas pipeline from Iran to India that would pass through Pakistan. Following the 2008 terrorist attack on Mumbai that prompted cross-border accusations and heightened tensions between Pakistan and India, Indian-controlled Jammu and Kashmir nonetheless held relatively peaceful state elections, in which voters chose a government committed to accommodation and negotiation, not separatism and violence.

SEPTEMBER 11 AND GREAT POWER RELATIONS

India's early hopes for peaceful relations with China, its neighbor to the north, were dashed by Chinese expansion into areas of India's northeastern Himalayan region. Tensions led to the Chinese invasion of India in 1962 to resolve what China viewed as "border disputes," but what India deemed outright aggression. India claims several territories now held by China—mostly Kashmiri land ceded to China by Pakistan—that are larger in area than

Switzerland. China, in turn, claims three times as much real estate to the east now in the hands of India. Efforts since 1998 to resolve these disputes finally yielded positive results in 2005, when both sides agreed to allow a cross-national committee to resolve this conflict. In 2006, a Himalayan border crossing reopened between the two countries for the first time since the Sino-Indian border war of 1962. Despite this recent thawing of border relations, growing bilateral trade, and China's claims to support India's bid for a permanent seat on the United Nations Security Council, the relationship remains fragile and complicated. India acknowledges China's claim to Tibet, but at the same time plays host to the Dalai Lama, his government-in-exile, and some 100,000 Tibetan refugees. China has stepped up military incursions into disputed Indian territory and has participated in the construction of naval facilities in both Bangladesh and Pakistan. China has also helped Pakistan keep pace with India's nuclear capabilities.

The September 11, 2001, terrorist attacks in the United States and subsequent war on terror launched by the United States have brought a new dynamic to India's dealings with China, the United States, and even Pakistan. Historically, India's relationship with the world's second-largest democracy has been cool at best. But like China, India saw the benefits of recasting its own struggle with Muslim insurgents as part of a larger global war on terror. The United States responded warmly, lifting sanctions in place since India's nuclear tests in the 1990s, expanding trade, and—to Pakistan's chagrin—increasing military sales. Most significantly, in 2005 U.S. President George W. Bush negotiated a nuclear cooperation deal with Prime Minister Singh that permits India to purchase nuclear technology for the first time in three decades, despite India's refusal to sign the Nuclear Non-Proliferation Treaty (see "Current Issues," p. 364). These actions have put Pakistan in an awkward position: after all, India's Kashmiri terrorists have been viewed by Pakistan as freedom fighters. But Pakistan has had little choice but to go along with the war on terror, and India has been generally impressed with Pakistan's recent efforts to rein in Kashmiri insurgents and facilitate peace efforts between the two countries.

Today, India's diplomatic relations with its neighbors and other powers in the region are for the most part more cordial than they have been at any time since independence. Trade and investment with both China and the United States are booming, and despite tensions stemming from the 2008 Mumbai terrorist attack, talks between India and Pakistan on resolving disputes and opening and expanding travel and trade links across the bloodstained region of Kashmir are under way. India is one of only a handful of nuclear powers and enjoys a growing economy and increasing influence in global forums. India—with good reason—sees itself, and is increasingly seen by others, as an emerging great power.

CURRENT ISSUES

NUCLEAR NEGOTIATIONS, COALITION POLITICS, AND U.S.–INDIAN RELATIONS

Perhaps no issue better captures the confluence of domestic and international politics for a rising great power than the controversial nuclear cooperation deal struck between India and the United States. Negotiations began in 2005 on an arrangement that would end the three-decade ban on India's access to peaceful nuclear technology and enriched uranium, a ban first imposed after India refused to sign the nuclear Non-Proliferation Treaty (NPT) in the 1960s and then developed and tested thermonuclear weapons in the 1970s and again in the 1990s in violation of the treaty. Like Pakistan and Israel, both of which have also refused to sign the NPT, India has long argued that it was unfairly excluded from the nuclear club and claims it maintains nuclear weapons only as a no-first-use deterrent against neighboring China and Pakistan.

The bilateral negotiations held benefits for both countries. The agreement promised India the right to purchase much needed fuel and technology for its civilian nuclear program and to legitimize its membership in the exclusive nuclear club. For the United States, the deal would strengthen ties with a key ally in the curbing of China's expansion and provide American companies access to lucrative nuclear and defense contracts in India. But while leaders in both countries saw the strategic promise of the agreement, domestic politics proved a different matter. Although American nonproliferation critics are many, the real political struggle came in India. The governing coalition forged by Prime Minister Singh's Congress Party in 2004 included a dozen small regional, caste-based, and left-leaning parties and depended on outside support from India's two main Communist parties to maintain its majority. Because the Communist parties are stridently anti-American, they opposed any warming of ties—particularly a strategic partnership—with the United States and rejected the deal from the outset.

Although the agreement did not require the approval of the Indian parliament, the Communist parties repeatedly threatened to abandon the Congress-led coalition and force a vote of no confidence if the government pursued the deal, which also required approval by the United Nation's International Atomic Energy Agency (IAEA), the 45-member Nuclear Supplier's Group, and the United States Congress. Prime Minister Singh spent three full years trying to bargain with, beg, and threaten his Communist party allies to no avail. Finally, in 2008, Congress abandoned the support of its recalcitrant erstwhile Communist partners, recruited a new parliamentary ally, a regional party, to take its place, and announced it would pursue IAEA approval. Amid charges of treachery and bribery, the new Congress-led coalition survived a vote of no confidence and forwarded the nuclear agreement to the IAEA and

United States Congress. Both bodies approved the deal, affording India access to peaceful nuclear technology and material.

IDENTITY POLITICS AND SECULAR DEMOCRACY

The Congress-led coalition's dependence on a regional political party to salvage its nuclear deal highlights the pivotal role of regional, ethnic, and caste-based politics in what Gandhi and Nehru envisioned would be a unified secular democracy. A spate of terrorist bombings and attacks in major cities across India in recent years offers a more troubling reminder of the politics-by-other-means to which local and sectarian militants are all too willing to resort. Bombings by Muslim extremists in New Delhi in 2005 and Varanasi in 2006 were followed by explosions at Muslim mosques in Mumbai that same year and Hyderabad in 2007. Over a period of three months in 2008, bombs rocked neighborhoods in Jaipur, Bangalore, and Ahmadabad, killing over one hundred and injuring hundreds more. The bombings in Ahmadabad, Gujarat state's largest city, threatened once again to stir the embers of the horrific violence that racked this state in 1992 and a decade later in 2002. Perhaps most dramatic was a sophisticated 2008 assault on Mumbai's city center carried out by a well-trained and well-armed group of Muslim terrorists with clear Pakistani ties. Although casualties were fewer than in the 2006 Mumbai bombings, the 2008 assault targeted luxury hotels and other venues frequented by wealthy Indian and Western elite. One can add to this grim tally of violence the persistent bloodletting in Kashmir and militant movements among disenfranchised tribal groups in eastern India.

This violence is both symbol and substance of the most pressing issue facing India today: Can pluralist politics prevail? Can Gandhi and Nehru's vision of a secular nation embracing all Indians and a democratic polity giving voice to all identities survive? Or will the rise of Hindu chauvinism, the pull of caste, the press of communitarian violence, and the stress of separatist demands fray India at its borders and tear it apart from the center?

Certainly there are reasons for grave concern. The embers from one sectarian clash hardly cool before the next spark is ignited. The Hindu uprising that destroyed the mosque in Ayodhya and the bloody siege at the Sikh Golden Temple in Amritsar compete with images of the charred corpses of Hindu pilgrims in railcars in Gujarat and the burning parapets of Mumbai's stately hotels. Each of these becomes the justification for yet another round of bloody reprisals and increasingly inflammatory political demands. And yet, the very survival of Indian democracy continues to offer its greatest hope. Despite the violence, Indian pluralist politics has given voice and legitimacy to a welter of demands and preserved relative peace in this multiethnic nation. As one observer notes in praise of Indian democracy, "All politics is local, and India has an awful lot of localities."[23]

NOTES

1. The Indian Constitution identifies 18 official or "scheduled" languages. A massive investigtion conducted by the Anthropological Survey of India from 1985 to 1992 identified 75 "major" languages and 325 distinct languages. See www.ansi.gov.in/people_india.htm (accessed 18 July 2008).
2. Stanley Wolpert, *India* (Berkeley: University of California Press, 1991), p. 14.
3. For a careful and thorough discussion of the caste system, its origins, evolution, and social and political consequences for India, see Susan Bayly, *The New Cambridge History of India: Caste, Society, and Politics in India from the Eighteeenth Century to the Modern Age* (Cambridge, UK: Cambridge University Press, 1999).
4. Francis G. Hutchins, *The Illusion of Permanence: British Imperialism in India* (Princeton: Princeton University Press, 1967), p. xi.
5. Wolpert, *India*, p. 55.
6. Yasmin Khan, *The Great Partition* (New Haven, CT: Yale University Press, 2007).
7. V. S. Naipaul, *India: A Million Mutinies Now* (New York: Penguin, 1990).
8. For a useful historical comparison of democracy and authoritarianism in India and Pakistan, see Ayesha Jalal, *Democracy and Authoritarianism in South Asia: A Comparative and Historical Perspective* (Cambridge, UK: Cambridge University Press, 1995).
9. Wolpert, *India*, p. 212.
10. "Batting for the Family," *Economist*, 27 September 2007.
11. Bhagwan D. Dua, "Presidential Rule in India: A Study in Crisis Politics," *Asian Survey*, 19 (June 1979), pp. 611–26.
12. Pradeep Chhibber and Ken Kollman, "Party Aggregation and the Number of Parties in India and the United States," *The American Political Science Review*, 92 (June 1998), pp. 329–42.
13. The following comparisons are taken from Susanne Hoeber Rudolph and Lloyd I. Rudolph, "New Dimensions of Indian Democracy," *Journal of Democracy*, 13 (2002), pp. 52–66.
14. See Freedom House's 2008 Indian Country Report at http://www.freedomhouse.org (accessed, 14 January 2009).
15. Arun Shourie, "Two Concepts of Liberty," *Economist*, 3 March 2005.
16. Kesavan Mukul, "India's Embattled Secularism," *Wilson Quarterly*, 27 (Winter 2003), p. 61.
17. Mukul, "India's Embattled Secularism," p. 63.
18. "Battling the Babu Raj," *Economist*, 6 March 2008.
19. Edward Luce, *In Spite of the Gods* (New York: Anchor Books, 2007), p. 78.
20. A number of the comparative figures for China and India in this and subsequent paragraphs are drawn from "The Tiger in Front," Survey: India and China, *Economist*, 3 March 2005.
21. Wolpert, *India*, p. 235.
22. Ishtiaq Ahmed, "The 1947 Partition of India: A Paradigm for Pathological Politics in India and Pakistan," *Asian Ethnicity*, 3 (March 2002), pp. 9–28.
23. "A Tarnished Triumph," *Economist*, 26 July 2008, p. 49.

GLOSSARY OF KEY TERMS ─────────────

Amritsar   Northern Indian city and location of the Golden Temple, Sikhism's holiest shrine.

Ayodhya   North-central Indian city where Babri Mosque was destroyed in 1992.

Bharatiya Janata Party (BJP)   Indian People's Party; Hindu nationalist party that governed from 1998 to 2004.

caste   Hindu hereditary social groupings.

Center   Term referring to India's national government and its capital in New Delhi.

Dalits   "Suppressed groups"; formal name of India's outcastes.

emergency rule   Right of Indian national government to suspend the constitution by declaring martial law.

Gandhi, Indira   Indian prime minister (1966–1977; 1979–1984) and daughter of Jawaharlal Nehru.

Gandhi, Mahatma (Mohandas K.)   Indian nationalist and leader of the Indian independence movement.

Gandhi, Sonia   Italian-born wife of Rajiv Gandhi and leader of the Indian National Congress Party.

green revolution   Technologically enhanced crops and cropping methods that dramatically improved production in India during the 1960s and 1970s.

Gujarat   Western Indian state in which Hindu-Muslim violence broke out in 2002.

Hindi   One of two national languages in India.

Hinduism   India's dominant religious tradition.

Hindutva   "Hindu-ness"; Hindu nationalism.

House of States   Upper house of Indian parliament, representing India's twenty-eight states and seven territories.

House of the People   Lower and more powerful house of Indian parliament.

import-substitution industrialization   Mercantilist strategy of development in which local production is protected from imports.

Indian National Congress (INC)   Major Indian political party, began as leading organization of Indian independence movement.

Kashmir   Contested region in northern India claimed by both India and Pakistan.

Kerala   Southwestern Indian state governed by Communists, famous for its high rates of literacy, low rates of fertility, and population growth.

license raj   India's highly bureaucratized and politicized mercantilist system of licenses, permits, and quotas governing virtually all aspects of the economy.

Modi, Narendra   Successful and controversial BJP chief minister (governor) of the state of Gujarat.

Mughals   Muslim invaders who ruled India for several hundred years beginning in the sixteenth century.

Muslim League   Indian Muslim independence organization.

nabob game   Strategy of British East India Company for controlling India by setting up puppet Mughal governorships, or nabobs.

Naxalism   Radical Maoist (or guerrilla Communist) insurgency in India.

Nehru, Jawaharlal   India's first prime minister (1947–1964) and successor to Gandhi as leader of the INC.

outsourcing   Moving the production of goods and services to another country to take advantage of cheap labor or other savings.

partition   Creation of the new states of Pakistan and India from the South Asian British colony of India in 1947.

presidential rule   State-level equivalent of emergency rule in India in which the national government takes temporary control of a state by imposing martial law.

raj   Hindu word for *rule*.

Sepoy Mutiny   1857–1858 failed revolt against the British, sponsored by the Indian aristocracy and carried out by sepoys, or Indian soldiers employed by the British.

Sikhism   Indian religious tradition combining elements of Hindu and Muslim beliefs.

Singh, Manmohan   Prime minister of India (2004–present).

untouchables   India's outcaste groups, including those who traditionally performed "unclean" duties and tribal aboriginals.

WEB LINKS

GOI Directory of Indian government Web sites **goidirectory.nic.in**

Government and Politics of South Asia: South and Southeast Asian Studies, Columbia University Libraries

    www.columbia.edu/cu/lweb/indiv/southasia/cuvl/govt.html

India Democracy **www.indiademocracy.com**

    A nonprofit, pro-democracy site facilitating communication between citizens and elected representatives.

Outlook **outlookindia.com** A popular weekly newsmagazine.

Parliament **parliamentofindia.nic.in**

The Times of India **timesofindia.indiatimes.com**

10 IRAN

Head of State: Ayatollah Ali Khamenei
(since June 4, 1989)

Head of Government: Mahmoud Ahmadinejad
(since August 6, 2005; declared winner in a
disputed election, June 2009)

Capital: Tehran

Total land size: 1,648,000 sq km

Population: 66 million

GDP at PPP: 753 billion US$

GDP per Capita at PPP: $10,600

Human development index ranking: 94

IRAN

INTRODUCTION

Why Study This Case?

Like many of the cases in this volume, Iran illustrates important dynamics of comparative politics. Most important, Iran is associated with what we think of as **Islamism**, or **Islamic fundamentalism**. When we speak of Islamic fundamentalism, we mean a belief that a literal interpretation of the faith should be the basis of the political regime. In other words, Islamic fundamentalism transforms faith into ideology.

In 1979, the authoritarian, secular Iranian monarchy fell to revolution, inspired in part by the charismatic leadership of the religious leader **Ruhollah Khomeini**. This Islamic revolution dramatically transformed all aspects of Iranian life, as Khomeini and his followers sought to create a **theocracy** in which the regime is dominated by a religious elite. In this "Islamic Republic," law and politics are expected to flow from the **Koran**, the main spiritual text of Islam. The Iranian revolution became a source of inspiration for Islamist movements around the world. As numerous countries struggle with Islamic fundamentalism, the Iranian revolution remains an important example of the power of Islam as a political vision.

When one looks more deeply, however, one finds that Iran is atypical and unrepresentative of the politics of Islam or even the politics of the Middle East. Contrary to what we might think, Iran is not an Arab country—the major ethnicity of Iran's population is Persian. Nor do Iranians speak Arabic, the common language of the Middle East; they speak, instead, **Farsi**. Indeed, Iranians see themselves as a distinct nation and look upon Arab countries as foreign and often with some degree of contempt. Iranians do not see themselves as part of a broader pan-Islamic or pan-Arabic movement.

The difference between Iranian ethnicity and Iranian national identity is further compounded by religion. Again, at first glance Iran's revolution might be seen as the first spark in the current wave of Islamic fundamentalism, and there can be no doubt that the revolution did inspire a new wave of radicalism and political violence across the region. But the international impact of the revolution was also tempered by the fact that Iranians practice **Shiism**, a minority form of Islam that differs from the rest of Islam in its belief regarding the rightful religious heir of the prophet **Muhammad**.[1] As a result, many followers of Islam around the world (especially fundamentalists) reject the Iranian theocracy for avowing a mistaken, even heretical, form of the faith. In spite of these divisions, Iran has certainly influenced modern debates about the relationship between politics and Islam, especially among Shiite groups elsewhere in the region (as in Iraq, Afghanistan, and Lebanon). For some, Iran remains an inspiration for political change; for others, Iran is an example of how religion and politics should not mix. Such conflicting views can be found not only among average Shiites (both inside and outside Iran) but also among Shiism's top clergy.

These complexities help shape Iran's role in the international system. In recent years, Iran has moved toward developing its own nuclear capacity, thus putting itself on a collision course with the United States and the European Union. Many observers fear that Iran might use nuclear weapons against Israel (which has its own nuclear arsenal), or that the regime might transfer weapons or weapons technology. Such tensions occur against the backdrop of domestic unease. In the 1990s, reformists sought to liberalize political, econonomic and social institutions in Iran. This goal translated into the election of president **Mohammad Khatami** in 1997, who spoke of a "dialogue of civilizations" in place of international conflict and an expansion of civil society. Hopes were high that Khatami's election would pave the way for dramatic political change. Religious conservatives, however, managed to beat back the reformers and limit Khatami's powers. The June 2005 election of the conservative Mahmoud Ahmadinejad as president dealt a serious blow to the reformers, and led to a new period of increased conservatism at home and confrontation abroad. This resulted in widespread support for reformist candidates in the 2009 presidential election, such that it appears that the top leadership chose to falsify the election results to ensure a second term for Ahmadinejad. Yet this has only deepened divisions over the future direction of the country. In spite of its unique institutions, Iran may give us a glimpse into the potential power of Islamic fundamentalism, as well as its limitations and the sources of resistance to it.

Major Geographic and Demographic Features

Iran occupies an important position in Middle East politics, yet it is in many ways an outlier in multiple senses of the word. Iranians do not belong to the wider Arab community of the Middle East; they have different national origins, with the national language being Farsi instead of Arabic. Iran itself is on the eastern periphery of the Middle East, sharing borders with Afghanistan, Pakistan, and several states that were once part of the Soviet Union. But its geographic position does not mean that Iran is insignificant. It is about the size of Alaska (somewhat smaller than Mexico) and has a population of nearly 70 million, which is larger than that of the United Kingdom. For both its size and its population, Iran ranks in the world's top twenty nations. Not only is it large, but its population is young. Close to half the population is under thirty. Compare this with Japan, for example, where the median age is forty-four. The youthful nature of Iran matters. A large percentage of the population has no memory of the country before the formation of the Islamic

Republic and has largely experienced only economic stagnation under the current regime. Related to this is the fact that the state must deal with a large influx of young people seeking higher education, employment, and housing, all of which the government has difficulty providing. This segment of the population currently represents the greatest challenge to the regime, and took to the streets in sometimes violent protests following the presidential election of 2009.

In addition to being young, Iran's population is diverse. Only about half the population is ethnically Persian. One quarter is Azeri, members of a Turkic-speaking people who are concentrated in the northwest of the country, near the borders of Armenia and Azerbaijan. The remaining quarter of the population is made up of several smaller ethnic groups, including Kurds, Arabs, and Turkmen. Some of these ethnic groups also follow Sunni rather than Shia Islam. These groups mounted various protests against the new government in the aftermath of the 1979 revolution; although such conflicts have largely subsided, there remain sporadic ethnic conflicts, particularly among the Azeri and Arab minorities.

As important as what lies above the ground in Iran is what lies beneath it. Iran is estimated to have the fourth-largest reserves of oil in the world, and it is the fourth-largest producer of oil. It also boasts one of the world's largest reserves of natural gas. As in many other countries, these resources have been both a boon and a curse. It was oil that drew imperial attention at the start of the twentieth century and helped foster modernization—as well as external intervention, domestic corruption, and eventually revolution. Oil has also helped keep the current regime in power, especially as prices have risen; however, one negative consequence of Iran's oil-derived wealth has been stagnation in other parts of the economy. Oil resources, moreover, themselves face limits. Poor relations with Europe and the United States have resulted in limited investment in oil and gas production, and a growing population will consume more of these resources at home.

Historical Development of the State

THE PERSIAN LEGACY AND THE ISLAMIC EMPIRE

Iranians trace their national and political origins back thousands of years, at least to the second millennium B.C.E. Around that time, a number of people migrated into the region from Central Asia, among them the ethnic group we now know as the Persians; Persian continues to be a common name used to describe the majority population of Iran. Up until 1935, the country itself was known as **Persia**. During the first millennium B.C.E., the Persians were able to extend their influence throughout the region, subduing other groups and creating the Achaemenid Empire in the process. Under the emperors Cyrus,

Darius, and Xerxes, the empire grew vast, stretching from modern-day India across much of the Middle East and becoming a major foe to the Greek city-states. This empire was noted for its wealth, technical sophistication, and relative political and religious tolerance. Destroyed by Alexander the Great, the Acheamenid Empire is an important symbol of Iranian might that still resonates with Iranians today. Although the empire collapsed after two centuries, the country continued to develop under a series of ruling dynasties; these kings, or shahs, ruled through the sixth century C.E.

The most dramatic transformation of Persia by outside forces occurred in the seventh century, with the arrival of Islam brought by Arabs from the Mid-

TIME LINE OF POLITICAL DEVELOPMENT	
Year	Event
1905–06	Constitutional revolution seeks to limit power of the monarchy
1921	Reza Khan seizes power
1925	Reza Khan proclaimed shah and changes his name to Reza Shah Pahlavi
1941	British and Soviet forces occupy Iran; the shah is forced to abdicate in favor of his son, Mohammad Reza Pahlavi
1951	Parliament votes to nationalize the oil industry
1953	Struggle between the shah and Prime Minister Mohammad Mosaddeq culminates in Operation Ajax, in which Mosaddeq is overthrown with U.S. help
1963	White Revolution begins
1979	Iranian revolution: the shah is desposed; Ayatollah Ruhollah Khomeini returns from exile; U.S. Embassy seized, and hostages held for 444 days
1980	Iraq invades Iran
1988	Iran-Iraq War ends
1989	Ayatollah Khomeini dies
1997	Reformer Mohammad Khatami elected president
1999	Pro-reform student protests lead to rioting and mass arrests
2002	Russia begins work on Iran's first nuclear reactor, at Bushehr
2005	Mahmoud Ahmadinejad elected President
2009	Ahmadinejad declared winner in a disputed election

dle East. Shortly after the death of the prophet Muhammad, in 632 C.E., his successors began to spread the faith through the region by military conquest. By 650, Persia was essentially under Islamic control. The new Islamic empire, under the Umayyad Dynasty (661–750 C.E.) and its successors, brought Persia into the Arabian fold. Although the conquerors adopted some Persian practices and institutions, differences between Persian and Arab culture remained. Arabic became the language of the state; Farsi, however, remained the tongue of the people. The population slowly converted from Zoroastrianism to the new faith. By the seventh century, the distinctions between Arabs and Persians within the Islamic empire were exacerbated by a growing schism within the faith led by the followers of Muhammad's son-in-law, Ali. The "party of Ali," or *shiat* **Ali**, had its stronghold in neighboring southern Iraq and became the state religion of Persia several centuries later.

Up through the eleventh century, Persia was part of several powerful Islamic dynasties that stretched across Central Asia and the Middle East. From the thirteenth to the fifteenth century, Persia, like much of the region, was devastated by the Mongols. Persia was not only economically devastated but also depopulated. Only with the death of the last major Mongol leader did a new independent Persian dynasty emerge.

DYNASTIC RULE AND THE ADOPTION OF SHIISM

The period from the sixteenth to the early twentieth century saw the rise of two long-standing Persian dynasties: the Safavids (1502–1736) and the Qajars (1794–1925). Under the Safavids, the country adopted Shiism as the state religion and tightly connected religion and state. Shiism deviated from dominant Sunni Islam not only in its views on the proper descendants of the Prophet, but also in its development of a messianic view. Shiism holds that the true descendant of Ali, known as the Hidden Imam, will reappear at the end of time to restore justice and equality to a corrupted world. In this regard, Shiism resembles Christianity. Shiism, moreover, emphasizes the martyrdom of the twelve true successors of Muhammad, most of whom died at the hands of Sunni rivals. Another similarity between Shiism and Christianity was the relationship between faith and state. In Shiism, the particular emphasis on the descendants of Ali returning at the end of time to rule made worldly politics in some ways irrelevant or even anathema to the faith. This may seem in complete contradiction to what we understand about Iran's "Islamic Republic," but it also indicates that for many Shia, an Islamic Republic is a contradiction in terms, an important element we will explore later on. Finally, the Safavids cultivated within Shiism's religious leaders (or ulema) a powerful higher clergy, known as ayatollahs, who are sometimes compared with bishops in Roman Catholicism. This, too, deviates from the more decentralized Sunni Islam; it is the clergy of Shiism who play a critical role in modern Iranian politics.

UNDERSTANDING ISLAM

Along with Judaism and Christianity, Islam is one of the three monotheistic faiths that trace their belief in one god to the biblical figure Abraham. Islam's central figure is Muhammad (c. 570–632 c.e.), known as the Prophet. In 610, he began to receive a series of revelations from God (Allah), which were delivered through the archangel Gabriel. These revelations were set down in the Koran, the central holy book of Islam. In these revelations, Muhammad came to understand that Judaism and Christianity, while originally prescribing proper relationships with God, had strayed from the true path. Facing persecution, Muhammad fled Mecca (in present-day Saudi Arabia) but eventually returned and took control of the city with the help of his followers. Mecca subsequently became the spiritual center of the faith.

Islam is built on five fundamental tenets, known as the pillars of Islam: the declaration of faith in Allah as the one God and Muhammad as his prophet; ritual daily prayers; almsgiving; fasting during the religious holy month of Ramadan; and the hajj, the pilgrimage to Mecca. Islam also comprises a system of religious laws, known as sharia, which regulates the conduct of believers.

In the centuries after Muhammad, Islam spread rapidly through the Middle East, Africa, Asia, and Europe. At the present time, nearly 1 billion people are Muslims (followers of Islam). As with other faiths, Islam is divided into several sects. Ninety percent of Muslims belong to the Sunni branch, which identifies with the Islamic leadership that succeeded Muhammad. Shiism breaks with Sunni Islam on this issue of leadership and relies to a greater extent on a clerical hierarchy of religious leaders (the imams and ayatollahs). Sufism, another branch of the faith, emphasizes mysticism and ritual as a means of making a connection with Allah. Many Sunnis do not recognize Shiites or Sufis as Muslims, branding them heretical and idolatrous.

Although Persia during the Safavid and Qajar eras was able to maintain its power in the face of regional rivals, such as the Turkish Ottoman Empire, it inevitably came under pressure from the expanding Western powers. In the early nineteenth century, Russia squeezed Persia from the north, seizing territories; the United Kingdom conquered neighboring India and attempted to gain control over Afghanistan. Thus, by the mid-nineteenth century, Persia faced a crisis that extended across the region: how to confront the Western powers, given their superiority in military and economic might? How could Persia modernize and still preserve its sovereignty?

FAILED REFORMS AND THE EROSION OF SOVEREIGNTY

In the last decades of the Qajar dynasty, the monarchy enacted various reforms, learned from the West, that were meant to modernize the state. The monarchy experimented with Western-style economic and political institutions even as it surrendered ever more sovereignty to the British and the Russians. Public animosity grew in the face of government weakness and the perception that the monarchy, ineffectual and corrupt, was selling off the country to Westerners. In 1906, religious groups and businesses protested in favor of limitations on the powers of the Qajar monarchy in what came to be known as the Constitutional Revolution. The protest resulted in an elected assembly that drew up the country's first constitution and legislative body, known as the **Majlis**.

The Constitutional Revolution, while important, did not live up to expectations. The monarchy quickly sought to abolish the constitution, relying in part on the Russian military to attack the Majlis. Ongoing battles between monarchists and constitutionalists opened the way for the United Kingdom and Russia to divide the country into formal spheres of influence in 1907, all but eliminating Persian sovereignty. With the outbreak of World War I, Persia became entangled in the conflict as troops from the Russian, British, German, and Ottoman empires fought each other and supported various Persian factions that were vying for power; some quarter of the population was killed.

Following World War I and the collapse of the Ottoman and Russian empires, the United Kingdom became the dominant foreign power and occupied much of the country. The embattled Majlis continued to oppose British imperialism, however, rejecting a 1919 agreement that would have granted the United Kingdom significant control over the state and the economy, including Persia's oil industry. One important observation to make at this point is that modern Iranian history is thus tightly connected to British imperialism, and even though the country never formally became part of the British Empire, these unequal relations sowed the seeds of Iranian animosity toward Britain that continues to this day.

Amid the ongoing political turmoil in Persia, a relatively obscure military officer came to political power. Born to a poor family, Reza Khan had distinguished himself as a superior military figure, rising rapidly through the ranks. In 1921, he marched into Tehran as part of a wider group of coup plotters, but he quickly outmaneuvered his allies and consolidated his rule. Although the United Kingdom did not directly plan the coup, it helped indirectly (if unintentionally) pave the way for the coup. From the outset, most Persians considered the coup was the direct result of an imperialist plot—a view that continues in some circles to this day. Interestingly, during the same period the United States was seen by many Persians as an important supporter of Persian independence. An American served as the country's treasurer in 1911, and U.S. diplomats and missionaries generally backed Persian independence and republicanism.[2]

THE CONSOLIDATION OF POWER UNDER THE PAHLAVI DYNASTY

Reza Shah Pahlavi, as Reza Khan eventually called himself, proved to be more than a mere puppet of the British. Once head of the armed forces, he quickly moved to consolidate his power, removing his fellow conspirators from office and neutralizing threats within and without Persia. Centralizing the military, he was able to quell several regional rebellions and to limit British and Soviet interference in the country's affairs. In 1923, the last shah of the Qajar dynasty appointed Reza Khan prime minister and promptly went into exile in Europe; in 1925, the Majlis formally deposed the Qajar dynasty and appointed Reza Khan the new shah.

As a monarch with limited constraints on his power, the shah pursued a course of dramatic Westernization, going far beyond the country's previous flirtation with Western innovations. This course included the abolishment of the aristocracy (other than the shah himself), bureaucratic reform, the institution of primary and secondary education as well as a university system, the development of road and rail systems, and the establishment of a number of state-owned businesses to develop monopolies in important domestic and export-oriented markets. Persia also exerted greater control over its burgeoning oil industry, which had been dominated by Britain since its inception. In addition, Reza Shah instituted national conscription as part of his effort to centralize military might and extend state control over what had been a fractious and tribal country. The shah complemented this political centralization with efforts to build a modern national identity, promoting the idea of a single people whose glory extended back thousands of years, drawing on the country's pre-Islamic history.

Finally, as part of his modernization, the shah greatly extended the rights of women, giving them the right to education, including at the university level. He also sought to root out traditional customs seen as holding back the emancipation of women. One important symbol was the head scarf (*hijab*) and public cloak (chador), which women wore in public as a sign of modesty and privacy. In 1934, inspired by similar reforms in Turkey, Persia forbade the wearing of the head coverings in schools, a proscription that was later extended to other public facilities. The shah's efforts in regard to women were part of a broader attack on Shiism and Islamic religious and educational institutions, which were seen as backward and of foreign (that is, Arab) origin.

Modernization came at the expense of democratization. The shah's objective was to rapidly develop the country along Western lines. Democratic institutions, such as the press and the Majlis, were curtailed, and religious and political opponents were jailed, exiled, or killed. By the eve of World War II, Iran, as the country was by then known,* had made significant progress in establishing modern political institutions and independence from foreign interference. Yet progress had come at the cost of increased repression of civic life and traditional institutions and identities.

---

*In 1935 the country renamed itself Iran, using the Iranian word for the country (Persia being a foreign name).

World War II again drew the country into international conflict. Reza Shah's friendly relations with Germany raised fears among the United Kingdom and Russia; in 1941, the two countries invaded Iran to open a land corridor between them and prevent a further drift of Iran (and its oil) into the Axis orbit. Reza Shah was forced to abdicate in favor of his son, Mohammad Reza Pahlavi, and to go into exile. As World War II gave way to the cold war, the United States, the United Kingdom, and the Soviet Union all sought to consolidate their power over the weakened country and its oil supplies. Political and religious activity also resurfaced in the face of the weakened state and regime.[3]

THE NATIONALIST CHALLENGE UNDER MOSADDEQ AND THE U.S. RESPONSE

In the aftermath of Reza Shah's abdication, republican and religious activity began to reassert itself; the new monarch, Mohammed Reza, was unable to thwart these advances. The Majlis and the ulema promoted the removal of Western influence over Iran, and many supported nationalization of the oil industry, which was under joint Iranian and British ownership. Nationalization was advocated in particular by the new prime minister, **Mohammad Mosaddeq**, who represented the **National Front**, a republican party that favored eliminating the monarch or reducing its power. The shah reluctantly conceded to nationalization, provoking British anger and leading to the withdrawal of Britain's technical support, essentially halting oil production. As the crisis deepened, Mosaddeq moved leftward, allying himself with the Marxist Tudeh Party and thus alienating his support among much of the ulema. He also grew more authoritarian in his politics, dissolving the Majlis in 1953 on the basis of a questionable referendum. The United States, which initially had been sympathetic to Iran's dispute with the United Kingdom, now began to see Iran through the lens of the cold war, fearing that Mosaddeq's nationalism would, in fact, lead to Communist rule in Iran (indeed, immediately after the war, the Soviet Union tried to create an independent pro-Soviet government in the north of the county).

With the support of the shah, the United States and the United Kingdom moved to overthrow Mosaddeq, through a covert program known as **Operation Ajax**. Several days of conflict between supporters of the prime minister and supporters of the shah, including rival elements of the military, finally culminated in a victory for the shah and his backers. In the aftermath of Operation Ajax, hundreds of National Front and Tudeh leaders and supporters were arrested, and several key leaders were executed. Much of the ulema, however, welcomed Mosaddeq's overthrow and the restoration of the monarchical power.[4]

The shah wasted little time in concentrating his power along his father's lines. Reza Shah had expended much of his energy developing an Iran independent of Western power, but his son balanced his quest for sovereignty with a new alliance with the United States. The United Kingdom receded as the main player in Iranian affairs as the United States became central to the development of Iran's economy, education, military, cultural, and civic life. Democracy, however, was deemed not worthy of emulation: the shah repressed opposition parties and built a powerful secret police (known by its acronym, **SAVAK**); he also marginalized the prime minister and Majlis. The short-lived and turbulent period of democracy thus ended.

AUTHORITARIANISM AND MODERNIZATION DURING THE WHITE REVOLUTION

After bringing the political system under his control, the shah revived the policy of top-down modernization that had earlier been promoted by his father, again marginalizing the ulema. These reforms, starting in 1963, were known as the **White Revolution**.[5] The policy included land reform, privatization of state-run industries, a literacy campaign, and the enfranchisement of women. Some reforms, in particular land reform and female enfranchisement, faced strong opposition from religious leaders and in June of that year led to rioting, which the government suppressed violently. A subsequent protest in 1964 over Iran's growing alliance with the United States was also quickly quelled. Associated with both protests was Ruhollah Khomeini, an ayatollah based in the holy city of Qom. Khomeini was already known for his writings that linked worldly politics to spiritual issues, an interest that extended back to the 1940s and set him apart from most Shia clerics. Khomeini quickly became an important symbol of opposition to the shah, which coincided with his rise to the rank of Grand Ayatollah, a position held by only a very few ayatollahs deemed worthy of emulation. Khomeini's growing power led the shah to expel him from the country (execution was too dangerous a move), and he settled in neighboring Iraq. From there he continued to criticize the Iranian regime and articulate a vision of an Iran governed by Islam, which culminated in his work *Islamic Government: The Governance of the Jurist (Velayat-e Faqih)*.

For the next fifteen years, the shah would rule without serious challenge. All remaining pretenses of democracy were swept away, leaving a state with power concentrated in the hands of the monarchy and enforced by the military and SAVAK. Rapid if uneven modernization continued, fostered by state policy as well as rising oil revenues (by the mid-1970s, upward of US$20 billion a year). Iran built a large military in response to the shah's desire to project the country as a major regional force and a "great civilization" to be reckoned with on the world stage.

All of the rapid changes did little to legitimize or support the shah's rule. Although billions of dollars in oil revenue flowed into Iran, much of it disappeared into the pockets of those in power or went to support the lavish lifestyle of the shah and his family. Economic improvements were not experienced widely across the population, and the influx of oil money led to inflation and the consequent erosion of the middle class. That so much disruption and misery was tied to oil, and that so much of the oil industry was directed and run by foreigners, helped foster the sentiment that the United States and other Western powers were plundering the nation, as many observers felt they had for the past century.

OPPOSITION TO THE SHAH AND THE IRANIAN REVOLUTION

The worsening of the economy during the mid-1970s eventually mobilized the public. In 1977, the new U.S. president, Jimmy Carter, with his greater emphasis on human rights, began to criticize the shah for his repressive practices. Hoping to pacify his ally, the shah carried out a limited set of reforms, freeing some political prisoners and allowing banned organizations, like the National Front, to reorganize. The Carter administration did not press the shah further, however, and in the eyes of many hopeful Iranians seemed to retreat from its earlier criticisms in favor of political stability.

As U.S. pressure on the shah flagged, Iranians found a second source of external opposition to his repressive rule in the form of the Ayatollah Khomeini. Still living in Iraq, in the Shiite holy city of Najaf, Khomeini had through his works elaborated a vision of an Islamic political system for Iran quite at odds with much of the Shia clergy. In particular, he argued that Islamic government should be constructed around the concept of **velayat-e faqih**; whereas a monarchy was a usurpation of Allah's rule on earth, a system of government by a clergy trained in Islamic jurisprudence would be a continuation of the political system first established by the Prophet. Since such a form of government was the only regime consistent with the will of God, secular forms, such as that of the shah, should be overthrown. Khomeini's writings began to attract a large following in Iran, where, despite his absence, his reputation continued to grow.[6]

The shah, Khomeini, and the United States were now on a collision course. In 1978, the Iranian government attempted a smear campaign against Khomeini, which only increased support for the ayatollah and touched off a series of protests. The government responded harshly, but this in turn only sparked a new round of conflict, often linked to the forty-day cycle of mourning that is central to Shia belief. Finally, three important events turned public protest into revolution. First, in August 1978 a fire at the Rex Cinema in Abadan killed some 400 people. Many latched on to the rumor that SAVAK had torched the theater to blame the religious opposition. Others suggested that protesters had been chased into the theater by the police and then set ablaze. The funerals for the victims became another flash point for massive public protest.

In response to the public protests, the shah declared martial law. Yet the protests continued. In September, a massive protest in Tehran in defiance of martial law called for the end of the monarchy and the return of Ayatollah

Khomeini. The army fired on the protesters, and some fired back. Hundreds of people were killed, and the violence took on increasingly religious symbolism, with allusions to martyrdom and the coming of the Hidden Imam.

The shah, realizing that even in exile Khomeini was a dangerous force, persuaded the Iraqi government to remove him to France. Rather than isolating him, however, the move to Europe only improved Khomeini's connections to Iran, the outside world, and the international media. By November, Tehran was racked by widespread public violence, and the shah, while increasing his reliance on force, feared for his political survival. A series of crackdowns and attempts at co-opting the opposition had no effect. The United States, too, vacillated in its support for the shah, criticizing the use of violence while continuing to give him its support.

In December 1978, millions of protesters took to the streets of Tehran in defiance of a government ban on such public gatherings. Military units began to defect. The shah fled to Egypt and was replaced by a provisional government with a tenuous hold on the country. On February 1, 1979, millions gathered to welcome the Ayatollah Khomeini as he returned to Iran.[7]

THE CONSOLIDATION OF AN ISLAMIC REPUBLIC

The revolution did not automatically mean that Iran would have an Islamic regime; as in Russia in 1917, many observers expected a democratic republic, not simply a change from one form of authoritarianism to another. But capitalizing on the political turmoil, his own charismatic authority, and personal ideology, Khomeini moved to undermine the secular provisional government. Outflanking the various political and religious factions that had sprung up during the revolution, Khomeini gained control of the government; he wrote a new constitution, which allowed for not only a president and a prime minister but also a *faqih* (religious leader with expertise in Islamic law) who would have supreme political authority. This position was filled by Khomeini until his death.

The **Islamic Republic of Iran** had a violent birth. The new government suppressed all opposition, including monarchists, members of Marxist and other secular political groups, ethnic minorities, and members of other faiths. From 1979 to 1980, perhaps thousands were executed in the name of "revolutionary justice." Student supporters of Khomeini also seized control of the U.S. Embassy, holding much of its staff for over a year (and leading to an ill-fated rescue attempt by the Carter administration).

Yet the violence paled in comparison with the **Iran-Iraq War**. As the Iranian revolution unfolded, in Iraq Saddam Hussein perceived these developments as a threat to his own rule over a country in which more than half the population was Shiite. Khomeini himself hoped to spread his Islamic revolution beyond Iran's borders, and Iraq was the logical next choice. At the same time, Iraq saw in Iran's chaos an opportunity to extend its power in the region

THE U.S. EMBASSY HOSTAGE CRISIS

On February 14, 1979, a group of Iranian students associated with a Marxist political group temporarily seized control of the U.S. Embassy in Tehran. From the perspective of many Iranians, the embassy represented the power behind the throne that had propped up the shah's rule and acquiesced in his despotic ways. Khomeini denounced the takeover and forced the students' retreat. On November 4, the embassy was stormed a second time, and sixty-six Americans were taken hostage. On this occasion, however, the students were followers of Khomeini and were inspired by the belief that the United States was preparing a counterrevolution that would restore the monarchy, akin to operation Ajax in 1953. Most observers believed that the seizure would not be a prolonged affair. Within a matter of days, however, Khomeini formally endorsed the takeover, helping to project the new regime's staunch anti-Americanism and sideline more moderate forces who sought better relations with the United States. The crisis lasted for 444 days, generating frustration and a deep animosity in the United States toward Iran while serving as a source of revolutionary pride for many Iranians. In April 1980, President Carter approved a military operation to rescue the hostages, only to have the mission scuttled after sandstorms, equipment failure, and a helicopter crash that killed eight servicemen. Only after Carter had been defeated by Ronald Reagan in the 1980 presidential election did Khomeini agree to allow the hostages to leave. To this day, the United States does not have formal diplomatic relations with Iran.

and seize territory. In September 1980, Iraq launched a full-scale invasion of Iran, initiating the Iran-Iraq war, which lasted until 1988.

The war caused widespread destruction on both sides. Iraq had superior firepower and the support of such countries as the United States, which feared the spread of the Iranian revolution. Iran, in contrast, had the greater population and its revolutionary fervor—using, for example, unarmed children to fight the Iraqis, promising them rewards in the afterlife for their certain martyrdom. In 1982, realizing that he had miscalculated his chance of success, Hussein sought to end the war; Khomeini refused, believing that this was the opportunity to carry his revolution to Iraq. In 1988, when the war finally ended, neither side emerged victorious, and nearly 1 million Iranians and Iraqis were dead. Shortly thereafter, Khomeini himself died, leaving the Islamic Republic to govern without its founder and spiritual guide.

POLITICAL REGIME

Since 1979, the Islamic Republic of Iran has sought to follow the ideas of Khomeini in creating a political system built around his idea of the *velayat-e faqih*, which would replace the sovereignty of men and women with the sovereignty of God as transmitted by the clergy. Yet Khomeini had come to power in the wake of a popular revolution that was driven by the public's demand for a political system that responded to their needs and desires. The new regime would thus have to reconcile the will of the people with what was seen as the will of God. Finally, as with the Russian Revolution of 1917, the new Iranian system was seen as a temporary set of institutions to serve until the return of the Hidden Imam, or true descendant of the Prophet. (Some Iranians, in fact, initially saw Khomeini as this figure, or as a sign that the end of times was near.) Since the death of Khomeini, however, the regime has faced the challenge of what Max Weber termed "the routinization of charisma." That is, how does a nation maintain the ideals of the leader once the leader is gone? The result is a political system quite unlike any other, a mixture of institutions that seek to balance the word of man with the word of God.

Political Institutions

THE CONSTITUTION

The Iranian constitution is a product of the 1979 revolution. Since that time, the only major changes to the document occurred ten years later, when Khomeini sought to ensure that the principles of the Islamic Republic would be maintained after his death. In its preamble, the constitution lays out the origins of the current regime, which is viewed as a revolt against the "American conspiracy" of the White Revolution. According to the constitution, the Islamic Republic exists not to serve the individual or mediate between diverse interests but to guide the people toward God (Allah). The Koran (the holy book of Islam) therefore serves not only as a spiritual text but also as the foundation for a unified national ideology that is to be embodied in the political system. Allah is sovereign over the Iranian people and state, and all political acts are expected to flow from the word of Allah. As the constitution itself states, "All civil, penal, financial, economic, administrative, cultural, military, political, and other laws and regulations must be based on Islamic criteria." This concept is consistent with religious fundamentalism in general, where sovereignty

---

ESSENTIAL POLITICAL FEATURES

- Legislative-executive system: semi-presidential theocracy
- Legislature: Majlis
- Lower house: Majlis
- Upper house: (none)
- Unitary or federal division of power: unitary
- Main geographic subunits: *ostanha* (provinces)
- Electoral system for lower house: single-member district majority
- Chief judicial body: Supreme Court

in the form of statehood and democracy is seen as blasphemous, with humans arrogating to themselves powers and rights that should reside only with God. The rule of law is heresy, as it is God's law (***sharia***) that should reign supreme. As such, the Iranian constitution and political institutions are (at least in theory) an attempt to express God's will rather than instruments of human will.

The Branches of Government

THE SUPREME LEADER AND THE PRESIDENCY

The particular nature of the Iranian constitution has resulted in a set of political institutions that are quite bewildering to outsiders but consistent with the *velayat-e faqih*. We can see this most clearly in the executive branch of the government. As in many other countries, Iran has a dual executive, with power divided across two offices. In most other cases, such divisions fall between head of state and head of government, with the former a monarch or president and the latter prime minister. The former reigns while the latter rules.

STRUCTURE OF THE GOVERNMENT

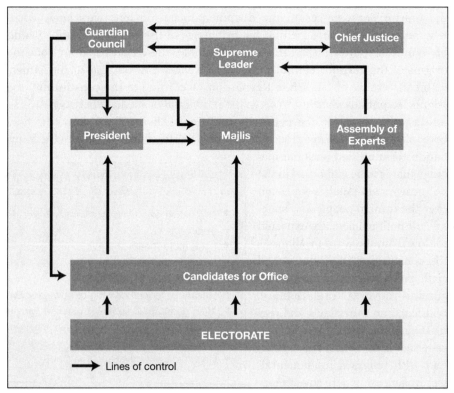

Iran's executive does not follow this pattern. The dominant executive is the **supreme leader**, a position created for Khomeini following the revolution as an expression of his charismatic power and political ideology. As befits the title, the supreme leader is the most powerful office in Iran, created to ensure that a senior cleric is at the helm of Iranian politics, directing both political and spiritual life. The supreme leader serves for life, though he can theoretically be removed for incompetence or failure to uphold his religious duty.

The powers of the supreme leader are numerous. First, he may decide who may run for the office of president, eliminating rivals in the process. He is also commander in chief of the armed forces and appoints the heads of the various branches of the military. The supreme leader also appoints the chief justice and even the directors of radio and television broadcasting. The supreme leader, while not directly involved in legislation, is given the power to supervise policy and, if necessary, call referenda. In some ways, the supreme leader may be seen as the head of state, embodying the people (through the word of Allah) and representing the nation in such areas as national defense. The supreme leader's role in policy is also much more that of reigning than ruling. Yet given the powers that reside with the office, it is hardly ceremonial. If anything, the supreme leader looks much more like a traditional monarch than any corresponding modern political executive.

Following Khomeini's death, the office of supreme leader was to be held by a high-ranking ayatollah, just as Khomeini had been. Even at the time of the revolution, however, few of the grand ayatollahs accepted Khomeini's notion of the *velayat-e faqih*, and Khomeini's heir apparent, Grand Ayatollah Hussein Ali Montazeri, was sidelined for his criticism of the regime's dictatorial nature and was under house arrest from 1997 to 2003. Since 1989, the supreme leader has been **Ali Khamenei**, the president of the country from 1981 to 1989. Khamenei was not a grand ayatollah, or even an ayatollah, as was designated by the constitution. A revision to the constitution, and quick promotion of Khamenei to ayatollah, resolved this problem. In spite of this, Khamenei lacks the charismatic or intellectual power of Khomeini or the religious authority of Iran's most senior clerics.

How is the supreme leader chosen? The role falls to the **Assembly of Experts**, a body of eighty-six members who are themselves popularly elected for eight-year terms. Candidates for the assembly are vetted in advance of elections, limiting the people's choice and ensuring that its membership is dominated by clerics who accept the political status quo.

If the supreme leader functions as a powerful head of state, the presidency is (confusingly) more akin to a head of government. Unlike the supreme leader, the president is directly elected and can serve only two four-year terms. Within his scope of responsibilities lie the budget, initiating legislation, and selecting a cabinet of ministers charged with directing various facets of policy. The president is also in charge of foreign policy, appointing ambassadors, signing treaties, and helping foster diplomatic relations. Given the president's lack of control over the military, however, his powers in this area remain circumscribed, and the supreme leader does not refrain from making his own foreign policy statements. In general, the president is charged with the task of executing the laws, making certain that specific policies are carried out. After 1979, there was an expectation that the president would be a nonreligious figure, more in keeping with an office concerned with "worldly" affairs. Since 1981, however, the position has been held primarily by clerics. The election of President Mahmoud Ahmadinejad in 2005 was a departure from this trend, with his background in higher education and local government rather than theology.

THE LEGISLATURE

The Islamic Republic retains one political institution from Iran's past. The legislature, or Majlis, is a unicameral body the members of which are directly elected on the basis of universal suffrage of men and women over the age of eighteen. Its 290 members serve four-year terms. As one might suspect, this Majlis, like its predecessors, has a limited amount of power. Its powers include initiating and passing legislation, overseeing the budget, and approving the members of the president's cabinet. Cabinet members may also be removed by a vote of no confidence, though the Majlis's power in this area does not extend to the president or to the supreme leader.

The inherent supremacy of God's law in the Iranian constitution raises questions about the very functioning of the legislature. Since man-made laws are liable to deviation from God's will, the role of the Majlis is technically to legislate in accordance with divine law. This condition raises the question of who is to ascertain whether legislation is consistent with religious law and to what extent that limits legislative authority.

These limitations can be seen in the presence of two additional bodies, the **Guardian Council** and the **Expediency Council**. The Guardian Council is made up of twelve individuals who serve six-year terms: six lawyers, who are nominated by the chief justice and approved by the Majlis, and six clerics specializing in religious law, who are appointed by the supreme leader. The powers of the Guardian Council are significant; among them is the power to review all legislation that derives from the Majlis, to "ensure its compatibility with the criteria of Islam and the Constitution."[8] It may send legislation back to the Majlis for revision if it finds it incompatible; if the Majlis is unable to revise the legislation to the Guardian Council's satisfaction, a third body, the Expediency Council, mediates. Members of the Expediency Council are appointed by the supreme leader for five-year terms; it is currently headed by Ali Akbar Hashemi Rafsanjani, who was the country's president from 1989 to

1997. The final decision of the Expediency Council cannot be overturned. The Guardian Council (and, to a lesser extent, the Expediency Council) serves as a kind of unelected upper house, with substantial powers to restrict the work of the Majlis.

THE JUDICIAL SYSTEM

The way in which political authority stems from religious tenets naturally has a profound effect on the nature of the law itself. The legal system in Iran, derived from religious law, or sharia, serves to defend itself against deviation—not to interpret the law or expand its boundaries, as is often the case in secular democracies. At the apex of this branch of government is a **chief justice**, a single figure whose qualifications require an understanding of sharia (making the appointment of a cleric necessary). The chief justice is appointed by the supreme leader for a five-year term. His role is to manage the judicial institutions and oversee the appointment and removal of judges. Beneath the chief justice is the Supreme Court, which serves as the highest court of appeal. Like the position of chief justice, this office is entirely staffed by high-ranking clerics chosen for their familiarity with religious law. It is worth noting, however, that in spite of, or because of, this system debates over the rule of law continue in Iran: for example, whether the supreme leader is beholden to the constitution. For now, the supreme leader appears able to operate largely free from constitutional constraints.

The Electoral System

In spite of the theocratic limitations, Iran seems to enjoy some elements of democratic participation. In particular, there are direct elections for the Majlis, the Assembly of Experts (which selects the supreme leader), and the presidency. The constitution gives the Guardian Council the power to oversee all elections, however, which in practice means that this unelected body may reject any candidate for each elected office. In the 2007 Majlis elections, the Guardian Council barred some 1,700 candidates from standing for office, eliminating all the candidates from some reformist parties. Of the 495 candidates for the 2006 Assembly of Experts election, only 144 were allowed to stand; in the 2005 election for president, only 8 candidates were allowed to run from a list of over 1,000 who applied. Though not specified in the constitution, women have not been allowed to run for the Assembly of Experts or presidency, though they do hold a handful seats in the Majlis and serve in local government.

Elections for all three institutions are based on a single-member district majority system. Candidates compete in districts for a majority of the vote (for the presidency, the country serves as a single district); if no single candidate wins a majority, a runoff is held between the two top vote getters. Interestingly, given the strong support for reform among the youth, the voting age has become a political tool. During the 1990s, the reformist-dominated Majlis lowered the legal voting age from sixteen to fifteen (the lowest in the world), seeking to enfranchise millions of voters they hoped would help consolidate their position. As reformers lost power, conservative forces raised the voting age to eighteen for the 2007 elections.

Local Government

Iran's history, like that of many countries, has been one of a struggle by the state to centralize power. Though the country is currently divided into thirty *ostanha*, or provinces; these bodies, like the local institutions below them, have limited authority, a condition that existed long before the current regime. Although the Constitutional Revolution of 1905–1906 was driven in part by local associations with the goal of creating representative local government, this goal was never realized. The 1979 revolution similarly made claims about the need for local government, though again no changes were instituted. After taking initial steps toward creating local government, the theocracy moved away from devolving power. The demands of institutionalizing the theocratic regime, going to war with Iraq, nationalizing industry, and quelling ethnic unrest drove the regime to centralize power even more. It rejected any notions of regional autonomy or federalism and suspended elections to the local and regional councils that were first started in 1980.

This situation, like much about politics in Iran, is in flux. In 1997, the government passed a law on decentralization that moved power away from the Ministry of the Interior. Prior to that time, the ministry had been responsible for local affairs, appointing regional governors and mayors. As a result of the new law, local councils were created at the village, city, and province level to manage local politics and the election of mayors. In a further departure from the past, these councils—over 100,000 offices in all—were directly elected. The first elections to the newly created council positions took place in 1999, with over 500,000 candidates competing at the local level for the first time in Iranian history. Though candidates have to be approved by the Majlis, this review does not appear to be as onerous as those conducted by the Guardian Council. In 2006, a number of reform and moderate candidates won local elections and mayoral seats, in what was seen as a rebuff to the new president, Ahmadinejad.[9] Still, local government remains an institution with limited power.

Other Institutions: The Revolutionary Guard and the Basij

Alongside the wide reach of state power and the role of the theocratic revolution in Iran, there are a number of institutions with political power that operate largely outside normal state authority. Of these, two merit particular mention: the **Revolutionary Guard** and the **Basij**, or People's Militia.

The Revolutionary Guard is a paramilitary force that emerged from the 1979 revolution. It originally comprised several thousand men from various militias and groups that had sprung up in response to particular events, and it was independent of the armed forces, which Khomeini mistrusted because of their role during the Pahlavi dynasty; it answered only to the supreme leader. As a "corps of the faithful," the Revolutionary Guard was assigned the immediate task of defending the new regime, destroying rival groups and movements, such as Marxists and supporters of greater ethnic autonomy. Later, during the Iran-Iraq War, the Revolutionary Guard expanded in size to fight on the front lines as a military force. It did this by forming a large people's volunteer militia, the Basij, in which young boys played a prominent role. With its members poorly trained and ill equipped but imbued with religious fervor, the Basij was known for its "human wave" attacks against the Iraqi front lines, sometimes even clearing minefields with its soldiers' own bodies.

The end of the war and the consolidation of the revolution undercut the justification for the Revolutionary Guard and the Basij, but both organizations have continued to play an influential role in Iranian politics, as political actors outside the state, controlled only by the supreme leader and his allies. The Revolutionary Guard remains a potent force, with its own ministry, army, navy, and air force units, and appears to have a hand in the development of Iran's nuclear program. The Guard has become an increasingly independent and direct player in Iranian domestic and international affairs as well, with its top leaders taking on important additional roles in the state and government. Given the Guard's hostility to reform and its military power, this is a worrisome development.

In contrast, the Basij is no longer a significant military force, though it has maintained its importance in other ways. Basij members serve in public works, doing disaster relief and other civil projects. More disturbing has been their role as a public-morality force, often taking responsibility for such things as preventing public displays of affection and seizing illegal satellite dishes. In recent years, this role has been transferred to a special police force; the Basij, however, remains a force that can be used to quell opposition to the regime, such as its attacks on protesters following the 2009 presidential election.

POLITICAL CONFLICT AND COMPETITION

For many reasons, political competition in Iran is a confusing matter to outside observers. The nature of the revolution and the role of religion in the course of that radical change constitute one factor, as they helped create political differences that do not easily fit on our usual palette of ideologies. In addition, Iran lacks institutionalized political parties, a result of the regime's desire to stifle dissent and safeguard the revolution against "un-Islamic" policies and ideas.

It was not always this way. In the immediate aftermath of the 1979 revolution there was an outburst of new political activity, and previously suppressed groups, such as the National Front and the Tudeh Party, reemerged. Out of this activity emerged two dominant parties. The first, the Islamic Republican Party (IRP), was closely allied with Ayatollah Ruhollah Khomeini and his desire to establish a theocracy. The second, the Liberation Movement, was more pro-Western and favored a more limited role for religion in politics. Numerous parties stood for the first postrevolutionary elections in 1980, but the electoral system eliminated virtually all groups but the IRP, which gained a majority of seats. Some independent parliamentarians and members of the Liberation Movement sought to resist this consolidation of power; others turned their weapons on the IRP, much of whose leadership was killed in a bombing in 1981. The government responded with increased repression of opposition groups, imprisoning and executing thousands of political activists while marginalizing the increasingly critical Liberation Movement.

With the 1984 and 1987 elections, the theocratic hold on the Majlis was made complete. In advance of the 1984 elections, all parties other than the IRP were banned. In 1987, even the IRP itself was eliminated.

The Rise and Fall of Political Reform

After 1987, political debate within the Majlis was limited primarily to economic concerns, with competition between those who favored a more free-market economic approach and those who supported more statist policies. (See "Society," p. 393, for a discussion of these different political tendencies.) Debates on the nature of the political system itself were not allowed. Change was afoot, however, made possible by the death of Khomeimi in 1989 and a worsening economy. In 1992, Majlis elections saw a victory for the free-market faction, many of whom in turn supported the 1997 presidential candidacy of the pro-reform Mohammad Khatami. His victory, gaining over 70 percent of the popular vote, surprised Iranians and outside observers alike. Finally, under Khatami the government rescinded its ban on political parties.

The reform period of the 1990s saw a dramatic diversification in political views and organizations, much of which called for improved relations with the outside world and democratic change, arguments spearheaded by intellectuals, students, and a number of clerics who had long opposed the idea of the *velayat-e faqih*. In 2000, reform groups coalesced to form the **Second Khor-**

dad Front (named after the date in the Iranian calendar for Khatami's 1997 election) to contest the Majlis elections. The Guardian Council used its power sparingly in disqualifying Khordad candidates, and the party went on to win a stunning 189 of the 290 parliamentary seats. In 2001, President Khatami was again overwhelmingly reelected with over 70 percent of the vote. Many expected that these twin victories would solidify reformist power and pave the way for a political transition not unlike the Soviet Union in the 1980s.

That belief was short-lived. While reformers controlled the Majlis and the presidency, these were relatively weak political institutions. Conservatives still controlled or had the support of the Guardian Council and the Expediency Council, the Revolutionary Guard and Basij, and of course the supreme leader. Soon after the elections, a wave of repression was directed against reformists. Numerous journalists and pro-democracy activists were arrested, and a number of pro-reform newspapers were shut down. In the Majlis, while reformers passed a wide array of legislation to limit state power and increase democratic rights, the bills were mostly vetoed by the Guardian Council. Meanwhile, President Khatami lacked the power and the political skills to outflank the conservatives and was increasingly seen as an impotent and indecisive leader.

Using their legal and coercive powers, conservatives effectively brought the reforms in Iran to an end. In the 2004 Majlis elections, the Guardian Council banned large numbers of Khordad candidates (including 80 standing members of parliament), and reformers called for an election boycott. With fewer reformists competing or turning out to vote, religious conservatives, campaigning under a variety of names, swept to power. As of the 2008 Majlis elections, reformers held only around 40 of the 290 Majlis seats, and voter turnout had dropped to about 50 percent, and even lower in Tehran.

The last piece in the struggle over reform was the presidency. In the 2005 presidential elections, former president Ali Akbar Hashemi Rafsanjani, who served from 1990 to 1997, was expected to return to power with the hope that his conservatism would be tempered by limited economic reforms and improved relations with the West—a model some have called "China lite."[10] To the surprise of many Iranians and outside observers, however, the presidency was won by the conservative mayor of Tehran, Mahmoud Ahmadinejad. His modest background and limited connection to those at the upper reaches of power, and his concern for such social issues as poverty and corruption, were seen as a marked contrast to Rafsanjani and other revolutionary elites who had grown wealthy since the revolution. Ahmadinejad's surprising win was thus a victory for those opposed to reform. However, Ahmadinejad's first term in office not only polarized conservatives and reformers, but also deepened splits within the conservative camp.

Civil Society

As might be expected, civil society in Iran has mirrored the changes and challenges of political competition. Over the past century, Iran has seen the rise of organized civil activity during periods in which the state was weak, as during the constitutional revolution in 1905–1906, immediately after World War II, and during the 1979 revolution. After the creation of the Islamic Republic of Iran, the nascent civil society was again stifled, viewed as anathema to the supremacy of religious rule and the need for national unity during the war with Iraq. Most civic organizations were either absorbed into the state or outlawed. This was consistent with the theocracy's emphasis on the notion of the **ummah**, or community, whose members were expected to act as a unified group that embodied and served the revolution. Plurality and autonomy were anathema to religious rule and revolutionary ideals.

After Khomeini's death and the end of the war, however, civil society began to reemerge, though it remained marginal and beleaguered. A handful of intellectuals, clerics, and others questioned the current regime and advocated reform, but this activity was frequently met with arrest, torture, and even death. One notable example is Ayatollah Hussein Ali Montazeri, whom Khomeini had handpicked to serve as supreme leader upon his death. Montazeri eventually fell out of favor, however, having criticized the government for human rights abuses. From 1997 to 2003 he was placed under house arrest, in part for suggesting that the supreme leader should be a popularly elected position and many of its powers transferred to the presidency. In spite of his arrest, however, he continues to speak out on political issues, most recently in favor of the Bahai religious minority, which has been subject to discrimination and violence since before the revolution.

In the 1990s, President Khatami made the invigoration of Iran's civil society a major plank of his campaign, and this cause was soon taken up by the media. New publications rapidly proliferated at all levels of society, from academic journals and independent publishers to magazines and newspapers. In the early 1990s, for example, Tehran had five newspapers; by 2001, there were over twenty. In entertainment as well, a new wave of films satirized or dramatized the country's social and political problems. Numerous civic organizations also sprang up, dealing with such issues as local government, human rights, the environment, women's rights, and poverty.

This flowering of civil society came under sustained attack. Supreme Leader Khamenei attacked the press as "the base of the enemy," and numerous publications were closed or physically attacked by government-sponsored militants. A 2000 law restricted the ability of the press to operate and new publications to form, and since 2003, over 100 publications have been closed; dozens of journalists have been arrested, and several were killed or died under suspicious circumstances.

Internet Usage in Three Middle Eastern Countries, 2000–2007		
Country	**Internet Penetration (% of population)**	**Growth 2000–2007**
Saudi Arabia	17%	2250%
Syria	8%	4900%
Iran	28%	7100%

Source: Internetworldstats.com

Similar pressure has mounted against nongovernmental organizations, with many being attacked, their offices destroyed, and an unknown number of their members detained, often without charges. After the student protests of 1999, many prominent student leaders were arrested and a number remain in prison. The overt use of repression has declined in recent years, but the 2009 presidential election led to a surprising resurgence of public protest, which was met with force. The extent to which this repression will continue over the long term is still unclear.

One area of civic activity in Iran that remains lively is Internet usage, which has exploded, growing faster than in any other country in the Middle East since 2000 and accounting for over half of usage in the Middle East. Of particular interest has been the expansion of blogs, frequently written by Iranian women, to whom few other outlets of expression are open. While most blogs focus on the personal lives of their authors, as in the West, many tackle social and political subjects that are not covered in the largely weakened media. Iran is now estimated to be one of the top ten countries in the world for numbers of blogs, and Persian is one of the top ten languages used in the blogosphere. This development of a virtual public discourse has not escaped the notice of the authorities, who have attempted to limit access to various websites and social networks, such as Facebook, Twitter, and YouTube, especially given their use by reformers during the 2009 presidential elections. Iranians have been able to find ways around these obstacles, but the state still has the ability to easily choke off internet access and text messaging. The internet revolution in Iran has been more influential in linking Iranians to the outside world than to each other.

SOCIETY

Ethnic and National Identity

Iran is distinct from other Islamic states in the Middle East, not only in its embrace of the minority Shia branch of Islam but also in that the majority population is ethnically Iranian (or Persian) rather than Arab. With their distinct language, history, and culture, ethnic Iranians view themselves as quite separate from the Arab states of the Middle East, contributing to a sense of nationalism that is in many ways much stronger than anything found elsewhere in the region. It was this nationalism that, in part, helped sustain Iran in its long war against Iraq, which was often portrayed by both sides as part of a struggle between Persians and Arabs that went back thousands of years.

In fact, as the legitimacy of the Islamic regime has waned, a form of Iranian nationalism has resurfaced, finding its roots in the myths of the pre-Islamic era. This nationalism draws on the history of the Achaemenid Empire and Zoroastrianism, a largely extinct religion that predates Islam by over a thousand years. Many Iranians, particularly the young, have embraced the symbols of Zoroastrianism and pre-Islamic ceremonies like Nowruz (New Year), some going even so far as to brand Islam an alien "Arab" faith that destroyed the Iranian empire and Iranian identity. A bomb blast at a mosque in Shiraz in 2008, which killed twelve, may have been carried out by supporters of one such fringe nationalist group.

At the same time, Iran is not the homogeneous state that its nationalism or distinctive identity might lead us to believe it is. While Persians make up a majority of the population, it is a bare majority. The rest of the population is composed of various other ethnic groups, some close to the Persian majority, others not. Among these groups, the two largest, the Azeris and the Kurds, are particularly important. This is not only because of their size but also because of their connection to ethnic kin outside Iran. In both cases, turmoil and political change in surrounding countries have affected these ethnic minorities and, as a result, the way in which Iran deals with its neighbors.

ETHNIC GROUPS

RELIGION

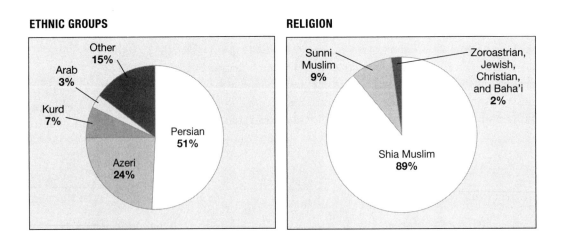

The largest and most important minority ethnic group in Iran is Azeri, who make up around one quarter of the population (perhaps more) and are concentrated in the north of the country. Like the majority Persians, the Azeris follow Shiism, but they speak a Turkic language related to the languages of Turkey and Central Asia. Historically, the Azeris resided entirely within the Persian Empire, but with the expansion of Russia in the nineteenth century their region was divided between the two countries. With the collapse of the Soviet Union in 1991, an independent Azerbaijan emerged on Iran's border, which helped foster a stronger ethnic identity among Iranian Azeris, and there have been occasional protests among Azeris in Iran, most recently in 2006. However, there is relatively little support for greater regional autonomy or unification with Azerbaijan, and Azeris have historically played a prominent role in all facets of Iranian life.[11]

The relationship with Kurds is more complicated. Less than 10 percent of the population, Kurds carried out an armed revolt against the new Islamic Republic of Iran in 1979. While suppressed, the rise of a largely autonomous Kurdish region in Iraq following the U.S. invasion has raised hopes and fears of a sovereign Kurdish state, something that makes neighboring Iran and Turkey nervous, fearing the loss of their Kurdish regions. Other minority ethnic groups, such as Baluchis and Arabs, also have complained of discrimination, leading to protests and sporadic acts of terrorism.

Ideology and Political Culture

In the absence of institutionalized political parties and free expression, it is hard to speak of any coherent spectrum of ideologies in Iran. A confusing array of terms is used—hard-liners, radicals, conservatives, traditionalists, reformers, pragmatists, technocrats. In spite of this confusion, we can speak of several loose political attitudes or tendencies, some of which are more ideologically coherent than others. As in other countries, these divisions tend to fall along issues of freedom and equality, though they combine in ways that are quite different from those commonly found in the West.

One major division is over the relationship between religion and the state. As we might expect, those known as "reformists" in Iran, whose political power rose and fell under the Khatami presidency, favor a reduced role for Islam in politics in favor of the rule of law and democratic reform. This group, whose orientation is more secular, also has unexpected allies among many clerics. For many Shiite religious leaders, the very notion of the *velayat-e faqih* runs counter to the basic tenets of Shiism. This **"quietist"** vision of Shiism, which dominated Iranian Shiism before the revolution, emphasizes that worldly political power cannot be reunited with Islam until the return of the Hidden Imam. This belief holds that the role of the faith is to act as an intermediary

Support For Sharia

In the way Iran is governed, do you think that sharia should play a larger role, a smaller role, or about the same as it plays today?

Answer	Percent
Larger role	34
Smaller Role	14
About same as now	45
Don't know	8

Source: Center for Common Ground Survey, 2008.

between the state and society until the return of the Hidden Imam, influencing spiritual and social values but not getting directly involved in politics, which is viewed as a corrupting influence on faith, something to be kept at a distance. In 2003, a number of reformist and quietist religious leaders signed a statement criticizing the regime, arguing that according to Islam, "no one has the right to rule or to control any institution without the approval of the nation. It is the rulers who must accommodate themselves to the wishes of the ruled, not the other way around."[12] Grand Ayatollah Montazeri, once the heir apparent to Khomeini, has made several similar statements. In contrast, political conservatives ("principalists," as they have recently called themselves) support the *velayat-e faqih* and oppose democratization or the return of faith to a primarily social, as opposed to political, role.

The second area of contention is over the relationship between the state and market. At the inception of the Islamic Republic there was a schism between those who saw the primary role of the revolution as bringing about a moral order, and those who saw the revolution as a means to bring about economic justice. Indeed, Khomeini emphasized both of these issues, viewing the revolution as a way to create a just social order that integrated faith, politics, and the economy. As we shall discuss shortly, however, just as religion has clashed with politics, so too has it led to divisions over the economy. Among conservatives there are those, such as former president Rafsanjani, who favor economic liberalization and better relations with the international community to increase trade and investment. Others, such as President Ahmadinejad, take a more populist line that opposes economic reform and liberalization in favor of reducing poverty and inequality (both of which have grown over the past decade). Quietists and reformers, too, while often in agreement on political reform, do not necessarily see eye to eye on economic changes.[13]

Past these debates we can observe more fixed elements of political culture. Iranian political culture is highly nationalist, with one survey showing that nearly 90 percent of Iranians indicate that they are very proud of their nationality. In addition, Iranians also indicate that religion remains a very important part of their lives while there is strong support for more democracy. These views are not contradictory; Iranian religiosity appears to tend more toward the traditional quietist view that would favor a greater separation between faith and state. This is important to consider; many observers of Iranian politics have assumed that one result of the Islamic Republic's fundamentalism would be to effectively alienate the public from religion by politicizing it. Certainly, among the younger generation and more educated there are some signs of disaffection, but it is also clear that Islam remains a central part of Iranian culture and national identity, and political change or democratization would not mean the secularization of the country along Western lines.

Finally, another enduring part of Iranian political culture is a complicated relationship to the West. Iranian history and consequent national identity is tightly linked to the rise of the West over two thousand years ago, where Iran, Greece, and Rome all commanded power and respect. In this way, Iranians may see themselves as equal participants in Western history in the way other peoples may not. At the same time, the frequent Western (and Arab) interventions in modern Iranian history have created a strong tendency toward seeing international politics in conspiratorial terms, such that every political event is the product of foreign powers with seemingly limitless power. For example, while Iranians will point to the United Kingdom and the United

IN COMPARISON   CLASH OF CIVILIZATIONS?

Thinking about Muslim and Western cultures, do you believe that violent conflict between them is inevitable, or that it is possible to find common ground?

Answer	Iranians (percent)	Americans (percent)
Conflict Inevitable	12	47
Possible to find common ground	64	50
Don't know	24	3

Source: Center for Common Ground Survey, 2008.

States for the rise of the Pahlavi dynasty, they may also argue that the West was "behind" the Islamic Revolution. Based on the author's observations in Iran in 2008, the United States (or Israel) is also viewed as the mastermind behind Al Qaeda, September 11, and even anti-American Sunni and Shiite insurgent groups in Iraq. At an even more extreme level, many Iranians continue to believe that the United Kingdom remains the dominant world power, concealed behind its "puppet," the United States. Indeed, Supreme Leader Khamenei singled out the United Kingdom as a mastermind of the 2009 protests, rather than the United States.

POLITICAL ECONOMY

Iran's economic system reflects the dilemmas of late modernization, authoritarianism, and war. It is also a good example of what is sometimes called the "resource trap," the situation that occurs when a resource paradoxically makes a country poorer rather than richer.

Iran's modern economic development lagged well behind that of the West, beginning only in the 1920s under the Pahlavi dynasty. This was not a late embrace of liberalism, however, but rather an attempt at top-down industrialization, following the mercantilist pattern adopted by many countries in the less developed world. Nor should such a path have been surprising; an attempt by the state to generate domestic wealth was a logical response and not unlike the Western powers' own history. Iran's mercantilist policies helped modernize the country, such that by the 1970s half the population was living in urban areas. At the same time, it led to social dislocation as the country made a rapid jump from an agrarian, isolated, and religiously conservative society in just a few decades.

Top-down mercantilist development led to similar problems in other less developed countries, though in Iran the problems were compounded by the discovery of oil. At first glance, one would expect oil reserves to be the salvation of any country, providing it with the resources to develop its infrastructure and generate new industries. In reality, the opposite tends to be the case. Oil is often more a curse than a blessing, especially when controlled by the state. Rather than directing resources toward the goal of development, leaders give in to a seemingly irresistible temptation, which leads to corruption as they siphon off the wealth to line their pockets or serve their own policy predilections. Moreover, since the public is eliminated as

LABOR FORCE BY OCCUPATION

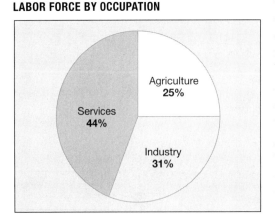

Agriculture
25%

Services
44%

Industry
31%

the major source of state revenue, those in power can effectively ignore the public and repress or co-opt any opposition. Interestingly, the resource trap may also explain the degree of women's rights; where oil is strong, the private sector is weak, limiting women's participation in the workforce and economic independence. The issue of "taxation without representation," for women and men, thus becomes meaningless—the state can do without either and is able to avoid having to make the trade-off. This became evident during the time of the White Revolution, when economic development coincided with growing inflation, inequality, and increased repression. Development, built on oil exports and Western imports, also fueled hostility toward Western materialism, or what was termed "Westoxication" or "Weststruckness" by one critical Iranian scholar of the era.[14]

Reflecting the economic factors that helped bring about the 1979 revolution, the new constitution explicitly stated that "the economy is a means, not an end." This stood in contrast to liberal capitalist systems, in which the quest for wealth and profit becomes "a subversive and corrupting factor in the course of man's development." The oil and other state-owned industries were to remain in the state's hands, with the profits redirected toward presumably more equitable goals. In addition, numerous private industries were nationalized after their owners fled the revolution. In many cases, their assets were turned over to several **bonyads**, or parastatal foundations. The objectives of the *bonyads* are ostensibly to help the disadvantaged, such as war veterans and the poor. Over time, however, the *bonyads* have become major economic players and often monopolies, controlling substantial assets and industries (for example, construction, pharmaceuticals, housing, and food) while operating independently of government oversight or taxation.[15] Thus between oil, the *bonyads*, and the state, the private sector is a small portion of the economy, perhaps less than 20 percent, and is made up of small-scale businesses.

Another important distinction in Iran's economic system is its history of autarky, or economic independence. Opponents of the Qajar and Pahlavi dynasties accused their leaders of selling the country to foreigners and exporting their oil wealth for the benefit of a few. Just as the 1979 constitution describes profit and wealth as corrupting influences, the postrevolutionary government has been wary of international economic ties. Oil could be exported to develop the economy, but the government, at least initially, sought a policy of greater self-sufficiency and more state ownership to secure the country from the effects of Westoxication.

The results of the post-1979 economic model have been poor. To be fair, Iran's economy was devastated by the long war with Iraq, which destroyed infrastructure, drained the national treasury, and killed many of the country's young men. By 1988, when the war ended, Iran's per capita GDP had fallen to just over half its 1979 level. Since that time, the economy has steadily rebounded, although only now is it returning to its level of some twenty years before. In addition, while oil prices have provided a windfall for the government, production itself has been stagnant, due in part to insufficient investment in the oil sector. Ironically, Iran must import and ration gasoline as it lacks the refining capacity necessary to meet domestic need. It is estimated that the poverty and unemployment rate are somewhere around 25 percent, and Iran's economic equality, a cornerstone of the revolution, is no better than that of the United States. Finally, compounding matters is the fact that the Iranian economy faces the challenge of providing employment for millions of young Iranians who enter the workforce each year. This economic marginalization of the young, in turn, increases their hostility to the regime and encourages emigration.

Solutions to these economic problems are not easy. Iran can expect that ongoing revenues from its oil reserves and the development of natural gas will help sustain the state budget. This, however, is not likely to diversify the economy or provide new sources of employment. Privatization and the liberalization of the economy are also difficult. The *bonyads* are loathe to give up their monopoly control over much of the economy, and tensions with the West have limited foreign investment, tourism, and international banking (including things we take for granted, such as credit cards). Until domestic and international obstacles are resolved, the economy is unlikely to improve, though high oil prices may help stave off needed reform.[16]

FOREIGN RELATIONS AND THE WORLD

Iran's foreign relations are a function of its revolutionary aspirations, the limits of that revolution, and the nature of power at the international level. After 1979, Iran's leaders believed that theirs was the first in a series of revolutions that would sweep the Islamic world. Like the Russian and Chinese revolutions before it, the Iranian revolution was thought to be the vanguard of a political movement that would extend beyond Iran's borders. In the early postrevolutionary years, Iran served as a beacon for Muslims everywhere, helping to give voice to their grievances against the West and against their own despotic rulers. Iran became associated with radical movements and terrorism, including the use of suicide attacks, which emerged first inside Iran during the struggles following the Iranian revolution. In the 1980s, Iran backed the Shiite group Hezbollah in Lebanon in its efforts against the occupying Israeli forces and rival Lebanese groups. Iran's long struggle against Iraq was also shaped by revolutionary fervor and the initial belief that Iraq was the logical next step in Iran's Islamic revolution.

Iran's hope to spread its vision of political Islam to the rest of the world faced several major obstacles. The first was Shiism itself, which is viewed by majority Muslims at best as an incorrect interpretation of the faith. For many Sunnis, Shiism is more than incorrect, but heretical and thus in some ways worse that Judaism or Christianity. These theological differences have limited the ability of the revolution to spread among the majority Sunni Muslim population worldwide. Only in a few countries, such as Iraq, Lebanon, and Afghanistan, do Shiites exist in significant numbers.

A second major obstacle to Iran's international vision was ethnicity. The obvious goal of the Iranian revolutionary policy was to spread the revolutionaries' vision within the Middle East, helping to overthrow secular leaders, establish Islamic states, and drive out Western influence in the process. But Iranians are not Arabs; their culture is not Arabic, nor is their language. Just as the revolution had difficulties speaking in terms of one Islam, it could not speak in terms of one Middle Eastern people. Here, too, Iran was the outlier. This was only reinforced by the Iran-Iraq War, in which Iran relied, in part, upon nationalistic fervor to maintain public support and Iraq's Arab but Shiite majority sided with their government against Iran. Although Iran failed to serve as the lodestar for revolution, many of the ideas and symbols of the revolution influenced a second wave of political conflict, beginning with the war in Afghanistan in 1980 and continuing through the emergence of Al Qaeda. Though Al Qaeda views Shiism as heretical, it owes much of its ideological justification for violence to the Islamic Revolution and the Shia tradition of martyrdom.[17]

Over the past twenty years, Iranian relations with the outside world, particularly the West, have oscillated between reconciliation and conflict. In the late 1990s, President Mohammad Khatami actively sought to improve international relations, speaking of a "dialogue of civilizations" in contrast to a "clash of civilizations." Greater domestic liberalization and an easing of tensions led to more international contact, from diplomats and civil society to Western tourism. In addition, the terrorist attacks on the United States in 2001 and the invasion of Afghanistan on Iran's border also seemed to provide an opportunity for engagement. While President George Bush spoke of Iran as part of an "Axis of Evil," the Iranian government also strongly opposed the Taliban in Afghanistan (who were hostile to that country's Shia population) and Saddam Hussein, their old nemesis who had invaded Iran in 1980.

However, both domestic and international factors brought Iranian-Western rapprochement to an end. Inside Iran, in spite of Khatami's call for improved relations, the supreme leader and many others inside the state were opposed to better relations with the United States, in particular, which they had long viewed as the "Great Satan." This limited the extent to which the president could realize his foreign policy. Second, Iran's ongoing pursuit of nuclear technology (discussed below) became of increasing concern after 2001, when many leaders in the international community began to worry that such technology could be transferred to terrorist or other non-state actors. This led to increased pressure on Iran from the international community, heightening tension. Third, the election of President Ahmadinejad further changed the tenor of relations with the outside world, as Ahmadinejad took a more confrontational line, using nuclear technology as a symbol of national pride while simultaneously taking a more openly hostile tone toward Israel. To be clear, both the nuclear program and hostility to Israel have a long history, but the combination of increased international tensions after 2001 and the combative tone of both President Bush and Ahmadinejad brought many of these tensions to a head.

Iran now finds itself in a complicated international situation. At one level, its place in the international community is higher than perhaps at any time since 1979. Its ongoing pursuit of nuclear technology has raised its profile dramatically and generated concern and divisions over how best to engage Iran. In addition, while the U.S.-led invasions of Afghanistan and Iraq put the Great Satan on its border, difficulties in both conflicts have given Iran much greater leverage than many expected. Indeed, early in the Iraq and Afghanistan wars, some observers in the United States (and some Iranians at home) expected that Iran would be next in the wave of regime change, with these invasions either prompting revolution inside Iran or paving the way for an invasion of Iran itself. Instead, American forces became bogged down in long-term conflicts. The Iraq War in particular seemed to play directly into Iran's hands. Not only was Saddam Hussein eliminated, but the war brought into power the majority Shiite population who had long been under the thumb of the Sunni minority. Shiite exile groups in Iran returned to Iraq and quickly dominated politics, while domestic Shiite insurgents appeared to benefit from Iranian funding and training, inflicting heavy casualties on U.S. and coalition forces. This shift in power, combined with the nuclear standoff and growing Iranian influence in places like Lebanon, Syria, and the Palestinian Territories, has led some commentators to speak of an emerging (if misleading) "Shia arc" of power across the region that threatens the west and Sunni Arabs alike.

As always, the situation is far more complex. While Iraq may have presented an opportunity for Iran to extend its power, there remain tensions between Arabs and Persians and Shia and Sunni that will continue to limit the kind of sway Iran can hold. Moreover, a continuation of violence and chaos among its neighbors has repercussions for Iran itself. For example, the overthrow of the Taliban in Afghanistan has meant a resurgence of opium production, the majority of which is trafficked across Iran. Organized crime and drug addiction have consequently risen in Iran, to the extent that Iran is now thought to have one of the highest per capita number of opium addicts in the world. Similarly, the rise of Shia power in Iraq led to violence by Sunnis who seek to reclaim their old position of authority. Ironically, these regional problems have required increased communication between the United States and Iran. The two countries do not have diplomatic relations, and even whether the two countries should talk at all was a source of controversy in the 2008 U.S. presidential elections. But in May 2007, U.S. and Iranian diplomats met in Baghdad to discuss Iraq's security situation, the first bilateral meeting since the Iranian Revolution. Could Iraq become the means through which the United States and Iran find common ground? This will, in large part, depend on whether the nuclear issue leads to compromise or military conflict.

CURRENT ISSUES

THE NUCLEAR PROGRAM AND THE DISPUTED PRESIDENTIAL ELECTION OF 2009

One of the most critical issues that confronts the international community at the present is Iran's apparent nuclear weapons program. How this issue is resolved will have profound repercussions, and any solution has been complicated by the presidential election of 2009.

Even before the 1979 revolution, as part of an extensive plan to develop nuclear energy for peaceful purposes, Iran showed interest in developing a nuclear weapon. By the mid-1980s, the Iranian leadership had begun to actively develop nuclear technology. Even though Iran is a signatory to the Nuclear Nonproliferation Treaty (NPT), it is clear that Iran has been developing the technology to produce enriched uranium, a necessary ingredient for making nuclear weapons. Furthermore, these actions have been undertaken without oversight by the International Atomic Energy Agency (IAEA), which oversees the NPT and obliges nonnuclear signatories to report any such activities and allow inspection. Under President Ahmadinejad there has been growing rhetoric about the progress of the nuclear program and the country's inalienable right to such technology, albeit for peaceful purposes (Iran does in fact suffer from a shortage of electricity). Whether Iran is currently working on nuclear weapons technology itself, however, is unclear.

The IAEA, the United States, the European Union, and Israel have all expressed concern about this project but have failed to find a clear solution. The United States and Israel have favored a much harder line toward Iran, both threatening the country with military strikes if the situation is not resolved. Over the past five years there have also been several attempts to strike a deal with Iran over this issue, promising improved relations in return for greater international oversight of its nuclear technology. Under President Obama, the United States government has dropped the earlier demand that Iranian work cease before negotiations could begin, something that appeared to open the door for negotiation and perhaps even a restoration of ties with the United States.

These hopes were dashed by the 2009 presidential election. Most observers conclude that the election results, showing Mahmoud Ahmadinejad winning over 60 percent of the vote, were fraudulent; there is speculation that in reality he placed third behind two reformist candidates. His main challenger (and the presumed winner), Mir Hossein Mousavi, drew widespread support for his relative moderation, past governmental experience (he served as prime minister under Khomeini), and his call to improve relations with the outside world. The stolen election galvanized Mousavi and his supporters, who took to the streets for days of mass demonstrations. The government responded with threats and violence, killing dozens. Irrespective of how this conflict winds down, the result is a compromised leadership, including the Supreme Leader, that will complicate any international negotiations. Iran may be headed for political drift, with dangerous implications at home and abroad.

NOTES

1. Elton L. Daniel, *The History of Iran* (Westport, CT: Greenwood Press, 2001); also Moojan Momen, *An Introduction to Shia Islam* (New Haven, CT: Yale, 1985).
2. For a discussion of Shiism in Iran and elsewhere, see Heinz Halm, *Shi'ism* (New York: Columbia University Press, 2004); also see, for example, W. Morgan Shuster, *The Strangling of Persia; story of the European diplomacy and oriental intrigue that resulted in the denationalization of 12 million Mohammedans: a personal narrative* (New York: Century Co., 1912).
3. For a discussion of this period and the increasing U.S. influence in Iranian politics, see Kenneth M. Pollack, *The Persian Puzzle: The Conflict between Iran and America* (New York: Random House, 2004).
4. Stephen Kinzer, *All the Shah's Men: An American Coup and the Roots of Middle East Terror* (New York: John Wiley & Sons, 2003).
5. Ali M. Ansari, "The Myth of the White Revolution: Mohammad Reza Shah, 'Modernization,' and the Consolidation of Power," *Middle Eastern Studies,* 37, no. 3 (July 2001), pp. 1–24.
6. Ruhollah Khomeini, *Islamic Government* (Tehran: Institute for Compilation and Publication of Imam Khomeini's Works, n.d.); see also Karen Armstrong, *The Battle for God* (New York: Alfred A. Knopf, 2000).
7. For an analysis of these events, see Charles Kurzman, *The Unthinkable Revolution in Iran* (Cambridge, MA: Harvard University Press, 2004).
8. From International Constitutional Law, www.oefre.unibe.ch/law/icl (accessed 14 July 2005).
9. Kian Tajbakhsh, "Political Decentralization and the Creation of Local Government in Iran: Consolidation or Transformation of the Theocratic State?" *Social Research,*

67, no. 2 (Summer 2000), pp. 377–404; also "Iranian President suffers defeat in local elections," *Al Jazeera,* 21 December 2006.

10. Afshin Molavi, "Buying Time in Tehran," *Foreign Affairs* (November/December 2004), pp. 9–17.

11. Nazrin Mehdiyeva, "Azerbaijan and Its Foreign Policy Dilemma," *Asian Affairs,* 34, no. 3 (November 2003), pp. 271–85.

12. Graham E. Fuller, "Islamist Politics in Iraq after Saddam Hussein," Special Report 108, United States Institute of Peace, August 2003, www.usip.org/pubs/special reports/sr108.html (accessed 11 July 2005).

13. Ali Banuazizi, "Iran's Revolutionary Impasse: Political Factionalism and Societal Resistance," *Middle East Report,* 191 (November/December, 1994), pp. 2–8.

14. Jalal Al-e Ahmad, *Weststruckness,* trans. John Green and Ahmad Alizadah (Costa Mesa, CA: Mazda, 1997).

15. Suzanne Maloney, "Islamism and Iran's Postrevolutionary Economy: The Case of the Bonyads," in Mary Ann Tétreault and Robert A. Denemark, eds., *Gods, Guns, and Globalization: Religious Radicalism and International Political Economy* (Boulder, CO: Lynne Reinner Publishers, 2004), pp. 292–334.

16. Jahangir Amuzegar, "Iran's Unemployment Crisis," *Middle East Economic Survey,* 41 (11 October 2004), www.mees.com (accessed 11 July 2005).

17. Michael Scott Doran, "The Saudi Paradox," *Foreign Affairs* XLVII, 41 (October 11, 2004), pp. 35–51.

GLOSSARY OF KEY TERMS

Assembly of Experts Elected body that chooses supreme leader.

Basij "People's militia" that serves as a public morals police.

bonyads Parastatal foundations made in part from assets nationalized after the Iranian revolution.

chief justice Head of the judiciary.

Expediency Council Appointed body that mediates between the Majlis and the Guardian Council over legislative disputes.

Farsi Language of Iran.

Guardian Council Appointed body that vets candidates for office and can overturn legislation.

Iran-Iraq War 1980–1988; conflict between the two countries started by Iraq.

Islamic Republic of Iran Name for postrevolutionary Iran.

Islamism or Islamic fundamentalism The belief that Islam should be the source of the political regime.

Khamenei, Ali Current Supreme Leader of Iran

Khatami, Mohammad President of Iran from 1997–2005.

Khomeini, Ruhollah First Supreme Leader of Iran from 1980 to his death in 1989.

Koran   Central holy book of Islam.

Majlis   Legislature of Iran.

Muhammed   Main prophet of Islam.

Mosaddeq, Mohammed   Prime Minister of Iran; deposed in 1953 by Operation Ajax.

National Front   Political party in Iran following World War II, which opposed the monarchy and favored greater Iranian control over natural resources. Outlawed after Operation Ajax.

Operation Ajax   U.S.- and UK-backed overthrow of Iranian Prime Minister Mossadeq in 1953.

Pahlavi, Reza Khan   Monarch of Iran from 1925 to 1941.

Persia   Name for Iran before 1935.

quietist   View within Shiism that rejects theocracy and the direct role of religion in the state.

Revolutionary Guard   Paramilitary force charged with defending the regime from domestic and internal enemies.

SAVAK   Secret police of prerevolutionary Iran.

Second Khordad Front   Reformist party that emerged in Iran to contest 2000 Majlis elections.

sharia   Religious law of Islam.

shiat **Ali**   "party of Ali," term from which the word Shiism derives.

Shiism   Minority sect of Islam that differs over the proper descendents of the Prophet Mohammed.

supreme leader   Chief spiritual and political leader of Iran.

theocracy   Rule by religion or religious leaders.

ummah   "Community," meant to refer to nation or Islamic community everywhere.

velayat-e faqih   Rule by Islamic jurists; Islamic Republic's political system that places power in the hands of clerics.

White Revolution   Policy of Shah to rapidly modernize and westernize Iran.

WEB LINKS

Iran Daily **www.iran-daily.com**Web site of the Supreme Leader Ayatollah Khamenei **www.leader.ir**

Islamic Republic News Agency **www.irna.com/en**

Middle East Economic Survey **www.mees.com**

Middle East Network Information Center, University of Texas, Austin **menic.utexas.edu/menic/Countries_and_Regions/Iran**

Ministry of Foreign Affairs, Islamic Republic of Iran **www.mfa.gov.ir**

Ministry of Foreign Affairs, Islamic Republic of Iran **www.mfa.gov.ir**

Web site of the Supreme Leader Ayatollah Khamenei **www.leader.ir**

11 MEXICO

Head of state and government:
President Felipe Calderón Hinojosa
(since December 1, 2006)

Capital: Mexico City

Total land size: 1,972,550 sq km

Population: 109 million

GDP at PPP: 1.34 trillion US$

GDP per capita at PPP: $12,500

Human development index ranking: 52

MEXICO

INTRODUCTION

Why Study This Case?

For over eight decades, stability was the feature that differentiated Mexico's political system from that of most of its Latin American neighbors and from its own turbulent pre-1917 history. Unlike the political atmosphere of most other third world countries, Mexico's post-1917 politics were relatively peaceful: power was transferred between leaders after regular elections, and the military was thoroughly subordinate to civilians. This stability resulted from a highly effective and remarkably flexible semi-authoritarian regime dominated by a single party, the **Partido Revolucionario Institucional (PRI)**. That model delivered impressive rates of economic growth but also produced an economy plagued by severe economic inequality and massive poverty.

In July 2000, the PRI's long tenure came to a sudden end, marking the start of a new era in Mexican politics. The decline of the PRI's political hegemony began in the early 1980s, when the Mexican economy narrowly averted bankruptcy. In response to a severe economic crisis, the PRI leadership started to dismantle the prevailing protectionist and statist economic model. Mexico opened up its economy to the world and began a transition to a neoliberal political economy. It quickly became one of Latin America's most open economies. The hallmark of this new era was Mexico's 1994 entry into the **North American Free Trade Agreement (NAFTA)** with the United States and Canada.

The economic crisis of the 1980s (and the PRI's response to it) created new sources of political opposition, and the party's power was seriously threatened for the first time in seventy years. In 1988, the PRI resorted to massive fraud to avoid losing the presidency, and it increased the use of fraud to prevent the opposition from taking control of state legislatures. In January 1994, armed Mayan peasants shocked Mexico when they seized control of a southern Mexican town. In March of that year, the PRI's presidential candidate was assassinated while campaigning for office, the first such political murder since 1928. There were allegations that the murder had been ordered by members of the governing party, and the inability of the government to solve the crime added to a sense of crisis. The emergence of a strong political challenge to the PRI, the presence of an armed guerrilla movement, and a high-profile political murder destroyed the image of Mexico's system as stable and peaceful.

The political turmoil was alarming to Mexicans and Americans alike. Participation in NAFTA only ratified a growing (but highly asymmetrical) interdependence between the U.S. and Mexican economies. Mexico and the United

States share a 2,000-mile border, and Mexican immigration to the United States has long provided a steady stream of labor that is vital to the U.S. economy. In addition, the United States is the chief consumer of Mexico's oil exports, and Mexico is now the United States' second-biggest trading partner, after Canada.

After two decades of political and economic crisis, the July 2000 victory of **Vicente Fox**, the first non-PRI president since 1917, provided new hope for Mexico's future, even as it raised new questions. Fox took power vowing to shake up the Mexican system but soon discovered that the PRI's loss of the presidency did not give him a blank check. The PRI maintained strongholds of political power in a variety of federal and state political institutions. The hotly contested elections of July 2006 revealed that six years after its democratic transition, Mexico was deeply polarized between left and right. The conservative **Felipe Calderón** won a razor-thin victory over a leftist candidate who was critical of free trade, and whose main priority was to address Mexico's endemic poverty. The election was so close that Calderón's opponent, Andrés Manuel Lopéz Obrador, demanded a recount, launched a legal challenge to the results, and has refused to concede to his opponent. Our study of Mexico will raise several important questions: Has Mexico had a democratic transition, or is it still best viewed as a semi-authoritarian regime? Has Mexico's embrace of a neoliberal economic model been a success, or has it merely exacerbated inequality and worsened poverty? Can the Mexican state defend itself against challenges to its authority? Is Mexico likely to remain a close and trusted ally of the United States?

Major Geographic and Demographic Features

Mexico's stunningly diverse geography includes tropical rain forests, snow-capped volcanoes, and rich agricultural regions. Historically, the two major mountain ranges that divide Mexico, the eastern and western Sierra Madres, have made transportation and communication difficult. Only 12 percent of Mexico's land is arable, and the most productive agricultural areas are in northern Mexico, close to the U.S. border. There, large and highly mechanized export farms provide much of America's winter produce. The proximity of Mexico's agricultural export to the U.S. market has been a major boost to Mexico's economic growth. Agriculture in southern Mexico is characterized by smaller farms and less efficient production. Mexico is well endowed with minerals and has major oil reserves.

With 109 million people, Mexico has the second-largest population in Latin America (after Brazil). Its population is racially quite diverse: about 60 percent are **mestizos**, people of mixed Spanish and indigenous blood; another 30 percent, living primarily in the central and southern parts of the country, are considered indigenous because they speak an indigenous language. The largest indigenous groups are the **Maya**, located in Mexico's far south (along the Guatemalan border), and the **Nahuatl**, concentrated in central Mexico. On Mexico's Caribbean coast is a large population of African decent.

Nearly three quarters of Mexico's population lives in an urban setting, a relatively recent change. Mexico City has dwarfed all other Mexican cities: it now has about 18 million residents. Population growth has slowed with economic development, but Mexico's large population still strains the country's resources. As a result, Mexicans still migrate in very large numbers. Many have left the impoverished countryside for the cities, often leaving the poor south for the wealthier north, especially the factory towns along the U.S. border. At the same time, a steady stream of Mexicans has migrated across the border to the United States.

Historical Development of the State

The history of the modern Mexican state can be viewed as a struggle between political order, which has almost always been achieved by authoritarian rulers, and periodic political anarchy.[1]

When the Spanish conquistador **Hernán Cortés** arrived in Mexico in 1519, he encountered well-established and highly sophisticated indigenous civilizations. The country had long been home to such peoples as the Maya, Aztecs, and Toltecs, who had relatively prosperous economies, impressive architecture, sophisticated agricultural methods, and powerful militaries. Within three years of their arrival, the Spanish conquerors had defeated the last Aztec leader, **Cuauhtémoc**; destroyed the impressive Aztec capital, Tenochtitlán; and decimated the indigenous population. By the early seventeenth century, the indigenous population had been reduced from about 25 million to under 1 million. The surviving indigenous peoples of Mexico, concentrated in the central and southern parts of the country, became a permanent underclass of slaves and landless peasants.

The Aztec Empire was replaced by the equally hierarchical, authoritarian, and militaristic Spanish Empire, which created a legacy very different from that imparted to the United States by British colonialism. Mexico was the richest of Spain's colonial possessions, and Spain ruled the distant colony with an iron fist, sending a new viceroy to the colony every four years. Colonial viceroys were absolute dictators: armed with the terror of the Spanish Inquisition, they were able to stamp out most political dissent. Lacking any civilian oversight, rampant corruption thrived in the colonial administration.

INDEPENDENCE AND INSTABILITY: THE SEARCH FOR ORDER

The struggle for independence can be viewed as a conflict over control of the state between the aristocracy loyal to Spain and the increasingly powerful and

TIME LINE OF POLITICAL DEVELOPMENT

Year	Event
1810–21	War of Independence fought against Spain
1846–48	One third of Mexico's territory lost in war with the United States
1910–17	Mexican Revolution
1917	Revolutionary constitution adopted
1929	Official revolutionary party created, later becoming the Partido Revolucionario Institucional (PRI)
1934–40	Presidency of Lázaro Cárdenas, during which land reform is promoted, the oil industry is nationalized, and the state is given a larger role in the economy
1939	Partido Acción Nacional (PAN) formed as a conservative opposition to the revolution
1968	Student protest movement against the Mexican government violently repressed
1981–82	Economic collapse caused by sudden drop in oil prices and Mexico's inability to pay its foreign debt
1988	Assumption of power by President Carlos Salinas de Gortari after elections widely viewed as fraudulent
1994	North American Free Trade Agreement (NAFTA) put into effect
	Rebellion of Zapatistas, indigenous peasants in the southern state of Chiapas
	PRI presidential candidate Luis Donaldo Colosio assassinated while campaigning, replaced by Ernesto Zedillo
2000	Election of PAN candidate Vicente Fox, marking the first defeat of the PRI in seventy-one years
2006	Felipe Calderón begins a six-year term as president

wealthy **criollos** (Mexican-born descendants of the Spanish colonists). Though inspired by the French and American Revolutions, the Mexican independence movement was mostly a response to the sudden blow that Napoléon's invading armies delivered to Spain. When Spain adopted a progressive liberal constitution in 1820, conservative Mexican elites accepted independence as the only means by which to preserve order and the status quo. The leading rebels and political conservatives agreed that an independent Mexico, declared in 1821, would preserve the role of the Catholic Church and implement a constitutional monarchy with a European at the head. **Mexico's War of Independence** lasted eleven years and cost 600,000 lives.

Mexico's independence was dominated by political conservatives who sought to preserve the economic and social status quo. As a result, independence did nothing to alleviate the poverty of Mexico's indigenous people and its large mestizo population. Indeed, the violence of the War of Independence and the elimination of the minimal protections of the Spanish crown worsened their plight. The power of the large landholders, or *latifundistas*, grew with independence, and the newly independent Mexico grew more economically disparate and politically unstable. Much of the turmoil and political chaos that plagued Mexico over the next half century was caused by a dispute between conservative monarchists and more liberal republicans. With the end of Spanish rule and the strong centralized government of the viceroy, Mexico was dominated by local military strongmen, known as **caciques**. Mexico's weak central state could not impose its authority.

Independent Mexico's first leader, Colonel Agustín de Iturbide, had himself crowned emperor in 1822 but was overthrown by **General Antonio López de Santa Ana**, Mexico's first in a series of **caudillos** (national military strongmen), and executed two years later. Santa Ana dominated the politics of Mexico for the next thirty years; despite his considerable power, however, he was unable to impose his authority over the local caciques or to prevent the secession of Texas in 1836. The impotence of a fragmented Mexico became even more apparent in the 1840s, when a rising imperial power, the United States, defeated the country in the **Mexican-American War** (1846–1848), which resulted in Mexico's loss of half its territory (present-day Arizona, California, Colorado, Nevada, New Mexico, Texas, and Utah) to the United States. In the aftermath of the defeat, Mexico's weakened government faced a massive uprising, known as **the War of the Castes**, by the indigenous Mayan population in the south. It took several years of fighting to subdue the rebellion.

Over the next several decades, Mexican liberals, led by a Zapotec Indian, **Benito Juárez**, attempted to centralize, modernize, and secularize Mexico. Juárez, who occupied the presidency on three separate occasions, imposed a fairly progressive constitution in 1857 and is today considered one of Mexico's first proponents of democracy. Juárez was unable to bring stability to Mexico, however. In 1864, Mexican conservatives, backed by French troops, imposed an ill-fated and short-lived monarchy ruled by an Austrian emperor, Maximilian, who was captured and executed in 1867. Juárez regained power, but his reforms alienated Mexican conservatives, and Mexico soon succumbed to a long dictatorship.

THE *PORFIRIATO*: ECONOMIC LIBERALISM AND POLITICAL AUTHORITARIANISM

From 1876 to 1910, Mexican politics was dominated by **Porfirio Díaz**, a general who had backed the liberal reforms of Juárez and fought to expel the French-imposed monarchy. Díaz assumed power in 1876 and had himself reelected repeatedly until 1910. Díaz ruled Mexico with an iron fist, imposing a brutal authoritarian regime (known as the *porfiriato*), which gave Mexico its first taste of stability since independence. Díaz was also responsible for Mexico's first real economic development and was the first Mexican ruler to impose the power of the state on remote areas.

THE REVOLUTION

The **Mexican Revolution** (1910–1920) can be viewed as a struggle between two groups attempting to seize control of the state. The first included middle-class Mexicans resisting the dictatorship of Díaz. The second included radical social reformers who sought agrarian reform, among other things.

In the first phase of the revolution, middle-class political reformers, led by the landowner **Francisco Madero**, defeated the Díaz dictatorship. Madero's victory promised democratic reforms and minimal economic change. The second phase of the revolution involved a struggle between these political reformers and advocates of radical socioeconomic change. The most famous revolutionary advocate of the poor was **Emiliano Zapata**, a young mestizo peasant leader. Zapata organized a peasant army in Morelos, south of Mexico City, to push for agrarian reform. In the north of Mexico, **Francisco (Pancho) Villa** had organized an army of peasants and small farmers.

The often contradictory aspects of the Mexican Revolution help explain why it was so protracted and so bloody: Mexico soon descended into political chaos, in which armed bands led by regional caciques fought one another over a period of ten years. About 1.5 million Mexicans (about 7 percent of the total population) died in the conflict, and thousands more fled north to the United States. Order was restored only in 1917, under the leadership of a northern governor, **Venustiano Carranza**. He defeated not only his supporters, who wanted a return to a dictatorship, but also Zapata and Villa, the more radical voices of the revolution.

The **constitution of 1917** reflected some of the contradictions of the revolution. The document was written not by peasants and workers but by middle-class mestizo professionals who had suffered under the Díaz dictatorship. That some of their values were largely "liberal" explains provisions that call for regular elections as well as harsh measures to weaken the Catholic Church. The constitution sought to prevent the reemergence of a dictatorship by devolving political power to Mexico's states, adopting federalism, and barring presidents and other elected leaders from reelection. Reflecting the power of the emerging mestizo class and the role played by indigenous Mexicans in unseating the dictatorship, the 1917 constitution provided elaborate protection of indigenous communal lands and called for land reform. It was also a nationalist document, prohibiting foreign ownership of Mexican land and mineral rights.

Although Carranza successfully seized power and fostered the new constitution, he was unable to implement many of the reforms or to stem Mexico's endemic political violence. His government was responsible for the murder of Zapata in 1919, and Carranza himself was assassinated by political opponents in 1920.

Mexico's next two elected presidents, Álvaro Obregón (1920–1924) and Plutarco Elías Calles (1924–1928), finally put an end to the political bloodshed and developed a political system capable of maintaining order. Obregón promoted trade unions but brought them under the control of the state. He also promoted land reform while tolerating the presence of haciendas. He managed to gain the support and recognition of the United States, which had feared the revolution as a socialist experiment. Most significant, he purged the army and weakened the revolutionary generals who had continued to meddle in politics. Calles consolidated state power by imposing the first income tax and investing in education and infrastructure. He vigorously enforced the constitution's limit on the power of the Catholic Church. The church was a major landowner, and its support for the dictatorship of Díaz and the enemies of the revolution made it a prime target for reform. Religious processions were banned, clergy could not appear in public in religious garb, the church could not own any property, and control over education was given to the state.

When Calles left power, he also left Mexico his most enduring legacy: the Revolucionario Partido Nacional, later renamed the Revolucionario Partido Institucional (PRI). From the outset, the PRI was conceived as a party of power and a party of the state. Its colors (red, white, and green) are the colors of the Mexican flag. Its goal was to encompass all of those who supported the revolution, and its members thus ranged from socialists to liberals. Moreover, it was designed to incorporate and co-opt the most important organizations in Mexican society, starting with the army. The PRI's main purpose was to end political violence by controlling the political system and the process of presidential succession. After decades of instability and violence, the revolution's leaders brought Mexico an unprecedented period of political peace.

STABILITY ACHIEVED: THE PRI IN POWER, 1917–2000

For decades, the PRI provided Mexico with the much-desired political stability that its founders had sought. Under the PRI, Mexico held national elections every six years, and new presidents took power without violence or military intervention. The PRI regime featured a strong president, directly elected for a single six-year term. Though not stipulated in the 1917 constitution, PRI presidents claimed the power to name their successors by officially designating the PRI candidate for the presidency; for over eighty years, no official PRI candidate ever lost a presidential election. During most of the PRI's tenure in office, the Mexican president enjoyed the reverence and aloofness of monarchical heads of state while possessing far more power than the typical democratic president. Most important, until 2000, Mexican presidents controlled the vast machinery of the PRI and used the state to dispense patronage. Unlike U.S. presidents, they faced no effective check on their power from the legislature, judiciary, or state governments, all of which were controlled by the PRI.

Under the PRI, regular elections were held for national, state, and local offices, and opposition parties actively contested these elections. During most of this period, there was no formal censorship of the press, and Mexicans were free to voice their opinions and criticize the government. Mexicans were free to live where they wanted, and according to their constitution, they were living in a democratic state.

But under its surface, the Mexican regime had clear authoritarian tendencies. The PRI held an inordinate amount of power. It won every presidential election between 1917 and 2000 and during that time won the vast majority of seats in the legislature and at the state and local level. The PRI dominated major trade unions and peasant organizations. Through its control of the state, the PRI dominated major pieces of the economy, including Mexico's vast oil wealth. The PRI became expert at co-opting possible sources of opposition, including the press and the weak opposition parties. Unlike many authoritarian regimes, the PRI did not often need to revert to harsh measures of repression; when necessary, however, the regime used a variety of tactics to stifle the opposition. Most notorious was the selective use of electoral fraud to preserve its political dominance, a tactic that was employed increasingly in the 1970s and 1980s as its grip on power began to erode.

Since the Mexican Revolution, scholars have struggled to characterize the Mexican regime. It is perhaps most accurate to view Mexico under the PRI as an authoritarian regime dominated by a single political party, but one that afforded far more civil liberties than its authoritarian counterparts elsewhere. Mexico held regular (though not always free and fair) elections, tolerated and even encouraged political parties (although those parties began to win office only in the 1980s), and formally protected basic civil liberties. Compared with most other authoritarian regimes, the PRI kept human rights abuses to a minimum. The PRI maintained its power almost exclusively through co-optation, inclusion, and corruption. Its unparalleled success meant that it did not often

CARLOS SALINAS AND THE POWER OF THE PRI

The history of Carlos Salinas illustrates well the workings of the PRI. Salinas, a Harvard-educated technocrat, rose steadily through the ranks and was appointed by his political patron, President Miguel de la Madrid Hurtado, to a top cabinet post. De la Madrid then handpicked Salinas for the PRI presidential nomination. In 1988, Salinas won the presidency in elections widely thought to have been stolen from the opposition. Despite a questionable popular mandate, Salinas continued de la Madrid's neoliberal economic reforms and signed the landmark 1994 NAFTA with the United States and Canada.

Mexican presidents traditionally completed their terms and once out of power scrupulously avoided the political limelight and were treated with considerable respect. The tradition was broken with Salinas, however, who found himself vilified after leaving office in 1994. His economic policies were blamed for the economic depression of 1994–1995, and his administration was accused of massive corruption. In March 1995, Salinas's brother Raúl was arrested and later sentenced to prison for the 1994 murder of a PRI deputy leader. Subsequent investigations revealed that the former president's brother had stashed millions of dollars in hidden bank accounts and had not paid taxes on most of that wealth. As a sign of the growing disarray within the PRI, Carlos Salinas then committed a political taboo by publicly attacking the policies of his handpicked successor, President Ernesto Zedillo. At the request of Zedillo, Salinas went into voluntary exile in Ireland. For many Mexicans, the Salinas episode was symbolic of everything that was wrong with PRI rule.

need to resort to brute repression. The Peruvian novelist Mario Vargas Llosa thus viewed the PRI regime as the "perfect dictatorship."[2]

THE SLOW EROSION OF PRI POWER, 1980–2000

By the early 1980s, the vaunted stability of the Mexican regime was called into question by a series of interrelated economic and political challenges to PRI rule. The economic crisis of the 1980s unleashed numerous challenges to the party's political hegemony. The conservative opposition in northern Mexico, long an advocate of free-market economic policies, began to seriously contest local and state elections. The PRI was then forced to revert to ever-increasing and ever-more-overt electoral fraud to deny power to the opposition. The watershed election of July 2000 ended the PRI's seventy-one-year control of the presidency. Vicente Fox, candidate of the conservative Partido Acción Nacional (PAN), handily defeated **Francisco Labastida** of the PRI, despite an expensive and elaborate PRI campaign.

POLITICAL REGIME

Political Institutions

THE CONSTITUTION

On paper, the Mexican regime does not differ markedly from that of the United States, although much more power is granted to Mexico's president. The constitution of 1917 calls for a presidential legislative-executive system; a separation of judicial, legislative, and executive power; and a system of federalism that gives Mexico's states considerable power. The seventy-one-year domination of the political system by the Partido Revolucionario Institucional (PRI), however, rendered this formidable constitution largely meaningless. Mexican presidents enjoyed near-dictatorial powers with few checks on their authority. Through their domination of the PRI, they not only controlled the judiciary but also handpicked state governors. The Mexican legislature might have served as a check on the PRI, but until July 1997 it was controlled by it. Elections at all levels were largely a charade, serving mainly to validate PRI appointments to elective offices. Even the president was not truly elected, since incumbent presidents ritually designated their successor. Campaigns were more celebrations of PRI's power than genuine political contests.

How, then, did the opposition manage to win local and state elections in the 1980s? And how did the opposition unseat the PRI in the 2000 presidential election? Part of the answer to these questions lies in the growing illegitimacy of the regime during the 1970s, when Mexico's economy began to deteriorate. But the erosion of PRI legitimacy was also the result of widespread outrage in reaction to the PRI's blatant and unabashed disregard for the rule of law in the 1980s and 1990s. As opposition to the PRI grew and as the PRI resorted more openly and more regularly to widespread electoral fraud, sectors of the party pushed for democratization. Seeking to polish its image, the PRI passed a number of reforms that favored the opposition.

One important set of reforms passed in 1993 changed the electoral law (implementing some element of proportional representation, or PR) to guarantee the

---

ESSENTIAL POLITICAL FEATURES

- Legislative-executive system: federal republic
- Legislature: Congreso de la Unión (National Congress)
- Lower house: Cámara Federal de Diputados (Federal Chamber of Deputies)
- Upper house: Cámara de Senadores (Senate)
- Unitary or federal division of power: federal
- Main geographic subunits: *estados* (states)
- Electoral system for lower house: mixed single-member district and proportional representation
- Chief judicial body: Suprema Corte de Justicia de la Nación (National Supreme Court of Justice)

presence of the opposition in the legislature. Other reforms passed under the last PRI president, **Ernesto Zedillo,** gave the legislature control over judicial appointments and imposed electoral safeguards that greatly reduced the ability of a government to steal an election.

The Branches of Government

THE PRESIDENCY

Because of their immense power and unchallenged authority, Mexican presidents have often been viewed as elected monarchs. The 1917 constitution created a far more powerful president than that conceived in the U.S. model. The Mexican president can issue executive decrees that have the force of law. He can directly introduce legislation in Congress and can veto legislation initiated by Congress. Until 1994, Mexican presidents had extensive power to appoint and remove judges. As late as 1982, President **José López Portillo** essentially decreed the nationalization of Mexico's banking system.

Mexican presidents serve a single six-year term. They must be at least thirty-five years old and native born and cannot be a member of the clergy or an active member of the military. During the seventy-one-year reign of the PRI, the power of the president was greatly enhanced by the tradition of hand-picking his successor, who was generally chosen from among the cabinet members. Mexican presidents also enjoyed enormous power because the state played a leading role in the economy. Control over key natural resources and infrastructure (for example, oil, electricity, and communications) historically put the key economic lever in the hands of the executive.

Mexican presidents appoint and preside over a large cabinet of ministers, who oversee the various government departments. In recent decades, the **Secretariat of Government**, which controls internal political affairs, and the **Secretariat of the Treasury**, which oversees the economy, have been the highest-profile cabinet posts and have often been stepping-stones to the presidency. The reorganized cabinet of Vicente Fox included nineteen cabinet secretaries, in addition to seven policy coordinators whose job was to ease communication among ministries.[3] In the first two years of Fox's administration, his inexperienced cabinet was characterized by chaos and confusion, a radical departure from the PRI era. Since Fox's historic victory in 2000, Mexico's presidents have lacked a majority in Congress. As a result, some of the constitutional checks on presidential power that were long absent in the Mexican system have become more effective. One sign of the waning of presidential power was Fox's inability to obtain his party's nomination for his favored candidate, Interior Minister Santiago Creel, in the 2006 elections.

STRUCTURE OF THE GOVERNMENT

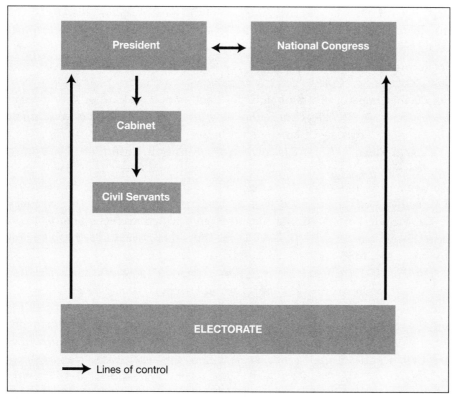

THE LEGISLATURE

Mexico has a bicameral legislature, called the National **Congress**, which is composed of a lower house (the **Chamber of Deputies**) and an upper house (the **Senate**).[4] The 500-member Chamber of Deputies has the power to pass laws (with a two-thirds majority), levy taxes, and verify the outcome of elections. Mexico's upper house is composed of 128 members, with three senators from each state and the **Federal District of Mexico City**, and an additional 32 senators selected from a national list on the basis of proportional representation. The upper house has fewer powers than the lower house, but it does have the power to confirm the president's appointments to the **Supreme Court**, approve treaties, and approve federal intervention in state matters.

Both houses have a committee system that on paper looks much like the U.S. system. In practice, however, Mexican legislators and the legislative committees lack the teeth of their northern counterparts because of one key difference: according to Article 59 of the constitution, Mexican legislators cannot be reelected to consecutive terms. As a result, from 1970 to 1997 only about

17 percent of Mexican deputies entered the lower house with any legislative experience, effectively depriving Mexico of the kind of senior lawmakers who dominate the U.S. system.[5] Most legislators were members of the PRI and could not afford to cross the leadership because they depended on the party for future political appointments. Even after the PRI's loss of the presidency in 2000, single-term legislators were reluctant to disobey their party leadership if they hoped to be nominated for another post in local or state government. Ironically, the PRI (whose founding principle was no reelection) is now the strongest advocate of ending term limits.

The Mexican legislature is currently in transition. Until 1988, the PRI regularly won over 90 percent of lower house seats and never lost a Senate seat. Between 1970 and 2003, it averaged 66.9 percent of the seats in the lower house, dwarfing the presence of its nearest rival, the Partido Acción Nacional (PAN, Vicente Fox's **National Action Party**), which averaged about 17 percent during that period.[6] In 1997, the two main opposition parties were able to form a coalition and take control of the lower house.

Before 1997, the lower house approved about 97 percent of the legislation submitted by the executive. That percentage dropped precipitously after 1990 and has continued to fall. Moreover, the number of laws originating in the legislature (instead of in the president's office) has increased dramatically. With its internal divisions and a president who did not enjoy complete control over deputies from his own party, the lower house resisted many of Fox's policies. Despite his inaugural pledge to respect Congress, Fox began his term acting very much like the PRI presidents in his relationship with Congress: he designed legislative proposals without any congressional input.[7] Fox's imperious behavior only emboldened the legislature. Congress blocked some legislation and radically altered other measures. For example, the lower house modified Fox's indigenous-rights bill, which emerged from the legislature so weakened that the Zapatista guerrillas rejected it. Fox's proposed reform of Mexico's tax structure was torpedoed by PRI and PRD (Partido de la Revolución Democrática) opposition, and Congress blocked his effort to negotiate a reduction of tariffs on imported sugar. Mexico's upper house even used its constitutional power to bar Fox from traveling to the United States in April 2002, complaining that the president was not paying enough attention to domestic politics. President Calderón has faced similar legislative opposition but has proved more adept at compromising with the opposition-dominated legislature.

Since Mexican legislators cannot be reelected and the majority of them are unlikely to receive presidential patronage, there is little to incline them to end the executive-legislative gridlock. The stubborn opposition to Fox by PRI and PRD legislators could have been predicted. The lukewarm support for Fox's legislative proposals by members of his own party was more surprising.

In short, Fox attempted to govern like the PRI presidents but without the benefit of the PRI's system of political control.

THE JUDICIAL SYSTEM

Mexico's judiciary is structured according to the U.S. model. Like the United States, Mexico has a Supreme Court as well as courts at the local and state levels. The eleven Supreme Court justices are appointed by the president and are confirmed by a two-thirds vote of the Senate. They serve terms of up to fifteen years. The Mexican judiciary has important formal powers, but under the PRI the Supreme Court never overturned any law, and it tended to view its jurisdiction in very limited terms. During the last PRI presidency, dramatic changes were introduced to give the Supreme Court far greater jurisdiction and power.[8] The Supreme Court can now determine the constitutionality of legislation upon the request of one third of the lower house, but it can strike down a law only if a supermajority of eight out of eleven justices agrees. The reforms have increased the independence of the judiciary by creating a seven-member Federal Judicial Council to oversee the administration of justice.

During the last years of PRI rule and in the early years of the Fox administration, the Supreme Court assumed a much more activist role. For example, it ordered President Zedillo's administration to release records relating to the banking industry, and it struck down Fox's attempt to privatize electricity generation. Despite this progress, Mexico's judicial system is severely hampered by a widespread perception that judges, especially at the local level, are corrupt. Both Fox and Calderón made it a priority to enhance the prestige and power of the beleaguered court system.

The Electoral System

During the last two decades of PRI rule, elections were widely viewed as corrupt. The 1988 presidential election was probably the zenith of PRI electoral fraud: over 30,000 ballot boxes disappeared; in an effort to cover up the thievery, the federal government declared the final ballots a state secret. Only in 1996 did the PRI succumb to pressure and create a truly independent **Federal Electoral Institute**, taking power away from the government-controlled Secretariat of the Interior. It also created the Federal Electoral Tribunal to adjudicate all electoral disputes. Mexico now has a more sophisticated and transparent electoral system featuring a national electoral register and voter identification cards, public funding for electoral campaigns, and strict limits on private contributions. Nevertheless, the bitterly contested presidential elections of 2006 raised new concerns about Mexico's electoral system and generated calls for further reform.

Voting is compulsory in Mexico, although enforcement of the law is sporadic. In part because of this law and in part because the PRI traditionally used its power to encourage electoral turnout, Mexican elections under the PRI had high turnout, usually between 60 and 70 percent. Since 2000, turnout has been closer to 60 percent.

Mexico's current electoral system for the legislature dates from reforms implemented by PRI president Miguel de la Madrid Hurtado in 1986. Mexico now has a mixed electoral system for the lower house, with 300 single-member districts (SMDs) and 200 proportional representation (PR) seats. Deputies in the lower house serve three-year terms. Mexico's electoral system for the upper house is unique. Senators serve six-year terms, and three are elected from each state and the federal district. The party with the most votes wins two Senate seats, and the party finishing second is automatically awarded the third seat. An additional thirty-two seats are allocated according to PR. Mexican presidents are directly elected every six years in a single round of voting. Elections to the Senate take place at the same time as the presidential elections. Parties must get at least 2 percent of the national vote in order to win seats from the PR lists.

Local Government

Despite being formally federal, Mexico operated very much like a unitary political system under the PRI. Excessive localism and a history of instability and political violence caused by the absence of a weak central authority favored the PRI's centralizing tendencies, despite the federalist constitutional rhetoric. Federal authorities controlled local elections, local budgets, local police forces, and so forth. Until 1997, the mayor of Mexico City was a cabinet member appointed directly by the president.

Mexico currently has thirty-two states and a Federal District of Mexico City, each with its own constitution and unicameral legislature.[9] States are subdivided into county governments (called *municipios*). State governors, county councils, and county presidents are elected directly, although until recently PRI leaders handpicked them. Until 1988, all governors were from the PRI, although in the 1980s only widespread electoral fraud prevented opposition victories. Indeed, some of the first serious opposition to PRI hegemony came at the local level, especially in Mexico's prosperous north, where unpopular PRI local leaders and state governors were successfully defeated by opposition candidates. The PRI's use of widespread electoral fraud at the local level helped ignite regional opposition to the party's heavy-handed centralist policies. The first opposition governor took power in 1989 in the state of Baja California Norte. In the 1990s, the PRI began to accept opposition victories in numerous local elections, and by the end of that decade opposition parties controlled seven governorships.

LOCAL RESISTANCE TO GLOBALIZATION

Mexico's federal government has enthusiastically embraced foreign investment as a way to provide jobs for Mexico's poor. No region needs jobs more than the poverty-stricken state of Oaxaca, home to many of Mexico's indigenous poor. But in December 2002, the city council of Oaxaca voted to prohibit the construction of a McDonald's restaurant in the city's historic and picturesque zocalo (town square). Oaxaca has long prided itself on its reputation as Mexico's culinary capital, and the zocalo has been an important venue for protests against federal policy. The city council responded to a grassroots protest movement that collected almost 10,000 signatures, another sign of the reemergence of an autonomous civil society after decades of PRI rule.

Mexican states have important powers, but their sovereignty is far more circumscribed by federal authorities, especially the federal bureaucracy, than is state sovereignty in other federal systems, such as in the United States, Canada, and Germany. The PRI regime limited local autonomy by retaining tight control over public funds, controlling about 85 percent of all revenues collected. Under Fox, this figure was substantially reduced, suggesting that local government will play an enhanced role in Mexico's future.

Although in the 1980s and 1990s state and local politics provided the first opportunities for Mexico's anti-PRI opposition, some local and state offices (especially in rural areas) remained PRI strongholds long after the party lost the presidency in 2000. A good example is the rural west-coast state of Guerrero, where the PRI retained a lock on state government until being ousted by the leftist PRD in the gubernatorial elections of 2005.

POLITICAL CONFLICT AND COMPETITION

The Party System

Under the Partido Revolucionario Institucional (PRI), opposition parties were mostly tolerated; some were even encouraged to exist to give superficial legitimacy to the PRI-dominated system. The PRI skillfully cultivated and selectively co-opted all the opposition parties, which were, in general, weak and divided until the 1980s. The PRI also periodically altered the election laws to increase the presence of the opposition in the legislature while using electoral fraud to retain control of the presidency and key governorships.

THE PARTIDO REVOLUCIONARIO INSTITUCIONAL

The PRI was founded in 1929 as a way of ending Mexico's often violent struggle for political power. From the start, the PRI was viewed as a party representing the interests of the Mexican state. During its long rule, the PRI became increasingly indistinguishable from the state, and the immense power of Mexico's presidents resulted from their effective control over both the party and the state.

A key element of the PRI's exercise of power was the use of **patron-client relationships**, in which powerful government officials delivered state services and access to power in exchange for the delivery of political support. The patron-client relationships operated from the top of the hierarchy, dominated by the PRI-controlled presidency, down to the very poorest segments of society. At the elite level, vast informal networks of personal loyalty, known as **camarillas** (political cliques), were far more important than ideology.

The PRI also maintained control over the state through its ability to mobilize and control mass organizations. During the presidency of **Lázaro Cárdenas**, worker and peasant organizations were created and then integrated into the PRI structure. By using the state to channel patronage to PRI mass organizations, independent mass organizations were rendered marginal and impotent. Mexico's business elite duly lavished the PRI with campaign donations. One notorious example was a 1993 dinner, hosted by President Carlos Salinas, at which two dozen of Mexico's top business leaders were asked to give US$25 million each to the PRI.

The PRI has no clear or consistent ideology other than political opportunism. Over the past century, it sought mainly to control political power, and PRI governments varied greatly with each presidency. For example, redistributive and nationalist economic policies implemented during the Cárdenas presidency (1939–1940) were directly contradicted by subsequent PRI presidents. All PRI leaders claimed to represent the legacy of the Mexican Revolution, but that legacy is ambiguous.

Given that PRI presidents supported very different types of political economic policies, why was there not more open dissent within the PRI? In part, dissent was not strong because the PRI wrote electoral rules that made it virtually impossible for dissident PRI factions to form new parties and win elections.

Beginning in 1982, the PRI slowly but steadily lost support in presidential, congressional, and local elections. Some of the decline was a direct result of Mexico's rapid urbanization: while rural Mexicans were particularly susceptible to local PRI bosses, urbanites were better educated, wealthier, and more politically independent. The PRI also suffered from a reduction in the state's ability to dispense patronage during tough economic times. The economic austerity policies of the 1990s, a cornerstone of the government's neoliberal policies, undoubtedly cost it a number of votes.

Ironically, the erosion of the PRI's political power in the 1990s was also a partial consequence of its attempt at democratic reform. Seeking to enhance its democratic legitimacy, the government in the 1990s spent over US$1 billion to implement a high-tech electoral system that greatly reduced electoral fraud.

Even with its historic defeat in the July 2000 presidential elections, the PRI controls more than half of Mexico's governorships. The PRI gained sixteen seats in the July 2003 midterm lower house elections, but its disappointing performance in 2006 continued the steady decline that had begun in the mid-1990s.

Since losing the presidency in 2000, the PRI has been rudderless. As a party designed to serve sitting presidents, it no longer has a clear leader. The official party leadership, the PRI legislative delegation, and PRI governors have all wielded considerable power and have produced what one observer has called "a hydra-headed behemoth."[10] Recent changes in the PRI structure, however, have led to the direct election of a party president.[11] Whether the PRI can transform itself from the perennial party of the state to an effective force of political opposition remains to be seen. Its 2006 presidential candidate, Roberto Madrazo, ran a lackluster campaign and was widely perceived as an old-style PRI machine politician.

THE LEFT

After the revolution, the PRI attempted to occupy the political space traditionally occupied by leftist parties, even though it usually pursued economic policies traditionally identified with the right. Because the PRI regime had its leftist phases, especially during the presidency of Lázaro Cárdenas, and because Mexico's foreign policy often supported leftist governments and leftist movements elsewhere in Latin America, there was little real political space to be occupied by leftist parties.

Nevertheless, parties of the left existed in Mexico, though most of them supported the PRI. Although the Communist Party was banned until 1979, the Popular Socialist Party (a moderate socialist party) and a few other leftist parties regularly won a few seats in the legislature. A serious leftist political force emerged only in the 1980s, when a leftist faction within the PRI, led by Michoacán governor Cuauhtémoc Cárdenas, bolted from the party.[12] Cárdenas, the son of the former president, then led the newly formed PRD (Partido de la Revolución Democrática) in a coalition of four opposition parties in the 1988 elections.

Bolstered by the high-profile leadership of Cárdenas and boosted by the PRI's loss of popularity, the PRD performed extremely well in the 1988 elections. Many observers believe that had there not been significant electoral fraud, the PRD would have won those elections. Despite this auspicious start, the PRD struggled as a leftist opposition party. It has been plagued by internal infighting and has been unable to capture enough voters outside its strongholds in Mexico City and the south.

The PRD clearly stands to the left of the PRI. During the 1980s and 1990s, it attacked the PRI's neoliberal reforms and neglect of poor Mexicans. It advocated more nationalist and protectionist policies than had traditionally been pursued by the PRI. The PRD candidates at the state and local level have had considerable success, and the PRD has controlled Mexico City's government since 1997, but the party's performance in the 2000 presidential elections was certainly a disappointment. Cárdenas won just over 16 percent of the presidential vote, and the PRD did only slightly better in elections to Congress. The 2000 elections left the PRD as a minor political force whose seats in Congress were not sufficient to build a majority, even if combined with the Partido Acción Nacional (PAN).

The PRD's prospects improved considerably after the 2003 legislative elections. With its allies on the left, it saw its support increase moderately, to about one quarter of the electorate, and it gained thirty-six seats, the biggest gain of any party. The PRD defeated the PRI in key gubernatorial elections in Guerrero and Baja California del Sur in February 2005, although the PRD still controlled only five of Mexico's thirty-two states. The PRD mayor of Mexico City, Andrés Manuel López Obrador, a charismatic populist, emerged as the front-runner in the 2006 presidential election but saw his lead slip away as the conservative opposition portrayed him as a dangerous radical who would threaten Mexico's prosperity and harm relations with the United States.

THE RIGHT

Mexico's main conservative party, the Partido Acción Nacional (PAN), was founded in 1939 by defectors from the PRI. It became the only opposition party to develop a strong organizational presence, especially in its strongholds in northern Mexico and the state of Yucatán. The party emerged as a conservative response to the leftist policies of the PRI during the late 1930s and early 1940s. It advocated Christian democratic ideas, opposing the PRI's anti-clericalism and supporting pro-business policies. Since its base of power was state politics, the PAN became an early advocate of state's rights and opposed the centralization of power that was a feature of Mexican politics under the PRI.

Like many conservative parties, the PAN has been divided historically between Catholic conservatives and more progressive technocrats. The more progressive wing has dominated the party since the late 1980s, but the PRI's adoption of neoliberal economic strategies during that decade threatened to steal the PAN's thunder. The PAN continues to be plagued by internal division, and PAN legislators have been much less willing to follow their own leadership than have PRI legislators.

In the 1990s, the PAN won the governorship of seven states. As the PRI fought harder to deny the PAN electoral victories, it unwittingly gave the PAN an issue that garnered support among Mexicans of all classes: the need to end corruption and guarantee free elections. PAN leaders now preside over one third of all Mexicans. Nonetheless, the PAN suffers from its geographic concentration of the vote (mostly in northern Mexico) and its relative weakness among rural voters, who continue to overwhelmingly support the PRI.

Vicente Fox was not a prototypical PAN leader and did not share much of the social conservatism that is typical of many PAN leaders. His roots were in local government, having served as governor of his home state after a stint in Congress. His charisma and his personal support network allowed him to overcome much opposition within his own party and helped expand the PAN's appeal to new voters. In the 2000 presidential campaign, Fox created his own campaign organization. That organization did not depend on the official PAN hierarchy, which was dominated by Fox's political rivals.[13] Once in office, Fox formed a cabinet that included no members of the PAN's traditionalist wing, and his closest advisers were non-PAN members. He had stormy relations with the more conservative "traditionalist" wing of the PAN, which dominates the legislature and the party hierarchy.

Fox's record in office has been viewed as a mixed bag, but on the whole his administration had trouble meeting the very high expectations that accompanied his historic victory in 2000. His administration delivered on some concrete reform promises.[14] Fox passed a transparency law to facilitate public oversight of government, and he restructured and purged Mexico's powerful and corruption-riddled Federal Judicial Police. He passed legislation to allow some 10 million Mexicans living abroad (many in the United States) to vote in elections. Some progress was made on health care and pension reform, and the Fox administration has been praised for containing inflation. These successes, however, were outweighed by numerous policy failures, due in large part to Fox's inability to work with the opposition-dominated legislature, as well as with the opposition within his own party. Fox failed to end the Zapatista rebellion in Chiapas, was unable to pass a badly needed tax increase to raise revenue for social spending and other public investment, and had a disappointing record on rooting out government corruption. After the PAN's drubbing in the 2003 legislative elections, when the governing party lost one quarter of its seats in the lower house, Fox's status as a lame-duck president was exacerbated, and his government was accused of losing focus.

Mexico's President Felipe Calderón has been involved in conservative politics his entire adult life. His father was a founder of the PAN, and Calderón became leader of its youth wing in his twenties. Calderón held a variety of elected political positions and twice served as a Federal Deputy. He served as party president in the 1990s when the PAN first began to mount a serious challenge to the PRI. Vicente Fox appointed him Secretary of Energy, an important cabinet post in oil-rich Mexico. In a 2005 internal party election, Calderón defeated President Vicente Fox's choice for the 2006 PAN presidential nomination. He narrowly defeated the leftist Manuel López Obrador in the bitterly contested 2006 presidential election. Since taking office, Calderón has generally proven to be a social conservative and a supporter of free-market policies. His campaign to defeat Mexico's drug cartels has delivered mixed results. The resulting violence has tarnished Calderón's previously high approval ratings in opinion polls.

Since the upsets of the 2000 election, the Mexican party system has been in flux. Recent data suggest that only about one quarter of Mexican voters have a strong identification with any party. Beginning in the 1990s, there was a significant partisan "dealignment," in which many voters abandoned the PRI. Not all of those voters have realigned themselves with other parties, however, and a large segment of the Mexican electorate remains "fluid."[15]

This fluidity can be witnessed in the legislative elections since 2000. The 2000 presidential elections were a clear victory for Vicente Fox, but the PRI emerged from the legislative elections as the dominant political force, though it suffered setbacks in its percentage of votes and in the number of seats it won in the lower house. The big loser in those elections was the leftist PRD, which was relegated to third place. The 2003 election dealt a severe blow to the governing PAN and signaled a comeback for the left: the PRD and its allies picked up thirty-six seats in the lower house. The PRI continued to suffer a loss of votes but was able to exploit the electoral system to win sixteen additional seats. The 2006 elections confirmed the steady rise of the PAN and PRD at the expense of the waning PRI. Like his predecessor, President Calderón has had to govern without a majority in the lower house.

Mexico has had a highly competitive electoral system since 2000. The current system has three major parties but operates as a two-party system in most of the country.[16] In Mexico's north and west, the PAN and PRI fight for votes, while in southern Mexico the PRD and PRI are chief rivals. Only in Mexico City and the surrounding areas do all three parties really compete on an equal footing. The PRI remains the only party with support in all regions, while the PRD and the PAN have more regionally concentrated bases of support.

A variety of smaller parties compete for, and regularly win, seats in the Mexican legislature. The most important of these is the Mexican Green Party (PVEM), an environment-oriented party that has little in common with its European counterparts. The PVEM was allied with the leftist PRD in the 1997 elections, then backed the conservative PAN in 2000. In 2003 and 2006, it ran in an alliance with the PRI.

SEATS IN THE CHAMBER OF DEPUTIES, 2003 AND 2006

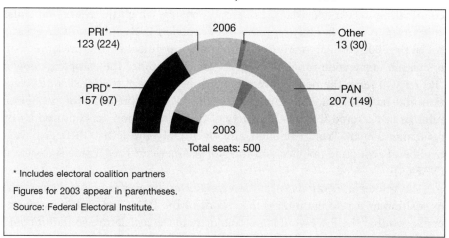

PRI*
123 (224)

2006

Other
13 (30)

PRD*
157 (97)

PAN
207 (149)

2003

Total seats: 500

* Includes electoral coalition partners

Figures for 2003 appear in parentheses.

Source: Federal Electoral Institute.

Elections

During most of the PRI's long reign, elections were more national celebrations of PRI power than competitive electoral campaigns. Every six years, the
country was decked out in the PRI's colors, patronage was dispensed on a
massive scale, and the PRI nominees (in effect, the presumed winners) toured
their constituencies and made speeches.

The 2000 presidential campaign broke with the tradition. The opposition
candidates (Cuauhtémoc Cárdenas, of the PRD, and Vicente Fox, of the PAN)
had announced their intention to run for the presidency several years before
the election, and both candidates were widely assumed to have a lock on their
parties' nominations. The PRI candidate, traditionally named quite late in the
six-year presidential term, was determined for the first time by a PRI primary
vote. As a result, several PRI candidates began campaigning for the nomination early in Zedillo's presidential term, with Francisco Labastida winning the
party primary in a hotly contested race.

The 2000 campaign was also the first to be governed by new electoral
finance rules, which not only sharply limited private contributions but also
provided candidates with public financing. Access to the media by all political parties was far more equitable than ever before. While PRI candidates still
enjoyed an advantage, the playing field was more level than it had been in
past elections. The first truly fair and competitive election was also the first
national campaign in which U.S.-style mudslinging was widespread. The PRI
portrayed Fox as a U.S. lackey, while Fox questioned Labastida's "macho" credentials. Some of the most negative campaigning took place between the two
PRI contestants for the nomination. The 2000 campaign was also the first

truly modern campaign in Mexican history. Television took on a pivotal role, culminating in two televised presidential debates, which the charismatic and engaging Fox won handily over the more wooden Labastida and Cárdenas.

In the 2000 campaign, Mexico's three major political parties presented voters with a fairly wide range of choices. The PRI, under the campaign slogan "Power will serve the people," represented the legacy of the Mexican Revolution and nationalism. The PAN shared the PRI's enthusiasm for neoliberal reforms but offered itself as the party of democratization, as captured by its campaign slogan "Ya!" ("enough already"). Only the leftist PRD criticized neoliberal economic policies and the North American Free Trade Agreement (NAFTA).

The midterm elections of 2003 were viewed by the government and the opposition as a referendum on the record of the PAN. Fox and his supporters hoped that the PAN would get a majority in the legislature so that it could implement its reform agenda without having to deal with a "do-nothing" lower house. The opposition sought a popular mandate for its strategy of opposing reforms that were seen as damaging to Mexico's economy and society. The results were not encouraging for the PAN, but gains made by the PRI and, especially, the PRD seemed to portend an especially competitive presidential election in 2006.

The 2006 presidential campaign was Mexico's first "normal" presidential contest. In 2000, the main issue had been democratization and the defeat of the PRI's semi-authoritarian regime. In 2006, Mexicans faced their first real choice between parties of the right and left. The early front-runner, Andrés Manuel López Obrador (of the leftist PRD) ran a campaign aimed at improving the plight of Mexico's poor. His main opponent, the PAN's Felipe Calderón, advocated a pro-business set of policies aimed at increasing employment. Calderón chipped away at López Obrador's initial lead by questioning his commitment to democracy and by portraying him as a dangerous leftist who would threaten Mexico's economic stability. The campaign was characterized by an unprecedented level of impassioned and negative attack advertisements, ending the relatively benign political discourse that characterized the political campaigns of the PRI era. The outcome of the 2006 election revealed a polarized and divided electorate; Calderón and López Obrador each won just over 35 percent of the vote, and Calderón won by a mere one half of a percentage point.

Civil Society

Under the PRI, Mexican groups and associations were often incorporated into the state in a system known as corporatism. The paternalistic PRI would then mediate among different groups while making sure that no one group chal-

DEMOCRATIZATION, IMPUNITY, AND THE EMERGENCE OF CIVIL SOCIETY IN GUERRERO

From 1929 to 2005, the PRI held power in the state of Guerrero, where international human rights organizations had long complained that the PRI government, the police, and the judiciary, in collusion with powerful landowners (caciques), were conspiring to repress all types of civic groups. A good example was the repression of a variety of environmental groups that sought to stop powerful logging companies from clear-cutting the forests of the Sierra Madre. Felipe Arreaga, an environmental activist who had been particularly successful in his opposition to powerful logging interests, had led a group of farmers who successfully blockaded logging trucks. Local landowners threatened Arreaga and his followers and accused them of being leftist guerrillas. Arreaga was jailed in November 2004 on what human rights groups claim were trumped-up charges of murdering the son of a wealthy landowner who opposed the activists. Arreaga's defenders claim he was jailed as a vendetta for having stopped lucrative logging projects favored by powerful landowners. After the defeat of the PRI state government by the leftist Partido de la Revolución Democrática (PRD) in early 2005, Arreaga was aquitted of all charges and released. The PRD has long claimed that hundreds of Guerrero activists were harassed and killed during the decades of PRI rule. Human rights activists are hopeful that the new PRD state government will signal a democratization of Guerrero politics and break the nexus linking powerful landowners, the judiciary, the police, and the state government.

lenged government power. The PRI was formally divided into three sectors (labor, peasants, and the "popular" middle class), each dominated by PRI-controlled mass organizations. It would be a mistake, however, to assume that the Mexican state could control all autonomous groups in society. To cite one example, the private-sector Confederation of Employers of the Mexican Republic (COPARMEX) became an important voice of opposition to the PRI, instead of supporting the governing party.

BUSINESS

Although the PRI successfully co-opted Mexico's private sector for decades, it can be argued that business groups later emerged as the most powerful source of opposition to PRI rule. Under the PRI, most private-sector interests were channeled into a variety of semi-official organizations, including the National Chamber of Industries and the National Chamber of Commerce. Until 1996, private-sector membership in these organizations was mandatory. Even though the PRI never gave business organizations formal representation within the governing party, business interests wielded power through more informal organizations and channels. The secretive Business Coordinating

Council (CCE), which represents some of Mexico's wealthiest capitalists, had close ties to the Fox government.

The relationship between the business sector and the PRI was complex and often contradictory. In general, the policies of the PRI favored the private sector, especially big business. At the same time, business leaders bitterly opposed attempts by some PRI presidents to enact the social agenda of the Mexican Revolution. In the 1970s, Presidents Luis Echeverría Alvarez and José López Portillo sought to expand the role of the state in the economy, and their policies damaged business-government relations. Although those policies were short-lived, they served to garner opposition to the PRI among northern business interests. The prospect of a PRD victory in 2006 clearly alarmed much of the business sector.

LABOR

The PRI actively supported the unionization of Mexican workers, but the unions were thoroughly integrated into the corporatist system. They received massive subsidies from the state, which made them politically pliant. They enjoyed privileged treatment under the PRI, in part because they were never able to incorporate much of the workforce (about 16 percent, at their peak) and because one third of their members were government employees. The labor movement in Mexico was highly centralized. The dominant labor organization, the **Confederation of Mexican Workers (CTM)**, was created by the PRI and became one of the main pillars of the governing party. The CTM was dominated for over fifty years, until his death in 1997, by Fidel Velázquez Sanchez, a PRI die-hard.

Unions independent of the PRI are a relatively new phenomenon. In 1997, Mexico's independent unions formed the National Union of Workers (UNT) to compete with the CTM. Since the mid-1990s, a series of laws and court decisions have weakened the grip of the formerly official unions. The neoliberal economic policies pursued by the PRI over the past two decades and the PRI's recent loss of national power have created new dilemmas for the CTM. Its membership has clearly suffered from the economic reforms, and its leadership no longer benefits from government patronage. On the one hand, democratic reforms promoted by the PAN are likely to give labor unions more autonomy and a greater ability to contest government policy. On the other hand, the PAN is even more committed to neoliberal economic reform than is the PRI.

THE MEDIA

The PRI maintained a political lock on the media by co-optation more than by coercion. Rather than imposing censorship, the government courted the favor of Mexico's media by purchasing advertisements in pro-PRI media outlets, giving supportive media voices cheap access to infrastructure, and bribing reporters outright. Mexico's largest media conglomerate, **Televisa,** was extremely close to the PRI. By the early 1990s, the PRI had loosened its control of the media somewhat. The government stopped bribing reporters, and the wave of privatizations created a more competitive media environment, allowing for criticism of the PRI.

SOCIETY

Ethnic and National Identity

Alan Riding has described Mexico as a nation proud of its Indian past but ashamed of its Indian present.[17] Under the Partido Revolucionario Institucional (PRI), Mexico glorified and embraced its indigenous ancestry and inculcated pride in the *mestizaje,* or blending of cultures produced by the conquest. Indigenous peoples who have not assimilated into *mestizo* Mexico have been politically marginalized and have been victims of Mexico's worst poverty, whereas Mexico's wealthy elite have tended to be lighter skinned and of European origin.

 The PRI's success in perpetuating the myth of *mestizaje* may help explain how it avoided the kind of ethnically based violence that has plagued Guatemala, its neighbor to the south, as well as other Latin American nations. But that myth was violently shattered on January 1, 1994, when a rebel army made up mostly of Mayan Indians, the **Zapatista Army of National Liberation (EZLN)**, occupied several towns in Mexico's southernmost state of Chiapas.[18]

ETHNIC GROUPS

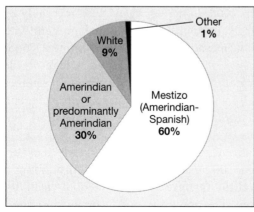

RELIGION

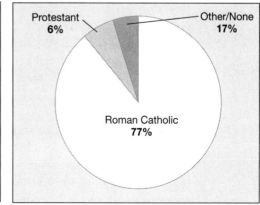

Many viewed the EZLN as solely an indigenous group seeking greater autonomy for Mexico's long-neglected Indian population. It soon became clear, however, that the EZLN included among its demands the democratization of the Mexican political system and an end to the neoliberal reforms that had ravaged the indigenous poor. Chief among the EZLN's concerns was the abrogation of Article 27 of the constitution of 1917, which had mandated land reform. On a more general level, the EZLN was reacting to the devastation caused by neoliberal trade policies that had exposed the inefficient peasant farmers to competition from cheaper foreign imports. The call for democratization was partly a response to the political lock that the PRI maintained on some of Mexico's poorest and most heavily indigenous regions.

The Zapatista uprising was surprisingly popular within Mexico and, together with the economic crisis, helped erode PRI political dominance and accelerate electoral reforms. In 1996, the Zedillo government signed the **San Andres Peace Accords** with the EZLN, promising protection of indigenous languages and granting indigenous communities political autonomy. These provisions were never implemented, however, and Vicente Fox, who claimed he could resolve the Chiapas conflict "in fifteen minutes," was unable to make peace with the Zapatistas. Fox's proposed constitutional amendment aimed at addressing some Zapatista demands was watered down by Congress, and the Zapatistas rejected the outcome. As of this writing, the standoff between the government and the Zapatistas continues with the EZLN controlling some remote communities.

Ideology and Political Culture

Perhaps the most important aspect of Mexican political culture is a profound distrust of the state and the government. Opinion research demonstrates that Mexicans have a far more negative view of their political system and state than do their U.S. counterparts. In 2000, Congress was viewed favorably by only 20 percent of Mexicans.[19] Mexicans' high level of disenchantment with their state and political system has been exacerbated by the government's poor response to many national crises over the past two decades. A high-profile split within the PRI, the massive electoral fraud of 1989, corruption charges against former president Carlos Salinas de Gortari, the Chiapas uprising, and the murder of the PRI's designated presidential candidate were all factors that helped to erode popular confidence in the Mexican system.

These scandals and decades of authoritarian rule may explain why a majority of Mexicans express little or no interest in politics, notwithstanding a temporary surge of interest around the historic 2000 presidential elections. Mexican men express far more interest in politics than do women, and interest in politics increases with levels of education and income. Mexicans on the left of the political system (supporters of the Partido de la Revolución Democrática, or PRD) generally express much higher levels of interest in politics than do Mexicans in the center and on the right.

A serious problem confronting Mexico's attempt to construct a stable democracy is the very low level of political efficacy (the belief that one can make a difference), as expressed in opinion polls. Whereas about one third of U.S. respondents claim to have no ability to influence political outcomes, over half of Mexicans express this view. One positive sign is that the 2000 PRI electoral defeat appears to have restored Mexicans' faith in the fairness of elections, and recent data show that levels of electoral efficacy have risen dramatically.

Unlike Communist regimes, which actively promote political mobilization, Mexico under the PRI was an authoritarian regime that sought to contain and limit popular participation in politics. Mexico's political culture continues to show the effects of decades of authoritarian rule: the country has very low levels of participation in politics, party membership, and political activism. Although there is some evidence of a steady increase in popular political activity since the 1980s, declining voter turnout has continued to be a concern. Turnout for the 2003 elections was only 41.7, percent down from 63.7 percent in 2000. The declines may be explained by the weakening of the PRI electoral machine, the return to "normal" politics after the excitement surrounding the 2003 elections, and the fact that midterm elections usually draw fewer voters.

During the authoritarian regime of the PRI, the majority of Mexicans professed sympathy for no political party. The erosion of PRI hegemony and the increasing competitiveness of elections have led far more Mexicans to identify with a political party. By 2000, the PRI and the Partido Acción Nacional (PAN) each enjoyed the support of about one third of the electorate, and the PRD was supported by about 10 percent. Opinion data show quite clearly that the Mexican electorate is anchored on the center right. The leftist PRD suffers from the fact that only about 20 percent of Mexicans identify themselves as being on the left. Although more Mexicans define themselves as being on the left or right than do U.S. respondents, Mexicans have been steadily gravitating toward the center.

The erosion of PRI political hegemony has also been accompanied by a dramatic shift in the social-class basis of Mexico's parties. Wealthy and middle-class Mexicans abandoned the PRI in droves between 1989 and 2000. By 2000, the PRI depended mostly on the support of lower-class Mexicans, though the PAN had nearly the same amount of support among poor voters. Indeed, one of the remarkable changes between 1989 and 2000 was the PAN's ability to garner support from all classes.

Opinion research reveals that most Mexicans favor democracy over author-itarianism. When compared with U.S. respondents, however, Mexicans are far more likely to define democracy in terms of equality than in terms of free-dom. The inability of democracy to remedy Mexico's staggering inequality or halt the violence of Mexico's drug wars could potentially undermine Mexican support for democracy.

POLITICAL ECONOMY

The leaders of the Mexican Revolution had a complex and often contradic-tory set of goals. Some of the revolutionaries were middle-class landowners who sought greater political democracy, others sought major socioeconomic (especially land) reform, and others were mostly interested in restoring polit-ical order while eliminating the dictatorship of Porfirio Díaz.

Between 1917 and 1980, leaders of the Partido Revolucionario Institu-cional (PRI) agreed on some main features of the Mexican economy. First, Mexico's industrialization would be encouraged through import-substitution policies, which employed high tariffs to protect Mexican industries and agri-culture. Government policies provided Mexican entrepreneurs with subsidized credit and energy and very low taxes. The PRI's ability to control labor and therefore labor costs also benefited Mexico's entrepreneurs. Second, Mexico was to have a capitalist economy, but the Mexican state played an important role in key sectors of the economy, though far less than in socialist economies.

Despite this general consensus, economic policies of the PRI presidents between 1917 and 2000 fluctuated a great deal. The nationalists, usually asso-ciated with the left wing of the PRI, placed more emphasis on redistribution of income, plenty of state social spending, and a strong state presence in the economy. Their economic policies tended to be strongly nationalistic, and they sought greater economic independence from the United States.

President Lázaro Cárdenas, who served from 1934 to 1940, was the most impor-tant advocate of economic naturalism. Cárdenas was a mestizo revolutionary gen-eral who became governor of the state of Michoacán. He used the PRI to organize and mobilize Mexico's workers and peas-ants, and he was the first president to imple-ment the land reform called for in the constitution of 1917. Cárdenas gave 180,000

LABOR FORCE BY OCCUPATION

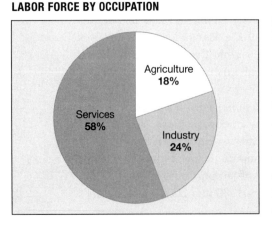

Agriculture
18%

Services
58%

Industry
24%

peasant communities grants of land, called *ejidos,* providing land to some 750,000 landless Mexicans. He integrated peasants and workers into state-controlled unions, and he strengthened the Mexican state by nationalizing the foreign-dominated oil industry and creating a state oil monopoly (**Pemex**). More than any other Mexican president, Cárdenas embodied the socialist aspects of the Mexican Revolution. At the same time, his policies won the PRI the enduring political loyalty of Mexico's workers and peasants. Future Mexican presidents never addressed the socioeconomic aspirations of the Mexican constitution as much as Cárdenas did, but the presidencies of Adolfo López Mateos (1958–1964), Luis Echeverría Álvarez (1970–1976), and José López Portillo (1976–1982) followed policies that mirrored the views of the PRI nationalist left.

The liberals—including Miguel Alemán Valdés (1946–1952), Gustavo Díaz Ordaz (1964–1970), Miguel de la Madrid Hurtado (1982–1988), and Carlos Salinas de Gortari (1988–1994)—favored economic growth over redistribution. They tended to favor freer trade, increased foreign investment in the Mexican economy, and better relations with the United States. President Díaz Ordaz strongly favored economic growth over distribution, and his policies favored big business and agricultural exporters. De la Madrid and Salinas undertook a major change in Mexico's political economic policies by liberalizing its statist economy, abandoning long-entrenched social commitments (like land reform), and entering the General Agreement on Tariffs and Trade (GATT) in 1986 and the North American Free Trade Agreement (NAFTA) with the United States and Canada in 1994. Since 2000, PAN presidents Fox and Calderón have continued these liberal economic policies.

THE DIMENSIONS OF THE ECONOMY

In terms of its aggregate wealth, Mexico is a relatively prosperous developing country and, compared with other developing countries, fairly industrialized. It is currently the world's eighth-largest exporter. Industry accounts for about one quarter of its GDP, and agriculture now accounts for only 8 percent. The country is also rich in natural resources, especially oil, which is its chief economic asset. Since the presidency of Lázaro Cárdenas, Mexican oil has been controlled by the state monopoly, Pemex.

From the 1940s to about 1980, the Mexican economy grew spectacularly, in what has often been called the **Mexican miracle**. Bolstered by the peace and stability of the PRI regime, and benefiting from a steady increase in U.S. investment, Mexico became more industrialized, urban, and educated. Its economy also became more heavily dependent on the United States. By 1962, the United States accounted for 85 percent of all foreign investment in Mexico. Mexico sent two thirds of its exports to the United States, and the same percentage of its imports came from the United States. The U.S.-Mexican economic relationship, however, was (and remains) asymmetrical: the U.S. economy is far more vital to Mexico than is Mexico's to the United States.

ECONOMIC CRISES OF THE 1970s AND 1980s

In the 1970s, Mexican presidents used the country's vast oil wealth to support massive government spending in an attempt to alleviate chronic inequality and poverty. The spending fueled inflation and began to erode the value of the peso, Mexico's currency. Mexico incurred vast debts from foreign lenders, who viewed the oil-rich country as a trustworthy borrower. By the 1980s, oil accounted for over two thirds of the value of Mexico's exports. A major drop in world oil prices in 1981 exposed the shaky foundation of Mexico's economy, and Mexico came close to defaulting on its international debt in August 1982.

The response by Presidents de la Madrid and Salinas was to abandon the decades-old mercantilist model of protectionism and state interventionism and embrace neoliberal economics, thus beginning a reversal of the country's political economy. By terminating the constitution's promise of land reform and opening up Mexico to a flood of cheap agricultural imports, the government in effect devastated many of Mexico's poorest peasants. The country's steady economic recovery in the late 1980s and early 1990s was upset in 1994 and 1995 by its most severe economic depression since the 1930s. In December 1994, the value of the Mexican peso collapsed, and the Mexican economy was saved only by the International Monetary Fund's largest bailout ever. Between 1994 and 1996, real wages dropped 27 percent, and an estimated 75 percent of Mexicans fell below the official poverty line.[20] Mexico had embraced free trade and globalization as a response to the economic crisis of the early 1980s, but its response had made it even more vulnerable to economic instability.

NAFTA AND GLOBALIZATION

The North American Free Trade Agreement has drastically reduced (and will soon eliminate) most tariffs on agricultural goods traded among Mexico, Canada, and the United States. As a result, Mexico has been flooded by U.S. products (such as corn and pork) that cost one fifth as much to produce as similar Mexican products. NAFTA has doubled the amount of food that Mexico imports from the United States, thereby lowering Mexican food prices but creating a massive crisis for millions of Mexico's farmers. About one fifth of Mexicans work in agriculture, and the vast majority are poor subsistence farmers who will be hurt the most by NAFTA competition. As a result, Mexico will lose millions of jobs in agriculture. NAFTA has also exacerbated the gap between the wealthy north and the impoverished south.[21]

In many other ways, however, NAFTA benefits Mexico. Manufacturing exports to the United States have skyrocketed, growing at an average rate of

75 percent annually since NAFTA went into effect.[22] Greater access to U.S. markets has been a boon to Mexico's fruit and vegetable producers, who now supply much of the U.S. winter market, although exports of agricultural goods have grown very modestly compared with those of manufactured goods. Cheaper imports have benefited a wide variety of Mexican producers and consumers.

Mexico's embrace of NAFTA has clearly created a more diversified economy. In the 1980s, oil made up about two thirds of the country's exports. Mexico now exports a wider variety of goods, but it is extremely dependent on the U.S. market, to which it sends 82 percent of all its exports.

Mexico's entry into NAFTA has attracted more direct U.S. investment in Mexico. Much of the investment has gravitated toward **maquiladoras**, factories that import materials or parts to make goods that are then exported. These factories, concentrated along the Mexican-U.S. border, account for about half of all of Mexico's exports, and they now generate more foreign exchange for Mexico than does any other sector, including oil.[23] The maquiladoras have added half a million jobs to Mexico's north, but some critics argue that the operations add relatively little to the Mexican economy, since most materials and technology are imported. Average maquiladora wages are above Mexico's minimum wage but far below the average wage in the manufacturing sector. The concentration of maquiladoras in Mexico's wealthier north has exacerbated the country's severe north-south income gap.

Whether NAFTA has created more winners than losers is a hot topic of debate within Mexico.[24] One result of the new pressures created by NAFTA has been the increased flow of Mexicans to the United States in search of employment. What is clear, however, is that NAFTA has dislocated millions of Mexicans and will create new political and economic challenges for future Mexican administrations.

ECONOMIC POLICIES AND ISSUES

Despite the Mexican Revolution's commitment to greater equality and the efforts of some reformist presidents to help the poor, Mexico was and is a country of massive inequality. The Mexican novelist Carlos Fuentes has called Mexico a country "where 25 people earn the same as 25 million."[25] The pre-1980s mercantilist policies were unable to address the persistence of massive poverty in Mexico, and the more recent shift to neoliberal policies has only increased the gap between rich and poor. In 2000, the poorest 40 percent of the population earned about 12 percent of Mexico's income while the wealthiest 10 percent earned about 40 percent, and the gap has widened since 1984.[26] *Forbes* magazine listed twenty-four Mexicans in its 1994 annual report on the "swelling roster of global billionaires." Only the United States, Germany, and Japan had more billionaires at the time. A year earlier, there were thirteen

Mexicans on this list, and in 1987, when the magazine first began compiling its list, there was only one.[27] These huge inequalities in income are mirrored by a variety of social indicators. For example, in 1998 infant mortality was four times higher among the poorest 20 percent of Mexicans than among the richest 20 percent, and the poorest 10 percent of Mexicans averaged only 2.1 years of education, whereas the richest 10 percent average over 12 years of education.[28]

The Mexican government has estimated that about one fourth of Mexicans lack enough money for food and clothing. One third of all workers earn less than the minimum wage (about US$4 per day). Poverty in Mexico is most pronounced in rural areas, still home to some 23 million people. Despite the legacy of land reform, most rural Mexicans cannot support themselves on their tiny plots of land, and many are forced to seek work as migrant laborers. Millions have migrated to already overcrowded urban areas, seeking employment and a better life, and millions more have emigrated to the United States for the same reasons.

Mexico's wealth is also geographically unequal. Northern Mexico is far wealthier than the central and southern regions. While the north is characterized by large-scale export agriculture (benefiting from proximity to the U.S. market), land use is much more fragmented in the south. Southern Mexico has a far poorer infrastructure, lower levels of education, and more poverty.

Another indicator of the degree of inequality in Mexico is the tremendous size and importance of the **informal sector**. A conservative estimate is that over 9 million Mexicans (perhaps as much as one third of the total workforce) are employed in the underground economy as informal vendors of goods and services. Mexican cities are full of *ambulantes* (street vendors), which local governments have fought unsuccessfully to regulate. These workers pay no taxes on their earnings but enjoy few protections and benefits.

Efforts to redress these inequalities through increased social spending have been hampered by Mexico's inability to collect taxes, especially when compared with wealthier industrialized countries. Attempts to raise taxes meet with widespread skepticism in part because Mexico's traditionally corrupt state is simply not trusted.

FOREIGN RELATIONS AND THE WORLD

Mexico's foreign relations have always been heavily molded by its complex relationship with the United States. In the political turmoil of the nineteenth century, Mexico lost half its territory to an expanding United States. Indeed, Mexico's humiliation at the hands of the United States has been a major theme in the Mexican psyche. Even Porfirio Díaz, whose dictatorship promoted closer ties to the United States, is reported to have lamented, "Poor Mexico! So far from God and so close to the United States." One goal of the Mexican Revolution (and the aim of much of its official rhetoric) was to restore the sovereignty and power of Mexico on the global stage. The Partido Revolucionario Institucional (PRI) leadership clearly sought a system that would restore stability to the Mexican system and prevent future attacks on Mexican sovereignty. In the early years of the revolution, foreign economic interests were sharply curtailed, and foreign oil companies were nationalized. Mexico under the PRI began to assert itself as an independent and autonomous state, gradually gaining the status of a regional power within Latin America.

During and after World War II, Mexico became a closer ally of the United States while still asserting an independent voice in its foreign policy. From the 1960s through the 1980s, Mexico opposed U.S. foreign policy in Latin America, fostered a close relationship with Fidel Castro's Cuba (a U.S. archenemy), and supported revolutionary movements in the regions that often opposed the United States.

Many Mexicans were proud that their country could act so independently of the United States in the arena of foreign policy. The economic catastrophe of the 1980s and Mexico's decision to abandon revolutionary economic policies and liberalize its economy made clear the limits to Mexican independence in its foreign affairs. In exchange for massive economic aid in the 1980s, Mexico was pressured to curtail its opposition to U.S. foreign policy in Latin America.

After the election of Vicente Fox in 2000, Mexico moved closer to the United States on most foreign policy issues.[29] Fox sought to work closely with President George W. Bush in the hope of gaining new agreements on immigration and trade. Since the 1994 North American Free Trade Agreement (NAFTA), Mexico's increased economic dependence on the United States has clearly limited its international assertiveness. That did not stop the Fox administration from opposing the U.S. invasion of Iraq in 2003, a stance that led to a cooling of U.S.-Mexican relations. Immediately after taking office in 2009, the U.S. administration of Barack Obama took steps to improve relations with Mexico and collaborate to stem growing drug violence.

Mexico today is clearly at a crossroads. With the consolidation of democracy and a more prosperous economy based on exports to the United States, Mexicans can feel proud of their accomplishments. At the same time, now that Mexico has vanquished authoritarian rule, it must deal with a number of historical problems. It must find a way to reestablish the legitimacy of the state (by reducing corruption), restore public order (by reducing crime and improving the judiciary), and perhaps most important, address the growing inequality between the winners and the losers in its political economic transition.

CURRENT ISSUES

CRIME AND CORRUPTION: THE COLOMBIANIZATION OF MEXICO?

The Mexican Revolution successfully strengthened state power and autonomy and ended endemic violence in Mexico. Yet the long domination of the Partido Revolucionario Institucional (PRI), its dependence on patron-client relations, its co-optation, and its electoral fraud all fostered a culture of corruption and lawlessness that now increasingly threatens the state and its capacity, autonomy, and legitimacy. The ability of the state to impose its authority has eroded because of the explosion of crime since the 1980s. In Mexico City, reported crimes doubled from 1993 to 1997, and an estimated 90 percent of all crime in the city goes unreported. Kidnappings have become alarmingly common; they rose almost 40 percent between 2005 and 2007. Well over six thousand Mexicans were killed in 2008 in violence associated with the war between the Mexican drug cartels themselves, and between the cartels and the Mexican state.[30] Statistics like these have led some to wonder whether Mexico could become a "failed state."[31]

The spectacular increase in crime has a variety of causes. To some extent, it coincides with the economic crisis that began in the 1980s and was exacerbated by the 1994–1995 economic depression. The governments of the 1980s and 1990s pursued painful neoliberal economic reforms while weakening the welfare state established by the PRI. The rise in crime rates may also be related to the steady decline in the PRI's hegemony and the decentralization and democratization of the political system. In the case of most postauthoritarian democracies, crime tends to flourish when the power of an authoritarian state is weakened and a painful economic transition is under way. The increase of drug trafficking has also been accompanied by a dramatic increase in violent crime.

What is perhaps most alarming from the perspective of the legitimacy of the state is that Mexico's various police forces (local, state, and federal) contribute directly to the problem. Mexican police are generally poorly trained and poorly paid, making them susceptible to corruption. Even worse, the police have been known to be involved in a wave of kidnapping and extortion crimes that have shocked the country. A survey in the 1990s showed that between 1981 and 1990, the proportion of Mexicans who thought it acceptable to accept a bribe or buy stolen goods rose from 32 percent to 55 percent.[32]

Over the past two decades, Mexico has seen an alarming rise in drug trafficking, driven by the growing market for illegal drugs north of the border and facilitated by a Mexican legal system that is both weak and corrupt.[33] Mexico has experienced a dramatic growth of drug-related gang violence and a steady stream of corruption scandals involving drug money. Shortly after his inauguration, President Calderón called on the army to combat the drug cartels, and in 2009 Calderón sent troops to replace corrupt local police forces in some cities along the United States border. The military response only emboldened the drug cartels, who initiated a campaign of assassination aimed at the police and anti-drug authorities. A series of discoveries in 2008 that implicated Federal anti-drug officials in the drug trade further damaged the government's image. The United States has been alarmed by the growing drug traffic across the U.S.-Mexican border: it is estimated that about 70 percent of all marijuana and cocaine entering the United States arrives through Mexico. U.S. attempts to undertake anti-narcotics operations in Mexico have been attacked as abridging Mexico's sovereignty, and U.S. criticism of Mexico's lackluster anti-narcotics efforts has often raised tensions between the two neighbors. Mexican officals counter that drug cartels take advantage of lax U.S. gun control laws to purchase most of their weapons north of the border. In 2009 the Obama adminisration acknowleged that Mexico's drug wars are a shared problem and vowed to work with Mexico to address the threat.

MIGRATION

There is a long history of Mexicans emigrating across the 2,000-mile U.S.-Mexico border.[34] Mexicans have long argued that the United States depends on Mexican immigrants and that their right to work in the United States should

IN COMPARISON	THE IMPORTANCE OF FOREIGN REMITTANCES TO THE MEXICAN ECONOMY

Do you receive money from relatives living abroad? Percent answering yes:

Country	Percent
Nigeria	38
Mexico	23
Russia	7
India	6
South Africa	5
Brazil	2
China	1

Source: Pew Center for the People and the Press, 2007.

be guaranteed through bilateral agreements. But many Americans have focused on the negative effects of Mexican emigration to the United States. Why has there been such a steady flow of Mexicans into the United States? Most of them come because of the higher standard of living in the United States, although the first wave of immigrants were also fleeing the violence of the Mexican Revolution. During the severe labor shortages of World War II, the United States established the **Bracero Program**, which allowed over 4 million Mexicans to work temporarily in the United States between 1942 and 1964. Today, there are almost 11 million Mexicans living in the United States (about 10 percent of Mexico's total population and 4 percent of the U.S. population). According to some estimates, the amount of foreign remittances sent to Mexico by Mexicans living outside the country has grown to almost US$20 billion annually, making it the largest single source of foreign exchange (even larger than revenue earned from oil exports).[35]

From 1965 to 1986, an estimated 5.7 million Mexicans emigrated to the United States, of whom 81 percent were undocumented.[36] The United States operated a "de facto guest-worker program," whereby border enforcement was tough enough to prevent a flood of immigration but not so strict as to prevent a steady flow of cheap and undocumented labor.[37] The costs of illegal immigration were raised just enough that only about one in three undocumented Mexicans could be caught and returned. Most emigrants who tried to enter the United States succeeded, although not on the first try. The U.S. attempt to enforce border control was largely symbolic, but it never threatened the availability of cheap labor. The dramatic growth of undocumented Mexican immigrants, especially after the economic crisis in Mexico during the early 1980s, became a political crisis in the United States during the 1980s and 1990s. The result was the 1986 U.S. **Immigration Reform and Control Act (IRCA)**, which imposed sanctions on employers of illegal aliens and toughened the enforcement of immigration laws. At the same time, it provided an amnesty for longtime undocumented workers and legalized about 2.3 million Mexican immigrants.[38] In the late 1990s, however, illegal immigration continued to skyrocket. In 2006, the U.S. administration of George W. Bush proposed tougher border controls as well as measures aimed at giving legal status to more Mexicans living in the United States.

NOTES

1. For a good overview of the development of the Mexican state, see Alan Knight, "The Weight of the State in Modern Mexico," in James Dunkerley, ed., *Studies in the Formation of the Nation State in Latin America* (London: Institute of Latin American Studies, 2002), pp. 212–52.
2. Quoted in www.libertyhaven.com/countriesandregions/latinamerica/mexicomyths. shtml (accessed 25 July 2005).

3. Pamela Starr, "Fox's Mexico: Same As It Ever Was?" *Current History* (February 2002), pp. 58–65.

4. For the best English-language overview, see Luis Carlos Ugalde, *The Mexican Congress: Old Player, New Power* (Washington, D.C.: Center for Stategic and International Studies, 2000).

5. Ugalde, *The Mexican Congress*, p. 102.

6. Ugalde, *The Mexican Congress*, p. 146.

7. Ginger Thompson, "Congress Shifts Mexico's Balance of Power," *New York Times*, 21 January 2002, p. A6.

8. Jodi Finkel, "Judicial Reform as Insurance Policy: Mexico in the 1990s," *Latin American Politics and Society*, 47, no. 1 (Spring 2005), pp. 87–111.

9. Wayne Cornelius, Todd Eisenstadt, and Jane Hindley, eds., *Subnational Politics and Democratization in Mexico* (San Diego, CA: Center for U.S.-Mexican Studies, 1999), and R. Andrew Nickson, *Local Government in Latin America* (Boulder, CO: Lynne Reinner, 1995), pp. 199–209.

10. Starr, "Fox's Mexico," p. 62.

11. Joy Langston, "Why Rules Matter: Changes in Candidate Selection in Mexico's PRI, 1988–2000," *Journal of Latin American Studies*, 33 (2001), pp. 485–511.

12. Kathleen Bruhn, *Taking on Goliath: Mexico's Party of the Democratic Revolution* (University Park, PA: Penn State Press, 1997).

13. Starr, "Fox's Mexico," p. 60.

14. For a good overview, see Chappell Lawson, "Fox's Mexico at Midterm," *Journal of Democracy*, 15 (2004), pp. 339–50.

15. Lawson, "Fox's Mexico at Midterm," p. 144.

16. Joseph Klenser, "Electoral Competition and the New Party System in Mexico," paper presented at the annual meeting of the Latin American Studies Association, Washington, D.C., 6–8 September 2001.

17. Alan Riding, *Distant Neighbors* (New York: Vintage, 1989), p. 199.

18. Three excellent overviews are Tom Hayden, ed., *The Zapatista Reader* (New York: Thunder's Mouth Press, 2002); Lynn Stephen, *Zapata Lives: Histories and Cultural Politics in Southern Mexico* (Berkeley: University of California Press, 2002); and Chris Gilbreth and Gerardo Otero, "Democratization in Mexico: The Zapatista Uprising and Civil Society," *Latin American Perspectives*, 28, no. 4 (July 2001), pp. 7–29.

19. Data in this section are drawn from Roderic Ali Camp, *Politics in Mexico*, 4th ed. (New York: Oxford University Press, 2003), ch. 3.

20. Paul Cooney, "The Mexican Crisis and the Maquiladora Boom: A Paradox of Development or the Logic of Neoliberalism?" *Latin American Perspectives*, 28, no. 3 (May 2001), pp. 55–83.

21. Rafael Tamayo-Flores, "Mexico in the Context of the North American Integration: Major Regional Trends and Performance of Backward Regions," *Journal of Latin American Studies*, 33 (2001), p. 406.

22. Tamayo-Flores, "Mexico in the Context of the North American Integration," pp. 377–407.

23. Cooney, "The Mexican Crisis and the Maquiladora Boom."

24. Thomas J. Kelly, "Neoliberal Reforms and Rural Poverty," *Latin American Perspectives*, 28, no. 3 (May 2001), pp. 84–103.

25. Quoted in Nicolas Wilson, "What's Wrong with This Picture?" *Business Mexico*, 4 (April 1997), p. 22.

26. Roderic Ali Camp, *Politics in Mexico*, 4th ed. (New York: Oxford University Press, 2003), p. 251.

27. John Summa, "Mexcio's New Sugar-Billionaires," *Multinational Monitor*, November 1994, http://multinationalmonitor.org/hyper/issues/1994/11/mm1194_09.html (accessed 23 July 2005).

28. "Rich Is Rich and Poor Is Poor," Survey: Mexico, *Economist*, 26, October 2002.

29. Stephen Morris and John Passé-Smith, "What a Difference a Crisis Makes: NAFTA, Mexico, and the United States," *Latin American Perspectives*, 28, no. 3 (May 2001), pp. 124–49.

30. Michael J. Mazarr, *Mexico 2005: The Challenges of the New Millennium* (Washington, D.C.: Center for Strategic and International Studies, 1999), p. 102.

31. Much to the chagrin of Mexicans, a 2009 study by the U.S. Pentagon warned that drug violence could turn Mexico into a failed state.

32. Mazarr, *Mexico 2005*, p. 103.

33. Victoria Malkin, "Narcotrafficking, Migration, and Modernity in Rural Mexico," *Latin American Perspectives*, 28, no. 4 (July 2001), pp. 101–28.

34. Douglas Massey, Jorge Durand, and Nolan Malone, *Beyond Smoke and Mirrors: Mexican Immigration in an Era of Economic Integration* (New York: Russell Sage Foundation, 2002).

35. "Rise Report in Remittances to Mexico," *Seattle Times*, 15 (April 2005), p. A14.

36. Massey, Durand, and Malone, *Beyond Smoke and Mirrors*, p. 45.

37. Massey, Durand, and Malone, *Beyond Smoke and Mirrors*, p. 45.

38. Massey, Durand, and Malone, *Beyond Smoke and Mirrors*, p. 49.

GLOSSARY OF KEY TERMS

Bracero Program   A World War II program that allowed millions of Mexicans to work temporarily in the United States.

caciques   Local military strongmen, who generally controlled local politics in Mexico in nineteenth-century Mexico.

Calderón, Felipe   Mexico's current president, elected in 2006.

camarillas   Vast informal networks of personal royalty that operate as powerful political cliques.

Cárdenas, Lázaro   Mexican President from 1934 to 1940 who implemented a radical program of land reform and nationalized Mexican oil companies.

Carranza, Venustiano   The Mexican Revolutionary leader who eventually restored political order, ended the Revolution's violence, and defeated the more radical challenges of Zapata and Villa.

caudillos   National military strongmen, who dominated Mexican politics in the nineteenth and early twentieth centuries.

Chamber of Deputies   The lower house of Mexico's legislature.

Confederation of Mexican Workers (CTM)   Mexico's dominant trade union confederation that was a main pillar of the PRI's authoritarian regime.

Congress   The name of Mexico's bicameral legislature.

constitution of 1917   The document established by the Mexican Revolution that continues to regulate Mexico's political regime.

Cortés, Hernán   The Spanish conqueror of Mexico.

criollos   Mexican-born descendants of Spaniards during the period of Spanish colonial rule.

Cuauhtémoc   The Aztec military leader defeated by the Spanish conquerors.

Díaz, Porfirio   A Mexican dictator who ruled from 1876 to 1910 and was deposed by the Mexican Revolution.

Federal District of Mexico City   Similar to the U.S. District of Columbia, this powerful Mexican district encompasses Mexico's capital city and contains most of its population.

Federal Electoral Institute   An independent agency that regulates elections in Mexico, created in 1996 to end decades of electoral fraud.

Fox, Vicente   Mexico's president since 2000, and the first non-PRI president in over seven decades.

Immigration Reform and Control Act (IRCA)   1986 U.S. immigration legislation that toughened American immigration laws while granting amnesty to many longtime undocumented workers.

informal sector   A sector of the economy that is not regulated or taxed by the state.

Juárez, Benito   A nineteenth-century Mexican president who is today considered an early proponent of a modern, secular, and democratic Mexico.

Labastida, Francisco   The first-ever PRI candidate to lose a presidential election, he was defeated in 2000 by Vicente Fox of the PAN.

latifundistas   Owners of *Latifundia* (huge tracts of land).

Madero, Francisco   An initial leader of the Mexican Revolution and a landowner who sought moderate democratic reform.

maquiladoras   Factories that import goods or parts to manufacture goods that are then exported.

Maya   Mexico's largest indigenous group, concentrated in the south of the country.

mestizos   Mexicans of mixed European and indigenous blood, who make up the vast majority of Mexico's population.

Mexican-American War (1846–1848)   The conflict between Mexico and the United States in which the United States gained one third of Mexican territory.

Mexican miracle   The spectacular economic growth in Mexico from the 1940s to about 1980.

Mexican Revolution   The bloody conflict in Mexico between 1910 and 1917 that established the long-lived PRI regime.

Mexico's War of Independence   A bloody eleven-year conflict that resulted in Mexico's independence from Spain in 1821.

municipios   County-level governments in Mexican states.

Nahuatl   Mexico's second-largest indigenous group, concentrated in central Mexico.

National Action Party (PAN)   A conservative Catholic Mexican political party that until 2000 was the main opposition to the PRI.

North American Free Trade Agrement (NAFTA)   A free trade agreement linking Mexico with the United States and Canada.

Partido Revolucionario Institucional (PRI)   The political party that emerged from the Mexican Revolution to preside over an authoritarian regime that lasted until 2000.

patron-client relationships   A system in which powerful government officials deliver state services and access to power in exchange for the delivery of political support.

Pemex   Mexico's powerful state-owned oil monopoly.

Portillo, José López   Mexican president from 1976 to 1982 who increased the role of the state in the economy and nationalized Mexico's banking system in an attempt to avert a national economic crisis.

Santa Ana, General Antonio López   Mexico's first great *Caudillo*, who dominated its politics for three decades in the mid-nineteenth century.

San Andrés Peace Accords   A 1996 accord that promised to end the Zapatista rebel uprising but was never implemented by the PRI government.

Secretariat of Government   A top cabinet post that controls internal political affairs and a post that was often a stepping-stone to the presidency under the PRI.

Secretariat of the Treasury   Mexico's most powerful economic cabinet minister.

Senate   The upper house of Mexico's legislature.

Supreme Court   Mexico's highest court.

Televisa   Mexico's largest media conglomerate, which for decades enjoyed a close relationship with the PRI.

Villa, Francisco (Pancho)   A northern Mexican peasant leader of the Revolution who, together with Emiliano Zapata, advocated a more radical socio-economic agenda.

the War of the Castes   A massive nineteenth-century uprising of Mexico's indigenous population against the Mexican state.

Zapata, Emiliano   The southern Mexican peasant leader of the Revolution most associated with radical land reform.

Zapatista Army of National Liberation (EZLN)   A largely Mayan rebel group that staged an uprising in 1994, demanding political reform and greater rights for Mexico's indigenous people.

Zedillo, Ernesto   Mexico's president from 1994 to 2000. He implemented political reforms that paved the way for fair elections in 2000.

WEB LINKS

La Jornada **www.jornada.unam.mx** A Mexican daily newspaper

Latin American Network Information Center: Mexico
www.lanic.utexas.edu/la/mexico An encyclopedic collection of links maintained by the University of Texas, Austin

Mexican government offices and agencies
www.mexonline.com/mexagncy.htm

Reforma **www.reforma.com** A Mexican daily newspaper

El Universal **english.eluniversal.com** A Mexican daily newspaper

Zapatista Army of National Liberation **www.ezln.org.mx**

BRAZIL

Head of state and government:
President Luiz Inácio Lula da Silva
(since January 1, 2003)

Capital: Brasília

Total land size: 8,511,965 sq km

Population: 192 million

GDP at PPP: 1.84 trillion US$

GDP per capita at PPP: $9,700

Human development index ranking: 70

BRAZIL

INTRODUCTION

Why Study This Case?

When Brazil successfully launched a rocket into space in October 2004, it became the first Latin American country to do so. Brazil has ambitious plans to sell rockets to the European Space Agency, adding to its already impressive list of high-tech exports. Brazil's successful entry into space exemplifies its many paradoxes. It is the ninth-largest economy in the world, with a dynamic industrial sector. It has strikingly modern cities, such as São Paolo and Rio de Janeiro. Recently Brazil's export-based economy has boomed, and its economic prospects seem limitless with the 2008 discovery of large offshore oil reserves. But it is also plagued by some of the worst poverty, inequality, and indebtedness on the planet, and its cities are burdened by sprawling slums and violence. One Brazilian economist dubbed Brazil "**Belindia**" to denote this odd combination of Belgium's modernity and India's underdevelopment.[1]

Brazil is a highly urbanized society, with over 80 percent of its population living in its cities (six of which have more than 2 million residents), but about half of its land consists of the sparsely populated **Amazon basin**. The Amazon rain forest is often considered to be the lungs of the world, and its rapid destruction has become a major focus for environmentalists. Within Brazil, the Amazon has until recently been viewed most often as a rich resource that needs to be more efficiently exploited to help reduce inequality and poverty and to enhance Brazil's *grandeza* (national greatness).

Given Brazil's history of extreme inequality and its large mass of poverty-stricken citizens, one might expect it to have experienced a mass revolution along the lines of Russia, Mexico, and China. At the very least, one might have assumed a history of political violence similar to that of South Africa during apartheid. But Brazilian history is mostly devoid of such organized violence. For the most part, the country's political elite have retained power skillfully, and Brazil's poor have remained politically disorganized. Since its independence from Portugal, Brazil has alternated between weak democratic regimes dominated by economic elites and authoritarian rule, usually presided over by the military. From 1964 to 1985, a military dictatorship quashed a growing mass movement and suspended most political freedoms. Nevertheless, Brazil experienced a gradual and remarkably peaceful transition to democracy in the mid-1980s, and today it is the world's fourth-largest democracy. Brazilian democracy is characterized by regular elections and broad civil liberties and has enabled a peaceful succession of power. In 2002, Brazilians elected a leftist president, **Luiz Inácio Lula da Silva**, known popularly as

Lula, Brazil's first working-class president (see "Lula," p. 465). Despite fears surrounding his election, democracy has proved remarkably durable, Brazil's economy has boomed, and da Silva was reelected to a second term in 2006.

Despite this admirable political record, serious questions remain about the long-term viability of Brazilian democracy. Can a democratic regime persist when there are extraordinarily high levels of economic inequality? Will the growing wave of crime and lawlessness erode confidence in democracy and the rule of law? Will Brazil's legacy of statism, clientelism, corruption, and political deadlock prevent democratic reforms?

Brazil is a fascinating case in part because of its relatively successful multiracial society. It has the largest African-origin population outside Africa. Despite a brutal history of slavery that lasted until relatively recently (ending in 1888) and persistent racism, Brazilian blacks are more comfortably integrated into society than are their U.S. counterparts. Brazilian society has also integrated Europeans (initially, Portuguese and later Italians, Germans, and Spaniards), Africans, indigenous Americans, and other immigrants with relatively little ethnic tension. Endowed with a gigantic and geographically insulated country and blessed with formidable natural resources, Brazilians have a strong sense of national identity that makes Brazil unlike many of its Latin American neighbors.

Major Geographic and Demographic Features

Brazil's immense size gives it special importance: slightly larger than the continental United States, it is the world's fifth-largest country and occupies almost half of the South American continent. With more than 190 million citizens it is home to one third of Latin America's population.

Brazil shares borders with ten other South American countries, but because most of its population has always been concentrated on its east coast, it historically has had surprisingly little interaction with its neighbors. Brazilians have often looked to Europe instead of their Latin American neighbors. (Brazil's main population centers are geographically closer to Europe than to some parts of South America.)

The concentration of population on the coast has been a major theme in Brazilian politics. In the 1950s, Brazilian leaders sought to shift Brazil's energy westward and open its vast Amazon frontier. In 1960, the capital was moved from the cosmopolitan, coastal Rio de Janeiro to the barren and isolated interior location of **Brasília**, where a futuristic planned city was created. Today Brasília has a population of about 2.5 million.

Brazil's Amazon has only 13 percent of its population but makes up over 60 percent of its landmass. In the 1960s, Brazil's military government began building roads west into the Amazon jungle, seeking to promote a demographic shift westward to alleviate the landless problem, exploit the natural resources of the region, and extend the power of the state into the hinterlands. Waves of impoverished northeasterners migrated to the Amazon to claim land and eke out a living, with mixed success. This colonization of the Amazon region came at a tremendous cost to the natural environment and to its indigenous inhabitants.[2]

Brazil is now overwhelmingly an urban country, but this is a fairly recent development. The economic miracle of the late 1960s and early 1970s drew much of Brazil's rural population into its already overcrowded cities. Immigrants from the countryside helped fuel Brazil's industrial growth but were forced to live in the sprawling **favelas** (urban shantytowns) that ring Brazil's cities. Nowhere is the phenomenon of rapid urbanization more apparent than in São Paolo, Brazil's industrial capital and largest metropolitan area, with about 20 million residents.

Industrialization has also exacerbated a geographic schism in terms of socioeconomic development. Brazil's southeast, originally the center of the coffee boom, has become wealthy, industrialized, and populous; the three southeastern states of Rio de Janeiro, São Paolo, and Minas Gerais now contain nearly half of Brazil's population, generate well over half of its wealth, and contain its most important cities. Meanwhile the northeast, the old center of sugar production, has become less populated and poorer. What once was the population center of Brazil now contains only 28 percent of its inhabitants and has the lowest per capita income. The region is now plagued with depleted soil, fierce international competition in the sugar market, and periodic droughts.

Historical Development of the State

THE RELUCTANT COLONY

Pedro Álvares Cabral first arrived in Brazil in 1500 when he was blown off course on his way to India. He claimed the territory for the Portuguese crown, but Portugal initially paid little attention to it. Unlike the Spaniards, who encountered sophisticated empires and vast mineral wealth in their Latin American colonies, the Portuguese found the land sparsely populated (by between 1 million and 6 million indigenous Americans), and it offered no apparent mineral resources. While the Spaniards focused much of their energy on populating and exploiting their newfound territories, the Portuguese crown continued to focus on the lucrative spice trade with the East, and they built few permanent colonies.

Despite this neglect, the Portuguese established trading posts along their new territory's coast. The early explorers discovered a hardwood that pro-

TIME LINE OF POLITICAL DEVELOPMENT	
Year	**Event**
1500	Portuguese arrive in Brazil
1690s	Gold is discovered
1763	Capital transferred from Salvador to Rio de Janeiro
1822	Pedro I declares Brazilian independence from Portugal
1822–89	Empire, a semi-authoritarian monarchical regime
1899–1930	First Republic, a quasi-democratic regime
1930	Military overthrows the republic and establishes authoritarian rule
1937–45	Rule of Getulio Vargas's Estado Nôvo (New State), an authoritarian regime
1945–64	Second Republic, a democratic regime
1960	The capital is transferred from Rio de Janeiro to Brasília
1964–85	Authoritarian military regime
1985–present	New Republic, a democratic regime
2003	Luiz Inácio Lula da Silva assumes presidency

duced a valuable red dye; its Latin name was Brasile, for which the new territory was named. In response to incursions by the French in the 1530s, the Portuguese crown attempted to take more permanent control of Brazil. The government doled out massive territories (often larger than Portugal itself) to *donatarios* (nobles) who were willing to settle the remote land and defend it from foreigners. Brazil's first capital was established in 1549 in the northeast coastal town of Salvador, also called Bahia.

The Portuguese crown's decision to cultivate sugar in Brazil first transformed the colony from a backwater into a more vital part of the Portuguese Empire. Brazil had unlimited rich land on which to cultivate sugar, but it lacked the necessary labor pool. Initial attempts to enslave the indigenous population backfired: the relatively small population was quickly decimated by European-borne disease, war, and harsh treatment, and the survivors fled deep into Brazil's interior.

By the late sixteenth century, the Portuguese had come to depend on African slaves to maintain the sugar economy. Between 1550 and 1850, between 3 million and 4 million African slaves were shipped to Brazil, and at that time Brazil's African population was far larger than its tiny white minority. Almost half of all Brazilians today have African ancestry.

Unlike the United States, Brazil soon developed a large **mulatto** population (Brazilians of a mixed white and black ancestry). Portuguese settlers also mixed with indigenous people in the interior, resulting in a smaller but still significant *caboclo* population.

The institution of slavery turned Brazil into the world's first great plantation export economy. The slave-based sugar economy generated massive wealth for the white minority and established a pattern that persists today: a tiny (mostly white) elite controls the vast majority of wealth while much of the population lives in poverty.

By the mid-seventeenth century, Brazil's sugar economy had begun a steady decline, caused, in part, by fierce competition from Spanish, French, and Dutch colonies in the Caribbean. The presence of the Portuguese crown was relatively small and was largely concentrated in the sugar-producing areas of the northeast coast.

THE GOLD AND DIAMOND BOOM AND THE RISE OF BRAZIL

The discovery of gold in the 1690s and diamonds in the 1720s forever changed the fate of Brazil. Mineral wealth was concentrated in the southeast and led to a demographic shift southward that has continued to this day; the central interior region, called Minas Gerais (General Mines), became the country's most populous area. The Portuguese began to establish settlements in the interior, and in 1763 the capital was moved south from Salvador to Rio de Janeiro. The seventeenth-century gold boom generated massive wealth, but much of Brazil's gold ended up in Europe.

By the end of the seventeenth century, the Portuguese Empire had weakened in the face of growing British, French, and Dutch power. The Portuguese crown reacted by attempting to tighten its control of its Brazilian colony, imposing unpopular taxes on the colonists. These measures provoked a rebellion in the gold-mining capital of Vila Rica in 1789, but unlike the outcome of rebellion in the United States, the Portuguese crown quickly crushed the uprising. Moreover, the colonial elites, frightened by Haiti's slave rebellion in 1791, were too fearful of the Afro-Brazilian majority to push for outright independence.

THE PEACEFUL CREATION OF AN INDEPENDENT BRAZILIAN STATE

Although Brazilian colonial elites did not advocate independence, the economic development spurred by mineral wealth created demands for increased autonomy and helped establish a distinct Brazilian identity. Furthermore, the colonial elites in the huge territory developed strong regional identities. Ironically, events in Europe more than colonial dissatisfaction paved the way for independence.

Napoléon Bonaparte's invasion of the Iberian Peninsula in 1807 was the catalyst for independence movements in Spanish America. Portugal's monarchy fled the invading French and moved the royal court to Brazil, a de facto recognition that Brazil had become the center of the Portuguese Empire. The arrival of the Portuguese monarch entailed transplanting the Portuguese state bureaucracy to Brazil, and Rio de Janeiro soon became a modern, cosmopolitan capital. Recognizing the importance of its colony, King João VI designated Brazil a kingdom, coequal with Portugal. The king returned to Portugal in 1821 after the end of the Napoleonic Wars, but he left his son Pedro on the Brazilian throne with instructions to support independence.

In this unusual manner, Pedro I became the leader of Brazil's transition to independence and spared the country the kind of bloody wars experienced by much of Spanish America. Pedro declared independence on September 7, 1822, and Portugal offered little resistance. Without its own armed forces and facing the prospect of rebellion by powerful regional elites, Brazil depended heavily on the British, who quickly became its major trading partner.

Emperor Pedro I promulgated a constitution in 1824 and did not behave as an absolutist monarch. Nevertheless, the constitution was essentially authoritarian with a very strong executive. In 1826, Pedro I inherited the Portuguese throne from his father, but shortly thereafter he returned to Portugal and left his own son, Pedro II, on the Brazilian throne. Pedro I's official abdication in 1830 greatly weakened the power of the central state and further enhanced the power of regional elites. Pedro II formally assumed the throne in 1840 from a caretaker regency when he was only fourteen years old, and he ruled Brazil until 1889.

Brazil's peaceful independence movement as well as the presence of reasonably enlightened monarchs during the nineteenth century were crucial to solidifying the Brazilian national identity and, most important, were essential for stemming the countless regional rebellions that plagued the country during its first half century of statehood. Under the Empire (1822–1889), the foundations were laid for a strong central state dominated by the monarch. Brazil was also fortunate to find a new export product to replace sugar and minerals: coffee cultivation began in the 1820s in central and southern Brazil, further drawing economic development southward toward the coffee capital of São Paolo. Bolstered by the continued importation of slaves (which continued until the British banned the slave trade in 1850), Brazil quickly became the world's leading coffee producer.

Although the emperor opposed slavery, the Brazilian state did little to end it, in large part because the economy depended so heavily on slave labor. When the monarchy finally decreed the abolition of slavery in 1888, the conservative Brazilian rural elite begrudgingly accepted the new reality rather than risk a U.S.-style civil war. Slave labor was partly replaced by a massive influx of immigration from Europe.

Politically, Brazil was remarkably stable during the nineteenth century (especially when compared with much of South and North America), in part due to the presence of a reasonably progressive monarchy that played a moderating role in Brazilian society. The monarchy promoted competition and alternation between Brazil's main conservative and liberal political parties. Pedro II purposely kept Brazil's military weak, fearing its involvement in politics, and he actively worked to limit the power of Brazil's Roman Catholic Church.

By the 1880s, the monarchy had a variety of opponents. Urban intellectuals, influenced by European positivism and republicanism, saw the monarchy as antiquated. Abolitionists, frustrated by the monarchy's prolonged acceptance of slavery, viewed it as a reactionary force. Powerful interests, including the military, the Catholic Church, and some regional elites, came to resent it. Faced with a military coup d'état in 1889, Pedro II chose exile instead of war, once again sparing Brazil from the violence that plagued the rest of Latin America.

REPUBLICANISM AND THE CONTINUATION OF OLIGARCHIC DEMOCRACY

Brazil's military overthrew the monarchy and established the Old Republic (1889–1930), whose motto, "Order and Progress" still adorns the Brazilian flag. It turned the republic over to civilian political elites (oligarchs) but replaced the monarchy as arbiter of Brazilian politics. A new constitution, modeled almost entirely on the U.S. Constitution, established a federal system composed of powerful states, a directly elected president, and separation of power between the branches of government. Voting was restricted to literate male adults, and only 3 to 6 percent of the population voted in elections.

Although the monarchy was abolished, political power continued to be held tightly by a somewhat expanded political elite. At the state level, the governorships were controlled by economic oligarchs and their network of local bosses (known as *coroneis*, or colonels). The most powerful states—São Paolo, dominated by the coffee oligarchs, and Minas Gerais, dominated by dairy farmers—competed and cooperated to control the presidency and the national legislature in an arrangement that has been called "the politics of the governors" and "the alliance of coffee and cream." Presidents selected their successors and then used a vast web of patronage and clientelism to deliver the vote.

During the First Republic, the state governments, particularly the most important states of São Paolo, Minas Gerais, Rio de Janeiro, and Rio Grande do Sul, became more powerful at the expense of the federal government. The weak federal government and the decentralization of power suited Brazil's powerful economic interests. The republic effectively mediated and contained political conflict between and within powerful economic interests while excluding all others. But by the early twentieth century, the elitist regime had alienated the growing urban middle class, who sought increased participation; the nascent industrial working class in São Paolo, who sought the creation of a welfare state; and immigrants inspired by radical European ideologies. Demands for political and economic reform were met with harsh repression. New forces of opposition weakened the Old Republic, but the increased infighting between regional leaders was the root cause for the regime's failure.

GETÚLIO VARGAS AND THE NEW STATE

In October 1930, the military once again intervened in politics, this time to end the First Republic. Military leaders installed **Getúlio Vargas**, an elite politician from Rio Grande do Sul who had been a losing candidate for the presidency. Vargas acted quickly to enhance the power of the federal government, replacing elected governors with his appointees. In 1933, a new constitution reduced the autonomy of individual states (revoking their power to tax, for example), while maintaining the elected president and congress. Vargas broke his pledge to hold democratic elections and in 1937 created a new dictatorial regime he called the **Estado Nôvo** (New State).

The Estado Nôvo was clearly inspired by fascist Italy and Germany, whose regimes featured a strong, authoritarian central state, as well as by Franklin Roosevelt's New Deal policies. But Vargas is best viewed more as a typical Latin American **populist** (similar in many respects to Argentina's Juan Perón or Mexico's Lázaro Cárdenas) than as a fascist or social democrat. Unlike both the monarchy and the First Republic, which largely catered to the agricultural elite, Vargas's bases of support included the urban industrialists, middle-class professionals, workers, and sectors of the military. Politically, Vargas favored a model of **state corporatism**, whereby all sectors of society were strongly encouraged to organize within state-controlled associations. Vargas viewed this system as a way to cultivate his base of support among different sectors of society while limiting the ability of civil society to challenge the state. Unofficial unions, groups, and parties were marginalized and harassed. Vargas viewed the state as a paternalistic arbiter of societal conflict.

The authoritarian Estado Nôvo was responsible for some of the first protections and welfare benefits for Brazil's urban workers, and Vargas's regime mobilized labor and raised wages. Vargas established state firms to promote industrialization in key sectors, such as steel, and imposed protectionist policies to shield Brazilian industry from foreign competition (import-

ARE POPULISTS ON THE LEFT OR THE RIGHT?

Latin American populism is hard to label on a left-right spectrum, and populism is a complex, contradictory, and controversial movement. Latin American populists usually challenged established agrarian elites, who had previously dominated politics. They mobilized and sought to improve the lives of urban workers as a way of promoting industrial growth. At the same time, populists were hostile to socialists and Communists, the traditional parties of the left. Unlike those groups, populist leaders advocated capitalist development with a large role for the state. Moreover, the authoritarian methods of populist leaders alienated many leftist intellectuals. Vargas's Estado Nôvo nicely illustrates the many contradictions of populism. His pro-worker rhetoric alarmed entrepreneurs, and his pro-industrial policies alienated traditional rural oligarchs. Vargas never implemented badly needed agrarian reform, and his regime effectively weakened the Communist and socialist left. Indeed, at the time some called Vargas the "father of the poor and the mother of the rich."[3] Key elements of Latin American populism were statism and nationalism, as well as the charismatic nature of the populist leaders. Vargas believed that state sponsorship of industrialization was a way to modernize and enhance the power and prestige of Brazil. The question of how to view populism is more than a historical debate. It has also informed the current controversy surrounding the presidencies of Venzuela's Hugo Chávez and Bolivia's Evo Morales.

substitution industrialization). As a result, Brazil experienced an industrial boom after 1930. Vargas modernized and professionalized the Brazilian military, creating the **Escola Superior de Guerra (Superior War College)**, an institution that further bolstered the confidence and autonomy of the military.

After 1945, pressure mounted for Vargas to convene free elections. In the aftermath of World War II, during which Brazil had sent troops to help defeat fascism in Europe, dictatorships fell out of favor. In October 1945, Brazil's military, emboldened by its enhanced role in the dictatorship and its successful contribution to the Allied war effort, deposed Vargas and convened elections.

THE DEMOCRATIC EXPERIMENT: MASS POLITICS IN THE SECOND REPUBLIC

During the Second Republic (1945–1964) Brazilians had their first real taste of democracy, and for the first time there was real competition for control of the state. The Brazilian masses, mobilized by Vargas during the Estado Nôvo, had become a force to be reckoned with. Suffrage was expanded dramatically (though only about one fifth of the electorate participated during elections), and new national parties, including the Communist Party of Brazil, attempted to appeal to voters.

In 1950, Vargas, the former dictator, was elected to the presidency in a deeply polarized election. He attempted to continue the populist policies of the Estado Nôvo but faced vigorous opposition that controlled the legislature and the press and stymied his policy proposals. In 1954, Vargas broke the deadlock by resigning and shortly after stunned the nation by committing suicide.

In the aftermath of Vargas's death, Juscelino Kubitschek, a follower of Vargas's, was elected president. Often considered Brazil's greatest president, Kubitschek was responsible for a number of grandiose public works, including the moving of Brazil's capital from Rio de Janeiro, on the coast, to Brasília, deep in the interior.

THE BREAKDOWN OF DEMOCRACY AND THE MILITARIZATION OF THE STATE

Following Vargas's dictatorship, democracy was established but never consolidated. Brazil's democracy was deeply polarized between supporters and opponents of Vargas's populist policies. Opponents of Vargas and his successors increasingly called on the military to end democracy to prevent a return to populism. They sought to reduce the role of the state in the economy. Supporters of Vargas and his successors increasingly viewed Brazil's democracy as weak, ineffective, and beholden to the country's wealthy elite. They increasingly advocated leftist policies that called for a growth in the role of the state in the economy through a wave of nationalizations.

This political polarization crystallized during the presidency of **João Goulart** (1961–1964), a minister of labor under Vargas. In the context of the cold war, the military and much of the right viewed Goulart as a dangerous leftist and a potential dictator who reminded them too much of Vargas. His term began inauspiciously, as the military insisted that the Brazilian legislature curtail the president's power before allowing him to take office. Goulart spent much of his first years in power, and a great deal of political capital, passing a national plebiscite that restored his full powers, further alarming his opponents. The political crisis also developed in the context of a severe economic crisis caused by rampant inflation and growing debt. In 1964, after Goulart attempted to rally workers and peasants to his defense and after he clumsily alienated the military by backing some mutinous officers, the Brazilian military, with U.S. support, once again seized power.

The military had intervened in Brazilian politics six times since 1889, but in each instance soldiers had quickly retreated to their barracks, leaving politics to civilian leaders. By 1964, the Brazilian military believed it was time to take control of the state and hold on to it. Encouraged by the United States and politicians on the right, Brazilian military leaders thought they possessed the leadership skills to preserve political order, the power to prevent a feared Communist revolution, and the technical skills to run the economy.

Brazilian military leaders presided over a regime that has often been described as **bureaucratic authoritarian**.[4] Military leaders suspended the constitution and then decreed a new authoritarian one, banned existing parties and replaced them with two official ones to contest local and congressional elections (eliminating direct elections for governors and the president), took control of trade unions, and severely restricted civil liberties. They sought to erase for good the populist legacy of Vargas. The presidency, held by a series of military leaders, issued numerous decrees that gradually stripped the political system of its democratic features. Torture, disappearances, and exile became commonplace, though they never reached the horrific dimensions experienced during bureaucratic authoritarian regimes in Argentina or Chile.[5]

Although it initially attempted to reduce the role of the state in the economy, the Brazilian military eventually adopted policies of state-led industrialization that were in many ways a continuation of Vargas's statism. The state spent lavishly on major infrastructure projects, including hydroelectric dams, a paved highway to penetrate the Amazon rain forest, and even a nuclear power program. Military rule coincided with the decade of sustained spectacular economic growth that averaged over 10 percent annually—known as the economic miracle.

GRADUAL DEMOCRATIZATION AND THE MILITARY'S RETURN TO THE BARRACKS

Beginning in the mid-1970s, faced with an economic crisis and growing domestic opposition, the military began to slowly loosen its political grip on the country while maintaining ultimate control. This process, known as *abertura* (gradual opening), coincided with the global energy crisis that hit Brazil particularly hard, raising its already high level of international debt. Inflation skyrocketed to levels that exceeded those under Goulart. The "official" oppo-

History of Regimes			
Regime	**Years**	**Type**	**Outcome**
Empire	1822–89	Quasi-democratic constitutional monarchy	Military coup
Old Republic	1889–1930	Quasi-democratic republic	Military coup
Provisional government	1930–37	Authoritarian republic	Gétulio Vargas seized power with military backing
Estado Nôvo	1937–45	Semi-authoritarian republic	Military coup
Second Republic	1945–64	Democratic republic	Military coup
Military regime	1964–85	Military dictatorship	Controlled, negotiated transition
New Republic	1985–present	Democratic republic	

sition party tolerated by the regime became more vigorous in its call for regime change and more successful in legislative elections.

Under the presidency of General João Figueiredo (1979–1985), political prisoners were released, censorship was reduced, and political parties were allowed to reemerge. These measures and the growing economic crisis led to a surge of opposition demands for direct presidential elections and democratic reform. The military's carefully laid plans for controlling the transition unraveled in 1984, when members of the pro-military party in the legislature backed a civilian democratic reform candidate, Tancredo Neves. He died shortly after his election and was replaced by the more conservative José Sarney, but the momentum of political reform could not be stopped. In 1987, a constituent assembly was elected to write a new democratic constitution, formally adopted in 1988.

Thus, democratization came gradually to Brazil and began when the military sought to begin a controlled process of reform. It was encouraged by a severe economic crisis, facilitated by political miscalculation, and supported by a widespread popular fatigue with military rule.

POLITICAL REGIME

Political Institutions

THE CONSTITUTION

Brazil has been a democracy since the adoption of its current constitution in 1988. The constitution was written in the waning days of the country's authoritarian regime and made important compromises in a number of areas. In many ways, the constitution is similar to that of the Second Republic. However, reacting to the long period of authoritarian rule, the framers of the current constitution established a set of rights that could not be amended or curtailed: for example, the principles of federalism, the separation of powers, and certain individual rights. Compared with previous documents, the current constitution imposes very strict limits and controls on the ability of the government to declare a state of siege or take wartime measures. Constitutional amendments are possible and can be initiated by the legislature (if one third of the members of either house agree), the state legislatures (if a majority of them agree), or the president. Such amendments can pass only with the support of separate two-thirds majority votes in both houses of the legislature.

A major debate raged during the writing of the constitution in 1987. Most members of the constituent assembly favored abandoning Brazil's traditional presidential system for a parliamentary model. The conservative president at the time did not want to see his own powers diminished, and he resisted vigorously but agreed to hold a plebiscite on the issue. In 1993, voters rejected the proposed parliamentary system. Brazilians were wary of losing their ability to elect their head of government directly after a period of authoritarian rule and distrusted their political parties, the linchpin of the parliamentary model.[6]

> ### ESSENTIAL POLITICAL FEATURES
>
> - Legislative-executive system: presidential
> - Lower house: Chamber of Deputies
> - Upper house: Federal Senate
> - Unitary or federal division of power: federal
> - Main geographic subunits: states
> - Electoral system for lower house: proportional representation
> - Chief judicial body: Supreme Federal Tribunal and Higher Tribunal of Justice

The Branches of Government

THE PRESIDENCY

As is the norm in Latin America, the Brazilian president is both head of government and head of state. The president and a vice president are elected for four-year terms and may serve a second term.[7] The Brazilian president has the line-item veto, allowing for the rejection of select aspects of legislation. The president has the power to initiate and push legislation through the legislature (about 80 percent of all legislation is initiated by the president) and is the only individual capable of initiating budgetary legislation. Presidents may veto legislation, but vetoes can be overridden by a simple majority in each house of the legislature. Presidents may issue decrees, but the legislature can overturn them; decrees become law for only 30 days, unless adopted by the legislature.

However, the formal power of Brazilian presidents has to date been weakened by the fragmentation of the legislature. Brazilian heads of government need to patch together legislative majorities from fractious and poorly disciplined political parties. Faced with the lack of legislative majorities, Brazilian presidents have often resorted to legislating by emergency decree, thereby circumventing the legislature altogether.[8] President Fernando Collor de Mello won the presidency in 1999 as an "outsider," and his political party held only 3 percent of the seats in congress. In his first year in office, he used 150 such emergency decrees to pass a variety of important economic reforms, whose dubious legality were justified by the president as a necessary response to an economic crisis and whose legality went unchallenged by Brazil's highest court.[9]

Perhaps the greatest power of Brazilian presidents comes from their ability to make appointments to the cabinet and top levels of Brazil's vast bureaucracy. The ability to appoint key ministers, especially the powerful minister of the economy (who controls economic policy and the budget), gives presidents enormous patronage power.

STRUCTURE OF THE GOVERNMENT

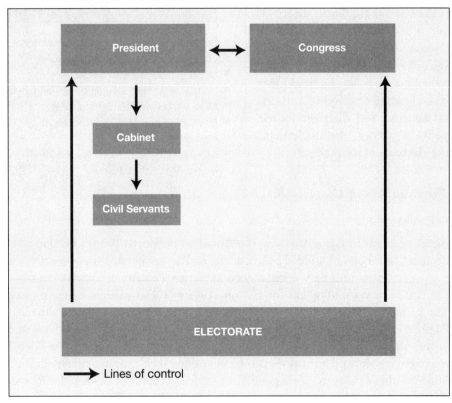

THE LEGISLATURE

Brazil's legislature, the **National Congress (Congresso Nacional)** is composed of two coequal houses. The 513-member **Chamber of Deputies (Câmara dos Deputados)** is the lower house (whose members are elected to four-year terms), and the 81-member **Federal Senate (Senado Federal)** is the upper house (whose members are elected for eight-year terms). There are no term limits for members of either house.

Both houses must approve all legislation before it is sent to the president; when the houses disagree on legislation, they convene joint committees to iron out differences. The legislature can override presidential vetoes with a majority vote of both houses and can, with a two-thirds vote in both houses, amend the constitution with the agreement of the president. As in the United States, the Senate has the power to try a president or cabinet members for impeachable offenses and must approve top presidential appointments.

The actual power of the Brazilian legislature is a complex matter. On the one hand, legislators do not play a key role in most policy making, for many

LULA

Brazil's president breaks with a long line of leaders who come from the powerful, wealthy elite. Luiz Inácio Lula da Silva, known as Lula, was born in the poverty-stricken rural northeast. The sixth of seven children, Lula was raised in a shack by a single mother. The family moved to a favela of São Paulo in search of employment when Lula was seven, and he immediately began to participate in Brazil's vast informal sector, shining shoes and selling candy to help support his family. By the age of twelve, Lula was working full-time in a screw factory, where he eventually began his involvement in the trade union movement. Lula's life bears many of the marks of Brazil's endemic poverty. Formally, he has only a fifth-grade education (though he earned his high-school equivalency and a technical degree). His first wife died in childbirth because she could not afford medical care.

In the 1970s, just as Brazil's union movement began a wave of strikes aimed at pressuring the military government to democratize, Lula became a local union leader, a position that earned him a prison term. In 1980, he was elected the first leader of the new Worker's Party (PT), a democratic socialist party. By the mid-1980s, Lula had become a member of congress and the best-known politician in Brazil. He was especially admired by Brazil's large underclass. Lula ran unsuccessfully for president three times and was defeated mainly because Brazil's upper-class politicians closed ranks to defeat what they viewed as a socialist threat. In the 2002 elections, Lula moderated his image, donned a business suit, and made an effort to reassure business leaders, the church, and the military, the sectors most frightened by his candidacy. To explain these changes he quipped, "I changed, Brazil changed." Despite a series of corruption scandals that tainted his first term in office, Lula was elected to a second term in 2006.

With his resounding victory in the 2002 elections, Lula becomes the first Brazilian president directly touched by the poverty afflicting so many of his fellow citizens. One of his inauguration goals was to ensure that every Brazilian got one plate of food a day. His election was in many ways as momentous as the election of Nelson Mandela in South Africa or Vicente Fox in Mexico.

reasons, including the dominance of the president, the weakness of the political parties, the individualism of legislators, and the relatively weak committee system. A persistent problem limiting the effectiveness of the legislature has been an inability to reach a quorum on key matters. Legislators often view their jobs as stepping-stones to more prestigious and lucrative occupations, such as state governor or top bureaucratic posts.

On the other hand, the constitution allocates significant power to congress, and Brazil's legislature has played an important, if not the leading, role from time to time.[10] Several high-profile congressional hearings (called parliamentary commissions of investigation) have exposed fraud and corruption, even at the highest level of government. In 1992, congress impeached President Fernando Collor de Mello on corruption charges, forcing his resignation. On the whole, congress has not achieved the popular legitimacy that might be expected given its formal power.[11]

THE JUDICIAL SYSTEM

Along with the legislature and executive branches, the judiciary is the third branch of government in Brazil. At the highest level is the **Federal Supreme Court (Supremo Tribunal Federal)**, whose eleven justices are appointed by the president and approved by a majority vote in the senate for a term not to exceed thirty years. The thirty judges of the Superior Court of Justice are similarly appointed and approved and also serve no more than thirty years. Brazil's federal judicial structure is replicated at the state and local level. The court system also features a Supreme Electoral Court (Tribunal Superior Eleitoral), an increasingly common institution in developing countries that is designed to prevent fraud. Most observers agree that elections in Brazil have been remarkably transparent and fair in large part because of the Electoral Court.

As is the norm in Latin America, Brazil employs code law, a rigid system in which judges apply the penal code rather than broadly interpret laws based on historical precedent. As a result, the Brazilian judiciary has less power than its U.S. counterpart, and the Supreme Federal Court has been reticent to challenge the ongoing use of presidential emergency decrees. During his first term, President da Silva enacted a series of measures that gave the higher courts more power, especially the provision that made higher court decisions binding on lower-level courts.

At the lower levels, the Brazilian legal system is regularly criticized as beholden to economic elites and riddled with corruption. Many poor Brazilians feel that they cannot be fairly represented within the system. A survey taken in 1996 reported that 96 percent of respondents believed that a poor person would be dealt with more harshly in the legal system than would a wealthy person.[12] In rural areas, for example, powerful landowners are often successful at influencing legal decisions to the detriment of the peasants. An old Brazilian expression summarizes this unequal access to the judicial system: "For my enemies, the law; for my friends, anything." There have been particularly harsh criticisms, backed by reports by international human rights organizations, of the judiciary's inability to hold Brazil's numerous security forces responsible for a host of human rights abuses.

The Electoral System

Brazil is an excellent example of how an electoral system can fundamentally influence the way in which legislatures and executives interact. As noted earlier, Brazil's democracy is characterized by a multiplicity of relatively weak parties. This has made it almost impossible for Brazilian presidents to gain the support of a stable legislative majority and has created a built-in conflict between the executive and the legislature. The electoral system is largely to blame.

All Brazilians over the age of sixteen can vote, and since 1988 illiterate citizens have been allowed to vote. Voting is mandatory for all literate citizens between the ages of eighteen and seventy. Partly as a result, Brazil has regularly enjoyed a turnout of around 70 percent in legislative and presidential elections. Presidents, state governors, and mayors of large cities must receive a majority of the vote in a first round of voting or face their strongest opponent in a second round. For senate races, the three candidates with the most votes win seats.

It is the electoral system used for Brazil's lower house (and for all state legislatures) that has been most controversial. In this highly unusual system, called **open-list proportional representation (PR)**, voters may choose either a party list (as in normal proportional representation) or write in names of candidates. Votes for each party (and for candidates associated with each party) are then tallied, and seats are allocated to each party proportionally. However, the determination of how seats are allocated to individual party members is based on the number of votes they receive. Candidates must therefore campaign under their own names (not just their party labels) and have an incentive to promote their own candidacies at the expense of their party colleagues. The system serves to weaken the power of political parties and the ability of those parties to enforce internal discipline. The fragmentation of parties is exacerbated by the fact that state-level parties, not the federal party hierarchy, determine the composition of party lists. The tendency has been for individual candidates to seek the backing of powerful state-level politicians, further enhancing Brazil's tradition of clientelism and pork-barrel politics. Moreover, unlike many systems that employ proportional representation, Brazil has no threshold for gaining seats, meaning that even the smallest political parties can easily gain representation in the legislature.[13]

While Brazil's electoral system for the legislature makes it hard to form legislative majorities, its system of electing presidents guarantees that presidents enjoy majority support. If no candidate wins a majority of the vote in the first round, a second round of balloting takes place between the top two first-round contenders.

Districts for both houses of the legislature are the twenty-six states plus the federal district. For the lower house, the number of legislators per district is determined roughly according to population and ranges from a low of eight to a maximum of seventy. This minimum allocation has overrepresented the least populated (and most conservative) sectors of Brazil and has underrepresented urban Brazil, but attempts to change the allocation have been blocked by representatives of all parties from the overrepresented regions.[14] The fact that each state also sends three senators to congress has, as in the United States, added to the overrepresentation of sparsely populated, rural, and generally more conservative states.

Local Government

Brazil is a large and diverse country, and since colonial times there has been a tension between control by the federal government and the desire for regional autonomy. For much of Brazil's history, local authorities have enjoyed considerable autonomy, but during the Estado Nôvo and the military regime, the pendulum swung decisively toward the federal government. During the transition to democracy, Brazil's first directly elected heads of government were the state governors chosen in 1982. Brazil's new democracy has firmly reestablished the principle of **robust federalism**, and Brazilian federalism devolves more power to the states than in most other federal systems.[15]

Each of Brazil's twenty-six states (plus the federal district) has an elected governor and a unicameral legislature. Since 1997, governors have been allowed to be reelected to a second term. Brazilian states are further divided into over 5,000 *municípios* (municipalities), similar to U.S. counties, that are governed by elected mayors and elected councils. Brazilian states have historically owned their own banks and have even run some industries. The constitution allocates to state and local governments a huge chunk of all federal tax revenue. State governors have largely been free to spend as they please, and many states have run up huge debts with the federal government. In 1998, the governor of the powerful state of Minas Gerais (former president Itamar Franco) stopped repayment of his state's massive debt (over US$15 billion) to the federal government, provoking a severe budgetary crisis. Brazil differs from most other federal systems in that the constitution of 1988 does not spell out specific spending responsibilities in areas such as health and education. Nor did it regulate the spending of state banks, which continued to fund excessive spending at the state level.

Governors and mayors of big cities thus have a lot of money to use to help federal legislators gain election. Those legislators, in turn, work at the federal level to promote pork-barrel federal spending on infrastructure projects for their states. Some of those expenditures have ended up in the pockets of corrupt local officials.

Beginning in the Collor de Mello administration, the federal government began to reassert itself vis-à-vis the states, intervening in (and in some cases privatizing) the state banking systems. The federal government forced some states to sell state-owned utilities and rein in state spending. During the two terms of President Cardoso, states and municipalities were forced to assume a greater portion of welfare spending. The 2000 Fiscal Responsibility Law further limited state and local spending by specifically preventing the federal government from refinancing state-government debt.[16] Nevertheless, much of Brazilian politics can still be seen as the politics of the governors, and Brazilian presidents must negotiate with powerful state governors much as they must horse-trade with the Brazil's fractious legislature.

Other Institutions: The Military and the Police

We have seen that Brazil's military played an important role in its domestic politics. From the late nineteenth century until 1964, the military acted mainly as an arbiter, intervening in politics to depose leaders it found unacceptable and then returning to the barracks, handing power over to the civilians. By the mid-1960s, however, the military no longer saw itself as a simple arbiter of domestic conflict. Its officer corps, trained at the influential U.S-supported Escola Superior da Guerra (Superior War College, or ESG) during the cold war, began to view its role as a domestic guardian of order against the "foreign" ideological threats of socialism and Communism. Many of these ideas were fused into a national security doctrine, which focused the military's attention domestically and deflected it from threats on Brazil's borders. Not only were the military elite trained in war strategy, but increasingly they also gained expertise in public administration and economics. By 1964, military leaders believed that Brazil's democratic regime, with its weak and polarized parties, had become chaotic and would be susceptible to Communist subversion. Between 1964 and 1985, Brazil's military held power directly, in an alliance with conservative business elites and technocrats and, at least initially, with the tacit support of the upper and middle classes. Military officials participated directly in key sectors of the economy, such as the nuclear industry and arms production.

Brazil's democratic transition began in the 1970s and was in large part led by the military, which after two decades of military rule was eager to leave economic problems to the civilians. Because military leaders controlled the transition to democracy, there were no attempts to bring Brazilian military officials to justice for destroying democracy or for engaging in widespread human rights abuses. The military was able to pressure the transitional government to pass a widespread amnesty for members of the armed forces.[17]

As a result, Brazil's military continues to be a powerful arm of the state with far more autonomy than in most other advanced democracies.[18] Article 142 of the constitution calls on the military to guarantee law and order. At the same time, democratic governments, beginning with that of President Collor de Mello, have cut military budgets (which are now among the lowest in Latin America), purged military leaders most closely connected to the authoritarian regime, redeployed troops away from population centers, and removed the military from cabinet and top bureaucratic posts. The military's national security doctrine was replaced by a new policy that focuses almost entirely on foreign threats, especially to Brazil's vast and porous Amazon borders. Some Brazilians who were victims of the military's human rights abuses have received compensation, which has further damaged the image of the military.

The two Cardoso administrations continued to assert state control over the armed forces by creating a single civilian ministry of defense to replace ministries that had existed for each branch. Upon his election, Lula tested the loyalty of the armed forces by canceling the costly purchase of fighter jets, which had been a pet project of the military. Brazil's military today plays a much smaller role in politics, and fear of a military coup against democracy has virtually disappeared. When the military exercises its muscle domestically, it is likely to be at the behest of the civilian government.

Brazil's police forces, however, have been the subject of a chorus of concern from human rights experts who have noted the high levels of "state violence" perpetrated against Brazil's poorest citizens. State governments control their own civil police forces (which mainly investigate crimes) and military police forces (which are uniformed and armed). The military police, like the military itself, are governed by their own judicial system, which has in practice allowed the police to act outside the law. Off-duty officers are often hired by business owners to kill homeless street dwellers, and many of the dead have been children. The large number of such killings has exceeded the number of deaths caused by the military during the two decades of authoritarian rule, leading one observer to call Brazil an "ugly democracy."[19] There are also serious concerns about the ability of Brazil's police to maintain a monopoly on violence. Brazil's murder rate is twice that of the United States, and private security guards outnumber the almost 500,000 military police.[20] A wave of gang violence further eroded public confidence in the police.

POLITICAL CONFLICT AND COMPETITION

The Party System and Elections

Brazil's party system has perhaps been the most vilified aspect of its democratic regime. The country has a fragmented multiparty system with weak and fickle political parties, due in large part to the electoral laws.[21] Twenty-one parties currently hold seats in the legislature, and seven gained over 5 percent of the vote in the 2006 election. Opinion research consistently shows extremely low levels of party identification and low public confidence in parties.[22] The weakness of political parties complicates a president's attempt to find a majority to support his legislative proposals. The president's need to bargain regularly with a number of small parties has only increased the pork-barrel aspects of the Brazilian political system and has often made it hard to implement tough decisions, such as reductions in state spending. It has also contributed to the numerous corruption scandals that have plagued the legislature.

Historically, Brazil's parties have been highly personalistic, that is, based on the leadership of a powerful or charismatic individual instead of an ideology. This feature has its roots in Brazil's patron-client politics. The military regime attempted to create a "modern" two-party system by fiat, but the two official parties did not survive the transition to democracy. Instead, the transition gave rise to an even greater proliferation of political parties. Today, the weakness of their ideological component is evident in the large number of party members who, after being elected, change affiliation or leave to create new parties.[23] This has most often occurred after the election of a president from another party, prompting legislators to switch to the governing party in order to assure their access to patronage. In the 2003–2006 legislature, 195 of 413 deputies switched parties, and over the past sixteen years 36 percent of legislators switched parties. In 2007, Brazil's courts upheld rules that will limit the ability of parliamentarians to switch parties.

Another serious problem is the sheer number of political parties and their lack of internal discipline. In 2006, twenty-one parties won seats, and the biggest party (the Brazilian Democratic Movement Party, or PMDB) won only 17 percent. Legislators respond far more to local barons, government incentives, and pork-barrel opportunities than to their party leadership. Since Brazilian electoral laws allow candidates to run as members of a party without approval of the party leadership (in Brazil, any elected member of the legislature is guaranteed a place on the ballot in the following election), there is little incentive for party loyalty. Moreover, Brazil's powerful federalism further weakens party cohesion: it is common for legislators to vote across party lines with members of their state delegations to support legislation of local interest. Lula's Worker Party (PT), which won only 16 percent of lower house seats in 2002, has been especially successful at recruiting opposition members to join the governing party.[24] After 2006, Lula pieced together a coaltion of legislative supporters that included fourteen parties.

There have been many proposals to improve the workings of Brazil's legislature, regularly reported to suffer from rock-bottom levels of popular trust and respect.[25] Proposals to enact a threshold that would limit representation to parties with over 5 percent of the vote, and thus reduce the number of parties, have to date failed in the legislature.

The most important conservative party, the Liberal Front Party (PFL), grew out of the two "official" parties tolerated during the military regime. It is a free-market, pro-business party, differing from parties of the center mainly in its opposition to land reform and its conservative stand on social issues. Today, the PFL is the third-largest party in the Chamber of Deputies and the largest part in the senate.

Two main centrist parties are the PMDB and the Brazilian Social Democracy Party (PSDB), to which former two-term president **Fernando Henrique Cardoso** belongs. Both parties include a mix of free-market conservatives and social democrats, and neither has a clear ideological orientation. The PMDB was the most important pro-democracy opposition party in the years of the transition and played a critical role in the move toward direct elections and a new constitution. Cardoso and other prominent PMDB members bolted to form the PSDB in protest over the PMDB's patron-client politics. The PSDB initially distinguished itself as a social democratic alternative to the PMDB, but since Cardoso's two terms in office it has been more closely associated with free-market reforms. Its candidate in the 2006 presidential election, Geraldo Alckmin, lost to Lula da Silva in the second round of voting.

The **Workers' Party (PT)** is currently the third-largest political party in congress, and it is the dominant party of the left.[26] The PT is led by the current president, Luiz Inácio Lula da Silva, whose decisive victories in the 2002 and 2006 presidential elections have boosted the party's profile. It was founded in 1980 mainly among unionized industrial workers but has grown to incorporate landless workers, rural unions, and other disaffected Brazilians. It has also attracted significant support from educated middle-class Brazilians. It claims to represent Brazil's poor, and it advocates social democracy. Unlike most of Brazil's parties, the PT has practiced a high degree of internal democracy and has had fewer defections and splits. Lula was elected in 2002 partly on the PT's reputation for honesty and clean government. Its reputation was badly tarnished, however, by a series of corruption scandals in 2005 and 2006, and it lost some seats in congress as a result.

The dominant cleavage in the Brazilian electorate has been regional, rather than by social class, with the rural conservative northeast often pitted against the more progressive and urban south and southeast. The 2002 presidential election generally followed this pattern with Lula most strongly supported in Brazil's southeastern urban areas while his opponent, José Serra, drew his vote disproportionately from the rural northeast. Interestingly, Brazil's severe class inequality does not appear to have affected the outcome of that race. Lula did equally well among poor and wealthy Brazilians. In the 2006 presidential elections, poor northeasterners shifted their support to Lula, due in large part to his targeted social spending. In legislatlive elections, however, the PT has been slower to make inroads in the northeast.

Despite some recent signs that the major parties are beginning to consolidate and that parties (especially on the left and in the center) are becoming more disciplined, the party system is badly fragmented. Despite Lula's resounding victory in the 2002 and 2006 presidential elections and despite the fact that his PT is the second-largest party in congress, Lula's party still controls only 15 percent of the seats in the lower house. Even with support from parties on the left and in the center, Lula has faced difficulties passing any legislation without a lot of compromise. Party fragmentation by itself rules out any radical policy shifts under the current president. While the Brazilian model has often been portrayed as inefficient and gridlocked, some scholars have begun to take a more nuanced view. According to this new perspective, skillful presidents must be master bargainers and coalition builders, forming majority legislative support from the plethora of parties. Unlike their predecessors, the two most recent Brazilian presidents (Cardoso and Lula) have excelled at that task.[27]

Civil Society

Democratization has led to a mushrooming of civil society that had been stifled during the military regime. Membership in urban and rural trade unions has grown quickly. The growth of decentralized Protestant religious groups, many with a conservative political agenda, has helped to reinvigorate civil society. A host of environmental, human rights, and women's groups has emerged as well.

Although the return of democracy has given rise to women's rights groups, women remain fairly marginal in Brazilian politics. Brazil's rapid industrialization has greatly increased the percentage of women in the workforce (now estimated at about 40 percent), but women are still paid far less than their

2006 Brazilian Legislative Election Results				
Party	Chamber of Deputy Seats	% of Seats	Senate Seats	% of Seats
Brazilian Democratic Movement Party (PMDB)	80	14.6	4	5
Liberal Front Party (PFL)	65	10.9	6	7.5
Workers' Party (PT)	83	15	2	2.5
Brazilian Social Democracy Party (PSDB)	65	13.6	5	6.0
Others	220	45.9	64	59
Total	513	100	81	100

Source: http://electionresources.org/br/deputies.php?election=2006 (accessed 2 June 2008).

male counterparts. Laws have been passed to try to increase women's representation. In 1998, congress stipulated that 20 percent of the seats in the federal legislature must be held by women. The presidency of Lula, whose PT has integrated numerous women's groups, has inspired new hopes for more equal representation.

Brazil's largest social movement is the **Landless Workers Movement (MST)**, a peasant organization that has fought for land reform. It has advocated legal change but has often supported and even organized peasant seizure of uncultivated, privately owned land.[28] This activism has been opposed, often violently, by Brazil's powerful landlords, often with the support of the police forces and with the tacit tolerance of the rural courts. Hundreds of MST workers have been killed for trying to address Brazil's extremely unequal landholding patterns. MST pressure resulted in a major redistribution of land to peasants.

Despite centuries of church support for the most conservative elements of Brazilian society, the Roman Catholic Church in Brazil played an essential role in mobilizing civil society to protest the military regime. Spurred by changes in Rome, especially the Second Vatican Council (1962–1965), much of the Brazilian church, including some of the hierarchy, embraced a new interpretation of the role of religion. **Liberation theology**, which developed in the 1960s among a group of Catholic intellectuals that included numerous Brazilians, held that the church should use its power and prestige to teach the poor how to improve their lives immediately, in both physical and spiritual terms. Liberation theology advocated organizing small neighborhoods called **Christian Base Communities**, often in rural areas or urban favelas, not only for prayer but also to learn and advocate political and social justice. These base communities were often led by "lay priests" who directly challenged the traditional church hierarchy. The National Conference of Brazilian Bishops was for a time a leading advocate of liberation theology and was a major advocate of democratization, land reform, and human rights.

SOCIETY

Ethnic and National Identity

Brazil has an extremely diverse population that has emerged from a blending of Native Americans, African slaves, and Europeans. Unlike much of Spanish America and the United States, there was far more intermarriage among racial groups in Brazil. Today, around 40 percent of Brazilians consider themselves to be of mixed race, and 80 percent claim some African ancestry. Brazilians have a complex vocabulary to describe the rainbow of skin colors, ranging from *preto* (black) to *mulato claro* (light brown). Despite the Brazilian myth of "racial democracy," there is an extremely strong association between race

ETHNIC GROUPS

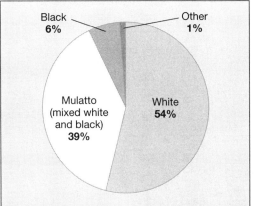

RELIGION

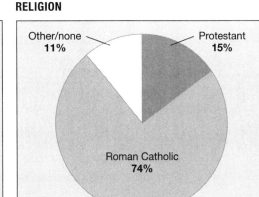

and wealth. Wealthy Brazilians tend to be lighter skinned, and blacks are disproportionately present among Brazil's poor.[29] Relatively few blacks are found at the highest level of business or government. Blacks or mixed-race Brazilians are twice as likely to be unemployed, and whites earn on average 57 percent more than do Brazilians of color.[30]

Race was not a political topic in Brazil until President Fernando Henrique Cardoso brought it to the national agenda in the 1990s. Cardoso (a sociologist who wrote a dissertation on race in Brazil) claimed that "Brazilians live wrapped in the illusion of racial democracy," and he began a national dialogue on affirmative action.[31] Cardoso enacted measures to redress the problem, including quotas for Afro-Brazilians in some government ministries and the diplomatic corps. President Lula da Silva redoubled the effort, creating a cabinet-level Secretariat for Promotion of Racial Equity, and appointing a record number of Afro-Brazilians to government posts, including the first-ever black Supreme Court justice.

The most controversial aspect of affirmative action in Brazil has been the imposition of admission quotas for Afro-Brazilians at some public universities. Admissions to Brazilian universities is fiercely competitive (only about 8 percent of college-age Brazilians attend university), and traditionally about 65 percent of those admitted attend exclusive private high schools that better prepare students for grueling college entrance exams. As a result, two thirds of those admitted typically come from the wealthiest 20 percent of the population.[32]

Racially based admissions quotas were first attempted in 2001 when the state of Rio de Janeiro adopted a 40 percent quota for state universities. Over 300 lawsuits were filed alleging that applicants with higher test scores were being denied application in favor of those with lower scores. To date, the courts have backed admissions quotas, and two other states have followed Rio

Confidence in Brazilian Institutions, 2007	
Institution	**% Expressing Confidence**
Political parties	20
Congress	29
Judiciary	30
Presidency	43
Armed Forces	41
Church	74

Source: www.Latinobarometro.org (accessed 2 June 2008).

de Janeiro's lead. Racial quotas have provoked a fierce debate within Brazil. Critics say that it is virtually impossible to know who is black in a country where 80 percent of Brazilians have some African ancestry. Some black students with high enough test scores to enter the university without quotas resent the new system. Average test scores have dropped at universities that have adopted the quotas. Critics of quotas say that it has increased racial tensions, and they believe that affirmative action policies that are less blunt would be more widely accepted and more effective. Defenders of quotas point to the dramatic increase in blacks at formerly mostly white universities. They argue that the debate about racial discrimination is healthy and long overdue. Supporters of affirmative action have proposed extending quotas to all universities and to boardrooms of private firms. To date, those proposals have failed to prosper in the legislature.

Brazil has also become a religiously diverse country after centuries of domination by the Roman Catholic Church. While the vast majority of Brazilians claim to be Catholic, Brazil has seen an extraordinary explosion of Protestants, especially Pentacostal movements, over the past two decades. In addition, many Brazilians (even white Brazilians) practice one of several Afro-Brazilian religions, such as Macumba, Candomblé, or Umbanda, often in addition to Catholicism.

Ideology and Political Culture

Despite very high levels of participation in elections, due in large part to mandatory voting, and despite the growth of civil society since democracy, a look at Brazil's political culture reveals serious concerns. Perhaps most alarming is the low level of support for democracy as a system of government. According to public opinion data, only about 43 percent of Brazilians viewed democracy as the best form of government when asked in 2007, well below the Latin American average.[33] Brazilians report very low levels of satisfaction with how democracy is working (only 30 percent of Brazilians were very or fairly satisfied with democracy in 2007), also well below the Latin American average. Research also shows that confidence in specific institutions, especially political parties and congress, is extremely low. Brazilians have been more willing to blame their legislators than their presidents for the persistence of corruption.

POLITICAL ECONOMY

Beginning with Estado Nôvo and continuing through the military regime, Brazil's political economy could be described as capitalist but also heavily statist. Over the years, Brazil's state, through the implementation of import-substitution industrialization (ISI) policies, has played a major role in the economy by limiting imports, regulating credit, controlling the currency, regulating wages, and even owning and operating sectors of the economy. Statist policies have often resulted in spectacular economic growth, as was the case during the so-called economic miracle (1967–1973), when annual growth rates averaged 11 percent. But statist policies have also been blamed for a number of serious problems that have long plagued the Brazilian economy.

Perhaps the most serious problem is inflation. An inflation rate of 90 percent was a major reason for the breakdown of democracy in 1964. The military regime was initially successful at reducing the inflation rate, but during

---

THE INFORMAL SECTOR: FAVELAS AND CABLE TV

Jardim Ângela is a typical favela on the outskirts of Brazil's largest city, São Paolo. A surprisingly large number of its residents enjoy cable television despite the fact that none of Brazil's cable companies have wired the area. The cable companies do not want to extend cable into the favela because most residents cannot afford the monthly fees. So entrepreneurs of the informal sector have installed pirated cable lines and charge a much lower monthly fee than the legal companies would. It is estimated that half a million poor Brazilians pay for pirated cable television. Rather than crack down on the illegal operations, Brazil's cable television industry has lobbied the government to pass laws that would effectively legalize such informal-sector services, hoping that they can at least gain some revenue from favela dwellers in a new partnership with the cable pirates.[34] It is recognition of both the important role of the informal sector and the inability of the Brazilian state to stop or regulate it.

LABOR FORCE BY OCCUPATION

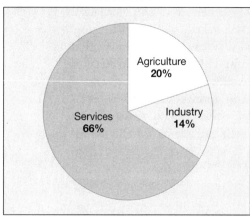

Agriculture
20%

Services
66%

Industry
14%

the military period inflation still averaged 20 percent and began to skyrocket in the 1970s due to a rise in oil prices, high interest rates, and heavy state spending. Inflation eroded wages and hurt Brazil's poorest disproportionately.

Another serious problem is Brazil's debt. Brazil's military regime borrowed heavily from international lenders, and despite rapid growth rates its foreign indebtedness grew. Its long-term foreign debt has almost doubled since 1990 and in 2000 was valued at 31.5 percent of the GDP.[35] An additional problem has been Brazil's public-sector debt, which escalated rapidly with the return of democracy and increased social spending.

Finally, there is the problem of unemployment. Despite rapid economic growth, a large sector of Brazil's population remain jobless, and that joblessness is a chief cause of the country's endemic poverty and inequality. As a result, a large portion of Brazil's population (perhaps as much as two thirds of the active workforce) makes its living in the informal sector (see "The Informal Sector: Favelas and Cable TV," p. 477).[36] As recently as 1995, one survey reported that over half of Brazil's workers did not contribute to the national social security system because they were not employed in a legally regulated job. The persistence of such a large informal sector deprives the state of needed tax revenue but, more important, deprives informal-sector workers of many welfare benefits.[37]

Democratization has addressed some but certainly not all of Brazil's economic problems. Democratic governments began a gradual reduction of the role of the state in Brazil's economy, but liberalization in Brazil has not been as extensive as in much of the rest of Latin America. Compared with its Latin American neighbors, the Brazilian state still has a relatively large presence in the economy. However, starting with the presidency of Fernando Collor de Mello (1989–1992), the role of the state in the economy has been curtailed and protective tariffs have been reduced. During Fernando Henrique Cardoso's two terms (1995–2002), a major policy of privatization of state assets was undertaken, ending the state monopoly in a number of key economic sectors, including energy and telecommunications. Under Cardoso, rules governing foreign investment in the Brazilian economy were liberalized.

Overall, aggregate economic growth since democratization has not attained the spectacular rates achieved during the so-called miracle. Between 1980 and 1990, average GDP per capita fell .41 percent, and between 1990 and 2000 it grew by an average rate of 1.13 percent. However, recent democratic governments have made excellent progress in taming inflation. During the two Cardoso administrations, inflation was eventually reduced to single digits (8.5 percent on average between 1995 and 2002). During the da Silva administration, continued fiscal conservatism and skyrocketing commodity export prices helped strengthen the economy. One sign that the international financial community approved of Lula's handling of the economy was that in 2008 Standard and Poor's rated Brazil's debt "investment grade" for the first time in its history.

Despite impressive records of aggregate growth, the most troublesome feature of Brazil's economy is its endemic poverty and persistently high levels of inequality. In 1998, the richest 20 percent of the population received 64 percent of the nation's income, while the poorest 20 percent earned only 2 percent, making Brazil the most unequal country in the world. Brazil's ranking in the 2004 United Nation's Human Development Index Ranking now stands at 70, well below Mexico (52) and Russia (57).

Nowhere is Brazil's poverty and inequality more evident than in education. In the first decade of Brazilian democracy, the average number of school years completed was only 3.8, and the vast majority of Brazilians never completed primary school. Only 1 percent of Brazilians attended university. The Cardoso administrations increased spending on Brazil's education system and produced a marked improvement, but a disproportionate amount of state spending continues to be directed toward a higher education system that benefits the economically advantaged.

Brazil's health-care system also reflects its massive poverty and inequality. Since 1987, all Brazilians have been formally entitled to public health care, but access and quality are very uneven. Brazil still has one of the highest infant mortality rates in the world; it has higher rates than China, Mexico, and Russia despite having a higher per capita GDP than those countries. Its life expectancy is lower than China's and Mexico's. About one third of the population lacks access to clean water.

Inadequate housing is yet another symptom and cause of poverty and inequality. The military regime did little to address housing needs, and despite increased spending on housing under the democratic governments, it is estimated that there are over 3,500 favelas (urban shantytowns) in Brazil, with populations ranging from several thousand to half a million.[38] Cardoso's administrations attempted to alleviate the housing crisis by distributing land to over half a million landless Brazilians, but the crisis remains acute.

The severe economic crisis of 1999, immediately following Cardoso's election to a second term, almost pulled Brazil into an economic depression. The Brazilian currency, the real, suffered a 42 percent devaluation, Brazil lost US$8 billion of its foreign reserves in one month, and inflation began to reemerge. The economy was rescued by two events: the International Monetary Fund provided a massive aid package, and Cardoso was finally able to pass a social security and pension reform package.

Despite a legacy of significant economic reform, Cardoso was less successful in other areas. His attempt to slim down Brazil's badly bloated state bureaucracy ran into serious opposition in the legislature. Public servants who run the state bureaucracy have been a relatively privileged labor elite, with a costly pension system that strains the Brazilian budget. Brazilians bear a relatively heavy tax burden that is nearly at European levels (about 40 percent of GDP) but has not been used to create a European-style welfare state.[39] Brazil does have a national social security system, but it does not cover the massive number of informal-sector workers.

The 2002 election of President Luiz Inácio Lula da Silva raised hopes for a fundamental resetting of economic priorities. Lula campaigned on a pledge to end hunger in Brazil. In office, he has steered a more cautious course. He has rejected further tax increases, though his administration has improved tax collection, and his ability to increase social spending has been constrained by Brazil's huge debt burden, commitments to state and local governments, and his inability and reluctance to reduce the state bureaucracy.

On the bright side, Lula's policies to reduce poverty have clearly had some success. Between 2003 and 2006, the percentage of Brazilians living in poverty dropped from 28.1 percent to 22.7 percent, the lowest rate in a quarter century.[40] Most important in this regard was the establishment of the **Bolsa Familia (Family Fund)**, which is worth discussing in some detail. During his 2000 presidential campaign, Lula da Silva pledged to end hunger. In 2003, President da Silva merged several antipoverty programs into the Bolsa Familia, which pays monthly small cash stipends (ranging from about $7 to $45 according to a family's income) to Brazil's poorest families on the condition that recipients' children attend school and receive medical attention. The payments are made by the federal government directly to a family debit card (usually to the mother of the family). By the end of 2006, the program had reached 11 million families (equivalent to a quarter of Brazil's population) and is currently the largest targeted welfare program in the world.[41] Together with other policies (for example, a 25 percent increase in the minimum wage), the result has been a dramatic drop in poverty and a reduction of inequality.

The program has paid political dividends as well. The president's political base had traditionally been in the wealthier and more industrialized southeast of Brazil, and residents of the impoverished north and northeast usually voted for conservative parties dominated by machine politicians. In 2006, however, voters in Brazil's impoverished north and northeast (where the Bolsa Familia benefited about half the population) overwhelmingly supported Lula (he won 77 percent of the vote there). Curiously, the Bolsa program translated into votes for Lula as president but not his party in the legislature. Lula benefited from the targeted cash transfer program, while his party was punished by voters for a series of corruption scandals.[42]

Brazil has become a dominant world exporter and currently has a large trade surplus. In 2006, its biggest exports were transport equipment and parts and metallurgical products, followed by soybeans, bran, and oil. Its export markets are fairly diversified, with the United States, China, and Argentina as the top three export destinations.[43]

FOREIGN RELATIONS AND THE WORLD

Until fairly recently, Brazil has not played the type of role in world politics that one might expect given the size of its territory and economy. Perhaps even more counterintuitive is that Brazil historically remained somewhat detached from its Spanish-speaking neighbors. With democratization, and especially since the presidency of Fernando Henrique Cardoso, its foreign policy has assumed a higher profile, and Brazil has become an informal leader of the developing world.

The biggest issue in Brazil's foreign affairs is trade relations. Brazil is a major exporter and has sought to create free-trade agreements with its neighbors and with Europe and the United States. To date, the most important trade agreement is **MERCOSUR** (Common Market of the South; MERCOSUL in Portuguese), founded in 1991 by Brazil, Argentina, Uruguay, and Paraguay. Brazil has supported the enlargement of MERCOSUR, and Chile and Bolivia are now associate members. These countries have virtually eliminated tariffs, and within the first decade of MERCOSUR's existence there was a spectacular increase in trade among its members. Given the power of its industrial sector, Brazil has reaped a windfall with this increased trade, and its trade with MERCOSUR members now accounts for about 11 percent of its total exports. The economic crisis in Argentina and Argentine-Brazilian disputes over currency valuation slowed the momentum of MERCOSUR in the late 1990s, but since then a slow recovery of MERCOSUR trade has taken place. Many believe that MERCOSUR will eventually be incorporated into a free-trade area of the Americas, which has been supported by some in the United States and Latin America.

Brazil has emerged as a world leader of attempts to create international agreements on nuclear proliferation, women's rights, environmental protection, and human rights. The Cardoso administration's successful effort to confront major multinational drug companies and to produce cheap generic medicines to treat AIDS has been a model for countries in Africa and elsewhere.

The election of Luiz Inácio Lula da Silva to the presidency in 2002 created new strains in the normally strong U.S.-Brazilian relations. The George W. Bush administration was wary of Lula's socialist ideology and irritated by his warm relations with the Venezuelan populist Hugo Chávez. However, U.S. fears proved unfounded, and Lula's administration has acted moderately on all fronts and has continued the fiscally conservative policies of his predecessor. Lula has honored all of Brazil's debt commitments and U.S.-Brazilian relations have improved considerably. In December 2002, Lula made an official state visit to the United States. The two countries worked together to address the political crisis in Venezuela and have even collaborated on Colombia despite Lula's strong opposition to U.S. policy there.

In November 2004, Brazil sent 1,200 troops to Haiti as part of a Brazilian-commanded United Nations peacekeeping mission, the biggest Brazilian military deployment since World War II. Brazil has also campaigned for a permanent seat on the United Nations Security Council.[44]

One example that highlights Brazil's complex international and domestic roles is in the case of the Amazon. In an era of growing concern about global warming, increasing attention has been paid to the rapid deforestation of the Amazon rain forest, about 60 percent of which lies within Brazil's borders. Environmental limits on development in the Amazon have long been controversial for Brazilians, many of whom view the region as a key to its economic development and who resent being told by foreigners how they should manage the rain forest. In the 1960s and 1970s, the Brazilian military operated under the motto "occupy so as not to surrender"—colonization and development of the Amazon would guarantee Brazilian sovereignty over it.

The 2002 election of President da Silva, who proclaimed himself to be Brazil's first "green president," was thus viewed as a watershed event. In power, his government has bitterly disappointed environmentalists while angering pro-development forces. Lula appointed Marina Silva, a lifelong advocate of rain forest preservation, as Environment Minister. The government established over sixty forest reserves, putting vast tracts of forest off limits to development. Enforcement of laws against illegal logging were more effectively enforced. Brazil proposed a plan in which the international community would pay Brazil to preserve the area.

Environmentalists have argued that deforestation has actually increased during the da Silva administration, and they have noted that forest preserves have been created but cannot be policed. They have warned that agricultural interests have increasingly dominated policy making, too readily yielding to pressure by powerful governors of pro-agricultural states. The 2008 resignation of Minister Silva, who was unable to stop the construction of hydroelectric projects and who lost out on other conflicts between environmentalists and pro-development forces, further convinced these skeptics.

Which view of the da Silva record on the Amazon is correct? His government has always been torn by the struggle between ministers who hold very different environmental agendas. The legislative coalition supporting Lula's government includes many who favor more rapid development of the Amazon. The rapid rise of agricultural commodity prices in 2008 may have tilted the balance within the da Silva administration toward those who want fewer restrictions on agriculture, and may explain the sudden spike in the rate of deforestation.

CURRENT ISSUES

Any assessment of Brazil's democratic regime must be mixed. Brazil has managed a difficult transition to democracy and has held regular, fair elections. The recent election of Luiz Inácio Lula da Silva, the first working-class Brazilian to hold the presidency, was clearly a turning point in Brazilian politics. Brazil's economy has undergone major reform and has weathered the severe economic crises of the 1970s and 1990s. Today, Brazil is a major industrial power and a major exporter. It has gained considerable prestige and influence in the world arena.

ECONOMIC INEQUALITY AND CRIME

Despite its many advances, Brazilian democracy faces a litany of challenges. First among them is the inequality and poverty that persist even as Brazil has taken enormous economic strides. It remains to be seen whether Brazil's state, even under the leadership of a president like Lula, can redirect its energy to improve the lot of its poor majority.

A related challenge is the epidemic of crime, which Brazilians regularly name as the country's most serious problem. Brazil's murder rate has doubled since democratization, and Brazil now has one of the highest rates of homicide by guns in the world (about 40,000 Brazilians die from gun violence each year). To a considerable extent, crime is a symptom of Brazil's endemic poverty, persistent inequality, and stubborn unemployment. Much crime in Brazil can be linked to the drug trade that has infested Brazil's favelas. Brazil's police have generally retreated from the favelas, where they are outnumbered and often outgunned.

In July 2004, President Lula da Silva enacted a tough new gun-control law, passed by Brazil's legislature after fierce opposition from the country's powerful arms manufacturers. The law tightened rules on gun permits and created a national firearms register, with strict penalties (including a four-year prison term) for possessing an unregistered gun. The Brazilian government has begun purchasing handguns turned in by civilians in an effort to reduce gun violence, and it called a referendum in October 2005 on a proposed ban on handgun sales. The measure was rejected, however, by 63 percent of voters.

Finally, Brazilians will likely need to consider a set of institutional weaknesses that have made it difficult to address its major socioeconomic challenges. As we have seen, Brazil's electoral laws have exacerbated its weak and ineffective political parties. Weak parties have served to increase pork-barrel politics and legislative gridlock. As a result, Brazilians are increasingly frustrated with how democracy works. Paradoxically, the presence of weak parties and a fragmented legislature makes it harder to reform the system.

POLITICAL CORRUPTION

Even in the context of Latin America, where political corruption is commonplace, Brazilian democracy has been exceptionally plagued by a nonstop series of high-profile corruption scandals. In the early 1990s, President Fernando Collor resigned rather than face impeachment for corruption. President Fernando Henrique Cardoso's administration, in an attempt to garner support for an amendment that would allow Brazilian presidents to run for a second term, was found to have offered bribes to legislators. The amendment passed and Cardoso was reelected. When President da Silva assumed the presidency in 2003 there were high hopes that the era of political corruption was over, since his Workers' Party (PT) enjoyed a reputation as a party of "clean government." Those hopes were soon dashed as the minority PT scrambled to achieve legislative support for the president's agenda. In the notorious Mensalão (monthy stipend) scandal of 2005 and 2006 the governing party was found to have paid opposition legislators to vote for the PT agenda, using funds from state-owned enterprises. President da Silva's chief of staff, communications director, and the entire top leadership of the PT were forced to resign, but Lula emerged unscathed and won reelection (his party lost seats in the legislature). Corruption charges have continued into da Silva's second term. In December 2007, the president of the Senate, a close ally of the president, was forced to give up his leadership post because of corruption charges. In 2008, a scandal erupted over misuse by top government officials of government-issued credit cards.

There are many possible explanations for the persistence of corruption in Brazilian politics, but many scholars blame the Brazilian electoral system, which favors a proliferation of weak parties in the legislature and a low level of accountability for individual legislators.

The prospects and challenges facing Brazil can be summed up by the comments of two political scientists:

> Brazil is a country with relatively few of the regional, nationalist, ethnic, linguistic, religious divisions and conflicts that pose a threat to democ-

racies, old and new, through most of the world. In this respect it is uniquely fortunate. But with the ninth or tenth largest economy in the world, Brazil is sixtieth or worse in international league tables of human development and is a strong contender for the title of world champion in social inequality. Can democracy be healthy, can it properly function, can it even survive in the long run, when, as in Brazil, a third of the population (some would put it much higher) live in conditions of extreme poverty, ignorance and ill health and are treated at best as second class citizens?[45]

NOTES

1. Marshall Eakin, *Brazil: The Once and Future Country* (New York: St. Martin's Press, 1998), p. 1.
2. Binka Le Breton, *Voices from the Amazon* (Hartford, CT: Kumarian Press, 1993).
3. Eakin, *Brazil*, p. 44.
4. For an excellent overview, see Alfred Stepan, ed., *Authoritarian Brazil* (New Haven, CT: Yale University Press, 1973).
5. The first attempt to document the abuses under military rule was conducted secretly by the Catholic Church and published as a book titled *Brazil, Never Again*, or *Brasil: Nunca Mais* (São Paolo: Archdiosis of São Paolo, 1985). It became an instant best seller.
6. A number of prominent political scientists have argued that presidentialism has not served Brazil's relatively young democracy well because it is less flexible and responds less well to crises. See, for example, Juan Linz, "Presidential or Parliamentary Democracy: Does It Make a Difference?" in Juan Linz and Arturo Valenzuela, eds., *The Failure of Presidential Democracy* (Baltimore: Johns Hopkins University Press), pp. 3–87.
7. In 1997, President Fernando Henrique Cardoso was able to push a constitutional amendment through the legislature that allows presidents and state governors to run for a second term. Cardoso became the first president to avail himself of that opportunity and was reelected in 1998.
8. Scott Mainwaring, "Multipartism, Robust Federalism, and Presidentialism in Brazil," in Scott Mainwaring and Matthew Soberg Shugart, eds., *Presidentialism and Democracy in Latin America* (New York: Cambridge University Press, 1997), pp. 55–109.
9. Bolivar Lamounier, "Brazil: An Assessment of the Cardoso Administration," in Jorge Dominguez and Michael Shifter, eds., *Constructing Democratic Governance in Latin America* (Baltimore: Johns Hopkins University Press, 2003), p. 281.
10. Angelina Cheibub Figueiredo and Fernando Limongi, "Congress and Decision-Making in Democratic Brazil," in Maria D'Alva Kinzo and James Dunkerley, eds., *Democratic Brazil: Economy, Polity, and Society* (London: Institute of Latin American Studies, 2003), pp. 62–83.
11. Juan Linz and Alfred Stepan, "Crises of Efficacy, Legitimacy, and Democratic State Presence: Brazil," in Juan Linz and Alfred Stepan, eds., *Problems of Democratic Transition and Consolidation* (Baltimore: Johns Hopkins University Press, 1996), pp. 166–89.

12. Fiona Macaulay, "Democratization and the Judiciary: Competing Reform Agendas," in Maria D'Alva Kinzo and James Dunkerley, eds., *Brazil since 1985: Economy, Polity, and Society* (London: Institute of Latin American Studies, 2003), pp. 93–96.

13. Predictably, Brazil's many small parties have resisted attempts at electoral reform, fearing that any such reform would likely impose a threshold and threaten their existence.

14. In 1989, the vote of one citizen of Roraima, a poor northern state, was the equivalent of thirty-three votes in São Paolo, Brazil's largest state. Timothy Power, "Political Institutions in Democratic Brazil," in Peter Kingstone and Timothy Power, eds., *Democratic Brazil: Actors, Institutions, and Processes* (Pittsburgh: University of Pittsburgh Press, 2000), p. 27.

15. Mainwaring, "Multipartism, Robust Federalism, and Presidentialism in Brazil."

16. David Samuels, *Ambition, Federalism, and Legislative Politics in Brazil* (Cambridge, UK: Cambridge University Press, 2003). See p. 161, on spending levels of federal and state governments.

17. Wendy Hunter, *Eroding Military Influence in Brazil: Politicians against Soldiers* (Chapel Hill: University of North Carolina Press, 1997), pp. 42–71.

18. Wendy Hunter, "Assessing Civil-Military Relations in Postauthoritarian Brazil," in Kingstone and Power, *Democratic Brazil*, pp. 101–25.

19. Anthony Pereira, "An Ugly Democracy?: State Violence and the Rule of Law in Postauthoritarian Brazil," in Kingstone and Power, *Democratic Brazil*, pp. 217–35.

20. Anthony Pereira, "An Ugly Democracy?" p. 230.

21. Scott Mainwaring and Timothy Scully, "Introduction: Party Systems in Latin America," in Scott Mainwaring and Timothy Scully, eds., *Building Democratic Institutions: Parties and Party Systems in Latin America* (Stanford, CA: Stanford University Press, 1995), pp. 1–35.

22. A comparative survey in 1997 found that Brazil had the lowest level of party identification in Latin America. See J. Mark Payne, Daniel Zovatto, Fernando Cavillo-Flórez, and Andrés Allamand Zavala, *Democracies in Development: Politics and Reform in Latin America* (Washington, DC: Inter-American Development Bank, 2002), p. 136.

23. Scott Mainwaring, *Rethinking Party Systems in the Third Wave of Democratization: The Case of Brazil* (Stanford, CA: Stanford University Press, 1999), pp. 140–45.

24. Michael Reid, *Forgotten Continent* (New Haven, CT: Yale University Press, 2007), p. 287.

25. "Laws for the Lawmakers," *Economist*, 8 November 2007, www.economist.com/world/americas/displaystory.cfm?story_id10104985 (accessed 30 December 2008).

26. William Nylen, "The Making of a Loyal Opposition: The Worker's Party (PT) and the Consolidation of Democracy in Brazil," in Kingstone and Power, *Democratic Brazil*, pp. 126–43.

27. Leslie Armijo, Philippe Faucher, and Magdalena Dembinska, "Compared to What? Assessing Brazil's Political Institutions," *Comparative Politics*, 39, no. 6 (2006), pp. 759–86.

28. On the MST, see Gabriel Ondetti, "Opportunity, and Protest: Explaining the Take-off of Brazil's Landless Movement," *Latin American Politics and Society*, 48, no. 2 (Summer 2006), pp. 61-94.

29. Timothy Power and J. Timmons Roberts, "A New Brazil?" in Kingstone and Power, *Democratic Brazil*, p. 249.

30. Jon Jeter, "Affirmative Action Debate Forces Brazil to Take Look at the Mirror," *Washington Post*, 16 June 2003, p. A1.

31. Mala Htun, "Racial Quotas for a 'Racial Democracy'," *NACLA Report on the Americas* (January/February, 2005), pp. 20–25.

32. Rodrigo Davies, "Brazil takes affirmative action in Higher Education," *The Guardian*, 4 August 2003, p. 4.

33. Data from www.latinobarometro.org (accessed 2 June 2008).

34. Todd Benson, "Cable Pirates Thrive in Brazil," *New York Times*, 10 November 2004, p. W1.

35. Edmund Amann, "Economic Policy and Performance in Brazil since 1985," in Kinzo and Dunkerley, *Brazil since 1985*, p. 135.

36. Timothy Power and J. Timmons Roberts, "The Changing Demographic in Context," in Kingstone and Power, *Democratic Brazil*, p. 246.

37. It also weakens trade unions and their ability to improve wages for Brazil's poorest workers.

38. Power and Roberts, "The Changing Demographic Context," p. 243.

39. "Bloated, Wasteful, Rigid and Unfair," *Economist*, 4, September 2004, p. 37.

40. Aleyei Barnonvevo, "Brazil Grows as Larger Economies Struggle," *International Herald Tribune* (31 July 2008).

41. Charles Blake, *Politics in Latin America*, 2nd Ed. (Boston: Houghton Mifflin, 2008), p. 180

42. Wendy Hunter and Timothy Power, "Rewarding Lula: Executive Power, Social Policy, and the Brazilian Elections of 2006," *Latin American Politics and Society*, 49, no. 1 (Spring 2007), pp. 1–30.

43. *Economist Factsheet, 2004*, www.economist.com/countries/Brazil/profile.cfm?folder5Profile-FactSheet (accessed 18 July 2005).

44. "A Giant Stirs," *Economist*, 10, June 2004 www.economist.com/world/americas/displaystory.cfm?story_id=E1_N5VNDD (accessed 19 February 2009).

45. Kinzo and Dunkerley, *Brazil since 1985*, p. 33.

GLOSSARY OF KEY TERMS

abertura   Gradual opening of Brazilian politics by the military during the 1970s, a process that eventually led to democratization.

Amazon basin   Vast and sparsely populated area of Brazil's interior that is home to the world's largest tropical rain forest.

Belindia   Term combining Belgium and India; used to decribe Brazil's unique combination of modernity and undervelopment.

Bolsa Familia (Family Fund)   Brazilian social welfare program that pays monthly stipends to families when their children receive education and health care.

Brasília   Brazil's futuristic capital city that was created in the barren interior in the 1960s by urban planners.

bureaucratic authoritarian   Form of authoritarian rule common in Latin America during the 1960s and 1970s (in Brazil, 1964–1985) in which military leaders and civilian technocrats presided over conservative, anti-Communist regimes.

caboclo   Brazilians of mixed European and indigenous ancestry.

Cardoso, Fernando Henrique   Brazilian president from 1995–2002, responsible for significant economic and political reform.

Chamber of Deputies (Câmara dos Deputados)   The lower house of Brazil's legislature.

Christian Base Communities   Small neighborhood groups of progressive Catholics who promoted liberation theology and political activisim.

da Silva, Luiz Inácio Lula   Brazil's current president, first elected in 2002, and a member of the leftist Worker's Party.

Estado Nôvo   The populist authoritarian regime of Getúlio Vargas between 1937 and 1945.

Escola Superior de Guerra (Superior War College)   The elite Brazilian military academy that professionalized the Brazilian military.

favelas   Brazil's sprawling urban shantytowns.

Federal Senate (Senado Federal)   The upper house of Brazil's legislature.

Federal Supreme Court (Supremo Tribunal Federal)   Brazil's highest judical body.

Goulart, João   Brazilian leftist president (from 1961 to 1964) whose removal by the military began a long period of authoritarian rule.

Landless Workers Movement (MST)   The large Brazilian social movement that has fought for land reform.

liberation theology   A radical doctrine within the Catholic Church advocating that the church should act to improve the social and political power of the poor.

MERCOSUR   A free-trade organization that includes Brazil and some of its neighbors.

mulatto   Brazilians of mixed white and black ancestry.

National Congress (Congresso Nacional)   Brazil's legislature.

open-list proportional representation (PR)   Brazil's electoral system for legislative elections in which voters may select individual candidates instead of a party list.

populist   A type of leader who appeals to the masses and attacks elements of the established elite. The term applies to Getúlio Vargas in Brazil.

robust federalism   Brazil's current constitution established a federal system in which states enjoy very strong power.

state corporatism   Political system in which citizens are encouraged to participate in state-controlled interest groups.

Vargas, Getúlio   Brazilian populist dictator who presided over the Estado Novo (1937–1945) and was later elected to office during the Second Republic.

Workers' Party (PT)   Brazil's most important leftist party, and the party of President da Silva.

WEB LINKS

InfoBrazil **www.infobrazil.com**
Articles on Brazilian politics and current events.
IUPERJ: Programa de Pós-Graduação em Sociologia e Ciência Politica, Instituto Univeristário de Pesquisas do Rio de Janeiro
www.iuperj.br/english/pesquisas_bancodedados.php.
An excellent source of online data.
Landless Workers Movement **www.mst.org.br**
Links to major Brazilian periodicals **newslink.org/sabra.html**
Latin American Network Information Center: Brazil
lanic.utexas.edu/la/brazil
An encyclopedic collection of links maintained by the University of Texas, Austin.
The Workers' Party **www.pt.org.br**

13 SOUTH AFRICA

Head of state and government:
President Jacob Zuma
(since May 9, 2009)

Capital: Pretoria is the seat of government;
Cape Town is the legislative capital;
Bloemfontein is the judicial capital.

Total land size: 1,219,912 sq km

Population: 44 million

GDP at PPP: 491 billion US$

GDP per capita at PPP: $11,100

**Human development index
    ranking:** 121

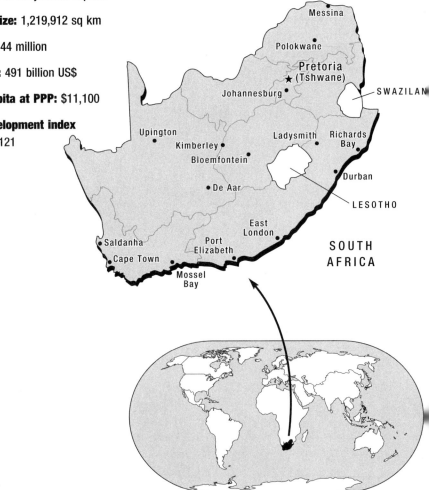

INTRODUCTION

Why Study This Case?

True to its remarkable modern history of tragedy and triumph, South Africa is a nation of paradox. The contradictions that constitute South African history and the remarkable capacity of South Africans to face and resolve them make this a fascinating case to study.

South Africa makes for a fascinating study for several other reasons as well. Like Russia, it in fact presents to students of comparative politics two cases in one. Prior to the early 1990s, South Africa's politics, society, and economy were dominated by the racist authoritarian system known as **apartheid**, or "separateness." In **Afrikaans**, the language spoken by the descendants of the first white settlers, the term refers to policies imposed by the ruling minority regime from 1948 to 1994 that systematically segregated races and privileged white South Africans. But with the collapse of the apartheid regime, the "new" South Africa of the past decade has been a fascinating petri dish of unfolding multicultural democracy.

South Africa's remarkable and relatively peaceful transition from oppressive minority rule to a broad-based democracy is an even more compelling reason to study this case. Refuting the mid-1990s doomsday predictions of incendiary race wars, the overwhelming majority of South African citizens chose reconciliation over revolution, opting for ballots over bullets as a means of resolving seemingly intractable political differences. This political miracle not only stands in contrast to Africa's dismal record of failed democracies and even failed states but also offers a powerful example to other nations of the world plagued by racial, ethnic, and religious strife.

South Africa has taken remarkble strides since its return to democracy in 1994. Politically, its democratically elected legislature has written and revised a constitution with broad political rights and civil liberties, and its government has convened regular nationwide elections. Socially, South Africans vanquished the world's most elaborate and overtly racist authoritarian regime and forged a common nation from its ashes. Economically, the government confounded its critics by avoiding the "easy" path of populist redistribution, instead cutting government expenditures and debt while delivering impressive gains in access to basic necessities for the country's poorest citizens.

Make no mistake, however; this tale of two South Africas cannot yet boast a fairy-tale ending. The decades of political violence, social partition, and economic deprivation that victimized over 80 percent of the population have left horrible and lasting scars. Compounding the legacies of racism and authoritarianism are a host of pernicious social problems, such as rampant violent crime, brooding racial tension, and the pandemic of HIV/AIDS. As if these challenges were not enough, the remarkable success of the new government has heightened expectations for rapid economic change and social equality, and there are concerns that democracy has been successful only because the postapartheid government faces no serious opposition.

South Africa's leaders must attempt to satisfy rising expectations and must balance decades of pent-up social and economic demands with the requirements of lenders and investors to maintain fiscal discipline and free markets. Without economic growth, the government will lack the very means to address South Africa's social and economic problems. The political temptation to promote affirmative action in the workplace must be weighed against the demands of the marketplace. Safeguarding the political rights of all groups in South Africa can at times necessitate overruling the will of the dominant black majority and resisting the temptation to dispense with democratic niceties.

How can the current government (or any government, for that matter) fare under such challenging circumstances? As one editorial asked, "How can a black revolutionary movement, forged by 40 years of struggle against white supremacy, transform itself into a multiracial ruling party, to run a sophisticated industrial economy? How can a new generation of leaders, without the aura of struggle, restrain the pressures towards populism and maintain a tolerant democracy when so many African governments have so noticeably failed?"[1] This case seeks to address these questions as well as the historical puzzle of why apartheid, enforced by such a small minority, managed to persist so successfully for so long and how its collapse and replacement came about under relatively peaceful circumstances.

Despite its unique history and political experience, South Africa faces many of the same issues and dilemmas as other developing countries. These include coping with the legacies of colonialism and racism, dealing with the policy trade-offs between freedom and equality, and managing the social and economic consequences of crime, poverty, and disease. The case of South Africa offers insights into these fundamental issues.

Major Geographic and Demographic Features

Historically, South Africa has been a harsh and isolated region. Ocean currents and the dearth of natural harbors impeded early European settlement of its coastline. Much of western South Africa (with the notable exception of the area around Cape Town) remains drought stricken and unsuitable for agriculture. South Africa's eastern coast and interior are subtropical and more suitable to agriculture, though the quality of the soil is generally poor. South Africa has no navigable waterways, a fact that until modern times made transportation and communication over the vast region very difficult. These factors limited the growth of a large population in precolonial South Africa.

Today, South Africa has about 44 million inhabitants. Unlike much of the rest of Africa, South Africa has seen its birth rates decline dramatically over the past twenty-five years, though considerable population growth is still created by emigration from South Africa's impoverished neighbors. Due to the experience of apartheid, it is common to think of South Africa's population as being neatly divided between blacks and whites. This gross simplification obscures a much more heterogeneous ethnic makeup. Three quarters of South Africans are black, but the ethnic composition of the black population is extremely diverse. About one quarter of black South Africans are Zulus, another one fifth are Xhosa (the ethnic group of former president **Nelson Mandela**), and about 18 percent are Sotho. The Tswana and Tsonga (and to a lesser extent the Venda and Ndebele) groups also have a significant presence in the South African population. Each of these ethnic groups has a different language and is concentrated in a different area. For example, Xhosas predominate in the western part of the country and in Cape Town and Port Elizabeth. Zulus are the dominant group in Durban.

Whites constitute about 10 percent of the population, and that population is also divided ethnically. Over half are **Afrikaners**, descendants of the Dutch, French, and German colonists who arrived in the seventeenth century and developed their own language (Afrikaans) and cultural traditions. Another 40 percent of South Africa's white population are descendants of English settlers who arrived in the eighteenth century. Even today these "English whites" favor English over Afrikaans and view themselves as somewhat distinct.

South Africans of mixed race account for 9 percent of the population. This group, largely concentrated in the Western Cape Province and KwaZulu-Natal, is widely referred to as **colored**. The majority of colored South Africans speak Afrikaans as their first language.

This diversity of the people is also shaped by urbanization. About half of South Africans (including most whites, Asians, and colored people) live in an urban setting. South Africa has five cities with over 1 million inhabitants: Cape Town (2.8 million), Johannesburg (2.2 million), Durban (1.3 million), Pretoria (1.3 million), and Port Elizabeth (1.1 million). Soweto, a large black township outside Johannesburg, has between 600,000 and 2 million inhabitants.

South Africa is truly a complex, polyglot nation. The 1994 constitution recognizes eleven languages, nine of which (Ndebele, Northern Sotho, Sotho, Tsonga, Tswana, Venda, Swazi, Xhosa, and Zulu) are spoken exclusively by blacks, and some of which are very closely related to one another. One characteristic of quite a few of the languages is the distinct clicking sound that eludes nonnative speakers. Quite a few blacks speak more than one African language. If there is a common language among South Africans, it is English.

Virtually all whites, Asians, educated blacks, and coloreds can speak at least some English. Almost all Afrikaners are bilingual in Afrikaans and English, and many South Africans of English descent (as well as colored South Africans) also speak some Afrikaans.

But language has often bitterly divided the South African people. Blacks long resisted the imposition of Afrikaans by Afrikaners, and the 1976 Soweto Uprising was ignited by the Afrikaner authorities' attempt to make Afrikaans the official language of instruction in schools. Colored South Africans, on the other hand, have recently fought to preserve the role of Afrikaans in the schools.

South Africa's neighbors have been an important focal point for many South Africans. As illustrated in the map of the region, South Africa is bordered to the north by Zimbabwe (formerly Rhodesia). Zimbabwe's transition to majority black rule, in 1980, was an inspiration to black South Africans. Botswana, also to the north, has been one of the most economically successful African nations. On its eastern border, Mozambique and Swaziland are extremely poor. Throughout much of the twentieth century, apartheid leaders frequently pointed to these neighbors (as well as much of the rest of Africa) as proof that blacks were incapable of governing themselves. Sparsely populated Namibia, a former German colony and later a United Nations protectorate, was long dominated by apartheid South Africa.

Historical Development of the State

The telling of history often reflects the perspective of those in power, so it is not surprising that South Africa's history has usually been told from the perspective of whites. Afrikaners often contend that southern Africa was largely uninhabited when their Dutch ancestors arrived at the Cape of Good Hope in 1652. The truth is far more complex. Hunters and herders populated South Africa when the Dutch arrived in the mid-seventeenth century. The Dutch East India Company officials who first established a fort in what is today Cape Town encountered tribes of Khoisans, whom they soon enslaved. When these native Africans died from disease and slavery, the Dutch settlers imported slaves, mostly from Southeast Asia.[2]

In the interior of South Africa, a variety of Bantu-speaking tribes were ending their centuries-long migration southward from central Africa, integrating with hunters and herders who had long inhabited the region. Among the largest of these tribes were the Zulu, the Sotho, and the Swazi kingdoms.

DUTCH RULE

While most of the colonial "scramble for Africa" took place in the nineteenth century, European domination of South Africa began almost two centuries earlier. Cape Town was initially settled by the Dutch East India Company to resupply ships heading to and from Dutch colonies in Indonesia. The early

TIME LINE OF POLITICAL DEVELOPMENT

Year	Event
1652	Arrival of the Dutch at the Cape of Good Hope
1795	Cape Town captured from the Dutch by the British
1880–81; 1899–1902	Boer Wars fought between the Afrikaners and the British
1910	Formation of the Union of South Africa, dominated by English-speaking South Africans
1948	Election of Afrikaner National Party and beginning of apartheid
1960	Banning of African National Congress (ANC)
1964	Nelson Mandela imprisoned
1990	Mandela released from prison
1990–93	Transition to democracy as the result of negotiations between Mandela and President F. W. de Klerk
1994	After historic multiracial elections, ANC majority government established under Nelson Mandela
1996	Democratic constitution approved
1999	Legislative elections won by ANC; Thabo Mbeki named president
2008	Thabo Mbeki replaced as president by Kgalema Motlanthe
2009	Jacob Zuma becomes president after ANC wins a fourth consecutive election

Dutch settlers, known as **Boers** (Afrikaans for "farmer"), quickly seized the fertile land of the Cape of Good Hope. The European residents of the Cape developed their own culture, based in their conservative Protestant **Dutch Reformed Church** and their unique language. The small and isolated Cape Colony was fairly prosperous until it was seized by the British Empire in 1795. The Dutch ceded formal control of the region to the British in 1814.

BOER MIGRATION

As Britain quickly began to integrate this new colony into its burgeoning empire, the arrival of waves of British settlers was seen as a threat to Boer society. Bristling under British rule, many Cape Colony Boers (and their slaves) undertook a migration into the interior of southern Africa that would later gain the status of heroic myth. During the **Great Trek** of 1835 the **voortrekkers** (Afrikaans for "pioneers") drove their wagons northeast to regain their autonomy and preserve their way of life. They met strong initial resistance from the Xhosa and other Bantu kingdoms, though whites had important technological advantages in these conflicts and were able to exploit the numerous divisions among the indigenous tribes.

A number of bloody battles ensued, most famously the 1838 Battle of Blood River between Zulu tribesmen and Afrikaners. During that conflict, a group of heavily outnumbered Afrikaners defeated the Zulus, with legend claiming that no whites were killed. Afrikaners still consider the Blood River anniversary an important religious holiday and celebrate it each year on December 16. By the early 1840s, Afrikaners were firmly ensconsed in South Africa's interior.

The exhausting exodus to escape British domination, along with the bitter fighting between Boers and blacks, was in the short term a Boer success. The Boers created two states, known as the Boer republics, in which slavery, strict segregation of races, the Afrikaans language, and the Dutch Reformed Church were protected by law.

Initially the British grudgingly tolerated the interior Boer republics. However, the discovery of massive deposits of diamonds (in 1870) and gold (in 1886) changed everything. English-speakers flooded into the interior, and the city of Johannesburg quickly became an English-speaking enclave in the Boer-controlled state of Transvaal. Transvaal President Paul Kruger attempted to limit the influence of the English by denying them the vote. In 1895, English diamond magnate Cecil Rhodes used the pretense of Boer discrimination against En-glish settlers and the presence of slavery in the Boer republics to incite a rebellion among the English. President Kruger declared war on England in 1899.

THE DEFEAT OF THE AFRIKANERS IN THE BOER WARS

Though outnumbered five to one, the Boers fought tenaciously to defend their independence during the **Boer Wars**. To defeat the well-armed and disciplined Afrikaners, the British pioneered the use of concentration camps, in which as many as 20,000 Afrikaners and 15,000 blacks perished. By 1902, the Boers had been defeated, and the Boer republics had become self-governing British colonies. In exchange for signing a peace treaty, the Boers were promised full political rights, protections for their language and culture, and the ability to deny blacks the vote in the former Boer republics. In 1910, these agreements were formalized in the **Union of South Africa**.[3]

THE RENAISSANCE OF AFRIKANER POWER

English and Afrikaners worked together to create a single British colony, and the first prime minister of the Union of South Africa was a former Afrikaner military leader. The Native Land Act of 1913 prevented blacks from owning land except in designated "reserves" (less than 10 percent of the total land of South Africa). Discrimination against blacks continued in the former Boer republics. Only in the largely English Cape Colony were coloreds and a small number of blacks allowed to vote. Nowhere in South Africa were rights of the black majority protected, and racial discrimination was the rule even in English-governed areas.

The first elections in the united country brought to power the South African Party (SAP), which included both English speakers and Afrikaners. But many Afrikaners, especially those in the former Boer republics, continued to deeply resent the English. The Afrikaners enjoyed full political rights, but the English controlled most of the country's wealth, especially its mineral profits and budding industry.

As has so often been the case throughout their history, the Afrikaners resisted this marginalization, but this time they did so within the political system. The formation of the **National Party (NP)** in 1914 was the most important step in their attempt to organize and mobilize the Afrikaner population. The NP demanded that Afrikaans be recognized alongside English and called for South Africa to secede from the British Empire. In the mid-1930s, NP leader Daniel Malan articulated the policies of white supremacy that later became the hallmark of apartheid. At the same time, Malan called for Afrikaner control of the state so that wealth held by the English could be redistributed to Afrikaners. Malan's goals appealed to the mass of poor white Afrikaner workers, who felt threatened by the better-off English as well as by the growing number of even poorer black workers (who vied for their jobs). The NP realized that if Afrikaners could be unified, they could not be denied power. In 1948, the NP was elected to office.

THE APARTHEID ERA

What distinguishes the apartheid era were the NP's two goals: consolidating Afrikaner power and eliminating all vestiges of black participation in South African politics. To a considerable degree, apartheid simply codified and intensified the racial segregation that existed in the mid-twentieth century. During an era when racial discrimination was being challenged in virtually every other country, Afrikaner leaders sought to construct elaborate legal justifications for it.

The Population Registration Act of 1950 divided South Africa into four racial categories and placed every South African into one of those categories (see "Hendrick Verwoerd and the 'Logic' of White Rule," p. 498). Once Africans were divided into races, the apartheid architects argued that blacks (about three quarters of the population) were not citizens of South Africa. According to the **Group Areas Act** of 1950, blacks were deemed to be citizens of ten remote "tribal homelands" (dubbed **Bantustans**), whose boundaries and lead-

---

HENDRIK VERWOERD AND THE "LOGIC" OF WHITE RULE

The leading ideologue and architect of apartheid was Hendrik Verwoerd, a professor at South Africa's leading Afrikaner university and prime minister from 1958 to 1966. Verwoerd argued that the population of South Africa contained four distinct "racial groups" (white, African, colored, and Indian) and that whites, as the most "civilized" racial group, should have absolute control over the state. Verwoerd and the advocates of apartheid further argued that Africans belonged to ten distinct nations, whereas the other racial groups belonged to only one nation each. By this logic, whites were the largest nation in South Africa and were therefore justified in dominating the state.

---

ers were decreed by the government. The Bantustans, somewhat akin to American Indian reservations, constituted only around 13 percent of South Africa's territory and were usually made up of noncontiguous parcels of infertile land separated by white-owned farms. The NP chose black leaders (often tribal chiefs) loyal to the party goals to head the Bantustan governments. All blacks in South Africa were in effect "guests" and did not enjoy any of the rights of citizenship. The 1971 Bantu Homelands Citizenship Act allowed the government to grant "independence" to any Bantustan, and though government propagandists defended the measure as an act of "decolonization," in reality it had little impact. Over the next decade, many Bantustans became "independent," though no foreign government would recognize them as sovereign countries.

Racial segregation in the rest of South Africa went even further. Members of each of the four racial groups were required to reside in areas determined by the government. The vast majority of blacks who lived and worked in white areas were required to carry internal visas at all times. Each year, failure to carry such a pass resulted in hundreds of thousands of deportations to a "homeland" that, more often than not, the deportee had never before set foot in. The apartheid authorities created new racial categories and designed separate residential areas for South Africans of Asian descent, or of mixed race, often forcibly relocating them. Other infamous laws reinforced racial segregation. The Prohibition of Mixed Marriages Act (1950) banned relations across racial lines, and the Reservation of Separate Amenities Act (1953) provided the legal basis for segregating places as diverse as beaches and restrooms.[4]

The apartheid system retained many of the trappings of a parliamentary democracy. Apartheid South Africa had regular elections, a fairly vigorous press, and a seemingly independent judiciary. The vast majority of South Africans, however, were disenfranchised and utterly powerless. The regime tolerated mild opposition on some issues but ruthlessly quashed individuals and groups that actively opposed apartheid itself.

FORCED RELOCATION AND THE BUILDING OF APARTHEID

One of the pillars of South African apartheid was the 1950 Group Areas Act, which prohibited South Africans of different races from living in the same neighborhoods. The practical implications were immediate and devastating: nonwhites were forcibly relocated to areas outside of South Africa's main cities. The most infamous example was Sophiatown, a vibrant black community in Johannesburg (often compared to New York City's Harlem) that was bulldozed in 1955. Its inhabitants were relocated to a settlement thirteen miles outside of the city that later became known as **Soweto**. Another example was District Six, a multiracial neighborhood in Cape Town with a large mixed-race (or colored) population. It was destroyed in 1966, and its colored inhabitants were relocated to the dusty Cape Flats fifteen miles outside of the city.

The apartheid regime met resistance from its very inception. The most important organization resisting racial discrimination was the African National Congress (ANC). Founded in 1912 it was a largely black organization that sought the extension of suffrage to blacks. The ANC was initially nonviolent and politically moderate in its calls for multiracial democracy. Under the leadership of Nelson Mandela, it led a series of nonviolent civil disobedience campaigns against apartheid laws.[5]

Fierce repression of this protest by the apartheid regime had several consequences. First, some blacks tiring of the nonviolent, gradualist approach of the ANC, created more radical organizations, such as the Pan African Congress (PAC), founded in 1959. Second, the apartheid leaders, alarmed by the growing resistance, banned the ANC and the PAC. Third, the repression (especially the government slaughter of protesters during the Sharpeville Massacre of 1960) persuaded ANC leaders to initiate military action against the apartheid regime. The government countered by arresting Mandela and other top ANC leaders in 1963 and sentencing them to life in prison. The ongoing repression led to the incarceration and murder of thousands of South Africans who actively resisted apartheid.

Although not all whites supported the apartheid system, the NP skillfully retained the majority's allegiance. For Afrikaners, the NP dramatically improved their political and economic status, making them dependent on the perpetuation of the status quo. The NP played on English-speaking whites' fears of black rule. Moderate white critics of apartheid were mostly tolerated, as they generally held little sway among the white population.

Though the NP subdued most domestic resistance to apartheid, the system faced growing hostility from abroad. The end of colonialism created independent African states that supported the ANC, and the United Nations condemned apartheid as early as 1952 and imposed an arms embargo on South Africa in 1977. Nevertheless, in the context of the cold war, South Africa was able to gain support (from the United States, in particular) by portraying its fight against the ANC as a struggle against Communism. Moreover, the world's major capitalist powers had lucrative investments in South Africa and were ambivalent about promoting black rule.

THE TRANSITION TO DEMOCRACY

There was nothing inevitable about South Africa's transition from apartheid to majority rule. Five categories of factors need to be considered to explain the momentous political shift that culminated in South Africa's first free elections in 1994.

1. *Demographic pressure and growing unrest:* The growth of opposition to apartheid had at its core a demographic component. The proportion of whites in the population had dropped from a high of 21 percent in 1936 to only 10 percent in 1999. Not only was the black population growing more quickly, but it was increasingly concentrated in urban areas, which were more subject to political mobilization. Most of these newly urban blacks lived in squalid conditions in South Africa's townships, the population of which doubled between 1950 and 1980. These demographic trends meant that despite largely successful efforts to deny blacks political power, their economic power and significance were rapidly expanding.

As a result of these changes, opposition to apartheid during the 1980s assumed dimensions previously unknown in South Africa. The creation of the **United Democratic Front (UDF)** in 1983 effectively united trade unions and the major black and white apartheid opposition groups. The number of protests, strikes, boycotts, and slowdowns grew, requiring ever-greater levels of repression by the apartheid regime. In July 1985, the government imposed a virtually permanent state of emergency, leading to massive arrests of suspected opposition members. In 1988, the government banned the UDF and the largest trade union confederation. The ANC, whose leadership was either in prison or in exile, waged a guerrilla war against the apartheid regime. That struggle was never able to dislodge the heavily armed white regime, but nor could the regime destroy the ANC or stop the escalating violence.

2. *Economic decline:* By the 1980s, the deficiencies in the apartheid economic model had become increasingly apparent. During this decade, South Africa's economy was among the most stagnant in the developing world, growing at an average rate of only about 1 percent. The apartheid economic system had clearly raised the standard of living for South Africa's whites, especially Afrikaners, but it had also led to serious distortions that were by now beginning to take a toll.

The apartheid state, with its convoluted and overlapping race-based institutions and its subsidies to the entirely dependent black "homelands," was costly and inefficient. The mercantilist apartheid policies of self-sufficiency and protectionism led to the creation of industries and services that were not competitive. The system of racial preferences and job protection that was a cornerstone of apartheid clearly hindered economic development and economic efficiency.

3. *Internal reforms:* By the mid-1970s, even leading Afrikaner politicians were convinced that apartheid was an anachronistic system that needed reform if it was to survive. The reforms that followed paved the way for a future transition to democracy. Prime Minister P. W. Botha, who took power in 1978, promised to dismantle apartheid and enacted some minor reforms. However, Botha was unwilling to push the reforms very far. The next leader, President **F. W. de Klerk** (1989–1994), repealed the Reservation of Separate Amenities Act, the Group Areas Act, and the Population Registration Act. De Klerk legalized black political parties, including the ANC and the PAC, and freed their leaders. The crisis of apartheid served to split the traditionally unified Afrikaner leadership, opening the window to reform.

4. *The changing international context:* During the 1980s, many countries imposed embargoes on South Africa, limiting trade and foreign investment, though powerful nations like the United States and the United Kingdom continued to trade with the regime into the 1990s. Of greater importance was the winding down of the cold war in the 1980s. On the one hand, it deprived the South African regime of a key source of international legitimacy: the decline of Communism weakened its claim that it was facing a Communist insurgency. On the other hand, the collapse of the Soviet Union and the Soviet bloc weakened the ANC sectors that promoted Communist revolution in South Africa.

5. *Skilled leadership:* Finally, South Africa's transition would likely not have occurred (or at the very least would not have been as peaceful or successful) had skilled leaders not managed the transition. F. W. de Klerk's role in forcing Prime Minister Botha's resignation and his courageous decisions to free Mandela and legalize the ANC were essential to the transition. De Klerk used his unblemished credentials as a National Party stalwart to convince NP die-hards to accept the transition. He was able to convince most Afrikaners that their interests would be safeguarded during and after the transition.[6]

Likewise, Nelson Mandela risked a great deal by negotiating the terms of the transition with the NP government. Mandela and the ANC leadership agreed to power sharing and numerous guarantees in order to assuage white fears and were able to restrain radicalized blacks who wanted quick redress for decades of abuse. Mandela's knowledge of Afrikaner language and culture (gained through decades of study in prison) undoubtedly helped him negotiate with his Afrikaner opposition. His ability to eschew bitterness and revenge

**NELSON MANDELA: DEMOCRATIC
SOUTH AFRICA'S FOUNDING FATHER**

The remarkable story of Nelson Mandela parallels the turbulent history of modern South Africa. Mandela's father was a Xhosa-speaking tribal chief in the Eastern Cape Province. Mandela was expelled from the University College of Fort Hare for demonstrating against racism but went on to earn a law degree and was one of the first blacks to practice law in South Africa. He became deeply involved in the ANC and was appointed one of its four deputy presidents in 1952.

Mandela helped move the ANC in a more radical direction after NP governments began construction of the apartheid regime in 1948. The ANC was banned in 1960 after it led nationwide protests against apartheid. In response to the Sharpeville Massacre of that same year (in which police massacred sixty-nine unarmed protesters), the ANC abandoned its strategy of nonviolent protest, and Mandela was named its first military commander. Mandela was sentenced to life in prison in 1964 and was held with other ANC leaders on Robben Island. From his cell, he was able to direct the antiapartheid struggle, learn Afrikaans, and write his autobiography.

When Mandela was released in February 1990, he immediately assumed the role of representative of the black majority in the negotiations for a democratic transition. After Mandela received the Nobel Peace Prize in 1993, his ANC won a landslide victory in the country's first multiracial elections; Mandela became South Africa's first black president. While in office, Mandela did much to heal the racial divide, taking special pains to respect the culture of the Afrikaners. His decision to step down in 1997 and make way for a younger generation of ANC leaders was another sign of Mandela's commitment to democracy.

after his twenty-seven-year prison term impressed even his strongest opponents. Still, the negotiations between the black leadership and the NP were protracted and difficult. De Klerk and Mandela faced serious opposition from radical sectors of their own camps. Nevertheless, an interim constitution was approved in 1993, paving the way for democratic elections and majority rule in 1994. In recognition of their important role in the South African transition, de Klerk and Mandela were awarded the 1993 Nobel Peace Prize.

POLITICAL REGIME

Political Institutions

During the apartheid regime, South Africa enjoyed a set of democratic institutions, but these applied only to the white population. Nonwhites had much more limited political rights or none whatsoever. As a result, few considered the country to be democratic. After the political transition in 1994, however, political rights were extended to the population as a whole, regardless of race. South Africa is now a democracy with broad political rights and civil liberties commensurate with those found in advanced democracies. Ironically, South Africa's long tradition of democratic institutions, albeit highly restrictive ones, helped smooth the transition to multiracial democracy. The architects of the 1994 transition did not need to create an entirely new democratic system from scratch but merely reformed existing democratic institutions and extended them to the entire population.

THE CONSTITUTION

The new democratic regime is fundamentally enshrined in the South African constitution, approved in 1996. This document reflects the delicate nature of the country's transition to democracy, in which new democratic rights had to be provided to the black majority while those of the white minority had to be protected.

The constitution attempts to balance majority and minority concerns carefully, affirming the basic values of human rights regardless of "race, gender, sex, pregnancy, religion, conscience, belief, culture, language and birth," a list far more detailed than that of most democratic constitutions. Eleven official languages are recognized. The constitution also upholds citizens' rights to housing, health care, food, water, social security, and even a healthy environment. Reacting to decades of apartheid authoritarianism, the constitution includes unusually detailed provisions limiting the powers of the state to arrest, detain, and prosecute individuals. Finally, it enshrines the principle of affirmative action, stating that in order to achieve greater equality, laws and other measures can be used to promote or advance individuals who have been discriminated against.

The constitution also firmly protects the rights of property, which ensured the white population that their property would not be seized by a black-dominated government. Perhaps most important, the constitution defines itself as the supreme law of the land: parliament must act within its confines, and the new Constitutional Court can strike down unconstitutional behavior. This is a departure from the past, when the parliament and the government reigned supreme and could

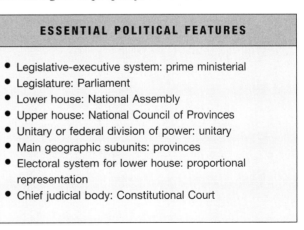

ESSENTIAL POLITICAL FEATURES

- Legislative-executive system: prime ministerial
- Legislature: Parliament
- Lower house: National Assembly
- Upper house: National Council of Provinces
- Unitary or federal division of power: unitary
- Main geographic subunits: provinces
- Electoral system for lower house: proportional representation
- Chief judicial body: Constitutional Court

change and reinterpret laws as they saw fit, with no higher legal power to restrain them.

The Branches of Government

The South African government is based on British institutions, with some variations. For most of the apartheid period, South Africa had a bicameral parliament and a prime minister, with a ceremonial president as head of state. Since 1994, the South African system has been transformed into one similar to that seen in many other democracies, with a bicameral parliament and a Constitutional Court. Interestingly, as a result of historic compromises between Afrikaner and English-speaking whites, South Africa has three capitals. The seat of government is located in Pretoria, the traditional heart of Afrikaner power and the center of the former Boer republics. Cape Town, where English influence was strongest, is the legislative capital. South Africa's judicial capital is located in Bloemfontein.

STRUCTURE OF THE GOVERNMENT

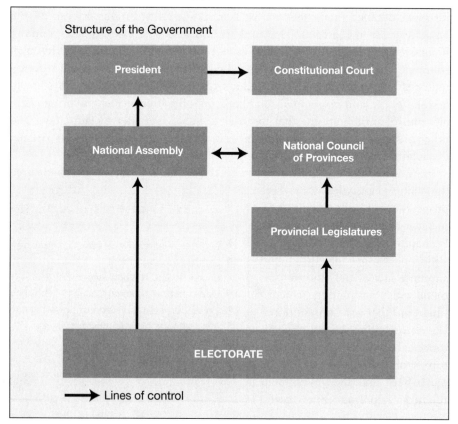

Structure of the Government

President → Constitutional Court

National Assembly ↔ National Council of Provinces

Provincial Legislatures

ELECTORATE

→ Lines of control

THE PRESIDENCY AND THE CABINET

The chief executive of South Africa is the president. This title is rather confusing, however, given that, like a typical prime minister, the president is chosen from the National Assembly, the lower house of the legislature, by its members and can be removed by a vote of no confidence. Yet, there is no division between the head of state and the head of government, as is found in most parliamentary systems, so the South African president serves in both capacities. Like most prime ministers, the president chooses a cabinet of ministers, signs or vetoes legislation presented by the National Assembly, and can refer legislation to the Constitutional Court as necessary. The president may also call national referenda, dissolve the National Assembly, and (in some situations) call new elections. If the president wishes to dissolve the National Assembly, a majority of the lower house must support the dissolution and three years must have passed since it was first elected. The president is unable to call snap elections as in other parliamentary systems.

The president is stronger than a typical prime minister. As head of state and head of government, the president can not only exert authority over the cabinet and government policy (like a typical head of government) but also speak on behalf of the nation and represent the country on the world stage (as a head of state does). Moreover, South African presidents can be removed by the legislature, but only with great difficulty. A vote of no confidence requires the support of two thirds of the members of the National Assembly and can be taken only on the grounds of a substantial violation of the law or constitution, serious misconduct, or an inability to perform the functions of the office—circumstances akin to an impeachment in a presidential system. Theoretically, the National Assembly cannot simply dismiss the president because it opposes a given policy. This provision remains untested, however, as a vote of no confidence has not yet been attempted. To date, the overwhelming power of the ANC in the National Assembly, combined with the prestige of Nelson Mandela as the first president, has given the office a great deal of authority.

However, the limits to the power of the president were evident in 2008 when President **Thabo Mbeki** was forced to resign after he failed to win reelection to the ANC leadership. Mbeki was replaced by Kgalema Motlanthe, a caretaker president who served until the 2009 general elections. As is the case in all parliamentary systems, South Africa's head of government serves at the behest of his political party and can be replaced by the party at any time.

THE LEGISLATURE

South Africa has a bicameral parliament. The lower and more powerful of its two houses, the **National Assembly**, currently has 400 members. Members serve for five-year terms, and they are charged with electing and removing the president, preparing and passing legislation, and approving the national budget. As in the United Kingdom, the lower house has a weekly "question time," when members can question the cabinet and the president. Question time can become a heated affair, with members of the opposition parties grilling the cabinet and casting aspersions on one another. Given the racial divisions in the country, however, such debate is also limited (for example, when one white member of parliament commented that a black member of the cabinet lacked intelligence, he was rebuked for using racial stereotypes).

The upper house is the National Council of Provinces. Its ninety members are indirectly elected by the nine provincial legislatures and include the premier of each province. Each province, regardless of its size or population, sends ten delegates. The power of the National Council depends on the type of legislation under consideration. When the National Assembly is dealing with national policy (such as foreign affairs or defense), the National Council has relatively little influence. When proposed legislation affects the provinces, however, the National Council can amend or reject measures, forcing the two houses to form a mediation committee to hammer out a compromise. Ultimately, the National Assembly can override the upper house with a two-thirds vote. In short, the National Council exists to ensure that local interests are heard at the national level, which is especially important when the provinces are distinguished by ethnicity, language, and culture.

THE JUDICIAL SYSTEM

Another important component of the transition to democratic multiracial rule in South Africa is the Constitutional Court. This body hears cases regarding the constitutionality of legislation on the separation of powers among the branches of government. Its eleven members serve twelve-year terms and are appointed by the president on the basis of the recommendations of a judicial commission. The commission is made up of government and nongovernment appointees who evaluate candidates' qualifications and take racial and gender diversity into account. To date, the court has shown a tendency for activism; in 1997, for example, it struck down the country's death penalty despite public sentiment in favor of capital punishment, and in 2002 it ruled that the government was obligated to provide treatment for persons with AIDS.[7]

The Electoral System

The current electoral rules in South Africa mark a significant departure from the past. Under apartheid, the country used the British single-member district, or plurality, system. As part of the transition to democracy, South Africa had to decide what election method would best represent the needs of a diverse public and help consolidate democratic legitimacy by creating an inclusive system. The result was the creation of an electoral system based on pure proportional representation (PR). Voters now cast their votes not for individual candidates but for a party, which is designated on the ballot by name, electoral symbol, and the picture of the head of the party (to ensure that illiterate voters are not excluded). To ensure the greatest possible proportionality, representatives are elected from a single nationwide constituency, and there is no minimum threshold for receiving seats in the legislature. The number of seats a party wins is divided proportionally to reflect the percentage of the total vote it receives. At elections, voters are given two ballots: one for the national legislature and one for their provincial legislature.

Overall, the electoral system in South Africa has successfully created an inclusive political atmosphere and has averted conflict and violence.[8] Electoral turnout has been very high, and in the 2009 elections turnout was over 77 percent. However, some critics have argued that the use of PR has created a disconnect between the National Assembly and the citizens. Because members of parliament are tied to their party instead of their constituency, they are not accountable to local communities. Political parties can stifle internal dissent and limit the independence of legislators by threatening to remove them from the party electoral list if they stray too far from the party's wishes. Critics inside South Africa have suggested that the country consider adopting a mixed electoral system, in which some percentage of the seats are filled by plurality while the remaining are filled by PR. This would give voters a local representative with whom they could identify, as well as the ability to cast their vote for a particular party.[9] After some discussion on electoral reform earlier in the decade, however, such suggestions have faded and the current system has become institutionalized. The ANC, in particular, has been unwilling to change an electoral system that has so far delivered it a huge majority.

Local Government

Below the national level, South Africa is divided into nine provinces, each with its own elected assembly. Members are elected for a term of five years (with elections for the national and provincial legislatures occurring simultaneously) and, in turn, elect a premier to serve as the province's chief executive. The provincial assemblies have their own constitutions, pass legislation, and send delegates to the National Council of Provinces.

It is difficult to call South Africa a federal state, however, and the concept itself is a politically charged issue. During the transition to democracy, the ANC in particular looked upon federalism with a great deal of suspicion. At that time, the National Party (NP), architects of apartheid, favored federalism as a way to limit the ANC's power, while some Afrikaners in fact hoped that a federal right to self-determination could pave the way for outright secession.

The Zulu-based Inkatha Freedom Party also called for self-determination—and an independent Zulu state. The 1996 constitution reflects these concerns by supporting regional and ethnic diversity. Still, the constitution gives the central government the ability to overturn local legislation relatively easily, and any powers not delimited by the constitution reside with the central, not the local, government. Provinces also have limited power to levy taxes, giving them little financial autonomy.

Since democratization, municipal governments have become increasingly important.[10] The ANC has suffered its most important defeats at the local level, where complaints about the delivery of services have boosted the fortunes of the Inkatha Freedom Party and the Democratic Alliance. In the 2009 provincial elections, the ANC lost control of Western Cape Province, and Democratic Alliance leader Helen Zille became premier.

POLITICAL CONFLICT AND COMPETITION

The Party System and Elections

During apartheid, few political parties existed, and the National Party (NP) dominated politics from 1948 until 1994. The main opposition was the weak Progressive Federal Party, which opposed apartheid laws and favored multiracial democracy within a federal framework. The enfranchisement of the nonwhite population has dramatically changed the political spectrum, though as in the past it remains dominated by one major party. National elections are held at least every five years, and those differences that do exist between the parties are driven as much by race and ethnicity as they are by ideology. Party identification is relatively weak in South Africa, and only about 60 percent of South Africans claim to identify with any party.[11]

Currently the dominant party, the **African National Congress (ANC)** led the struggle against white rule starting in 1912. During the ANC's long period underground and in exile, it developed an ideology strongly influenced by Marxism, favoring the nationalization of land and industry. Economic equality was seen as a necessary mechanism in overcoming racial discrimination. The ANC cultivated relations with Communist countries, such as the Soviet Union and China, and at home formed an alliance with the much smaller South African Communist Party (which still operates within the framework of the ANC). Many white South Africans, including some opponents of apartheid, were troubled by the ANC's demands for radical political and economic change. Since winning power in 1994, however, the ANC has stood for racial and gender equality and a strong state role in the expansion of economic opportunities for nonwhites, but it has also embraced property rights to provide jobs, education, and social services to the much poorer black majority. As such, its ideology is unclear, encompassing a mixture of social democratic and liberal views, a lingering sense of militancy, and an emphasis on unity. The ANC increased its share of the vote in each of the first three democratic elections, but saw its share of the vote decrease slightly in 2009.

SOUTH AFRICA'S NEW PRESIDENT AND THE POWER OF THE ANC

South Africa's new president is likely to be very different from the aloof, intellectual Thabo Mbeki. Jacob Zuma is the ANC's most prominent Zulu politican, and has been the leader of the ANC left. Unlike the scholarly Mbeki, Zuma grew up poor and received no formal education. He became involved in the ANC in the 1960s, and was sentenced to ten years in prison in 1963 (he served time at Robben Island with Nelson Mandela). After his release, he became a top ANC leader in exile. After the return of democracy, Zuma quickly rose within the ANC hierarchy, culminating in his 1997 appointment as executive Deputy President (Mbeki's number two).

Zuma's rise to power within the ANC has been clouded in controversy. In 2005, Zuma was charged with raping a young woman in his home. Zuma admitted to having unprotected sex with the woman, whom he knew to be HIV-positive, but claimed the relationship was consensual. Zuma was acquitted of the charges, but his statement under oath that he had showered after sex to reduce his risk of contracting the HIV virus infuriated many South Africans.

In 2005, Zuma was fired after he was accused of corruption and racketeering in a government arms procurement scandal. Charges were brought against Zuma in 2007, but they were dropped in April 2009, shortly before the elections. Zuma has claimed that the corruption charges are politically motivated. Zuma has strong support among South Africa's labor unions, among Zulus, and generally among those frustrated with the pace of change under Mandela and Mbeki. Unlike Mandela and Mbeki, Zuma is considered an economic populist who is less likely to continue the pro-business and pro-growth economic policies pursued by the ANC to date.

In December 2007, Zuma easily upset Thabo Mbeki in elections for the ANC presidency (he won two thirds of the internal party vote). Zuma's victory virtually guaranteed that he would become president after the April 2009 general election. The prominence of Zuma points to a broader issue: the dominance of the ANC and the weakness of the opposition. This raises concerns about possible abuses of power. The ANC has generally acted with caution to avoid antagonizing opposition parties and South Africa's various ethnic and religious minority groups. South Africa has yet to experience political alternation. Other democracies, like Japan, have been dominated by a single political party. Nevertheless, the dominance of a single party may threaten democracy in the long run.

The overwhelming preponderance of ANC power raises concerns. Some observers fear that the party has so easily embraced democracy after its long struggle in part because the party has done so well. Were the ANC to face losing power, it might not look upon the democratic process so favorably. These concerns were heightened in particular by Thabo Mbeki's tenure in office, as his rhetoric and that of the ANC grew increasingly intolerant of those who challenge it.

In general, however, the ANC's record in office has been positively evaluated by most South Africans, who give it high scores for managing the economy, improving health care, and promoting racial equality. South Africans have been most critical of the ANC's record on job creation, crime reduction, and reduction of the gap between rich and poor.

Since late 2007, the ANC has become badly divided between a populist wing, led current president **Jacob Zuma** (see "South Africa's New President and the Power of the ANC," p. 509) and backed by trade unions and the party rank and file, and the more technocratic wing, dominated by former president Mbeki. Zuma's successful challenge to Mbeki in the bitterly contested party leadership election of December 2007 led to the first significant split in the ANC. After winning the ANC leadership, Zuma began to replace Mbeki loyalists with his own supporters in key party posts. Zuma was able to force the resignation of Mbeki in September 2008, but Zuma could not become president because he was not a member of the legislature. The ANC appointed Kgalema Motlanthe, an ally of Zuma, as a caretaker president to serve until the 2009 general elections.

Zuma's rise to the leadership of the ANC, and his ablility to force Mbeki's resignation, prompted the creation of the **Congress of the People (COPE)**, a breakaway party led by Mosiuoa Lekota, a former defense minister under Mbeki. COPE has the potential of becoming the first genuine black opposition party to the ANC, but in the 2009 elections it was hurt by internal divisions and lack of funds. Despite these problems, COPE was able to win over 7 percent of the vote and thirty seats in the legislature, making it South Africa's third largest political party. Its success, along with that of the Democratic Alliance, deprived the ANC of a two-thirds majority in the lower house, weakening the ANC's ability to amend the constitution and pass some types of legislation.

The overwhelming presence of the ANC in parliament dwarfs the opposition parties. Among them is the **Democratic Alliance (DA)**, successor to the old Progressive Federal Party. The DA is primarily liberal, favoring a small state, individual freedoms, privatization of state-run firms, and greater devolution of power to local governments. In the 2004 elections, the DA won 12 percent of the votes and 50 seats. In the 2006 local elections, the DA beat the ANC in Cape Town (the only local municipal council not controlled by the

ANC), winning about 15 percent of the vote nationally. **Helen Zille**, a liberal journalist during apartheid and the white mayor of Cape Town, became DA leader in 2007. Under her leadership, the DA has been an increasingly outspoken opposition to the ANC. Public support for the DA has grown since the 1994 elections, but its primary base of support remains the white and mixed-race population. To become a viable challenger to the ANC, it will have to broaden this base dramatically. In 2006, only 3 percent of South Africans said they identified with the DA. In the 2009 elections the DA increased its votes to over 16 percent and won control of Western Cape Province (the only one not controlled by the ANC).

The **Inkatha Freedom Party (IFP)**, played an ambiguous role in apartheid and post-apartheid politics. The IFP, founded in 1975 by Zulu chief Mangosuthu Buthelezi, challenged apartheid institutions but also participated in local government in the KwaZulu "homeland," one of the remote areas created to remove blacks from desirable areas and deprive them of basic citizenship. During the 1980s, animosity grew between the IFP and the ANC: the ANC saw the IFP as having been co-opted by the government, while the IFP viewed the ANC as dominated by ethnic Xhosas who did not represent Zulu interests. The animosity soon erupted into violence, which was

South African National Assembly Elections, 1999, 2004, and 2009

	1999		2004		2009	
Party	**% of Vote**	**Seats Won**	**% of Vote**	**Seats Won**	**% of Vote**	**Seats Won**
African National Congress	66	266	70	279	66	264
Democratic Alliance	10	38	12	50	17	67
Congress of the People	–	–	–	–	7	30
Inkatha Freedom Party	9	34	7	28	5	18
New National Party	7	28	2	36	–	–
Others	8	34	9	36	7	21
Total	100	400	100	400	100	400

Source: Independent Electoral Commission of South Africa, www.elections.org.za (accessed 25 April 2009).

abetted by the apartheid regime as a way to weaken both sides. After the first democratic elections, however, the ANC was careful to bring members of the IFP into the government cabinet, helping to diffuse much of the tension between the two parties. The IFP was embarrassed in 2004, however, having failed to do well even in the elections for KwaZulu's provincial legislature, and the party left the national government. Fears that the IFP could represent a threat to the stability of the country have disappeared. The long-term viability of a Zulu political party is doubtful since Jacob Zuma, a Zulu, became president in 2009. In the 2009 elections the IFP continued its steady decline, winning under 5 percent of the vote and only eighteen seats in the lower house.

Aside from those four main parties, few actors show much influence in South African politics. The now defunct National Party, which created apartheid and ran the country for over four decades, tried unsuccessfully to recast itself as a multiracial party and renamed itself the New National Party (NNP).

Voting in South African elections is still heavily influence by race.[12] In the 1999 elections, for example, 95 percent of blacks voted for the ANC, Inkatha, or other predominantly black parties, while 81 percent of whites supported the DA or other mostly white parties. Only colored and Indian voters more evenly split their votes among black and white parties (40 percent of coloreds and 34 percent of Indians backed white parties).

Civil Society

The exclusionary nature of the apartheid regime was built upon the policy of destroying black opposition, which it carried out by weakening any form of organized resistance. Black civil society in South Africa was crushed to an extent not seen elsewhere in colonial Africa, with traditional institutions undermined, co-opted, and repressed wherever possible. Yet even with such pressure, antiapartheid nongovernmental organizations (NGOs) continued to form and were vital in organizing the resistance that would help bring about democracy.

In the aftermath of apartheid, however, civil society in South Africa has remained weak for a number of reasons. One major problem is simply the legacy of the past: having had civil society effectively stifled for decades, South Africans have found it hard to create civic values. This is not unusual; with the fall of highly repressive regimes (like Nazi Germany or the Soviet Union), new democracies often experience a civil vacuum, in which the public is unfamiliar with and mistrustful of civic participation. A second problem lies with the ANC itself. During the transition period, the ANC relied heavily on a variety of NGOs to build public support. After 1994, the ANC co-opted many of these formerly autonomous groups, bringing them under its direction. This, too, has stunted the emergence of an independent civil society.

With the exception of political protest, public activism remains low in South Africa. A 2007 study of seven southern African countries showed that the South Africans' civic and political participation was among the lowest in the region.[13] This may be an inevitable reflection of a relatively new democracy, but it may also point to a long-term detachment of South Africans from public life, a detachment that could hinder further growth of democracy.

Given these problems, what elements of civil society (if any) play a prominent role in South Africa? One is organized labor, in particular the **Congress of South African Trade Unions (COSATU)**, formed in 1985 to promote workers' rights and oppose apartheid. In postapartheid South Africa, COSATU remains powerful in defending labor interests.[14] Like many other organizations that were involved in the battle against apartheid, COSATU is strongly tied to the ANC, through what is known as the Triple Alliance, which links COSATU, the ANC, and the South African Communist Party. In spite of this alliance, COSATU is openly hostile to the government's liberal economic policies, and this hostility has generated friction. COSATU has complained about the consistently high rate of unemployment that has weakened the union movement (only a small minority of South Africa's workforce is unionized). It has also been vocal in opposing the government's weak criticism of the Mugabe regime in neighboring Zimbabwe. COSATU has considered severing its ties to the ANC, but like other civic actors, it fears that doing so will result in its political marginalization.

A second important element of civil society is the media. Since 1994, electronic and print media have expanded substantially, making for a relatively well informed public. South Africans place a high degree of trust in the media, more so than they place in any of the state institutions, perhaps due in part to the ethnic integration of television and other outlets. In 2008, concerns

ETHNIC GROUPS

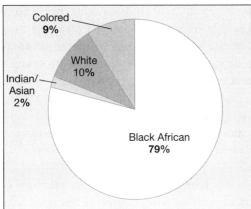

RELIGION

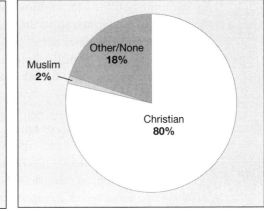

were raised when individuals close to the ANC leadership purchased one of South Africa's four main media groups.

Finally, the AIDS epidemic has recently led to the formation of numerous groups that have challenged the government's weak response to the crisis. Ironically, this horrible epidemic may help foster a new and positive wave of civil activism.

SOCIETY

Given the ethnic diversity of South Africa's inhabitants, as well as the colonial and national policies of systematic racial discrimination, it is no surprise that South African society has been (and in many ways remains) significantly divided along racial and ethnic lines. In fact, one of the most tragic effects of apartheid was that the social policy of racial segregation was compounded—indeed, was reinforced—by political persecution and economic discrimination.

What is surprising is the extent to which both groups and individuals in contemporary South Africa identify with the South African nation and express patriotism toward the state. Unfortunately, this shared national identity has not easily been translated into domestic peace or tolerance among the country's various groups. Despite South Africa's ability to avoid much of the ethnic violence and civil war that plagues other portions of the continent, there is much truth to former President Thabo Mbeki's indictment that South Africa remains in many ways two nations: one, wealthy and largely white; the other, poor and largely black.

Racism in the Rainbow Nation

Race relations have come a long way since Nelson Mandela issued his famous call for a multiethnic "rainbow nation." Public opinion research demonstrates that most South Africans think that race relations are improving, but a number of highly publicized recent incidents have challenged the idea of a rainbow nation. In 2008, after the administration of the formerly all-white Afrikaner University of the Free State decided to integrate dormitories, angry white students produced a video of a mock initiation in which black students (portrayed by black staff members) were humiliated. A discovery of a whites-only restroom in a police station, a shooting rampage by a racist youth gang (in which four backs were killed), and the barring of white journalists from a meeting with Jacob Zuma (the current president) are other disturbing examples that racism remains a potentially explosive problem in South Africa.

The challenge for South Africa as it moves from a political culture of racism to one of reconciliation is to forge the varying notions of South African identity into a common, multicultural concept of what it means to be South African, one that reconciles national unity with democratic pluralism.

Ethnic and National Identity

As should be clear, South Africa is truly a multiracial and multiethnic society. Under apartheid, government not only enforced policies of separate racial development but also used its "homelands" policy to divide and conquer the country's many ethnic and tribal groups. Although Bantustans (homelands) were legally dissolved in 1994, many citizens (particularly urban blacks) had never identified with or even visited their alleged homeland. Nonetheless, black Africans, particularly rural blacks, remain in many ways tribal in their social relations and political behavior, with tribe or ethnic group remaining their primary identification.

Like black South Africans, the white population has a long history of ethnic division, stemming from the colonial-era conflict between the Afrikaners and the British. A century of sporadic violence between the Afrikaners and the English culminated in the 1910 establishment of the Union of South Africa. The English minority dominated the Union politically, economically, and culturally. In fact, it was the fear of English dominance that inspired the formation and growth of the Afrikaner National Party (NP) and its policies of cultural and racial purity during the first half of the twentieth century. Apartheid allowed Afrikaners to separate the minority whites from the majority blacks and to culturally dominate the white English subculture.

But whereas racial and tribal groups were fastidiously segregated under apartheid, language has rendered the multiethnic fabric of South Africa far more complex. Indeed, linguistic differences have brought groups together and pushed them apart. Nine languages spoken exclusively by blacks are now enshrined in the constitution. Though violently resisted by blacks during apartheid, Afrikaans remains the preferred tongue of not only Afrikaners but also most colored South Africans. As is true in many polyglot former colonies, the English language serves to some extent to unify the country's citizens.

Similarly, religion has both unified and divided South African society. More than two thirds of all South Africans, including most whites and coloreds and nearly two thirds of blacks, identify themselves as Christian, and over three quarters describe themselves as religious.[15] The Dutch Reformed Church (sometimes called the National Party in prayer) played a particularly important role in unifying Afrikaners (first against the British, then against black Africans) and providing divine justification (at least in the eyes of its members) for their separate and superior status.

As with racial discrimination in America, the dismantling of legal racism in South Africa and the national strides taken toward reconciliation have not fully eliminated racial prejudice or distrust. Levels of black-on-white violence and even black-on-black violence climbed during the 1990s, particularly in the townships, with murder rates in South Africa now nearly ten times higher than those in the United States.

Despite persistent racial tensions, South Africans enjoy a remarkably high level of nationalism and patriotism. And while the apartheid state essentially excluded all nonwhites from political life, citizenship is now universally shared. However, legacies of division and exclusion combined with a perceived inability of the African National Congress (ANC) government to deliver socio-economic benefits have dampened citizen participation and increased levels of political apathy since the dissolution of apartheid. Recent polls show that support for democracy, trust in government, and satisfaction with government policy have all declined in recent years.[16]

Ideology and Political Culture

Although it may be troubling for the future of South African democracy, a relative decline in levels of political interest since the tumultuous early 1990s should not be surprising. Since the fall of apartheid, political ideologies have also become less pronounced and more pragmatic. In the old South Africa, Afrikaner politicians and intellectuals combined and refined political and theological ideas to form an ideology of racist authoritarianism. Like many other movements of resistance in colonial and postcolonial settings, the ANC and other revolutionary opponents of apartheid (including the South African Communist Party) adopted radical socialist principles of economic egalitarianism and revolutionary political violence. Now the ANC government has reached out to both white capitalists and black voters, embracing liberal capitalism, promoting electoral democracy, and handily winning two national elections.

Likewise, differences among the very disparate political cultures of apartheid South Africa—not just between ruling whites and oppressed blacks but also between the subcultures of Afrikaners and English and even between the Zulu and the Xhosa—have narrowed. Many South Africans have genuinely embraced the new culture of social inclusion and political participation and have supported efforts to integrate former adversaries and divided communities.

Certainly the highest-profile effort of bridge building was the **Truth and Reconciliation Commission**. Convened in 1995 and led by **Archbishop Desmond Tutu**, the commission was charged with two goals: (1) establishing the "truth" of crimes committed (on all sides) from the time of the 1960 Sharpeville Massacre through the outlawing of apartheid in 1994 and (2) using that truth as the essential foundation for healing the deep wounds of the era. The commission was given the authority to hear confessions, grant amnesty

Levels of Trust in South Africa, 2006
Percent expressing a lot or some trust in: The President: 69% Parliament: 55% Electoral Agency: 57% Ruling Party: 61% Courts: 68% Police: 48% Source: Etannibi Eo Alemika, "Quality of Elections, Satisfaction with Democracy, and Political Trust in Africa," *Afrobarometer Working Paper*, no. 84 (December 2007), available at www.afrobarometer.org (accessed 13 June 2008)

to those who were deemed to have told the complete truth, and provide recommendations for promoting long-term reconciliation (including reparation payments). While the commission uncovered a great deal of horrific "truth," much controversy surrounded the final report. Though not surprising given the enormity of the crimes, genuine reconciliation has remained elusive.

Nonetheless, many observers remain optimistic that ANC-governed South Africa can overcome the tragedies of the country's history as well as its current social and economic woes, including endemic crime and violence. They argue that both the South African people and political culture have shown a remarkable capacity to avoid conflict even in the face of serious economic and social problems. Scholars note "countervailing sources of stability" in South Africa's political culture, including a pervasive tradition of collective decision making (known as *ubuntu*), the ANC's proven pragmatism and political discipline, and the "prudential caution" of whites and blacks forged during the period of transition. Perhaps most important, with the rise of a new black capitalist class, the country has seen the gradual emergence of a multiracial elite.[17]

There are many signs that South Africa's political culture supports democracy. According to a 2006 public opinion study, 64 percent of South Africans are satisfied with how democracy works, and a similar percent of respondents think democracy is preferable to all other systems.[18] South Africans express strong support for the protection of civil liberties and minority rights, and almost 70 percent of South Africans reject the notion of one-party rule. South Africans are split fairly evenly between those who believe the government is responsible for improving the well-being of the population, and those who believe that individuals are primarily responsible for themselves.

LABOR FORCE BY OCCUPATION (2007 est.)

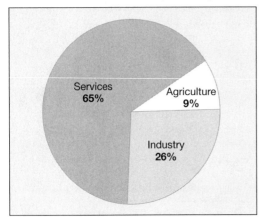

Services 65%

Agriculture 9%

Industry 26%

POLITICAL ECONOMY

One cannot separate the political and social challenges confronting South Africa today from its economic challenges. Having vanquished the demon of apartheid, South Africa faces massive unemployment, growing income inequality, and persistent poverty among South Africa's poorest.

The African National Congress (ANC) government must adopt policies that can both ameliorate these problems without alienating its broad and disparate constituencies and preserve South Africa's nascent democracy and fragile civil liberties. Moreover, successful democratic transition has not guaranteed the economic transformation of South Africa's. In fact, it has in some ways made it more problematic, as issues of equality—delayed in the name of promoting political freedom—have taken on more significance.

To its credit, the government has made strides in improving the economy by curtailing debt, reversing inflation, and expanding exports. It has also improved employment opportunities and income for the growing black middle class; for South Africa's poor it has greatly expanded access to basic necessities, such as water, electricity, and housing. By African standards, the South African economy is highly developed. Its companies have also become major investors elsewhere in the region.[19] South Africa's economy is also highly diversified, although still fairly dependent on the country's large mineral resources, particularly gold and diamonds.

Historically, both British- and Afrikaner-controlled governments sponsored political economic systems that favored their own. In the early twentieth century, government policy facilitated English ownership and control of mines and other industries, even in Afrikaner-dominated regions of the country. Squeezed by wealthier and more highly skilled English workers from above and by cheaper black labor from below, Afrikaners sought political power in large part to redress what they saw as economic oppression.

With this power, the National Party (NP) promoted essentially mercantilist policies of import substitution to promote local, and more specifically, Afrikaner industry. Though those policies were initially adopted to nurture an Afrikaner capitalist class, by the 1970s the international economic sanctions imposed on South Africa gave the state little option but to substitute local production and markets for those lost abroad. During its tenure, the NP government intervened extensively in the marketplace, imposing high tariffs and other trade barriers on imports, bestowing lucrative government contracts on favored firms, establishing state-owned enterprises (SOEs) in such key industries as weapons, steel, and energy production, and using oligopolist profits from gold and diamond exports to fuel industrialization.

Throughout the 1970s, the South African economy thrived and Afrikaners prospered. At the same time, the absence of economic opportunity for black Africans and the prohibition against the formation of black trade unions kept black labor costs artificially low, encouraging foreign investors eager to take advantage of the cheap labor and relative stability that authoritarian South Africa promised. During the 1980s, however, foreign firms and countries faced growing moral and legal pressures to divest their South African interests. At that time, too, multiracial trade unions (including the COSATU) were legalized and began demanding higher wages. Finally, the government began to face a shortage of skilled labor. Limiting access to education for blacks meant that the economy could not depend on a large pool of educated workers. These pressures dealt severe—and some would say ultimately fatal—economic blows to the apartheid state.

Given the history of policies benefiting the English and the Afrikaners, many observers expected that the victorious ANC would adopt interventionist policies to redress the discrimination and exclusion that blacks had experienced for generations. Not only would such policies promise to be popular with the ANC's majority black constituency, but this kind of progressive state intervention, designed to redistribute wealth and promote greater equality, would also be in harmony with the long-standing socialist ideological heritage of the ANC. White property owners feared that a great share of their economic assets would simply be seized by the state. This, then, would be state manipulation of the market by the left rather than the right—but state intervention all the same.

The ANC's approach to the economy was much less radical than expected, and in many ways it pursued a liberal political economic model. In 1994, Nelson Mandela announced the Reconstruction and Development Plan (RDP), which focused on meeting the basic needs of South Africans living in poverty. The ANC argued that safe drinking water, housing, electricity, jobs, affordable health care, and a safe environment had to take precedence over economic growth.

Within two years, however, the ANC government had recognized that the huge costs of the RDP were unsustainable in the absence of substantially more foreign investment and more rapid economic growth. In addition, the recent failure of Communism in Eastern Europe and the Soviet Union and the increasing popularity of neoliberal market solutions within international development circles helped turn the ANC leadership away from its socialist roots. In 1996, the government adopted a plan of liberal macroeconomic structural adjustment known as **Growth, Employment, and Redistribution Program (GEAR)**. GEAR called for opening trade, privatizing SOEs, and

otherwise limiting the role of the state in the marketplace in an effort to stimulate growth and attract foreign investment. These policies have paid dividends: growth rates under the ANC have been steady, if not spectacular, and
a vast improvement over apartheid-era governments.

Not surprisingly, this dramatic shift in redistributive priorities and interventionist policies has angered the ANC's longtime allies on the left, COSATU
and the South African Communist Party. In labor protests against GEAR,
COSATU leaders have called the GEAR privatization of the SOEs "born-again
apartheid" and have predicted devastating consequences for South Africa's
working poor. The government finds itself in the position of, on the one hand,
being praised by the International Monetary Fund for promoting GEAR privatization and delivering steady rates of economic growth (about 5 percent in
2007) but, on the other hand, being under attack from its erstwhile anti-
apartheid allies.

Facing this catch-22, the government is trying to please all sides: The ANC
government remains committed to land reform and basic health care and
funds programs to provide water, electricity, phones, and housing to the poor;
the government also continues to woo foreign investment by cutting inflation,
lowering taxes, and keeping a lid on its spending in order to promote economic growth. It has targeted key industries and manufacturing sectors, offering low-interest loans and other incentives for investment. As in other
developing economies, the government has promoted microcredit, or small-
loan initiatives designed to assist the very poorest in starting businesses. So
far, GEAR and related policies have borne some fruit, in the form of increased
growth rates that, it is hoped, will help reduce unemployment over the coming decade. But there are still serious obstacles to be overcome.

Chief among these is persistent income inequality. Despite the ANC government's affirmative action efforts and the emergence of a small but growing black middle and upper class, the white minority still dominates the
economy. South Africa has one of the highest levels of income inequality in
the world. Moreover, while the rising income of some blacks and the government's redistribution efforts have led to a decline in inequality between
races, overall inequality among all South Africans continues to increase. The
danger is that a white economic elite will simply be replaced by a black
one, with income redistribution no better (and perhaps worse) than before
apartheid. The ANC has been especially unsuccessful in redistributing land,
which remains overwhelmingly concentrated in the hands of the white minority; by 2007, only 5 percent of land had been redistributed to blacks, far short
of the goal of 30 percent initially established by the ANC.[20]

South Africa continues to suffer from extremely high rates of unemployment. In 2007, that rate was about 25 percent, but the figure for young blacks
was closer to 40 percent. While some have blamed South Africa's rigid labor
laws, COSATU and others have questioned the government's commitment to

job creation. South Africa's growth rate has simply not been high enough to generate enough employment. The persistence of massive levels of poverty is an equally vexing problem facing South Africa. About half of all South Africans are below the official poverty level. When asked to identify the greatest problem facing South Africa, the largest percentage of respondents (39 percent) cited unemployment, followed by the persistence of poverty (11 percent).[21]

The ANC's main approach to affirmative action has been its policy of **Black Economic Empowerment (BEE)**.[22] The goal of BEE is to increase the presence of disadvantaged South Africans (including coloreds and Asians) in a number of areas of the economy, including ownership of business, access to corporate management, training, and access to government procurement. Beginning in 2007, the government adopted a number of codes creating targets for each of these areas. State organizations and enterprises, and private sector firms that wish to do business with the state, must show progress on meeting some combination of these goals. New state agencies have been developed to rate organizations and enterprises using "scorecards" that award points for meeting individual targets.

To date, the results of BEE have been mixed. A small group of blacks (called "BEE-llionaires") with close ties to the ANC has benefited enormously from the policy, but this has only served to increase the gap between wealthy and poor blacks. Critics of the policy claim that inequality in the educational system and massive unemployment are the root cause of inequality in South Africa. Others fear the system will become cumbersome and a burden on the private sector.[23]

A final challenge worth noting is the loss of human resources through the emigration of skilled workers. The brain drain is sometimes called "white flight" because a high proportion of those leaving are young white professionals who are increasingly skeptical of their prospects in their native South Africa. The brain drain is particularly noticeable in the English-speaking population, whose ties to the country are not as old as those of the Afrikaners. It is estimated that nearly 50,000 whites have emigrated from South Africa since 1994.[24] To develop and diversify its economy, South Africa needs not only to create but also to retain its most skilled workers, both black and white.

FOREIGN RELATIONS AND THE WORLD

As South Africa's domestic institutions and politics are still in transition, so, too, are its relations with the outside world. Under apartheid, South Africa was largely isolated from the outside world, limited in its economic and diplomatic ties. This isolation helped reinforce a siege mentality among the white population and directed much of the politics of the country inward. Relations with the rest of Africa were particularly hostile, often limited to military skirmishes with neighboring countries that harbored or supported the African National Congress (ANC). With the move to multiparty rule, South Africa was able to break out of its isolation, rebuilding ties in the region and in the international community as a whole.

As can be expected, however, the realities of this transition have been somewhat more complicated. For most observers, this has been most obvious in the often prickly relationship between the ANC and members of the international community, whether they are other governments, intergovernmental organizations, or nongovernmental organizations (NGOs). Former President Thabo Mbeki bristled at suggestions that his government was derelict in its response to the AIDS crisis and in addressing some of the main issues involved, such as sexual assault. ANC leaders (including Nelson Mandela) have accused the international community of double standards and racism, treating South Africa as if it were still a colony of the imperial powers. Ironically, in some ways this defensiveness is reminiscent of the rhetoric of the apartheid-era National Party (NP), which also angrily rejected criticism from the international community. Perhaps this should not be surprising. In spite of the wide ethnic, economic, and other divisions among South Africans, surveys have found a deep vein of patriotism that has persisted over the past decade, with more than 90 percent of those surveyed saying that they are proud to be South African.[25] Such strong patriotism is less likely to tolerate external criticism, especially if it originates in the developed world.

Yet when we shift our focus from the international community to Africa alone, our perspective of South Africa changes. In the international community, South Africa is still a struggling country that confronts a series of major obstacles. But in Africa, South Africa is a regional powerhouse. On the economic front, its economy alone makes up nearly 45 percent of all of sub-Saharan Africa's GDP. By virtue of this large GDP and its vibrant private sector, South Africa has become central to trade and investment on the continent. South African exports to other African countries have risen substantially over the past decade, fostered in part by the lowering of trade barriers across the region. South Africa has also become a major investor in many neighboring countries. South African multinationals now play an important role in retail, banking, telecommunications, and other sectors in the region. As a result of this dominant economic presence, there has been a growing resentment of what is seen as a kind of South African imperialism, the effects of which are thought to be undermining local African businesses and increasingly controlling the regional economy.[26] Inside South Africa, these actions have also been criticized as running counter to the goals of economic development within South Africa itself. Furthermore, at the other end of this relationship, the far better economic conditions in South Africa have attracted millions of illegal immigrants over the past decade, fueling xenophobia among the South African population and mistreatment of immigrants by the police, immigration officials, and the public as a whole.

South Africa's regional power has expanded in the diplomatic sphere as well. An important element of this growing influence is the country's role in the formation of the **African Union (AU)**, which replaced the Organisation of African Unity (OAU) in 2002. In many ways inspired by the European Union, the AU seeks to depart from the OAU in pursuing greater political and economic integration across the continent. As the first head of the AU, Thabo Mbeki sought to position the organization as a mediator between African states and the advanced democracies. Mbeki also helped create the **Southern African Development Community (SADC)**, a thirteen-member body that is also concerned with regional economic integration and cooperation in southern Africa.

A cornerstone of regional integration and cooperation has been the **New Partnership for Africa's Development (NEPAD)**. NEPAD proposes that the developed world's support for African countries would, unlike past aid or loan programs, be tied to commitments to the rule of law and democracy. Progress toward this goal is to be monitored by the AU. If the AU is able to show progress in tying aid to economic and political progress in the region, it will no doubt boost the organization's power and with it the regional and international authority of South Africa.

Finally, South Africa has been directly involved in peacekeeping and peacemaking in the region. In recent years, the South African government has worked at brokering an end to civil conflicts in the Congo, Angola, Liberia, and Burundi, and it has troops on the ground as peacekeepers or observers in several African countries.

Thus South Africa's role in the region has been transformed from pariah to continental leader and mediator with the advanced democracies. But this power comes with its own costs. In many ways, South Africa has become a regional hegemon: that is, a dominant power that is able to set the rules for the region, adjudicate disputes between countries, and punish those who fail to go along. That South Africa has not only the most powerful army on the continent but also a sophisticated arms industry (as a legacy of apartheid) only reinforces this authority.

That power comes with a certain degree of contradiction is true for any important actor in the international system; in that respect, South Africa is no different from any other country with more power than its neighbors. What complicates matters for South Africa, however, is the way in which its new regime has been built on moral authority: that is, the need for democracy, multiethnicity, and tolerance. As a result, South Africa has been at the forefront of promoting democracy in the region through its own diplomatic efforts and through participation in the AU and the SADC. Yet its efforts have often been viewed in the region as patronizing, not unlike the behavior of the advanced democracies toward South Africa that Mbeki often condemned. This view is reinforced by the perception of double standards. In the economic realm, some observers see South Africa's economic relations with the continent as one of domination. NEPAD, too, has been criticized by some Africans as an attempt to bring a neoliberal version of GEAR to the rest of Africa, thereby primarily benefiting South African economic interests.[27]

In the diplomatic sphere as well, South Africa's calls for greater democracy in the region have rung hollow in the face of its support for Zimbabwe, whose deepening authoritarianism was faciliated, in part, by South African diplomatic and economic support (see "Current Issues," below). As with many other countries around the world, South Africa has found that its increased international power has led to a clash of morality, stability, and self-interest.

CURRENT ISSUES

CRIME AND CORRUPTION

Crime is regularly cited by South Africans as among the most serious problems facing the country. Crime rates skyrocketed after the transition to democracy, but rates started to drop after peaking in 2003. Pernicious inequality and endemic poverty have certainly contributed a serious crime problem. The rate of violent crime in South Africa, including murder, rape, and vehicle hijackings, is extremely high. Nearly 20,000 South Africans are murdered each year, a rate nine times greater than the U.S. average. Carjackings, often resulting in death or serious injury, are commonplace and have increased dramatically since 1994. Unemployment and poverty, particularly in the townships, and corruption in the police force exacerbate this problem. Crime not only undermines the social fabric but also deters domestic and international investment and diverts to security resources that could be spent elsewhere.[28]

Public opinion research has shown a steady growth of public concern about corruption since 1994, fueled in part by a number of high-profile corruption scandals that affected the governing ANC.[29] The data show that local governments are viewed as particularly corrupt (almost half of respondents view them as corrupt), while about a quarter of respondents view the president and the legislature as corrupt.

Faced with growing public concern over corruption, in 1999 President Mbeki established an elite crime-fighting unit: the Directorate of Special Operations, popularly known as the Scorpions. The unit was well funded and highly trained, and it had its own staff of investigators and prosecutors. Its motto became, "loved by the people, feared by the criminals." It quickly became a popular and highly effective unit, achieving conviction rates much higher than the regular police force. The Scorpions ran into trouble, however, when the force began to investigate corruption within the ANC government.

When they brought corruption charges against then former vice president Jacob Zuma, which led to Zuma's firing, Zuma's supporters claimed that the Scorpions were merely attempting to limit opposition within the ANC. A bitter political rivalry and turf war broke out between the police and the Scorpions. Despite widespread public opposition in 2008 Zuma's supporters passed legislation that reintegrated the Scorpions into the police force, effectively disbanding the unit.

ZIMBABWE: SOUTH AFRICA'S TROUBLED NEIGHBOR

Since the fall of apartheid, South Africa has sought to develop a role as an important regional actor, leading both by economic example and by moral example. But over the past decade, this position has been caught up in the politics of its neighbor Zimbabwe.

Like South Africa, Zimbabwe (formerly known as Rhodesia) is a former British colony in which a small white elite once dominated the black majority. Just as the African National Congress (ANC) fought a guerrilla campaign against the South African government, in Zimbabwe a movement known as Zimbabwe African National Union (ZANU), led by Robert Mugabe, struggled to end white rule. After years of violent conflict, the government agreed to open elections in 1980, which ZANU won. As in South Africa, the transition from white rule was predicated on allowing the white minority to maintain its economic domination over the country. Unlike South Africa, however, the transition led to conflict among different indigenous African ethnic groups and thousands of deaths.

The ZANU victory served as an inspiration for South Africans opposed to apartheid. Over time, however, it also became a more negative example. During the 1980s, ZANU (merged with its main rival, the Patriotic Front, to become ZANU-PF) consolidated power in the hands of the party and President Mugabe. Economic mismanagement and corruption followed, undermining political authority. In the late 1990s, as public opposition grew, a new party rose to challenge ZANU-PF, known as the Movement for Democratic Change (MDC). Fearing the MDC and seeking to shore up his own authority, Mugabe turned on both the MDC and the white landowners, who controlled most of the farmland in Zimbabwe. Mugabe encouraged his supporters to seize white-owned land and to harass and kill members of the MDC. The international community condemned these tactics, but Mugabe dismissed the criticism as the machinations of imperialist oppressors.

The South African government, however, took a different position. President Thabo Mbeki and the ANC expressed its support for Mugabe even in the face of increasing repression, and the South African government extended financial support when the rest of the international community had withdrawn its aid. In 2005, Zimbabwe held parliamentary elections that were widely regarded as rigged. Yet the South African government declared the elections free and fair, as it had done in response to similar elections in 2002. After Mugabe refused to accept his apparent defeat in the 2008 presidential elections, Mugabe inisted on a second round of elections and again began to harass the oppposition. In response, South Africa's government continued to advocate constructive engagement and quiet diplomacy and appeared to many to be coddling Mugabe.[30] When the MDC leader Morgan Tsvangirai withdrew from the second round of presidential elections because of state-sponsored violence against his party, South Africa opposed United Nations sanctions against its neighbor.

South Africa has long received immigrants from its poorer neighbors, and the flow increased after the end of apartheid. The crisis in neighboring Zimbabwe resulted in the arrival of hundreds of thousands of new immigrants: an estimated 3 million to 5 million who reside mostly in South Africa illegally, and who find employment in the informal sector. The growing visibility of immigrants has caused resentment among South Africans, and in 2008 a wave of anti-immigrant violence shocked the nation. Dozens of immigrants were killed, and foreign-owned shops were destroyed.[31]

Why would democratic South Africa coddle a neighboring dictatorship? Different factors may be at work. Some observers argue that the ANC and the ZANU-PF share a bond in the struggle against white rule. Both have since chafed at what they see as the lecturing of the international community, a reaction that also characterized Mbeki's intransigence on AIDS. Others emphasize that the South African government, concerned about the complete breakdown of authority in Zimbabwe, would rather back Mugabe than face chaos on its border.

But the South African government's position is not shared by everyone in the ANC. The COSATU has strongly supported the MDC and condemned Mbeki's support, whereas such national figures as Nelson Mandela and Archbishop Desmond Tutu have called for Mugabe to step down and have indirectly or directly challenged ANC policies on the matter.

THE DEVASTATION OF HIV/AIDS

It is estimated that nearly 12 percent of South Africans over the age of two are HIV positive, one of the highest rates in the world, and some 600 South Africans die of the disease every day. Despite increasing access to affordable drugs, most of those infected will die of the disease. Besides being a human and social tragedy, this situation will and already has had huge consequences for the economy. The AIDS pandemic will cut an estimated 5 percent from South African GDP growth each year over the next ten years. The health-care system is underfunded and grossly inadequate, and corporations are increasingly wary of investing in personnel, given the mortality odds facing their employees. Compounding this problem is a high degree of stigma attached to those with AIDS, as well as the questionable handling of the issue by Thabo Mbeki and other ANC politicians: They questioned the causal link between HIV and AIDS and resisted conventional drugs and drug protocols prescribed in the West, citing scientifically dubious theories and charging the West with racist views of African sexuality. Pressure from international and domestic activist groups and from Nelson Mandela (whose son died of AIDS) is slowly raising awareness and the level of treatment, but treatment remains limited in the face of this devastating epidemic.[32]

Only in 2003 did the government develop a comprehensive strategy to test and treat those affected. Mbeki's firing of deputy health minister Nozizwe Madlala-Routledge, who played a major role in changing government AIDS policy, raised new doubts about the president's commitment to fighting the epidemic. Madlala-Routledge was fired because she traveled to an international AIDS conference without government permission.

NOTES

1. Anthony Sampson, "Men of the Renaissance," *Guardian* (London), 3 January 1998, p. 19.
2. For a discussion of South African history, see Leonard Thompson, *The History of South Africa* (New Haven, CT: Yale University Press, 2001).
3. For more on this conflict, see Thomas Packenham, *The Boer War* (New York: Random House, 1979).
4. African History: Apartheid legislation in South Africa, http://africanhistory.about.com/library/bl/blsalaws.htm (accessed 30 December 2008); contains a detailed list of the apartheid legislative acts.
5. For more on the emergence of the struggle against apartheid and Mandela's role in it, see Nelson Mandela, *Long Walk to Freedom: The Autobiography of Nelson Mandela* (Boston: Little, Brown, 1996).
6. For de Klerk's own perspective on the transition from apartheid, see F. W. de Klerk, *The Last Trek: A New Beginning* (New York: St. Martin's Press, 1999).
7. J. L. Gibson and J. A. Caldeira, "Defenders of Democracy? Legitimacy, Popular Acceptance, and the South African Constitutional Court," *Journal of Politics*, 65, no. 1 (February 2003), pp. 1–30.
8. Andrew Reynolds, "Constitutional Engineering in South Africa," *Journal of Democracy*, 6 (1995), pp. 86–99.
9. For a good overview of the debate, see Louise Vincent, "Of No Account? South Africa's Electoral System (non) Debate," *Journal of Contemporary African Studies*, 24, no. 1 (January 2006).
10. Howard Lehman, "Deepening Democracy? Demarcation, traditional authorities, and municipal elections in South Africa," *The Social Science Journal*, 44 (2007), pp. 301–17.
11. 2006 Afrobarometer, www.afrobarometer.org (accessed 13 June 2008).
12. The data are taken from Karen Ferree, "The Microfoundations of Ethnic Voting, Evidence from South Africa," *Afrobarometer* working paper no. 40, June 2004.

13. Robert Mattes, "Democracy Without the People: Political Institutions and Citizenship in the New South Africa," *Afrobarometer* working paper no. 82, November 2007, p. 24.

14. On COSATU, see Sakhela Buhlungu, "Gaining Influence But Losing Power? COSATU members and the Democratic Transformation of South Africa," *Social Movement Studies*, 7, no. 1 (May 2008).

15. Ronald Inglehart et. al., eds., *Human Beliefs and Values: A Cross-Cultural Sourcebook Based on the 1999–2002 Value Surveys* (Mexico City: Siglo XXI, 2004).

16. Those data are cited in Robert Mattes, "South Africa: Democracy without the People?" *Journal of Democracy*, 13 (2002), pp. 22–36.

17. Daniel O'Flaherty and Constance J. Freeman, "Stability in South Africa: Will It Hold?" *Washington Quarterly*, 22 (Autumn 1999), and "Africa's Engine," *Economist*, 15, January 2004.

18. These data are drawn from the 2006 *Afrobarometer*, available at www.afrobarometer.org (accessed 13 June 2008).

19. "Africa's Engine," *Economist*, 15 January 2004.

20. "The Promised Land," *Economist*, 24 April 2008.

21. 2006 Afrobarometer, www.afrobarometer.org (accessed 13 June 2008).

22. A good overview of BEE is Stefano Ponte, Simon Roberts, and Lance van Sittert, "Black Economic Empowerment," Business and the State in South Africa," *Development and Change*, 38, no. 5 (September 2007).

23. Jeffrey Herbst, "Principled Pragmatists and Innovators Build a New South Africa, *Foreign Affairs*, 86 no. 1 (January/February 2007).

24. "If Only the Adults Would Behave Like the Children," *Economist*, 21 April 2005.

25. David Mattes, "Understanding Identity in South Africa: A First Cut," *Afrobarometer Working Paper* no. 38 (June 2004), www.afrobarometer.org/papers/AfropaperNo38.pdf (accessed 3 August 2005).

26. See Chris Landsberg, "Promoting Democracy: The Mandela-Mbeki Doctrine," *Journal of Democracy*, 11 (2000), pp. 107–21.

27. Henning Melber, "South Africa and NEPAD—Quo Vadis?" *Policy Brief*, 31 (June 2004), Centre for Policy Studies, www.cps.org.za/cps%20pdf/polbrief31.pdf (accessed 3 August 2005).

28. For more on murder, see Rob McCafferty, *Murder in South Africa: A Comparison of Past and Present* (Claremont, South Africa: United Christian Action, 2003). www.christianaction.org.za/newsletter_uca/murder_southafrica.doc (accessed 30 December 2008).

29. "Resurgent Perceptions of Corruption in South Africa," *Afrobarometer Working Paper* no. 43, June 2006.

30. Linda Freeman, "South Africa's Zimbabwe Policy: Unraveling the Contradictions," *Journal of Contemporary African Studies*, 23, no. 3 (May 2005).

31. "Nowhere Left to Go," *Economist*, 20 May 2008.

32. Adele Baleta, "South Africa President Criticized for Lack of Focus on AIDS," *Lancet* (14 February 2004), p. 541.

GLOSSARY OF KEY TERMS

African National Congress (ANC)   South Africa's major anti-apartheid liberation movement, and the governing party since the return of democracy in 1994.

African Union (AU)   An organization of African nations pursuing greater political and economic integration across the continent.

Afrikaans   The language of South Africa's Dutch settlers (Afrikaners).

Afrikaners   White South Africans who speak Afrikaans and are descendants of the Dutch, French, and German colonists.

apartheid   The Afrikaner-dominated racist authoritarian regime in South Africa that was in power from 1948 to 1994.

Bantustans   Tribal homelands established by the apartheid regime to deprive the black majority of South African citizenship.

Black Economic Empowerment (BEE)   South Africa's affirmative action program that aims to create a new class of black owners and management through a series of quotas and targets.

Boers   Term describing the early Dutch settlers in South Africa; also used to describe Afrikaners.

Boer Wars   Epic battle between the Boers and the British that culminated in the defeat of the Afrikaners and their integration into the Union of South Africa.

colored   Widely used term in South Africa to describe citizens of mixed race, largely concentrated in and around Capetown.

Congress of the People (COPE)   A new South African political party formed by defectors from the ANC.

Congress of South African Trade Unions (COSATU)   South Africa's most important trade union confederation, closely linked to the governing ANC.

de Klerk, F. W.   Last president of the apartheid regime; he negotiated the transition to democracy with the ANC.

Democratic Alliance (DA)   South Africa's main opposition party.

Dutch Reformed Church   Conservative protestant church that has historically been central to Afrikaner culture.

Great Trek   Epic migration of Afrikaners into the interior of South Africa to escape British colonization.

Growth, Employment, and Redistribution Program (GEAR)   The 1996 liberal macroeconomic structural adjustment plan that moved the ANC toward a more market-friendly political policy.

Group Areas Act   Centerpiece of apartheid legislation that divided South Africans into four racial categories and required strict segregation of housing along racial lines.

Inkatha Freedom Party (IFP)   Small Zulu political party that is currently party of the opposition to the ANC.

Mandela, Nelson   Long-imprisoned leader of the ANC who became South Africa's first post-apartheid president.

Mbeki, Thabo   South Africa's former two-term president who was forced to resign in 2008 when he failed to win the election as the ANC leader.

National Assembly   South Africa's legislature.

National Party (NP)   Now defunct party that created apartheid and dominated politics during the apartheid era.

New Partnership for Africa's Development (NEPAD)   The African Union program that attempts to tie foreign development aid to a commitment to democracy and the rule of law.

Southern African Development Community (SADC)   A thirteen-member African regional economic and cooperation community, of which South Africa was a founding member.

Soweto   A township created during apartheid to house blacks who were forcibly removed from Johannesburg.

Truth and Reconciliation Commission   Post-apartheid body established to document apartheid-era human rights abuses and to give reparations to victims and amnesty to perpetrators who confessed to crimes.

Tutu, Archbishop Desmond   Anti-apartheid activist and leader of South Africa's Anglican church who chaired the Truth and Reconciliation Commission.

Union of South Africa   The 1910 name given to the British colony that integrated British and Afrikaner colonists after the Boer Wars.

United Democratic Front (UDF)   Unified anti-apartheid coalition created in 1983 from the major black and white opposition groups.

voortrekkers   Afrikaner pioneers who migrated into South Africa's interior to escape British colonists.

Zille, Helen   Current leader of South Africa's main opposition party, the Democratic Alliance.

Zuma, Jacob   Current president.

WEB LINKS

African National Congress **www.anc.org.za**

African Studies Internet Resources: South Africa, Columbia University Libraries **www.columbia.edu/cu/lweb/indiv/africa/cuvl/SAfr.html**

The Democratic Alliance **www.da.org.za**

Inkatha Freedom Party **www.ifp.org.za**

Institute for Democracy in South Africa **www.idasa.org.za**

Overview of Soweto township **www.soweto.co.za**

South African Government **www.gov.za**

Truth and Reconciliation Report **www.gov.za/reports/2003/trc/index.html**

14 NIGERIA

Head of state and government:
President Umaru Musa Yar'Adua
(since May 29, 2007)

Capital: Abuja

Total land size: 923,768 sq km

Population: 138 million

GDP at PPP: 292.7 billion US$

GDP per capita at PPP: $2,000

Human development index ranking: 158

NIGERIA

INTRODUCTION

Why Study This Case?

Nigeria stands out in ways that are both impressive and disheartening. First, Nigeria is noteworthy for its sheer size: it is the most populous country in Africa. Second, unlike many other African countries, Nigeria is blessed with a great deal of natural wealth, from oil to agriculture. Following independence from British rule in 1960, those assets would have been expected to make Nigeria a major regional, if not global, actor.

Yet exactly the opposite happened, and Nigeria has become renowned for all that can go wrong. For most of the time since independence, the country has been under military rule. Those long periods of military dictatorship coincided with widespread corruption, with oil revenues and other resources siphoned off to line the pockets of those in power. In spite of earning billions of dollars in oil exports, Nigeria has become one of the poorest and least developed countries in the world. It would seem to be an excellent example of a country in which natural resources have been used by those in power to buy supporters and repress the public.

Yet the long era of military rule may now be at an end. In 1999, Nigeria returned to civilian rule, and since then a fragile democratic system has taken hold. Still, much remains to be done. Nigeria lacks the rule of law and continues to be recognized as one of the most corrupt countries in the world. The state also has questionable control over the monopoly of violence, both in terms of civilian control over the military and the country's widespread criminal and political violence. The standard of living for the average Nigerian remains very low, far below what the country's wealth should ensure. If it is to succeed, the country must confront these challenges while facing a large foreign debt, incurred while billions of dollars in oil revenue have been stolen by those in power.

If the legacy of its military rule were not enough of a challenge for Nigeria, a second concern derives from its sheer size. Nigeria is a diverse country encompassing numerous ethnic groups, whose local interests have been reinforced by corruption and federalism. For the past thirty years, military rule has largely kept fractiousness in check, but tensions and violence have surfaced with democratic rule. Most disturbing is a growing ethnic rift between the Muslim north and the Christian and animist south. At a time when many global conflicts center on religion and religious fundamentalism, the prospect of increasing tension among faiths in Nigeria leads some observers to worry that in the long run the country will be ungovernable and will return to authoritarianism, civil war, or both. Is Nigeria doomed to be a failed state?

Nigeria thus provides a fascinating, if daunting, example of the possibilities and potential limits of state power and democracy. Can the change from military rule to democracy help bring stability and prosperity to Nigeria? Or are the problems of state capacity and autonomy such that democracy cannot help improve them—and might even make them worse? We will consider these tensions as we investigate Nigeria's political heritage, current institutions, and political prospects.

Major Geographic and Demographic Features

One of Nigeria's most impressive features is its sheer size. Nigeria is the largest country in Africa in terms of population and among the top ten in the world. Lying along the western coast of the continent, Nigeria has a diverse climate and geography. The Niger-Benue river system divides the country into distinct regions. The north is relatively arid and known for its grasslands, while the south is characterized by tropical forests and coastal swamps. Nigeria's geography and climate (particularly in the south) are favorable to agriculture, such that nearly one third of the land is arable—compared with only 15 percent of the land in China and 20 percent of the land in the United States. Until oil became a major export commodity, cocoa and nuts were a major source of foreign trade.

Nigeria's best-known region is the **Niger Delta**. The Niger River enters the sea at that point, creating a vast swampy area of over 5,000 square miles. It is the third-largest wetland in the world, after the Netherlands and the Mississippi Delta, and home to an enormous range of plants and animals. The Niger Delta is also home to approximately 30 million people, who traditionally have been engaged in farming and fishing. The complicated topography of the area has limited interaction, integration, and assimilation, thus fostering a large variety of ethnicities; by some estimates, over a dozen groups speaking about twenty-five languages inhabit the Delta. It is also one of the poorest regions of the country, with limited infrastructure and development.

But the Niger Delta is also the source of Nigeria's oil and the vast majority of the country's exports. Oil production in the Delta has contributed to the national corruption spoken of earlier, and at the local level, too, its effects have been profound. The first and most commonly cited local effect is environmental degradation. In the nearly half century since oil production began, there have been more than 4,000 spills, whose effects on the wetlands and population are a source of intense domestic and international controversy.[1] Oil production has also abetted ethnic conflicts in the region, with groups on occasion attacking oil facilities in order to draw attention to their demands or seek ransoms. Finally, oil production has exacerbated intergroup hostility in the Delta as some groups have perceived that others have benefited disproportionately from the industry.[2] Given the importance of oil to Nigeria, the problems of this region significantly affect the security of the country as a whole.

The diversity that marks the Delta is mirrored across the country as a whole. Nigeria is home to some 250 ethnic groups. Dominant among them are the **Hausa** and the **Fulani**, who are overwhelmingly Muslim and concentrated in the north; the **Igbo** (also spelled "Ibo"), who are predominantly Christian and concentrated in the southeast; and the **Yoruba**, who inhabit the southwest and whose members are divided among the Christian, Muslim, and local animist faiths.

Nigeria's large population is a function of its growth rate. In the past twenty years, the country's population has doubled, with the result that nearly half the population is now under the age of fourteen. According to some projections, the country will increase by another 40 million people in the next decade, with Lagos becoming one of the ten largest cities in the world.[3] The presence of a large, rapidly growing, ethnically and religiously diverse population will complicate development, stability, and governance.

Historical Development of the State

Like most other less-developed countries, Nigeria has a history marked by local political organization, imperial control, and recent independence and instability. Contrary to common assumptions, however, precolonial Nigeria was neither undeveloped nor unorganized. Rather, the region was marked by varying degrees and kinds of political and social organization, some of which were highly complex and wide ranging. Although we cannot explore each of them in depth, we can point to some of the earliest and most powerful examples.

Nigeria was the setting for several early kingdoms. Over two thousand years ago, the members of the Nok society, located in what is now central Nigeria, fashioned objects out of iron and terra-cotta with a degree of sophistication unmatched in West Africa, though little else is known about their civilization. As the roots of today's dominant ethnic groups began to take shape, new forms of political organization also emerged. Around 1200 C.E., the Hausa to the north established a series of powerful city-states, which served as conduits of north-south trade. In the southwest, the Yoruba kingdom of Oyo extended its power beyond the borders of modern-day Nigeria into present-day Togo. This kingdom grew wealthy through trade and the exploitation of natural resources, facilitated by its location along the coast. In the southeast, the Igbo maintained less centralized political power, though they, too, had a

TIME LINE OF POLITICAL DEVELOPMENT

Year	Event
300s B.C.E.	Jos plateau settled by the Nok people
1100s C.E.	Hausa kingdom formed in the north; Oyo kingdom formed in the southwest
1472	Portuguese navigators reach the Nigerian coast
1500s–1800s	Slave trade develops
1807	United Kingdom bans the slave trade
1809	Sokoto caliphate founded
1861–1914	Britain acquires Lagos and establishes a series of Nigerian protectorates
1960	Nigeria achieves independence and creates the First Republic
1966	After a military coup, the Federal Military Government is established
1967–70	In Nigerian Civil War, Biafra fails to win independence
1975	General Olusegun Obasanjo comes to power and initiates a transition to civilian rule
1979	Elections bring Shehu Shagari to power, establishing the Second Republic
1983	Muhammadu Buhari seizes power
1985	Ibrahim Babangida seizes power
1993	Transition to civilian rule (the Third Republic) fails; Sani Abacha seizes power
1995	Activist Ken Saro-Wiwa executed
1998	Abacha dies; Abdulsalam Abubakar succeeds him as the military head of government
1999	Military rule ends and the Fourth Republic is established; Olusegun Obasanjo elected president
2000	Sharia law adopted by twelve northern states
2000–02	Ethnic and religious clashes leave several thousand dead
2003	Obasanjo reelected to a second term as president
2007	Obasanjo steps down; Umaru Yar'Adua elected in first civilian transfer of power

precedent of earlier kingdoms and would come to play a central role in modern Nigerian politics.

ISLAM AND THE NIGERIAN NORTH

The fortunes of these three dominant ethnic groups (the Hausa, the Yoruba, and the Igbo) and other peoples in what is now Nigeria changed dramatically as contact with peoples, politics, and ideas from outside West Africa increased. The first important impact came not from Europe, however, but from the Middle East, with the spread of Islam. By the eleventh century, Islam had found its way into the Hausa region of northern Nigeria, carried along trade routes linking the region to North Africa and beyond. By the fifteenth century, Islam had brought literacy and scholarship to the region through the Arabic language, though the religion and its influences remained largely confined to the Hausa elite. By the late eighteenth century, however, an increase in contact with Islamic regions led to an increase in conversions to the faith. The religion's growing influence was solidified by the leadership of Usman dan Fodio (1754–1817). A religious scholar, Usman played an important role in spreading Islam among the Hausa and Fulani. Usman found widespread support among the peasantry, who felt oppressed under the city-states' warring monarchies and saw in Islam's message a promise of greater social equality. Their embrace of Islam in turn alarmed those in power, eventually precipitating a conflict between the city-states and Usman. Following an initial conflict, Usman declared jihad against the Hausa city-states in 1804 and by 1808 had overthrown the ruling monarchs, establishing what became known as the Sokoto caliphate. The Sokoto caliphate became the largest empire in Africa at the time and provided a uniform government to a region previously racked by war. Islam would now play a central role in western Africa and in the eventual establishment of an independent Nigerian state.

EUROPEAN IMPERIALISM

As Islam and centralized political organization spread across the north, the south experienced similarly dramatic effects with the arrival of the European powers. As far back as the late fifteenth century, Europeans had begun arriving along Nigeria's coast, purchasing from indigenous traders agricultural products as well as slaves (often captives from local wars). From the seventeenth to the nineteenth century, Europeans established several coastal ports to support the burgeoning trade in slaves, with the United Kingdom becoming the major trading power. During that time, more than 3 million slaves were shipped from Nigeria to the Americas. In 1807, the United Kingdom declared the slave trade illegal and established a naval presence off Nigeria's waters for enforcement, though an illegal trade continued for another half century. The precipitous decline in the region's major export contributed to the collapse of the Oyo Empire and to warfare among the Yoruba, which in turn paved the way for an expanded British presence in the interior. The colonial presence further expanded as British industrialization generated ever-greater demand for resources, such as palm oil, cocoa, and timber. That demand radically changed the nature of agricultural production and encouraged the greater use of local slavery to produce these goods. At the same time, British missionaries began to proselytize in the coastal and southern regions, converting large numbers of Igbo and Yoruba to Christianity.

By 1861, the British had established a colony at Lagos, and by the 1884–1885 Berlin Conference other European powers had recognized the United Kingdom's "sphere of influence" along the coast. Fearing French and German encroachment in the interior, the United Kingdom quickly joined the European powers' **"scramble for Africa"** by asserting its authority far inland. Through a combination of diplomacy, co-optation, and force, the United Kingdom established control over both the north and the south. In many areas, the British relied upon a policy of indirect rule. For example, as the Sokoto caliphate was brought under British control, local leaders were allowed to keep their positions, co-opted as part of the new state bureaucracy. Furthermore, **sharia**, or Islamic law, was respected in noncriminal matters, and in that region Christian proselytizing was prohibited. Such policies helped limit local resistance but increased the power of some ethnic groups over others, giving them greater authority within the imperial administration. In areas where indirect rule was less successful, as among the Igbo, resistance was much more significant. In 1914, the various protectorates in the area under British control were unified under the name "Nigeria", though the country remained highly decentralized administratively, reflecting its distinct regional differences.

Following unification, Nigeria experienced dramatic change under British imperial rule. The British developed a modern infrastructure and constructed ports, roads, and railways to facilitate economic relations. Agricultural production continued to play an important role in exports. Within Nigerian society, development meant the establishment of Western educational policies and institutions, especially in regions where Christian missionaries were active. In general, indirect rule meant the development of a new elite more Westernized and more conscious of the complexities of imperialism. The creation of a colonial legislative council and local elections for some of the seats introduced the idea of democratic representative institutions, no matter how limited.

It might be thought that the development of a Westernized elite would serve to perpetuate imperial control. Instead, exposure to Western ideas often served as the foundation for resistance as Nigerians embraced the heretofore alien concepts of nationalism and sovereignty. Such ideas were not easily planted in Nigeria's complex political terrain. For some activists, anti-colonialism meant a greater role for Nigeria and other African states in the Commonwealth of Nations (the loose affiliation of former British colonies opposed to complete independence). For others, it meant a reassertion of pre-colonial political structures that had been destroyed or weakened by British rule. As economic development, urbanization, and state centralization increased the integration of Nigeria as a whole, however, there began to emerge the tentative notion of a Nigerian nation and state that could be independent from colonial rule.

Following World War II, Nigeria saw the rapid expansion of various civil society organizations, ranging from political parties and ethnic movements to labor unions and business movements. Among the numerous political leaders who emerged during this time was Benjamin Nnamdi Azikiwe (1904–1996). Born in northern Nigeria, Azikiwe studied and taught in the United States before returning to Nigeria in 1938. He established a daily newspaper and in 1944 helped found the National Council of Nigerian Citizens (NCNC), which advocated national unity and self-government. While the NCNC sought to appeal to all Nigerians, it drew heavily from the Igbo, while other political parties, such as the Northern People's Congress (NPC) and the Action Group Party (AGP), were backed by Hausa Muslims and the Yoruba, respectively.

The British government attempted to deal with the rising tide of Nigerian activism, strikes, and competing demands by reforming the local constitution, creating regional assemblies, and formalizing the decentralized nature of imperial rule through a system of federalism. Executive power remained in the hands of a British governor, but increasingly authority devolved on the local level. Thus, while Nigerian nationalism became a potent force among some political elites, the decentralization of power reinforced regional tendencies. By the late 1950s, an array of constitutional reforms had effectively created autonomous regions in the north, west, and east, with the goal of eventual national independence while remaining within the British Commonwealth. The new federal political structure consisted of three regions (Northern, Western, and Eastern), a directly elected **House of Representatives**, a Senate whose members were indirectly elected by the regional assemblies, a prime minister, and a governor general, who served as the representative of the British monarchy. Azikiwe was appointed governor general. On October 1, 1960, Nigeria formally gained its independence (creating what is known as the **First Republic**), absent much of the violence and destruction that plagued decolonization elsewhere. It also enjoyed ongoing industrialization, strong exports, and the promise of oil revenues, whose potential was just beginning to be explored.

INDEPENDENCE, CONFLICT, AND CIVIL WAR

The relative peace and the promises of an independent Nigeria quickly experienced tension, however. Elections in 1959 had given the NPC nearly half the seats in the House of Representatives, leading it to form a coalition with the NCNC. That coalition battled over some of the most essential questions regarding Nigerian statehood, including the scope of central versus local powers and national versus regional identity. Meanwhile, the AGP fragmented as a result of internal disputes and electoral setbacks. The infighting eventually spread across the Western Region, which the AGP controlled, leading to riots, the collapse of the regional legislature, emergency rule, and a conspiracy by some AGP leaders to overthrow the central government.

The dynamics of the Action Group crisis were not unique to the Western Region. Various groups across Nigeria demanded that the federal system be further decentralized to make way for additional states, while other groups and leaders opposed such tactics, fearing these actions would undermine their own territorial authority or even lead to the breakup of the country. Fragmentation was of particular concern to the NPC. As the Northern Region was allocated over half the seats in the House of Representatives, the NPC feared that any restructuring of federalism would undermine its power. Such concerns even extended to the national census, which each side hoped would bolster its allocation of seats. Sharply contested elections and electoral alliances were marked by ethnic tensions and electoral discrepancies. Economic differences sharpened the ethnic conflict, with each group viewing the state as a means to siphon off wealth for its own people.

In the violent aftermath of the contentious 1965 regional assembly elections in the Western Region, two thousand people died. In the midst of the increasing disorder, a group of army officers, primarily Igbos, staged a coup d'état, assassinating the prime minister, the leaders of several political parties, and a number of military officials from the north. The coup leaders suspended the constitution, banned political parties, and called for a unitary government and the end to northern domination. But the coup failed to impose order, setting off civil war instead. Conflict erupted between northern and Igbo troops, and the coup leaders were in turn overthrown, and many of them were killed. Many Igbo living in the north were also massacred, and Igbo leaders who had supported the coup and an end to federalism as a way to weaken northern power now believed that their people and region had no future in a multiethnic Nigeria.

In May 1967, the Igbo-dominated Eastern Region seceded from Nigeria, declaring itself the **Republic of Biafra**. Although the Biafrans were outnumbered and outgunned, they held off the Nigerian military for three years, helped in part by international supporters, who believed that the Nigerian government was conducting a genocidal war against the Igbo. Azikiwe, who had been dismissed from his post by the military government, became a prominent supporter of Biafran independence. In 1970, Biafra was defeated. Although the defeat did not lead to the Igbo extermination that many had feared, the war itself exacted huge costs in terms of military and civilian life: estimates range from 500,000 to 3 million fatalities.[4]

THE MILITARY ERA

The armed forces brought an end to the Nigerian Civil War, but their role in the politics of Nigeria was just beginning (see "Nigerian Heads of Government," p. 546). The 1966 countercoup in response to the takeover by Igbo army officers established the Federal Military Government (FMG), which initially claimed that it would soon return power to civilian control. General Yakubu Gowon, who came to head the FMG in 1966, argued that in advance of any such transition, Nigeria needed to undergo dramatic state and economic reform. Dominated by none of the three main ethnic groups, the FMG broke Nigeria into a number of federal states, hoping to weaken regional and ethnic power. The government also sought to move the country away from its reliance upon agriculture by stimulating industrialization through a policy of import substitution. This shift was made possible in part because agricultural exports were declining in favor of oil, which was emerging as a major source of revenue. By the 1970s, Nigeria had become one of the top ten oil-producing countries in the world. The result was rapid if uneven development of the country in numerous areas.

The FMG had come to power with a certain degree of public support, given its call for an end to divisive ethnic-based politics and the creation of an effective state. Yet in reality, military rule simply replaced one form of patronage with another, tapping oil revenues as a way to enrich those in power and their supporters. By the mid-1970s, Gowon's political authority had deteriorated in the face of public animosity in reaction to widespread corruption, crime, and stagnating economic development. In 1975, Gowon was overthrown in a bloodless coup that brought General Murtala Muhammed to power. Muhammed began to crack down on corruption and took the long-delayed steps necessary for the return of civilian rule, thereby becoming widely popular with the public. But within a year, Muhammed himself was assassinated in a failed coup attempt, which brought to power General **Olusegun Obasanjo**, who continued Muhammed's plans for the restoration of civilian rule. A new constitution enacted in 1979 ushered in the **Second Republic**, under which the old parliamentary system was replaced by a presidential system, in the hope of strengthening central authority and preventing a breakdown like the one that had occurred a decade earlier. Democratic elections were held in 1979, and Obasanjo willingly retired from political and military life; subsequently, he became active with various intergovernmental and nongovernmental organizations (NGOs), such as the World Health Organization and Transparency International. Obasanjo's apparent respect for the rule of law while in power and his prominent international role thereafter have made

OLUSEGAN OBASANJO: GENERAL, PRESIDENT, AND CHICKEN FARMER

Olusegun Obasanjo, a Christian of ethnic Yoruba descent from southwestern Nigeria, was a career soldier before serving twice as Nigeria's head of state, first as military ruler (1976 to 1979) and then as elected president for an unprecedented two terms from 1999 to 2007. Despite first coming to power in a military coup and only reluctantly leaving the presidential office at the end of his constitutional term limit in 2007, Obasanjo is nonetheless rightly seen as a champion of democracy and reform in Nigeria. He presided over the voluntary transition to civilian rule in 1979 at the end of his first (unelected) stint in office—a promise often made by Nigeria's coup leaders but heretofore never kept. He was imprisoned by General Sani Abacha during the 1990s and released only after Abacha's sudden death in 1998. He and other opponents of Abacha formed the **People's Democratic Party (PDP)**, successfully won the presidency in the following year's election, and earned reelection in 2003. The constitution permits the president to hold office for no more than two terms of four years each, and efforts by some of Obasanjo's closest allies (not surprisingly, those who reaped political and monetary benefit from his rule) to push through a constitutional amendment allowing Obasanjo to remain in power longer failed in 2006. Obasanjo claimed he would prefer to return to his "beloved chicken farm" and left office willingly, though he remains an influential power broker in the party and state.[5]

him one of the most prominent Nigerians of the last twenty years and favored his return to politics.

The 1979 presidential elections resulted in a victory for the northerner Shehu Shagari (narrowly defeating the perennial candidate, Azikiwe) and the reemergence of several traditional parties that had dominated Nigeria before military rule. Shagari's civilian government faced numerous obstacles. In addition to the ethnic factionalism that continued to plague politics, state revenues declined dramatically in 1981 after a drop in oil prices. The resultant economic recession fostered unrest, and the government was burdened by the use of public spending and corruption to award supporters and buy off the public. Inflation and foreign debt increased, and capital fled. When the Shagari government sought to stay in power in 1983 by rigging elections, the military re-entered the picture.

After 1983, Nigeria experienced another decade and a half of military rule, a period dominated by two men: General **Ibrahim Babangida** and General **Sani Abacha**. Babangida, an ethnic Gwari and a Muslim, had the unenviable task of dealing with Nigeria's mounting economic crisis. He implemented a structural-adjustment program backed by the International Monetary Fund and the World Bank that dramatically worsened the lives of average Nigerians by cutting back on public spending. In politics, too, while Babangida asserted that he would restore civilian rule, he increased tension by packing the military government with northerners, only deepening regional and ethnic resentments. In the late 1980s, Babangida sought to initiate a civilian transition under his control, even to the point of creating new political parties and platforms. Under growing public pressure, presidential elections for this **Third Republic** were held in 1993, but Babangida quickly annulled the results, an action that set off a wave of public protests, strikes, and the fear of a new civil war. Babangida stepped down in the face of the unrest, installing a caretaker civilian government. Within three months, Babangida's second in command, Sani Abacha, a northerner, had taken the reins of power for himself in yet another military coup.

Abacha's government lacked many of the skills that had allowed Babangida to remain in power for such a long time. While Babangida sought to co-opt his opponents as much as possible, using force only as a last resort, Abacha regularly employed violence as a means of public control. Political leaders and activists involved in the 1993 elections and ensuing crisis were arrested, and Abacha used his North Korea–trained Special Bodyguard Unit to repress and murder critics of the regime. In 1995, a number of civilian and military officials were imprisoned for allegedly plotting against Abacha, among them former President Obasanjo. The writer and environmentalist **Ken Saro-Wiwa**, a critic of the regime and of the Shell company's role in Nigeria, was also arrested and executed for his opposition to the regime (see "Ken Saro-Wiwa: Playwright and Environmental Activist," p. 549). Saro-Wiwa's execution led to Nigeria's expulsion from the Commonwealth of Nations and to sanctions by the United States and the European Union. Not only did Abacha repress the Nigerian people, but it is estimated that during his rule he also stole as much as US$6 billion from the state. This dark period ended suddenly in 1998, when Abacha died of a heart attack (some observers suspect that he was poisoned). Perhaps realizing the dangers of military rule, the general who succeeded Abacha rapidly carried out a democratic transition and released all political prisoners. In 1999, free presidential elections were held, bringing Obasanjo to power again as head of the **Fourth Republic**.

POLITICAL REGIME

Nigeria's uneven record of governance presents a compelling study of political regimes and a sober lesson in the challenges facing postcolonial countries struggling to institutionalize stable government. Nigeria has experimented with an assortment of political regimes and experienced more than its share of political turmoil in less than fifty years of independence. The country has vacillated between authoritarian military regimes and democratic civilian republics (both parliamentary and presidential) and has had a variety of federal, state, and local political arrangements.

The most prominent form of governance in independent Nigeria has been **patrimonialism**, in which the personal rule of an authoritarian leader has been shored up by the economic privileges he bestows upon a coterie of loyal followers. Not surprisingly, the divisiveness, corruption, and illegitimacy of patrimonialism has meant that the bullets of military coups, rather than the ballots of electoral democracy, have more frequently determined Nigerian regime shifts and changes in government. Each of those shifts has shared at least two features: each new regime has come to power promising improved governance, and each has largely failed to deliver on its promise. Whether military or civilian, authoritarian or democratic, no regime has worked particularly well in Nigeria. On a brighter note, the current Fourth Republic, ushered in with the transition to civilian democracy in 1999, has successfully sponsored three elections (including the first-ever transtion from one civilian government to another in 2007), kept the military in its barracks, and survived longer than any of its democratic predecessors. Perhaps most important, Nigerians seem willing to keep trying. As one observer noted, "Although they have badly botched it up when they achieve democratic rule, Nigerians refuse to settle for anything less."[6]

Because of that tenacity, even though military regimes have ruled Nigeria nearly twice as long as civilian republics, over the years Nigerians have developed a number of important components of successful democracy. These include a diverse and vigorous media, an educated and often critical elite, outspoken human rights organizations, a growing middle class, and a respected legal profession and judiciary. In short, Nigerians have sought to establish the rules and procedures of an effective political regime, but political instability, ethnic disunity, and bureaucratic corruption persist. Long periods of authoritarian oppression have alternated with shorter periods of what appears to be democratic chaos.

The primary focus of the following discussion is the nature of the current civilian democratic regime, but it also touches on the more prevalent authoritarian regimes that preceded it. For, like its two predecessors, if this dem-

---

ESSENTIAL POLITICAL FEATURES

- Legislative-executive system: presidential
- Legislature: National Assembly
- Lower house: House of Representatives
- Upper house: Senate
- Unitary or federal division of power: federal
- Main geographic subunits: states
- Electoral system for lower house: single-member district plurality
- Chief judicial body: Supreme Court

ocratic regime is unable to deliver on its promises and devolves into corruption and chaos, history has shown that authoritarian rule will likely replace it. Nigerians may dislike military rule, but they have also shown little patience for bad democracy.

Political Institutions

THE CONSTITUTION

Since independence, Nigeria has been governed by six constitutions (after having been governed by four during the colonial era). The problem for Nigerian political leaders has not been coming up with rules of good governance but, rather, abiding by them.[7] Well-meaning leaders have oftentimes sought in good faith to revise legal norms to better accommodate both the developmental and the democratic aspirations of the Nigerian people, as well as the realities of their ethnic and religious differences. Too often, however, neither military rulers nor civilian elites (nor foreign multinational corporations, for that matter) have felt bound by those rules.

The British established colonial Nigeria's first constitution in 1922 and then rewrote it three times to reflect the decentralized federal arrangements they imposed to accommodate the colony's regional economic and ethnic divisions. Nigeria's first national constitution, promulgated in 1960, reflected the colonial imprint in at least two important ways. First, like all former British colonies, independent Nigeria established itself as a constitutional monarchy with a Westminster-style parliamentary democracy: the British monarch remained the head of state, legislative authority was placed in the hands of a bicameral parliament, and executive power was vested in a prime minister and cabinet. Second, the federal nature of the Nigerian state was further institutionalized with the codification of the regional division of Nigeria into the Hausa- and Fulani-dominated North, the Igbo-dominated East, and the Yoruba-dominated West.

In 1963, after only three years of independence, Nigeria reconstituted itself as a republic, replacing the queen of England as head of state with its own elected but largely ceremonial president. The revised parliamentary system ostensibly remained in place over the next decade and a half, though military rule for most of that period precluded its functioning. When the military finally acceded to civilian rule in 1979, the constitution of the Second Republic established an American-style presidential system with a directly elected president (as both head of state and head of government), a bicameral legislature, and a separate constitutional court. Subsequent constitutions (of 1989, 1995, and 1999) have retained the presidential system. Nigeria's current Fourth Republic, established in 1999, is thus a federal democratic republic with a presidential executive and a bicameral legislature.

STRUCTURE OF THE GOVERNMENT

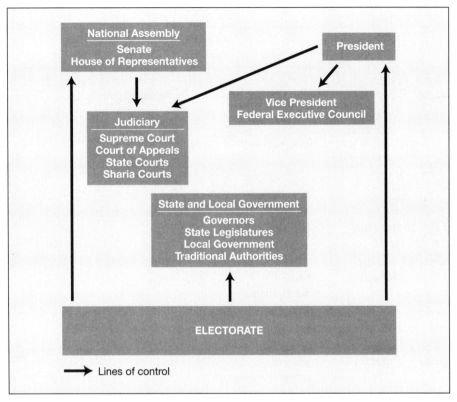

The Branches of Government

THE EXECUTIVE SYSTEM

Nigeria's frequent leadership changes are in large part a consequence of the substantial social, economic, and political challenges facing this postcolonial country. Those changes and challenges have in turn fostered the personal rule of authoritarian leaders and hampered efforts to institutionalize more legitimate executive rule. As the table "Nigerian Heads of Government" (see p. 546) indicates, in its five decades of independence, Nigeria has been ruled for most of three decades by patrimonial strongmen. Elected civilian rule has been infrequent, consistently giving way to military rulers. Generally speaking, military and civilian rulers alike have possessed substantial, if frequently short-lived, political power. Nigeria's current president, **Umaru Yar'Adua**, is only the fourth democratically elected executive to govern Nigeria and the first to succeed a democratically elected president. An ethnic Fulani Muslim from Northern Nigeria and trained chemist, Yar'Adua served as a popular governor of a Northern state, but came to office in 2007 amid charges of election fraud as the handpicked successor to Obasanjo.

Nigerian Heads of Government

Name (Tenure)	Ethnicity (Religion)	Office	Path to Power	Regime Type
Abubakor Tafawa Balewa (1960–66)	Hausa-Fulani (Muslim)	Prime minister	Elected (indirectly)	Parliamentary democracy (First Republic)
Johnson T. U. Aguiyi-Ironsi (1966)	Igbo (Christian)	Military head of government	Coup	Authoritarian military rule
Yakubu Gowon (1966–75)	Tiv (Christian)	Military head of government	Coup	Authoritarian military rule
Murtala Muhammed (1975–76)	Hausa-Fulani (Muslim)	Military head of government	Coup	Authoritarian military rule
Olusegun Obasanjo (1976–79)	Yoruba (Christian)	Military head of government	Coup	Authoritarian military rule
Shehu Shagari (1979–83)	Hausa-Fulani (Muslim)	President	Elected (directly)	Presidential democracy (Second Republic)
Muhammadu Buhari (1983–85)	Hausa-Fulani (Muslim)	Military head of government	Coup	Authoritarian military rule
Ibrahim Babangida (1985–93)	Gwari (Muslim)	Military head of government	Coup	Authoritarian military rule
Ernest Shonekan (1993)	Yoruba (Christian)	Interim head of government	Appointed	Civilian puppet rule (proposed Third Republic)
Sani Abacha (1993–98)	Kanuri (Muslim)	Military head of government	Coup	Authoritarian military rule
Abdulsalam Abubakar (1998–99)	Gwari (Muslim)	Military head of government	Assumed power	Authoritarian military rule
Olusegun Obasanjo (1999–2007)	Yoruba (Christian)	President	Elected (directly)	Presidential democracy (Fourth Republic)
Umaru Yar'Adua (2007–present)	Fulani (Muslim)	President	Elected (directly)	Presidential democracy

As in the U.S. presidential system, the president of Nigeria is directly elected by the people and nominates his or her own running mate, who automatically becomes vice president if the president is elected. The president also appoints ministers to the Federal Executive Council, or cabinet, which is charged with initiating and implementing the policies and programs of the federal government. In a nod to Nigeria's ethnic challenges and in an effort to avoid favoritism (if not clientelism), the constitution requires the president to appoint ministers from each of the states of the Nigerian republic. This quota system, what Nigerians refer to as the **federal character principle**, is also used with federal appointments and civil service positions in the government bureaucracy.[8] Each ethnic group is allotted a certain portion of federal positions based on its regional population. The federal character principle may have spread the spoils of office among the various groups but has done little to prevent corruption. Bribery, waste, and rent-seeking remain the norm in Nigeria's largely dysfunctional civil service, which "absorbs most of the budget but delivers little in the way of service."[9]

THE LEGISLATURE

Although in practice the president and his cabinet initiate budgetary legislation and most other important bills, the constitution designates the National Assembly, Nigeria's federal legislature, as the highest lawmaking body. This bicameral legislature consists of a lower House of Representatives and an upper Senate, with both representatives and senators serving four-year renewable terms. Elections for both houses are held the week preceding the presidential election.

The House of Representatives contains 346 seats, with each member representing an individual district. The 109 seats in the Senate are divided among Nigeria's thirty-six states and the federal district of Abuja. Despite their appointed constitutional roles, both chambers of the National Assembly have served as little more than rubber stamps for the executive branch, even during periods of democratic rule. This circumstance is in part a result of the same party controlling both branches of government, but it is also a result of the legislature's lack of experience, expertise, and staff support. In recent years, however, the National Assembly has demonstrated less compliance in passing budgetary bills and has become more vocal in expressing the demands of regional and even local interests.

These regional disagreements speak to the huge political challenge an increasingly democratic Nigeria faces in overcoming its seemingly intractable ethnic divisions, as we discuss later in this case. Some critics have argued that a parliamentary system might better address Nigeria's challenges of cultural pluralism, by reducing conflict between the executive and legislative branches. Others have called for a unicameral legislature or even the rotation of the presidency and other key executive posts among the dominant ethnic groups, as is done with civil service appointments.

THE JUDICIAL SYSTEM

Nigeria inherited a colonial legal system that combined British common law with an assortment of traditional or customary laws that the colonial government had permitted to handle local matters (including sharia, which predominated in the Northern Region). This legacy fostered a court system and rule of law that historically, even during periods of military rule, retained a degree of independence and legitimacy. However, the Abacha military dictatorship (1993–1998) flouted this independence, routinely ignoring legal checks and using an intimidated judiciary to silence and even eliminate political opponents. Although Abacha frequently used the courts to persecute many of his enemies (including those alleged to have plotted coups against him in 1995 and 1997), the most infamous case of "judicial terrorism" was the 1994 Abacha military tribunal that resulted in the execution of the noted playwright and activist Ken Saro-Wiwa.[10]

With the return to democratic rule, an effort has been made to reestablish the legitimacy and independence of the judiciary. The 1999 constitution established a Supreme Court, a Federal Court of Appeals, and a single unified court system at the national and state levels. The rule of law has been further strengthened under the Yar'Adua government, which launched an anticorruption campaign in 2007. But although the courts have had some success prosecuting former state officials for enriching themselves in office and addressing electoral fraud at the state level, their anticorruption campaigns have faltered as they draw closer to those who are still in office or remain politically influential.

The constitution also permits individual states to authorize traditional subsidiary courts, giving these customary legal systems significant judicial clout. The most controversial of the traditional systems have been the Islamic sharia courts, which now function in twelve of the predominantly Muslim northern states. As discussed later in this case, Nigerians have contended heatedly and, in some cases, violently over the role and jurisdiction of the sharia courts.

The Electoral System

As in the United States, Nigerians directly elect their president and separately elect members of both chambers of their legislature, the National Assembly. But unlike the system in the United States, in Nigeria presidents, senators, and representatives all serve four-year terms, with elections for all three offices held in the same year. In an effort to ensure that the president serves with a national mandate, Nigeria's constitution requires that the winning presidential candi-

---

KEN SARO-WIWA: PLAYWRIGHT AND ENVIRONMENTAL ACTIVIST

Kenule Benson Saro-Wiwa was born in 1941 to an Ogoni family, members of an ethnic minority of southern Nigeria, on whose land in the Niger Delta rich oil reserves were discovered. By the 1980s, Saro-Wiwa had become known internationally for his novels and plays, many written in Nigerian pidgin, or "rotten" English. At the same time, Saro-Wiwa became increasingly involved in political efforts to force the Shell oil company and the Nigerian government to take greater responsibility for the environment and share a greater portion of the oil wealth with the Ogoni, whose lands the oil rigs were despoiling. With others, Saro-Wiwa founded the Movement for the Survival of the Ogoni People (MOSOP) in 1990. MOSOP challenged the government's revenue-sharing formulas, which kept the bulk of the oil wealth flowing to national government coffers. With allied groups, MOSOP also disrupted production, compelling Shell first to curtail oil extraction in the Ogoni region and ultimately to abandon its operations there altogether. By interfering in this "stream of petroleum revenues that fed the dictatorship,"[11] MOSOP raised the ire of General Sani Abacha's military government, which in 1994 ordered a brutal crackdown on Ogoni activists and sympathetic Ogoni villages. Saro-Wiwa and other activists were arrested on trumped-up charges and brought before a special military tribunal. The show trial returned a verdict of guilty, and in November of 1995 the government hanged all nine of the defendants despite an international outcry and efforts to intervene by international human rights groups and the leaders of dozens of countries.

---

date obtain both an overall majority of votes and at least 25 percent of the ballots cast in at least two thirds of the states. This requirement became an issue of contention in the 1979 election, when the Supreme Court was called upon to determine what constituted two thirds of Nigeria's then nineteen states (there are now thirty-six). Ultimately, the court ruled that Shehu Shagari's victory in twelve states—not the thirteen demanded by the opposition—sufficed, and Shagari was named president. The constitution holds that if no candidate succeeds in winning a majority of total votes and obtaining the two-thirds threshold in the first round, a second round of voting takes place a week later, pitting the top two candidates against each other in a runoff.

All 360 seats in the House of Representatives are contested in single-member districts apportioned roughly equally by population. The 109 members of the Senate are also elected from single-member districts, with each of the thirty-six states divided into three districts. The federal district, or "capital territory," of Abuja elects one senator in a single-seat constituency for the 109th seat. These winner-take-all single-member districts have allowed just three parties to dominate both chambers of the National Assembly. Several other smaller parties have managed on occasion to win seats in the House. The success of the smaller parties reflects the geographic concentration of ethnic groups willing to vote in blocs large enough to win a plurality of votes in the less-populous lower-house electoral districts, such as the districts dominated by the Kanuri minority of northeastern Nigeria.

Local Government

Constitutionally, Nigeria is a federal republic with national, state, and local levels of governance. Although Nigeria's military governments sought to establish a unitary system, the gaping ethnic divisions within the country have prevented governments of all stripes from truly unifying the nation and centralizing political authority. These divisions reflect the ethnic diversity of Nigeria and the legacy of colonial rule.

In 1970, the Federal Military Government divided the republic into twelve states following the Nigerian Civil War, which nearly split the country permanently. The number of states grew to nineteen in 1976, thirty by 1991, and thirty-six by 1996, plus the Federal Capital Territory. The number of local government units has varied even more substantially, reflecting the uncertainty of how federalism should be constituted in Nigeria. The democratic government elected in 1979 doubled the number of local authorities to more than 700. In 1983, the military government downsized the number to 300, but it has since increased to nearly 800.

With a history of interregional instability and suspicion and relatively weak state capacity, the countervailing demands of centralization and devolution will certainly persist in Nigeria. On the one hand, the national government's control of the lion's share of oil revenues has provided the patrimonial glue that keeps the local regions dependent upon the center. But as increasingly diverse and articulate voices have entered an increasingly democratic political arena, the calls for enhanced state and local autonomy have grown louder. Those demands range from expanded state control over the budget (and for the oil-rich Niger Delta, local control over its oil revenues) and a separate military for each region to full-fledged dismemberment of Nigeria.

To date, local and even state governments have enjoyed little autonomy from the national government and have no means of generating revenue. Put simply, the central government controls the purse strings, and the Nigerian purse depends almost completely upon oil revenues. Not surprisingly, as oil revenues have expanded, so has the public sector at all levels and the levels of corruption associated with that patronage. At the same time, the expansion of oil revenues has led to increased disputes over the percentage—known as the **derivation formula**—that should accrue to the oil-producing localities.[12]

Other Institutions: The Military

Although the Fourth Republic has managed to sponsor three successive and relatively peaceful democratic elections, independent Nigeria's tumultuous history cautions us not to become too confident that the military will remain in its barracks. Nigeria's experience with military-in-government (military officers as political leaders) has left a deep impression on Nigerian politics. It is not a coincidence that most of Nigeria's most powerful leaders (including former coup leader and recent president Obasanjo) boast a military background. As is the case elsewhere in postcolonial Africa and in much of the developing world, the military has served as one of the few stable avenues of meritocratic social mobility; it has long been able to attract many of Nigeria's best, brightest, and most ambitious.

This avenue has been particularly important for the ethnic Muslims of northern Nigeria, who have been educationally and economically disadvantaged in comparison with southern Nigerians. Although the south is the source of Nigeria's oil, for many years the north controlled the army and used that control, in the form of military dictatorships, to redistribute oil wealth. Time will tell whether Nigeria's military is prepared to make its most recent withdrawal from public life permanent.

POLITICAL CONFLICT AND COMPETITION

The Party System

Politics in oil-rich, patrimonial Nigeria has been described as a "contest of self-enrichment."[13] Whether these political contests have been fought with ballots or bullets, the stakes are indeed high, the competition fierce, and corruption and violence all too common.[14] Not surprisingly, political parties and the party system have fared best under democratic regimes and have withered during periods of military rule. Political parties first began forming during the colonial period and did so quite naturally along ethnic lines even as early advocates of democracy sought to establish multicultural and issue-based platforms. Although the names of the dominant parties have changed over time, the parties that emerged during each era continued to reflect the ethnic divisions, despite efforts of democratic and even some military regimes to establish cross-ethnic national parties.

It makes more sense to discuss Nigeria's parties in terms of their ethnic identity and, therefore, their geographic location than to try to place them on a left-right political continuum. This regional party identity has exacerbated ethnic tensions and complicated efforts to establish democratic institutions and legitimize national party politics. Moreover, most state and local contests are also dominated by the region's dominant party, a circumstance that allows the party to control the state assembly and effectively capture the seats in the national Senate and House of Representatives as well. This reminds us that in Nigeria all politics is in the first instance local, and that in communities, ethnicity and clientelist networks have traditionally meant everything.

Although democratic elections under Nigeria's Fourth Republic offer hope for the establishment of cross-ethnic parties with national appeal, strengthened democracy has also given stronger voice to persistent sectarian and even local separatist demands. The centrifugal push of communal violence between the Muslim north and the Christian south and growing violent contention over the spoils of the oil-rich Niger Delta weaken the centripetal pull of national electoral contests too often plagued by political corruption.

Elections

Colonial-era parties survived through the First Republic (1960–1966) but were banned from the onset of military rule until Olusegun Obasanjo, as leader of a military coup, seized power in 1976. Obasanjo legalized the establishment of political parties in 1978, and some 150 parties were formed in that year alone. In 1979, Obasanjo's elected successor, Shehu Shagari, sought to impose order on this political cacophony by compelling the formation of nationwide parties. The constitution of the Second Republic specified that any successful presidential candidate must win at least one fourth of the vote in at least two thirds of the states. The election commission required that all parties open membership to all Nigerians and that the parties' leadership come from at least two thirds of the states. In all, five parties were deemed viable contenders in the 1979 and 1983 elections. Military coups in 1983 and 1985 (in part the result of the widespread corruption and failure of the Second Republic) once again banned political parties.

Ibrahim Babangida, the military ruler from 1985 to 1993, charged his National Election Commission with reforming the party system to produce a two-party system. But fears that such a system would lead to a dangerous political division between the Muslim north and the Christian south led the commission once again to approve five parties. Dissatisfied, Babangida dissolved the commission and established two national parties, one neatly placed "a little to the left of center and one a little to the right."[15] The government built headquarters for each party, gave each one start-up funds, and even named them (the Social Democratic Party and the National Republican Convention). Babangida called for local elections in 1990 and announced plans to hand over power to civilians with a presidential election in 1992.

Although the election was postponed until 1993, it took place fairly. But because the winner was a southern (Yoruban) civilian distrusted by the northern military generals, the military nullified the results and charged the apparent victor with treason. The military installed an interim puppet president, who was quickly pushed aside by General Sani Abacha. Abacha called for elections in 1996, and his military government certified five parties—all loyal to him. Not surprisingly, all five nominated Abacha as their candidate for president.

Abdusalam Abubakar, Abacha's military successor, dissolved the five parties and called for presidential elections in 1999. In another effort to foster political parties with a "federal character," the election commission approved only parties that maintained well-established national organizations. Nine parties qualified for local elections, and the three parties with the highest votes in those elections were permitted to participate in the national legislative and presidential elections. Not surprisingly, each of those parties once again reflected its regional base in one of the country's main ethnic groups: the People's Democratic Party (PDP), representing the northern Hausa; the All People's Party (APP) of the eastern Igbo; and the Alliance for Democracy (AD) of the western Yoruba.

Democracy advocates are hopeful that the 1999 election has marked a watershed for Nigerian national politics. PDP supporters—with strength in the Muslim north, home of many of Nigeria's military leaders—chose to support Obasanjo, a retired general but a southern Christian Yoruban. The AD chose to throw its support behind the APP contender rather than field its own candidate. Obasanjo won with nearly two-thirds of the vote, and a "relieved public" overlooked the many flaws in the election and largely accepted the results that ushered in the Fourth Republic.[16]

The two most recent elections have followed this trend of both growing democracy and persistent concerns with electoral corruption. The 2003 election, the first sponsored by a civilian government in twenty years, returned Obasanjo to office. In 2007, Obasanjo stepped down as required by the constitution, marking the first ever succession of democratically elected executives in Nigerian history. This cleared the way for Umaru Yar'Adua, Obasanjo's handpicked candidate to succeed him, winning a landslide victory with purportedly 70 percent of the vote (see "Results of Nigeria's Recent National Elections," p. 554). As in the 2003 elections, the PDP swept not only the presidential election but also contests for the two chambers of the legislature and state assembly races held in the same month. The victory was marred, however, by opposition and foreign observer charges of widespread electoral corruption and fraud in electoral contests at all levels. Yar'Adua's two chief rivals for the presidency sought to annul the election results,[17] and even foreign observers concluded that the elections were so badly rigged that they "lacked even the pretense of democratic plausibility."[18] After a nearly yearlong investigation, an appeals court concluded that the margin of victory was wide enough that, despite shortcomings, even a fully clean election would have still brought Yar'Adua to office.

In spite of three consecutive affirmations of the democratic process in Nigeria and the high expectations of the Nigerian people, endemic government corruption, communal and gangster violence, and persistent economic misery have tested Nigerians' patience for democratic rule. When asked in 2005 if the present system of elected government "should be given more time to deal with inherited problems," only 55 percent of Nigerians said yes, compared with 58 percent in 2003 and nearly 80 percent in 2000. Support for the democratic system remains strong, but governments of the Fourth Republic must start delivering on promises of better times if they hope to avoid the fate of the earlier republics.

Civil Society

Neither the British colonial government nor the series of military authoritarian regimes has been able to squelch Nigeria's rich tradition of activism and

Results of Nigeria's Recent National Elections					
Region **Ethnicity** **Party** **Election Year**	**North** **Hausa** **PDP**	**East** **Igbo** **APP/ANPP***	**West** **Yoruba** **AD/AC****	**Other** **parties**	**Total**
Presidential Vote (%)					
1999	62.8	37.2	no candidate	—	100
2003	61.9	32.2	no candidate	5.9	100
2007	69.8	18.7	7.5	5.0	100
Senate Seats					
1999	65	24	20	0	109
2003	73	28	6	0	107***
2007	87	14	6	2	109
House Seats					
1999	212	79	69	0	360
2003	213	95	31	7	346***
2007	260	61	31	4	356

*The APP renamed itself the All Nigeria People's Party after a merger with a smaller independent party in 2003.

**The Action Congress is the result of the 2006 merger of the Alliance for Democracy and several smaller parties.

***Contested returns from some districts reduced the total number of candidates seated in both the Senate and the House in the 2003 election.

IN COMPARISON	CHOOSING BETWEEN A GOOD DEMOCRACY AND A STRONG ECONOMY	
	Good Democracy (percent)	Strong Economy (pecent)
Nigeria	59	40
India	56	41
Mexico	53	41
China	50	44
Brazil	50	46
South Africa	40	58
Russia	15	74

Source: Pew Center for the People and the Press, 2007.

dissent. Even Abacha's oppressive dictatorship in the 1990s could not fully muzzle what one foreign observer referred to as Nigerian citizens' "defiant spunk."[19] In Nigeria's relatively short postcolonial history, a wide variety of formal interest groups and informal voluntary associations has emerged and persisted. Under the relaxed environment of the Fourth Republic, these groups and organizations have proliferated and strengthened. Some of them, particularly professional associations and other nongovernmental organizations (NGOs), have drawn their support from across Nigeria's cultural spectrum and have functioned in ways that promote national integration. Others, particularly those based on ethnic and religious identities, are among the most resilient of groups and in some cases serve to fragment Nigerian society.

Formal and informal ethnic and religious associations were the first groups in Nigerian society and remain the most cohesive. Some of these groups have long served as important vehicles of mutual trust for promoting the economic interests of their members, for example, by mobilizing savings or investing in a business. Others have formed to protect or promote the ethnic or local interests of a particular minority group. In the early years of independence, some groups provided the foundation for the subsequent formation of political parties. Among the most important of these issue-based minority associations are those that have emerged in the Niger Delta to protect the interests of ethnic and other groups in the region. The **Movement for the Survival of the Ogoni People**, or **MOSOP**, established by Ken Saro-Wiwa in the 1990s to defend the interests of the Ogoni, employed a variety of legal and extra-legal political tactics to secure more financial benefits with fewer environmental costs from foreign-operated oil interests in the Niger Delta. As conditions in the region worsen and more and broader constituencies feel they have a right to a portion of the oil revenues, groups in the Niger Delta have more readily turned to violence. Most notorious among these is the **Movement for the Emancipation of the Niger Delta (MEND)**, which has developed a reputation for "bunkering" (illegally siphoning off) oil, kidnapping foreign oil workers, and even launching daylight attacks on oil facilities in the region. The lines dividing ethnic and environmental political associations, insurgent separatist movements, youth fraternities (or cults), and common gangs are blurring in this complex and troubled region.

Likewise, the volatile potential of conflict between Christian and Muslim religious institutions and groups persists. However, this has been mitigated by the numerous divisions and differences within each religious tradition. Although Muslims of the north share a common faith and have banded together in defense of certain interests (such as the maintenance and expansion of the scope of sharia law), there are numerous schisms within the faith as well. For example, the Tijaniyah variety of Sufi Islam, practiced among lower-class Hausa Muslims, is quite distinct and in many ways at odds with the orthodox Sunni Islam practiced by the Hausa and Fulani Muslim elite. In fact, some liberal Muslim groups favor secular government and oppose the implementation of sharia. Christian-based politics in the south is similarly far from monolithic.

Modern civic associations such as trade unions and professional organizations played a prominent role in the anticolonial struggle and have been relatively active in promoting their particular, and at times more collective, interests since the time of independence. Unions representing workers in the all-important petroleum industry—for example, the National Union of Petroleum and Gas Workers (NUPENG)—have been particularly influential. Formal associations such as those representing legal, medical, and journalism professionals have begun to articulate the political interests of Nigeria's growing professional class. Particularly since the end of military rule and the establishment of the Fourth Republic, NGOs promoting issues such as development, democracy, and civil rights have exerted more influence in Nigerian politics.

SOCIETY

Ethnic and National Identity

It should be quite clear by now that one of the central factors defining Nigerian politics is group identity. Ethnicity is a powerful force, given the historical rivalry among Yoruba, Igbo, and Hausa and Fulani peoples. In addition, nearly one third of the population belongs to none of those groups, further complicating the ethnic map. This diversity has created significant problems for the consolidation of democracy, as there are temptations for each group to see politics in zero-sum terms. That is, an electoral victory by a Hausa candidate, for example, is viewed as a blow to the interests of the Yoruba, and vice versa. Such centrifugal tendencies were largely responsible for the collapse of civilian government in 1966 and of course for the Nigerian Civil War. Subsequent military leaders often sought to play on the fears of ethnic conflict as a justification for authoritarianism, arguing that democracy only exacerbated the fault lines between regions and peoples. Changes in the federal structure (creating more territorial divisions) and the executive system (replacing a parliamentary system with a presidential one) similarly reflected the desire to weaken local authority and shift more power to the center. Even the capital was moved, in 1991, from Lagos to Abuja, a city built from scratch in the center of the country.

How has the transition to democracy affected ethnic relations? Since the end of military rule, communal violence has risen, as the state is no longer able to suppress the public as it pleases and as the struggle for control over the state has returned to the populace. Since the return to civilian rule in 1999, it is estimated that such conflicts have taken thousands of lives and displaced over a million Nigerians. This violence often has economic motives, with its origins in conflicts over access to state funds, oil revenues, jobs, or other resources. Moreover, it is frequently asserted that political elites capitalize on these conflicts as a way to build their base of support, even to the point of inciting conflict through words and actions (such as paying supporters to attack rival groups).

ETHNIC GROUPS

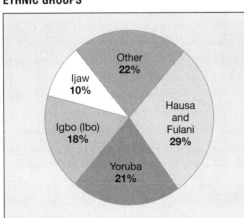

RELIGION

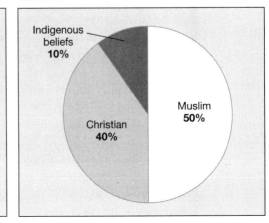

The conflicts also have a religious component. In recent years, there has been a deepening fissure between Muslims, who are concentrated in the north, and Christians and animists, who are concentrated in the south. The catalyst has been the role of sharia, or Islamic law. Under British rule, Islamic law was preserved in the north and continued to serve an important, if limited, role. The practice was continued under independent Nigeria, and by the 1980s Islamic groups had begun to press the Ibrahim Babangida government to allow for the expansion of sharia in the north as well as in higher courts, where it then had no authority.

While the repression of Sani Abacha's regime froze much of that activism, it quickly revived with the onset of civilian rule. Muslim leaders and the Muslim public saw the expansion of sharia as a way to overcome the corruption of the military era and reassert their rights in a democratic system. Some political leaders also clearly saw the issue in a more cynical light, as a way to garner public support. Shortly after the 1999 elections, a dozen northern states made sharia the primary law, extending it to criminal and other matters. This legal system includes an extreme punishment for adultery and apostasy (leaving the faith): death by stoning. The imposition of sharia has touched off some of the worst violence under civilian rule; in one incident in 2000, clashes between Christians and Muslims in the town of Kaduna left 2,000 dead. In 2006, sixteen Christian churches in another northern city were burned down during a riot. The tension over sharia also grabbed international attention when two women were sentenced to be stoned to death for committing adultery. Although the verdicts were eventually overturned by higher courts, the seeming incompatibility between secular national law and an expansive regional use of sharia remains a serious and potentially destabilizing issue.[20]

Ideology and Political Culture

Could the conflicts between north and south, between Christian, Muslim, and animist, lead to civil war, another military coup, or the dissolution of the country itself? Perhaps. As we have seen, political parties in Nigeria tend to be built around individual leaders and ethnic groups, meaning that ideology plays a limited role compared with more narrow communal concerns, in contrast to a country like South Africa, where ideology plays a much stronger role in the party system. Similarly, it is commonly asserted that Nigerians have a low sense of patriotism or pride in their state, presumably a result of their stronger local identity and the legacy of military rule. The Nigerian novelist and political activist Chinua Achebe once described Nigerians as "among the world's most unpatriotic people," which, he argued, was a serious impediment to prosperity and democracy.[21]

In spite of these concerns, however, there are aspects of Nigerian political culture that continue to lend support to the state and the democratic regime. A 2005 survey of Nigerians showed that despite the tensions and disappointments that have followed the return of civilian rule, nearly 65 percent continued to support democracy and reject military rule (though this is down from a high of 84 percent in 2000). Nigerians also express strong opposition to a political system dominated by a single party or leader, an attitude quite different from that in many other African democracies, where such domination is common. Over time, Nigerians have come to base their support for democracy less on economic performance and more on trustworthy leaders and similar factors—quite the opposite of what is expected in less-developed countries with weakly institutionalized democracy.[22] Moreover, in contrast to Achebe's assertion, surveys show that Nigerians exhibit a high degree of pride in their broader national identity. Those views, if sustained, may help limit communal tension and build ties across ethnic and religious divisions.

POLITICAL ECONOMY

The misfortune of the Nigerian economy has been a constant theme throughout our discussion. The economic difficulties that Nigeria has faced since independence are not unusual among less-developed countries, but they are particularly egregious given that Nigeria is one of the world's largest oil producers and has earned hundreds of billions of dollars from its steady export of the product, making up 90 percent of its foreign-currency earnings. In fact, Nigeria's economic difficulties exist not in spite of its oil resources but in large part because of them. Nigeria's predicament is an excellent example of what scholars sometimes refer to as the **resource curse**. Natural resources that are abundant and state controlled often serve to support authoritarian rule by giving the ruling regime the means to buy off the public and pay for repression. It is also argued that natural resources tend to distort an economy by diverting it from other forms of development. This situation can be seen in other oil-producing economies, such as Iran.

Each of these factors is evident in the development of Nigeria's political economic system. Like other less-developed countries, in the years following independence Nigeria opted for a system of import substitution, creating tariff barriers and parastatal industries with the objective of rapidly industrializing the country. This ambitious program was made possible by oil sales, which during the 1970s benefited from high prices. However, these programs suffered from policies directing resources toward certain industries for political reasons, without a clear understanding of whether the investments would be profitable. For example, US$8 billion was spent in the attempt to create a domestic steel industry that in the end produced barely any steel.[23] The decline in oil prices in the 1980s and the subsequent economic crisis and substantial foreign debt led Nigeria to initiate a policy of structural adjustment that moved the country away from import substitution, although the economy remained highly regulated and closed to trade.

The limited reforms also did not address the fact that the country remained dependent upon oil exports and that the revenues from those exports were in the hands of the military. As the public suffered from the effects of structural adjustment, such as unemployment and inflation, the regime of Ibrahim Babandiga used its financial resources to co-opt some opponents while repressing others. Economic reforms also facilitated this patrimonialism, as newly liberalized markets or privatized state assets could be doled out in return for political support—not unlike the "insider privatization" that plagued Russia in the 1990s.

By the time of Sani Abacha's government, corruption had reached such heights as to be described by one scholar as outright "predation" under an "avaricious dictatorship."[24] The Nigerian economy not only suffered from the outright theft of state funds, but also became a center for illicit activity, including narcotics trafficking, human trafficking, money laundering, and perhaps best known, the so-called 419, or advance-fee, scams (see "419 Scams," p. 561). One might argue that corruption should not be a central focus if it has helped provide funds for economic development, but the reality is that little of this wealth was reinvested in the country. Over the past thirty years, Nigeria has had a negative GDP growth rate and has suffered from a high degree of income inequality. It boasts the dubious distinction of being one of the world's most corrupt countries (surpassed only by Bangladesh and Haiti) as well as a nation with one of the world's lowest life expectancies. Nigeria ranks 159th out of 177 countries on the United Nation's Human Development Index. Corruption, inequality, and poverty are clearly connected.

The Fourth Republic thus faces an enormous challenge in righting the Nigerian economy and breaking with the practices of previous regimes. The Obasanjo and Yar'Adua governments have taken several important steps, developing a wide-ranging reform program known as the **National Economic Empowerment and Development Strategy (NEEDS)** and launching an impressive anticorruption campaign. The NEEDS program has tackled several important areas. First, it has increased the transparency of government finances, for example, by auditing the accounts of various levels of government to oversee how money is being spent and by making the findings available to the public. Second, it has prompted the government to

LABOR FORCE BY OCCUPATION

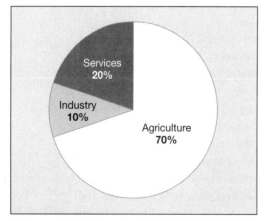

Services 20%

Industry 10%

Agriculture 70%

419 SCAMS

Many readers of this case have received an e-mail message stating that if they provide financial support up front, they will receive a share of a large sum of money from overseas. Those offers are known as 419, or advance-fee, scams. Such confidence games, long known as Spanish-prisoner cons, date back to sixteenth-century Europe. What is notable about the recent permutation, however, is the frequency with which the scam has originated in Nigeria: indeed, the term "419" stems from the Nigerian legal code banning such activities. The Nigerian scams appear to have begun in the 1980s, around the time of the decline in oil prices, and were tolerated, if not abetted, by the government. The most common version is an unsolicited letter from a Nigerian claiming to be a senior civil servant. The letter writer is seeking a partner in whose account he can deposit several million dollars, money that supposedly was overpaid on a government contract. The partner is offered a share of the funds for his or her assistance but first must help defray the cost of a number of bribes or licenses. Gullible (and greedy) recipients of such letters have sent substantial amounts of money to Nigeria, billions of dollars, according to some estimates. In some cases, individuals have been lured to Nigeria to complete the supposed transaction, only to be kidnapped or killed. In addition to defrauding unwitting marks, the cons have deterred prospective legitimate investors, who are unwilling to risk having to distinguish between a business opportunity and a scam.

In recent years, the Nigerian government has cracked down on the 419 scams, with the Economic and Financial Crimes Commission seizing over $700 million between 2003 and 2004 and arresting over 500 people. With the proliferation of e-mail, however, it has become much easier for scam artists to distribute their bogus stories of covert wealth, and they have moved on to new territory, focusing new variants on eBay customers, for example. Nigerian expatriates have apparently moved the scams abroad, to Europe and South Africa. The 419 scams demonstrate the lack of the rule of law in Nigeria, as well as how that condition, facilitated by globalization, can spill over into the international system.

address the corruption problem and improve the rule of law, for example, by creating an Economic and Financial Crimes Commission to pursue theft and money laundering (and seizing over US$500 million in the process).[25] Under the Yar'Adua administration, this commission took some impressive steps in tackling Nigeria's endemic corruption, arresting seven former state governors for the missappropriation of funds. NEEDS also focuses on the country's inadequate infrastructure, seeking to boost electricity production, improve transportation, increase telecommunications, and expand access to sanitation and clean drinking water. The goal, then, is to reform the state while expanding basic social expenditures across Nigeria. If successful, NEEDS could dramatically improve the lives of average Nigerians and increase domestic business and foreign investment.

The long-term success of NEEDS will of course hinge on one critical factor: oil. As oil prices have risen, the Nigerian government has found itself in a better financial position, but as we know from the past, such windfalls reap no long-term benefits if they are stolen or spent unproductively. Realizing this, the government has earmarked some of the oil revenues for a stabilization fund that can be drawn from if and when oil prices fall. The government has also taken on corruption within the oil industry. But huge problems remain, reflecting the enormous impact that the oil industry has on Nigeria.

FOREIGN RELATIONS AND THE WORLD

Nigeria's foreign policy has undergone several shifts in emphasis since independence, reflecting international and domestic influences. The country's gradual transition from colonialism has meant that it did not undergo revolution or a protracted war of independence, either of which might have dramatically reshaped its relationship with the outside world. As a result, during the cold war Nigeria remained clearly within the pro-Western camp and retained its ties to the United Kingdom through membership in the Commonwealth of Nations. However, Western sympathy for the Biafrans during the 1967–1970 Nigerian Civil War and the West's refusal to provide arms to defeat Biafra steered Nigeria toward nonalignment. Nigeria has also sought to play an important regional role by helping to lead several international governmental organizations focused on Africa. One such body is the Economic Community of West African States (ECOWAS), with a membership of fifteen West African countries. ECOWAS was created as an instrument of regional integration, not unlike the European Union in its early stages. The process of economic integration has been slow, however, although ECOWAS has actively met its obligation to intervene in armed conflicts in member states. Thus it has dispatched peacekeeping troops to help resolve civil conflicts in Liberia and Sierra Leone. As the largest ECOWAS member state by far, Nigeria has borne the brunt of the peacekeeping efforts. Nigeria has similarly been active in deploying peacekeepers for far-flung UN missions, as in Lebanon and along the Indian-Pakistan border. In spite of these important responsibilities, Nigeria's international relations declined steadily under the Sani Abacha regime, and by 1995 the country had been suspended from the Commonwealth and subject to sanctions by the European Union and the United States following the execution of Ken Saro-Wiwa. With democratic elections, however, Nigeria has once again gained status as a regional and, increasingly, a global actor.

In the coming decades, it is likely that Nigeria will become more important on the international scene. Whether this change will contribute to global security and prosperity, however, is an open question. One main reason that Nigeria may grow in importance takes us back to a recurrent theme of this case, and that is oil. It is estimated that Nigeria has some 34 billion barrels of oil reserves. Whereas that is only a fraction of the reserves of major oil-producing states, such as Saudi Arabia, it nevertheless makes Nigeria one of the world's major producers. The vast majority of Nigerian oil is exported to Europe, Asia, and North America, making it an important trading partner. Instability in the Middle East and economic development in Asia may further push Nigeria into the forefront of energy production. For example, India and particularly China have shown increased interest in investing in Nigeria's oil industry, raising the possibility that the country will find itself caught in a political struggle as the United States, Europe, and Asia vie for access to its oil. Recognizing its increased status on the world stage, Nigeria has been pushing for representation as a permanent member of the United Nations Security Council, which currently has no permanent African member (the permanent members are the United States, the United Kingdom, Russia, China, and France).

A second factor is regional. As the most populous country in Africa, Nigeria stands to play a key role on the continent in helping to bolster democracy and stability. In addition to its role in ECOWAS, Nigeria has long been an important player in the Organisation of African Unity (OAU), which was created in 1963. Within the OAU, Nigeria was a strong opponent of white rule in Rhodesia (now Zimbabwe) and South Africa and with its own transition to democracy has stressed its commitment to democratic rule in Africa. This attitude can be seen in the recent transformation of the OAU. In 1999, its members agreed that the body should broaden its responsibilities to actively pursue a process of greater regional integration (not unlike the original intentions of ECOWAS in West Africa). In 2002, the OAU officially renamed itself the African Union (AU) and declared a new mandate for its member states, known as the New Partnership for Africa's Development, or NEPAD. The primary goals of NEPAD are to eradicate poverty, sustain growth, integrate Africa into the process of globalization, and empower African women.

To that end, the AU and NEPAD have broken with past practices by serving as an intermediary between international donors and African states and holding the latter accountable for enforcing the rule of law and making certain that foreign aid is properly spent. Nigeria and South Africa have become the leading members of the African Union, with Nigeria taking a strong line on supporting democracy on the continent. For example, as Zimbabwe's government under Robert Mugabe slid deep into authoritarian rule over the past decade, Nigeria supported the country's suspension from the Commonwealth of Nations, and both Obasanjo and Yar'Adua have been openly critical of Mugabe's dictatorial rule. Both Nigeria and South Africa can be expected to grow in influence across the continent, with the former benefiting from its size while the latter benefits from its more developed economy. Some observers of Africa have called Nigeria and South Africa the China and Japan of Africa.

Finally, Nigeria's presence in the international system will depend to a great extent on how its democracy fares. A slide toward authoritarian rule will undoubtedly weaken the country's regional and international moral authority and in the process damage institutions like the AU and NEPAD. Another worry is that the history of conflict between northern and southern Nigeria could embroil the country in the current international struggle against violent Islamic extremism. Recent clashes among Nigerian Muslims, Christians, and animists have their impetus in disputes that date back many generations. As in many other parts of the world, however, local ethnic or religious conflicts might become radicalized and internationalized and drawn into the loose ideology of Al Qaeda and its supporters. What role, if any, such groups may have in Nigeria is unclear, although their presence in Africa is long-standing. Al Qaeda staged devastating attacks on U.S. embassies in Kenya and Tanzania in 1998, and its operatives may have been active in nearby Liberia before and after 2001. Nigeria's widespread criminal activities may also be attractive to terrorists, as a means of raising funds and laundering money. Some observers express concern that the long-standing ethnic and religious tensions in Nigeria will provide a platform for terrorist activity, especially attacks on the country's oil facilities. Terrorist concerns will only be heightened if state capacity weakens under ineffectual democracy or illegitimate authoritarianism. Because of these concerns, the United States has significantly increased its military support for West African countries, including Nigeria. Closer ties with the United States increase the risk of exacerbating tensions in Nigeria's Muslim community, however, and so could play directly into the hands of terrorists.[26] Nigeria will undoubtedly become more connected to the globalizing world in the coming decade, but such a connection will require balancing domestic tensions with regional and international pressures. It will not be easy.

CURRENT ISSUES

NIGER DELTA

Nowhere do Nigeria's multitude of complex political, social, economic, and environmental problems and prospects converge more acutely than in the oil-producing Niger Delta. Home to some 31 million Nigerians who comprise more than 40 distinct ethnic groups and over 250 dialects, this region also produces over 2 million barrels of crude oil a day and has the potential to produce up to 3 million barrels. Tragically, corrupt national and local politicians steal or squander the lion's share of oil revenues; local militias and gansters siphon oil, kidnap oil workers, and wreck production facilities; and millions of gallons of oil and other effluents contaminate the Niger's delicate tropical ecosystem (the wasteful and illegal "flaring" or burning off of natural gas alone is by some estimates the world's single-largest contributer of greenhouse gas and wastes US$500 million in potential gas revenues each year).

Although the region has been troubled for many decades, in the past few years impoverished communities in the Delta have become increasingly angry and restive. With the reestablishment of democracy in 1999, politicians began to arm local gangs to rig elections for them. International oil producers who operate in Nigeria, such as Shell and Chevron, have worsened matters by regularly providing payments to local leaders as tribute for operating in their community. This practice has increased conflict between ethnic groups in the Delta and between community leaders and unemployed youth, with each group vying for a share of the funds. A result has been the spread of armed militias, often linked to political parties, battling—often violently—over oil. Among their activities are "bunkering" (illegally siphoning oil from pipelines— perhaps as much as 40 percent of all that is produced), seizing or destroying facilities and kidnapping foreign oil-industry workers for ransom, and staging attacks on rival groups. Solving this conflict will not be easy; it will require more effective policing, local governance, central control over the actions of foreign oil producers, and addressing the economic and environmental demands of the local population most directly affected and deeply harmed by these activities.

NOTES

1. Ike Okonta and Oronto Douglas, *Where Vultures Feast: Shell, Human Rights, and Oil* (San Francisco: Sierra Club Books, 2001).
2. *The Niger Delta: No Democratic Dividend* (New York: Human Rights Watch, 2002).
3. *World Urbanization Prospects: The 2003 Revision Population Database* (New York: United Nations, 2004).
4. Charles R. Nixon, "Self-Determination: The Nigeria/Biafra Case," *World Politics*, 24, no. 4 (July 1972), pp. 473–97.
5. "A Troubled but Lingering President," *Economist*, 4, August 2005.
6. Blaine Harden, *Africa: Dispatches from a Fragile Continent* (Boston: Houghton Mifflin, 1990), p. 247.
7. Julius O. Ihonvbere, "How to Make an Undemocratic Constitution: The Nigerian Example," *Third World Quarterly*, 21 (2000), pp. 343–66.
8. The 1999 constitution states that the "composition of the Government of the Federation or any of its agencies and the conduct of its affairs shall be carried out in such a manner as to reflect the federal character of Nigeria and the need to pro-

mote national unity, and also to command national loyalty thereby ensuring that there shall be no pre-dominance of persons from a few states or from a few ethnic or other sectional groups in that government or in any of its agencies." See E. Ike Idogu, "Federalism and Ethnic Conflict in Nigeria," *Journal of Third World Studies* (Spring 2004).

9. "A Reporter's Tale," *Economist,* 26 February 2004.

10. For the term *judicial terrorism,* see Shu'aibu Musa, "Shades of Injustice: Travails of Muslim Activists in Nigeria in the Hands of Successive Regimes," paper presented at the International Conference of Prisoners of Faith, London, 17 February 2002 (London: Islamic Human Rights Commission, 2002), www.ihrc.org.uk/file/02feb17drmusaSHADES%20OF%20INJUSTICE.pdf (accessed 3 November 2005).

11. Howard French, *A Continent for the Taking* (New York: Alfred A. Knopf, 2004), p. 38.

12. Idogu, "Federalism and Ethnic Conflict in Nigeria."

13. French, *A Continent for the Taking,* p. 27.

14. Ike Okonta, "Nigeria: Chronicle of a Dying State," *Current History* (May 2005), pp. 203–08.

15. Harden, *Africa: Dispatches from a Fragile Continent,* p. 306.

16. Peter M. Lewis, "Nigeria: Elections in a Fragile Regime," *Journal of Democracy,* 14 (2003), p. 133.

17. These two opposition candidates were Muhammadu Buhari from the All Nigeria People's Party (formerly the APP) and Atiku Abuabakar from the Action Congress (a party resulting from the 2006 merger of the Alliance for Democracy and other small parties).

18. "It All Looks Horribly the Same," *Economist,* 28 February 2008.

19. French, *A Continent for the Taking,* p. 42.

23. Vincent O. Nmehelle, "Sharia Law in the Northern States of Nigeria: To Implement, or Not to Implement, the Constitutionality Is the Question," *Human Rights Quarterly,* 26, no. 3 (2004), pp. 730–59.

21. Chinua Achebe, *The Trouble with Nigeria* (London: Heinemann, 1983).

22. Bratton and Lewis, "The Durability of Political Goods?" Afrobarometer Working Paper no. 48 (April 2005).

23. "A Tale of Two Giants," *Economist,* 13 January 2000.

24. Peter Lewis, "From Prebendalism to Predation: The Political Economy of Decline in Nigeria," *Journal of Modern African Studies,* 34, no. 1 (March 1996), pp. 79–103.

25. International Monetary Fund, "Nigeria: 2005 Article IV Consultation Concluding Statement," International Monetary Fund, March 25, 2005. www.imf.org/external/np/ms/2005/032505.htm (accessed 27 February 2006).

26. Princeton N. Lyman and J. Stephen Morrison, "The Terrorist Threat in Africa," *Foreign Affairs* (January/February 2004), pp. 75–86.

GLOSSARY OF KEY TERMS

Abacha, Sani   Oppressive Nigerian military dictator from 1993 to 1998 who came to power in a miliary coup.

Babangida, Ibrahim   Military ruler of Nigeria from 1985 to 1993 who sought to establish the failed Third Republic.

derivation formula Formula for distributing percentage of oil revenues between national and local government in Nigeria.

federal character principle Nigerian quota system designed to ease ethnic tension by requiring the president to appoint ministers from each Nigerian state.

First Republic Nigerian parliamentary democratic regime that followed independence (1960–1966).

Fourth Republic Nigeria's current presidential democratic regime, established in 1999.

Fulani Predominantly Muslim ethnic group located in northern Nigeria.

Hausa Predominantly Muslim ethnic group concentrated in northern Nigeria.

House of Representatives Lower house of Nigerian parliament.

Igbo (Ibo) Predominantly Christian ethnic group concentrated in southeast Nigeria.

Movement for the Emancipation of the Niger Delta Militant separatist group from the Niger Delta.

Movement for the Survival of the Ogoni People (MOSOP) Ethnic association founded by Ken Saro-Wiwa to promote interests of ethnic Ogoni in the Niger Delta.

National Economic Empowerment and Development Strategy (NEEDS) A wide-ranging Nigerian reform program designed to stem government corruption and enhance economic infrastructure.

Niger Delta World's third-largest wetland and source of Nigerian oil and economic and ethnic conflict.

Obasanjo, Olusegun Military ruler from 1976 to 1979 and two-term elected president, from 1999 to 2007, of Nigeria.

patrimonialism Arrangement whereby a ruler depends on a collection of supporters within the state who will gain direct benefits in return for enforcing the ruler's will.

People's Democratic Party (PDP) Political party that has dominated Nigerian politics since its 1998 formation; its base is in the Hausa Muslim ethnic group of northern Nigeria.

Republic of Biafra Ill-fated effort by Nigeria's Igbo-dominated eastern region to secede in 1967.

resource curse Abundant natural resources distorting an economy by preventing diversification.

Saro-Wiwa, Ken Noted Nigerian playwright and environmental activist, executed in 1995 for his defense of the land and peoples of the Niger Delta.

"scramble for Africa" Late nineteenth-century race by European countries to expand influence and establish imperial control over the majority of African territory.

Second Republic Short-lived Nigerian democratic regime, from 1979 to

1983, in which the former parliamentary system was replaced by a presidential system.

sharia   System of Islamic law.

Third Republic   Democratic regime proposed by General Ibrahim Babangida in 1993, but precluded by General Sani Abacha's military coup in the same year following annulled elections.

Yar'Adua, Umaru   Current president (2007–present) of Nigeria.

Yoruba   Ethnic group largely confined to southwest Nigeria whose members are divided among Christian, Muslim, and local animist faiths.

WEB LINKS

African Studies Internet Resources: Nigeria, Columbia University Libraries
   www.columbia.edu/cu/lweb/indiv/africa/cuvl/Nigeria.html
Economic and Financial Crimes Commission **www.efccnigeria.org**
The Guardian (Nigeria) **www.ngrguardiannews.com**
IRIN News.org UN Office for the Coordination of Humanitarian Affairs
   www.irinnews.org
Niger Delta Development Commission
   www.nddconline.org/The_Niger_Delta
Nigeria Direct: Official Government Gateway **www.nigeria.gov.ng**

INDEX

Page numbers in *italics* refer to charts and maps. Page numbers in **boldface** refer to keyword definitions.